Business

PRINCIPLES, PRACTICES, AND OPPORTUNITIES

Second Edition

James A. Senn

Prentice Hall, Upper Saddle River, New Jersey 07458

Acquisitions Editor: David Alexander
Editor-in-Chief: P. J. Boardman
Assistant Editor: Audrey Regan
Editorial Assistant: Shane Gemza
Marketing Manager: Nancy Evans
Production Coordinator: Cindy Spreder
Managing Editor: Katherine Evancie
Senior Manufacturing Supervisor: Paul Smolenski
Manufacturing Manager: Vincent Scelta
Design Director: Pat Smythe
Interior Design: Ann Beurskens for GTS Graphics
Cover Design: Cheryl Asherman
Illustrator (Interior): GTS Graphics
Photo Research: Melinda Reo, Melinda Alexander, Diane Austin, Teri Stratford
Composition and Prepress: GTS Graphics
Cover Art: Marjory Dressler

Copyright ©1998, 1995 by Prentice-Hall, Inc.
A Simon & Schuster Company
Upper Saddle River, New Jersey 07458

ISBN 0-13-857715-3

This book was designed to be useful and accessible
to the reader. Prentice Hall and the author gratefully
acknowledge those companies that have allowed use
of their brand names and registered trademarks in a
manner that supports this.

Library of Congress Cataloging-in-Publication Data

Senn, James A.
    Information technology in business : principles, practices, and
opportunities / James A. Senn. — 2nd ed.
        p.   cm.
    Includes bibliographical references and index.
    ISBN 0-13-857715-3
    1. Business—Data processing.   2. Information storage and
retrieval systems—Business.   3. Information technology.   I. Title.

HF5548.2.S4366   1997
650′ .0285—dc21   94-47029
                                                            CIP

Prentice-Hall International (UK) Limited, *London*
Prentice-Hall of Australia Pty. Limited, *Sydney*
Prentice-Hall Canada, Inc., *Toronto*
Prentice-Hall Hispanoamericana, S.A., *Mexico*
Prentice-Hall of India Private Limited, *New Delhi*
Prentice-Hall of Japan, Inc., *Tokyo*
Simon & Schuster Asia Pte. Ltd., *Singapore*
Editora Prentice-Hall do Brasil, Ltda., *Rio de Janeiro*

Printed in the United States of America
10   9   8   7   6   5   4   3

To Tyler

(To whom every encounter is an opportunity)

With an easy laugh and a warm smile—

essential assets for the journey ahead—

you'll always capture Grand Pa's attention.

ABOUT THE AUTHOR

Jim Senn is known internationally as a dynamic speaker on management, corporate strategy, and information technology. He is Director of the Information Technology Management Group, well known for its many activities that facilitate and promote research and communication between information systems professionals, executives, researchers, and organization managers. The group is international in its focus and interacts with executives around the world on a continuing basis.

Senn is also Professor of Information Systems in the College of Business Administration at Georgia State University in Atlanta. Under his six-year leadership as Chairman of the Department of Computer Information Systems at Georgia State University, the department gained widespread international recognition for its programs and activities. It received an overall national ranking by *Computerworld* as the number two program (second to the Massachusetts Institute of Technology) in the United States and was identified as having the top curriculum in the nation.

Senn interacts widely with businesses in many countries. He is the author of several leading books on information systems and systems development that have been translated into multiple languages for use in many countries. He has written numerous articles and papers appearing in leading professional and academic publications. He is also a highly regarded facilitator at corporate and technology planning sessions and frequent interviewer of leaders and executives. Their views are often included in his regularly appearing column about business strategy and his numerous articles and papers. He addresses audiences around the world on strategies for personal and corporate success.

Brief Contents

Contents

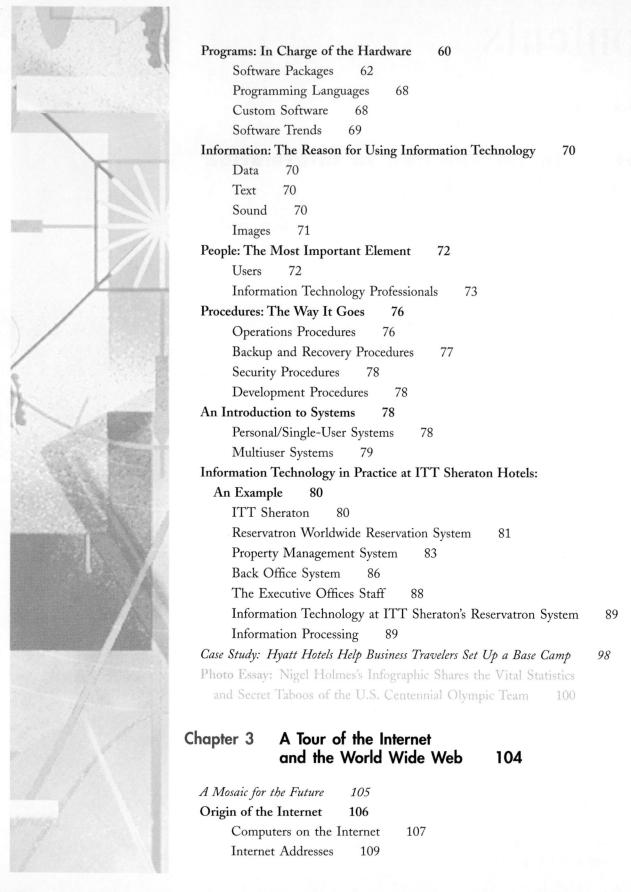

Part 2 Tech Talk

Chapter 4   The Central Processor and Memory   146

Part 3 Single-User Systems

Chapter 12   Developing Shared IT Applications   546

Chapter 13   Business Information Systems and Information Technology in Industry   608

Part 5   IT Issues and Opportunities

Chapter 14   Issues in Information Technology   658

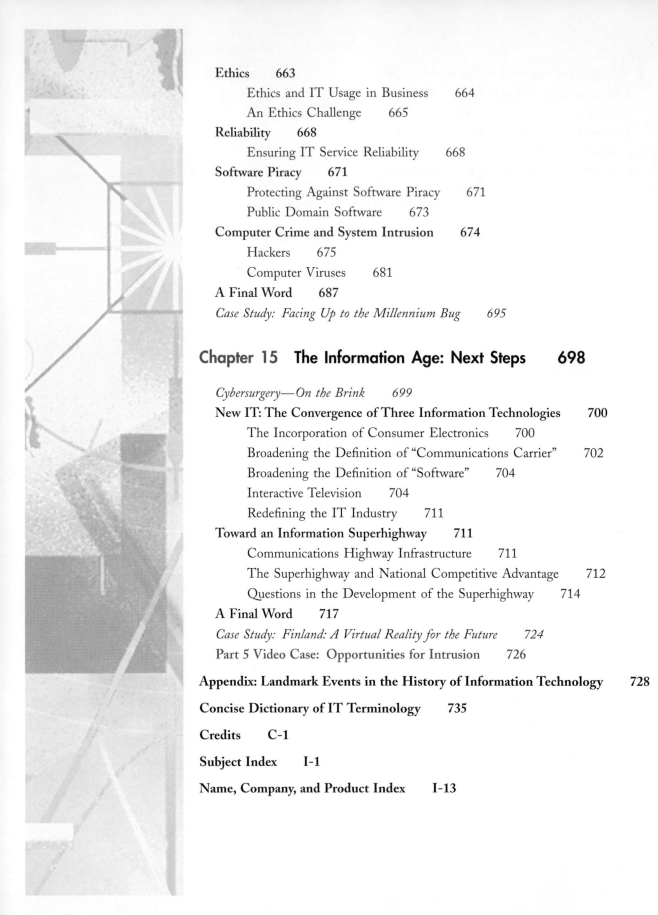

Preface

You've overheard it . . . probably said it yourself: "The Internet makes everything different." These frequently repeated words crystallize the feelings of many about the most important influence on business life since the introduction of microprocessors in 1971. It's evident that the Internet, the near seamless and worldwide web of networks, is a pivotal force that is triggering leaders to consider new possibilities and redefine expectations in business. It is unlocking new sources of enlightenment and entertainment, not to mention communication and commerce, in daily life. Even more important, perhaps, is the realization that Internet-led innovations are emerging daily, with no end in sight.

The Internet—the Net—is causing us to change the way we look at information, the nature and delivery of products and services, and the ways we keep in touch. The very content of these items has changed as well. In many instances, they incorporate colorful graphics, sound, video, and animated images. These forms are commonplace on the Net and elsewhere, dramatically augmenting everyday text. For many people these multimedia forms are rapidly becoming the norm in important communications.

What does this all mean? A myriad of scenarios is emerging; however, one thing is certain. Those who have a firm grasp on the capabilities of the Internet, multimedia, and the characteristics of the underlying information technology are most likely to influence, or at least capitalize on, their application to the world around them—business or personal.

The Internet and multimedia are among the most visible icons in the continuing evolution of information technology in business. Those companies and individuals having the *know-how* to combine their resources in *computers* and *communication systems*—the principal elements of information technology—are the most likely to be successful in their endeavors. Moreover, their application of the *principles* of IT, in combination with an awareness of the best *practices*, provides the greatest *opportunity* for their success. However, it's no surprise to anyone in business today that many of yesterday's practices—division of labor (not career development and job enrichment) and an education for a lifetime (rather than a lifetime of education), for example—no longer apply. It is precisely this realization that has led so many companies to rethink, or *reengineer*, their previously sacred business practices.

The Second Edition

This book's title, *Information Technology in Business: Principles, Practices, and Opportunities*, reflects the basic realities and promise of information technology in business, both globally and locally. It suggests the book's distinguishing characteristics:

- Focus on **information technology**
- Emphasis on **problem solving**
- Examination of actual **business experiences**
- Application to **professional practice**

This second edition includes extensive discussions of the practical uses of information technology (IT) in business internationally, a distinguishing characteristic of the very successful first edition. You'll recognize the many examples of business practice throughout the book, all chosen to show how the world's best-known firms are capitalizing on IT to serve their stakeholders effectively. Because IT is not just for big business, as you know, I've also included many examples that illustrate the impact of IT in creating opportunities for small business and individual entrepreneurs: artists, athletes, entertainers, inventors, journalists . . . the list is almost endless.

New Chapters Expand Principles and Practices

This edition features comprehensive new chapters on the Internet—including its most widely used resource, the World Wide Web—and on multimedia technologies. Drawing on these chapters, I incorporate applications of the Net, the Web, and multimedia into many of the company practices described throughout the rest of the book.

This book is organized into five parts. The first module, "An Introduction to Information Technology," introduces the principles of information technology and describes the reasons for its extensive use in all types of businesses. You'll find the Internet chapter in this module (in Chapter 3), introduced early so it can be used in all the chapters that follow.

"Tech Talk," the second part, describes in detail the components of computers, including hardware and programs. A vast array of business uses of these IT components is described through illustration. If you're already familiar with the technical aspects of IT, this part will be useful to review the most recent developments in IT.

Part 3, "Single-User Systems," examines the productivity tools people find most useful: spreadsheet programs, database systems, word processing, desktop publishing, presentation systems, and computer graphics. This part also discusses the development of single-user systems, including selection of both computer and communication hardware as well as personal productivity programs. I've created an entire chapter on multimedia to describe how companies are capitalizing on the power of graphics, audio, video (and more) to streamline their operations and augment services for their customers. This chapter also illustrates, step by step, how to build a multimedia presentation using widely available authoring tools. This chapter will assist you in getting your students up to speed in doing electronic presentations.

"Multiuser Systems," Part 4, explores the way businesses interconnect many users, within departments and across work groups, and throughout an enterprise. End-users also share IT resources that are distributed across miles, countries, or continents. Developing shared databases and shared applications places special requirements on the know-how of IT professionals, as this part also discusses.

Part 5, "IT Issues and Opportunities," explores important challenges surrounding the use of information technology, including the issues of ethics, personal privacy, and IT security. The final chapter examines the emerging developments that will take us to the next steps in the Information Age.

New Features Highlight Practice

The themes of principles, practices, and opportunities are integrated into the hundreds of company illustrations spanning the chapters of this book. I further highlight the themes in each chapter with special insert features:

- **Rethinking Business Practices** explores the way companies have changed their way of conducting business by challenging conventional practices and capitalizing on their information technology capabilities
- **Information Technology in Practice** discusses innovative and effective applications of IT that are making people and organizations more successful

In these features you'll find a candid (and sometimes gritty) discussion of company practices related to the chapter's focus. For instance, you'll see how intranets are used at Visa, the well-known bank card company, and how Europcar, the European car rental company, used IT to restructure its business practices throughout Europe. Another feature will discuss why Xerox chose to outsource its existing worldwide information systems applications to EDS. Then there's the story of how Cable Network News (CNN) protects against illegal use of the programs it broadcasts around the world.

Chapter Cases

Each chapter ends with a story of real companies and real people in the form of a comprehensive case. For example, you'll see how the nationwide tool company, Snap-on Tools, is using intranets to keep its dealers up to date, making them both more successful. ESPN's highly successful SportsZone on the Internet is also explored. Then there's the emergence of digital cash and the story of how one company, Amsterdam-based DigiCash, is making its mark around the world. Or take the case of doing business from scenic Carmel, California, home of well-known necktie maker Talbott Ties. You will see how Talbott uses IT to support its roving sales force and yet ensure that its customers obtain the products they want when they need them.

New technology uses are featured in the cases as well. The use of data warehouses by SNCF, the French national railroad, is discussed at the end of Chapter 11. Another case focuses on the troublesome millennium bug. Most IT professionals are watching, as you surely are, to see how this problem gets resolved.

Video Cases

Each part of the book concludes with a media case that is supplemented by a news clip from the ABC News/Prentice Hall Video Library or the *Wall Street Journal* video library. I think you'll find these timely and topical cases can be used to spur discussion on some of the key IT issues for today—and for tomorrow. Will people grow to shop on-line? What will become of the Network computer? What does Bill Gates go to see at Comdex, the giant computer trade show? For that matter what does *he* expect for the future of IT? These are among the questions posed in the combination of cases ending each section of the book and in the video footage available to instructors using the book.

Critical Connections

Critical thinking is an important part of solving problems and capitalizing on opportunities. A special Critical Connection feature emphasizes problem solving. Each chapter introduces a challenge facing an individual or company and draws on the principles and practices discussed in the chapter. At the end of the chapter, these experiences are revisited and conclusions are drawn. Each Critical Connection concludes with a series of discussion questions. Like the other examples throughout the book, Critical Connections focus on a wide variety of businesses from small single-owner start-ups to multinational corporations like McDonald's and Levi Strauss.

Reality Checks

I often find it useful to step back from what I'm doing, or what I'm reading, to consider the ramifications of what's happening. For this reason I've included a series of Reality Checks in every chapter. Each Reality Check is a personal assessment of a particular principle, practice, or opportunity, and is drawn from a vast array of IT experiences in the worlds of business, government, and research.

Photo Essays

The "mind's eye" augments written descriptions by allowing us to visualize experience. To further share the experiences of people and companies, I've created a series of photo essays that tell stories through photographs, images, and display screens. Each photo essay tells a step-by-step story in pictures. For example, in Chapter 2 you'll see how Nigel Holmes, the inventor of infographics, uses this powerful medium to describe Olympic athletes in *Sports Illustrated* magazine. In Chapter 10, you'll see how a company can use Lotus Notes to manage important projects when team members are in different parts of the world. The Federal Express photo essay in Chapter 11 takes you behind the scenes to show how the successful overnight carrier uses IT to honor its slogan (When it's absolutely, positively, gotta be there . . .) repeating the company's "overnight success" every day. Check out the other photo essays too. They're both fun to read and informative.

The Appendix: Landmark Events in the History of Information Technology time line uses a variety of photographs to trace the key events leading up to IT as we know it today. And, if you're buying a new model PC to replace your current one, be sure to check out the PC Buyer's Guide.

Group Projects and Applications

Since people often learn best when they learn from each other and through the firsthand gathering of information, you'll find a set of group projects included in every chapter. The project descriptions focus on a current topic relevant to the subject of the chapter. Each describes a topic for investigation, divides up the responsibility among group members, suggests a means for assembling information, and presents an approach to present results to the class. The projects require team members to get into the field, visiting companies or interviewing businesspersons.

Net_Work Projects Explore the Internet

Elements of the Internet are woven throughout this book. However, of special significance are the Net_Work projects included in each chapter. These projects, which can be completed by individuals or teams, are designed to showcase the many capabilities and features of the Internet and the World Wide Web. Net_Work projects will visit corporate and government sites, utilize the search engines to locate information, teach how to download software and documents, explore the multimedia possibilities provided by plug-ins—even venture into cybercruiting to see the career opportunities that are posted at various Web sites. Net_Work projects begin in the first chapter where the specific capabilities to use the Internet from your campus are identified.

Additional Learning Aids

Each chapter includes a variety of other learning aids designed to assist readers in testing their understanding and ability to apply the principles and practices described in the chapter. Included in each chapter are:

- A detailed outline that previews the chapter's contents
- Learning objectives that focus readers on *understanding* key concepts and frameworks
- An opening vignette describing a practical use of information technology in business
- A running marginal glossary of key terms introduced in the chapter
- A chapter summary keyed to learning objectives
- Key terms useful for review
- Review questions that test understanding of the chapter
- Discussion questions that raise thought-provoking, often controversial, issues
- Suggested readings for pursuing topics introduced in the chapter

Learning System Resources

Instructors using *Information Technology in Business: Principles, Practices, and Opportunities, 2nd ed.,* will be provided with a complete system designed to facilitate education and learning in the dynamic field of IT. Each component of this system has been carefully crafted to ensure that the learning experience is rewarding and effective for instructor and student alike. They are available to instructors who adopt this book for their classes and have their bookstore order from the publisher.

INSTRUCTOR'S RESOURCE MANUAL   The Instructor's Resource Manual is a complete tool for preparing college lectures. It includes one chapter for each chapter of the text and contains a chapter overview, teaching tips, learning objectives, lecture outlines, and solutions to all questions in the text.

TEST ITEM FILE   A printed Test Item File is also available to adopters. More than 1,000 multiple choice, true/false, and short answer/essay questions are included. Tests are arranged on a per-chapter basis.

PRENTICE HALL CUSTOM TEST   A computerized version of the printed Test Item File allows instructors to design and create tests as well as maintain student records and provide online practice testing for students. Windows PH Custom Test is a PC-compatible software package.

POWERPOINT PRESENTATION SLIDES   Also available to adopters are PowerPoint presentation slides. These slides, created in PowerPoint 4.0 for Windows 3.1 and Windows 95 (or later versions), outline each chapter of the text and incorporate tables and graphs as well.

VIDEO LIBRARY   Video cases, consisting of interviews, critical analyses, and network news reports drawn from the library of ABC News and *The Wall Street Journal,* are available to instructors who adopt this book for their classes and have their bookstore order it from the publisher. The cases are chosen because of their widespread applicability to business and their usefulness and appeal to students, and draw on such ABC News programs as *Nightline, World News,* and *This Week with David Brinkley.* The video clips accompany the media cases that conclude each part of the text.

   A video guide, to assist instructors, is included in the Instructor's Resource Manual.

ACETATES   A set of 100 color acetates is provided to facilitate in-class lectures. These acetates are adapted from the four-color art in the textbook.

WORLD WIDE WEB SITE   New to this edition is a Web site which supports the text. The site, located at http://www.prenhall.com/senn contains a section for students and a section for instructors. The student section includes photo essays, technology updates, and additional part-ending cases, as well as Web links to companies mentioned in the text and an interactive study guide organized by chapter. The instructor section contains password-protected access to the instructor's manual and other teaching resources.

Additional Student Learning System Resources

To further augment learning, two powerful resources are available to adopters of this book.

IT Works CD-ROM: Courseware for Information Technology   *IT Works CD-ROM* is an innovative multimedia educational tool that can be used one-on-one with students to demonstrate basic computer concepts and applications. It employs sound, motion video, colorful high resolution graphics, and animation.

   IT Works CD-ROM consists of four modules:

- Inside the Computer Explorer. This Explorer examines the computer's system unit, inside and out (front and rear). The student simply clicks on a component to learn more about it.
- Peripherals Explorer. This Peripherals Explorer activity introduces students to common input/output devices, storage devices, and storage media which might be configured with a PC.
- Online Explorer. This Explorer simulates going online. The student can "log on" and learn to navigate the Internet, America Online, and a BBS.

- Applications Explorer. The Applications Explorer gives the student a lesson on the different classes of software programs available. They can explore various applications in four categories: productivity, multiuser applications, home/personal, and system software.

Acknowledgments

The fact that this book is characterized by so many descriptions of actual IT applications and experiences is a result of the tremendous support and involvement of companies and their leaders as well as a seasoned research team.

Business Leaders   A large number of business executives from North America, Europe, and Asia participated in the development of this project by sharing first-hand with the author their business experiences and insights, as well as those of their companies and employees. They were willing to discuss their successes (as well as other experiences that became "significant learning events"). A large number are identified through their company names in this book. I appreciate their support and candor.

I'm also indebted to the many businesses that allowed me to use their logos as well as their stories.

Research Support   The book benefited tremendously from the skilled researchers who helped conduct research, assemble information, and prepare notes and narratives to bring about the business discussions appearing in the text. I'm indebted to key research assistance from Melissa Morris, Melinda Alexander, Diane Austin, Linda Muterspaugh, Teri Stratford, Cathy Luce, Sherry Fowler, Suzanne Scully, John Blatt, Kristen Knutson, and Harry Knox.

Nigel Holmes provided personal documents—sketches, drawings, and final copy—for the photo essay on infographics.

Learning System Support   The supplements for this book were developed with the assistance of many. Their efforts will enable students and instructors alike to seek and achieve a practical and forward-looking knowledge of the opportunities emanating from the effective use of information technology in business.

The most important event in creating the vision and concept for this book was a focus group convened early in the process. Members of the group included:

Frank Davis
Bloomsburg University

Adolph Katz
AK Associates & Fairfield University

Donald L. Dawley
Miami University

Robert T. Keim
Arizona State University

Richard Fenzl
Syracuse University

John Pagliarulo
Rockland Community College

Barry Floyd
California Polytechnic State University

John F. Sanford
Philadelphia College of Textiles and Science

The reviewers kept the manuscript's contents on track with their their helpful comments and suggestions during the development and delivery of this project:

Theresa Adams
DeKalb College

Theo Addo
San Diego State University

Gary R. Armstrong
Shippensburg University

Anitesh Barua
University of Texas at Austin

Luverne Bierle
Iowa Central Community College

Catherine J. Brotherton
Riverside Community College

Bruce Brown
Salt Lake Community College

Donald L. Dawley
Miami University

Lois T. Elliot
Prince George's Community College

Mary Helen Fagan
Salisbury State University

Edward Fisher
Central Michigan University

Stephen Haag
University of Minnesota–Duluth

Wade M. Jackson
Memphis State University

O. K. Johnson
University of Utah

Ernest A. Kallman
Bentley College

Adolph Katz
AK Associates & Fairfield University

Robert T. Keim
Arizona State University

Mohammed B. Khan
California State University–Long Beach

Constance A. Knapp
Pace University

Kenneth A. Kozar
University of Colorado–Boulder

Gerald F. Mackey
Georgia Institute of Technology

Tony L. McRae
Collin County Community College

Pat Ormond
University of Utah

King Perry
Delaware County Community College

Tom Philpott
University of Texas at Austin

Armand Picou
The University of Central Arkansas

John F. Sanford
Philadelphia College of Textiles and Science

John R. Schillak
University of Wisconsin–Eau Claire

Vincent J. Skudrna
Baruch College

Blair A. Smith
University of Phoenix, Colorado Campus

Ronald W. Stimson
Eastfield College

Susan Silvera
Los Angeles Trade-Technical College

Ajay S. Vinze
Texas A&M University

Fred Wells
DeKalb College

Prentice Hall David Alexander, P. J. Boardman, and Sandy Steiner were the essential ingredients in the ultimate evolution of this book's second edition. They not only facilitated the many steps needed to produce this book, but carried on the vision and spirit that made the first edition so successful. Their efforts augmented the original team consisting of Valerie Ashton, Joe Heider, Will Ethridge, Steve Rigolosi, and P J. Boardman.

Katherine Evancie managed the entire production effort, ensuring that there were no loose ends. Her commitment to schedule, balanced with a healthy respect for the project's purpose, was instrumental in the final result.

Mary Fernandez provided all-important support from the field, playing a role that was more essential in the completion of this edition than will ever be known. Only time will tell what other projects may result from her insights, vast experience, and most important of all, her sincere interest in ensuring peak performance.

On the home front, my wife Elaine played the essential role of "Chief of Staff," keeping this and all other projects in their proper perspective. Whether our adventures take us across town or around the globe, as they so often do, I can always count on her wisdom, organization, and friendship being close at hand.

CHAPTER 1

Information Technology: Principles, Practices, and Opportunities

CHAPTER OUTLINE

Information Technology Keeps You On-the-Go and On-Schedule

Welcome to the Information Age

The Evolution of the Information Age • The Characteristics of the Information Age

What Is Information Technology?

Computers • Communications Networks • Know-How

The Principles of Information Technology

The Functions of Information Technology • The Benefits of Information Technology • IT at Work: Caterpillar's Virtual Reality • The Opportunities for Information Technology • Information Technology Is All Around Us, Improving Our Lives • The Responsibilities of Using Information Technology

The Career Side of Information Technology

Information Technology as a Career • Information Technology as an Aid to Your Career

Case Study: Information Technology Outruns Runners of the New York Stock Exchange

LEARNING OBJECTIVES

When you have completed this chapter, you should be able to

1 Describe the six characteristics of the Information Age and discuss the role of information technology as the principle tool of the Information Age.

2 Explain the three primary components of information technology.

3 Identify the six information-handling functions and the four benefits of information technology.

4 Summarize the principles of business reengineering, emphasizing the potential benefits to people and businesses.

5 Discuss the types of opportunities that information technology offers to people.

6 Describe the responsibilities of people who use information technology.

Information Technology Keeps You On-the-Go and On-Schedule

Every day you step in front of your personal computer, touch the keyboard, and watch the screen as it blinks momentarily. In seconds, you've captured your schedule of events: meetings, locations, and times—not just for the day, but for the next several months. And you can take it with you.

You do not transfer your schedule to paper or to the pages of a diary or calendar. Instead, you transmit it, without using wires, to your Timex Data Link wristwatch. This watch performs pretty much like a standard wristwatch, but it has these additional features:

- Software that accepts wireless transfer of your personal schedule from your personal computer.
- Digital readout that displays date, time, and notes on its face.
- Search-by-date ability.
- "On-board" address book complete with names, addresses, telephone numbers, and optional comments.
- Sound—an alarm that signals any appointment noted in your personal schedule.
- Software that enables you to maintain both calendar and address book on your personal computer and in an instant transfer those details to your wristwatch.

The Timex Data Link is the first, but it certainly won't be the last, wristwatch to maintain personal calendars, address books, schedules, and more. By the way, this watch keeps accurate time. The price? It lists at $99.

Whether the Timex Data Link wristwatch is a necessity, luxury, or novelty depends on your personal situation. It certainly exemplifies the creative way both businesses and individuals are using information technology to influence their routine activities.

In the past decade and a half, we've witnessed the introduction of stunning new products based on information technology, including

- The personal computer
- The cellular telephone
- Magnetic resonance imaging (MRI)

- Videoconferencing
- Wireless computers
- The Internet and World Wide Web

Each of these innovations is changing the way we work, live, or play.

Businesses are capitalizing on developments in information technology to move information fast enough to coordinate many activities simultaneously—producing greater efficiency and accuracy in responding to customer needs. Here are some examples:

- Rosenbluth Travel Agency, headquartered in Philadelphia, transformed itself from a regional travel agency in 1980 into one of the four largest travel agencies in the United States, with annual sales over $1.3 billion, in just 10 years. Aggressive use of information technology enabled Rosenbluth to interconnect approximately 500 sales offices and 2,500 staff members. Business volume, driven by excellent customer service provided by agents with instant access to up-to-the-moment information, made Rosenbluth a national player.

   In the 1990s, Rosenbluth again seized on the latest information technology—this time to springboard into more than 40 countries spanning Europe, the Middle East, Asia, and the Pacific. The company's 1,400 offices are grossing more than $6 billion in annual sales.

   Rosenbluth does more than write airline tickets. To satisfy customers in a business whose essence is negotiating the best service and rates, good information is crucial. Rosenbluth provides excellent travel management reports and cost analyses as well as reliable reservation management and travel counseling.

- Mullen Advertising Agency of Boston, comprising some 150 employees, depends on videoconferencing to work with its clients. Writers, artists, and account executives can meet electronically, often on a moment's notice, with clients in various industries, including textiles, footwear, publishing, automobiles, and computer software. Without leaving their offices, each party can see and hear the other parties and share drawings, photographs, or advertising layouts on paper or on the display screen of a computer.

- Faragut Mortgage Co. services more than $2 billion in loans every year from its offices in Martinez, California. Keeping track of mortgage fluctuations at this 100-person company is a challenge met through desktop computers. Every morning, Faragut's staff members review information on mortgage rate changes that the company receives electronically from its financial sources and enter these changes into Faragut's computers. New rate sheets are prepared as often as necessary, but getting these often-revised rate sheets to the more than 700 independent mortgage brokers who are Faragut's customers presented a challenge. Letters and phone calls were out of the question—the volume was much too large. Faragut's solution was to transmit its rate sheets to Xpedite Systems, a company located in San Francisco that provides a broadcast faxing service. Upon receiving a rate sheet from Faragut's computer, Xpedite's computer immediately transmits it to each of Faragut's 700 brokers over ordinary telephone lines.

But make no mistake about it—the same information technology that offers these tremendous advantages can be misused, either through carelessness or through outright underhandedness. So we find companies moving information electronically at lightning speed and responding to customers at a snail-like pace, and electronic interlopers eavesdropping on private conversations or snooping into sensitive records.

- Over one Thanksgiving weekend, an intruder entered a communications network at the General Electric Co., boring through the system's security protection. GE officials were particularly concerned because the break-in involved a system containing proprietary company information. This breach of security sent a chill through the corporate community about the dangers of on-line access and made executives wonder whether their own systems were adequately protected.

This book explores the role of information technology (IT) in today's world. As we will see, the applications of IT are virtually limitless. IT can turn ordinary products into smart products, such as the wireless watch. But in most cases, IT transforms the way people work and play.

A working knowledge of the principles, practices, and opportunities of IT will help you succeed in whatever career you choose. Practically every professional, manufacturing, or service career requires some knowledge of information technology. Working in the field of information technology itself, where specialists develop new types of IT and new uses for existing IT, requires both a good understanding of the technology and insight into the most effective ways in which people can benefit from its use.

The pages that follow relate many instances of how people and companies are developing and using IT today and planning for its application tomorrow. Although a number of these examples come from different areas of society, most are taken from the business world. In today's quality- and productivity-conscious, globally competitive environment, it is businesspeople who are driving the development of IT. IT is providing business opportunities that could not have been imagined only a few years ago. As you progress through this book, you'll read a series of special features describing how companies, large and small, and people are capitalizing on information technology. Features titled *Information Technology in Practice* relate examples of successful IT use. Those headed *Rethinking Business Practices* detail how capitalizing on IT resulted in changes in corporate practices.

Our journey into the world of IT begins with a description of the Information Age and a discussion of what it means for us.

Welcome to the Information Age

We live in a society where information is an essential resource and knowledge is valuable. Only in the last 30 to 40 years have information and knowledge been recognized as assets a society needs to develop and manage. With that realization, the Information Age began. To better appreciate the social transformation wrought by the Information Age, let's take a brief look at how it evolved.

The Evolution of the Information Age

Until the 1800s, long before the day of the data link watch, the great majority of the world's people led lives that revolved around agriculture. During the **Agricultural Age,** entire families worked in partnership with the land to provide enough food for themselves (Table 1.1). This is still the case in many developing countries today.

Agricultural Age
The period up to the 1800s, when the majority of workers were farmers whose lives revolved around agriculture.

TABLE 1.1 *The Evolution of the Information Age*			
	AGRICULTURAL AGE	INDUSTRIAL AGE	INFORMATION AGE
Time Period	Pre-1800s	1800s to 1957	1957 to present
Majority of Workers	Farmers	Factory workers	Knowledge workers
Partnership	People and land	People and machines	People and people
Principal Tool	Hand tools	Machines	Information technology

As new tools and techniques gradually improved and extended the land that farmers could exploit for growing crops or grazing their herds, it became possible to produce more food with fewer hours of labor. Now most farm families could produce more food than they needed for themselves, enabling them to barter or sell farm products in return for other goods and services. This led to the expansion of the nonagricultural sector and the evolution of society into the next stage.

Industrial Age
The period from the 1800s to 1957, when work processes were simplified through mechanization and automation.

With the coming of the **Industrial Age**—first to England in the early 1800s, slightly later to other countries—workers were assisted by machines, which greatly extended their capabilities. A partnership developed between people and machines. As the nineteenth century progressed, machines became the primary tool for the majority of workers. With the simplification of more and more processes through mechanization and automation, the number of people working in manufacturing and industry increased. By the middle of the twentieth century, the great majority of workers in advanced societies had shifted from farming to industry.

Information Age
The period that began in 1957, in which the majority of workers are involved in the creation, distribution, and application of information.

In the **Information Age,** which began in the United States in 1957, the first year that white-collar workers outnumbered blue-collar workers, both agriculture and manufacturing are still important. But most of today's workers are involved in the creation, distribution, and application of information. These **knowledge workers** now outnumber those employed in agriculture and manufacturing throughout the developed world. In the Information Age, the partnership is one of people with other people, and the principal tool is information technology.

knowledge workers
Workers involved in the creation, distribution, and application of information.

Knowledge workers are found across many different professions. Stockbrokers, bankers, accountants, financial planners, and risk managers come to mind immediately. Other types of knowledge workers are telecommunications specialists, physicians, attorneys, systems analysts, computer programmers, journalists, and medical researchers.

Knowledge workers often depend on front-line service workers for data. The counter attendants at McDonald's are not knowledge workers, but they do capture data for those who are when they enter the details of your order into a cash-register-like computer terminal. Those data are used by knowledge workers to manage inventory, order supplies, and schedule workers. Knowledge workers, in fact, use information generated throughout the organization: on the front line, in the back office, and in the executive suite.

The Characteristics of the Information Age

Six characteristics distinguish the Information Age from previous ages:

1. An information-based society has arisen.
2. Businesses depend on information technology to get their work done.

3. Work processes are being transformed to increase productivity.
4. Information technology provides the means to rethink—that is, *reengineer*—conventional business processes.
5. Success in business is largely determined by the effectiveness with which information technology is used.
6. Information technology is embedded in many products and services.

Underlying all of these characteristics is the central importance of data and information processing in the day-to-day activities of most people in the industrialized world.[1]

AN INFORMATION SOCIETY.   The Information Age came about with the rise of an information society that depends on information technology. In an **information society,** more people work at handling information than at agriculture and manufacturing combined. This is true in the United States (Figure 1.1), as well as in Great Britain, Australia, and Japan—just a few of the countries that are information societies.

Person-to-person communications and IT links between individuals and businesses are important features of an information society. Effective use of IT enables a group of people working together to accomplish more than those same individuals could working alone.

DEPENDENCE ON INFORMATION TECHNOLOGY.   As we will see throughout this book, an information society depends on knowing when and how to use computers. Equally important are the capabilities to communicate information and to interconnect people through information technology.

information society
A society in which more people work at handling information than at agriculture and manufacturing combined.

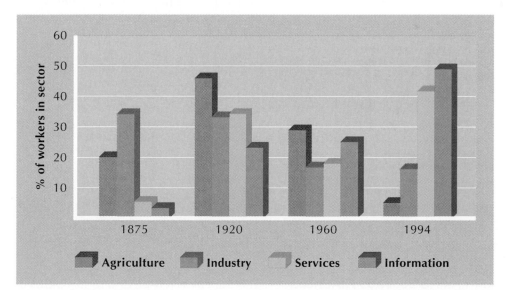

FIGURE 1.1
U.S. Workforce by Sector
In the U.S. information society of the 1990s, more people work at handling information than at agriculture and manufacturing combined.
SOURCE: United States Department of Labor.

---

[1]*Data* are facts—details that describe people, places, objects, and events. In and of themselves, they have little value. When a set of facts about an item or issues of interest are gathered and synthesized into a useful form, they become *information*.

Too often, we seek magic solutions to the problems and challenges that confront us. Some of us keep looking for that magic pill that will enable us to eat all the fattening foods we want without gaining weight or risking our health. Others of us seek a way to use all the gasoline we want without creating air pollution or depleting the supply of natural resources.

In the same way, many people have come to expect that their business problems will disappear if they learn how to use a word-processing system or how to transmit data electronically. But solutions to real-world problems are never that easy.

Similarly, success in the Information Age requires more than knowing how to use a computer. It also requires understanding information technology's principles and practices and the opportunities that IT can provide—as well as its limitations.

Working hard and having the right information are important, but they take you only so far. The true advantages of IT are realized when you use that information in a way that creates opportunity, produces results, and opens the way to new opportunities. The knowledge that allows you to do the right thing at the right time can create tremendous advantages for you. ■

TRANSFORMATION OF WORK. In addition to its startling new tools, the Information Age is characterized by the transformation of earlier tools and work processes so that they lead to more productivity and effectiveness. Consider, for example, the transformation of agricultural work processes during the Industrial Age through mechanization. First, tractors that pulled plows, cultivators, and harvesters replaced horses and oxen. Then many agricultural era tools were further mechanized to become self-propelled, so that not even a tractor was needed to pull them. The result of all this mechanization was a vast improvement in productivity. More work could be accomplished in the same number of labor hours. In the Agricultural Age, it might have taken a family of four with one ox two weeks to plow a field; with mechanization, the work could be accomplished by one person in a day or two.

Today, information technology is generating new knowledge about what, when, and where to plant and how to care for the crops as they grow. Through information technology, the productivity of both farmers and the land is further increasing.

This farm example illustrates how work is transformed. New tools and work processes are combined with earlier tools and activities in ways that raise their productivity and effectiveness. **Work processes** are the activities that workers perform, the way they perform them, and the tools they use. **Productivity** is a measure of the amount of work that can be accomplished with a certain level of effort—that is, the specific level of output that is produced with a specific amount of input. **Effectiveness** is the extent to which desirable results are achieved.

RETHINKING BUSINESS PRACTICES. The fourth characteristic of information technology is the capability it provides to rethink conventional business practices. When businesses introduced IT into their firms, they typically sought to use computer processing to automate routine tasks that workers had been performing manually. The ways of conducting business did not really change, they just speeded up, so that more business transactions were conducted more quickly. If the activities of a business were a mess as a result of disorganization or faulty procedures, automation accomplished nothing more than *speeding up the mess.*

work processes
The combination of activities that workers perform, the way they perform those activities, and the tools they use.

productivity
The relationship between the results of an activity (output) and the resources used to create those results (inputs).

effectiveness
The extent to which desirable results are achieved.

Properly used, information technology does more than simply speed up routine activities. It allows companies to rethink conventional ways of doing business. It provides the opportunity to reengineer what is being done in a company or an entire industry. **Reengineering,** a concept that entered management vocabulary in 1990 with the publication of a *Harvard Business Review* article by professor and consultant Michael Hammer, involves

- Rethinking business practices
- Introducing radical change to benefit both a business and its customers
- Focusing on business processes

Business processes are collections of *activities,* often spanning several departments, that take one or more kinds of input and create a result that is of value to a company's *customers.* The acceptance and processing of a customer's order for manufactured goods is a typical business process. In processing the order, the company's sales, inventory, manufacturing, shipping, and accounting departments all play a role. The activities they carry out make up the order fulfillment business process.

The first step in reengineering is to take a fresh look at a business process to see if it is fulfilling its objective and to determine whether it can be carried out in less time, using fewer steps, fewer resources, or fewer people. Reengineering does not seek incremental improvements of, say, 10 to 15 percent. Rather it seeks 100 to 200 percent improvements in the overall activity—a huge leap in performance.

The *Rethinking Business Practices* feature entitled "Ford Motor Co.'s Pioneer Experience in Reengineering" illustrates how a well-established global automobile company reshaped a basic business process.

reengineering
The reshaping of business processes to remove barriers that prohibit an organization from providing better products and services and to help the organization capitalize on its strengths.

business processes
Collections of activities, often spanning several departments, that take one or more kinds of input and create a result that is of value to a company's customers.

Carelessly applied, reengineering is nothing more than a euphemism for cost reduction through layoffs or through making employees work harder or make do with less support. You'll undoubtedly notice many situations where changes are called "reengineering," but where the sole purpose is to reduce costs, lower the head count, or speed up work. "Reengineering" is also used as a buzzword for minimal improvements achieved through minor adjustments to existing job steps.

Calling a change reengineering does not make it authentic reengineering. ■

During the Industrial Age, greater productivity was attained by separating a work process into component tasks, with different workers specializing in each of the tasks. This is called **division of labor.** Today, greater productivity is achieved by connecting different workers so that they can share the same information to produce a joint result. Information Age work is accomplished through

division of labor
Separation of a work process into component tasks, with different workers specializing in each of the tasks.

- **Teamwork**—people working together to accomplish a team outcome rather than an individual job.
- **Interconnection**—individuals communicating, regardless of distance, to exchange ideas, experiences, and insights.
- **Shared information**—communication networks making information available to several people simultaneously, instantaneously, or whenever they need it.

Continual concerns in the Information Age, therefore, are: Is the needed information available? Can it be made available to appropriate staff members directly?

RETHINKING BUSINESS PRACTICES

Ford Motor Co.'s Pioneering Experience in Reengineering

Ford Motor Co., a worldwide manufacturer of automobiles that is headquartered in Dearborn, Michigan, helped awaken executives around the globe to the advantages of rethinking business practices through information technology. In the early 1980s, when the auto industry was in the midst of a recession, Ford sought ways to reduce its costs and improve the value of the company to its shareholders. Among the areas it examined was its large accounts payable department. More than 500 persons in North America alone were involved in receiving and processing invoices from Ford's many suppliers and issuing checks to pay invoices.

Ford turned to information technology to more effectively automate its accounts payable process. Paying invoices may seem a mundane task. But when more than 500 people and hundreds of millions of dollars per month are involved, doing this task right is downright essential. Company managers sought to reduce both the time it took to manage accounts payable and the size of the department.

After developing a plan to downsize the staff by some 20 percent, Ford's leaders decided to delay executing it until they compared it with the best practices of other companies—a process known as *benchmarking*. They were shocked to find that while they were seeking to reduce their accounts payable department to fewer than 400 people, the accounts payable staff at the Japanese auto manufacturer Mazda consisted of just 5 people. Mazda had a much different corporate culture—one characterized by group morning exercises and singing of songs, as well as consensus decision making—but Ford executives doubted that these cultural differences could account for the dramatic difference in accounting staffs.

Where Ford's leaders did find vast differences was in Mazda's business processes for managing accounts

Ford Motor Company

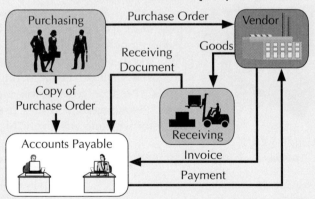

INFORMATION TECHNOLOGY INFLUENCES SUCCESS. The fifth characteristic of the Information Age is closely linked to the third: Information technology is to the Information Age what mechanization was to the Industrial Age.

It was hard to succeed in the Agricultural Age if you didn't understand the capabilities and limitations of the horses, land, and farm implements you used. Likewise, in the Industrial Age, you had to know how to use and care for your machines. In the Information Age, the most successful people are those who know how to make the most of information technology. That involves more than just

payable. This stimulated them to rethink their own processes for managing accounts payable and to reengineer them (see illustrations). Reengineering replaced paper purchasing orders with a system that sends purchasing information to suppliers electronically. Today, when merchandise from suppliers arrives at Ford's shipping dock, workers immediately use their computer workstations to look up information on the shipment. If the details of the arriving parts and materials agree with corresponding details in Ford's electronic file, the shipment is accepted and an entry to that effect is made in the computer.

Details of the arriving shipment are reviewed electronically in the accounting department, with automatic matching of arrival information with purchasing details. After this verification, a check is automatically prepared and sent to the supplier.

Reengineering permitted Ford to tell its suppliers to skip sending paper invoices. It also eliminated paper documents in the accounting process, relying on information technology to manage purchases, receipts, and payments electronically. Thus, Ford changed the rules of payment from "We pay when we receive an invoice" to "We pay when we receive the goods."

Reengineering a Process at Ford
➤ Original objective was to reduce A/P by 20%

- Purchasing
- Purchase Order
- Vendor
- Goods
- Receiving
- 500 A/P Clerks vs. Mazda Corp.'s 5
- Accounts Payable
- Invoice
- Payment
- Spend most of time investigating mismatches
- Rather than improving efficiency, decided to eliminate need

After Reengineering
An "Invoiceless" Payables System

- Purchasing
- Purchase Order
- Vendor
- Goods
- Receiving
- Matches goods received with purchase order
- Database
- Accounts Payable
- Issues checks when goods received

knowing how to key data into a computer or how to print reports. Success requires knowing what IT can do to improve your personal performance (quality, speed, and efficiency, for example) and how it can enhance your business's products and services in ways that add to their value for customers.

EMBEDDED INFORMATION TECHNOLOGY. In the Information Age, information technology is often a component of products and services. This is what *embedded* information technology means: IT that is integrated with the other components of products and services. Products and services with embedded technology are sometimes called *knowledge-based* because knowledge about their function and performance are embedded within them.

The Timex Data Link watch, for instance, is more than just a timepiece. The information technology embedded within it transforms the watch, giving it new features and capabilities that would be impossible for a traditional watch. The integration of information technology into the navigation and guidance system of a giant passenger aircraft or an electronic camera does the same thing—adds features and advanced capabilities to a traditional system.

An important point: Information technology is valuable only if the recipients find the capabilities it provides desirable. Value may consist of convenience, quality, reliability, or novelty—any characteristic the consumer feels is useful. IT embedded within an aircraft navigation system is universally considered valuable. So is the information technology in point-and-shoot electronic cameras. About the data link watch . . . we will have to wait for consumers' value verdict.

The pervasiveness of knowledge-based products, services, and activities in today's society has so thoroughly changed the way we act that we often take this technology for granted. Consider the introduction of information technology into the personal travel industry (Figure 1.2). Before computerized reservation systems were available, travel agents had to call an airline directly to make a reservation, providing the passenger's name, address, and telephone number verbally. Tickets were written by hand. Advance seat assignment was impossible. Either you got on the plane and took the first seat available, or you were assigned a seat at the gate just prior to boarding.

IT has not only enabled travel agents to be more effective but has also changed the nature of the services they provide. In addition to placing reservations and accepting payments, agents can now handle the advance assignment of seats, request special accommodations for a client, and keep track of the number of miles a passenger has flown during the course of a year—all through an information system. Furthermore, a traveler's preferences in automobiles, hotels, and special services are entered into the computer network as part of that traveler's personal profile. Personal travel is much easier today . . . and we take it for granted.

information technology (IT)
A term used to refer to a wide variety of items and abilities used in the creation, storage, and dispersal of data and information. Its three main components are computers, communications networks, and know-how.

data
Raw facts, figures, and details.

information
An organized, meaningful, and useful interpretation of data.

knowledge
An awareness and understanding of a set of information and how that information can be put to the best use.

What Is Information Technology?

By now, you probably have a good idea of what the term *information technology* means, but a formal definition should be helpful. **Information technology** refers to a wide variety of items and abilities used in the creation, storage, and dispersal of data and information as well as in the creation of knowledge. **Data** are raw facts, figures, and details. **Information** refers to an organized, meaningful, and useful interpretation of data, while **knowledge** is the awareness and understanding of a set of information and how that information can be put to the best use.

A simple example will clarify these distinctions. At a retail store, a specific customer order identifies the customer, the item(s) the customer purchased and in what quantity, and the price. These details are the raw data. At the end of a business period, the details of all customer orders are assembled, summarized, and compared with expected orders. This information tells managers whether the store's performance is better or worse than anticipated. This information may be combined with another set of information to create the knowledge that some customers are shopping at another store because of the competitor's new low-price

AT THE TRAVEL OR TICKET AGENT'S OFFICE
Maintain profile
of customers indicating
seating and dietary requirements,
payment details, and
frequent flier number

AT THE HOTEL, RESORT, OR CONVENTION CENTER
Maintain list of traveler's preferences
(pillow type, size of bed, smoking/
nonsmoking) and payment
details; provide automatic
baggage handling to and from airport

EMBEDDED INFORMATION TECHNOLOGY

AT THE AIRPORT
Ease passenger check-in and
baggage handling, purchase of
duty-free goods, and receipt of
messages; order on-board
services (such as in-flight
movies, music and
entertainment package);
allow self-service check-in

ON THE AIRCRAFT
Use telephone and fax, notebook computers,
and information services such as
investment databases

AT THE AUTO RENTAL AGENCY
Maintain list of client's preferred
automobile size, color, and
features; provide routing directions and maps, entertainment,
meal and lodging coupons based
on destination; allow automatic
or self-service check-in

FIGURE 1.2 *Embedded IT in Personal Travel*
The travel industry has used IT to increase the number and quality of the services it offers.

Bell Atlantic

At Bell Atlantic, Dialing 411 Gets Directory Assistance by Computer

At Bell Atlantic, the 411 directory assistance operator who answers your information requests may be a computer. This automated system—which will soon be introduced at other telephone companies—was developed to reduce the cost to both directory assistance callers and Bell Atlantic. Relying on computer speech technology to answer the 2 million daily information calls, the system asks the caller for the name and city and state of residence of the person or company whose number is being requested, and then hands the call over to an operator, who looks up the number.

Bell Atlantic's call-processing system detects and filters out the inevitable "ahs" and "ums" accompanying caller requests. It also knows to wait if the caller pauses or hesitates. But if the pause is too long, it will hand the caller over to an operator, who can provide needed assistance.

This system eliminates several seconds from every information request—a substantial time savings considering the large number of directory assistance calls the company receives every day.

program. This knowledge may cause the store's managers to change their pricing strategy. We'll see many examples throughout this book of the role good information can play in improving a business's performance.

Data and information are processed by information technology components. As Figure 1.3 shows, information technology comprises three primary components: computers, communication networks, and know-how. Combining these components in certain ways creates opportunities to be productive, effective, and successful.

FIGURE 1.3
The Forces of Information Technology
The three components of information technology are inseparable. Computers and communications are of little use without know-how.

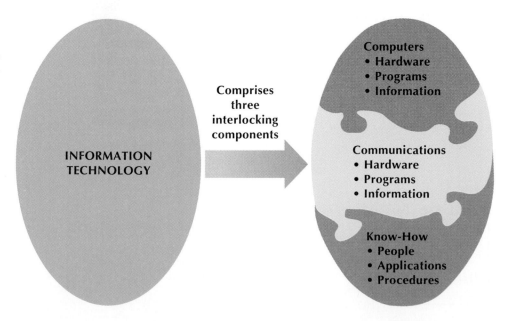

Computers

A **computer** is any electronic system that can be instructed to accept, process, store, and present data and information. The computer is now ubiquitous in the daily lives of many people around the globe. In fact, it is difficult to think of *any* field that does not involve or is not affected by computers.

Computers don't always look the way you think they should. An automated teller machine (ATM), for instance, may not fit your image of a computer. But this cash dispenser is a computer, and it is connected to a bigger one. The microwave and the self-focusing camera also are (or use) small computers.

Computers come in four sizes: microcomputers, midrange/minicomputers, mainframes, and supercomputers.

computer
An electronic system that can be instructed to accept, process, store, and present data and information.

MICROCOMPUTERS. The **microcomputer** (often called a **personal computer** or a **PC**) is the most common type of computer. Relatively compact, it is often found on a tabletop or desktop. Six common types of microcomputers are illustrated in Figure 1.4. Brand names that may be familiar to you are IBM, Apple, Compaq, Dell, Hewlett-Packard, Gateway, NEC, Zenith, Group Bull, and Toshiba—all sold around the world. If you do not know microcomputers by name, you probably know them by what they do: word processing, electronic

microcomputer/ personal computer/PC
A computer that is relatively compact and usually found on a table or desktop.

FIGURE 1.4 *Six Types of Microcomputer*

At one time, most microcomputers were found on desks or tabletops, but in the last decade, there has been an explosion of handheld and portable—sometimes even wearable—micros.

a) Hewlett-Packard desktop microcomputer with color monitor and printer.

b) IBM Thinkpad notebook computer.

c) Apple Macintosh Powerbook 170 laptop computer.

d) Hewlett-Packard palmtop computer.

e) Grid Systems Corp. pen-based laptop computer.

f) Apple Newton Message Pad.

spreadsheets, desktop publishing, account balancing, management of personal and business finances, creation of visuals for use in presentations, sending and receiving messages over an electronic mail system . . . the list goes on.

The Apple Macintosh microcomputer occupies a special place in computer history. Before the advent of the Mac, people had to enter command words to use a computer. The Mac was the first microcomputer to feature graphic means of interacting with computers. By pointing a device called a *mouse* at an *icon*—a graphical picture on the computer screen representing the desired command— and clicking the mouse, the user can execute a command.

The Macintosh was also the first microcomputer to divide the display screen into windows. Each *window* is a section of the display screen that shows a program in use. One or several windows can be open—that is, appear—on the screen at the same time. The entire computer industry is now adopting both the "point-and-click" graphical format and the windows capabilities introduced by the Macintosh. (*Note:* The term *microcomputer* in this book always refers to both IBM-compatible and Apple Macintosh microcomputers.)

notebook computer, laptop computer
Smaller versions of microcomputers that are designed for portability. All of their components, except a printer, are included in a single unit.

Notebook computers and **laptop computers** are small versions of microcomputers (about the size of this textbook) designed for portability. People can easily carry these PCs wherever they go. Unlike desktop PCs, which may have detachable components, notebooks and laptops include all their components (except a printer) in a single unit.

palmtop computer
The smallest and most portable computer, typically used for a limited number of functions, such as maintaining a personal calendar or address file.

The **palmtop computer,** a quite recent version of the microcomputer, is growing in popularity. About the size of a pocket calculator, the palmtop is the smallest and most portable computer yet made. Palmtops are used today for only a small number of functions, such as maintaining personal calendars, name-and-address files, and electronic worksheets. But PC designers are building more and more power into these devices, so it may not be long before they are an essential tool carried in every knapsack, book bag, or briefcase.

pen-based computer
A tabletlike computer controlled with a special pen.

Pen-based computers are tabletlike devices with computer capabilities. As their name suggests, they are controlled with a special pen. Touching the pen to a position on the screen is similar to checking a box on a form. In other forms of pen-based computing, handwriting and drawings can be sensed and worked on by the computer.

personal digital assistant (PDA)
A portable computer generally used as a personal aid.

Pen-based computers are used in many situations in which information must be recorded in a standardized form. For example, law enforcement authorities use them to write electronic tickets for traffic violations, and insurance agents prepare damage claims on the spot by sketching details of the scene on the screen.

midrange computer/ minicomputer
A computer used to interconnect people and large sets of information. More powerful than a microcomputer, the minicomputer is usually dedicated to performing specific functions.

Another new type of microcomputer, the **personal digital assistant (PDA),** is small enough to be carried anywhere. Most PDAs have a pen-based capability. Even though they weigh less than a pound (454 grams), they are fast and powerful. PDAs allow you to sketch ideas on the screen and jot down notes during a meeting. If you want to send a fax to someone, the PDA will retrieve the person's telephone number, dial it, and send the fax over the telephone line to which it is connected.

mainframe
Larger, faster, and more expensive than a midrange computer, this computer is used for several purposes simultaneously.

Like the other types of microcomputers, the PDA is a *personal* aid. It can provide substantial benefits to individuals who need to maintain up-to-the-minute meeting schedules and "to do" lists.

MIDRANGE/MINICOMPUTERS AND MAINFRAMES.   The computers most often associated with business, especially large business, are **midrange computers** (also called **minicomputers**) and **mainframes.** These types of computers interconnect

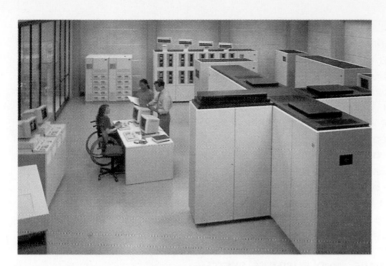

FIGURE 1.5
IBM ES/9000 Mainframe
In a mainframe computer room, cables and cooling lines are mounted below the floor. Operators sit at a workstation with a monitor and a keyboard.

people and large sets of information. The interconnection may be on an enterprise level—that is, across the many organizations or departments of an entire organization—or at the department level.

Mainframe computers (Figure 1.5) are generally larger, more expensive, and faster than midrange computers and permit the interconnection of a greater number of people. Mainframes also typically store larger volumes of data and information.

Midrange/minicomputers (Figure 1.6) are usually dedicated to performing specific functions. For example, midrange computers are used to control complex manufacturing processes or to operate a hotel's reservation system.

One of the great advantages of mainframe systems is that they can be used for several purposes simultaneously. As minicomputers have become faster and more powerful, however, organizations have learned to utilize these specific-function computers to perform activities that once had to be run on a mainframe.

FIGURE 1.6
Digital Equipment Corp.'s VAX 8800 Midrange Computer
The terms *midrange computer* and *minicomputer* are used interchangeably. DEC's VAX series is one of the most successful midrange systems.

SUPERCOMPUTERS.   The most powerful of all computers, supercomputers were designed to solve problems consisting of long and difficult calculations (Figure 1.7). Since they can perform many millions of calculations per second, scientists find them highly useful for predicting weather patterns, preparing models of chemical and biological systems, mapping the surface of planets, and studying the neural network of the brain. Businesses use supercomputers to create and test new processes, machines, and products. Today, for example, when aircraft manufacturers design a new airplane, they use a supercomputer to simulate the wind and weather conditions that planes encounter, and then "fly" the new plane under various simulated conditions before they attempt to build it. All of this happens in the supercomputer. Many automakers also design new vehicles on a supercomputer and then test them by simulating different driving conditions (including accidents) to evaluate the structure and safety of their designs before they invest resources in manufacturing the actual vehicles.

hardware
The computer and its associated equipment.

program
A set of instructions that directs a computer to perform certain tasks and produce certain results.

software
The general term for a set of instructions that controls a computer or communications network.

system
A set of components that interact to accomplish a purpose.

HARDWARE, SOFTWARE, AND BUSINESS SYSTEMS.   Computers and the equipment associated with them—monitors, printers, keyboards, and peripheral devices—are called **hardware.** This hardware can do nothing on its own. Rather, each component must be equipped with a **program** consisting of instructions that tell it how to carry out a particular task or set of tasks. **Software** refers to the instructions that manage the hardware. The computer will not function correctly unless it is properly programmed—that is, unless the software for all of its components is correct.

A **system** is a set of components—people, computers, other businesses, governmental agencies—that interact to accomplish a purpose. Systems are all around us: education systems, transportation systems, inventory systems, for example. And everyone in the world lives according to an economic system—although not the same one.

Any business is also a system (Figure 1.8). Its components—marketing, manufacturing, sales, research, shipping, accounting, and human resources—all work together to create a product or service that benefits customers and therefore the

FIGURE 1.7

Cray 3 Supercomputer
Seymour Cray of Cray Computer Corp. with the Cray 3, one of the most powerful supercomputers in the world. At one time, Cray produced more than half the supercomputers sold worldwide. Future generations of the supercomputer may sit on a desktop.

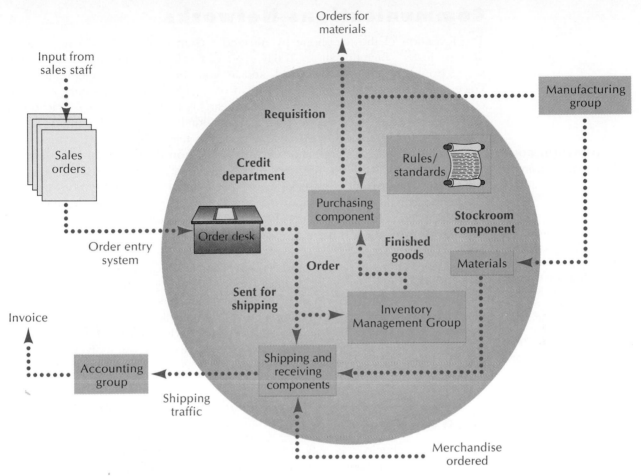

FIGURE 1.8   *A Typical Business System*
A system is a set of components that interact to accomplish a purpose. The business system shown
here includes not only people and departments but also procedures for conducting the business
efficiently.

employees and shareholders of the organization. Each of these components of a
business is itself a system.

Contemporary businesses depend heavily on **information systems,** the systems by which data and information flow from one person or department to
another. Information systems encompass everything from interoffice mail and telephone links to computer and communications systems that generate reports. They
serve all the systems of a business by linking the different components together
so that they work effectively toward the same goal.

information system
A system in which data and
information flow from one
person or department to
another.

Worried about using computers? Don't be. You are undoubtedly using some types of computer, knowingly or unknowingly. Computers may be devices, large or small, that you
use directly, often through a keyboard or touch pad. Or,
the computer may be embedded in another device or appliance. Use the device or appliance and you also use the
computer. ■

Communications Networks

The invention of the telephone by Alexander Graham Bell in 1876 did a great deal to foster communication. Today, you can call someone anywhere in the world from anywhere in the world, and as you speak into the telephone, your voice will reach its destination in less than one second. When the person on the other end of the line talks, you will also hear his or her words in a fraction of a second, whether the voice is coming from Britain, continental Europe, Japan, Russia, South Africa, or any other country across the globe.

An integral part of information technology is **communication**—the sending and receiving of data and information over a communications network. A **communications network** consists of a set of stations at different locations that are interconnected through a medium that enables people to send and receive data and information. Telephone wires and cables are common communications media. **Data communication** is the transmission of data and information through a communications medium.

Communications networks are revolutionizing business products and services as well as our personal lives. Airlines use communications networks to communicate with one another and share information on passenger reservations, meal requirements, and baggage handling. Public networks like America Online, Minitel, CompuServe, Prodigy, the Internet, and the World Wide Web—all of which offer a wide variety of shopping and other types of services—allow individuals to correspond with others electronically through their PCs. You will see many other uses of data communication in the IT practices we'll be examining.

communication

The sending and receiving of data and information over a communications network.

communications network

A set of stations, consisting of hardware, programs, and information, that are linked together as a system that transmits and receives data or information.

data communication

The transmission of data and information through a communications medium.

Know-How

Information technology is only as good as the user's *know-how*. In other words, you have to *know how* to explore and take advantage of the opportunities this technology creates. Information technology **know-how** consists of

know-how

The capability to do something well.

- Familiarity with the tools of IT
- Possession of the skills needed to use these tools
- An understanding of when to use IT to solve a problem or to capitalize on an opportunity

We'll use a simple analogy to demonstrate what this means.

You probably know someone who is a whiz at technical details—maybe concerning cars, sports, electronics, or medicine—but can't put those details into a language and perspective that other people can understand. The whiz is too focused on the technical specifics to see the big picture—the human, day-to-day use of the technology.

Let's say you go to a ballgame with a "technician." He knows who holds all the records; how fast the players run; how often they score; whether they perform better on rainy, sunny, or windy days; and the odds that they will attempt a risky play. But he is so caught up in these details that he loses sight of the game being played. There is a time and a place for statistics, but most fans prefer the company of an expert who knows the fundamentals but doesn't overwhelm them with details.

Like sports fans who concentrate so hard on memorizing stats that they lose sight of the actual game, people who focus too much on the technical details of IT often fail to grasp the big picture. The big picture encompasses what information technology can do today and what it might be able to do tomorrow. It involves knowing when an approach will work *and* when it won't.

Think of IT as you would an automobile. If you're a mechanic, you have to know how to diagnose an engine problem and how to take the engine apart to replace or repair parts. If you're not a mechanic, you don't need to know how to disassemble an engine and put it back together again. All you're interested in is what the automobile will do for you. This could be providing transportation for yourself or your business, or presenting an opportunity to open a store that sells car-care products. Most users of IT are like the people who are not mechanics. They don't need to know the internal workings of IT. All they're interested in is reaping its benefits. And for this, they simply need the know-how to use IT.

The Principles of Information Technology

It is always rewarding to have the right answer to a question. In fact, anticipating questions and identifying answers can be an effective way to solve problems. It is also a method many people use in studying for examinations: They attempt to identify the questions that they'll be asked and then master the answers to those questions. But *what happens when the question has not been anticipated correctly or when it changes?* The known "answer" may no longer apply; in fact, it may be downright counterproductive to solving the problem or answering the new question correctly. This is precisely the danger of focusing on answers exclusively.

The most effective way to learn a subject is to master the basic facts of that subject and to understand the principles underlying those facts. A *principle* is a fundamental rule, guideline, or motivating idea that, when applied to a situation, produces a desirable result. Focusing on principles rather than on a particular situation or set of facts prepares you to deal with a variety of problems and opportunities.

The first principle of information technology describes the purpose of IT: ***Information technology's great usefulness is as an aid in solving problems, unlocking creativity, and making people more effective than they would be if they didn't apply IT to their activities.***

Equally important to the effective application of information technology is the principle of high-tech/high-touch. It says: ***The more "high-tech" the information technology you're considering, the more important it is to consider the "high-touch" aspects of the matter—that is, "the people side."*** A related principle stresses this: ***Always fit information technology to people rather than asking people to adjust to information technology.***

The Functions of Information Technology

What exactly can IT do? As Figure 1.9 shows, IT performs six information-handling functions: capture, processing, generation, storage and retrieval, and transmission. The way these functions are applied determines the impact IT will have.

CAPTURE. It is often useful to compile detailed records of activities. This process, called data **capture,** is performed when it is expected the data will be useful later.

capture
The process of compiling detailed records of activities.

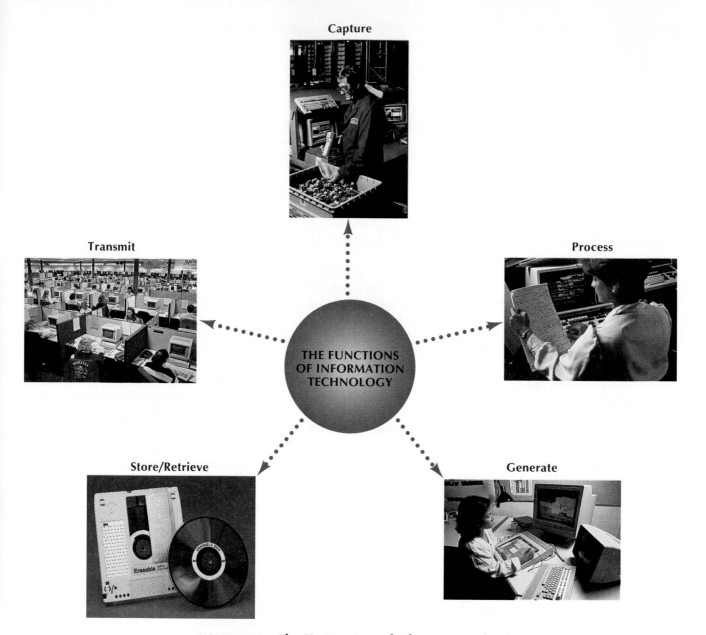

FIGURE 1.9 *The Six Functions of Information Technology*
The six functions of IT—capturing, processing, generating, storing and retrieving, and transmitting—may take place sequentially. In many cases, however, two or more functions take place simultaneously.

Here are some common examples of data capture:

- Whenever a book is checked out of the library, the name (or identification number) of the borrower and the title (or call number) of the book are captured.
- The theater box office records the assignment of every seat to an attendee as it is sold.
- A monitor records the pulse, heart rate, and white blood cell count of a hospital patient.

- When Madonna performs live, her singing is sometimes captured and transferred to a cassette tape or compact disc (CD) for listening at a later time.
- The voice and data recorders in aircraft cockpits capture the pilots' conversations and record flight data about the aircraft's location and performance.

PROCESSING.   The activity most often associated with computers, **processing,** is usually the purpose for which people and organizations purchase computers. The processing function entails converting, analyzing, computing, and synthesizing all forms of data or information.

One of the earliest business applications of computers, **data processing,** focuses on taking data (raw numbers, symbols, and letters) and transforming them into information. An example of data processing is calculating the balance in a checkbook by taking the starting balance for the month, adding all deposits and subtracting all checks written (that is, the data), and determining the current balance.

Information processing is the transformation of any type of information into a different type of information. Text (reports, correspondence), sound (voice, music, tones), and images (visual information such as charts, graphs, drawings, and animated drawings) can all be processed. **Multimedia systems,** which are one type of information processing, have recently captured interest. These systems process multiple types of information simultaneously—for example, an animated presentation displayed on a computer screen will use information retrieved from within the computer, perhaps accompanied by music, voice, or other types of sound.

Other types of processing include these:

- **Word processing**—the creation of text-based documents, including reports, newsletters, and correspondence. Word-processing systems allow people to enter data, text, and images into a computer and transform them into a useful and attractive format.
- **Image processing**—converting visual information (graphics, drawings, and photos) into a format that can be managed within a computer system or transmitted between people and other computers. A process called *scanning* converts a print or film image into a form that a computer can use. (We discuss scanners in Chapter 5.)
- **Voice processing**—the transformation and transmission of spoken information. Currently, voice information is most frequently entered into a computer system through a telephone, but other systems that enable people to speak directly into a computer system to instruct it to take specific actions are emerging.

GENERATION.   Information technology is frequently used to generate information through processing. **Generation** of information refers to the organization of data and information into a useful form, whether as numbers, text, sound, or visual image. Sometimes the information is regenerated in its original form. At other times, a new form is generated—for example, recorded musical notes are "played" as sounds with rhythm and pauses (that is, as music).

STORAGE AND RETRIEVAL.   **Storage** enables computers to keep data and information for later use. Stored data and information are placed on a storage medium (for example, a magnetic disk or CD-ROM optical disk—discussed in Chapter 4) that the computer can read when it needs to. The computer converts the data or

processing
The process of converting, analyzing, computing, and synthesizing all forms of data or information.

data processing
The process of handling data and transforming them into information.

information processing
A general term for the computer activity that entails processing any type of information and transforming it into a different type of information.

multimedia system
A computer system that can process multiple types of information simultaneously.

generation
The process of organizing information into a useful form, whether as numbers, text, sound, or visual image.

storage
The computer process of retaining information for future use.

information into a form that takes less space than the original source. For example, voice information is not stored in voice format, but rather in a specially coded electronic form that takes less space and that the computer can manage.

Retrieval entails locating and copying stored data or information for further processing or for transmission to another user. The computer user must keep track of the medium where the data or information is stored and make it available to the computer for processing.

retrieval
The process by which a computer locates and copies stored data or information for further processing or for transmission to another user.

transmission
The computer process of distributing information over a communications network.

TRANSMISSION.   Sending data and information from one location to another is called **transmission.** As noted earlier, telephone systems transmit our conversations from a point of origin to a destination. Computer systems do precisely the same thing, often using telephone lines. Computer networks can also send data and information through other media, including satellites and light beams transmitted along plastic or glass optical fibers. The *Information Technology in Practice* feature entitled "Japan's AUCNET Electronic Market" illustrates how the ability to transmit information can change the way dealers buy and sell some types of automobiles.

Modern communications networks enable us to send information down the hall or around the world in an instant. PCs, mainframes, and supercomputers can be connected electronically to transmit data and information to and from one another, using the network to overcome distance barriers.

There are two common forms of information transmission:

- **Electronic mail** (known as **e-mail**)—the acceptance, storage, and transmission of text and image messages between users of a computer system. Typically, e-mail messages are entered through a computer keyboard and viewed on the receiving party's computer monitor (eliminating the need for sending paper messages). E-mail messages can be sent between individuals or broadcast to a large number of people simultaneously.
- **Voice messaging** (sometimes called **voice mail**)—a form of voice processing in which callers leave spoken messages entered through their telephone receiver. The voice information is transmitted, stored, and retrieved ("played") by the recipients.

THE SIX IT FUNCTIONS AT WORK: THE U.S. EXPORT BUREAU.   Before a company can sell and ship its products outside the United States, it must obtain a federal license to do so. The United States Bureau of Export Administration processes more than 130,000 export license applications annually. Information technology is at the center of the Bureau's operations. Rapid access to the information contained in the application is essential to the quick approval U.S. companies need to compete successfully against exporting firms in other countries.

The approval process works like this: The authorization request, consisting of information identifying the exporting company, its customer(s), and the nature of the goods it intends to export, is submitted to the Bureau either in written form (on paper) or electronically over a communications network. This information is stored in the Bureau's computer in its Washington, D.C., office. Within two weeks, one of the Bureau's 500 export agents in Washington reviews the details of the application on a computer display screen and determines whether to grant export authorization. If all application information is complete and correct and the export is a permissible one, authorization is granted. Written approval is sent to the applicants who applied in writing, and electronic approval is transmitted to those who applied over the Bureau's communications network. However, the process does not end there. Periodically, export agents randomly select export authorizations and perform an audit on the company to determine if all of the statements it made during the application process were accurate and complete.

This example illustrates the six functions of information technology:

- **Capture.** Incoming documents are accepted either electronically over the Bureau's communications network or in the form of paper documents that are captured electronically (scanned) for storage in the Bureau's computer.
- **Processing.** The details of pending applications are highlighted on a video display screen for review by agents. After applications are approved, the Bureau audits randomly selected applications. All of this is processing.
- **Generation.** Notices of approval or disapproval, as well as requests to audit company records, are generated by the Bureau's system.
- **Storage and retrieval.** All applications are stored and can be retrieved for display on the reviewing agent's video display screen. After review, details of approval or disapproval are stored with the initial application.
- **Transmission.** Exporters can electronically transmit their applications via a network to the Bureau and, after an agent has reviewed their application, can receive an electronically transmitted notice of approval or disapproval.

The Benefits of Information Technology

Computers linked through communications systems offer four major personal and business benefits to users: speed, consistency, precision, and reliability (Figure 1.10).

SPEED. "Split-second thinking" is an ability we admire in others and would like to have ourselves. What exactly is split-second thinking? Clearly, the term implies *speed*—if a ball bounces in front of the car you're driving, you step on the brake pedal instantly to avoid hitting the child you suspect is chasing after the ball. You have only a fraction of a second to decide on and take the proper action. That's split-second thinking. Most tasks, however, take even the quickest thinkers longer than a split second. For instance, no one can write a sentence or add a list of 15 deposits and withdrawals from his or her checking account in a split second.

Computers, on the other hand, do *everything* in fractions of seconds. They are very much faster than people could ever hope to be at a myriad of tasks. They

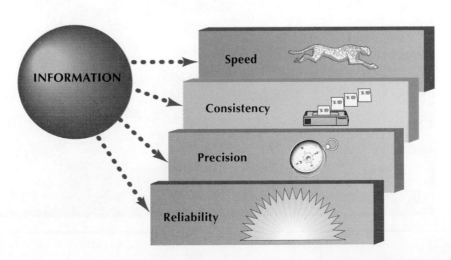

FIGURE 1.10
The Benefits of Information Technology

INFORMATION TECHNOLOGY IN PRACTICE

Japan's AUCNET Electronic Market

It's not a video game, but it blinks and beeps like one. The system has a color display screen and a joystick for controlling movement on the screen. It connects to a satellite network to send and receive color images, video, sound, and text. But instead of playing video games, AUCNET is used for buying and selling used cars in Japan.

In Japan, where traditions endure for centuries, there are two fixed traditions in the auto industry. One is selling autos door-to-door. The other is selling used cars through auction, where the price is determined by the buyers, not the sellers. AUCNET was created to introduce information technology into this public bidding process and to capitalize on a business opportunity.

AUCNET is an electronic network linking thousands of car dealers throughout Japan to create an Information Age electronic market for selling used cars. Unlike in traditional auctions, neither buyer, seller, nor car need be at the same location. Because AUCNET relies on a satellite link, the buyers and sellers can be anywhere in Japan.

Founded in 1984 by Masataka Fujisaki, owner of businesses in both the auto and computer software industries, AUCNET began as a system in which photographs of cars were stored on video disks and the disks then shipped to participating dealers, where they were used along with computer and communications technology in weekend auctions. Through the bidding process conducted over the network, a price was agreed on and the terms of sale arranged.

Initially, Japan's used-car dealers' association resisted AUCNET because it was feared the system would undermine local auction exchanges. However, AUCNET quickly demonstrated the viability of electronic markets. Seeing the new opportunities offered by the network, more than 500 Japanese dealers signed up right away, and the dealers' association was forced to recognize that AUCNET was a permanent fact of life. Membership has grown dramatically since the mid-1980s.

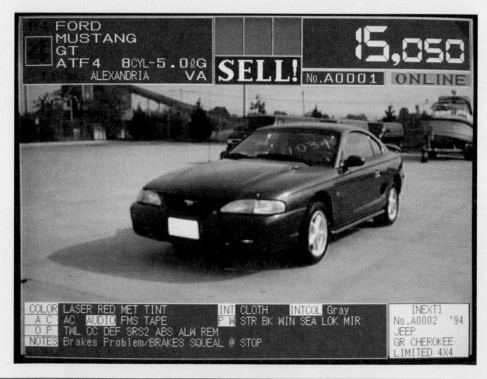

In 1989, Fujisaki decided to hook up to Japan's first commercial communication satellite. Today, photographic images of used cars, together with descriptive details and inspection information (certifying the car's condition), are instantly sent from AUC-NET's headquarters directly to the display screens of all participants in the network. From their computer displays, more than 5,000 used-car dealers throughout Japan participate in the regular weekend auctions in which several thousand automobiles are sold. A typical bid process and sale takes less than 30 seconds, even though the participants are hundreds of miles apart. Moreover, both buyer and seller find the bid prices to be fair, another factor attesting to the public's respect for the quality and value of vehicles bought and sold this way.

There are several keys to AUCNET's success:

- High-quality displays show photographs of the vehicles for sale, which is important to Japanese buyers, who are much more concerned than American buyers about a vehicle's appearance and more likely to reject cars with nicks, scratches, or dents.
- Detailed descriptions of the vehicle's condition and maintenance history are offered.
- The ratings of certified inspectors, who use rigorous inspection and evaluation standards to rate used cars on a 1-to-10 quality scale, are provided. This information is essential to creating the trust necessary to get people to buy and sell in an electronic, rather than a face-to-face, market.
- The system offers a communications network that is fast, reliable, and accessible to participating dealers anywhere in Japan.
- It's easy to use.

AUCNET is expanding at a rapid rate. Fujisaki launched an auction network for buying and selling motorcycles, a very important means of transportation in Japan, and ever-popular cut flowers. In 1994, AUCNET expanded to the United States, where Fujisaki patented his system for the electronic auctioning of used cars.

can perform complex calculations, recall stored information, transmit information from one location to another, and move objects around a computer screen almost instantaneously.

CONSISTENCY. People often have difficulty repeating their actions exactly. Indeed, doing something once is not nearly as difficult as doing it the same way, and with the same result, repeatedly.

Computers excel at repeating actions *consistently*. Whether running a spell checker built into a work processor or playing multimedia animation for training purposes, a computer will carry out the activity the same way every time.

PRECISION. In addition to being fast and consistent, computers are extremely *precise*. They can detect minute differences that people cannot see. In manufacturing an automobile, for example, the precise placement of a part, as directed by a computer, may make the difference between long use and early wear. Computers excel in managing the smallest differences . . . in being precise.

RELIABILITY. With speed, consistency, and precision come reliability. When you know that the same procedure will be followed, rapidly, consistently, and precisely, you can expect *reliability of results*—that is, you can depend on getting the same result again and again. You can also count on computers and communications networks to be available and properly functioning when you need them—which is another kind of reliability, *reliability of use*.

In general, computers are very reliable. Many personal computers have never needed a service call. Communications networks are also very reliable and generally available whenever needed. You are seldom unable to use your telephone because the public telephone network is out of service. Usually, phone service is disrupted only when a bad storm has downed a line in your area or when power lines have been damaged by workers.

IT at Work: Caterpillar's Virtual Reality

Caterpillar, Inc., of Peoria, Illinois, is the world's leading manufacturer of the giant earthmoving equipment used in road building, digging, and construction. The firm designs and builds equipment in today's Information Age very differently from the way it did in the Industrial Age. Today, Caterpillar test-drives its machines *before* it builds them—an advantage made possible by virtual reality.

Virtual reality is the illusion of reality created by a computer. In Caterpillar's case, a supercomputer controls the projection of 3-D images on the four walls within a simulator—a 10-by-10-foot sound cave—and a high-quality sound system carries the noises created by the actions and motions of a mockup of a newly designed piece of equipment.

This is the system Caterpillar uses as a proving ground for all its new equipment designs. A mockup of the new machine (see Figure 1.11) is created on a screen displaying full-size images of the earthmover's frame, body, engine, shovel or blade, and hydraulic lines. Images of gauges and dials are shown on the dashboard, just as they will appear when the machine is built. The virtual roads, trees, buildings, people, and vehicles surrounding the earthmover are visible through the machine's window. From the operator's seat, the driver can turn the steering wheel and manipulate the levers to guide the machine ahead, backwards, or sideways

FIGURE 1.11
Virtual reality testing has enabled Caterpillar to build equipment that is easier to use, with just the right features to do the intended job.

as it moves the earth. As the driver turns the steering wheel, the machine also turns. Changes in direction and speed are visible through the window as buildings, trees, and people appear nearer or more distant. The sounds of the powerful engine and the people around the vehicle, as well as sounds of moving rock, dirt, and sand, are clearly audible. The driver can stand up in the operator's compartment and move over to look out the windows.

Unlike the more popular virtual reality systems you may be familiar with, including those used with arcade games, no helmet, visor, or special gloves are needed to create the illusion, though lightweight glasses worn by the driver do enhance the images and ensure the proper perception of depth and dimension.

Virtual reality testing has enabled Caterpillar to build equipment that is easier to use, with just the right features to do the intended job. The ability to test designs this way before the equipment is built has helped Caterpillar maintain its position as the largest builder of earthmoving equipment in the world, even in the face of some very tough foreign competition.

Caterpillar's virtual reality story demonstrates the four benefits of information technology:

- **Speed.** Each action by the driver of the virtual earthmoving machine is sensed immediately and in a split second converted into motion that is displayed on the driver's screen. Since human senses can detect even an instant's delay, anything less than instant response would result in a contrived look and feel.
- **Precision.** Each time a lever, button, shift, or wheel is moved, the direction, length, and speed of the movement is detected and the exact result computed and communicated to the visual display.
- **Consistency.** Identical motions and instructions from the driver trigger the same actions by the system every time.
- **Reliability.** Caterpillar can count on the availability of the virtual reality development system and on its ability to produce proper and accurate results.

 You have probably heard some lurid stories about computer failures—maybe even told a few yourself. Remember, though, it's important to distinguish between the inability to get the results you want from the computer and the failure of the computer (or the network) itself.

Early in the computer era, the failure rate of computers was high because the components used in the systems burned out after only a few hours of use. Today, however, we have extremely reliable computers and communications networks that operate for years without a hitch. Some systems—called *fail-safe* or *nonstop systems*—even include duplicate components, so that if one component malfunctions, the other will take over to keep the computer running.

Consider this example. How often has the National Aeronautics and Space Administration (NASA) failed to bring back a space shuttle because a computer system failed? Despite many days of flight under the most grueling conditions in outer space, the shuttles almost always return on time.

Nonetheless, computers are not perfect. Computers and networks on some university campuses fail more often than others do. Generally, the cause of failure is excessive use. Because they are called upon to process a heavier load than anticipated when they were designed and implemented, the systems become overloaded and break down. ▓

The Opportunities for Information Technology

IT provides many opportunities to help people and to solve problems.

HELPING PEOPLE.   "How can I be more effective? More productive? More creative?" Asking these kinds of questions regularly will challenge you to perform at your best and fulfill your potential.

Other questions focus your attention outward: "How can I help other people? How can I work toward providing affordable health care to all and jobs to all those who want them? How can I help to safeguard the environment, protecting the air, water, and land from pollution and saving endangered species from extinction? How can my business improve the society in which I live?" These are questions of tremendous importance and challenging complexity. The *Information Technology in Practice* feature entitled "IT Opens New Doors for People with Disabilities" will give you some idea of the difference information technology has made in the lives of disabled people.

This book will shed light on IT's potential role in improving society. It will also describe many opportunities to use IT to assist people both in their personal lives and in their careers.

problem
A perceived difference between an existing condition and a desired condition.

problem solving
The process of recognizing a problem, identifying alternatives for solving it, and successfully implementing the chosen solution.

SOLVING PROBLEMS.   A **problem** is the perceived difference between an existing condition and a desired condition—for example, the study time you wish you had to prepare for an exam and the time you actually have to prepare. Problems can be as dramatic as accidents that cause serious harm or as mundane as traffic hassles. Dramatic or mundane, all problems can be challenging.

Problem solving is recognizing a problem, identifying alternatives for solving it, and successfully implementing the chosen solution. Information technology presents many opportunities to help people identify and solve problems. Using a word-processing program to prepare term papers and a spreadsheet program to analyze financial cases may help you solve a study-time problem, for example, because these programs enable you to accomplish more in a given amount of time. We will examine the problem-solving process in detail in Chapters 6, 7, 9, and 12.

Problems are usually perceived as causing trouble, harm, even destruction. But there is a brighter side to problems: they often create opportunities. Out of a difficult situation arises the chance to formulate innovative ways of dealing with the difficulty—to do something new, different, and better. In the business world, successful executives see problems as opportunities to create a distinct advantage in a product or service.

At one time, all automobile fenders rusted eventually and doors dented easily and stayed that way unless the car's owner undertook expensive repairs. These problems were seen as opportunities by the innovators of fiberglass fenders (which do not rust) and high-impact plastic for auto bodies (the kind in which a dent immediately pops back out).

Or take the problem of automobile tire wear. Many people are too busy to notice when the tread on their tires is worn down—a problem. Opportunity— tire manufacturers are developing technology that involves inserting into a new tire a microprocessor that senses wear and signals the driver it is time to replace the tire. Thus, the problem of unnoticed worn tires turned out to be an opportunity to develop a new product: smart tires.

Because we are surrounded by a seemingly endless stream of problems, we are also in the midst of an unending series of opportunities. ▪

Information Technology Is All Around Us, Improving Our Lives

Information technology is everywhere. Here are some ways in which IT touches on and improves our lives every day—though we are usually not aware of it (Figure 1.12).

TELEVISION.   ABC, CBS, NBC, and FOX in the United States; CNN around the world; the BBC in Britain; and TF TV in France all rely heavily on graphics and animation to illustrate weather patterns, present sports results, and report the news. These graphics are produced on power microcomputers. Whether they are showing the movement of storm clouds across a region or the results of a public opinion poll, graphics grab our attention in a way words might not.

SHIPPING.   Couriers and package carriers around the world rely on information technology. DHL, TNT, Airborne Express, Federal Express, and United Parcel Service use computer systems to keep track of every package they pick up and deliver. Their worldwide communications networks allow them to determine instantly the origin, current location, and destination of a package.

PAPERWORK.   Despite early predictions, the age of the paperless office is not yet upon us. Most businesses still send, receive, and store huge quantities of paper. Some, however, are taking steps to lighten their paper load. For example,

a) Stock trading is no longer done only on the trading room floor. The London Stock Market's "Big Bang" system allows stockbrokers to do all their trading electronically, through PCs and computer workstations.

b) Airlines around the world, including American, British Airways, and Lufthansa, use computer-controlled training systems to duplicate the interior of a cockpit and to simulate conditions identical to those that occur during real flights.

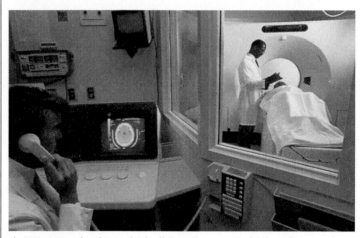

c) CAT scan technology, which allows physicians to look under a patient's skin without performing surgery, has become an important weapon in early cancer detection.

d) Robots used in manufacturing facilities throughout the world perform monotonous tasks tirelessly and precisely.

FIGURE 1.12   *The Uses of Information Technology in Business*

whenever any correspondence about policies, claims, or premiums arrives at Texas-based USAA Insurance's mailroom, the sheets of paper are entered directly into the company's computer system using a scanner. An electronic image of the correspondence can then be seen on the desktop display screen of any customer service agent (CSA) connected to the company's data communications network.

INFORMATION TECHNOLOGY IN PRACTICE

IT Opens New Doors for People with Disabilities

Illinois Bell   Like other Illinois Bell employees, financial strategist Dorsey Ruley uses a computer workstation to retrieve electronic mail, write and send messages, and order printouts of work. The only difference is that Ruley is a quadriplegic—one of the many workers with disabilities who are using adaptive information technology to lead more productive lives.

In Ruley's case, the information technology takes the form of a voice-recognition system, a combination of hardware and software that lets him direct the computer by speaking into a headset rather than by typing on a keyboard or clicking a mouse. Ruley trained the system to recognize his voice by pronouncing several hundred words into the headset. The system memorized those words, and will continue to memorize any new words he uses, up to about 35,000 words.

Another type of keyboard replacement uses special switches that respond to eye or tongue movements. A sip-and-puff device, which looks like a wheelchair-mounted straw, is one example. Other types of adaptive technologies include

- Monitor enhancements, such as magnification software that produces large-type screen displays for users with limited vision.
- Voice-output systems, software and hardware devices that read text and screen displays out loud.
- Keyboard enhancements, such as Braille keyboards and overlays that help workers keep their hands centered on the keyboard.
- Augmented communication technologies, such as devices that translate screen prompts and other visual displays into audio signals for the visually impaired and devices that translate audio signals into visual displays for people who are hearing and speech impaired.

Prices for adaptive technology devices, which range from less than $100 for a specialized keyboard to about $5,000 for Ruley's voice-recognition system, continue to drop in the face of technical advances and increased demand. Without this kind of technology, many disabled people would have much poorer lifestyles. With it, they can work in almost every field, ranging from word processing to computer programming, law, and counseling.

Specially equipped personal computer technology has allowed Marilyn Hoggatt to begin work as a part-time facilities administrator at Northeastern State University in Tahlequah, Oklahoma. Hoggatt says: "The [wheel]chair is my legs, the computer is my hands."

When a customer telephones with an inquiry, the CSA can display the previous correspondence on the workstation simply by punching a few buttons. Several CSAs can display an image of the same correspondence simultaneously. The result is quicker service for the customer and less paper for the company.

MONEY AND INVESTMENTS. Stock markets around the world are in transition. On some trading floors, paper is disappearing. In fact, the trading floor itself is disappearing in some places. The London Stock Market launched a system known as "Big Bang" that makes it possible for stockbrokers to do all their trading electronically (Figure 1.12a). Brokers interconnected through a data communications network submit and receive bids using their PCs and computer workstations. Electronic trading will displace floor trading at investment markets around the world in the near future.

AGRICULTURE. Several chemical and fertilizer companies now offer a planning service that combines their expertise in agriculture with effective use of information technology. Company advisors employ sophisticated computer programs to help farmers analyze alternative uses for their land. These programs evaluate different planting and fertilizing strategies while estimating crop sensitivity to rain and other environmental conditions. Each strategy can be analyzed to determine which will yield the most desirable results in terms of productivity and profits.

TAXATION AND ACCOUNTING. People don't like to pay taxes, and they don't like filling out forms either. Nothing can be done about the first dislike, but the Internal Revenue Service (IRS) has installed a system that allows people to file their federal tax returns electronically using the PC in their home or office. Use of the electronic filing service has grown substantially every year since its inception in 1989.

Some pioneering public accounting firms have developed the capability to file IRS tax returns electronically. H&R Block was the first to combine the IRS electronic filing process with its own Rapid Refund program. The happy result: Block's customers can receive a refund the same day they file their return.

EDUCATION. IBM Corp., the largest computer company in the world, distributes multilingual computer packages for use in the countries in which it does business. These packages, called "Write to Read" and "Exploring Measurement, Time, and Money," help young and old to acquire basic skills in reading and math. Microcomputers present the information in forms tailored to the student's needs and keep track of his or her progress.

TRAINING. Some companies are using information technology in their employee training programs. For instance, insurance adjusters in training at State Farm Insurance can view damage scenes (automobile accidents or natural disasters) on a computer display screen. The screen allows them to scrutinize photographs and images of the damage from any direction to estimate the extent of the repairs needed. Interacting with the computer, the trainees ask questions and retrieve information about the damage. They get answers only to the questions they ask, however. At the end of the training session, the trainees receive suggestions about other questions they should have asked and further views of the damage they should have checked to produce a more accurate analysis.

Lufthansa, SwissAir, JAL, British Airways, SAS, American, Delta, United, and other airlines around the world conduct pilot training through flight simulators (Figure 1.12b). These computer-controlled training systems duplicate the cockpit of a plane and simulate conditions pilots encounter during real flights. They allow pilots to practice corrective actions under simulated emergency conditions they hope they will never have to face in the air.

THE HOME. France Télécom, the French telephone company, stopped handing out telephone directories to its customers several years ago. Instead, it gives them computer terminals connected to a communications network. Today, Minitel, as the network service is called, has become a major vehicle for obtaining a wide variety of goods and services: airline reservations, theater tickets—and telephone numbers. Minitel is available to every household in France and is included free with telephone installation. The service is so successful that France Télécom now exports a version of Minitel to Europe and North America.

HEALTH AND MEDICINE. It will come as no surprise that hospitals and clinics use computers to keep records and generate invoices. They also use computers to diagnose and treat patients' problems. For example, the CAT scanner is an imaging device that enables physicians to look beneath the patient's skin (Figure 1.12c). As the scanner passes over the patient, it displays an image of bone and tissue structures on a computer screen. The CAT scanner has become invaluable in identifying cancer and other conditions that benefit from early treatment.

MANUFACTURING. Robots have moved from the realm of science fiction to the factory floor over the last few decades. Automobiles made around the world, whether by Daimler-Benz, Peugeot, Ford, GM, Chrysler, Honda, or Toyota, are touched by robots at some point in the manufacturing process (Figure 1.12d). Robots do the monotonous jobs that people don't want, such as spraying paint and welding seams.

JOURNALISM. Reporters and journalists rely heavily on word processors to prepare news articles and write their columns. Few use typewriters anymore. The graphics people who design the illustrations that accompany the text also use computers. At the offices of *USA Today,* the national U.S. newspaper sold throughout North America, Europe, and the Middle East, charts and graphs are produced on a PC that uses a special illustrator software program. Computer stores make this package (Adobe Freehand) available to anyone for only a few hundred dollars.

ENERGY. A gas pump that accepts credit cards is operating in France and the United States today and is coming soon to other countries. To use it, you just place your credit card in the automated pump's reader and your vehicle begins fueling up. The pump's built-in computer notes the cost of the fuel pumped, transmits the details of the transaction over communications lines to your bank or credit card agency, and prints a receipt for you. You never have to wait for an attendant or go into the station. Automated gas pumps don't reduce the amount of fuel your vehicle consumes, but they do reduce the time and energy you burn in fueling up.

Large office buildings consume huge quantities of energy in both summer and winter. Thanks to information technology, this energy usage is better managed than ever before. Using a system of thermostats and sensors interconnected through a communications network, a computer constantly monitors temperatures around the clock, controlling heating and cooling devices to maintain the pre-specified comfort level. At the end of the workday and on weekends, the system automatically adjusts the temperature, thus conserving additional energy. Some systems can also determine when a room is no longer occupied, and shut off lights.

SPORTS.   Auto racing draws enthusiasts around the world. In all the auto circuits, including Formula 1, Indianapolis, IMSA, and NASCAR, computers are an integral part of race cars and a central element in racing strategy. Today's race cars are fitted with on-board computers and communications capabilities. Data regarding rate of fuel use, engine functions, braking patterns, and speed are monitored, displayed in the driver cockpit, and transmitted from the race car to the crew in the pits. These data provide information that can influence racing strategy and determine whether a team wins or loses.

The Responsibilities of Using Information Technology

Implicit in using IT are three fundamental responsibilities:

- **To be informed.** Users have to know how computers and networks can be applied in different situations and the capabilities and limitations of IT in those situations.
- **To make proper use of IT.** Users need to take responsibility for employing IT in desirable and ethical ways that help people and do not infringe on their privacy, rights, or well-being.
- **To safeguard.** Users must take responsibility for protecting data and information that are in a computer or transmitted over a network against intentional or accidental damage or loss. They also need to guard against the failure of all processes that rely on information technology.

An important principle follows from these responsibilities: ***People who use information technology have the obligation to consider both the upside and the downside of introducing IT into any situation.***

The Career Side of Information Technology

Some careers demand a detailed knowledge of the intricacies of computers and communication systems. Most business careers, however, require only a good understanding of what can and cannot be done with IT and what should not be done with it.

Information Technology as a Career

Careers in the technical side of information technology span the gamut from writing computer programs and installing hardware to determining users' needs. We'll examine these roles in Chapter 2. Already the demand for information technology

Ernst & Young's Hot-Desking Nomads

Ernst & Young

In Chicago, Ernst & Young's consultants book small offices when they are in the company building. When they leave for the day, they take all their belongings with them because the office will be assigned to someone else the next working day. The practice of assigning a different temporary office to certain employees every day they come in is known as *hot-desking*.

Ernst & Young's consultants, like most people in most consulting, sales, and customer service companies, spend at least 70 percent of their time in the field. Since computer and communications systems allow them to stay in touch with headquarters and with their customers, the company's managing partners decided that setting aside an office for every single consultant was an unnecessary cost of doing business.

Permanent offices may soon be an anachronism in companies whose employees spend most of their time in the field.

specialists is substantial throughout the world, and it is growing rapidly. In many countries, there is a severe shortage of IT professionals. In the United Kingdom, for example, the shortage of people with IT skills may force British companies to relocate in countries where such specialists are available. As one business manager said in a conversation with the author, "Companies can now base themselves wherever in the world the relevant IT skills are and use international networks to transmit data from there."

As in other fields, good "people skills" and the ability to communicate ideas effectively are critical ingredients for success in the field of information technology.

Information Technology as an Aid to Your Career

Information technology can help you in whatever career you pursue. Knowing how IT is used in organizations, acquiring demonstrable IT skills, and being able to list your IT accomplishments on your résumé will give you a solid advantage when you are competing for a job. So be sure to learn how to use a PC, do word processing, solve problems on a PC, and communicate electronically. In business as well as in the arts, the sciences, education, medicine, law, and government, information technology—computers, communications networks, and know-how—is an essential tool.

You don't have to wait until you start your career to begin using information technology. You can start right now.

SUMMARY OF LEARNING OBJECTIVES

1 **Describe the six characteristics of the Information Age and discuss the role of information technology (IT) as the principal tool of the Information Age.** The six characteristics of the Information Age are (1) the evolution of an information society in which more people work at handling information than at agriculture and manufacturing combined; (2) the dependence of businesses on information technology; (3) the transformation of work processes to increase their productivity and effectiveness; (4) the capability IT provides to rethink (reengineer) conventional business practices; (5) the importance of IT for business success; and (6) the embodiment of IT in many products and services.

2 **Explain the three primary components of information technology.** The three components of information technology are (1) computers—electronic systems that can be instructed to accept, process, store, and present data and information; (2) communications networks—the interconnection of different locations through a medium that enables people to send and receive information; and (3) know-how—the familiarity with the tools of IT, the skills needed to use these tools, and the understanding of when to use them.

3 **Identify the six information-handling functions and the four benefits of information technology.** The six information-handling functions of IT are (1) capture, or the compilation of detailed records of activities; (2) processing, or the conversion, analysis, computation, and synthesis of all forms of data or information; (3) generation, or the organization of information into a useful

form, whether as text, sound, or visual image; (4) storage, or the maintenance of data and information for future use; (5) retrieval, or the locating and copying of stored data or information; and (6) transmission, or the sending of information from one location to another.

The four benefits of IT are speed, consistency, precision, and reliability.

4 **Summarize the principles of business reengineering, emphasizing the potential benefits to people and businesses.** Reengineering emphasizes rethinking of business activities and introducing radical changes that benefit both a company's customers and its employees. Reengineering seeks to capitalize on the capabilities of information technology in a sensible and beneficial way to improve performance while using fewer steps, fewer resources, and fewer people.

5 **Discuss the types of opportunities that information technology offers to people.** IT can aid people in their personal lives as well as in their careers. It also helps them to see the opportunities created by problems and to formulate solutions that capitalize on those opportunities.

6 **Describe the responsibilities of people who use information technology.** IT users have three fundamental responsibilities: (1) to be informed—to know the capabilities and limitations of IT; (2) to make proper use of IT—to employ it in a desirable and ethical manner; and (3) to safeguard—to protect data and information against damage or loss.

KEY TERMS

1   At Bell Atlantic, Dialing 411 Gets Directory Assistance by Computer

Bell Atlantic   While Bell Atlantic believes that using computer speech technology to assist in 411 information calls will improve the company's productivity and reduce costs, it recognizes that some people will be uncomfortable with the computer's questions. Hence, it has built in an "old-fashioned alternative." If at any time during the call the person wants to speak to a human operator, all he or she has to do is press zero.

Although it does not currently plan to replace its telephone operators with computers, Bell Atlantic does not rule out that possibility in the future. The company's goal is to use information technology for what it does best and reserve employees for the kind of work better done by people.

Questions for Discussion

1. As a telephone company customer, what advantages and disadvantages do you see in Bell Atlantic's system?

2. How would you determine whether computer speech technology offers sufficient benefits to warrant its additional use?

3. Should Bell Atlantic entirely replace its directory assistance operators with information technology if such a move would make the company more competitive by reducing costs *and* the company believes its customers will feel comfortable with such a change?

2   Ernst & Young's Hot-Desking Nomads

Ernst & Young   Ernst & Young's consultants, and other hot-desking businesspeople people, need not lose touch with events at the office or within the company. Call forwarding, whereby telephone calls made to one number are transferred to another, permit the intended recipient to talk with callers regardless of his or her location. When a consultant is unable to take a call, voice-mail systems record the caller's message and the consultant can later retrieve it from any telephone.

Wireless cellular telephones allow the businessperson to make or receive calls whether inside an automobile, on a train, or walking the streets. Notebook computers small enough to fit into a briefcase come equipped with fax machines so messages can be sent or received anywhere.

Given IT's capabilities, people need never be out of touch. In many types of businesses today, the large office with its vast assemblage of employees may already be obsolete.

Questions for Discussion

1. What does hot-desking imply for the costs of running companies and delivering services to customers?

2. The biggest impediment to the hot-desking revolution is management resistance. The majority of managers gauge their value and prestige at least partly by the size of the permanent office they are assigned. How can companies overcome this resistance?

3. Do you think hot-desking is a fad or a long-term trend made possible by information technology that will render ordinary offices obsolete? State the reasons underlying your answer.

Net Work

Are You Networked?

Your institution probably provides a way for you to use the Internet through its computer center, through one of its academic departments, or through a local Internet service provider (i.e., a company whose business is providing an Internet connection for a fee). Chapter 3 discusses the Internet in detail. To prepare for that discussion, you should establish an Internet account through your institution now.

When you have established an Internet account (required both to ensure that no one else can use the Internet under your name and to keep track of the time you're on the network), your institution or service provider will give you the information you need to use the system. Record that information here so you will have a convenient reference for your network's characteristics.

- Your user name/ account number   _____
- Your password   _____
- The name the institution has assigned to its computer   _____

- Terminal emulation required so your computer will interact with the network properly (e.g., VT100; the computer center or service provider must give you this information)   _____

- If using telephone dial-up access, choose one from each of these five parameters:
  —Transmission speed: 300/1200/2400/ 4800/9600/14400/28800
  —Parity: None/Even/Odd/Mark/Space
  —Data bits: 7/8
  —Stop bits: 1/2
  —Port: Com1/Com2/Com3/Com4

- Telephone number(s) to gain access to the Internet (if you're using dial-up access)   _____

- Telephone number(s) to call if you need help (a service often known as a *help desk*)   _____

- Name of communication software you must first start on your PC before you can use the Internet _____
- Name of the Internet browser program you'll run on your computer (e.g., Netscape or Exchange) _____

- The address (called a uniform resource locator—URL) of your institution or service provider's home page. It will appear similar to this: http://www.college.edu _____ (URLs are discussed in Chapter 3)

GROUP PROJECTS AND APPLICATIONS

Project 1

With a partner from your class, make arrangements to visit one of the following businesses:

- Neighborhood restaurant
- Retail store in the mall or downtown area
- Copy center

Plan to interview the proprietor or staff and observe how customers or clients are served. Then do the following:

- Identify the roles played by information technology in the way business is conducted.
- Find out how IT has changed a particular business activity or process.
- Brainstorm ways that IT might be used to improve, or reengineer, other business processes or activities.
- Present a report of your findings and recommendations to the class.

Project 2

Consult the help wanted ads in your weekend newspaper and summarize the characteristics of jobs open in your local job market. Then do the following:

- Estimate the percentage of ads that focus on (1) information technology occupations, (2) other occupations that require some IT skills, and (3) jobs that require no IT training. Bring in a sample of each of these three types of ads and estimate the entry-level salary range for each type.
- Based on your estimates, what is your overall view of the importance of information technology in making career choices?
- Include a section in your report identifying the limitations you will face if your peers have a higher level of IT know-how than you have.

Project 3

As a class project, develop a file of real-world examples of IT in business. Your examples might focus on the following topics:

- Improving customer service
- Improving delivery time
- Improving quality
- Reaching new customers
- Increasing sales to existing customers
- Developing relationships with suppliers

Cast your net wide as you search for examples. Look in the business pages of your local newspaper; in business magazines such as *Fortune, Forbes,* and *Business Week;* and in on-line or Internet-based publications. You might also want to write up examples that you've heard about through friends, relatives, or co-workers.

Each member of the class should bring in two examples for the file. Attached to each example should be a brief summary, along with complete information regarding its source.

REVIEW QUESTIONS

1. Distinguish between the Agricultural, Industrial, and Information Ages. What developments brought about the onset of the Industrial and Information Ages?

2. Define knowledge workers. What is their relation to the Information Age?

3. What is meant by the term *information society?*

4. "The Information Age does not replace the activities of earlier ages. It transforms them." Explain this statement.

5. What are the six characteristics of the Information Age?

6. Define information technology. How are information technology and computers related?

7. Describe the characteristics of reengineering. In what ways does reengineering seek to improve business? Who benefits from reengineering?

8. What is the role of information technology in the reengineering of business?

9. Distinguish among data, information, and knowledge.

10. Identify the four types of computers.

11. How are hardware and software different? How are they related?

12. What role do communications networks play in an information society?

13. "Know-how" is neither a computer nor a data communications network. Why, then, is it a component of information technology?

14. Describe the principle of high-tech/high-touch.

15. What six functions does information technology perform? Briefly describe each one.

16. Describe four benefits of information technology.

17. What is meant by the term *problem?* By *problem solving?*

18. What three responsibilities does information technology create for its users?

DISCUSSION QUESTIONS

1. How might the illustration of a business process in Figure 1.8 be changed by applying the principles of business process reengineering described in this chapter? Apply these principles to two different situations: (1) a system that depends on paper documents from the sales staff and (2) one that depends on the electronic submission of sales orders.

2. Discuss how the AUCNET system might be applied to the sale of new cars. What factors would make such a sales method functionally possible? What concerns would have to be met in order for consumers to feel comfortable using such a computer- and communications-based system?

3. Ford Motor Co. was highly pleased with its reengineered system for processing accounts payable.

But how do you think this redesigned accounts payable process was perceived by Ford's suppliers? What factors would likely determine whether they were pleased with the reengineered business process? Do you think suppliers benefited from the change?

4. Bell Atlantic Corp. of Philadelphia, one of the "Baby Bells" created by the breakup of the original AT&T in 1984, recently earmarked $2 billion for Project 2000, which involves the complete revision of 400 computer applications that support more than 120 business functions. Use what you have already learned about IT and its functions to explain why many IT professionals are now engaged in similar projects.

5. "Computers don't make difficult things easier, they make impossible things possible." Do you agree or disagree with this adage? Explain your answer.

6. Procter & Gamble routinely searches databases of public information to discover the names of new parents and then mails these parents coupons and samples of P&G's disposable diapers in the hope of winning them over to P&G's baby products for the next two years. Is this a responsible use of IT? Comment on the ethical or legal issues involved in this form of "micromarketing."

7. How do you think the Information Age will change your personal and work life? What characteristics of the Information Age will have the greatest influence on your career?

SUGGESTED READINGS

Champy, James. *Reengineering Management: The Mandate for New Leadership*. New York: Harper Business, 1995. A sequel to the innovative book that focused management's attention on business process reengineering (see Hammer and Champy, *Reengineering the Corporation,* below). Here the author provides guidelines that managers need to lead, organize, inspire, deploy, measure, and reward the new work created when firms reengineer.

Davenport, Thomas H. *Process Innovation: Reengineering Work Through Information Technology*. Boston: Harvard Business School Press, 1993. An insightful discussion of how information technology can be applied to introduce innovation in management thinking about conducting business. This book shows how the challenge of process innovation affords maximum use of IT's potential.

Davis, Stan, and Bill Davidson. *2020 Vision: Transform Your Business Today to Succeed in Tomorrow's Economy*. New York: Simon & Schuster, 1991. An excellent discussion of the ways computers and data communications networks are reshaping the structure of modern business, allowing firms to improve existing products and services and create new ones.

Hammer, Michael, and James Champy. *Reengineering the Corporation: A Manifesto for Business Revolution*. New York: Harper Business, 1994. The book that defined the revolution in business process thinking. Hammer and Champy explore the principles of reengineering and share their firsthand experiences of how some of the world's best-known companies applied those principles to change the way they do business—to the benefit of customers, employees, and shareholders.

Toffler, Alvin. *Powershift*. New York: Bantam Books, 1990. A groundbreaking book in which Toffler, one of the leading futurists, describes how knowledge is creating tremendous shifts in power at the local and global levels.

Zuboff, Shoshana. *In the Age of the Smart Machine: The Future of Work and Power*. New York: Basic Books, 1988. An in-depth examination of how information technology is spreading across the business landscape and transforming the nature of work. Zuboff demonstrates the benefits of "informating" (empowering working people with overall knowledge) and points out the problems that can occur when IT is used merely to automate jobs.

CASE STUDY

Information Technology Outruns Runners of the New York Stock Exchange

NYSE In 1792, 24 stockbrokers and merchants gathered under a buttonwood tree on New York City's Wall Street in Lower Manhattan and signed a document describing their agreements on doing business. The Buttonwood Agreement was the first document describing membership requirements and self-regulatory details for the New York Stock Exchange.

Steeped in its 200+ years of tradition, the New York Stock Exchange (NYSE) is a storied symbol of the energy and competitiveness of securities markets. Here buyers and sellers trade shares of stock, each share representing ownership in one of the world's best-known companies—AT&T, Coca-Cola, General Electric (GE), General Motors, Procter & Gamble, Wal-Mart. A peek inside the Corinthian-columned building where the NYSE does business reveals a paper-strewn trading floor where some 500 million buy-and-sell transactions take place on an average day.

Transactions are initiated when a customer or member firm of the NYSE telephones an order to buy or sell shares to a clerk in a brokerage firm's booth at the edge of the trading floor. After completing a paper order form, the clerk summons a "squad"—a runner who scrambles to the middle of the floor where the traders congregate. The squad (short for "message squad") gives the order to a trader, who executes it—buying or selling the desired stock at the best negotiated price. When the trading order is completed, the broker jots the details on a scrap of paper and summons another squad to run the paper back to the booth, where the clerk takes it and calls the customer to confirm the transaction. Shortly after the transaction is completed, the name of the stock and the price paid for it appear on the lighted overhead electronic tape that displays Exchange transactions for all to see.

The 150 runners who scamper across the Exchange floor throughout the day are as much a tradition as the trading floor itself. Many executives in leading broker-

age firms actually began their careers as runners, using the job to learn the trading business and to become acquainted with the member firms that make up the Exchange.

Since the volume of trading has risen more than 10-fold over the past decade, reducing trading time and increasing efficiency are constant concerns of the Exchange's members and management. They are acutely aware that competing stock exchanges are continually trying to lure business away from the Exchange

with claims of greater efficiency and faster trades. Hence, a new generation of information technology is being introduced at the NYSE. The traditional runners will be replaced by hand-held computers and portable telephones. Calls will be made from the booth directly to floor traders, who will also be able to receive buy-and-sell orders over their hand-held computers. Traders will be able to enter trading details directly into the Exchange's system, and those details will be transmitted immediately to the booth and to the electronic tape for all to see.

By eliminating runners in favor of this electronic system, the Exchange will shave some 30 seconds off the average transaction—a significant time savings considering that most trades are completed in just 2 or 3 minutes. The mountain of paper produced each day will be eliminated as well.

Observers wonder whether the NYSE is doing enough to capitalize on information technology. They note that rival exchanges, such as the Nasdaq—a NYSE neighbor—have been so successful at using IT that they are able to compete with the NYSE in attracting new members and additional business.

Observers also point out that some exchanges, such as the London Stock Exchange, have virtually eliminated the trading floor. Buy-and-sell transactions take place on interconnected computer display screens, where brokers match buyers with sellers, so that neither trading floor nor slips of paper are necessary.

Questions for Discussion

1. If you were a floor trader at the NYSE, would you be pleased to see this information technology introduced and the runners eliminated?

2. Since its primary competitors have eliminated the trading floor by matching buyers with sellers over computer networks, should the NYSE seek to do likewise? Why or why not?

3. What role does IT play in the transfer of data and information and in the overall operational performance of the NYSE?

4. Describe how an all-electronic trading process could by conducted by the NYSE. Include in your description how such a process would affect the way customers inform brokers about their desires to buy or sell a particular stock, the handling of the transaction by the trader, the transfer of money between buyer and seller, the reporting of transaction details to the NYSE, and the display of trading results on the Exchange's electronic tape.

CHAPTER
2

A Tour of a Computer System

CHAPTER OUTLINE

IT Helps Combine Journalism and Art at the Associated Press

Hardware: Computing, Storing, and Communicating

Programs: In Charge of the Hardware

Information: The Reason for Using Information Technology

People: The Most Important Element

Procedures: The Way It Goes

An Introduction to Systems

Information Technology in Practice at ITT Sheraton Hotels: An Example

Case Study: Hyatt Hotels Help Business Travelers Set Up a Base Camp

Photo Essay: Nigel Holmes's Infographic Shares the Vital Statistics and Secret Taboos of the U.S. Centennial Olympic Team

LEARNING OBJECTIVES

When you have completed this chapter, you should be able to

1   Identify the five components of a computer system.

2   Explain the four categories of hardware and their functions.

3   Discuss the relationship between hardware and software.

4   Differentiate between an operating system and an application program.

5   Identify eight types of software packages.

6   Explain the four components of information.

7   Distinguish between the users of information technology and IT professionals.

8   Describe the four types of procedures used in computer systems.

9   Explain the difference between single- and multiuser systems.

10   List the 13 information-processing activities associated with the 6 information-handling functions of IT.

IT Helps Combine Journalism and Art at the Associated Press

Since it was founded in the 1840s, the Associated Press (AP) has been a principal supplier of news to the world's newspapers. Every day, from its headquarters in New York City's Rockefeller Center, AP sends out a wealth of information—some 20 million words, equivalent to half the content of the *Encyclopaedia Britannica*—to its 8,500 member newspapers, government agencies, television and radio stations, and private news agencies around the world.

Words and photos are two forms of information AP provides to all its subscribers. Karl Gude, AP's art director, provides another form—*infographics*—to more than 900 newspapers. Infographics combine *information* and *graphics* (that is, pictures or illustrations) in ways that bring ideas to life. Each day, Gude and his staff create a dozen infographics on breaking news or topics of special interest—education, problems of the elderly, personal safety, starvation. The infographics do four things for newspaper readers:

- They identify the topic.
- They illustrate key facts about the topic.
- They provide information.
- They explain the information in visually attractive formats that are easily comprehended.

Though a personal computer is used to create the infographics, artists usually begin by sketching their ideas on paper in pencil. Then the infographics are scanned into a PC and illustration software is used to embellish and refine them—adding lines, color, and shading to create dimensions and perspectives.

Once the basic drawing is complete, brief text explanations of the images are entered through the computer's keyboard. Words or phrases to be emphasized get styled in a special color. Because artists are working with a computer almost from the beginning of the creative process, they can send and receive

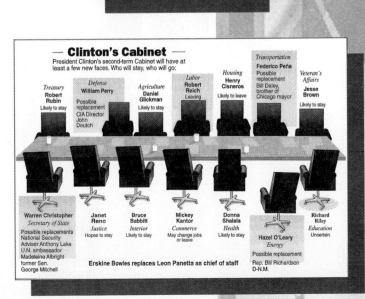

— Clinton's Cabinet —
President Clinton's second-term Cabinet will have at least a few new faces. Who will stay, who will go:

Treasury
Robert Rubin
Likely to stay

Defense
William Perry
Possible replacement CIA Director John Deutch

Agriculture
Daniel Glickman
Likely to stay

Labor
Robert Reich
Leaving

Housing
Henry Cisneros
Likely to leave

Transportation
Federico Peña
Possible replacement Bill Daley, brother of Chicago mayor

Veteran's Affairs
Jesse Brown
Likely to stay

Warren Christopher
Secretary of State
Possible replacements National Security Adviser Anthony Lake U.N. ambassador Madeleine Albright former Sen. George Mitchell

Janet Reno
Justice
Hopes to stay

Bruce Babbitt
Interior
Likely to stay

Mickey Kantor
Commerce
May change jobs or leave

Donna Shalala
Health
Likely to stay

Hazel O'Leary
Energy
Possible replacement Rep. Bill Richardson D-N.M.

Richard Riley
Education
Uncertain

Erskine Bowles replaces Leon Panetta as chief of staff

sketches, rough drawings, and completed infographics electronically. The photo essay at the end of this chapter shows the step-by-step creation of infographics.

The computer and programs that Gude and the staff use to create infographics are available to the general public at retail stores across the nation. Because these tools are easy to handle, users can focus on the best way to present information graphically rather than on mastering the intricacies of a difficult piece of technology.

As the story of Karl Gude and infographics at the Associated Press suggests, information technology enables us to accomplish what we need to get done more quickly and more effectively. Gude doesn't have to know all the technical details of computers to do his job. All he needs is a general understanding of how computers work and what they can do for him.

To see what a computer can do to make you more productive, you need to become familiar with its primary components. This chapter's guided tour of a computer system will give you a working knowledge of the basics so that you can avoid some of the problems that often trip up new computer users. An informed computer user is an effective user.

Computer systems are made up of five components: hardware, programs, information, people, and procedures (see Figure 2.1). We'll discuss each component—and the know-how you'll need to acquire to use it effectively—in turn, starting with hardware.

FIGURE 2.1

The Five Components of a Computer System

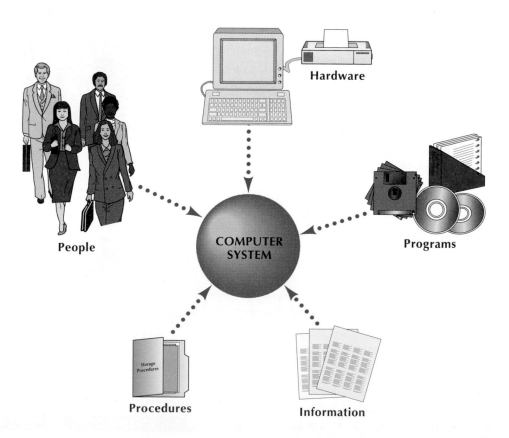

People

Hardware

COMPUTER SYSTEM

Programs

Procedures

Information

Hardware: Computing, Storing, and Communicating

The terms *computer* and *computer system* are often used loosely. We need to be more specific for this tour. As you learned in Chapter 1, a *computer* is any electronic system that can be instructed to accept, process, store, and present data and information. *Computer system* refers to a computer *and* all the hardware interconnected with it.

Hardware, or **computer hardware,** is the general term for the machines (sometimes called the **devices**) that carry out the activities of computing, storing, and communicating data. As Figure 2.2 shows, computer hardware falls into four categories of components:

hardware/computer hardware/devices
The computer and its associated equipment.

- Input devices
- Processors
- Output devices
- Secondary storage devices

These components are part of most computer systems, regardless of their cost or size. (Some computer systems are designed to store all data and information internally and thus do not include secondary storage devices.)

Input Devices

Input has two meanings: (1) as a noun, it refers to the data or information entered into a computer; (2) as a verb, it means the process of entering data or information into the computer for processing, storage and retrieval, or transmission.

Seven different devices are commonly used to enter data or information into a computer:

1. **Keyboards.** Keyboards (Figure 2.3) containing the letters of the alphabet, numbers, and frequently used symbols (such as $, &, and #) are the most common input devices. In some parts of the world, keyboards consist almost exclusively of symbols rather than alphabet letters. In Japan, for example, a popular keyboard contains the 5,000 symbols representing characters of the Kanji alphabet. The Kanji keyboard thus is much larger and contains many more symbols than the keyboards used in North and South America and Europe.

input
The data or information entered into a computer or the process of entering data or information into the computer for processing, storage and retrieval, or transmission.

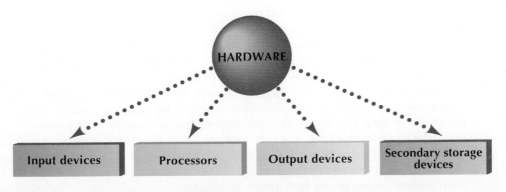

FIGURE 2.2
The Four Categories of Hardware

a) The standard keyboard for the IBM PS/2.

b) The Apple Macintosh extended keyboard.

c) The Microsoft Natural Keyboard.

d) A multilingual keyboard, with both English and Chinese numbers and characters.

FIGURE 2.3 *Keyboards*

Most keyboards also have a numeric keypad. Arranged in a layout similar to that used on handheld calculators, numeric keypads are useful for entering data quickly.

2. **Point-of-sale terminals.** A variation on the standard business cash register, these terminals typically do not contain alphabet letters. Rather, they consist of a numeric datapad and special-purpose function keys, such as those for a sale, a refund, or a void (Figure 2.4). The numeric keypad is used to enter details of a purchase (such as a product or stock number), the cost of the product (if that information is not automatically retrieved from the computer when purchase details are entered), and the amount of money tendered for a cash purchase or the account number for a purchase by a credit or debit card.

3. **Mouse.** On the underside of the mouse is a ball that rotates as the mouse is moved, causing the corresponding movement of a pointer (a large arrow) on the display screen. A "click" of a button on the top side of the mouse lets the user invoke a command or initiate an action (Figure 2.5). A computer system can be controlled by pointing the mouse at commands on the screen rather than by entering them through the keyboard.

4. **Image scanners.** Image scanners (Figure 2.6) can enter (that is, *input*) both words and images (including drawings, charts, and graphs) directly into a computer. A light illuminates the information one section at a time, and the information under the light is recognized and read into the computer. Image scanners range in size from those that fit into the palm of your hand to those the size of a newspaper page. Once in the computer's memory, images can be modified or combined with other information.

FIGURE 2.4
*Point of Sale Terminal
in a Supermarket*

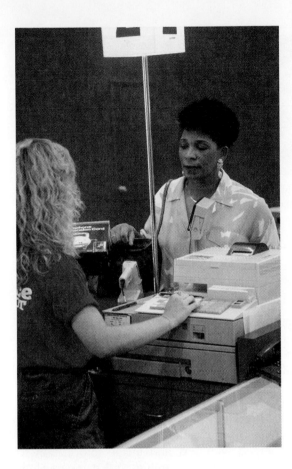

5. **Bar code scanners and wands.** Manual input of data or information takes time and is subject to error. Many retail stores have found that the scanning of *bar code* information on a package is a faster and more accurate process than entering the same information through a keyboard (Figure 2.7). A **bar code** is a computer-readable code consisting of bars or lines of varying widths or lengths. As the **wand,** a hand-held scanner, is waved across the bar code on the package, it recognizes the special letters and symbols embedded in the bar code and inputs this information directly into a PC, midrange computer, or point-of-sale terminal. There the code is translated into product and

bar code
A computer-readable code consisting of bars or lines of varying widths or lengths.

wand
An input device used to read a bar code and input this information directly into a computer.

FIGURE 2.5
*Two Variations on the
Mouse*

a) The Microsoft mouse, with its simple and functional design, is now the bestselling mouse in the United States.

b) A variation on the standard mouse, designed by Logitech for children.

FIGURE 2.6
Image Scanners

a) Hewlett-Packard's DeskScan III flatbed scanner permits scanning of full-color, large-size documents in a few minutes.

b) Logitech's ScanMan 256 hand-held scanner permits the scanning of smaller documents and is frequently used as an alternative to more expensive flatbed models.

price information. Some stores, such as supermarkets, use a fixed scanner at the checkout counter instead of a wand. In this case, the package containing the bar code is passed over a scanner mounted under a piece of glass.

6. **Microphones.** Often used in multimedia systems, microphones capture voices or other sounds for use in computer processing (Figure 2.8). The microphone is attached to a computer by a cable that transmits the sounds.

7. **Prerecorded sources.** Tape recorders, cassette decks, record players, and stereo amplifiers can be connected to a computer that captures sounds as they are played (Figure 2.9). This method of input allows high-quality music and voice reproductions to be merged with text and image information to produce multimedia presentations for education, training, and marketing.

Input devices can be either internal or external. For instance, some PCs and older terminals include the display screen and keyboard in a single case. In contrast, mice, scanners, wands, and microphones are usually separate devices, attached to the computer by a cable. This setup is changing, however, with the development of wireless input devices (e.g., the wireless keyboard and mouse).

FIGURE 2.7
Bar Code Scanning

a) Bar code scanning is a fast and efficient way of inputting data. Here, a department manager uses bar codes to replenish inventory in her stock room.

b) Bar code scanning at checkout allows clerks to move customers much more quickly than cash registers do. It also permits managers to change the price of a product in an instant and to keep track of inventory.

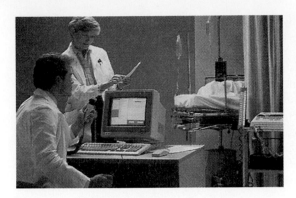

FIGURE 2.8
A Microphone in a Medical Diagnosis System
The computer captures the words spoken by the doctor into the microphone, then processes them to help him determine the best treatment for a patient.

The Processor

The center of action in a computer is the **processor,** also called the **central processing unit (CPU).** In microcomputers, the processor is a **microprocessor**—a central processor contained on a single computer chip.

A *chip* is a collection of electronic components in a very small, self-contained package. Chips perform the computer's processing actions, including arithmetic calculations and the generation of lines, images, and sounds. Some chips are general purpose and perform all types of actions. Others have a special purpose. Sound chips, for example, do exactly what their name suggests: they generate signals to be output as tones.

processor/central processing unit (CPU)
A set of electronic circuits that perform the computer's processing actions.

microprocessor
The smallest type of processor, with all of the processing capabilities of the control unit located on a single chip.

FIGURE 2.9
Prerecorded Sources as Input
Many products that are often considered "consumer electronics" are being used in multimedia systems. Video is provided by videocassette recorders attached to the computer, and stereo sound comes from compact disc players.

SYSTEM BOARD.   The processor/CPU can take several forms. Microcomputers contain a specific microprocessor chip as their CPU. This chip is put into a protective package, then mounted onto a board contained within the computer. This board is called a **system board** or **mother board** (Figure 2.10). The system board also contains other chips and circuitry that carry out processing activities.

Larger computer systems may have separate cabinets or freestanding units that contain the chips and circuits that make up the CPU. At one time, all mainframes and supercomputers had separate units housing the central processor. Today, thanks to the continued miniaturization of chips and circuits, separate units are not always necessary. Even in the most powerful central processors, chips and circuits can be integrated onto a few boards.

MEMORY.   Both system boards and separate processing units include space for memory, sometimes called **primary storage** or **main memory** because it is used by the central processing unit to carry out all computing activities. No processing takes place in memory—memory stores data, information, and instructions. When data enter the computer as input, they go into main memory until they are processed. After processing, the results—information—are retained in memory.

At any given time, a section of memory can hold either data and information or processing instructions. The allocation of memory at the time a program is running will determine whether a particular location will hold an instruction or a unit of data or information. We discuss the CPU and primary memory fully in Chapter 4.

**system board/
mother board**

The system unit in a microcomputer, located on a board mounted on the bottom of a computer base.

**primary storage/
main memory**

Storage within the computer itself. Primary memory holds data only temporarily, while the computer executes instructions.

FIGURE 2.10
*A Microcomputer System
Board*

The system board is often referred to as the *motherboard.* In PCs, the CPU is a single microprocessor chip that is installed on the system board.

The *Rethinking Business Practices* feature entitled "Sea-Land's Use of Handheld Computers" illustrates how microprocessors and storage can be combined to produce small, but powerful, portable computers.

Output Devices

People use computers to generate **output**—the *results* of entering and processing data and information. Output falls into two categories: (1) information that is presented to the user of the computer; and (2) information in the form of computer commands that are input to another device.

Common forms of output are reports, schedules, budgets, newsletters, and correspondence. These results can be printed out, displayed on a computer screen, and sometimes played through the speaker built in or attached to a computer (Figure 2.11).

output
The results of inputting and processing data and information returned by the computer, either directly to the person using the system or to secondary storage.

INPUT DEVICES   OUTPUT DEVICES

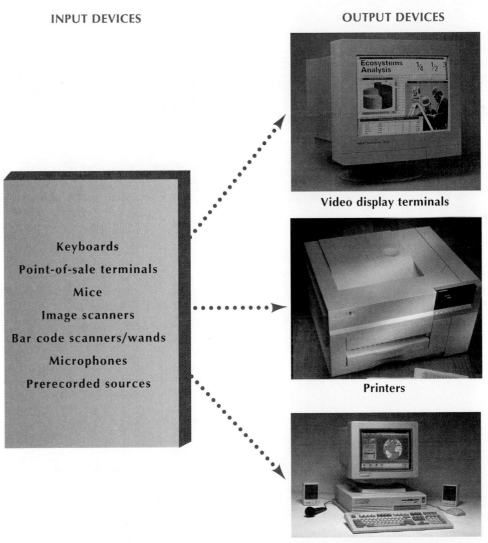

FIGURE 2.11
The Relationship Between Input and Output Devices

Video display terminals

Keyboards
Point-of-sale terminals
Mice
Image scanners
Bar code scanners/wands
Microphones
Prerecorded sources

Printers

Speakers

Data enter the computer
as input . . .

. . . and are transformed via
processing into output for the user

RETHINKING BUSINESS PRACTICES

Sea-Land's Use of Handheld Computers

Sea-Land Service, Inc.'s port facility at Charleston, South Carolina, is a showcase for the shipping company's planned use of information technology at 17 other port facilities. A growing business (daily truck traffic in and out of Sea-Land's facility doubled in just three years) can turn from an opportunity into a problem if expansion results in slower customer service or delays in delivering and picking up freight. The Charleston yard is divided into a series of rows and slots (see photo), and a combination row-and-slot number serves as a container's "address." With space for 3,500 tractor trailer–size containers in the yard, locating the right container or the optimal spot to store an incoming container is a challenging task.

A new terminal automation system (TAS), the result of a carefully formulated reengineering plan, has changed the way Sea-Land runs its container business at the Charleston yard. The old system was successful, but the new system has provided both improvements and new opportunities. Lower costs are only one of the benefits the company and its customers receive from the system.

Each container entering or leaving Sea-Land's Charleston shipyard is inspected for damage. Under the old system, drivers signed a paper inspection form describing the condition of the entering or departing container. Typically, the process, including wait time, required 50 to 60 minutes per driver.

Gate forms were counted manually and information from the form was entered into a terminal and transmitted by a communications network to a mainframe computer in Jacksonville, Florida. Having accurate information necessitated careful checking of details as they were keyed, since the form was the only record of container condition and location.

The key to Sea-Land's terminal automation system today is the handheld computer. The visual inspec-

Output from computer processing that is entered as input to another device can perform various functions, including

- **Control a printer.** Computer output can tell a printer when and what to print, including the location of text or images on a sheet of paper, film, or transparency. The dimensions of the image and the shades and colors used in the printout (if the printer prints in color) can also be determined.
- **Direct a display.** Computers can display words, graphics, and shapes, either simultaneously or one at a time, on the computer display screen, sometimes called a *video display terminal (VDT)* or *monitor.* These displays can be animated, so that words and shapes move across the display screen. With animation, ideas can be demonstrated rather than described.

tion of the container still occurs in much the same way—but that's about all that has been retained of the old system. When a driver arrives at the gate entrance to the terminal, the cargo's container number is entered directly into the handheld computer (see photo). Details—the container's owner, its contents, condition, and storage location—are retrieved and displayed on the com-

puter screen. An inspection form is created, which the driver signs, and the form is transmitted electronically to the company's central computer system. The manual shuffling of forms and the need to enter details through a keyboard have been eliminated.

Sea-Land's automated terminal system is so easy to use that a training period of less than an hour is all new gate agents need to become comfortable with the handheld computer and the system.

The benefits of TAS for the company include swifter movement of containers in and out of the shipyard and a substantial decrease in the time it takes to load and unload ships. Since containers can be located faster, ships can enter and leave the port more quickly, resulting in lower costs and higher revenues. Reengineering through information technology has made it possible for Sea-Land to handle doubled cargo levels in half the time, opening up the opportunity for even more spectacular growth in the future.

Sea-Land's use of information technology has not only improved productivity in the Charleston shipyard, it has built new business. Customers acknowledge that they do more business with Sea-Land than with other terminal operators because of the company's ability to get their drivers in and out of the terminal faster, which means each driver can be responsible for more loads per day.

- **Control another device.** Output from computers can direct the actions of other computers and machinery. Devices such as computer-controlled manufacturing lathes, automobile ignition systems, and CAT scanners (which physicians use to look beneath the skin of a patient to view tissue and bone structures) accept computer output as their input—that is, instructions that guide the actions they perform.
- **Generate sounds.** Computer output can direct the computer itself to play music, simulate the sound of a jet powering up its engine, or replicate a human voice announcing train stops or telephone numbers. Driven by the need to cut costs while increasing responsiveness to callers, many businesses are augmenting their telephone switchboards with computer-generated voices that answer information inquiries or instruct callers on how to reach a certain party.

- **Initiate transmission of information.** Because computers are often connected to data communications networks, output is frequently sent over a communications link to another destination or to multiple destinations simultaneously.

Input and output devices are discussed in more detail in Chapter 5.

Video games—both those found in arcades in your local shopping mall and the Super Nintendo Entertainment System in your home, apartment, or dorm—are computers. They don't look like the PCs you find on desks and tables, but they do have all the characteristics of computers that we've discussed so far. They use input, do processing, and generate output. (They are not connected to computer networks—at least not yet—so they cannot transmit information from one location to another.)

A video game's *input* activities are the instructions that control the movement of the characters and vehicles as you use a joystick, button, steering wheel, or foot pedal. *Processing* takes place before your eyes as the computer translates your actions into the characters' activities. The *output* is what you see on the display screen and hear from the speakers. Processing also determines whether you

a) BASF 3.5″ diskettes.

b) Conner-Pancho 2.5″ hard disk.

c) Optical disk (in protective packaging) with Optimem optical disk drive.

d) 3M 2400-foot magnetic tape reels.

e) BASF EXTRA TR-3 QIC 3020 magnetic tape cartridges.

FIGURE 2.12 *Secondary Storage Media*

have made good moves, assigning (or subtracting) points accordingly. If the computer chip inside senses that you have not made good moves, it will zap, trip, crash, or destroy you. When you have made too many mistakes, or when you have used up your allotted time, the chip will end the game. ■

Secondary Storage Devices

Computers that run multimedia and other complex programs require lots of storage capacity. For this reason, computer systems have several secondary storage options. Secondary storage provides enormous capacity to store data, information, or programs outside of the central processor.

The most widely used types of **secondary storage** (Figure 2.12) are

- **Diskettes**—flexible, flat, oxide-coated disks on which data and information are stored magnetically (hence, they are sometimes called **magnetic disks**). Diskettes are either 3½ inches (the current standard size) or 5¼ inches across (the old standard size). Diskettes are removed from the computer when the user has finished using the data or information they contain. The data remain on the diskette.
- **Hard disks**—inflexible magnetic disks. Ranging from 2½ to 14 inches across (with standard sizes of 2½ and 3½ inches), hard disks can store more data than diskettes can and provide for more rapid storage and retrieval of data and information. Hard disks are usually mounted inside the computer and, unlike diskettes, are not easily removed.
- **Optical disks**—a storage medium similar in design to the compact discs (CDs) played on stereo systems. Many optical disks are **read only,** meaning that they can only be played—that is, data, information, and instructions can be read from them but not written onto them. This is why optical disks are sometimes known as **CD-ROM disks** (compact disk–read only memory). Other types of optical disks allow the writing of information under certain circumstances. (More on the characteristics of optical disks is coming in Chapter 5.)
- **Magnetic tape**—used to store large quantities of data and information, often as a second copy of data or information that exists elsewhere. Unlike diskettes, hard disks, and optical disks, which are circular, magnetic tape is linear and comes in reels or cartridges.

Information is written to or read from each type of secondary storage medium by a read/write unit contained in a **drive.** The drive rotates the medium during the read/write process. Disk and tape drives read information magnetically, in much the same way that stereo systems read information from cassette tapes. Optical drives use a laser beam to read information—just like an audio CD player.

Peripheral Equipment

If you listen to computer professionals or systems engineers discussing the components of a computer system, you may hear them refer to "peripherals." **Peripheral equipment** is a general term for *any device* that is attached, either physically or in wireless fashion, to a computer system—that is, to a PC, midrange, mainframe, or supercomputer. Peripherals include input devices, output devices, and secondary storage units. Any device that is ready to communicate with the computer is said to be *on-line.* One that is not ready to communicate is *off-line.*

secondary storage
A storage medium that is external to the computer, but that can be read by the computer; a way of storing data and information outside the computer itself.

magnetic disk
A general term referring to two types of disk: flexible/floppy disks and hard disks.

read only
A type of disk that information can be read from but not written onto.

CD-ROM disk
Short for "compact disk–read only memory": an optical medium that permits storage of large amounts of information. CD-ROM disks can only be written to and cannot be erased.

drive
The device containing a secondary storage medium's read/write unit.

peripheral equipment
A general term used for any device that is attached to a computer system.

Kao's IT Keeps Everyone in Touch

Kao

Kao Corp. is a $7 billion supplier of soap, cosmetics, and other consumer products that is headquartered in Japan. All of its 7,200 employees, regardless of their position or experience, are expected to contribute to the company's purpose, which is to create and apply innovative technologies to produce products that are useful to society and that offer real value to consumers. Employees are encouraged to grow and share knowledge among themselves and to be familiar with the company's performance and its plans.

Two operating strategies support Kao's objectives. One is job rotation. To instill a sense of creativity and curiosity in its employees, Kao rotates people through various jobs (quite unusual in tradition-bound Japan). Job rotation expands employees' knowledge of the company and promotes knowledge sharing across the firm.

The second strategy is to make information technology an important tool of knowledge creation and creativity. All employees at Kao have desktop computers, which they can use to review company databases. The databases provide users in every department of the company with data and information on forecast sales, daily retail sales, inventory levels, and customer comments. The terminals are also linked to marketing and planning databases. Every store that sells Kao products is equipped with a pen-based computer for data collection, analysis, and simulation.

At Kao, knowledgeable employees are key to creative work and opportunity.

---

software
The general term for a set of instructions that controls a computer or a communications network.

program
A set of instructions that directs a computer to perform certain tasks and produce certain results.

operating system
A combination of programs that coordinates the actions of a computer, including its peripheral devices and memory.

disk operating system (DOS)
An operating system whose components reside on a disk and are brought into computer memory as needed.

Programs: In Charge of the Hardware

Today's general-purpose computer systems can perform many different tasks, moving between tasks in an instant. Because of the versatility of computers, businesspeople can create drawings and illustrations, write correspondence, prepare detailed financial analyses, maintain accounts payable, and control inventory—all on the same system.

The secret to the versatility of computers is programs. By itself, hardware is nothing but a collection of apparatus. Computer hardware is useless without software or programs. Though the terms *programs* and *software* are often used interchangeably, their meanings vary slightly. **Software** is the general term for a set of instructions that controls a computer or a communications network, while a **program** is a specific sequence of instructions that tells a computer how to perform a particular action or solve a problem. For example, a communications program instructs the hardware how to send or receive information.

At the center of a computer's activities is the **operating system,** a combination of programs that coordinates the actions of the computer, including its peripheral devices and memory. Historically, one of the most common operating systems is **DOS,** a single-user personal computer operating system. DOS is an acronym for **disk operating system,** which means that the operating system's components reside on a disk and are brought into computer memory as needed. Today, most desktop microcomputers rely on **Windows.** This single-user PC **graphical user interface (GUI)** allows multitasking, which means that several programs can be operated concurrently, each in its own window or section of the computer screen. (An **interface** is the means by which a person interacts with a computer.) Using the GUI (pronounced "gooey") to interact with the DOS operating system, the individual directs the computer through the window created by the software. A mouse is used to point to and click on an icon that will activate a program. Without the GUI interface, it would be necessary for the user to enter a command word to start processing. Most people prefer using GUI interfaces to entering DOS commands. Figure 2.13 explains Windows in more detail.

Other popular operating systems are NT and OS/2 for PCs; UNIX for PCs, midrange systems, and mainframes; and MVS and VM, multiuser operating systems for the IBM mainframe computers used in business. Whether used on a PC, midrange, or supercomputer, all operating systems perform the same function:

Windows

A single-user operating system that allows several programs to be operated simultaneously.

graphical user interface (GUI)

A link to an operating system that allows users to use icons rather than command words to start processing.

interface

The means by which a person interacts with a computer.

FIGURE 2.13 *Sample Windows Interface: Windows 3.11 (top) and Windows 95*

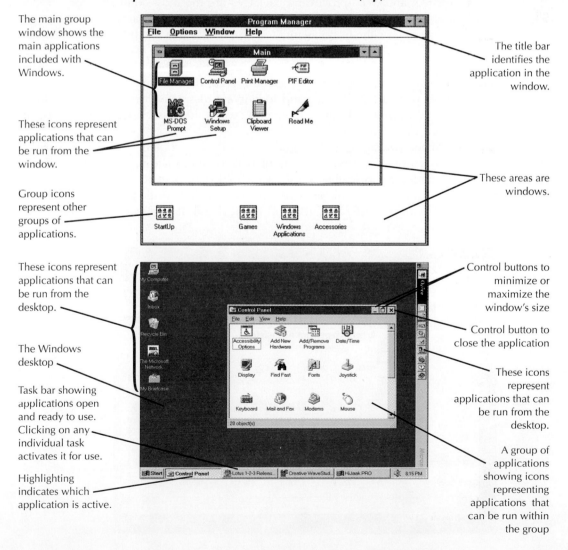

The main group window shows the main applications included with Windows.

These icons represent applications that can be run from the window.

Group icons represent other groups of applications.

The title bar identifies the application in the window.

These areas are windows.

These icons represent applications that can be run from the desktop.

The Windows desktop

Task bar showing applications open and ready to use. Clicking on any individual task activates it for use.

Highlighting indicates which application is active.

Control buttons to minimize or maximize the window's size

Control button to close the application

These icons represent applications that can be run from the desktop.

A group of applications showing icons representing applications that can be run within the group

they enable people to interact with the computer and to control the movement, storage, and retrieval of data and information.

Another type of software is the **application program** (**application,** for short). An application program is actually several programs working together. The illustration program Karl Gude uses to create infographics is an application program. Likewise, the programs a bank uses to process charges, payments, and adjustments to an individual's credit card account are application programs.

application program/application

A program or a combination of programs written for a specific use.

Software Packages

software package

An application that focuses on a particular subject, such as word processing, and is sold to businesses and the general public.

Many of the applications used on computers today are purchased as **software packages,** applications that focus on a particular subject. All software packages are accompanied by **documentation,** which is an instruction manual for the software. The most frequently used software packages allow users to do spreadsheet analysis, word processing, and desktop publishing; to create illustrations and graphics; to manage databases; to communicate with other computers; and to manage information systems.

documentation

An instruction manual that accompanies software. Also, a technical, detailed written description of the specific facts of a program.

Spreadsheet and word-processing packages are the most common types of software purchased today. However, with the increased use of computers, other types of packages are growing in popularity (e.g., packages that teach foreign languages).

SPREADSHEET PROGRAMS. Employees at all levels of the organization—whether large or small, profit or nonprofit—spend a great deal of time reviewing business activities, recognizing problems, and identifying alternative ways to correct those problems. As we pointed out in Chapter 1, when addressed effectively, problems can become opportunities.

spreadsheet

A table of columns and rows used by people responsible for tracking revenues, expenses, profits, and losses.

Spreadsheet packages are designed to assist in problem solving. A **spreadsheet** consists of rows and columns of data or information. The intersection of each row and column (called a *cell*) can hold data or text, as Figure 2.14 illustrates. New information can be keyed in over old information, so the data in the spreadsheet can be easily updated and recalculated. It is also easy to instruct the

FIGURE 2.14

Worksheet Created with Spreadsheet Software

Spreadsheet software allows a user to change data and perform recalculations easily. For example, if rent were to increase to $12,000 per quarter, the spreadsheet software would automatically adjust both total expenses and gross profit to reflect that change.

	A	B	C	D	E	F	G
1			**Arts Management Associates**				
2			*Operating Summary*				
3							
4			1st Qtr	2nd Qtr	3rd Qtr	4th Qtr	Year Total
5	Sales		$78,000	$81,000	$76,000	$92,000	$327,000
6							
7	Expenses						
8		Salaries	$41,000	$41,000	$42,500	$42,500	$167,000
9		Rent	$11,000	$11,000	$11,000	$11,000	$44,000
10		Telephone	$1,405	$1,386	$1,599	$1,675	$6,065
11		Office Supplies	$1,015	$764	$832	$901	$3,512
12		Miscellaneous	$1,200	$1,324	$855	$862	$4,041
13	Total Expenses		$55,620	$55,474	$56,586	$56,938	$224,618
14							
15	Gross Profits		$22,380	$25,526	$19,414	$35,062	$102,382
16							
17							

software to add the contents of columns, determine percentages, and calculate trends.

Spreadsheet packages make the people using them more effective because they automate time-consuming and error-prone tasks like the adding and subtracting of columns of numbers. Users are thus able to spend more time analyzing conditions and opportunities. Spreadsheets are discussed in detail in Chapter 6.

WORD-PROCESSING PROGRAMS.   Correspondence (including letters, memoranda, and reports) is an important part of both business and personal life. **Word-processing (WP) programs** allow you to enter, change (edit), move, store, and print text information (Figure 2.15). Many programs will also check your spelling, evaluate your grammar, and verify your punctuation.

Because word-processing programs allow text to be stored and retrieved, they are frequently used to prepare tailor-made versions of correspondence and project proposals. The user can make the necessary changes to a stored document and print a new copy for distribution. Relieved of the task of rekeying an entire document manually, the user gains time to perform other, more important activities.

Software manufacturers are adding new features to word-processing programs all the time. For example, many now provide the capability to insert graphics into the body of the text. In effect, word-processing software and desktop publishing software are converging.

DESKTOP PUBLISHING PROGRAMS.   **Desktop publishing (DTP) programs** combine text and image-handling features with the capability to design documents. These programs give users more flexibility in positioning of text and images (whether drawings or photographs) on a page than word-processing programs do. They also allow people to choose from a wide range of type styles and sizes to enhance the appearance of a document.

Desktop publishing was made possible by the introduction of powerful PCs and high-quality software and printers. Many organizations rely on a desktop publishing program to prepare newsletters, brochures, project proposals, advertisements, menus, and theater programs (Figure 2.16).

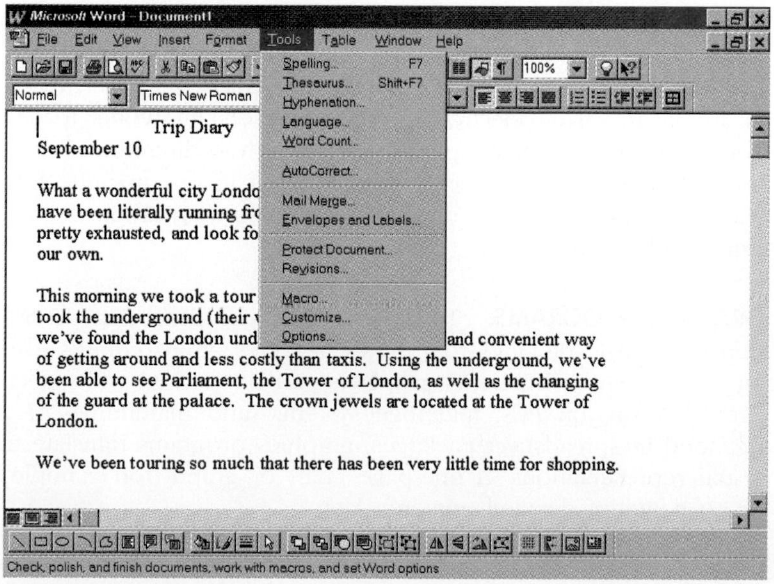

word-processing (WP) program
A program that allows the user to enter, change (edit), move, store, and print text information.

desktop publishing (DTP) program
A program that combines text and image-handling features with document-design capabilities.

FIGURE 2.15
Sample Word-Processing Options
In addition to allowing the user to lay out words in an aesthetically pleasing format, word-processing software also checks spelling, grammar, and punctuation. Many newer programs offer graphics capabilities as well.

FIGURE 2.16
Desktop Publishing Capabilities

Desktop publishing programs provide a great deal of flexibility in positioning text and images on a page. After the document designer has placed all the items in the desired locations (left), the document can be printed out and used as a master for making copies. Alternatively, the DTP system can be used to create a computer file that is sent on disk to a printer for printing (right). This process is more common with full-color publications.

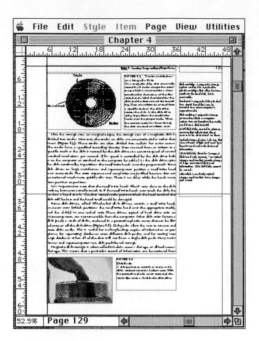

During the early days of information technology, the coming of the "paperless office" was proclaimed. Ideas would be entered through a keyboard and viewed on a computer screen, making it unnecessary to print the information. Some people even speculated that the general means of distribution of information throughout society would be magnetic disks, with newspapers, advertisements, magazines, and books being read on computer screens.

People *are* putting their thoughts down on computers. But they aren't generating any less paper. In fact, computers have led to a dramatic increase in paper use. It turns out we are unwilling to give up the printed word. In fact, when preparing a report or document, we tend to print it repeatedly to view changes and adjustments. (Of course, continual printing brings with it the social responsibility to recycle the excess paper generated.)

In an effort to reduce this stubborn reliance on paper, more and more organizations are using electronic communications networks to send messages and documents that recipients print out only at their discretion. Perhaps one day, most business communication will be carried out in this manner. But we have a long way to go before this kind of electronic communication becomes the norm and print is obsolete. ■

GRAPHICS PROGRAMS.   To present data in a form that describes trends, tracks performance levels, and compares categories often requires using charts, graphs, and maps. These **business graphics** can be created with special graphics packages that run on PCs, midrange systems, and mainframes (Figure 2.17). Often included in spreadsheet packages, graphics programs translate tables of data into visual representations. A one-page chart or graph, for example, may summarize many pages of detailed numeric data.

Graphics software programs prepare graphics more quickly and accurately than traditional manual methods. They not only help the user be more precise in draw-

business graphics
Charts, graphs, and maps that are created using special graphics packages that translate data into visual representations.

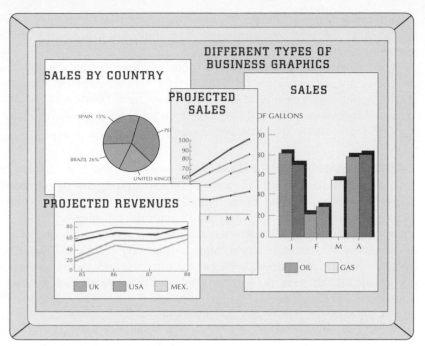

FIGURE 2.17
Sample Graphics Program
Graphics programs translate mountains of data into an easy-to-read, aesthetically pleasing format.

ing a chart or map but also offer color, shading, and even the illusion of three dimensions to enhance the presentation. We examine and illustrate the uses of graphics software fully in Chapters 6 and 8.

ILLUSTRATION PROGRAMS.   To draw images, create special effects, and translate ideas (rather than data) into visual form, people use **illustration programs.** These programs are the electronic equivalent of the artist's box of brushes, pens, and other devices. They turn the computer screen into a drawing board on which artists can bring their ideas to life (Figure 2.18). A finished illustration can be stored, retrieved, changed, and sent to a printer or similar device.

Illustration packages enable an artist to create any type of illustration with greater speed and precision than are possible by hand. Yet artistic creativity still

illustration program
A program in which the computer screen becomes a drawing board on which artists translate their ideas into visual form.

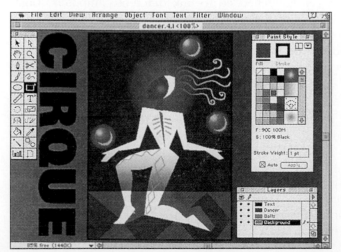

FIGURE 2.18
Illustration Program Capabilities
Illustration programs are like an electronic toolbox containing brushes, pens, boxes, circles, and color palettes.

originates with the user. The PC is but a tool that increases productivity; it is not a substitute for creativity and know-how. Illustration programs are discussed in detail in Chapter 8.

The *Information Technology in Practice* feature entitled "South Africa: Change in Government, Innovation in Voting" relates how graphical illustrations, sound, and computer processing were combined to help South Africa's citizens choose a new leader—one in a series of tremendous political changes that has transformed that country over the last decade.

database management program

A program that allows users to store information as interrelated records that can be retrieved quickly.

DATABASE MANAGEMENT PROGRAMS.   Businesses have a constant need to store and retrieve data and information. **Database management programs** let users store information as interrelated records that can be retrieved quickly. A *record* is a set of data pertaining to an item of interest. Information about a student, for example, is stored in a student record. Each record is composed of various *fields*, a collection of characters representing a single type of data. Thus, every student's record contains an address, a telephone number, and a date-of-birth field. A collection of related records (say, the freshman class or all biology majors, depending on how the database is organized) is called a *file*. The collection of all records about all students constitutes the **database.**

database

A collection of data and information describing items of interest.

With a database, information about an item can be retrieved according to a certain specified characteristic of the item. For example, a human resources manager could ask a database system to select the records in an interviewee database and print a list of all interviewees who live in Houston and are experts on international commerce in the European Community (Figure 2.19). A utility company could use a database to keep a record of all the houses, apartment buildings, and businesses to which it provides electricity.

Like all other software, database management programs handle the storage, retrieval, changing, and formatting of the information for the individual user. Many packages are available for use on every size of computer. We will develop your familiarity with database management systems in Chapters 7 and 11.

communications program

A program that manages the interaction between a computer system and a communications network and the transmission of data, programs, and information over the network.

COMMUNICATIONS PROGRAMS.   Data communication is an integral component of information technology and many computing applications. **Communications programs** manage the interaction between a computer system and a communications network and the transmission of data, information, and programs over the network. They provide the versatility needed to link different computers. Communications programs also establish the rules of data transmission and automatically manage electronic conversations to ensure users follow established rules. In addition, they control modems, the devices that allow computer-to-computer dialogue. In Chapter 10, we examine data communication from several different viewpoints.

information system/management information system (MIS)

A business information system designed to produce the information needed for successful management of a structured problem, process, department, or business.

INFORMATION SYSTEMS PROGRAMS.   Programs created to manage business activities made up the bulk of the software industry prior to the PC boom in the late 1970s and early 1980s. Most businesses acquired their first computers to process data for payroll management, production management, personnel records management, inventory control, and accounting procedures. Today, these applications still account for huge expenditures of business funds in both large and small organizations. Businesspeople often refer to these business management applications as **information systems** or **management information systems (MIS).**

INFORMATION TECHNOLOGY IN PRACTICE

South Africa: Change in Government, Innovation in Voting

When South Africa launched its first fully democratic elections, there were enormous challenges to be met. In this country of 39 million people, most of whom had never been allowed to vote before, it was necessary both to show people how to vote and to give them the information they needed about each candidate and political party to cast an informed vote. The landmark election that transformed South Africa's politics and government also occasioned a great innovation in communication.

Margot Sandenbergh and her thirteen-person company, Sandenbergh Pavon, Inc., of Johannesburg, developed a strategy that involved using some 30 kiosks that could be displayed at more than 70 sites around the country, primarily in rural townships. Each kiosk housed a microcomputer, color monitor, sound card, and audio speakers. The kiosks' touch screens not only displayed high-resolution graphics but also provided users with the means of interacting with the computers and accessing the voter information they contained.

Intended to overcome many first-time voters' fear and uncertainty, Sandenberg's kiosks were designed to be easy to use as well as informative. They reached out to voters, audibly beckoning them to "Come play me." By touching a candidate's image on the display screen, people could see and hear a one-minute video in which the candidate made a political pitch. The audio portion was broadcast in any of the country's 11 languages selected by the voter. Through a combination of text, high-resolution graphics, animation, full-motion video, and sound, the views of candidates from Nelson Mandela's African National Congress as well as from the 18 other political parties were presented.

Thus, voters came to know every candidate's views on important issues, and the information was presented in an entertaining and reassuring manner. Sandenbergh's multimedia kiosks also urged people to vote, emphasizing that their votes were confidential.

When two political parties changed their names late in the campaign, the necessary adjustments to the kiosks' presentations were quickly made. And when the Inkatha Freedom Party decided to join in the election at the last minute, Sandenbergh was able to film the party's candidate and electronically transfer the video and an accompanying recorded message to each of the kiosks scattered around the country.

South Africa's multimedia voter kiosks were so successful that the United Nations Economic, Scientific, and Cultural Organization (UNESCO) and the European Community, which provided the financial sponsorship that made them possible, are today seeking to create similar projects across Africa and Europe.

FIGURE 2.19
Records of Text and Data in a Job Database
Each employee has his or her own individual record, which includes three fields: the employee's name, date of hire, and job title. Together, these records constitute a job database.

NAME	DATE HIRED	JOB TITLE
Sally Thomas	10/2/88	Customer service representative
Morgan Fairfield	5/4/91	Advertising director
Bert Renoso	3/2/76	Customer service manager
James Jones Earl	2/5/78	Quality control supervisor
Ramon Vasquez	6/3/85	Customer service representative
Betty Lin	1/4/65	Operations manager

Record of information

Fields

Database

Information systems differ in an important way from spreadsheet packages and the other types of software we've discussed so far. Information systems focus on business processes (such as the processing of customer orders, the accounting process, the inventory management process, and increasing organizational productivity), while the other types of software focus on solving problems, aiding personal decision making, and increasing personal productivity. We explore information systems in depth in Chapter 13.

Programming Languages

computer programming language
A series of commands or codes that a computer can translate into the electronic pulses that underlie all computing activities.

Computer programs are not written in everyday language or as lines of text. Rather, they are created using a **computer programming language**—a series of commands and codes that the computer can translate into the electronic pulses that underlie all computing activities. When programmers write instructions in a programming language, they are telling the computer how and when to carry out arithmetic operations, read data from secondary storage, store data, and display or print information.

utility programs/utilities
Special programs used to perform tasks that occur repeatedly during processing.

Some tasks are performed so frequently during processing that it would be extremely inefficient to code these activities into the program again and again. For this reason, programmers use special **utility programs** (sometimes called **utilities**) to perform such functions as sorting records and copying programs from one medium to another. Utilities can either be bundled into an operating system or purchased as software.

Many programming languages have been developed to suit the needs of people tackling different types of problems, with some more popular in business than others. One of the most commonly used business programming languages today is COBOL (Common Business-Oriented Language). Other common programming languages are C, C++, and BASIC.

All the computer software packages discussed in the preceding section are written in a computer programming language. They eliminate the need for the user to know a programming language or how to write a program.

Custom Software

custom software
Software written specially for a particular business.

Not all software is prewritten and sold in package form. In fact, much of the software used in businesses is **custom software,** software designed for a particular firm by systems analysts and programmers (discussed later in this chapter). Applications software is the most common type of software developed by custom programmers (who write the application in a programming language). Custom applications may be developed by *in-house programmers,* who are employed by the company for which the application is developed, or by *contract programmers,* who are outside experts hired by the company to develop a certain program. The design and development of custom software is discussed in Chapter 12.

Software Trends

Two trends are changing the sources of computer software:

- **Greater use of prewritten software packages.** You can buy software to fit virtually any category of need, either from a computer retail store (such as CompUSA, Computer City, MicroCenter, Egghead Software, or Office Depot) that specializes in selling software or both software and hardware, or from a firm that develops and distributes software (such as IBM or Dow Jones Software). When selecting software, you need to first determine your requirements and then evaluate the features and price of a particular software package.
- **Greater use of prewritten components.** One of the most fundamental trends in computer software today is the move away from writing software from scratch toward using prewritten components (frequently called *objects* in IT parlance). Under this approach, developers acquire and assemble components to create an application. (Note: The objects and components are created by specialists who write the software in a fashion that makes it reusable.)

Advances in the power and capabilities of computer hardware, coupled with the skyrocketing demand for information technology at home, on campus, and at work, have led to advances in software development practices. Traditional software development practice is to use programming languages to create programs consisting of lengthy sections of computer instructions. Every time someone wants a new application written, the programmer has to write a separate programming procedure.

As you can imagine, many procedures are used repeatedly between applications. These procedures may be as subtle as date and time logging and customer account number validation routines in corporate accounting systems, or as visible as sound generation and graphics display modules in multimedia applications. There is no reason to keep writing these routine procedures over and over, regardless of which programming language is being used.

Object-oriented programming has evolved to simplify this situation. You might liken these new ways of developing software to the way consumer products have been manufactured for many years. A VCR, for instance, consists of the main circuit board, the tape transport mechanism, and the chassis. Each of these components, in turn, consists of smaller components: the circuit board, for instance, is made up of chips and diodes.

Objects are independent software blocks that can be used in many different applications without changing the program code. The software equivalents of the VCR's circuit boards and chips in an accounting application are the invoice object and its component parts, the date module, the item analysis module, and the invoice tax and total module. Each object contains data and processing procedures (for example, how to determine and validate the date of the invoice). Using objects in application development reduces the time and effort put into creating an application because each object can be reused, avoiding the need to write it from scratch.

object-oriented programming
Software development combining data and procedures into a single object.

object
A focal point about which data and information are collected; used in object-oriented databases.

A growing number of applications, both custom and commercial, are being written using object-oriented programming, and this will probably become the dominant programming method used by information technology professionals in the future. Both individuals and companies using software developed through object-oriented programming should benefit by getting better software more quickly. (We'll see how objects work in Chapter 12.)

Information: The Reason for Using Information Technology

information

An organized, meaningful, and useful interpretation of data.

As you already know, **information** is an organized, meaningful, and useful interpretation of data. Using information, you determine conditions, assess whether a problem has occurred, evaluate alternative solutions, and select actions. But information is not composed solely of data. It may also include text, sound, and images. As Figure 2.20 shows, information technology helps us make the most effective use of information in any or all of these forms.

Data

data

Raw facts, figures, and details.

The raw facts of a situation are **data.** Data can be numbers, letters, or symbols, or any combination of the three. Some examples of data are the average points scored by a team's leading player, the number of subscribers to a magazine, the attendance at a rock concert, the midday price for a corporate stock, and the number of English majors in the College of Arts and Sciences. Each piece of data describes a fact, a condition, an event, or the results of that event.

Text

Text is written (narrative) information. It may be typed, printed, or handwritten. When you scan a newspaper, flip through a magazine, read a letter, or look at the fine print on a rental agreement, you are using text information.

Sports scores and statistics on athletic achievements tell only part of the story of a game. That's why newspapers and magazines always include a narrative highlighting key plays. Without this narrative information, you couldn't possibly get the full story of the game.

Sound

spoken information

Information that is conveyed by sound.

The same sports statistics that you can read in a newspaper may be broadcast to you by an announcer at the game. This is **spoken information**—information conveyed by sound. Have you ever called directory assistance to obtain a phone number and heard the number spoken in a humanlike—but definitely not human—voice? This, too, is spoken information—information conveyed by sound from a computer.

Virtually any sound can be captured in a computer system, transmitted over a network, or output through a computer-controlled device. It is now quite common for sound input to originate from people speaking into microphones connected to a computer. For example, when a telephone directory system asks you to say the name of the city and then the name of the party for whom you are seeking a telephone number, your voice response is sound input to the system.

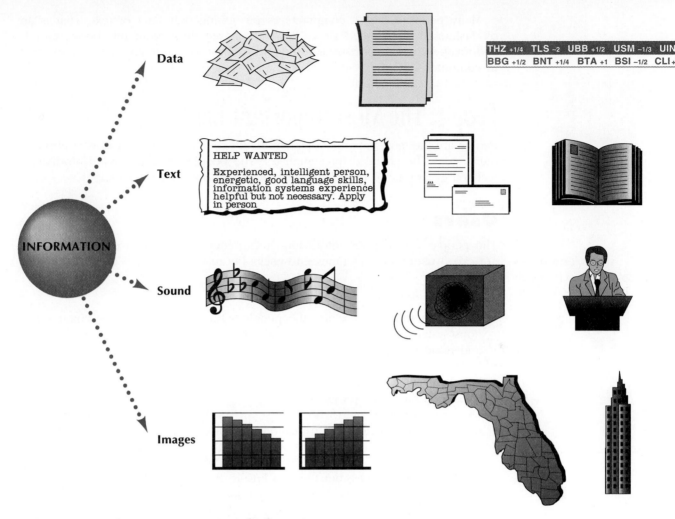

FIGURE 2.20 *The Four Components of Information*

Data do not become information until they are organized logically and usefully. Information may also include text, sound, and images.

Images

An image is information in visual form. Images may be used to summarize data, as in charts and graphs. They may also take the form of lines, drawings, or photographs. Karl Gude's infographics combine data, text, and images. Many multimedia presentations, which incorporate all four of the components of information, use animation to move words and images across the screen.

Most of the world's major league sports have a "hall of fame" where outstanding athletes and officials are honored. At the Football Hall of Fame, you will find computer-controlled multimedia displays of great plays made in the game down through the decades. Sound and image information stored on optical disk is retrieved to re-create these memorable events for the viewer—right down to the athletes' grunts and groans and the cheers from the crowd. Best of all, the computer-managed displays can be maintained forever, providing a vivid historical record of the sport.

Many people think of computers as processing only data or text. That is an old-fashioned and limited view. As you will see throughout this book, sounds and images are as important as—and used almost as frequently as—data and text in computer systems.

People: The Most Important Element

People are the most important element in any computer system, for without them, there would be no need for computers. The people associated with information technology are its users and information technology professionals.

Users

users/end-users
The people who use IT in their jobs or personal lives.

The people who employ information technology in their jobs or personal lives are called **users,** or sometimes **end-users** because they are the ultimate users of a computer system.

There are four types of users (Figure 2.21):

- **Hands-on users.** These are the people who use computers or communications systems directly, interacting with them to enter data, do processing, store and retrieve information, transmit details, or produce output.
- **Indirect end-users.** These individuals do not directly operate a computer but benefit from IT as the recipients of reports, electronic messages, communications, or multimedia presentations.
- **User managers.** People who have supervisory responsibility for activities that involve or are affected by information technology are known as user managers. Manufacturing managers, editors, and hospital administrators, for instance, may be in charge of departments or work groups that use IT. These managers may not use IT themselves, but they do ensure that their staff members have reliable computer and communication capabilities. It is increasingly rare, however, to find a user manager who is not a hands-on user.
- **Senior managers.** These managers incorporate the capabilities of information technology into an organization's products, services, and overall competitive strategies. They also evaluate the organization's dependence on IT and identify the problems that could arise if appropriate operating procedures (discussed later in this chapter) are not established or followed. The *Information Technology in Practice* feature titled "CIO Becomes Key Advisor to CEO" discusses a relatively new senior management position in IT.

The retailing industry provides a good example of how information technology can span all levels of management and strongly influence a company's operations. Wal-Mart, the ($100 billion!) U.S. discount retailer, has become the world's most successful firm of its type through its use of IT. At the store level, cashiers (hands-on end-users) enter sales data into point-of-sale terminals by waving a bar code scanner across a package's bar-coded price and stock numbers. The price of the item is then retrieved from the store computer and appears on the point-of-sale terminal display. At the same time, the sale of the item is recorded.

Store and department managers who receive reports of store and department sales and inventory levels are indirect end-users. They may not operate a computer directly, but they do rely on the information captured and generated through the company's information system to make decisions. User managers help to ensure that Wal-Mart maintains remarkably low inventories (only about 10 per-

FIGURE 2.21
*The End-Users of
Information Technology*

a) Hands-on users use IT directly, interacting with computers to perform their jobs.

b) Indirect end-users do not operate computers directly, but benefit from IT as the recipients of reports or multimedia presentations.

c) User managers supervise people or activities that involve or are affected by IT.

d) Senior managers incorporate IT's capabilities into their organizations' products, services, and overall competitive strategies.

cent of the company's square footage is devoted to inventory, compared to an industry average of 25 percent). The firm's senior managers, including the chief executive officer and corporate vice presidents, use IT to monitor store-by-store sales daily, a key step in ensuring that sales goals are being achieved.

Together, senior and user managers have extended the reach of Wal-Mart's IT beyond the company. The majority of Wal-Mart's 5,000 vendors now receive point-of-sale information through an electronic link. They use this information to determine what goods are selling and to keep Wal-Mart sufficiently—but not overly—stocked to meet its sales needs. Yet the entire process begins with the activities of the hands-on end-user who enters the details about each item sold at a Wal-Mart store.

Information Technology Professionals

Information technology professionals are responsible for acquiring, developing, maintaining, or operating the hardware and software associated with computers and communications networks. The following IT professionals have the highest profile:

information technology professional
A person who is responsible for acquiring, developing, maintaining, or operating the hardware associated with computers and communications networks.

INFORMATION TECHNOLOGY IN PRACTICE

CIO Becomes Key Advisor to CEO

If information is the lifeblood of the Information Age organization, it stands to reason that information managers are pretty important people. That's why hundreds of the world's top corporations have created the position of chief information officer (CIO) or senior vice president of IT, a corporate officer who reports directly to the CEO.

CIOs' backgrounds tend to vary. Some have extensive technical training, while others have MBAs but little or no technical expertise. All share a keen awareness of what IT can do for business. What else does it take to be an effective CIO? DuWayne Peterson, a leading IT consultant and former CIO for Merrill Lynch & Co., lists five requirements:

1. *The knowledge that business strategy is the rudder that steers IT planning.* Sometimes a company's IT strategy calls for an entirely new vision of its business. The CIO of Simon & Schuster, for ex-

ample, is charged with leading the giant publisher into the new world of electronic publishing. At other companies, the strategic goals are

less radical but equally challenging. The CIO at Levi Strauss & Co. is charged with using IT to help the company delegate authority and responsibility to its 32,000 employees around the world. This has meant setting up computer networks that help store managers and suppliers maintain proper inventory levels without intervention from headquarters.

2. *A strong vision of what IT can do to achieve strategic objectives.* In the past, banks resigned themselves to the idea that customers come and go. As a result, most banks used IT for processing transactions in separate checking, savings, loan, and credit card accounts. To-

day, however, banks realize that retaining customers will make their business more profitable, so competition for loyal customers is heating up. BANK ONE Corp. initiated a strategy that has become a banking trend: winning customer loyalty

- **Programmers**—use programming languages to create computer and communications network software.
- **Systems analysts**—work with users to determine the requirements an application must meet. As part of their job, they may specify the purchase of a software package that gets the job done or order the development of custom software.
- **Systems designers**—formulate application specifications and design the features of custom software. In some organizations, the roles of programmer, systems analyst, and systems designer may be filled by one person called a **programmer/analyst.**
- **Project managers**—coordinate the development of a project and manage the team of programmer/analysts.
- **Network specialists**—design, operate, and manage computer communications networks.

programmer/analyst
A person who has joint responsibility for determining system requirements and developing and implementing the systems.

by pursuing "relationship banking." At the heart of BANK ONE's campaign is a strategic application featuring a computer system that integrates 17 systems to create a comprehensive customer profile that can be used to market personalized services. With the help of SBS, BANK ONE's marketing department can identify customers who might need suggestions on financing a college education or preparing for retirement.

3. *The technical ability to develop an IT structure that will provide low-cost, responsive services for all, as well as individualized services for individual business units.* Kmart provides a good example. One of its CEO's first moves was to ask the senior vice president of information systems for advice on how to carry out a new merchandising strategy. At the time, the managers of Kmart's 2,400 stores made all buying and restocking decisions—a practice that led to overlapping orders, missed volume discounts, and sometimes empty shelves and lost sales. Five years later, a new satellite-based system lets headquarters track sales at all stores and coordinate the ordering process.

Kmart

4. *The ability to analyze business processes and au-*

tomate them to make them more efficient. This process, called *reengineering,* is transforming the face of U.S. business, which has recognized the need to become more efficient in the face of fierce global competition. At Eastman Kodak Company, for example, a recent reengineering project was the implementation of a software system that would integrate order processing with manufacturing, distribution, and operations.

5. *Effective human resource management programs and skills that produce well-trained IT workers and end-users.* To train workers, CIOs set up IT training programs for employees at all levels. At UNUM Life Insurance Co., for example, the CIO is retraining mainframe programmers to use PC software development tools and teaching end-users to perform a wider range of "quasi-technical" roles.

All of this adds up to one big job that requires excellent management skills—a fact that is not lost on business analysts.

- **Trainers**—work with end-users, helping them to become comfortable with and skilled at using hardware or software.
- **Computer operators**—oversee the operations of computers in **data centers** (sometimes called **computer centers**), facilities where large and midrange computer systems are located. These systems are shared by many users who are interconnected with the system through communications links. Computer operators also perform support activities, such as starting applications, loading magnetic tape, and any other job that will ensure the smooth operation of computer facilities.

These IT professionals usually work for businesses that use computers or communications technology but do not design and manufacture the hardware they use. IT professionals in the business of manufacturing computers or computer-

data center/computer center
A facility at which large and midrange computer systems are located. These systems are shared by many users who are interconnected with the system through communications links.

IT Simplifies Life for Price Waterhouse Auditors

If you're thinking of becoming a global auditor, be prepared for a challenging career. Your job will be to go over a corporation's financial statements with a fine-tooth comb. Is the corporation following generally accepted accounting practices? Are its figures accurate? Do the statements show any evidence of fraud? And (since you'll be working on-site) are you sure you've packed every tool you might need to do your job completely and accurately?

The more than 12,000 professionals working for New York–based Price Waterhouse used to have to pack an extra suitcase or two to hold the firm's 40-plus printed volumes of accounting guidelines. Now, however, Price Waterhouse arms its auditors with some of the newest IT "weapons." One such weapon is a high-powered laptop computer suitable for double-checking the figures on complicated financial statements. Others are a portable CD-ROM drive for the laptop and a CD-ROM disk containing every guideline contained in the 40-plus volumes. CD-ROM is lighter, more durable, and easier to search than a paper-based source. By typing in a keyword, auditors can retrieve relevant data from all the firm's 40 volumes of guidelines in an instant.

related components (such as communication cables and electrical power supplies) generally fall into two categories: **computer engineers,** who design, develop, and oversee the manufacturing of computer equipment; and **systems engineers,** who install and maintain hardware.

computer engineer
An IT professional who designs, develops, and oversees the manufacturing of computer equipment.

systems engineer
An IT professional who installs and maintains hardware.

Procedures: The Way It Goes

Good procedures are essential whether an application runs on a PC or a super-computer or is used by one person or a large number of people. A **procedure** is a step-by-step set of instructions—a process—for accomplishing specific results. Procedures, people, and applications together make up the know-how of IT.

There are four primary categories of procedures: operations, backup and recovery, security, and development (Figure 2.22). All are "people procedures" that help avert problems and provide guidance in dealing with any problems that do arise.

procedure
A step-by-step process or a set of instructions for accomplishing specific results.

Operations Procedures

Operations procedures refer to the execution of an application. Typically, operations procedures describe

- How a system or application is used.
- Who is authorized to use the system and to what extent.
- How often certain applications are to be used.
- Where results of processing—the output—should go.

operations procedure
A procedure that describes how a computer system or application is used, how often it can be used, who is authorized to use it, and where the results of processing should go.

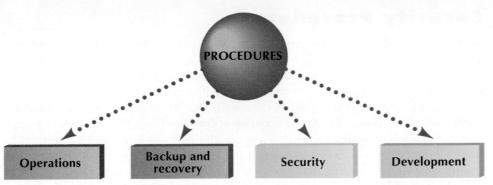

FIGURE 2.22
The Four Types of Procedures

At Wal-Mart, for instance, strict procedures govern what information will be shared with suppliers and under what circumstances. The guidelines also describe the form in which information is to be shared, indicating when raw data should be distributed and when only summary forms should be released.

If you use a PC, you probably follow a set of procedures for starting it up and shutting it down. Operators of mainframes in computer centers or midrange computers in offices must do the same thing. These procedures ensure that information will not be lost and that electrical components will not be damaged.

Depending on the application, operations procedures can be very simple ("Always make a backup copy of the day's work before shutting down the system") or quite involved ("At the end of every month, make a backup copy of all databases, a copy of all transactions, and reset all account totals to begin the next month").

Backup and Recovery Procedures

After several days' work creating a high-impact graphic, you don't want to risk losing it because a power line goes down or a diskette gets misplaced. As a general rule, you should assume that sooner or later something will happen to cause your work to be lost.

Backup procedures describe when and how to make extra copies (called **backup copies**) to protect yourself against loss of data, information, or software. Should any of these be lost or accidentally changed, they can then be restored from the backup copy. **Recovery procedures** describe what actions to take when data and information or software must be recovered.

backup procedure
A procedure that describes how and when to make extra copies of information or software to protect against losses.

backup copies
Extra copies of information or software made to protect against losses.

recovery procedure
An action taken when information or software must be restored.

A fundamental "principle" of personal life has been humorously phrased in the form of Murphy's Law: If something can go wrong, it will. There are corollaries to this principle, including these:

Nothing is as easy as it looks.

Everything takes longer than you think.

If you determine that there are exactly four ways in which something can go wrong, a fifth way will suddenly put in an appearance.

Nature always takes the side of the hidden flaw.

Applied to information technology, Murphy's Law dictates that you should *always* assume that data, information, and software sooner or later will be accidentally erased, damaged, or lost. Therefore, make backup copies of *everything*. ∎

Security Procedures

security procedure

A procedure designed to safeguard data centers, communications networks, computers, and other IT components from accidental intrusion or intentional damage.

Security procedures are designed to safeguard data centers, communications networks, computers, and other IT components from accidental intrusion or intentional damage. Backup copies protect against loss; security procedures prevent actions that could lead to that loss. Common security procedures entail limiting access to certain databases and creating secret passwords that users must input into the computer to perform certain functions. **Security software** allows IT managers to restrict access to files and databases, to disk drives, and even to input/output devices.

security software

Software that is designed to protect systems and data.

Of particular importance is protection against *viruses*—hidden programs, residing on disk or in memory, that can alter (without any users realizing it) the way a computer operates or modify the data and programs stored on the computer. The virus copies itself onto other programs or to diskettes inserted into the system, thereby spreading itself from one computer to another—just as a biological virus spreads from one person to the next. If undetected for a long period of time, a virus can do a great deal of damage to stored information. The *Information Technology in Practice* feature titled "Continuous Performance—Virus-Free" offers some tips on how to protect your computer from virus damage. (We discuss viruses in more detail in Chapter 14.)

Development Procedures

development procedure

A procedure that explains how IT professionals should describe user needs and develop applications to meet those needs.

Development procedures tell IT professionals how to describe user needs and develop applications to meet those needs. These procedures may also prescribe when and how software should be acquired and put into use. The IT professional involved in a development process should begin by examining the business situation, and then evaluate alternative methods for improving that situation or capitalizing on an opportunity. In some firms, these findings are recorded according to specific *documentation procedures*.

It's the development procedures that will determine how successful an application will be. (We'll talk more about development procedures in Chapter 12.)

An Introduction to Systems

Let's explore some of the differences between IT in personal systems and in multiuser systems. (Recall that a *system* is a set of components that interact to accomplish a purpose.)

Personal/Single-User Systems

A graphics illustrator using a desktop computer to create drawings and images has a powerful personal tool at hand. Karl Gude uses a PC to create his infographics. To him, the PC is a very personal tool, loaded with his favorite software and outfitted with equipment that enables him to translate his ideas onto paper. Because Gude is the sole user of his PC, it can truly be considered a *personal* system. It is also a **single-user system:** one that is not connected with other computers or shared by other people.

single-user system

An IT system that stands alone, meaning it is not interconnected with other computers or shared by other people.

The most important benefit of personal systems is their ability to be customized to enhance the productivity and effectiveness of the person using them. In Gude's system, effectiveness takes the form of being able to represent information in a creative and digestible format, while productivity derives from the system's ability to develop illustrations much more rapidly than he could by hand.

Multiuser Systems

People whose work requires them to exchange information find they can do so most quickly and effectively on computers that are interconnected. **Multiuser system** is the general term for a system in which more than one user shares one or more systems of hardware, programs, information, people, and procedures. The multiuser system has three purposes: (1) to increase the productivity and effectiveness of the people using the applications, (2) to increase the productivity and effectiveness of the organizations in which the applications are used, and (3) to improve the services provided to those who rely on the users of multiuser applications.

multiuser system
A system in which more than one user shares hardware, programs, information, people, and procedures.

All of the following are reasons to use multiuser systems:

- **To share a computer**   *Example:* American Airlines, Delta Air Lines, and TWA interconnect thousands of travel agents by allowing them to share a centralized mainframe system to book reservations for their customers. United Airlines and American Airlines have similar shared computer systems.
- **To share hardware**   *Example:* Artists working on separate projects at the *New York Times* share a printer on which they can produce their illustrations. Each artist's computer is connected to the printer through a communications cable.
- **To share software**   *Example:* Rather than requiring students to purchase individual copies of a multimedia biology education program, the University of Minnesota acquired a license from the manufacturer to allow many students to use the software. Students can share the software on a special network set up in the laboratory. The network interconnects separate PCs to a more powerful central PC on which the software is stored and made accessible to the separate student PCs.
- **To share information**   *Example:* Medical personnel at the Stanford Medical Center and at Massachusetts General Hospital can review all the diagnostic, test, and treatment information about a critically ill patient, including X-rays, because it is all stored in a single database maintained at the hospital chosen by the patient.
- **To share communications**   *Example:* Product designers in a company can stay in touch with one another, regardless of their geographic locations, by means of an electronic mail system. Both IBM and Digital Equipment Corp. interconnect their employees around the globe through their worldwide messaging networks. At Coca-Cola Co., employees use the same network to send and receive messages through their desktop, laptop, or notebook computers.

You can readily see how important multiuser systems are in manufacturing plants. Automobile makers in Japan, South Korea, throughout Europe, and in the United States rely on multiuser systems to interconnect production and assembly equipment, including robots. Networking allows activities to be synchronized so that all actions take place at the right time.

Multiuser systems are neither more nor less valuable than single-user systems. They just offer a different set of benefits. (We discuss single-user systems in detail in Chapters 5–8 and multiuser systems in detail in Chapters 9–13.)

INFORMATION TECHNOLOGY IN PRACTICE

Continuous Performance—Virus-Free

Once upon a time, most people associated the name "Michelangelo" with the famous Renaissance artist. That was before computer experts sounded the alarm about a different *Michelangelo,* a computer virus that was set to "go off" on March 6, the artist's birthday.

As the text discusses, a computer virus is a rogue computer program, a tiny saboteur that sneaks into your computer when you use an infected disk or program. Once inside your machine, the virus copies itself to other files it comes into contact with. Its effects can range from the distressing—the monitor displays "Your computer is now sick"—to the devastating—the system "crashes" as the virus clogs the computer's memory, or all your files are wiped clean, erasing thousands of hours of work. (*Michelangelo* has the latter effect.)

The first known computer virus was created by a University of Southern California student in 1983 to demonstrate the inadequacy of microcomputer security. But no one paid much attention to the security problem until July 1987, when officials at the Hebrew University in Jerusalem learned that a computer virus

was poised to erase any computer program executed on Friday the 13th. That virus, dubbed *Friday the 13th* or *Jerusalem B,* was the first computer virus to be named.

Today, computer viruses are considered to be chilling acts of computer vandalism. More than 1,500 computer viruses have already been identified, and another 50 surface every week. Computer viruses have been discovered in every type of computer and computer network around the world. They have been found in shrinkwrapped software and preformatted disks sold by major companies, as well as on the special diagnostic disks used by service technicians.

Microcomputers are the most vulnerable to viruses because most are not protected by the security measures that guard their larger cousins. That's why businesses that depend on PCs have issued instructions like these for safe, virus-free computing:

- *Perform regular backups.* Making a practice of storing backups of all your disks and your operating system on a write-protected set of disks

Information Technology in Practice at ITT Sheraton Hotels: An Example

Now that you've had a tour of the computer and been introduced to its capabilities, let's see how it all fits together. Here's an example of PCs, mainframes, and communications networks working together to accomplish the day-to-day activities of a worldwide hotel system. Note how single-user and multiuser systems work together.

ITT Sheraton

ITT Sheraton, headquartered in Boston (Figure 2.23), owns or operates more than 400 hotels around the world. Each hotel has a unique personality. Some are in downtown areas and cater to conventioneers and business travelers, while others

(disks that can't be written to by another program) won't keep the viruses away, but it will help you restore your system if it comes under virus attack.

- *Install and use an antivirus package.* These software packages work in one of two ways. Either they scan your computer system for the "signatures" of known viruses, or they use artificial intelligence techniques to warn you that your system has obeyed instructions to copy unusual instructions (a potential virus) to program files. Because just a few viruses account for almost 80 percent of all infections, this practice will go a long way toward protecting your system.

- *Know the source of your programs.* Many common viruses are spread when users download games and other programs from bulletin board systems (BBSs; see Chapter 10) or share pirated copies of software programs, many of which have been intentionally infected with viruses. Although the reputable BBSs and software distributors scan their systems for viruses, most corporations and all prudent end-users scan every program and disk themselves before using it. In addition, many corporations forbid employees to share disks or use disks from home on their office PCs.

- *If you think your computer has a virus, don't panic.* Save what you are working on and turn off your PC. Use your write-protected backup of the operating system to restart the computer and run your antivirus software at least twice. Once you are certain the system is "clean," you can use your backup to restore your hard disk.

Taken together, these measures should help you stay one step ahead of the virus vandals. Meanwhile, the computer industry is working on more permanent cures. The System 7 operating system for Macintosh computers is already immune to two of the most vexing viruses that damage key files, and Microsoft Corporation is releasing a read-only command that will keep viruses from copying themselves from program to program.

are in resort areas and specialize in ensuring that vacationing guests can unwind and relax. Whatever a Sheraton hotel's characteristics, an important factor in its ability to meet its customer's needs is ITT Sheraton's property management system. This system is integral to providing services to guests and running day-to-day hotel operations.

Reservatron Worldwide Reservation System

Most guests make an advance reservation through Reservatron, ITT Sheraton's worldwide computer and communication system that is operated from the company's Boston headquarters. Potential guests place a toll-free call to Reservatron to check on the rates and availability of guest rooms at their chosen hotel. Reservation agents must have information at their fingertips telling them not only whether rooms are available, but also the type of room (single bed, double bed,

CRITICAL CONNECTION 3

| McKesson Corp. | McKesson Corp.: "Wearable" Computers Streamline the Retailer-Distributor Link |

When you've got a splitting headache, you won't be pleased to find the drug-store shelf bare of aspirin. This, in a nutshell, summarizes the importance of *distribution*—the wholesale link between manufacturer and retailer. Few companies do distribution better than McKesson Corp., a San Francisco–based distributor of drugs and health-care products.

In the pre-IT era, McKesson's customers ordered goods by telephone. Banks of telephone order takers completed order forms and warehouse workers walked about handpicking the requested items off the shelves. The system was slow, expensive, and error-prone.

McKesson responded in the early 1970s by forging computer network links with manufacturers and retailers. Today, a retailer's employee walks through the store carrying a computer the size of a cellular phone. One swipe of a handheld laser scanner over a bar-coded shelf label and—presto—an order is beamed to a McKesson warehouse. At the warehouse, a central computer radios the order to a revolutionary "wearable" computer strapped to a worker's forearm. This wearable computer combines a portable computer with a two-way radio (for receiving and sending order information), a handheld laser scanner (for choosing items from warehouse shelves), and a three-inch screen that displays, among other things, the shortest route through the warehouse. When the worker has filled the order, the wearable computer sends a message back to the central computer, which creates an electronic bill for the retailer.

or suite), its location (oceanfront or mountain view, for example), and the daily rate. Rates vary according to the type of room, the season or dates of rental, and whether the guest is part of a convention or other large group booking rooms at the hotel. ITT's reservation system also keeps track of information of this nature for each hotel.

Potential customers can contact ITT Sheraton's toll-free number (800-325-3535) for making reservations from anywhere in the world. When a reservation is made by phone, a reservation agent takes the call. All agents ask what location the caller is interested in. If the caller knows the city, but not a specific Sheraton hotel within the city, the agent can call up a listing of all hotels in that city and information about their location. After the customer chooses a hotel and it is verified that a room is available there on the desired dates, details of the reservation are entered into the Reservatron database. The agent notes the name of the guest and all pertinent information, including address, dates and length of stay at the chosen hotel, and any special requirements. Reservatron issues a confirmation number that uniquely identifies the guest and the specific reservation (Figure 2.24a and b). (Business travelers may have several reservations for different

FIGURE 2.23
ITT Sheraton Headquarters

hotels on various dates entered for them in the system, and this unique number is Reservatron's way of keeping them separate.)

Reservatron communicates with a computer system at each Sheraton hotel. It retrieves information about the availability of rooms in order to respond to an inquiry from an individual guest. Likewise, details of reservations made through the reservation system are automatically passed to the local hotel through the communications link. (If a guest makes a reservation at the local hotel, or "walks in" to obtain a room on a specific day, this inventory information is also transmitted to Reservatron.)

Property Management System

Besides being connected to Reservatron, the ITT Sheraton headquarters system, each hotel in the Sheraton chain operates its own independent systems. A property management system that runs on a local network of computers at the hotel's front desk enables the staff to check in guests, registering them for the room, rate, and length of stay described in their reservation (Figure 2.25). All guest information originally entered through the Reservatron system is available to local hotel staff members. Front desk personnel can also enter additional details or make changes using the personal computer or workstation attached to the local hotel system.

During a guest's stay, the property management system keeps track of charges incurred by the guest in the hotel's restaurants and other facilities. At the guest's departure, a final bill is prepared and printed at the front desk (Figure 2.26). This bill reflects whether the guest is paying in cash or by credit card. Or the bill may be charged to a group account, which is paid later. All these details, entered into the property management system by the front desk attendant, are noted on the final printed statement.

FIGURE 2.24
ITT Sheraton Phone
Reservations

Property management involves more than just running the hotel's front desk. The property management system supports other areas of the hotel, using the database of information maintained in the system. For example, the hotel telephone operator interacts with the database to answer callers' inquiries about the room number of a guest. Entering the name of the guest on a personal computer, the operator retrieves the room number from the system's database. (If the caller is not certain how the name is spelled, the operator enters a name by spelling it as it sounds, and the system displays all guests' names that sound similar, regardless of how they are spelled.) The operator also uses the property management system to key in messages callers leave for guests. The system keeps track of messages in the databases, noting when they are picked up by the guest.

The property management system also helps the hotel's housekeeping department, which is responsible for cleaning and servicing guest rooms (Figure 2.27a and b). At the beginning of each day, a printer linked by a communication line to the property management system computer prepares a list of rooms to be serviced by each maid. Throughout the day, maids update the room database by entering the number and status information for each room as they clean it. They do this through the keyboard of a Touch-Tone telephone. The status information informs front desk staff when rooms have been serviced and are ready for new guests.

FIGURE 2.25
ITT Sheraton's Property Management System

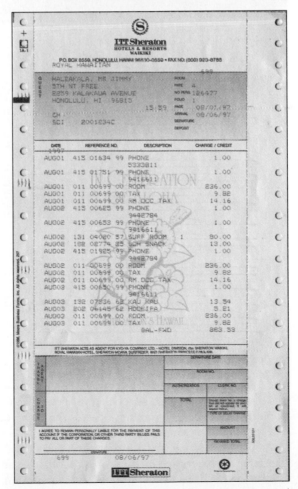

FIGURE 2.26
The Property Management System Updates Billing

FIGURE 2.27
The Property Management System Helps Maintain the Housekeeping Department

Back Office System

The hotel's property management system is visible to guests because they come into contact with it during check-in, throughout their stay, and at checkout time. Behind the scenes is another system, the back office system, which manages the hotel's overall operations.

At the end of each day, information from the property management system is transferred electronically to the back office system. Using desktop workstations linked to the back office system, the accounting staff reviews the previous day's work. Auditors check transactions for accuracy, and other staff members prepare the final bills to be mailed to groups that charged expenses.

Not all hotel transactions originate at the front desk. Some originate in banquets and special events (receptions, weddings, and business meetings). Back office staff members use desktop computers to enter these transactions into the database.

Still other transactions result from the purchase of supplies and services needed to keep the hotel running. Bills and invoices for these transactions are also submitted to the accounting staff, who enter details about them into the computer and prepare them for payment. Later, printed checks to suppliers are prepared on the back office system.

Juliette Reeves, the administrative coordinator for the Executive Offices of ITT Sheraton, is an effective information manager who works well with people. She believes in communicating face-to-face with managers, hotel staff members, and her own staff, but she also finds computers an invaluable tool for doing her job and for helping others to do theirs.

Juliette uses her PC to do five tasks: word processing, maintaining spreadsheets, maintaining departmental databases, doing departmental budgeting, and communicating electronically.

WORD PROCESSING. Juliette prepares many memos, letters, proposals, and reports, some of which are sent to people within the hotel, and others of which are sent to the business community, to potential guests, or to former guests. She prepares most of her written documents using word-processing software. Some of these documents are printed and mailed, while others are sent electronically over a network that connects management and staff of the hotel.

Juliette's office is currently extending its word-processing capabilities to include desktop publishing, which will enable the staff to prepare and print brochures and literature describing Sheraton hotels and the services they offer. These brochures will include photographs and graphic illustrations printed in color from a printer attached to her system.

SPREADSHEETS. Juliette routinely prepares and reviews guest occupancy projections, budgets, and proposals to enhance or repair specific facilities in the hotel. To keep this information accurate, she continually reviews and updates a spreadsheet containing the relevant categories of information.

Particularly important to Juliette and hotel managers are the "what if" analyses they perform using the spreadsheets. What if hotel occupancy increases by 10 percent next year? What if International Services Corp. requests a special price for the month-long use of a set of meeting rooms? By entering possible changes into the spreadsheets, Juliette is able to determine the likely effects of these changes.

DEPARTMENTAL DATABASES. Although ITT Sheraton's property management database contains a great deal of information on guest activities, facilities, operations activities, and maintenance, Juliette's department needs other information, which she maintains in separate databases on her PC. For instance, a special database contains personal information on managers and staff members (addresses and telephone numbers, e-mail addresses, employment histories). This database can also be used to retrieve the travel schedule of managers who are visiting corporate headquarters in Boston, attending planning meetings, or traveling on behalf of Sheraton. It can also be used to prepare a directory of all ITT Sheraton employees.

This special database resides only on Juliette's PC. It is maintained using a personal computer database management software package.

DEPARTMENTAL BUDGETING.   Although the property management system maintains a great deal of information on sales and guest activities, Juliette uses a software package running on her PC to maintain the hotel corporation's financial budget. This application includes information on actual and planned revenues, receipt of money, and expenses.

Periodically, Juliette prepares detailed listings itemizing all the department's expenditures. Whenever she needs to determine the balance of a specific account, she can display or print a summary listing. She can even retrieve the details of a particular transaction for review.

ELECTRONIC COMMUNICATION.   A communications network links all the PCs in the Executive Offices together. Thus, Juliette, like every other manager and staff member in the Executive Offices, as well as individual hotel departmental managers (such as the front desk, housekeeping, banquet, and sales managers), can send and retrieve messages or information about Sheraton's activities and plans.

Because the back office system is connected to the property management system, Juliette can access any information contained in the property management system. She can display or print this information, transferring it from the property management system to her PC. Transferring information makes it unnecessary to rekey data or information into the computer.

The Executive Offices Staff

Tanaka, Judy, Miguel, Tatiana, Roshawn, Carol, and Ruth are on the administrative staff at ITT Sheraton's Executive Offices. All of them have a personal computer on their desk. Most use IBM-compatible computers equipped with DOS, Windows, and a variety of PC application packages for word processing, desktop publishing, spreadsheets, and graphics, though Tatiana and Ruth use Apple Macintosh computers. Everyone's computer is outfitted with the same software, using versions either created for IBM-compatibles or for the Macintosh.

All members of the administrative staff have customized their PCs to meet their needs. All the PCs have a color monitor, keyboard, mouse, diskette drive, and internal hard disk. Many also have a CD-ROM drive. The PCs used by Roshawn and Carol have been set up to go right into the word-processing program when they are turned on. The others are set up so that the staff member must specify which application to use after turning the computer on.

In addition to a PC, Carol, along with several of the managers, has a notebook computer. The notebook, which is equipped with many of the same types of application software the PC has, can connect with a telephone line to send and receive information, including faxes. Its small size and portability mean it can easily be carried about so that Carol can enter information or connect with the hotel computers whenever the need arises.

All the personal computers used by the Executive Offices staff can be operated as stand-alone systems. Each is also connected to the hotel's computer network (Figure 2.27a).

Information Technology at ITT Sheraton's Reservatron System

ITT Sheraton operates a large complex of mainframe and midrange computers. These multiuser computers at the corporation's computer center serve several purposes. One midrange computer, for example, is dedicated to the management of regional activities. Other, general-purpose midrange computers are shared by many people on the headquarters staff.

In addition to being the nexus of the worldwide reservation system, the computers in the computer center contain software that is shared by managers, planners, and other staff members. Shared mainframe software is usually expensive and requires capabilities that are beyond PCs or midrange computers. The administration also maintains centralized databases on Sheraton's franchisees, facilities (buildings and equipment), employees, operating agreements, and finances. This information is accessible to some headquarters department administrators and staff members, who need it to operate their departments.

The ITT Sheraton corporate applications and databases reside on large systems, rather than PCs, because of the large volume of records that must be maintained. Large-scale applications require high-speed computing capabilities and large memory storage capacities. Mainframe computers can provide this capability while also providing access to large groups of people who wish to use the applications and databases.

Information Processing

Chapter 1 introduced you to the 6 information-handling functions of IT: capture, processing, generation, storage and retrieval, and transmission. At ITT Sheraton Hotels, 13 information-processing activities are associated with these 6 information-handling functions.

CAPTURE

Input: Inputting is entering data into the system for processing. A reservation agent entering guest information through a PC, and a housekeeper entering room and cleaning details through use of a Touch-Tone telephone, create transactions that are treated as *input* to the reservation and property management systems, respectively.

Upload/Download: Many hotel personnel receive information from another location that is part of the hotel or reservation network. For example, the administrative coordinator in the Executive Offices can download guest history information from the property management system. Likewise, reservation systems operators at headquarters upload information on conventions and room allocations at a local hotel. Sending information from a PC to a central mainframe is called **uploading.** Transferring information from a central system to a desktop computer is called **downloading.**

PROCESSING

Compute: Computing is calculating results through addition, subtraction, and other arithmetic functions. For example, the front desk system computes the total

uploading
The process by which information is sent from a PC to a mainframe.

downloading
The transfer of information from a central system to a desktop computer.

bill to be paid by each guest on checkout. This tabulation adds up all charges incurred during the stay, deducting any adjustments, credits, or advance payments.

Update: Adding, deleting, or changing details (such as guest name, balance due, or method of payment) in records in the database is known as updating. Records can be updated in one of two ways. In **batch processing,** all transactions are grouped and processed at one time. For instance, all the day's guest records are processed at one time to produce a report of revenue for the day. In **real-time processing,** each transaction is processed as it occurs. For example, if a guest calls Reservatron and adds several days to a planned stay at a hotel, the change is added directly into the database through a terminal in real time.

batch processing
The grouping and processing of all transactions at one time.

real-time processing
The processing of each transaction as it occurs.

Classify: To classify is to categorize or group information according to a particular characteristic. For instance, the sales office groups customers by their company to determine the names of Sheraton's biggest customers worldwide.

Sort: When information is arranged into a useful sequence (perhaps alphabetical or numerical order), it is said to be sorted. For example, the executive office of a local hotel prints an alphabetical listing of all employees, their departments and titles, and their telephone numbers.

Summarize: In this processing activity, a large volume of data is reduced into a concise, easily used format that contains sufficient detail to meet the user's need. Average annual occupancy rates, for instance, are a summary of the number of rooms occupied, day by day, over the course of one year.

GENERATE

Output: This activity consists of preparing a report to be printed or displayed for an intended recipient. For example, each day the front desk manager prepares a printed report that lists all charges and taxes associated with each guest.

Issue: This activity involves producing and printing a document. For example, the accounting department issues checks to pay suppliers, and the reservation system issues reservation confirmations that are mailed to guests who have booked a room in advance.

STORAGE AND RETRIEVAL

Inquire: This activity involves satisfying a request for information through computation or retrieval of stored information. For example, the front desk manager may ask the system to produce a list of all guests scheduled to arrive on a specific day.

Store: Storing is retaining information for future use by recording the details on disk or diskette (for long-term storage) or in memory (for short-term storage). Guest history databases are generally recorded on magnetic disk for long-term retention.

Retrieve: Retrieving is locating and obtaining information specified in an inquiry. For example, a reservation agent may retrieve the record of a specific guest to verify or change occupation dates.

TRANSMIT

Transmit: Distributing information over a communications network is known as transmitting. For example, ITT Sheraton headquarters regularly transmits reservation details to local hotels over its communications network. At local hotels, e-mail networks are often used to send messages to staff members, either individually or collectively.

 SUMMARY OF LEARNING OBJECTIVES

1 **Identify the five components of a computer system.** The five components of a computer system are (1) *hardware,* the machines (devices) that carry out the activities of computing, storing, and communicating data; (2) *programs,* the specific sequences of instructions that tell computers how to perform specific actions; (3) *information,* organized, meaningful, and useful sets of data; (4) *people,* the end-users of IT or IT professionals; and (5) *procedures,* the step-by-step processes or sets of instructions for accomplishing specific results.

2 **Explain the four categories of hardware and their functions.** The four categories of hardware are (1) *input devices,* used to enter information or data into a computer; (2) *processors,* sets of electronic circuits used to perform the computer's processing actions, including arithmetic calculations; (3) *output devices,* used to present information to the user or to input information into another device; and (4) *secondary storage devices,* used to augment the computer's primary memory.

3 **Discuss the relationship between hardware and software.** By itself, a computer is merely a collection of computer apparatus. To be useful, hardware needs software or programs. *Software* is the general term for a set of instructions that controls a computer or communications network. A *program* is a specific sequence of instructions that tells a computer how to perform a particular action or solve a problem.

4 **Differentiate between an operating system and an application program.** An *operating system* is a combination of programs that coordinates the actions of a computer, including its peripheral devices and memory. It enables people to control the movement, storage, and retrieval of data and information. An *application program* consists of several programs working together.

5 **Identify eight types of software packages.** Eight types of software packages are (1) spreadsheet programs, (2) word-processing programs, (3) desktop publishing programs, (4) graphics programs, (5) illustration programs, (6) database management programs, (7) communications programs, and (8) information systems programs.

6 **Explain the four components of information.** The four components of information are (1) *data,* the raw facts of a situation; (2) *text,* or written (narrative) information; (3) *sound,* or spoken information; and (4) *images,* or visual information.

7 **Distinguish between the users of information technology and IT professionals.** *Users* are people who use information technology in their jobs or personal lives. There are four types of users: hands-on users, indirect end-users, user managers, and senior managers.

IT professionals are responsible for acquiring, developing, maintaining, or operating the hardware and software associated with computers and communications networks. Some high-profile IT professionals are programmers, systems analysts, systems designers, project managers, network specialists, trainers, and computer operators.

8 **Describe the four types of procedures used in computer systems.** The four types of procedures used in computer systems are (1) *operations procedures,* which describe how a computer system or application is used, who is authorized to use it, how often it can be used, and where the results of processing should go; (2) *backup and recovery procedures,* which describe when and how to make extra copies of information and the steps to take when information or software must be recovered; (3) *security procedures,* which are designed to safeguard data centers, communications networks, computers, and other IT components from accidental intrusion or intentional damage; and (4) *development procedures,* which explain

how IT professionals should describe user needs and develop applications to meet those needs.

9 **Explain the difference between single- and multiuser systems.** A *single-user system* is one that stands alone and is not connected with other computers or shared by other people. *Multiuser system* is the general term used to describe a system in which more than one user shares hardware, programs, information, people, and procedures.

10 **List the 13 information-processing activities associated with the 6 information-handling functions of IT.** The information-processing activities performed by IT are (1) input, (2) upload/download, (3) compute, (4) update, (5) classify, (6) sort, (7) summarize, (8) output, (9) issue, (10) inquire, (11) store, (12) retrieve, and (13) transmit.

KEY TERMS

1 Kao's IT Keeps Everyone in Touch

Kao Kao knows that when its suppliers and the retail stores that sell its products are successful, the company also benefits. That is why Kao decided to extend its practice of sharing critical data and information to unlock creativity and enhance performance to critical suppliers and customers.

The payoff? Kao is able to fill orders for the 280,000 stores it serves in 24 hours or less—faster than any other firm in the industry. Yet the company makes fewer errors (0.1 percent) than any of its competitors.

Kao's product database is part of an information system that supplies customer service operators with photos and information on products. Telephone service operators also use the database to capture customer comments from the 50,000 phone calls it receives annually. These details are used by research and marketing staff members to identify new-product and product-improvement opportunities.

Questions for Discussion

1. How does Kao's use of information technology enable it to share data and information internally and externally?

2. What characteristics of IT, when combined with knowledgeable employees, have enabled Kao to fill orders so quickly?

3. What are the benefits of making photos and product information available on-line to the company's telephone operators?

2 IT Simplifies Life for Price Waterhouse Auditors

Price Waterhouse The financial statements an auditor examines are important for at least three reasons. First, they present a "snapshot" of the corporation's financial health. Second, they influence the actions of investors and competitors. And third, they establish the firm's tax liability, which helps determine how much money the government has to work with.

Questions for Discussion

1. Price Waterhouse's new IT system has not come cheap. The firm spent several million dollars on CD-ROM drives alone, in addition to the expense it incurred creating a database of the accounting guidelines and ordering a "pressing" (copying) of the CD-ROMs (for about $2 a copy). By way of comparison, each paper volume costs less than $2 to print and bind. Why do you think the national director of audit technology for Price Waterhouse estimates that CD-ROM technology actually repaid the investment in one year and will save the firm substantial sums in the future?

2. The accounting guidelines Price Waterhouse issues for its auditors sometimes need to be updated, and CD-ROM disks cannot be updated. How, then, can the use of CD-ROM be an advantage?

3. Clients often ask Price Waterhouse auditors questions that can be answered only by consulting more than one volume of guidelines. How might the use of CD-ROMs reduce worries that an auditor might give incomplete answers?

3 McKesson Corp.: "Wearable" Computers Streamline the Retailer-Distributor Link

McKesson Corp. McKesson estimates that its wearable computers have increased the productivity of its warehouse workers, reduced inventory levels, and cut order errors by 70 percent—all important considerations in an industry that operates on very narrow profit margins. Moreover, McKesson's investment in IT lets it offer its retail customers such value-added services as improved inventory control, better recordkeeping, and even more accurate profit-and-loss statements.

Questions for Discussion

1. Imagine that you are the CIO at McKesson in the 1970s. How would you try to convince the CEO to approve a multimillion-dollar investment in a networked computer system?

2. Using what you have learned about personal versus multiuser systems, how would you classify McKesson's wearable computers?

3. Major retailers such as Kmart and J. C. Penney are among the more than 100,000 organizations worldwide that have adopted electronic data interchange (EDI), a standard way of representing and transferring order-related data electronically. These retailers benefit because the system eliminates the paperwork involved in communicating with any manufacturer using EDI. The manufacturers benefit because the giant retailers provide them with updated sales and inventory information that is useful in planning production. What does EDI mean for distributors like McKesson? For competition in the retail industry?

Net Work

The Internet Access Providers

Providing access to the Internet has become a business. While use of the Internet itself is free—the costs being paid by organizations that maintain the Net's computers and communications links—getting access to it usually requires the payment of a fee to an access provider.

Many companies have been established to provide this service. To gain a better understanding of their costs and services and how they compete with one another, conduct a survey of Internet providers in your area by completing the following table (extending its size to accommodate the number of companies you survey). Be sure to consider telephone companies and cable companies servicing your area as well.

CHARACTERISTIC	COMPANY #1	COMPANY #2	COMPANY #3	COMPANY #4	COMPANY #5
Name of company					
Minimum monthly charge for service					
Hours of time included in monthly service charge					
Hours service is available (Monday–Friday; weekends)					
Additional charges (if any) for high-speed transmission service					
Additional charges (if any) for usage during peak times of the day					
Number of subscribers company has					

CHARACTERISTIC	COMPANY #1	COMPANY #2	COMPANY #3	COMPANY #4	COMPANY #5
Is service accessible through a local (toll-free) call?					
Other services company provides					
Other factors that distinguish the company					

Based on your survey, which companies do you feel best meet your Internet needs? Why?

GROUP PROJECTS AND APPLICATIONS

Project 1

With a partner or small group, visit a local business that uses information technology. Each member of your group should interview a person who uses information technology or manages one of the company's information technology applications.

Questions to Ask IT Users:

- Which software programs or IT applications do you use on a daily basis?
- What are your job responsibilities? Have the IT applications you use helped you become more efficient at your job?
- How did you learn to use IT in your job?

Questions to Ask IT Professionals:

- What are your responsibilities in managing the company's IT application(s)?
- What procedures do you follow on a daily basis?

- What types of support do you offer to the company's IT users?

Each group should summarize its interviews and present the results to the class.

Project 2—
Group Research Project

People in charge of IT systems must implement a series of security procedures to safeguard the system. Following is a list of words commonly used by network security specialists:

- Firewall
- Password
- Trojan Horse
- Digital signature encryption
- Hacker
- Trapdoor
- Antivirus program

With a partner or group, research each of these terms. What does each term mean? How is it related to network security?

REVIEW QUESTIONS

1. What is the hardware in a computer system? List and describe the four categories of hardware.

2. What are the most common types of input devices? Why are there different types?

3. What is the purpose of the central processing unit? By what other names is this hardware component known?

4. What is the purpose of memory? Why is the memory in the central processor sometimes called primary storage?

5. Discuss the different actions that can be triggered by computer output.

6. What is secondary storage? What is its relation to primary storage?

7. Distinguish between the characteristics of four types of secondary storage.

8. Why are some devices called peripheral equipment? What does "peripheral" mean?

9. What are the two types of software? What is the purpose of each?

10. List and briefly describe the eight most popular types of software packages.

11. What is a computer programming language? What is the most commonly used programming language in business?

12. How do custom software and package software differ?

13. Identify the two most important trends in the acquisition and development of computer software today.

14. How does the object-oriented approach to software change development practices?

15. What benefits are gained by the use of prewritten software components?

16. What is information? What are the four components of information?

17. What is meant by the term *user*? List and explain the four types of users.

18. Name the categories of information technology professionals. What function does each perform?

19. Discuss the types of procedures needed to manage and use information technology. Why is each needed?

20. How do single-user and multiuser systems differ? Is one type better than the other? Explain.

21. Describe each of the following information-processing activities: input, upload/download, compute, update, classify, sort, summarize, output, issue, inquire, store, retrieve, and transmit.

DISCUSSION QUESTIONS

1. Make a list of the IT-based systems and applications you encounter in a typical day and discuss how IT affects your activities. Do you agree that people are the most important component of these computer systems? Explain your answer.

2. Look over the list you made for question 1 and list the different types of input devices you encoun-

tered. Why do you think there are so many different types of input devices besides the keyboard?

3. Why do you think that accounting departments were the first to install mainframe computers back in the early days of computing?

4. At Employers Health Insurance in Green Bay, Wisconsin, IT professionals spend 6- to 12-month

"sabbaticals" in user departments interacting with users. The company's next move will be to assign IT managers to each of its business units, where they will present courses on how computer applications are developed. What benefit do these programs offer to Employers Health Insurance?

5. St. Agnes Medical Center of Fresno, California, has created a network that supports both critical pa-

tient-care applications and office productivity applications. Users can log onto the network from any PC in the medical center. Why do you think so many organizations like St. Agnes are developing computer networks of microcomputers?

SUGGESTED READINGS

Communications, Computers, and Networks. Scientific American, special issue, September 1991, pp. 62–164. An issue devoted entirely to network applications of information technology. Contains 12 in-depth articles written by leaders in the IT field.

Computers and the Family. Newsweek special report, Summer 1995. A report on the way information technology can be used in everyday family life. Includes special features on software for kids, shopping for software, and acquiring on-line services for children.

Making High Tech Work for You. Fortune, special issue, 1994. Explores a wide range of practical applications of information technology, emphasizing people and professions. Topics span the full range of IT, including computers, software, and networks, as well as a glimpse into the rapidly approaching future.

Penzias, Arno. *Ideas and Information: Managing in a High-Tech World.* New York: Norton, 1989. An excellent source detailing how information technology will shape work in the future, written by the director of research for AT&T Bell Labs.

Poole, Ithiel de Sola. *Technologies Without Boundaries: On Telecommunications in a Global Age.* Cambridge, MA: Harvard University Press, 1990. An exploration of the dramatic changes wrought by information technology that will affect business and politics and revolutionize culture and society in the twenty-first century.

Vincent, David R. *The Information-Based Corporation.* Chicago: Dow Jones Irwin, 1990. An important work showing how IT can help businesspeople on the front lines make decisions and solve problems, and how firms that have invested in IT can make the most of their investments.

Hyatt Hotels Help Business Travelers Set Up a Base Camp

Hyatt Hotels   Hyatt Hotels, operator of over 100 hotels in the United States and Canada, knows that its principal customers—business travelers—want the comfort and service they've grown to expect in a good hotel: pleasant rooms, adequate space, telephone and cable television (including Cable News Network—CNN) in the room, and a well-lit working area equipped with table or desk. But Hyatt believes these basics are no longer enough.

The lodging industry in which Hyatt competes consists of many well-run chains with familiar nameplates. Competing hotels set up business in similar locations: near airports and in the centers of major cities throughout North America, as well as in resort areas. Since they closely compete on price and service, hotel managers are forced to monitor the room rates, facilities, and services of their competitors constantly. No innovative idea goes unnoticed, and it won't be long before competitors are matching it.

Hyatt Hotels conducted a survey of frequent business travelers to determine how the hotel chain could better serve their needs. Three out of four travelers said that today they are expected to work more and produce more on their business trips. Visiting customers or making sales quotas is only part of the job. They must also stay in close contact with their home offices and other customers, as well as prepare proposals or write reports. As a result, the survey revealed, hotel guests are spending more time working in their rooms.

In an attempt to provide better services to its traveling guests while maintaining its competitive position vis-à-vis other hotels in major cities, Hyatt created the Hyatt Business Plan, which offers business travelers extra work-related resources in their rooms.

For an additional $15 per day, the Business Plan provides a spacious room equipped with office-style conveniences suitable for the businessperson who wishes to establish a base camp away from the office. The package includes 24-hour access to printers and photocopiers; complimentary and unlimited local, toll-free,

and credit-card telephone access; and voice mail and computer jacks to connect with phone lines.

While Hyatt's room plan is a recent innovation, the offering of business services is nothing new in the hotel industry. For two decades now, hotels have operated business centers. Usually located near the hotel's lobby or meeting rooms, these centers are staffed by personnel who will make photocopies, send or receive fax messages, ship packages, or prepare documents on desktop computers for guests. Hotel staff members do all the work, charging the guest a nominal fee that is billed to their account.

Hyatt has found that Business Plan rooms and its staff-operated business centers can happily co-exist because each appeals to a different type of traveler. The business center is used mostly by guests who do not travel with notebook computers, while those who do tend to prefer Business Plan rooms.

Hyatt's competitors have not been sitting by idly, watching Hyatt gobble up this lucrative business. They are responding with their own programs:

- Marriott Hotels' Rooms That Work program, developed with Marriott's telecommunications partner AT&T and the office equipment maker Steelcase, offers rooms equipped with a large computer table and desktop computer, telephone with computer jack, mobile writing desk, and adjustable chair with lumbar support.
- Hilton Hotel Corp. offers a SmartDesk plan that provides guests with a room that has a full-size desk, a desktop computer with color monitor and built-in fax and telecommunications capabilities, and dual-line telephones.
- ITT Sheraton provides rooms outfitted with telecommunications capabilities and in-room fax machines.
- Westin Hotels offers Guest Office rooms, each equipped with combination printer-fax-copiers, dual speakerphones, adjustable chairs with lumbar support, and complimentary local calls and long-

distance access.

- Holiday Inn's Select program provides business guests with voice mail, computer communications links, and businesslike work areas with good lighting.

Hyatt and other leading hotel chains are working hard to respond to the needs of business guests who rely increasingly on information technology. Hotels today offer more than just a place to sleep, dine, and meet guests. Indeed, they are becoming the business traveler's base camp—an office away from the office.

Questions for Discussion

1. If Hyatt's guests are able to plug their computers into a telephone line and dial into a computer at their company headquarters, which of the six information-handling functions associated with information technology can they use?

2. List and describe the five components of IT that hotel guests equipped with a notebook computer in Business Plan rooms can use.

PHOTO ESSAY

NIGEL HOLMES'S INFOGRAPHIC SHARES & THE
Vital Statistics & Secret Taboos
OF THE U.S. CENTENNIAL OLYMPIC TEAM

By the time the United States assembled its team of Olympic athletes for the Centennial Games, more than 600 persons had been named to compete in the various sports. Each individual had a story to tell, and each had his or her own unique characteristics.

Managing editor Bill Colson had the idea that citizens should know more about the athletes who would represent the United States in the Centennial Games. Who are these people? What do they do? What do they like? What are their personal attributes?

Since gathering this information on 649 athletes was thought to be virtually an impossible task ... Colson decided to accept the challenge. A team of interviewers and researchers was assembled, and off they went. The facts were assembled.

Then Colson contacted Nigel Holmes, long associated with *Time* magazine, to create an infographic suitable for sharing the profiles of the athletes. This photo essay describes how Nigel Holmes created an infographic to connect all the facts about the U.S. Olympic Team.

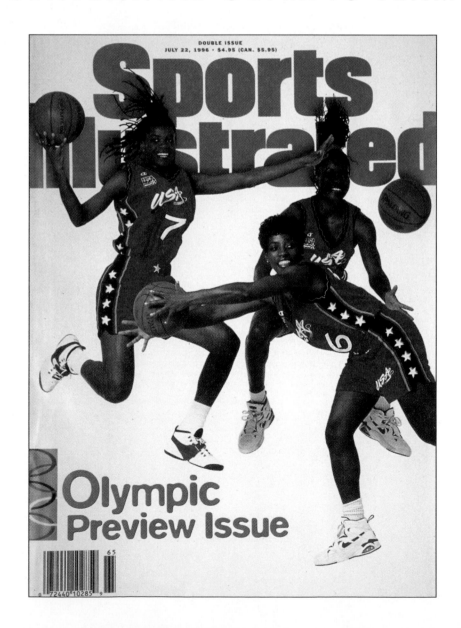

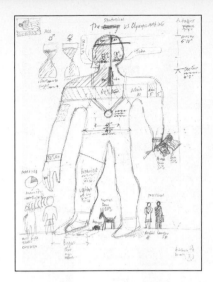

While writer Jack McCallum assembles the details, *Sports Illustrated*'s editor began readying the layout. The sheer volume of details, describing the characteristics of more than 600 Olympic athletes, could best be managed by a colorful graphic that would both illustrate and draw the reader to the image. Because the facts span everything about athletes from their ages, to how they train, to their sizes, and even something about their favorite pets, the graphic needed to have plenty of space, yet show the details in a meaningful way. It was decided to use a human figure to relate the details of the Olympic athletes. Nigel Holmes then sketched by hand an athletic-looking human figure, showing points where facts could be presented.

Holmes then transferred the ideas from his earlier sketch to a full-size magazine layout page. He organized the redrawn page to show information in a top-to-bottom flow corresponding to the way that it was expected that people would read the illustration.

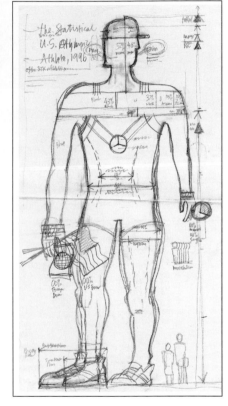

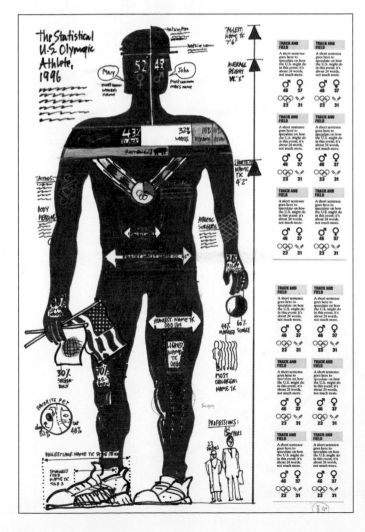

Next, the first of several color sketches was prepared. More details were added, pinpointing both the facts that would be presented and their location within the illustration. Holmes chose to use attention-getting icons with some facts (such as the athlete's favorite pet or tendency toward particular political parties) and simple graphics with others (including details of marital status and profession). Except for personal names, a single, clean type style was used throughout.

Sample facts on each sport were prepared, using a color printer, and pasted on the side of the color sketch to check size, proportions, and color usage.

The human eye can quickly determine when an illustration is out of proportion. Hence Holmes checked and rechecked for this, using a series of photographs and drawings. A 35mm color slide of Athenian black-vase figures was prepared along with several other Polaroid™ photos that served as references for size and proportion.

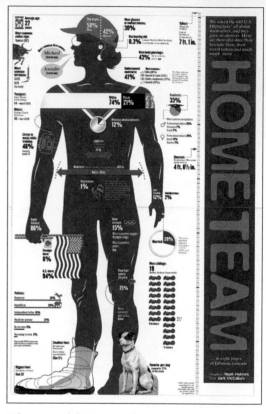

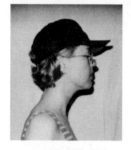

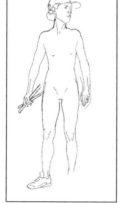

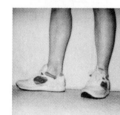

Holmes created the image on his computer, creating the human form that would serve as the principal feature in this infographic. Highlights were added to convey muscle tone and shape.

A special drawing was prepared to assist in contrasting the biggest shoe size, size 22 belonging to basketball player Shaquille O'Neal, and the smallest size, 5½ for gymnasts Dominique Moceanu and Kerri Strug.

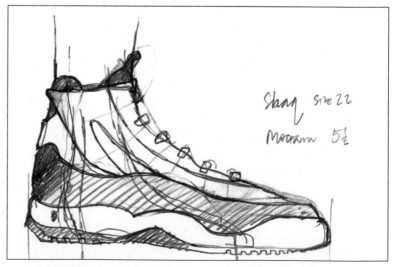

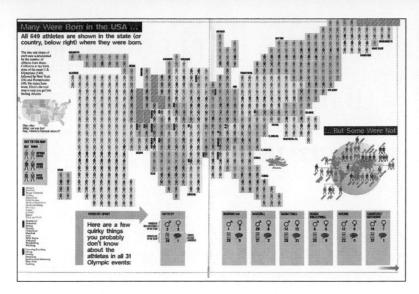

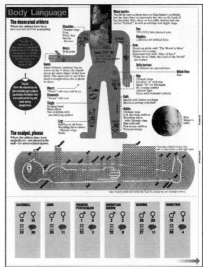

Finally, Holmes combined the infographic, text, headlines, and descriptive information for the story on the magazine page. Working at his computer console, he positioned descriptive details around the human form in relation to the idea they illustrate. Clip art was pasted in to add flags, radios, earphones, and other details to the illustration. Colors were also added, according to the choices made when the original sketches were prepared. Holmes's final version of the infographic was produced on his color printer, ready for use by *Sports Illustrated*'s production staff.

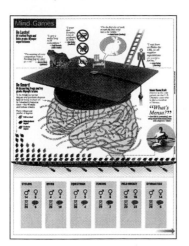

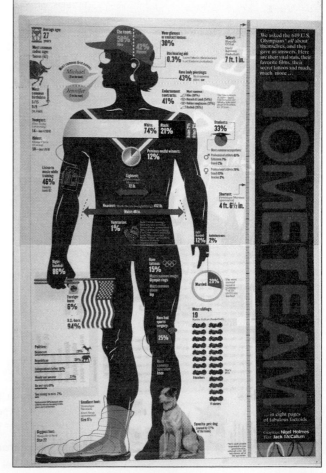

When the story appeared in *Sports Illustrated*, the infographic occupied two entire pages. Nigel Holmes's skillful design, layout, and color usage conveys the details of the U.S. Olympic team and draws readers into the facts about the team.

CHAPTER 3

A Tour of the Internet and the World Wide Web

LEARNING OBJECTIVES

When you have completed this chapter, you should be able to

1 Explain how individual computers and server computers interact on the Internet.

2 Describe the two types of capabilities of the Internet.

3 Identify the 11 principal communication and retrieval capabilities of the Internet.

4 Summarize how the Internet knows the location of a particular user on the Net.

5 Describe the use of pages on the World Wide Web.

6 Explain the purpose of hyperlinks and their role on the World Wide Web.

7 Describe the characteristics of browser software and relate them to the different types of information that can be included in a home page.

A Mosaic for the Future

A young, restless innovator, fueled by pizza, Oreo cookies, Bach, shredded newspapers, and algorithms, looked inside the computer organization he was with in 1990. He looked at the leading computer manufacturers of the day. He was not seeing the future!

The Internet had emerged out of the academic and scientific communities. Some said it was loaded with opportunity. Others said it was loaded with problems. To Marc, the Internet was "a giant hole in the middle of the world." The software to access it was at least 10 years behind what was running on the desktops of offices all over America. To tease out any useful information, you had to enter detailed commands by hand. This was the past, not the future.

One night late in 1992, Marc and a colleague at Illinois' National Center for Supercomputing Applications (NCSA) sat at a table at the Espresso Royale café in Champaign-Urbana discussing the capabilities and limits of the Internet and the World Wide Web. They wrestled with the idea of making the Web easily accessible. "Let's go for it," they decided.

Between December 1992 and March 1993, Marc and Eric, complementing each other in marathon code-writing sessions, completed a mere 9,000 lines of program instructions (for comparison, Microsoft needed 11 million lines to create Windows 95!). But that was all they needed to produce the most rapidly propagated software program in computer history. In writing Mosaic, the first graphical interface for the Internet's World Wide Web, Marc Andreessen and Eric Bina changed forever the world of information technology, for Mosaic made the World Wide Web widely accessible to ordinary people.

As time passed, the pair brought in other young programmers to work on additional features that would extend Mosaic's reach. By the time Andreessen graduated from the University of Illinois in December 1993 and left NCSA, some 40 programmers were plugging away at Mosaic software.

Andreessen attracted the attention of Jim Clark, founder of the innovative computer company Silicon Graphics, located in California's Silicon Valley, south of San Francisco. Fascinated by the possibilities of Mosaic's graphical browser program, Clark signed up Andreessen and formed a new company, Mosaic Communications, to produce the next generation of graphic software to access the World Wide Web. Eric Bina also became part of the new company, as did others who had worked at NCSA.

After hearing rumors of a possible legal challenge from NCSA over intellectual property rights to Mosaic, Andreessen and Clark dropped the notion of using ideas from their first software program. Instead, they started from scratch, rethinking and redesigning the software capabilities needed to utilize the World Wide Web even more effectively than Mosaic had.

Their new program was Netscape, which became the name of their company. It included many more features than Mosaic and had richer graphic layouts, as well as all-important security safeguards. To ensure that the greatest number of people would use Netscape, the company gave the software away on the Net. Within a few months, Netscape had captured 70 percent of the market for browser software on the Internet. When the company went public in 1995, investors fought to acquire its shares. The opening price was $24. By the end of the first day of public trading, Netscape was going for $87 a share.

Only a few years ago, the Internet interested few people. Today, it's hard to read a newspaper, watch a television program, or even get into a business discussion without hearing about the Internet or its most popular graphical component, the World Wide Web. If you're still unfamiliar with the Internet and wonder whether you're missing out on something . . . you are!

Internet/Net
A communication network that is itself a connection of many other networks.

The **Internet**—commonly called the **Net**—is a communication network that is itself a connection of many other networks. Hence the name: **inter**connection of **net**works.

The Internet is used on a frequent basis by some 30 million people today, and more and more gain access to it every day. It is radically changing people's daily lives. In fact, enthusiasts believe the Internet is the most profound invention since the printing press—or at least since the computer itself was invented. It has given birth to a good many IT applications. For example, electronic mail—written messages sent electronically over communication links—was born on the Internet. Knowledgeable people are convinced that the Internet will be the foundation of the future U.S. Information Superhighway. In this chapter, we will examine the origin and evolution of the Internet, see what it can do today, and consider its future.

Origin of the Internet

The value of a network lies as much in *whom* it connects as in *how* it connects. The Internet, a network of networks, originated back in the 1960s, when the U.S. Department of Defense established the network to provide researchers and government officials with access to such IT resources as radio telescopes, weather analysis programs, supercomputers, and specialized databases. From this origin as a vehicle for the exclusive use of government and educational institutions, the Internet has expanded prodigiously. Today, over half of all U.S. Internet addresses belong to people who got them through a private employer or a commercial access provider.

More than 150,000 new users join the Internet each day. Host computers are added daily, and the number of networks interconnected on the Internet doubles

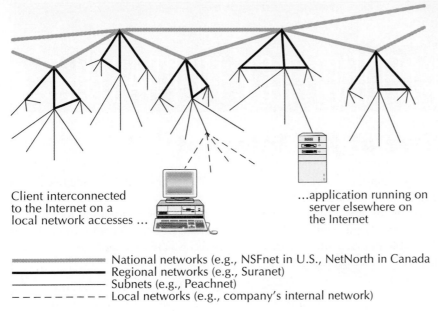

FIGURE 3.1
Structure of the Internet

Client interconnected to the Internet on a local network accesses ...

...application running on server elsewhere on the Internet

National networks (e.g., NSFnet in U.S., NetNorth in Canada)
Regional networks (e.g., Suranet)
Subnets (e.g., Peachnet)
Local networks (e.g., company's internal network)

every year. The rate of growth will likely peak in the not-too-distant future because at current growth rates, everyone on planet Earth would be connected to the network by the year 2002!

The U.S. government, through the National Science Foundation, paid a decreasing share of the operating cost of the Internet through 1995, when all government funding was phased out. The bulk of the cost to operate the Internet is paid by the users. For example, universities and other institutions pay for operating their host computers and interconnecting them to the network. There is, however, no charge for sending a message from one computer to another.

The *Information Technology in Practice* feature entitled "Vinton Cerf: Father of the Internet" introduces the man who has done more than anyone else to democratize the Net.

Computers on the Internet

The software an individual uses to access the Internet is running on his or her **client computer.** The client computer communicates with a **server computer** to access data and information. **Client-server computing** (Figure 3.1) is a characteristic of the Internet: Through the Internet, client computers interact with server computers, transmitting and receiving data and information. Data and information transmitted by the server computer are processed by the software running on the client computer (Figure 3.2).

client computer
The computer that accesses the information stored on a server computer.

server computer
The computer that contains data and information that can be accessed by a client computer.

client-server computing
A type of computing in which all data and information retrieval requests and responses pass over a network. Much of the processing is performed on the server computer, and the results of that processing are transmitted to the client computer.

Client Computer
(Individual User)

Server Computer
(on the Internet)

FIGURE 3.2
Client/Server Computing

Request for Data and Information

Response from Server

INFORMATION TECHNOLOGY IN PRACTICE

Vinton Cerf: Father of the Internet

Vinton Cerf is known as the "Father of the Internet" for his pioneering work in developing information technology to support the network and for his unending efforts to help the Internet grow. Cerf started with the principle that anyone should be able to talk to anyone else. Then he developed the TCP/IP protocol on which the Internet is built. This protocol greatly facilitated the Internet's growth by making networks open and thus permitting interconnection among them. Today, the ability to "surf on the Internet"—to ride freely from network to network the way a surfer rides from wave to wave—gives Internet users an endless wave of connectivity.

Cerf, who is part of the executive management team at MCI, headquartered in Washington, D.C., remains very active in the field of information technology. In a recent interview, he shared his thoughts on the surprises, capabilities, and possibilities of the Internet:

I guess the surprises come because the spread of the system has been so rapid in unexpected quarters. And so when I get e-mail from people who are in obscure places around the world saying, "Hi, I'm on the Net," I'm always surprised. When I get e-mail from somebody in China and somebody in Africa, I'm always stunned. . . . Those are the kinds of surprises that are happening now, and of course the new applications that have come along, like Internet Multimedia and World chat, are surprises just because I almost invariably underestimate the amount of human creativity there is out there, especially with millions of people trying things.

The Internet makes it far easier for the individual voice to be heard than any other communication medium ever has. The most interesting question now is: How will we take advantage of the opportunities provided by the Net?

SOURCE: "Poet-Philosopher of the Net," *Educom Review,* Vol. 31 (May–June 1996), p. 38.

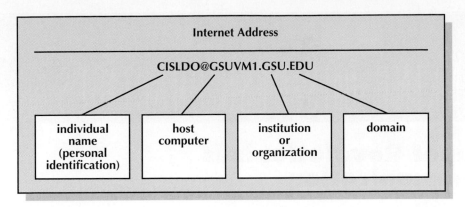

FIGURE 3.3
Internet Addresses

The *Rethinking Business Practices* feature entitled "Visa's Intranet Revolutionizes Internal Communication" describes how this worldwide credit card company has capitalized on the Internet's powerful capabilities for internal communication.

Internet Addresses

Everyone on the Internet has an address from which to send and receive messages. An Internet address has four parts: (1) the user's personal identification, (2) the name of the host computer, (3) the name of the institution or organization, and (4) the domain name (Figure 3.3).

The university or business that provides your access to the Net will assign you a personal identification name. This personal ID is often some combination of your name and the name of the network serving your location or work group within the organization. The university or business also connects one or more of its computers—called a *host computer*—to the Internet. Each host computer is given a unique identification code, which is included in your address.

The Network Information Center is the central authority responsible for assigning a range of addresses to an organization. The organization itself is responsible for assigning a specific host computer to one of the addresses within its range. Each organization also belongs to a domain that identifies the nature of its networks. Domain codes typically identify the type of organization—commercial (com), educational (edu), or government (gov)—or its country location—Australia (au) (Figure 3.4).

Domain	
Name	**Explanation**
.AU	Country code for Australia
.COM	Commercial organization
.EDU	Educational institution
.GOV	Government organization

FIGURE 3.4
Internet Domains

RETHINKING BUSINESS PRACTICES

Visa's Intranet Revolutionizes Internal Communication

The Internet's universal reach makes it possible to establish communications instantly with a server anywhere in the world. It's not surprising, then, that Net enthusiasts tend to focus on linking up with distant locations.

Yet, another advantage of the Internet is capturing the attention of business, and that is its ability to break down the communications walls *inside* companies. Companies are creating *intranets,* or networks that run inside the company, using the Internet's capabilities to do so.

Visa International, Inc., the worldwide credit card company, was having trouble keeping its customer contact directory (two four-inch-thick volumes) up-to-date. With 19,000 member banks, Visa found that its directory was out of date as soon as it was published because of the normal volume of personnel and telephone changes at the banks. Visa International executives Cathy Basch and Deborah McWhinney saw the Internet as an opportunity to solve this problem. They established an internal intranet Web site to house the directory so that quick changes could be made to the listings anytime. Now, whenever any of Visa's 1,200 employees access the directory from their desktop computers, they know they are getting the most up-to-date information. Visa is looking into setting up other intranets to help service its member banks.

Visa's intranet is shielded from outside access by "firewall" security software—a program that establishes a barrier that Internet users outside the company cannot penetrate. Thus, many types of information can be posted on Visa's internal Web sites that would never be published on the Internet.

Other international companies, such as the auto manufacturer Ford, the information technology service group EDS, and France's Cap Gemini Sogeti, are using intranets to link project teams scattered across the globe so they can share information, including drawings and design information. Hypertext links within Web pages can bring together scattered information for easy access. At the same time, an intranet can be used to disseminate knowledge within the organization. Thus, a project team member can post a report on the project, linking it to his or her home page, and others in the company can add their knowledge or experience to the report.

Because intranets draw on the power of the Web, they are much more sophisticated than e-mail. Entire documents can be posted on an intranet. The document's pages may contain colorful graphics and high-resolution photographs, and if the need arises, audio and video segments can be linked to the document—all available for viewing with a click of the mouse.

Because intranets use the infrastructure of the Internet, multiple communication paths from one site to another are available, making access reliable. Furthermore, since intranets can interconnect many different types of computers, the problem of isolated islands of information is overcome.

How widespread are intranets? Software builder Netscape claims that most of its Web server software is bought for use *inside* companies.

Capabilities of the Internet

There are two main things you can do on the Internet:

- **Communicate.** You can contact and exchange information with friends and organizations anywhere in the world. The Internet's special features allow you to participate in conversations, sharing ideas, opinions, and news with other users.
- **Retrieve.** You can access a broad range of data and information from other computers, or simply *sites,* on the network. You can also retrieve copies of information—including narratives, photographs, sound, and video—and bring them right into your own computer. The Internet's retrieval capability includes software. That is, computer software can be located and delivered immediately from commercial software manufacturers or from individuals who create and share software. Not too long ago, overnight delivery of software was considered immediate. Now *immediately* means *instantly:* you get copies of software, documents, and messages as soon as you ask for them.

A variety of capabilities (sometimes referred to as *Internet tools*) support communication and retrieval on the Internet (see Table 3.1).

Communications Capabilities

The principal communications features of the Internet are e-mail, user groups, chat sessions, mailing lists, and Telnet.

e-mail/electronic mail
A service that transports text messages from a sender to one or more receivers via computer.

E-MAIL. **E-mail**—short for **electronic mail**—is the most widely used function of the Internet. Anyone can transmit a message to anyone else on the Internet

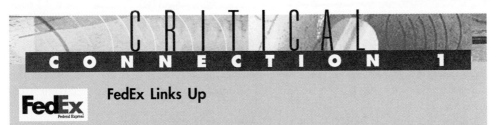

FedEx Links Up

For Federal Express Corporation, keeping track of the more than 2 million packages it carries on an average day is no small feat. As a status tracking aid, the company includes an identification number on the label that accompanies every package. When customers want to know whether a package has been delivered, all they need to do is call FedEx and provide the package tracking number. Within moments, information on the package is displayed on the customer service representative's computer display screen and the customer's question can be answered.

In order to provide even better service, FedEx has established a site on the Internet's World Wide Web. Now customers can contact the company on the Web, enter the package tracking number themselves, and see the tracking and delivery information displayed on their workstation screen. More than 30,000 customers use the Internet to track their packages every day.

TABLE 3.1 *Internet Capabilities*		
INTERNET CAPABILITY	TOOL	DESCRIPTION
Communication	Electronic mail (e-mail)	Sends and receives messages between locations on the Internet.
	Usenet	Worldwide discussion format where notices can be posted for anyone to view.
	Chat sessions	Interactive discussions in which parties on the network exchange ideas and observations electronically.
	Mailing lists	Each mailing list has subscribers who receive messages as part of an ongoing discussion of the list's topic.
	Telnet	A means of communicating with the user's own system at a home location by way of the Internet.
Retrieval	FTP (file transfer protocol)	Used for transferring files containing documents or software between computers on the Internet.
	Archie	A search database of documents and software at FTP sites suitable for transfer to the user's computer.
	Gopher	Searches the Internet for textual information using a hierarchy of menus.
	Veronica	Searches the Internet using a user-supplied keyword and connects to the appropriate Gopher computer.
	WAIS	Locates files in databases using keywords.
	World Wide Web (WWW)	Searches and retrieves information in a variety of forms (including audio and video) using hyperlinks.

simply by including the intended recipient's e-mail address in the message. Anyone who sends you a message over the Internet must supply your address. The network processes your address to determine where you are located on the Internet and then routes the message to your computer. (More on electronic mail in Chapter 10.)

Your computer need not be on in order for someone to send mail to you because the network to which you are attached will retain any messages directed to you in storage. Thus, the network acts as your "electronic mailbox." When your computer is on and interacting with the network, you can ask it to display the messages currently in your mailbox.

An e-mail message can be directed to a group of recipients, large or small, so that each member of the group receives the same message at virtually the same time.

An e-mail message may be a sentence or two intended to communicate an idea or trigger an action. Or it may be an entire document of several pages containing graphical illustrations.

Usenet/User's Network
A system of worldwide discussion groups, not an actual physical network.

USENET.   **Usenet**—short for **User's Network**—is a system of worldwide discussion groups. It is not an actual physical network. Rather, it is like a bulletin board—an electronic bulletin board—where notices can be posted for anyone to view. For example, there are Usenet discussion groups on physical fitness, computer technology, job listings, personal résumés, diabetes, *Star Trek* shows and movies, the Beatles . . . almost any topic you can imagine. If no discussion group exists for the topic you're interested in, you can start your own.

Usenet discussion groups are regularly added and removed from the Internet. The system administrator at a particular host site determines whether to carry a Usenet discussion group originating at that site.

CHAT SESSIONS.   A live, interactive discussion—meaning all parties to the discussion are actually on the network, interacting through their computers—is known as a **chat session.** For example, members of a consulting project team who cannot be at a single location at the same time might use the Internet's chat capability to exchange ideas through their PCs linked to the Internet. Each will see the others' comments simultaneously and be able to respond immediately, keying comments into the computer (Figure 3.5). The comments will appear simultaneously on the other members' computer display screens.

MAILING LISTS.   Mailing lists interconnect people who choose to participate in an ongoing discussion on a particular topic. The messages might be comments and opinions; announcements; discussions of new products, tools, or services; book, article, theater, movie, or music reviews; or just about any other information of interest to a group of persons.

You join a mailing list by subscribing electronically. Information submitted by any group member is automatically sent to you and stored by the host computer to which you are attached. You are then electronically notified that you have received information.

There are thousands of mailing lists on the Internet. You can join as many as you want—and have time to read.

You may be confused about the Internet's communication services at this point, thinking they all sound rather similar. But there are important differences for the user.

E-mail is delivered to your electronic mailbox automatically and the messages wait there until you are ready to read them. With e-mail, you have very little control over what you receive. Anyone who has your e-mail address can send you whatever he or she wishes.

A mail list will also deliver messages that appear automatically in your electronic mailbox, but this service is selective. You have to subscribe to a mailing list to get the messages.

Usenet groups and chat sessions are services that do *not* deliver messages to your mailbox. Instead, you must sign on to Usenet groups and chat sessions each time, and then receive and send messages on the display screen of your computer while you're using it. Usenet is a bulletin board you access and contribute to, while chat sessions are live, interactive discussion sessions that feel like conversations. ■

TELNET.   The essence of the "network of networks" concept, **Telnet** is the network capability that permits remote sign-on from whatever computer you are currently using. Any computer in the Internet can be accessed from any other computer in the Internet. If you are away from your college or organization, you can use Telnet to communicate with your own system back at your main location.

chat session
A live interactive discussion where all parties are actually on the network, interacting through their computers.

Telnet
The means users employ to communicate with their own systems through the Internet when they are away from their home location.

FIGURE 3.5

A Chat Session

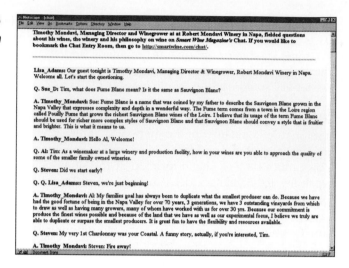

Timothy Mondavi, Managing Director and Winegrower at at Robert Mondavi Winery in Napa, fielded questions about his wines, the winery and his philosophy on wine on *Smart Wine Magazine's* Chat. If you would like to bookmark the Chat Entry Room, then go to http://smartwine.com/chat/.

Lisa_Adams: Our guest tonight is Timothy Mondavi, Managing Director & Winegrower, Robert Mondavi Winery in Napa. Welcome all. Let's start the questioning.

Q. Sue_D: Tim, what does Fume Blanc mean? Is it the same as Sauvignon Blanc?

A. Timothy_Mondavi: Sue: Fume Blanc is a name that was coined by my father to describe the Sauvignon Blanc grown in the Napa Valley that expresses complexity and depth in a wonderful way. The Fume term comes from a town in the Loire region called Pouilly Fume that grows the richest Sauvignon Blanc wines of the Loire. I believe that its usage of the term Fume Blanc should be used for richer more complex styles of Sauvignon Blanc and that Sauvignon Blanc should convey a style that is fruitier and brighter. This is what it means to us.

A. Timothy_Mondavi: Hello Al, Welcome!

Q. Al: Tim: As a winemaker at a large winery and production facility, how in your wines are you able to approach the quality of some of the smaller family owned wineries.

Q. Steven: Did we start early?

Q. Q. Lisa_Adams: Steven, we're just beginning!

A. Timothy_Mondavi: Al: My families goal has always been to duplicate what the smallest producer can do. Because we have had the good fortune of being in the Napa Valley for over 70 years, 3 generations, we have 3 outstanding vineyards from which to draw as well as having many growers, many of whom have worked with us for over 30 yrs. Because our commitment is produce the finest wines possible and because of the land that we have as well as our experimental focus, I believe we truly are able to duplicate or surpass the smallest producers. It is great fun to have the flexibility and resources available.

Q. Steven: My very 1st Chardonnay was your Coastal. A funny story, actually, if you're interested, Tim.

A. Timothy_Mondavi: Steven: Fire away!

All you need do is use the Telnet capability and provide it with your Internet address. Telnet takes care of finding the system and connecting you to it.

Retrieval Capabilities

Communication is the first reason for using the Internet. The other reason is to retrieve information. Enormous amounts of data and information are stored throughout the vast networks that make up the Internet. However, since the Internet is huge, continually evolving, and operating without any central governing body, how can you know what information is out there? There is no master directory listing all the information that can be retrieved by users. So how do you know where to go to get what you want?

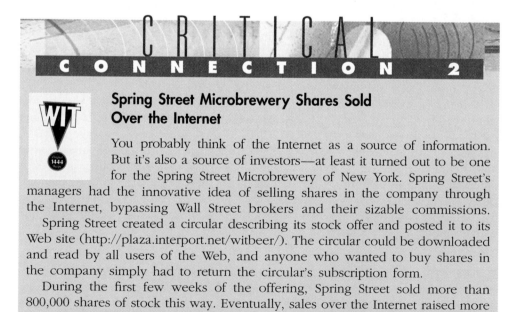

CRITICAL CONNECTION 2

Spring Street Microbrewery Shares Sold Over the Internet

You probably think of the Internet as a source of information. But it's also a source of investors—at least it turned out to be one for the Spring Street Microbrewery of New York. Spring Street's managers had the innovative idea of selling shares in the company through the Internet, bypassing Wall Street brokers and their sizable commissions.

Spring Street created a circular describing its stock offer and posted it to its Web site (http://plaza.interport.net/witbeer/). The circular could be downloaded and read by all users of the Web, and anyone who wanted to buy shares in the company simply had to return the circular's subscription form.

During the first few weeks of the offering, Spring Street sold more than 800,000 shares of stock this way. Eventually, sales over the Internet raised more than $1.5 million for the company.

There are four ways to retrieve information on the Internet: anonymous FTP and Archie, Gopher and Veronica, WAIS, and the World Wide Web.

ANONYMOUS FTP AND ARCHIE. You can transfer data and information from other computers connected to the Internet to your computer. For example, IBM, like many computer vendors, uses the file transfer protocol information retrieval capability to make notes and tips, as well as new versions of software, available to its personal computer customers by way of the Internet. **File transfer protocol (FTP)** is an Internet method that allows you to connect to another computer on the Net and transfer its files to your computer (Figure 3.6). The electronic files can contain anything that it is possible to store in a computer: data, pages of text (including entire books and newspapers), graphical images, photographs, music, recorded speeches, and software—including freeware and shareware (programs that the authors give away or allow users to try without a charge, while retaining ownership).

Other computers besides IBM's permit transfer of files on the Internet. The first step is to connect to the FTP site by entering its address into your computer so the Net can process it and make the connection. If the site is private, meaning the owner controls who can retrieve files, you must transmit a password. Many

file transfer protocol (FTP)
An Internet method that allows you to use a password to connect to another computer on the Net and transfer its files to your computer.

FIGURE 3.6
Internet Retrieval Tools

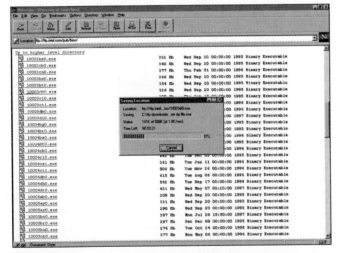

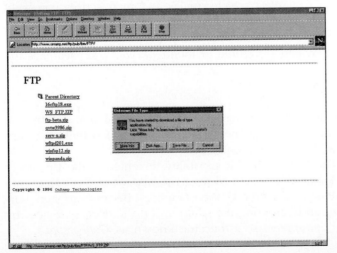

anonymous FTP site
A public FTP site that does not require you to use a special password to gain access.

Archie
A server that lists the contents of anonymous FTP sites.

keywords
A string of letters or words that indicates the subject to be searched.

Gopher
A server that organizes descriptions of information located on the Internet in the form of easy-to-use hierarchical menus.

Veronica
An internet program that uses keywords to search Gopher menus.

Wide Area Information Servers (WAIS)
A retrieval method that searches databases on the Internet and creates a menu of articles and manuscripts containing the keywords provided.

FTP sites, in fact, are public, so anyone can retrieve their files. To use these public or **anonymous FTP sites,** you simply enter the password *anonymous* and retrieve the files from the site.

If you don't know the address of an FTP site, you use Archie to find what you need. An **Archie** server contains a list of the contents of all anonymous FTP sites. There are many Archie servers on the Internet. Archie software, on your client computer, will search an Archie server using a string of letters or words, called **keywords,** that you enter to describe the subject you are interested in. Archie's response is a set of addresses for FTP sites containing information matching the keywords—addresses that you can use to connect to the FTP site to retrieve the information.

GOPHER AND VERONICA.   **Gophers** are servers that organize descriptions of information located on the Internet in the form of easy-to-use hierarchical menus. Through Gopher, you locate and connect with an Internet computer by choosing from a series of menu descriptions that progressively narrow your search until you locate the Internet computer you are seeking. Once you have it, you can read, print, transfer, or transmit the file's text information.

Gopher computers have a search capability, called **Veronica,** which is similar to the FTP's Archie. Veronica is an Internet program that uses keywords to search Gopher menus. Once you tell Veronica the keywords, it will search all Gopher server menus, and when it has completed the search, it will provide you with a menu of items it has found. Selecting any items from the menu will automatically connect you to the Gopher site containing that information.

WAIS.   The third way to search the Internet uses **Wide Area Information Servers (WAIS),** a retrieval method that will search the contents of databases on the Net for you. WAIS servers keep track of the location and contents of hundreds of databases on the Internet, and every document in a WAIS database is fully indexed on every word and phrase. (In contrast, Gopher servers only index by menu title.)

To conduct a search using WAIS, you enter the name of the database you wish to search and a set of keywords. Using your information, the WAIS server will search every work in every article in the specified database, producing a menu of articles and manuscripts containing the keywords you provided. Entries are listed in order of occurrence of the keywords, with articles containing the most occurrences listed first. You can select which articles and manuscripts you want shown on your display screen.

The essential difference between WAIS and the other search methods is that, unlike Archie and Veronica, which search file or menu *names,* WAIS searches the *contents* of the files.

Gophers? Archie? Veronica? You may be amused by the strange names for these Internet search capabilities. Here's how they came about.

The Gopher search capability, invented at the University of Minnesota, is named after the mascot of the university's athletic teams—the Golden Gophers. Because gophers burrow underground, the portion of the Net searched by Gopher servers soon became known as *Gopherspace.*

Archie is named after the comic book character of the same name. Soon after this search mechanism was created, the developers of a search mechanism for Gopherspace extended the fun by creating Veronica, an acronym for Very Easy Rodent-Oriented Net-wide Index to Computerized Archives, named for Archie's girlfriend in the comic book.

There's also a lesser-known search tool called *Jughead,* named for yet another character in the same comic book. Jughead, which stands for Jonzy's Universal Gopher Hierarchy Excavation And Display, was developed at the University of Utah by Rhett "Jonzy" Jones. This tool is used to search a single Gopher server. You might say Veronica searches across Gopherspace, while Jughead burrows deeper into Gopherspace! ▨

WORLD WIDE WEB.   The **World Wide Web (WWW)**—known to most users as simply **the Web**—is a set of interconnected electronic documents, called **Web pages,** that are linked together over the Internet. Web software searches the Web to find pages containing keywords you enter. Special keywords in the pages of Web documents, called **hyperlinks,** connect, or link, documents to one another. Recognized on your computer display screen as words and symbols highlighted by color, underline, or blinking words and symbols, hyperlinks are your connection to other documents on the Web (Figure 3.7). By using Web software to follow the links in a document, you can jump to related information in any file on the Web. When you click on a hyperlink, the Web software processes the address contained in the hyperlink, connects to the location, and displays information from the linked location. Clicking on successive hyperlinks enables you to jump from location to location to obtain the information you want.

The Web is the fastest-growing part of the Internet. For many people, the Web *is* the Internet, for that is the only part of the Net they use.

The *Information Technology in Practice* feature entitled "Internet Accessibility: Opportunities for Everyone" illustrates the many ways the Internet's World Wide Web can be used by people from all walks of life. The next section of this chapter tells you how to browse the Web to get the most from its capabilities.

Table 3.2 summarizes the retrieval methods we have just discussed.

World Wide Web (WWW)/the Web

A set of interconnected electronic documents linked together over the Internet.

Web pages

Interconnected electronic documents.

hyperlinks

Words and/or symbols highlighted by blinking, color, or underline that connect one document to another related document on the Web.

FIGURE 3.7
Hyperlink Structure

WWW pages. . . . .

Hyperlinks between
pages. . . . .

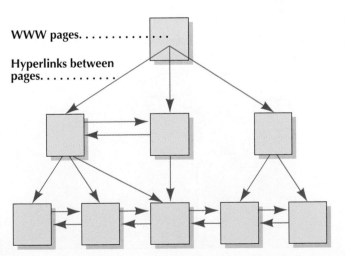

INFORMATION TECHNOLOGY IN PRACTICE

Internet Accessibility: Opportunities for Everyone

Eighteen coffee houses in San Francisco have gone on the Internet, installing terminals to allow their customers to interact with the network. Like jukeboxes, these Internet terminals accept quarters. Each quarter pays for four minutes of use, during which customers can send messages across the world or down the street to another coffee house, enter an electronic discussion on their favorite topic, or read through an electronic newsletter. Wayne Gregori, founder of SF Net, the firm that builds and programs café terminals, says, "We specifically target cafés in low-income areas. We're trying to get the have-nots on the computer."

Electronic entrepreneurs are taking to the Internet the way settlers once took to the offer of free land in the West after the Civil War. One such entrepreneur, Carl Malamud, created Internet Multicasting service, a weekly radio program distributed over Internet Talk Radio since 1993. Network users whose computers are equipped with speakers can download the program to their computers and listen to all or a portion of it whenever they have time.

As the Internet has grown, business users have become accustomed to its capabilities and have learned how to capitalize on them commercially. The Commercial Internet Exchange is a public data internetwork that offers unrestricted commercial connectivity without violating the restrictions against commercial traffic that prevail on some portions of the Internet.

Software Tool and Die (ST&D), a Brookline, Massachusetts, consulting firm that specializes in software development, has linked up to the Internet to provide consulting and programming services. It is not necessary for ST&D's people to ever meet customers face-to-face because they can converse with them easily through e-mail and can transfer files quickly over the other Internet communications services. ST&D also runs a public access bulletin board that makes software and services available.

Electronic entrepreneur Carl Malamud.

An Internet coffee house in San Francisco.

TABLE 3.2 *Internet Retrieval Methods*

RETRIEVAL METHOD	WHAT IT DOES	HOW IT DOES IT	WHAT IT GETS
FTP (file transfer protocol)	Transfers files between computers on the Internet.	User enters address of FTP site along with password for private site or "anonymous" for anonymous FTP site.	Copy of file is transferred over the Internet to user's computer.
Archie	Searches for documents and software at FTP sites.	Searches index of anonymous FTP sites for files (indexed by title and keyword). User types in keyword describing the files wanted.	Displays a list of FTP addresses showing where the files are available. User can enter addresses to transfer file from FTP site.
Gopher	Searches for textual information.	Searches menus of contents of interconnected Gopher servers. User types in keyword describing information wanted.	Displays menus listing contents of server located through the search. User chooses from successive menus until the desired file is found. Located files can be transferred, read, printed, or transmitted to another user.
Veronica	Searches for text information residing on Gopher computers.	Searches for text that appears in Gopher menus. User types in keywords relating to the document to be found.	Displays a menu containing the results of the search. User selects a choice from the menu to connect to the desired Gopher site.
WAIS	Searches for documents in specified databases.	Searches index to large text and document databases. User types in name of database and keywords relating to information to be found.	Results are listed in order by the number of keyword occurrences. User clicks on entry to display the desired document.
World Wide Web (WWW)	Searches for electronic pages.	Searches Web pages on the Internet. User types in keyword identifying information to be found.	Results are listed in order by number of keyword occurrences. User clicks on hyperlink to jump from location to location.

Browsing the World Wide Web

Graphical browser software, introduced in the early 1990s, triggered widespread use of the Web by individuals, universities, companies, and government. With interest in the Web skyrocketing, it was inevitable that there would be a tremendous growth in Web pages. This section of the chapter describes how to browse WWW pages, the HTML language, browser software, URL addresses identifying Web sites, and Net search tools.

Browsing the Web's Many Pages

Electronic pages are the most distinguishing characteristic of the Web. Here we discuss the characteristics of Web pages and tell you how to access these pages using browser software.

WEB PAGES. Pages in a Web document are specially formatted files that can display text, graphical, and image information. They can also include clips of audio and video information, which readers can play if their computers are equipped with the necessary hardware and software.

home page
The first page of a Web site, which identifies the site and provides information about the contents of electronic documents that are part of the site.

The **home page** is the first page you see when you access a Web site. It identifies the site and provides information about the contents of electronic documents that are part of the site (i.e., a table of contents or map). Often the home page uses graphical symbols, or icons, to supplement text in describing other information that is part of the Web site. The home page contains links to other pages.

Figure 3.8 shows the home page for the City of Paris, France. Notice how quickly you can identify the subject of this page—Paris. The city's name stands out because of its size, attractive color, and bracketing images of prominent statues in central Paris. Text information in the middle of the page further identifies the Web site and offers helpful information on accessing other information at the Paris Web site.

The City of Paris home page also contains links to other information. Eight of these links are visible, each a word or phrase underlined to signify that it is a hyperlink. For example, if you wanted to view this home page in the French language, you could click on the hyperlink *Vr.Française.* Or if you wanted a table of contents for the City of Paris document, you would click on *Contents.* Each of the page's hyperlinks works in the same way.

Images, or icons, are also used to signify hyperlinks on Web pages. Clicking on the image activates the hyperlink. The four images at the bottom of the City of Paris home page are hyperlinks that serve the same purpose as the text hyperlinks for *The City, Its Culture, Tourist Information,* and *Paris Kiosque.* These icons are also activated by a click of the user's mouse.

CREATING WEB PAGES USING HTML.   A Web page's features take shape when the user specifies the location and appearance of the information. A set of commands—**hypertext markup language (HTML)**—specifies the position, size, and color of text, the location of graphic information, and the incorporation of sound and video (Figure 3.9). HTML commands also identify the words or images that will serve as hyperlinks to other documents. When the computer processes files containing HTML commands, it creates and displays the page and prepares the hyperlinks.

hypertext markup language (HTML)
A set of commands that specifies the position, size, and color of text, the location of graphic information, and the incorporation of sound and video. HTML commands also identify the words or images that will serve as hyperlinks to other documents.

HTML consists of a series of *tags* that set off sections of text that will appear on a Web page. Used in pairs, the tags mark the beginning and end of an HTML section (such as the head, title, or body areas of a page). Tags are recognized by their angle brackets (<>). An initial tag identifies the beginning of a section

FIGURE 3.8
Home Page for the City of Paris, France

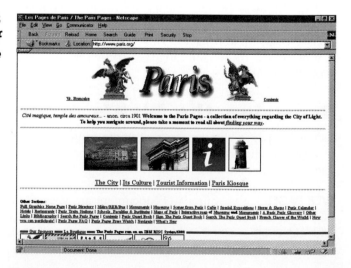

TAG	DESCRIPTION
Structure	
<HTML> ... </HTML>	Identifies the document as an HTML document and its beginning and end.
<HEAD> ... </HEAD>	Identifies the head, one of two parts of an HTML document.
<BODY> ... </BODY>	Identifies the body of the document, the other part of an HTML document.
<TITLE> ... </TITLE>	Identifies the document's title.
<!- ... ->	Sets off a comment within a document. (Browser software does not display comments on a Web page.)
Block Elements	
<H1> ... </H1>	Identifies a first-level heading (the highest level) within the document. It is customary to use a level 1 heading as the first element in the body of an HTML document.
<H2> ... </H2>	Identifies a second-level heading within the document.
<H3> ... </H3>	Identifies a third-level heading within the document.
<H4> ... </H4>	Identifies a fourth-level heading within the document.
<H5> ... </H5>	Identifies a fifth-level heading within the document.
<P> ... </P>	Sets off paragraphs within the document.
<CENTER> ... </CENTER>	Centers the block (the content between the tags) on the page when it is displayed.
<TAB>	Describes the number of spaces to indent: e.g., <TAG INDENT = 5> will indent the text 5 characters until the end of the paragraph (no closing tag is required).
Hypertext Links	
<A> ... </A>	Marks the start (HREF) or end (NAME) of a link: e.g., <A HREF=url>text to be highlighted as hyperlink</A>.
In-line Images	
<IMG>	Used to place an in-line image into the page at the designated location: e.g., <IMG SCR=../image.gif"> where SCR indicates the file name, image.gif, containing the image to be embedded (there is no closing tag).
Formatting	
<P>	Start a new paragraph; insert a blank line.
 	Start a new line.
<HR>	Insert a ruler line.
<B> </B>	Boldface type.
<I> </I>	Italic type.
<U> </U>	Underline.
<PRE> </PRE>	Maintains formatted space. (HTML will remove extra spaces, tabs, and blank lines except when instructed to retain preformatted spacing by the <PRE> tag.)
&	Inserts special character.

FIGURE 3.9 *Common HTML Tags*

(<HEAD>), and a second tag, which includes a slash (/), signifies the end of the section (</HEAD>).

The basic structure of a page will conform to this standard sequence:

```
<HTML>
 <HEAD>
    This is the section of the document where the purpose of the page is
    described. The comments here are not intended to be displayed by the
    browser; they are for informational purposes only.
 </HEAD>
 <BODY>
    This is the section of the document that contains the information and graph-
    ical images the browser will display. It also contains hyperlinks to other
    Web pages.
 </BODY>
</HTML>
```

Creating a Web page consists of preparing a document that includes the tags and a combination of text, hyperlink references, and graphics. Figure 3.9 lists the most common HTML commands used in creating Web pages.

The HTML commands describing a page are stored on a Web server. When retrieved by browser software, they are processed to create the page and its links, which are shown on the user's display screen (Figure 3.10).

Software developers have created tools to assist people in preparing Web pages (Figure 3.11). Some of these tools provide example HTML segments that users can modify to create the page they want without writing the HTML from scratch.

 Plenty of books are available that will familiarize you with HTML and help you create your own pages on the Web (see *Suggested Readings* at the end of the chapter). Alternatively, you can use the Web itself to retrieve information on HTML and page construction. For example, you may want to visit the following Web locations:

http://nearnet.gnn.com/gnn/netizens/fieldguide.html
(provides a field guide to home pages)
http://nearnet.gnn.com/gnn/netizens/construction/html
(includes a home page construction kit) ■

Browser Software

Web browser

Client computer program designed to locate and display information on the World Wide Web.

To take advantage of the graphical nature of the Web, you need a browser program.[1] **Web browsers** are client computer programs designed to locate and display information on the World Wide Web. With a Web browser you can display Web pages, jump between Web pages, using hyperlinks, and search the Web for pages of topical interest. It was when graphical Web browser programs were introduced in the early 1990s, making the creating and viewing of electronic pages possible, that interest in the Web shot up. Individuals, universities, companies, and governments began to use Web pages to display information and invite communication with people on the Internet.

[1] A variety of browser programs are available. Many can be downloaded from the Internet and loaded on a PC or workstation. Some are available without charge.

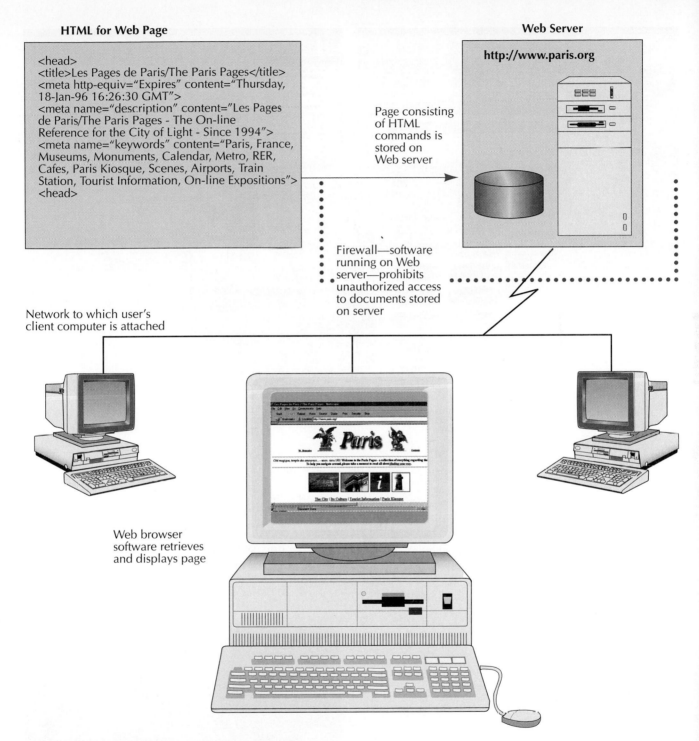

HTML for Web Page

```
<head>
<title>Les Pages de Paris/The Paris Pages</title>
<meta http-equiv="Expires" content="Thursday,
18-Jan-96 16:26:30 GMT">
<meta name="description" content="Les Pages
de Paris/The Paris Pages - The On-line
Reference for the City of Light - Since 1994">
<meta name="keywords" content="Paris, France,
Museums, Monuments, Calendar, Metro, RER,
Cafes, Paris Kiosque, Scenes, Airports, Train
Station, Tourist Information, On-line Expositions">
<head>
```

Web Server

http://www.paris.org

Page consisting of HTML commands is stored on Web server

Firewall—software running on Web server—prohibits unauthorized access to documents stored on server

Network to which user's client computer is attached

Web browser software retrieves and displays page

FIGURE 3.10 *World Wide Web Page Structure*

A page displayed on a PC connected to the Web is the result of a creation using HTML that is stored on a Web server, retrieved and transmitted over interconnecting networks, and viewed on a PC using a Web browser.

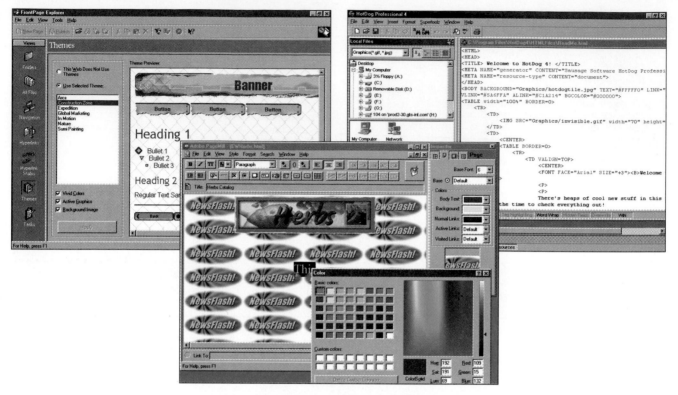

FIGURE 3.11 *WWW Development Tools*

Web browsers are typically activated by clicking on an icon that is associated with the program (Figure 3.12).

Two types of browsers are used with the Web: text-based and graphical. **Text-based browsers** display only text information, either a line at a time or a full screen at once (Figure 3.13). *Line browsers,* the simplest type of text-based browser, display information by writing one line after another on the display screen. As the screen fills, all lines scroll up and the new line is added at the bottom of the screen.

text-based browser

A type of browser used with the Web that displays only text information, either a line at a time or a full screen at once.

FIGURE 3.12
Browsers Client Program

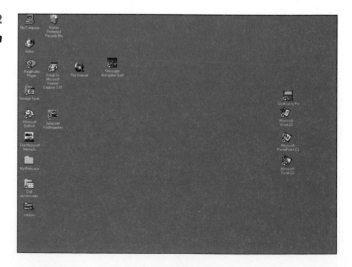

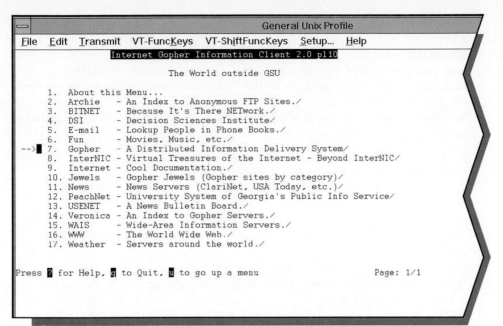

FIGURE 3.13
Text-based Line Browser Used to Access the Internet

A *screen browser,* as its name suggests, uses the entire display screen and can write information anywhere on the screen. Although the software for a screen browser is more complicated than that for a line browser, since it must know the characteristics of a specific display device and how to determine positions on the screen, users of the Web find information displayed by screen browsers easier to use because they see a full screen of information at once rather than individual lines appearing one after the other.

Today, regular users of the Web typically rely on a graphical screen browser. The distinguishing characteristic of a **graphical browser** is its capability for displaying both text and images (called *in-line images*) within a page. The image may be an icon, a photograph, or a drawing. Some pages also include animated images.

Graphical browsers display a window consisting of the display and nine principal components (Figure 3.14):

graphical browser
A type of browser used with the Web that displays both text and images within a page.

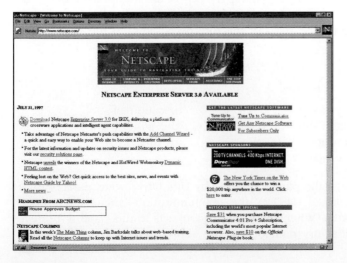

FIGURE 3.14
Netscape Graphical Browser

1. **Title bar**—displays the name of the browser and the page currently displayed.
2. **Menu bar**—contains the browser commands for creating, editing, navigating, and invoking special actions involving the page currently displayed.
3. **Net site**—displays the address of the Web site providing the page currently displayed.
4. **Toolbar**—contains icons that represent frequently used commands included in the menu bar, such as

   Forward—moves ahead to pages in the history list.
   Backward—moves back to pages in the history list.
   Open file—makes a file ready to use.
   File store—writes a copy of the current file to storage.
   History list—keeps track of all WWW pages visited in a particular session, thus providing the capability for a user to jump directly to any of those pages.
   Print—prints a copy of the page currently displayed.
   Home page—returns to the home page of the site at which the user is connected to the WWW.

5. **In-line image**—graphics embedded (at the page creator's option) in the page to enhance its appearance and visually convey information about the nature of the page.
6. **Hyperlinks**—icon or text links (usually signified by an underline or different color) that can be selected to jump to another page.
7. **Status bar**—displays the address of the highlighted link.
8. **Activity indicator**—an icon that signals the user that an activity, such as locating a WWW site or transmitting information from another location, is in process.
9. **Scroll bars**—allow the user to move the window up or down for viewing information.

WWW's URL Addresses

Uniform Resource Locator (URL)
A document's address on the WWW.

As with all Internet locations, each Web page location has its own address. The **Uniform Resource Locator (URL)** is the document's address on the WWW, so named because it is a consistent system for identifying Web sites that all page developers use. In Figure 3.8, http://www/paris.org is the address for the home page of the Paris Pages.

The URL is determined on the basis of the Internet address of the site. Its general format is:

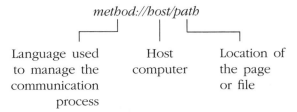

method://host/path

| Language used to manage the communication process | Host computer | Location of the page or file |

Hence, a browser pointed at the page identified by URL http://www.paris.org uses the hypertext transfer protocol (HTTP), the communication language employed by WWW clients and servers. When the browser connects to this page, it retrieves a file called *paris* in a directory named *org* (the abbreviation for organization).

American Airlines' Internet Ticket Auction

American Airlines had been offering last-minute ticket specials to customers of a local cable station in the vicinity of its Dallas, Texas, home base. When it learned that people were watching the announcements on TV and then using e-mail to tell their friends about the specials, American decided it had stumbled upon a new marketing channel.

In 1996, the airline began auctioning tickets over the Internet. Announcements of available tickets are posted on the Internet for 24- and 40-hour periods, during which Net users can bid on the tickets. American periodically posts the high bid during the auction period. At the end of the period, the highest bidders get the right to purchase the available tickets.

Navigating the WWW

To take advantage of what the WWW has to offer, you must know how to navigate from page to page. This is actually quite easy. You merely point the browser to a specific URL location, or, if you do not know the URL, you ask the Web to search for information or scan a directory.

SEARCHING WITH SEARCH ENGINES.   To find information on the Web when you do not know its location—that is, its URL—you start a search by invoking a program, called a **search engine,** from within the browser to scan the network. The search is guided by a keyword or phrase that you enter (Figure 3.15). For instance, if you want to search for information on World Cup Soccer, you simply enter the phrase "world cup soccer" (in any combination of upper- and lower-case letters) when prompted to do so by the search engine.

search engine
A program invoked from within the browser that scans the network by using a keyword or phrase.

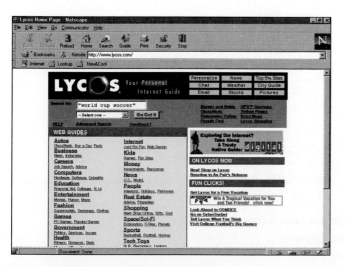

FIGURE 3.15

Home Page for the Lycos Search Engine

Many different search engines are available on the Web, most without a fee. These search engines go by such names as *WebCrawler* (which can be found at http://www.webcrawler.com), *Lycos* (http://www.lycos.com), and *Infoseek* (http://www.infoseek.com).

directory
A listing of information by category.

DIRECTORIES.   A Web **directory** is a listing of information by category. To find information in the directory, you choose the most important category by clicking on the category name, and continue through successive choices, each with more specific options, until you find what you're looking for.

Yahoo! is one of the most widely used directories. When you reach *Yahoo!* (http://www.yahoo.com), you see a subject list, including Arts, Business and Economy, Computers and Internet, Education, Entertainment, Health, and so forth (Figure 3.16a). If you're interested in a topic related to Business and Economy, you click on this *Yahoo!* area and a more detailed subject list will appear (Figure 3.16b).

The key to using both search engines and directories effectively is to plan in advance. Know what subject list is likely to contain what you're looking for and the keywords that will most accurately describe the topic.

surfing
Moving among a number of networks that are linked together, or internetworked.

internetworked
The linking of several networks.

To say that you are **surfing** the Web or the Net is a common way of expressing that you are moving among a number of separate networks that are linked together—that is, **internetworked.** In the ocean, when you ride a surfboard from wave to wave, you are moving across the water's surface. In surfing the Web or Internet, you are moving across networks, skipping from page to page or site to site. ∎

a) Home Page for the Yahoo! Directory

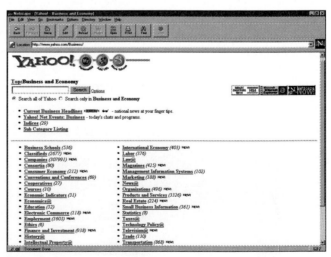

b) A Yahoo! Directory Listing

FIGURE 3.16   *Web directories help locate information on the Internet by topic and keywords.*

USING THE INTERNET'S OTHER CAPABILITIES.   Search engines can also scan for Gopher, FTP, newsgroups, and other sites to locate information, and the browser can retrieve, transmit, or view the files as they are located. Files at these locations have addresses that use the URL conventions outlined in this section. For example, the address of an FTP file will be ftp://(name of FTP file or site), while that of Gopher will be gopher://(name of Gopher site or file).

Internet Information

If you want more information on the Internet, check out your local bookstore and you will be sure to find a variety of books on its features and capabilities. The *Internet Yellow Pages,* for instance, lists available services and databases. Directories describing the thousands of mailing lists on the network are also available. The Internet's popularity has also spawned numerous newsletters and periodicals, including *The Internet Business Journal, The Internet Letter,* and *Internet World* (Figure 3.17). Each provides tips on network capabilities and pointers to interesting sites.

A Final Word

The World Wide Web and the Internet are still in their infancy, so you can be sure that many innovative uses for them will emerge in the next few years. People will certainly find clever new ways to capitalize on their capabilities for incorporating sound, video, animation, and high-resolution graphics. We can only guess at what will result.

FIGURE 3.17
Internet and World Wide Web Books and Magazines

SUMMARY OF LEARNING OBJECTIVES

1 Explain how individual computers and server computers interact on the Internet. A client computer—the computer on an individual's desktop—requests data and information from a server computer on the network. The requested data and information are transmitted to the client computer, where the recipient uses them as he or she wishes.

2 Describe the two types of capabilities of the Internet. The Internet supports communications and retrieval capabilities. Its communications capabilities allow the exchange of information between senders and receivers virtually anywhere in the world. Through the Internet's retrieval capabilities, individuals have access to data and information from other networks connected to the Internet.

3 Identify the 11 principal communication and retrieval capabilities of the Internet. The Net's communications capabilities are e-mail, Usenet, chat sessions, mailing lists, and Telnet. Its retrieval capabilities are FTP, Archie, Gopher, Veronica, WAIS, and the World Wide Web (WWW).

4 Summarize how the Internet knows the location of a particular user on the Net. Everyone on the Internet has a unique address. That address consists of four components: a personal identification, a host computer identification, the name of the institution or organization, and the domain name. All Internet messages are routed to a location according to these address components.

5 Describe the use of pages on the World Wide Web. Each WWW location consists of a series of pages or documents that contain text, graphics, images, and audio or video information. They may also contain links (called *hyperlinks*) to other pages. The home page is the main page at a specific location. All other pages are linked to the home page.

6 Explain the purpose of hyperlinks and their role on the World Wide Web. Hyperlinks (or hypertext) are keywords that connect WWW locations. When a hyperlink is activated by clicking on the linked word, a jump to the connected location occurs without any need to use menus or other means to access the location. Pages containing hyperlinks are the most visible characteristic of the World Wide Web.

7 Describe the characteristics of browser software and relate them to the different types of information that can be included in a home page. Browsers are client software programs that connect with servers on the Internet. Most WWW browsers are graphical, meaning they can display icons, graphics, and images. Individuals use the browser by clicking on hyperlinks or icons or by entering addresses (URLs) on the Internet. The browser, in turn, makes the interconnection, transferring information from the network to the display screen of the client computer.

KEY TERMS

CRITICAL CONNECTIONS

1   FedEx Links Up

When FedEx executives saw how successful the company's package tracking site on the Internet was with customers, they wondered if they could use these same capabilities to enhance communication within the company. They quickly set up some internal intranet sites, and their fast success let to the establishment of others. Soon there were more than 60 intranet sites within FedEx. Today, the thousands of desktop computers on employees' desks are all being equipped with Web browser software to enable internal communication.

Questions for Discussion

1. What possible uses for the intranet can you think of for FedEx?

2. How would you determine whether Federal Express is benefiting from its intranet sites?

3. If customers can access Federal Express's tracking system on the Internet, do you think they can also access the company's intranet sites? Why or why not?

2   Spring Street Microbrewery Shares Sold Over the Internet

When the Securities and Exchange Commission (SEC), which oversees the trading of stocks in the United States, got wind of the Spring Street offering over the Internet, the company voluntarily stopped trading to give the SEC time to investigate this novel practice.

After completing its review, the SEC made only a minor adjustment to Spring Street's stock offering: investors would now have to send their payment to a third party—an escrow agent—rather than directly to Spring Street. Spring Street's managers also agreed to make financial information on the company and its stock's trading history available to the SEC and others. In effect, the SEC, through its review of Spring Street, has endorsed trading on the Internet.

Questions for Discussion

1. Are the risks of purchasing stocks over the Internet different from those assumed when buying through

a broker? What does a broker do for a buyer in return for collecting a commission?

2. Do you think stock trades over the Internet are a potential threat to traditional trading centers like the New York Stock Exchange? Explain the reasoning behind your answer

3 American Airlines' Internet Ticket Auction

| American Airlines |

American Airlines has also started sending out e-mail messages about last-minute fare specials. To receive these messages, you must register at American's Web site (http://www2.amrcorp.com/cgi-bin/aans).

The airline's Internet auction has sold tickets ranging in price from one-tenth to one-half their original value. All types of tickets are available through this auction: first- and business-class tickets, as well as tickets to resorts and exotic locations. American has found the Internet auction an effective way to lower ticket costs since it permits the airline to deal directly with customers, cutting out the travel agent's commission. It has also proved an effective way to sell tickets that would otherwise go unused.

Questions for Discussion

1. Do you think the Internet is a good vehicle for selling surplus tickets at the last minute?

2. How can the Internet help reduce the airline industry's costs of selling and distributing tickets?

3. Do you think other airlines will follow American into the Internet auction arena?.

Net_Work

URLs Find Home

In this exercise, you'll journey onto the Internet's World Wide Web, using the browser's rich capabilities. As you visit different Web sites, you'll see dramatic differences between the way each site's designer has chosen to display information.

To get started, sign on to the Internet. Click on the appropriate icon to activate the browser software. If you're using either the Netscape Navigator or Microsoft Explorer browsers, you'll see one of these icons on your computer:

As soon as the browser is loaded and the Internet connection made, you'll see a home page display. The address for the home page shown on the screen can be found on the browser's location line, near the top of the screen.

| Netsite: http://www.lycos.com/ | ▼ |

Compare the address shown on the location line with the home page address—the URL—for your institution or service provider.

1. If your institution's home page URL is different, enter that URL in the location line (check your notes from the Net_Work application in Chapter 1, where you recorded the URL). Do this by clicking on the location line and keying the URL over the original URL. A new home page will appear on the screen. Move the vertical scroll bar on the right side of the page up or down to view the information clearly.

2. To see a different home page, enter the URL for Netscape Navigator: http://www.netscape.com.

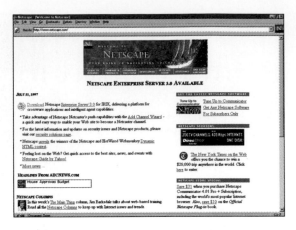

3. You can jump back and forth between the two home pages by clicking on the browser's Back or Forward button near the top of the display.

4. What are the differences between the home pages? Consider the size and style of the text information and note the use of color. What does the graphic image on Netscape's home page convey? Does the home page of your institution or service provider include graphics (perhaps a mascot, seal, or logo)?

5. What hyperlinks are embedded in each page? Hyperlinks are usually identifiable as text that is underlined or set off in a different color or as an icon.

6. Try the hyperlinks to see where they take you. Click on a hyperlink and you'll jump to a new page. You may see hyperlinks on the new page as well. Click on another hyperlink to see where that takes you.

7. Now go back to your starting point, in one of two ways:
   a. Click and the previous display will appear. Do this several times and you'll see each of the preceding screens, until you come to your starting point.
   b. Click on and the browser will jump directly to the home page.

8. Visit some other interesting Web sites, checking their contents and their design. Which ones stand out in your mind and why? Which are the easiest to navigate? The most difficult? Which appear to have useful information?

You might want to visit these sites:[2]

The U.S. Library of Congress: http://lcweb.loc.gov

The Smithsonian: http://www.si.edu

The White House: http://whitehouse.gov

The U.S. Bureau of the Census: http://www.census.gov

The Government of Canada: http://debra.dgbt.doc.ca:80/opengov/

The Government of Mexico: http://www.presidencia.gob.mx

9. For each site you visit, explore the hyperlinks. Behind each link you'll find some interesting features. For example, you can send an e-mail message to the White House, view one of the Smithsonian's collections via its on-line images, test your knowledge of French as you explore information on Canada's legislative bodies, or get a glimpse of Mexico's rich heritage.

10. When you're done, don't forget to sign off. Click on File on the menu bar. Then on the File menu, click Exit.

The wide world of the Internet awaits your next sign-on!

[2]Web sites can be "busy" because of high use, in which case you might see an informative message displayed on your screen. Also, Web site operators may move their home page to a different URL, sometimes linking the old page to the new (when they do not, a message may state that the URL is no longer used).

GROUP PROJECTS AND APPLICATIONS

Project 1

At one time, there were only a few Net search engines. In recent years, however, many new engines have been created. Most regular Net users have a favorite search engine. Which one do you like best? To find out, perform the following group activity with three or four members of your class.

Your goal is to answer *one* of the following questions:

- Which three companies in the United States spend the most each year on advertising? The most on public relations?
- In what year was the novel *Tom Jones* published? Who wrote it? Name two other English literary works also published that year.
- Which New Jersey counties use the 201 area code? Which three New Jersey towns have the highest per capita income?
- In which museum is Edvard Munch's "The Scream" displayed? Which museum owns the largest collection of paintings by Grandma Moses?

Each member of your group should use a different search engine to find the answer to the question you've chosen. Some search engines to try:

- *Alta Vista*   http://www.altavista.com
- *Excite!*   http://www.excite.com
- *Infoseek*   http://www.infoseek.com
- *Lycos*   http://www.lycos.com
- *WebCrawler*   http://www.webcrawler.com
- *Yahoo!*   http://www.yahoo.com

How long did each member of your group take to find the answer? Compare your answers with those of other groups. How do the various engines and directories differ? Are some more appropriate for particular types of research than for others? Report on the results of your searches to the class.

Project 2

Subscribers to Usenet groups often become members of a "virtual community" in which they exchange ideas and sometimes develop friendships. Groups of four or five students should subscribe to and monitor the activities of a Usenet group for a period of two weeks. Choose any topic in which the group is interested, from the standard to the unexpected.

At the end of two weeks, report to the class on the activities of your Usenet group. Is the group popular? What topics is it discussing? Have you begun to correspond with anyone?

Project 3

Very few companies have been able to make money through the Internet. Setting up and maintaining a Net site can be expensive. Free sites, such as search directories, are presently supported by advertising, but advertisers may not be willing to advertise on the Net in the future unless they see a return on their investment.

Form a team and visit a local company that has a home page on the Internet. Interview someone in the information technology or advertising department about the company's Internet philosophy. Some questions you might ask:

- Who designed the company's site—a company employee or an outside expert?
- Who maintains the site? Who is in charge of answering any e-mail that comes through the site?
- Does the company advertise on the Net? If so, where? Who designed the advertisements? How much do the ads cost?
- How many "hits" does the company get on its ads? In other words, how many people see the ad each week or month? Has the company been able to make a direct connection between its sales revenue and its Internet ads?
- What are the company's plans for using the Internet in the future?

Prepare a two- to five-page written summary of the interview.

REVIEW QUESTIONS

1. Was the Internet developed by public or private organizations? Who pays for the cost of operating the Internet today?

2. What is the significance of the name *Internet?*

3. Describe the characteristics of client and server computers. What is the relationship between client-server computing and the Internet?

4. What are host computers? How are host computers involved in the Internet?

5. How is an Internet address determined? Who assigns Internet addresses?

6. Describe the two types of activities possible on the Internet.

7. What are the characteristics of each of the five communications capabilities of the Internet?

8. Describe the similarities and differences among Gopher, Veronica, and Archie retrieval tools.

9. What is an FTP site? A WAIS server?

10. What is the most distinguishing characteristic of the World Wide Web?

11. How do text-based and graphical browsers differ? Do they have the same purpose?

12. When is HTML needed for use of the WWW? Who uses HTML?

13. How does a URL enable a WWW user to find and retrieve information?

14. Describe the importance of pages for the World Wide Web. What contents are included in a page?

15. What is a home page? How is a home page created?

16. Describe the purpose of a search engine. Who uses a search engine? What information must be provided before a search engine can work?

17. What is the difference between a search engine and a directory?

18. Why is using the Internet sometimes called *surfing?*

DISCUSSION QUESTIONS

1. The Internet is in its infancy; it exploded onto the business scene relatively recently. Hence, companies are still learning how to capitalize on its features. What characteristics of the Internet do you feel are most important to business and why? Do you think *every business,* from the largest corporations to the smallest "mom-and-pop" stores, will soon be Internet users? Why or why not?

2. What features of intranets do you believe underlie their rapidly growing use in business? What advantages does an intracompany intranet offer that cannot be obtained through use of ordinary e-mail?

3. Businesses have developed another use of the intranet to link selective business partners over the Internet. Access to these *extranets* is controlled in the same way as intranets so that only authorized companies can view company information. Develop three examples illustrating when a company might want to establish extranets to interconnect with outside companies.

4. The Net's FTP capabilities make it possible to transfer files containing digital information between virtually any locations. What are examples of ways in which businesses could use this capability to service their customers? Do you think companies can deliver their products by means of FTP? Why or why not?

SUGGESTED READINGS

Berghel, Hal. "Cyperspace 2000: Dealing With Information Overload," *Communications of the ACM 40* (February 1997). The author, a respected research scientist, examines the technology revolution brought about by the Internet, with implications for the way it will change daily living into the next century. The credibility of the Internet is examined from different dimensions in order to compare its impact to such other historical inventions as the printing press and the compass.

Martin, Michael H. "The Next Big Thing: A Bookstore?" *Fortune 134* (December 6, 1996): 68–170. This article, part of a special information technology issue covering the Internet, describes how business is using the Net to do more than exchange information. Companies, including amazon.com, who have come into existence to serve customers over the Net are discussed in this and the accompanying articles.

Nelson, Stephen L. *Microsoft FrontPage.* Microsoft, 1997. Describes the creation of Web pages using Microsoft's popular FrontPage construction software. The guide includes do's and don'ts as well as helpful hints that lead to functional and attractive Web pages.

Udell, Jon. "Net Applications: Will Netscape Set the Standard?" *Byte 22* (March 1997): 66–72,ff. This forward-looking article describes the manner in which Netscape will change its browser software in the future, promising to further change the world of computing. The evolution of Netscape software to link groups of individuals is discussed. Examples from business demonstrate the expected benefits of these advances.

Yourdon, Edward. "Java, the Web, and Software Development," *Computer 29* (August 1996): 25–30. What's the big deal about the Web? According to this distinguished computer pioneer, it marks the birth of dynamic computing on rented components. Seven key issues for developers of full-scale Internet applications are discussed.

Zimmerman, Paul H. *Web Page (Essentials).* Que Books, 1997. A practical and comprehensive book describing the creation of Web pages. Projects in the book guide readers through creation of pages, adding hyperlinks, and effective use of color and graphics.

C A S E
S T U D Y

The Snap-on Intranet

Snap-on   Snap-on, Incorporated, is among the best-known suppliers of hand and diagnostic tools for the automotive industry in the world. Headquartered in Kenosha, Wisconsin, and founded in 1920, the company has developed a successful, worldwide dealer network of more than 5,000 independent businesspersons who are authorized by Snap-on to sell the company's tools.

Snap-on sometimes refers to its dealer marketing strategy as a Store Without Walls. The name has its origin in the characteristic location of the dealer's "store"—a gleaming white van that serves as place of business, warehouse, and delivery system. Snap-on dealers visit their customers in the van, fully stocked with many products that can be delivered on the spot. More than 1 million automotive technicians are visited by Snap-on vans each week, making the company the leading dealer van network in the world.

Snap-on is perennially rated by industry experts as one of the top 10 franchises in the United States, partly because of its status as the leading seller of hand and power tools, tool storage equipment,

and diagnostic and shop equipment. Franchisee achievements are another factor in the high rating. Snap-on recognizes that its high ranking and success are due just as much to the efforts of its franchisees as to the quality of its products. From the franchisee's view, good tools are not the only reason to affiliate with Snap-on. Other important benefits include the company's efficient and reliable product delivery and support services,

training programs, dissemination of important sales information, and assistance in improving productivity and sales effectiveness. Snap-on also provides financing, equipment leasing, and insurance to its franchisees.

Always searching for more effective ways to make its dealers successful, Snap-on recently sought to increase its ability to keep franchisees informed about the company's latest products, current sales, and product promotions, as well as to share successful franchisee business strategies. It also wanted to encourage and support intrafranchise communication because it recognized that the best sales strategies and competitive insights often come from day-to-day contact with customers in the field. By putting dealers directly in touch with one another, the company believed it could improve everyone's business success. The challenge for Snap-on was

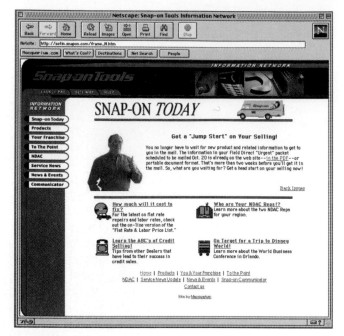

3. **Updates on sales and marketing.** Here is where franchisees obtain details of Snap-on's marketing programs, promotional programs, and sales contests. This intranet service also disseminates customer information and details of changes in customer- and business-related demographics in sales regions.

4. **Forums for franchisees.** This service details the best practices used by salespersons in the field to identify prospective customers as well as successful selling strategies. It also describes effective tactics for coping with late invoice payments. This service is used both for communication among franchisees and for sending messages to designated Snap-on employees.

5. **News and special events information.** Franchisees avail themselves of this service to learn about special marketing, advertising, and Snap-on's motorsports program.

Why did Snap-on's executives choose to develop an intranet to meet the company's communication needs? After investigating the capabilities of the Internet and the World Wide Web, Snap-on's information technology staff quickly recognized these benefits of an intranet:

- It handles widespread geographic distribution of franchisees.
- It ensures convenient access for everyone with a PC, Internet access, and appropriate authorization to interconnect with Snap-on.

to come up with a method of intrafranchise communication that was low-cost, yet flexible enough to link everyone together.

After exploring a variety of communication alternatives, Snap-on determined it could meet its objectives best by creating an intranet that would be accessible exclusively to franchisees through personal computers and available communication (telephone) services. The Snap-on intranet was designed to use the capabilities of the public Internet and a secured World Wide Web site to disseminate important information to all franchisees and allow them to communicate electronically with one another.

Dealers who have signed on to the Snap-on Tools Information Network can click on icons representing the system's principal services. For example:

1. **Information on Snap-on products and services.** The parent company provides highlights of new products and other changes to its product list. This service also includes candid comparisons of Snap-on product features and those of its principal competitors. The tips on how to pitch Snap-on tools against the competition are particularly well regarded by franchisees.

2. **Tips for franchisee management.** This service consists of on-line "training rooms" consisting of tips and training designed to assist franchisees in managing their businesses.

- Costs are low. Since Snap-on handles all development and maintenance of the intranet, there is no cost to customers other than Internet access. Creation of pages for the intranet has also proved relatively low cost, since the company already had the necessary hardware and software technology.
- The intranet controls access to information that Snap-on needs to keep secret from competitors. "Firewalls," in the form of security software, prevent unauthorized individuals from entering Snap-on's site. At the same time, Snap-on users can reach virtually anywhere on the Internet.

Snap-on's intranet seems to have an exciting future. Interviews with company officials and franchisees, with complete audio and video, as well as demonstrations of products and services, could become available over the intranet. In essence, the intranet ensures that Snap-on's Store Without Walls™ will include the capability for communication without barriers.

Questions for Discussion

1. What types of information can be delivered over Snap-on's intranet that cannot be provided through printed brochures and reports?

2. If you were a Snap-on franchisee, how would you feel about the use of the company intranet to deliver important sales- and product-related information?

3. What benefits of the Internet prompted Snap-on to take the intranet route to developing a communications link to each dealer?

PHOTO ESSAY

Tripod
D E V E L O P S A
WEB SITE

A producer, a designer, an editor, and a programmer are charged with creating a Web site. Sometimes these are all different people; sometimes it is a single developer wearing all these hats. In any case, there are steps in the development of Web media that will greatly enhance their effectiveness and usability.

In this case a team at Tripod (http://www.tripod.com) is creating a site about cooking called the Kitchenette. Here are some of the steps in the development of this area of the Tripod Web site.

1 The best place to start when you are designing a Web site is with a site map. This helps you understand the size of the project, and also helps you start thinking about how the pieces fit together. This stage is called site architecture, and it is critical to developing an easy-to-use, easy-to-navigate Web site.

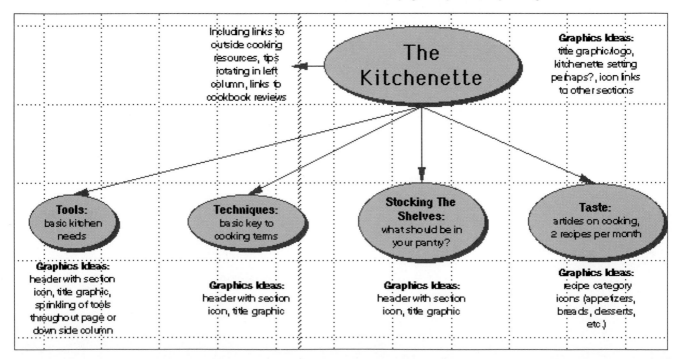

Including links to outside cooking resources, tips rotating in left column, links to cookbook reviews

The Kitchenette

Graphics Ideas: title graphic/logo, kitchenette setting perhaps?, icon links to other sections

Tools: basic kitchen needs

Techniques: basic key to cooking terms

Stocking The Shelves: what should be in your pantry?

Taste: articles on cooking, 2 recipes per month

Graphics Ideas: header with section icon, title graphic, sprinkling of tools throughout page or down side column

Graphics Ideas: header with section icon, title graphic

Graphics Ideas: header with section icon, title graphic

Graphics Ideas: recipe category icons (appetizers, breads, desserts, etc.)

2 Just as an architect wouldn't start building a house without a blueprint, it's always a good idea to sketch out your ideas before bringing them to the computer screen. Grab a piece of blank paper and roughly sketch out how all the pieces fit together and what the underlying structure of the page layout will be — this helps the translation of ideas into Web pages go more smoothly and ensures that everyone is working off the same diagram of what the end result would ideally look like. Of course, you should be flexible and understand that some ideas may need to be adjusted to function within the medium of the Web.

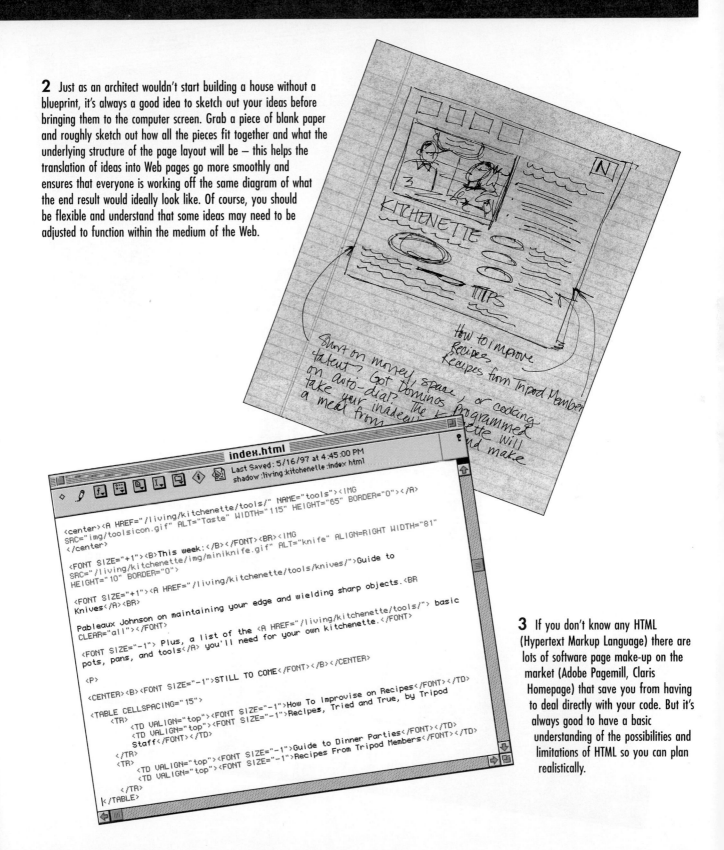

3 If you don't know any HTML (Hypertext Markup Language) there are lots of software page make-up on the market (Adobe Pagemill, Claris Homepage) that save you from having to deal directly with your code. But it's always good to have a basic understanding of the possibilities and limitations of HTML so you can plan realistically.

4 Your most basic page structure is laid out in HTML, with no color or graphics. It is helpful to view the page in this limited fashion because you can be sure that what you are communicating comes across even on low-end browsers or if the viewer has images turned off, as many do. It is a good reminder that what you are principally trying to do is communicate a message. Pretty graphs and animations are icing on the cake!

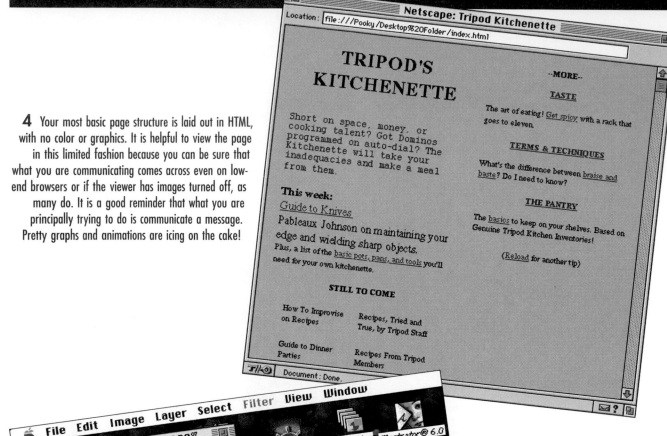

5 That having been said, everyone loves icing! Giving the page a visual identity through the use of color, typography, and images can greatly enhance the message you are trying to convey. Here, a comic of a woman and a man is created in Adobe Photoshop. It is critical to keep Web graphics small and as few as possible in the interest of download time. Tripod strives to keep all pages to a total of 35K of images. Using graphics with a limited palette (or using as few colors as possible) is a good way to keep file sizes small. This is why all of the images here are illustrations; these are easier to reduce to a limited palette.

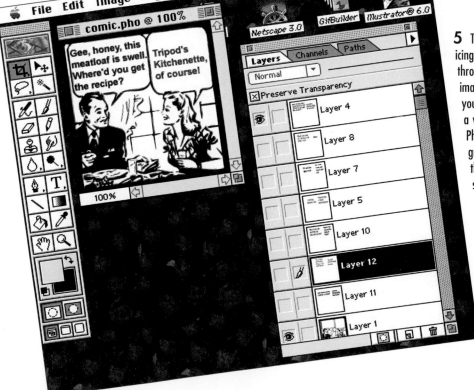

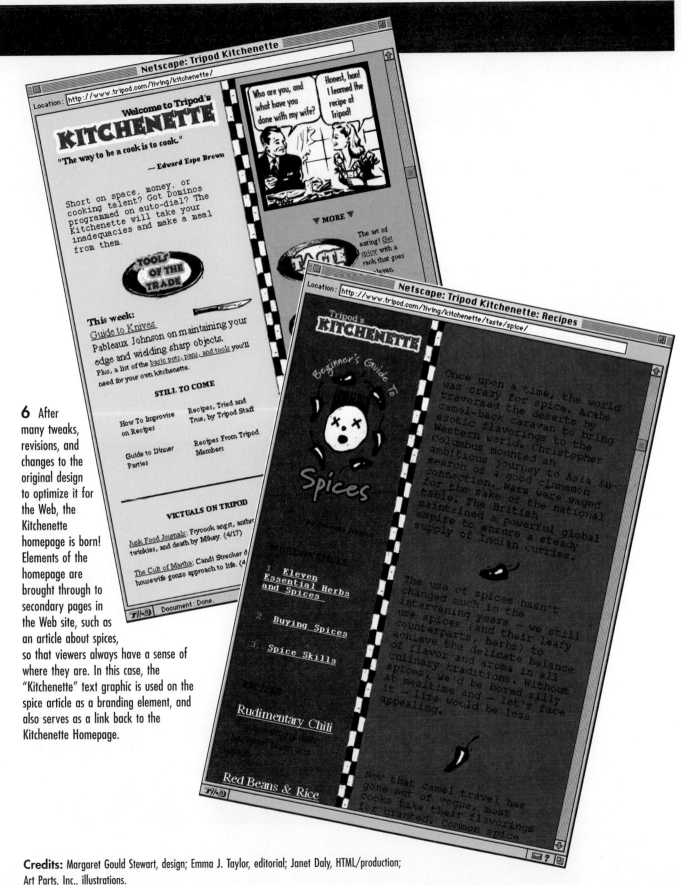

6 After many tweaks, revisions, and changes to the original design to optimize it for the Web, the Kitchenette homepage is born! Elements of the homepage are brought through to secondary pages in the Web site, such as an article about spices, so that viewers always have a sense of where they are. In this case, the "Kitchenette" text graphic is used on the spice article as a branding element, and also serves as a link back to the Kitchenette Homepage.

Credits: Margaret Gould Stewart, design; Emma J. Taylor, editorial; Janet Daly, HTML/production; Art Parts, Inc., illustrations.

Opportunities for Investing in the Internet

Shopping On-line: The Other Side of the Growing Internet

Distance and time . . . the most formidable barriers in business. Companies that can overcome geographic distance can serve customers virtually anywhere. If they can minimize the time between contact with customers and response to their requests, they might well have a new business opportunity.

The Internet has exploded into the lives of ordinary citizens as well as large and small businesses. As the largest network (or, more accurately, network of networks) in the world, the Internet is indeed a means of leaping over time and distance barriers. To many people, the Net is a vehicle for sending and receiving e-mail around the world. To others, it's a source of information and entertainment—the reason millions surf the Net every single day.

Entrepreneurs On-line   But to an increasing number of entrepreneurs, the Net is an opportunity to grow a business and build a company. In the process, they are creating new models for doing business. Consider the following companies that *began their life* on the Net:

- *amazon.com*. Lists more than 1 million book titles in its inventory. Often sells at a discount and promises fast delivery (gift wrapped, if requested). (http://www.amazon.com)

- *CDNow*. Lists thousands of popular compact discs that can be purchased over the Web and shipped direct to the purchaser's door. (http://www.cdnow.com)
- *CNN Interactive*. Includes the latest-breaking news and top stories of the day, along with audio interviews and video for many of the events it covers. (http://www.cnn.com)
- *Hot Hot Hot*. It may not be *your* thing, but thou-

sands of chili lovers from all over the world visit this company to buy from its inventory of more than 150 exotic hot sauces. (http://hothothot.com)

- *Virtual Vineyards.* Stocks several hundred different varieties of wine, including those that are difficult to get outside of California. Keeps track of repeat customers and their purchases to provide future assistance. (http://www.virtualvin.com)

Secrets to Success   What do all these Net businesses have in common? An idea and courage, at a minimum. Both are essential to building a successful business. Doing the same thing as someone else or having a potentially valuable idea without the willingness to take risks will probably not bring commercial success.

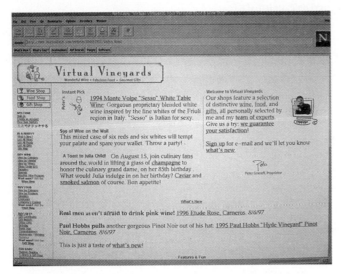

It pays to advertise on the Web, too. As you would expect, there are plenty of advertisements that pointedly promote a company or its product. But the more effective advertising is to appear repeatedly in the list of favorite Web sites included in the home pages of so many Web surfers. Remember, often you only have to click on the company name in a list and the hyperlink will take you right to the company's home page. Getting other people to advertise for you . . . that's the best advertising tactic of all.

Trust is an important element, too. Who repeatedly buys from a business that they do not trust? (Remember, every business needs repeat customers to succeed.)

Undoubtedly, there are other elements necessary to entrepreneurial success on the Net, though they can't yet be named so easily. After all, business on the Internet is just starting to grow.

Not every business on the Internet is profitable. In fact, it is estimated that for every one that is profitable, two others are not. Still, companies that have established a presence on the Net are gaining valuable experience and perhaps planting the necessary seed to grow a successful enterprise.

Many have created virtual communities whose members can surf in *whenever* they wish from *wherever* they are. The company's Web site may be a cozy hangout where ideas are easily exchanged electronically. Some offer contests, give-aways, and drawings. Bookseller amazon.com, for instance, holds regular drawings for a year's supply of books, gives away computer mouse pads to its regular customers, and keeps customers informed about publication of new books by their favorite authors. Wine merchant Virtual Vineyards has an excellent guide to wines and a cellar of fine wines not normally available outside of its home state of California. Smart Games offers thousands of dollars in cash prizes to those who score well on its Challenge CD-ROM game, a promotional tactic the company believes is responsible for sales in excess of $1 million for the CD.

Questions for Discussion

1. Look ahead five years. Do you think it will be common then for consumers to shop for products and services on-line? Why or why not?

2. What products and services do you think people will buy on-line, either over the Internet or through some other communications link? Why?

3. What products or services would *you* personally *not* consider buying over the Internet? Give your reasons.

CHAPTER 4

The Central Processor and Memory

CHAPTER OUTLINE

The Microprocessor Reaches Adulthood

The Central Processing Unit (CPU)

Control Unit • Arithmetic/Logic Unit (ALU)

Memory

Memory Size • RAM and ROM • Flash Memory • PCMCIA Card Memory

Inside the System Unit

Processor Chips • Memory Chips • Ports • Add-in Boards • Plug and Play

The Processing Sequence

The Machine Cycle • Registers

Processor Speed

Determining Processor Speed • Increasing Computer Speed

Case Study: DigiCash Makes Money Electronic

Photo Essay: The Making of a Microprocessor

LEARNING OBJECTIVES

When you have completed this chapter, you should be able to

1 Describe the components and purpose of the central processing unit (CPU).

2 Distinguish between primary and secondary storage and between RAM and ROM.

3 Describe the chips and boards that can be used to augment the CPU and main memory.

4 Explain the process by which computers use registers to process data.

5 List and explain the three determinants of processor speed.

6 Describe six ways of increasing processing and computer speed.

The Microprocessor Reaches Adulthood

Where do you find microprocessors? Walk through your home and take a count. The VCR, camcorder, TV, microwave oven, telephone, answering machine, and, of course, the PC, all contain microprocessors. And don't forget to include the stove, dishwasher, blender, and coffeemaker. Then there's the camera, radar detector (in your car), security system, and, of course, a few video games. You could probably add to this list.

The microprocessor has come a long way since November 15, 1971, the day on which the first computer on a chip—the Intel 4004—was manufactured. In a space of less than 30 years, the microprocessor has progressed from a pioneering invention to a necessity.

The 4004's development began when Busicom, a Japanese calculator manufacturer, asked Intel, then a two-year-old company, to design a set of 12 chips for its programmable calculator. Busicom gave Intel $60,000, an investment in both the company and the expected chip set.

After studying Busicom's functional requirements, Ted Hoff, the Intel project director leading the effort, determined the company could provide the requested capability with just four chips, one of which would be a general-purpose programmable processor ... a microprocessor. Aware of the vast potential of such an invention, Intel promptly returned Busicom's money to ensure that it would remain the microprocessor's sole owner.

Intel's 4004 opened the doors to a new world of computing, for on this single chip, measuring a fraction of a square inch, were 2,300 transistors that could run at a speed of 108 kHz.

What invention has changed day-to-day living more significantly in the twentieth century than the microprocessor? The microprocessor may be even more important than the radio, television, and the computer itself. Next time you stroll through a building, the easier question to answer may be "Where *don't* I find microprocessors?"

Chapter 2 explored the five components of a computer system: hardware, programs, information, people, and procedures. By this point, you should have a good sense of how these elements work together to help individuals and businesses perform more productively and effectively.

This chapter and the next will take a closer look at hardware components by building on what you learned in Chapter 2. We begin by taking a tour of the central processor to see what makes computers compute. You'll see how computers remember information and execute instructions. (Today's microprocessors, like Ted Hoff's original invention, rely on these fundamental principles.) In the final section of the chapter, we show how and why computers differ in processing speed. We'll conclude our discussion of hardware in Chapter 5, where you'll learn more about input and output devices and secondary storage.

By the time you finish these two chapters, you'll have a good working knowledge of how a computer functions—an important part of the know-how you will need to use information technology productively and effectively.

The *Information Technology in Practice* feature entitled "Remembering Elvis at Graceland" illustrates how a working knowledge of IT can help a visitor appreciate the intricate entertainment provided at the storied home and final resting place of Elvis Presley.

The Central Processing Unit (CPU)

central processing unit (CPU)/processor
The computer hardware that executes program instructions and performs the computer's processing actions.

integrated circuit/chip/microchip
A collection of thousands or millions of transistors placed on a small silicon chip.

transistor
An electrical switch that can be in one of two states: open or closed.

integrating
The process of packing more transistors onto a single chip.

Recall from Chapter 1 that a computer is any electronic system that can be instructed to accept, process, store, and present data and information. At the heart of the computer's hardware is the **central processing unit (CPU),** sometimes called the **processor,** which executes program instructions and performs the computer's processing actions.

The CPU is a collection of electronic circuits made up of thousands—millions in some computers—of transistors placed onto integrated circuits. **Integrated circuits** are also called **chips** or **microchips** because the transistors are etched onto a small silicon chip. Each **transistor** is an electronic switch that can be in one of two states: open or closed. (Numerically, a switch's closed state is described by the number 0, its open state by the number 1.)

Decreasing the size of transistors allows more transistors to be packed onto one chip. This process, called **integrating,** brought about the "PC revolution" in the 1980s and is driving many of the advances in information technology today. Integrating makes it possible to place more and more of the CPU's components onto a single chip, thus eliminating the need for separate chips. Integrating greatly increases the speed of the computer.

Because processing is electronic, you cannot see what happens inside a processor. If you open the cover, you will not see moving parts, just as you do not see the electricity moving when you turn on the lights in a room.

Processors are designed and constructed in different ways. The processor for a PC is a single microprocessor chip. For larger systems, the processor consists of multiple circuit boards, each containing many chips. Figure 4.1 shows the two parts of the processor—the control unit and the arithmetic/logic unit.

INFORMATION TECHNOLOGY IN PRACTICE

Remembering Elvis at Graceland

Elvis Presley, the King of Rock and Roll, died in August 1977. Yet, he lives on in Graceland, his home near Memphis, Tennessee, where some 700,000 visitors flock every year for a glimpse into his everyday life.

When Graceland was first opened to the public, visitors saw everything just as Elvis left it in 1977: facilities, grounds, a seemingly endless display of Elvis memorabilia. Graceland's management system was also out of the 1970s. Staff members hand-stamped tickets to each of the events offered and manually sorted them into blocks for each tour group. They often had to work late into the evening to prepare tickets, reservations, and tour schedules for the next day. The process was both time-consuming and error-prone—management of Graceland was in a primitive state.

Today, a visitor to Graceland notices immediately that information technology is an integral part of running Elvis's home. A combination of Apple Macintosh and IBM-compatible computers is evident throughout the estate's ticket offices as well as in its corporate and accounting offices. An electronic reservation system not only issues tickets but keeps track of the planned activities of visiting guests as well. Touch-screen terminals located around the estate's offices put the systems' capabilities within easy reach.

An on-line reservation system tracks group sales and the services requested by guests. Tickets are prepared quickly, even for large groups. Visitors no longer have to wait up to three hours to book their tours.

A sophisticated inventory system tracks sales and inventory in the gift shop and distribution center so that guests will always be able to find the records, scarves, photo albums, and other bits of popular memorabilia they want.

August is a particularly busy month at Graceland since fans return year after year to be at the estate on the anniversary of Elvis's death. Graceland's information technology smoothes the August rush for fans and employees alike. Management of even the most popular attractions—a museum of Elvis's personal mementos and stage costumes, his extensive automobile collection and the *Hound Dog II* and *Lisa Marie* airplanes—is nearly flawless.

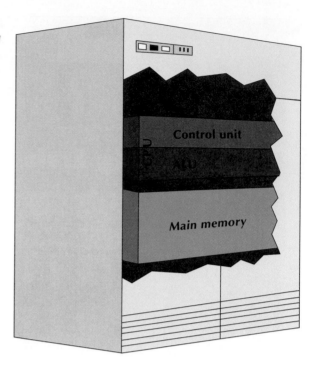

FIGURE 4.1

The Components of the CPU

In microcomputers, the control unit and the arithmetic/logic unit (ALU) are found together on a single microprocessor chip (see Figure 4.11). In larger systems, the control unit and ALU are usually found on separate boards. Note that main memory is *not* a part of the CPU.

Control Unit

control unit
The part of the CPU that oversees and controls all computer activities according to the instructions it receives.

instructions
Detailed descriptions of the actions to be carried out during input, processing, output, storage, and transmission.

Computers "think" by using the on/off pulses of electric current. You might liken the **control unit,** the part of the CPU that oversees and controls all computer activities, to the human brain, which oversees and controls all of our actions, whether we are working, playing, or exercising.

All computer activities occur according to instructions the control unit receives. **Instructions** are detailed descriptions of the actions to be carried out during input, processing, output, storage, and transmission. A typical instruction might be to add two numbers together, to retrieve information for processing, or to print the results of processing. A wide range of instructions is embedded in such computer applications as retrieving the details of a specific transaction or transmitting data over a communications network.

The control unit does not actually execute the instructions, just as the brain does not actually do the working, playing, and exercising that make up many of our daily activities. Rather, it directs other processing elements to do so.

Arithmetic/Logic Unit (ALU)

arithmetic/logic unit (ALU)
The part of the CPU that performs arithmetic and logical operations.

The other component of the central processor is the **arithmetic/logic unit (ALU).** The ALU contains the electronic circuitry that performs arithmetic operations and logical operations, the two activities that underlie all computing capabilities.

Arithmetic operations include addition, subtraction, multiplication, and division. When a university's computer tallies the number of credit hours in a student's schedule on a transcript, it's doing arithmetic. So is the post office's computer system when it sorts letters by the postal code in an address.

Logical operations compare one element of information to another. The comparison determines whether one item is greater than, less than, or equal to the other. The outcome of a logical comparison usually determines what type of processing occurs:

- **Greater than (>).** The ALU compares two values to determine if one is greater than the other. For example, if the number of reservations for a specific flight on an airplane is greater than the number of seats on the plane, the computer will show that the flight is oversold. Actions can then be taken to ensure that all passengers reach their destination—perhaps another flight will be scheduled or passengers will be assisted in making reservations at another airline.
- **Less than (<).** The ALU compares two values to determine if one is less than the other. For example, if the number of students registered for a class is smaller than the number of seats in the auditorium where the class is to be held, then the class is still open for registration.
- **Equal to (=).** The ALU compares two values to determine if they are equal or not. For example, if the amount of money submitted to a utility company for payment is equal to the amount of money owed, the computer will change the amount owed to show a zero balance.

Arithmetic and logical comparisons are possible because of computers' memory capability. But what exactly is memory?

Memory

When the electronic calculator was introduced in the 1930s, it was viewed as a breakthrough because of its memory capability. Earlier mechanical calculators did not have the capacity to store data and information, but electronic calculators did—and so do their descendants, the various kinds of computer. This memory, which is composed of computer chips, can be used repeatedly by different applications.

The CPU interacts closely with memory, referring to it both for instructions and for data or information. However, memory is separate from the CPU.

As Figure 4.2 shows, memory space in a computer is used in five different ways:

1. To hold the computer's operating system program (e.g., DOS, OS/2, UNIX, VM)—the software that oversees processing and acts as an interface between the hardware and the applications programs.
2. To hold application programs—word-processing, spreadsheet, order-entry, and inventory control programs.
3. To hold data and information temporarily (in "virtual memory"), receiving from input devices data or information that is processed and sent to output devices during processing.
4. To store other data or information needed in processing in the *working storage* area.
5. To provide additional space as needed for programs or data. If the computer has more memory than is needed for a particular application, the excess memory will go unused but remain available. Since the amount of memory needed may change during the processing of an application, it is useful to have excess memory.

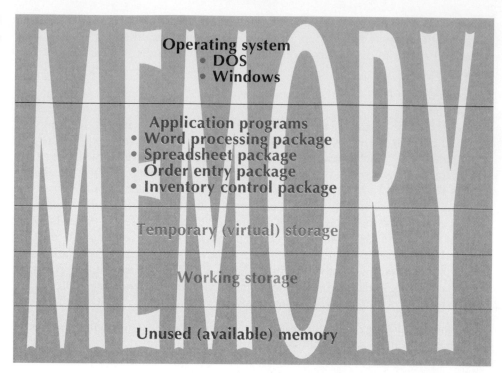

Operating system
* DOS
* Windows

Application programs
* Word processing package
* Spreadsheet package
* Order entry package
* Inventory control package

Temporary (virtual) storage

Working storage

Unused (available) memory

primary storage/
primary memory/
main memory/
internal memory
Storage within the computer
itself. Primary memory holds
data only temporarily, as the
computer executes
instructions.

secondary storage
A storage medium that is
external to the computer, but
that can be read by the
computer; a way of storing
data and information outside
the computer itself.

byte
A storage location in memory;
the amount of memory
required to store one digit,
letter, or character.

kilobyte/K-byte/KB/K
One thousand bytes.

megabyte/
M-byte/MB/meg
One million bytes.

Now we need to distinguish between primary storage and secondary storage. **Primary storage**—also known as **primary memory, main memory, internal memory,** or simply "memory"—is storage within the computer itself. It holds data only temporarily, as the computer executes instructions. **Secondary storage** is memory that augments the primary memory. It is used to store data long-term. Typically, only a portion of the data in use resides in primary memory during processing. The remainder is kept in secondary storage until needed.

Memory Size

Computers vary widely in the amount of primary memory they have. The size of this internal memory is measured by the number of storage locations it contains. Each storage location, or **byte,** has a predetermined capacity. In simplest terms, a byte is the amount of memory required to store one digit, letter, or character.

Bytes are generally measured by the **kilobyte** (also written **K-byte, KB,** or **K**)—which is a thousand bytes;[1] **megabyte** (**M-byte, MB,** or **meg**)—a million bytes; **gigabyte** (**G-byte, GB,** or **gig**)—a billion bytes; and **terabyte** (**T-byte** or **TB**)—a trillion bytes. Thus, a computer with "6 meg" has 6,000,000 bytes of memory.

Personal computers have memory capacities in the megabyte range. For example, most desktop PCs have a main memory capacity of 2 to 128 megabytes. Memory capacities for midrange, mainframe, and supercomputers are substantially higher.

Each byte is identified by a memory **address** that allows the computer to determine where an element of data or information is stored. (In some cases, a group

[1]Although users of information technology generally equate K with 1,000, doing so is not strictly accurate. A kilobyte of memory is actually 1,024 bytes. If you hear someone referring to 640K of memory, the component actually has 655,360 (calculated as 640 × 1024) memory locations. Reference to 8 megabytes means the memory actually has 8,192,000 memory locations (i.e., 8,000K × 1024).

of bytes may have an address.) As Figure 4.3 shows, memory addresses are similar in principle to the addresses of a house or building—they distinguish one location from another and make each one easy to find.

Figure 4.4 shows precisely how data are represented electrically using bits and bytes.

RAM and ROM

Two types of main memory are *random-access memory* and *read-only memory,* with two variations on each type.

RAM. Main memory, the largest area of memory within the computer, is composed of **random-access memory,** or **RAM,** chips. "Random access" means that data or information can be written into or recalled (read) from any memory address at any time. With RAM, there is no need to start at the first location and proceed one step at a time. Information can be written to or read from RAM in less than 100 billionths of a second. However, RAM stores data and information only as long as the computer is turned on. The electrical currents that comprise the data and information cease when the power is turned off.

Two types of RAM are widely used. *Dynamic RAM (DRAM)* is the major memory component in virtually every computer. DRAM chips hold data and information "dynamically." This means that the computer does not hold data and information indefinitely. Rather, this means it must continually refresh the DRAM cell electronically—several hundred times per second. In contrast, *static RAM* chips retain their contents indefinitely, without constant electronic refreshment. They are faster than DRAM, but are not as compact, and they use a more complicated design.

gigabyte/G-byte/GB/gig
One billion bytes.

terabyte/T-byte/TB
One trillion bytes.

address
An identifiable location in memory where data are kept.

random-access memory (RAM)
Memory that permits data or information to be written into or read from memory only as long as the computer is turned on.

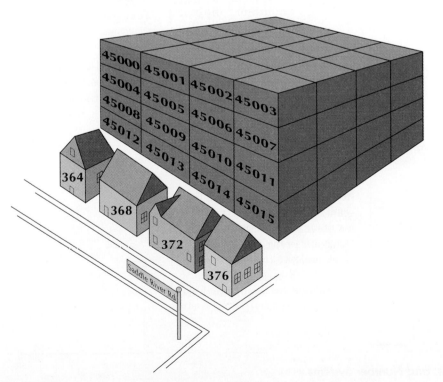

FIGURE 4.3
Addresses in Computer Memory
In main memory, bytes are identified by a memory address that allows the computer to determine where an element of data or information is stored.

Bit: **0**   o r   **1**

a) Computers use bits and bytes to process and store data. Because they run on electricity, computers know only two things: on and off. This two-state system is called a **binary system**. Using single digits called **bits** (short for *bi*nary digi*ts*), the computer can represent any piece of data. The binary system uses only two digits, 0 and 1. The 0 corresponds to the "off" state, the 1 to the "on" state.

Bits

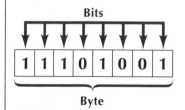

Byte

b) Single bits can't store all the numbers and characters that need to be processed and stored. For this reason, seven or eight bits are usually grouped together into bytes. Each byte generally represents one character.

When a character is entered through the keyboard, the processor accepts the character into main memory and translates it into coded form. It simultaneously shows the character on the display screen.

Character	EBCDIC	ASCII
A	1100 0001	100 0001
B	1100 0010	100 0010
C	1100 0011	100 0011
D	1100 0100	100 0100
E	1100 0101	100 0101
F	1100 0110	100 0110
G	1100 0111	100 0111
H	1100 1000	100 1000
I	1100 1001	100 1001
J	1101 0001	100 1010
K	1101 0010	100 1011
L	1101 0011	100 1100
M	1101 0100	100 1101
N	1101 0101	100 1110
O	1101 0110	100 1111
P	1101 0111	101 0000
Q	1101 1000	101 0001
R	1101 1001	101 0010
S	1110 0010	101 0011
T	1110 0011	101 0100

Character	EBCDIC	ASCII
U	1110 0100	101 0101
V	1110 0101	101 0110
W	1110 0110	101 0111
X	1110 0111	101 1000
Y	1110 1000	101 1001
Z	1110 1001	101 1010
0	1111 0000	011 0000
1	1111 0001	011 0001
2	1111 0010	011 0010
3	1111 0011	011 0011
4	1111 0100	011 0100
5	1111 0101	011 0101
6	1111 0110	011 0110
7	1111 0111	011 0111
8	1111 1000	011 1000
9	1111 1001	011 1001
!	0101 1010	010 0001
$	0101 1011	010 0100
&	0101 0000	010 0110

c) Two standard systems for representing data have been developed. **EBCDIC** (pronounced "eb-see-dick"), short for Extended Binary Coded Decimal Interchange Code, uses eight-bit bytes to represent a character. In EBCDIC, the capital letter S is represented by 11100010. **ASCII** (pronounced "ass-key"), short for American Standard Code for Information Interchange, uses seven-bit bytes to represent a character. In ASCII, the capital letter S is represented by 1010011. All characters—including upper- and lower-case letters—have a unique code in each system. EBCDIC is generally used in mainframes, ASCII in microcomputers.

H =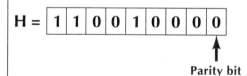

Parity bit

d) A special bit called a **parity bit** is sometimes used to detect errors in the transmission of data. If a bit is lost during transmission, the total number of bits will be wrong, and the computer will be alerted that there is something wrong with a particular byte.

Decimal	Binary	Hexadecimal
0	0000	0
1	0001	1
2	0010	2
3	0011	3
4	0100	4
5	0101	5
6	0110	6
7	0111	7
8	1000	8
9	1001	9
10	1010	A
11	1011	B
12	1100	C
13	1101	D
14	1110	E
15	1111	F

e) Sometimes computer professionals find it easier to convert binary values to another number system, the **hexadecimal number system**. This system uses the digits 1–9 and the letters A–F. One hexadecimal digit is the equivalent of four bits. For example, hexadecimal B, which represents the number 11, may be easier to deal with than the binary number 1011, which also represents the number 11.

FIGURE 4.4 *Bits, Bytes, and Number Systems*

RAM chip technology is changing rapidly, both in capacity and packaging. RAM chips are now available in 1M, 4M, 8M, and 16M. Soon to come are 32M and 64M versions.

ROM.   Like RAM, **read-only memory,** or **ROM,** offers random access to a memory location. However, ROM chips hold data and information even after the electrical current to the computer is turned off. Unlike the contents of a RAM chip, the contents of a ROM chip cannot be changed. Whatever is inserted into a location in a ROM chip when it is manufactured cannot be altered.

Typically, the start-up programs that run automatically when computers are first turned on are written into ROM. Since these programs—which perform housekeeping checks, like ensuring that a keyboard is attached or that memory is functioning—are written into ROM, the instructions can be read again and again, but can never be changed.

There are several variations on ROM. *Programmable read-only memory (PROM)* chips, first developed as a tool for testing a new ROM design before putting it into mass production, *can* be modified from their manufactured state, but only once. These modifications are not reversible. Data or information in *erasable programmable read-only memory (EPROM)* chips can be erased by bathing the chip in ultraviolet light, a process that dissipates the electric charges that created the original data or information values. *Electrically erasable programmable read-only memory (EEPROM)* chips are reprogrammed by electronically reversing the voltage used to create the data or information (rather than by using ultraviolet light).

Figure 4.5 summarizes the different types of memory chips.

read-only memory (ROM)
A type of storage that offers random access to memory and can hold data and information after the electric current to the computer has been turned off.

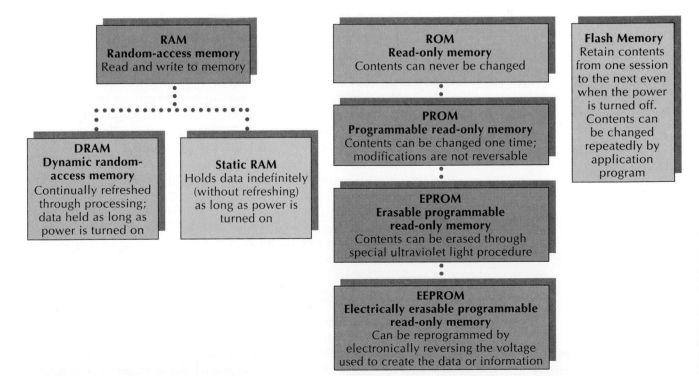

FIGURE 4.5 *Types of Memory Chips*

You won't see EPROM or EEPROM chips in business applications like spreadsheets or course registration systems. Generally, they are used only by engineers and designers who develop devices that contain embedded computers. When Hewlett-Packard develops a laser printer, for instance, its designers write the codes that control the printer's functions, paper-handling features, and type styles into EPROM or EEPROM. Using these special forms of ROM, they can rewrite the code without having to remanufacture the chip. When the design is complete and the printer goes into mass production, the EPROM or EEPROM is replaced with a ROM chip containing the final instructions.

When you turn on your computer, a power-on self-test brings all components to life. ROM chips are a key component of this test.

When the electrical (or battery) power to a computer, large or small, is turned on, the first thing the computer does is check itself to ensure its components are connected and in working order. To **boot** the system thus means to turn on the power and let the built-in self-test run. Booting the system—that is, lifting the system by its bootstraps—also activates the system's components to load the operating system into memory, ready for use. (The expression "to pull oneself up by the bootstraps" is an old adage that means "to take the initiative.")

The location of the beginning of the boot program is stored permanently in a set of ROM chips that contain the computer's basic input/output system (**BIOS**). Thus, in the start-up procedure, the CPU invokes the ROM BIOS boot program, which, in turn, runs the power-up self-tests and loads the operating system from disk storage. ■

boot
To turn on the computer system and let the built-in self-test run.

BIOS
The computer's basic input/output system.

Flash Memory

flash memory
Memory that retains its contents even when electricity is turned off.

Flash memory is memory that retains its contents even after the electrical power is turned off. Unlike with RAM, data and information stored in flash memory when the computer is on can be saved from one session of computer use to the next. Unlike with ROM, data and information held in flash memory can be erased and new details written in place by the application program.

Because of flash memory's flexibility in storing and changing all types of data and information, there is growing interest in expanding its applications. Flash memory chips are already commonly used in laptop and notebook computers to augment main memory storage, and they are increasingly utilized to augment or replace hard disk drive storage in both laptop and desktop units. Flash memory is also the principal component of PC memory cards.

PCMCIA Card Memory

PCMCIA card/PC card
A card designed to expand a computer's memory.

The Personal Computer Memory Card International Association (PCMCIA) was established in 1989 to formulate standards for the manufacture of memory cards for personal computers. The first cards manufactured according to the standards were designed to expand the memory of personal computers. Known originally as **PCMCIA cards,** and now as **PC cards,** these memory units are 2 by 3 inches

(5 × 8 cm) in size and several millimeters thick. Since they are about the size of a credit card, they are often also called "credit card memory."

PCMCIA cards use flash memory, which is faster, more power-efficient, and more shock-resistant than either hard disk or diskette storage. Because of these features, PCMCIA memory cards, designed initially for use in laptop and notebook drives, are being used in desktop systems as well.

Ever since the introduction of portable laptop and notebook computers, developers have sought to expand the capabilities of these computers without adding size, weight, or devices that consume excessive power. They have also sought a means to allow customization of portable computers. To customize a desktop computer, users can add a card or adapter board. This is not possible with laptop and notebook computers because they have neither cases that can be opened nor expansion slots inside.

Slots for PCMCIA cards (Figure 4.6) have become the means for expanding the capabilities of laptops and notebooks. Already a wide variety of credit card adapters are available. By inserting the appropriate PCMCIA card, users can add to a laptop or notebook computer an external disk drive, CD-ROM, fax/modem, network interface, speakers, cellular telephone (Figure 4.7)—the list of options becomes more extensive all the time. Thus have PCMCIA cards made it possible for people to personalize their laptop and notebook computers.

FIGURE 4.6   *Slots for PCMCIA Cards Expand the Capabilities of Laptops and Notebooks*

FIGURE 4.7
PCMCIA cards enable users to add to
a laptop or notebook computer an
external disk drive, CD-ROM,
fax/modem, or telephone.

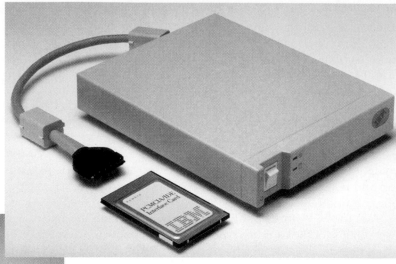

PCMCIA cards can instantly change a notebook computer's personality. For instance, if you want it to connect your notebook PC to a network, you merely insert a PCMCIA card that provides a connection to a local area network.

If you later decide to run a multimedia application that requires both extra memory and a CD-ROM unit, you can change your notebook's personality again. Pull out the network card (it slips right out) and push a PCMCIA memory card into one slot and a CD-ROM interface card into a second slot. (Most laptops have at least two PCMCIA slots.)

PCMCIA cards allow people to continually change the features of their laptop computers without using any tools at all—not even a screwdriver. ▨

The *Rethinking Business Practices* feature entitled "New Energy Emerges from the Power of Competition" illustrates how companies under competitive pressure, like Carolina Power and Light, can capitalize on the memory and processing capabilities of computers to streamline the way they carry out day-to-day activities.

Inside the System Unit

board
A hardware device onto which chips and their related circuitry are placed.

Both the CPU and memory units can be augmented by combinations of chips and boards. A **board** is a hardware device onto which chips and their related circuitry are placed. To show you how the hardware components fit together, Figure 4.8 takes you under the hood of a PC.

RETHINKING BUSINESS PRACTICES

New Energy Emerges from the Power of Competition

CP&L Companies selling electricity have been monopolies for generations, but that situation is changing fast in the United Kingdom and the United States, and will soon change in other countries as well. For some countries, privatization means these enterprises will no longer be owned by the government but by shareholders who will seek appreciation of their investments and profits. For others, deregulation of the industry is bringing about competition among electrical utilities, thereby changing the rules of success.

When a product is an indistinguishable commodity—like electricity—consumers view all versions of it as virtually the same and differentiate companies offering the product by their price and service. So companies selling electricity under the recently rewritten rules encouraging competition are rethinking the way they do business in order to reduce their costs and provide increased services. Carolina Power & Light Company found out it could do both simultaneously by redesigning key business processes.

Take customer service. As in most companies, Carolina Power's customer service staff was divided into specialized groups. One group handled billing, another dealt with the turning on and off of electrical service, and still others were responsible for inquiries and special requests. Although Carolina Power's executives long sought continual improvements in these day-to-day operations, they knew that such improvements would not satisfy customers in the new competitive environment. To find out what customers thought most needed changing, they decided to ask them directly.

They learned that what people wanted most was to have to make only one call to the company for all kinds of inquiries, adjustments, and changes in service. It turned out that the service setup with specialized departments was not only failing the customer but was also costing the company more than necessary. There were two problems: mindset and unconnected systems. Carolina Power's executives were determined to fix both by rethinking business processes.

The company found that by connecting and redesigning portions of its computer and communications systems it could handle all customers' needs on-line. Today, reviewing customer billing details, immediate posting of payments, changing of customer information, and scheduling of service calls

can all be done through a single phone call—while the customer is still on the phone. The same system is also used by Carolina Power's marketing representatives, engineers, and service dispatchers.

Rethinking its business processes resulted in a bonus to the company: Carolina Power found it could provide the simpler and faster service customers demanded using fewer resources than under its old system. Service representatives now access information in seconds. Fewer people are needed to provide the improved response. The information systems department, for example, needs fewer people to maintain the systems, so the customer service group has been reduced by more than 25 percent (some 100 people).

Rethinking its customer service business process has not only directly benefited both customer and company, it has also catalyzed reengineering in Carolina Power's other activities. New services are being planned, among them automatic meter reading, remote activation of services, and remote diagnosis and maintenance of facilities. More significantly, Carolina Power has begun to think beyond the meter, seeking to capitalize on the electrical "wire" running into the customer's house and its IT capabilities. Soon the company's one million customers will be able to choose telephone and fax services, security systems, homeshopping services, and cable TV from this reengineered electricity company.

---

system unit
The hardware unit that houses a computer's processor, memory chips, ports, and add-in boards.

system board/ mother board
The system unit in a microcomputer, located on a board mounted on the bottom of a computer base.

In all computers, the processor is housed inside a hardware unit called the **system unit.** On mainframe or midrange systems, the system unit is typically a cabinet filled with circuit boards (Figure 4.9). On microcomputers, a single **system board** (also known as a **mother board**) is mounted on the bottom of the computer case and attached to an electrical power supply that generates the current needed to operate the computer. The system board of a PC contains a processor chip, memory chips, ports, and add-in boards, in addition to the circuitry that interconnects all these components (Figure 4.10). System units in larger computers can also contain all these elements.

FIGURE 4.8
Under the Hood of a Personal Computer

Inside this IBM personal computer are a disk drive, circuit board (with a microprocessor chip), and power supply. The display terminal, keyboard, and printer are all attached by plug-in cables.

FIGURE 4.9
Amdahl 6390 Mainframe System Unit

The system unit of mainframe computers is typically a cabinet filled with circuit boards.

Processor Chips

The dream of a "computer on a chip" envisioned placing all the processing capabilities of the control unit and ALU on a single computer chip. The dream became a reality with the invention of the **microprocessor,** the smallest type of processor. A microprocessor is sealed in a protective package and connected to a system board with pins (Figure 4.11). Microprocessors gave rise to microcomputers, which use microprocessors for their CPU.[2]

microprocessor
The smallest type of processor, with all of the processing capabilities of the control unit and ALU located on a single chip.

[2]The terms *microcomputer* and *personal computer* are often used interchangeably. *Microcomputer* is the accurate technical term. *Personal computer* refers to the way microcomputers are used.

INTEL AND MOTOROLA MICROPROCESSORS.   The most popular processor chips are manufactured by Intel for IBM-compatibles and by Motorola for Apple Macintosh and Commodore Amiga computers (Table 4.1). These chips have evolved over time, with each new chip including more capability and greater speed than its predecessor.

Programs are written to work with a specific microprocessor chip. Thus, the software packages written to run on Apple computers, which use Motorola chips, cannot be used with IBM-compatible computers, which use Intel chips, without making substantial changes. However, software developers, ever mindful of people's desire to use the same software on both IBM-compatibles and Macintoshes, are finding ways to develop software that will run on both families of chips.

POWERPC MICROPROCESSOR.   The diversity of microprocessors has arisen for two reasons: (1) the objective of some manufacturers to achieve power and speed for a specific set of applications; and (2) the goal of some manufacturers to carve out their own niche in the marketplace, and with it a business advantage.

People using information technology, however, want to be able to focus on the application rather than on the underlying microprocessors, and software designers have tried to accommodate them. This has been most evident in the case of Apple Computers, which use Motorola microprocessors, and IBM-com-

FIGURE 4.11
*The Intel Pentium
Microprocessor Chip*
Because of the speed with which it
executes instructions, the Intel
Pentium microprocessor chip is
often used in processing-intensive
applications.

TABLE 4.1 *Evolution of Intel and Motorola Microprocessors*

MICROPROCESSOR	SPEED (MHZ)*	COMPUTERS USING THIS CHIP	WORD SIZE (BITS)†	BUS WIDTH†
Intel 8088	8	IBM PC	16	8
Intel 8086	8	IBM-compatibles	16	16
Intel 80286 ("286")	8–12	IBM-compatibles	16	16
Motorola 68000	12–20	Apple Macintosh Commodore Amiga	32	16
Motorola 68020	12–33	Apple Macintosh II	32	43
Intel 80386 ("386")	16–33	IBM-compatibles	32	32
Motorola 68030	16–40	Apple Macintosh SE/30 Apple Macintosh IIci, fx	32	32
Motorola 68040	25–33	Apple Macintosh, Quadra Engineering workstations	32	32
Intel 80486 ("486")	25–66	IBM-compatibles	32	32
Intel Pentium	66 and up	IBM-compatibles	32	64
Intel Pentium II	233 and up	IBM-compatibles	32	64

*The higher the megahertz (MHz), the faster the microprocessor.
†Discussed later in this chapter.

patible computers, which use Intel microprocessors. Since software designed to run on one computer could not be run on the other, separate programs had to be supplied. Thus, even a program with the same name (e.g., Microsoft's Word word-processing program) would be written in two different versions—one for the Macintosh and another for IBM-compatible PCs.

The PowerPC microprocessor, a product of the combined efforts of Motorola, Apple, and IBM, was designed to combine high-speed processing power with the ability to run both Apple Macintosh and IBM-compatible software. Both IBM and Apple have developed their own lines of computers based on the PowerPC microprocessor, regularly referred to as simply the *PowerPC*. Both can run their own operating systems (e.g., Apple's System 8 Operating System and IBM's OS/2 or MS-DOS), or they can run on software written specifically for the PowerPC that does not use either Apple or IBM operating systems.

With its smaller size, lower heat dissipation, and substantially lower price, coupled with its ability to run a wide range of existing software, the PowerPC is an impressive alternative to Intel's Pentium. (See Figure 4.12 for a comparison of the two chips. The SPEC of 92 referred to there is a floating point speed benchmark that is used for comparison just as MIPs, or millions of instructions per second, is a benchmark for comparing two processors.)

OTHER MICROPROCESSOR CHIPS.   In 1992, Digital Equipment Corp. (DEC) introduced the Alpha chip, a high-speed microprocessor intended to open a whole new era in microcomputers. The Alpha chip uses a 64-bit design (in contrast to the 32-bit design used by the rest of the industry) and RISC architecture

FIGURE 4.12

Comparing the First PowerPC and Pentium Microprocessors

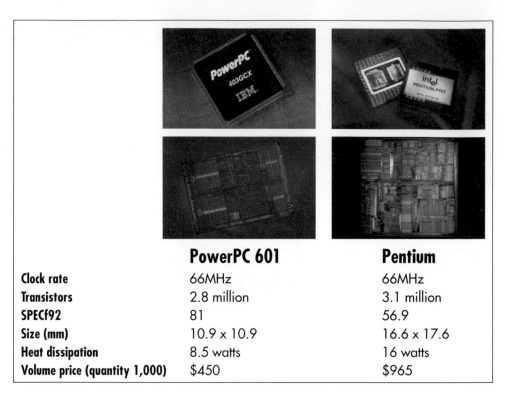

	PowerPC 601	**Pentium**
Clock rate	66MHz	66MHz
Transistors	2.8 million	3.1 million
SPECf92	81	56.9
Size (mm)	10.9 x 10.9	16.6 x 17.6
Heat dissipation	8.5 watts	16 watts
Volume price (quantity 1,000)	$450	$965

CRITICAL CONNECTION 1

Rockwell

Rockwell Fashions PC for Trekkers

There are times when even powerful notebook or laptop computers the size of a book are not small enough to do the job. Technicians who work on aircraft, elevators, building air-conditioning systems, and water systems often must maneuver in tight spaces. Under these cramped conditions, the fact that large technical volumes can be stored on the hard disk of a PC, ready for retrieval at the stroke of a key or the click of a mouse, is meaningless because they don't have enough space to use a keyboard, move a mouse, or, often, even squeeze in the PC to begin with.

Rockwell International, the electronics giant headquartered in Seal Beach, California, has created a wearable PC, dubbed the *Trekker PC,* to solve this problem. This Pentium microprocessor-powered PC unit is so compact that it can be worn on a belt or slung over the shoulder. There's no bulky monitor, either. Instead, the Trekker PC relies on a miniature "heads-up" VGA (video graphics array) that is mounted on a headband computer display and hangs in front of either eye, enabling the technician to look directly at the information.

This innovation did not completely solve the problem because flipping through the pages of the technical manual still required using a mouse. Rockwell fixed that difficulty by devising a mouse for its Trekker that is worn on the wrist, so it can be easily activated in tight quarters.

(discussed later in the chapter). With speeds in excess of 200 MHz, it is several times faster than any other available microprocessor. The Alpha chip is used in the full range of DEC's computers, from desktop units to midrange and mainframe systems. Although DEC would like to see its Alpha chip become an industry standard (so far, the chip is used only in DEC computers), it faces challenges from many other vendors who have developed their own high-speed microprocessors, among them Hewlett-Packard, MIPS, Silicon Graphics, and Sun Microcomputers. These companies' computers are widely used and play an important role in business applications, though they are not anywhere near as common as desktop computers based on Intel and Motorola microprocessors.

People choose notebook computers mostly for their processing and storage capabilities. However, battery power is also an important factor, especially if the purchaser expects to use the notebook on airplanes, in meetings, or at other times where it cannot be connected to an electrical outlet. Depending on their characteristics, notebook computers run from one to eight hours on a single battery charge.

Manufacturers of notebook computers have developed a special feature called **hibernation mode,** to minimize power usage and thus increase the time a battery charge will last. During hibernation mode, all computer tasks are suspended and memory data, as well as the details of processing, are stored on the hard disk. The computer turns off, meaning no battery power is used. When the power turns on again, the computer automatically restores programs and data, resuming the task that was in process.

This power-saving feature is often automatically invoked when the cover of a notebook computer is closed, when its battery power gets low, or when the notebook is not used for a period of time. As notebook computers grow in popularity, you'll see many more features developed to extend battery life. ∎

hibernation mode
The time during which all tasks are suspended and memory data and processing details are stored on the hard disk.

Memory Chips

Originally, memory chips were installed onto the system board, eight chips at a time, by connecting the chip to the system board with pins. Memory chips now often come in modules. A **single in-line memory module,** usually called a **SIMM,** is a multiple-chip card (Figure 4.13) that is inserted as a unit into a predesignated slot on the system board. SIMMs of 1M, 2M, 4M, 8M, 16M, and 32M are common.

Installed memory is the amount of memory included by the computer's manufacturer on its memory board. **Maximum memory** is the highest amount of memory that a processor can hold.[3]

The *Information Technology in Practice* feature entitled "Sears Enhances Service with Notebook Computers" shows how one company uses high-speed notebook computers equipped with PCMCIA cards and communications capabilities to stay competitive in the service business.

single in-line memory module (SIMM)
A multiple-chip memory card inserted as a unit into a predesigned slot on a computer's system board.

installed memory
The amount of memory included by a computer's manufacturer on its memory board.

maximum memory
The most memory that a processor can hold.

[3]Three memory allocation ranges are found in microcomputers. *Conventional memory* is the memory managed by the operating system and in which application programs run. Once conventional memory was limited to 640K, but this barrier was crossed with the introduction of Windows 95. ROM-based instructions, the computer's operating system, and application and communications programs run in conventional memory. A limited number of operating systems use *expanded memory*—the usable memory beyond the old 640K threshold, up to 1 megabyte. Application software may also use expanded memory. *Extended memory* starts at 1 megabyte and extends upward to 16 or 32 megabytes. This memory is freely available to application programs. (*Note:* These three memory allocation ranges pertain to the Intel line of chips, the most frequently used chips in PCs today.)

INFORMATION TECHNOLOGY IN PRACTICE

Sears Enhances Service with Notebook Computers

The combination of powerful microprocessors, expandable RAM memory capacity, and PCMCIA cards is leading to the automation of field service in many companies. Equipped with notebook computers, sales and service representatives are working more productively and effectively than they did under more traditional systems.

Sears, Roebuck and Co., the large Chicago-based international retailer, provides service for the products it sells, ranging from routine maintenance to repairs of damaged or worn products. Often the work is performed at the customer's home or business. Sears knows that field service is a competitive business—someone who needs service on a Sears product doesn't have to call Sears because there are plenty of other options. Sears' management looked for a way to gain an edge in this competitive market and found it in information technology. In terms of productivity and customer satisfaction, the most effective "tool" in the Sears service technician's arsenal today is not the screwdriver or the wrench, but the portable notebook computer.

Often companies that provide home service are unable to tell customers in advance what time of day the service technician will arrive, making it necessary for the customer to take the entire day off from work. Frequently, two trips are required—one to diagnose the problem and order the correct part, and another to install the part—meaning the customer must take two days off from work.

To provide one-stop service, Sears has armed its technicians with notebook computers equipped with programs developed in-house that allow the technicians to receive their daily work orders from the service center, order parts, obtain timely information from service managers, and report on their service calls. At the end of the workday, instead of filling out and dropping off numerous forms, the technicians simply plug into a phone line and download all information directly into Sears' mainframe computer.

After initially testing the system in four areas around the country, Sears found that it eliminated paperwork and improved the efficiency of its service operations. Work orders are dispatched much faster. Under the old system, when an emergency repair request came in, a service representative had to phone around to locate a technician who might be in or near the customer's area and available to do the work. Now a glance at the computer screen tells the dispatcher the location of every technician and which ones are available to do a job.

During a pilot test in California, the system proved its value. An earthquake had caused a gas leak at the Chatsworth service center, which would have put the technicians working out of the center out of business for the day. Yet because Sears could communicate with its technicians through their notebooks, most service technicians were able to complete their daily routes after dispatching was transferred to another Sears service center.

Sears is relying on its new dispatching system to give the company a significant edge in the service business. Hence, high-speed notebook computers equipped with PCMCIA cards and communications capabilities are standard equipment for all of Sears' 10,000 technicians.

FIGURE 4.13
Single In-line Memory Modules
Intel's SIMM memory modules are inserted as a unit into a predesignated slot on the system boards of selected IBM, Compaq, Hewlett-Packard, and Zenith computers.

Ports

Any device that is not part of the CPU or the system board must somehow be attached to the computer. **Ports** are the connectors through which input/output devices and storage devices are plugged into the computer (see Figure 4.14).

When an input/output device needs to be plugged into the system unit and there is not a built-in port for it, a special add-in circuit board is plugged into an **expansion slot** on the system board. All systems have a practical limit to the number of ports that can be added.

Add-in Boards

Virtually all desktop microcomputers as well as midrange and mainframe computers have an *open architecture,* meaning that additional boards, called **add-in boards,** can be plugged into them by way of expansion slots to customize the computer's features and capabilities. Computers that do not have this capacity are said to have a *closed architecture.*

Table 4.2 lists several types of boards available to be added to microcomputers today. The variety of add-in boards continues to expand as computer manufacturers find ways to meet users' demands for more and more capabilities.

The combination of desktop computers and customizing add-in boards is helping medical schools to improve training in areas of medicine difficult to explain through the usual classroom methods of instruction. For example, the American Heart Association, in an effort to encourage doctors and medical students to study preventive medicine, has been offering medical schools, community health groups, and practicing physicians a computer-based multimedia interactive application that focuses on the workings of the heart and bloodstream. Users load the system onto Apple or IBM-compatible computers outfitted with add-in boards that provide sound and animation capabilities. The system lets users see the effect on the heart of high cholesterol levels in the bloodstream by providing an animated view of that organ that shows just how it pumps blood into arteries. Another system developed by High Techsplanations of Rockville, Maryland, allows surgeons to practice prostate surgery without cutting up cadavers (Figure 4.15).

Marketing professionals are also using add-in boards for market research and target marketing.

port
A connector through which input/output devices can be plugged into the computer.

expansion slot
A slot inside a computer that allows a user to add an additional circuit board.

add-in board
A board that can be added to a computer to customize its features and capabilities.

FIGURE 4.14

Ports on a Microcomputer System Board

Most input, output, and storage devices must be plugged into ports on the system board.

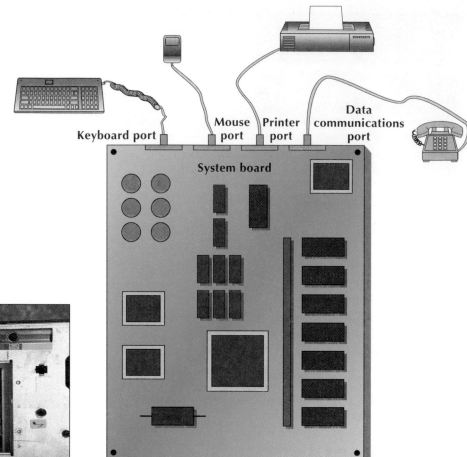

Keyboard port

Mouse port

Printer port

Data communications port

System board

TABLE 4.2 *Types of Boards That Can be Added to Microcomputers*	
BOARD FUNCTION	**DESCRIPTION**
Accelerator board	Increases speed of computer.
Controller board	Allows different printers and storage devices to be attached to a computer.
Co-processor board	Includes special chips that speed up the system's overall processing capabilities.
Display adaptor board	Permits the use of computer displays by providing interconnection with the processor board.
Emulator board	Allows the computer to act like another type of device, usually a terminal.
Fax modem board	Enables the computer to send and receive facsimile images, data, and information.
Memory expansion board	Extends the computer's memory capacity by adding additional sockets for memory chips.
Modem board	Enables the computer to interconnect with a telephone line to transmit and receive data and information.
Multifunction board	Includes several different functions (e.g., memory expansion and printer and display connectors).
SCSI adaptor	Provides an interconnection for a variety of peripheral devices, including scanners and CD-ROM units. Also interconnects disk drives using a SCSI interface (rather than the more common IDE interface).
Sound board	Contains chips and circuitry that translate data and information into sound output, including music.
Video capture	Enables the computer to capture full-motion color video and accompanying sound for processing and storage.
Voice board	Provides the capability to translate stored data and information into spoken output.

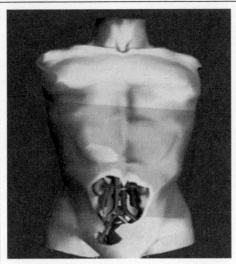

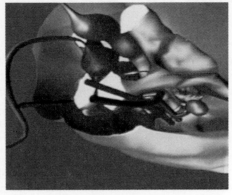

FIGURE 4.15
Surgical Simulation Using Add-in Boards
High Techsplanations recently launched a "virtual reality surgical simulator" to help surgeons learn how to operate on the prostate gland.

b) . . . to reveal details of the inner workings of the kidneys, bladder, urethra, and prostate.

a) Using the program, a medical student can strip away the pelvic bone of a computer-generated torso . . .

CRITICAL CONNECTION 2

BSW International

Add-in Boards and CADD: The Trump Cards for BSW International

Take an ordinary but high-powered computer, augment it with a stack of add-in boards, plug in a variety of high-resolution input and output devices, and what do you have? *The* tool of the modern architect—one that has been working well for BSW International in Tulsa, Oklahoma, where CADD (computer-aided design and drafting) has been the software of choice since the late 1970s.

CADD is important, says BSW general partner David Broach, because it increases the company's productivity in its specialty—designing hundreds of stores for such retailing chains as Wal-Mart and Pier 1 Imports. CADD, by letting architects modify an existing design rather than starting from scratch, can cut the time needed to design a store from a month to as little as 24 hours.

One of BSW's more unusual clients was Hallmark, which turned to the CADD masters at BSW when it embarked on an ambitious program of construction and renovation. Even though Hallmark couldn't reap the greatest benefits from CADD because many of its stores feature different designs, it wanted the convenience and cost savings of dealing with an architectural firm that could handle many projects simultaneously. Without CADD, Hallmark would have had to deal with at least 10 architectural firms to meet its goals.

Plug and Play

Inserting or removing memory, chips, or boards, as well as storage or peripheral devices, changes the configuration of a computer. In the past, computer users had to "inform" (or "tweak") the computer of a change, either through entering commands or changing switch settings inside the computer. Plug-and-play capability is making that step unnecessary, and simplifying computing in the process.

plug and play
The ability to install devices into a computer when the computer itself makes any necessary internal adjustments.

With **plug-and-play** capability, users can install devices into or remove them from a desktop computer and the computer itself will sense the change and make any necessary internal adjustments. For example, if you plug a modem into a communication port, the computer will sense that it has been plugged in. Or if extra memory is plugged in, the computer will sense that it has been added. In either case, you can begin using—that is "playing"—immediately, without doing any "tweaking." It's easy to see why plug and play, long a feature of Apple Macintosh computers, is quickly becoming the norm on all computers.

The Processing Sequence

By this point, you may be wondering exactly how a computer processes data. To understand this process, you need to know something about the machine cycle and the role of registers.

CRITICAL
C O N N E C T I O N   3

Comdisco   ### Comdisco Helps Clients Guard Against Memory Loss

Comdisco, Inc., of Rosemont, Illinois, is widely known as a provider of computer backup services, which are essential to companies that cannot risk *any* loss of computer operating capability during a disaster. Recently, Comdisco has begun treating the theft of computer chips as a new category of disaster.

High-tech thieves, often operating as organized gangs, have been targeting computer chips—both microprocessors and memory chips. Until recently, most victims of stolen chips were manufacturers, assemblers, and suppliers (the largest theft was of some $9 million of chip components from a southern California electronics firm). Now, however, companies are encountering an increasing rate of theft of computer memory from their desktop systems. Computer chips are so small that they can be pried from computer system boards and stuffed into a briefcase or knapsack. Their high value and the ease of selling them—"hot" chips often find their way into legitimately sold notebook and desktop computers—makes them an attractive target. The fact that it is practically impossible to distinguish similar types of chips from one another is compounding the problem.

The Machine Cycle

All the functions of processing are directed by the control unit, which works with the ALU and memory to perform four steps:

1. **Fetch**—obtain the next instruction from memory.
2. **Decode**—translate the instruction into individual commands that the computer can process.
3. **Execute**—perform the actions called for in the instructions.
4. **Store**—write the results of processing to memory.

Collectively, these four steps are known as the **machine cycle.** The first two steps, in which instructions are obtained and translated, are called the **instruction cycle (I-cycle),** and the last two steps, which produce processing results, are known as the **execution cycle (E-cycle)** (Figure 4.16).

Registers

To execute the machine cycle, the control unit depends on **registers,** temporary storage areas in the processor (*not* in the main memory). Registers, which can move data and instructions more quickly than main memory can, momentarily hold the data or instructions used in processing as well as the results generated. They also assist the ALU in carrying out arithmetic and logical operations.

machine cycle
The four processing steps performed by the control unit: fetch, decode, execute, and store.

instruction cycle (I-cycle)
The first two steps of the machine cycle (fetch and decode), in which instructions are obtained and translated.

execution cycle (E-cycle)
The last two steps of the machine cycle (execute and store), which produce processing results.

register
A temporary storage area in the processor that can move data and instructions more quickly than main memory can, and momentarily hold the data or instructions used in processing as well as the results that are generated.

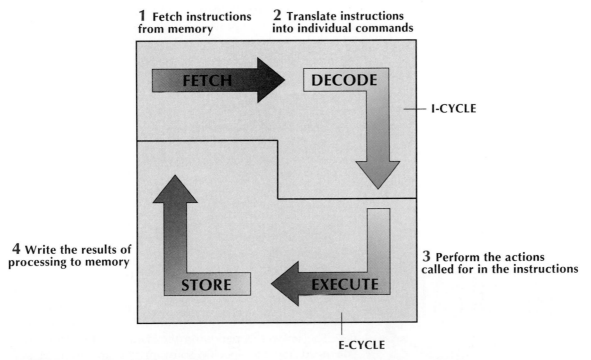

FIGURE 4.16 *The Machine Cycle*

The machine cycle is divided into two cycles. During the instruction cycle (I-cycle), instructions are obtained and translated. During the execution cycle (E-cycle), the results of processing are produced.

There are four types of registers:

1. **Storage registers** temporarily store data that have been moved from memory and are awaiting processing or that are about to be sent to memory.
2. **Address registers** contain the address of the data to be used in executing an instruction.
3. **Accumulators** hold the results of computation as each arithmetic operation occurs. From the accumulator the results are moved into main memory or to another register for additional processing.
4. **General-purpose registers** hold data, addresses, or arithmetic results.

Registers are like staging areas. They are a place where preparations are made so that an activity will go smoothly once it is underway. Consider the planning of a group trip. The organizer will tell members of the group to arrive at a specific location by a particular time. Some people will arrive earlier than others, of course, but all should be assembled at the specified location by the time the trip is due to begin. This is how registers work. They assemble all the data instructions so that the computer can perform its next machine cycle quickly and without a hitch.

Processor Speed

As noted in Chapter 1, one of the main reasons people use information technology is speed. Computers can perform millions of calculations per second consistently, accurately, and reliably.

Computer speeds are measured in **milliseconds** (thousandths of a second), **microseconds** (millionths of a second), **nanoseconds** (billionths of a second), or **picoseconds** (trillionths of a second). Processors and processor chips tend to operate at microsecond and nanosecond speeds, though new chips are emerging with picosecond capabilities. Secondary storage and input/output devices function at millisecond speeds.

Another way of describing speeds is by the number of instructions the processor can execute per second. **Millions of instructions per second,** or **MIPS,** ratings range from approximately 1–50 MIPS for a typical desktop PC, to 200–400 MIPS for a mainframe, to even higher speeds for supercomputers. Computer speeds are constantly increasing; consumers expect every new computer model to have a higher MIPS capability.

Computing speed can also be measured in **megaflops,** or millions of floating point operations per second. *Floating point operations* is a technical term that refers to the floating of decimal point from calculation to calculation. *Megaflops* is a measure of how many detailed arithmetic calculations can be performed per second.

millisecond
One thousandth of a second.

microsecond
One millionth of a second.

nanosecond
One billionth of a second.

picosecond
One trillionth of a second.

millions of instructions per second (MIPS)
The number of instructions the processor can execute per second—a measure of processor speed.

megaflops
Millions of floating point operations per second—a measure of how many detailed arithmetic calculations the computer can perform per second.

MIPS and megaflops are best used as bases of comparison. Rather than worrying about absolute measures of speed, people need to ask themselves: Will the system I choose do the work I need it to do in an acceptably speedy manner? The answer depends on the nature of the processing you need and the specific software you are using. A system used for word-processing applications need not be as powerful as one intended to process thousands of business transactions per second. The number of people simultaneously using a computer system will also influence decisions about required speed. ∎

OPPORTUNITIES

Geographic Information Systems Put Marketers on the Map

Linda Brown, research analyst for Colorado-based Eagle Marketing Services, Inc., uses mapping software to support the company's database and direct-mail services. The software helps Brown identify the response rate to direct mailings by zip code. "A mapped comparison of good response areas becomes a tool for our salespeople," she says. "They can tell advertisers about the number of potential buyers in any zip code."

What do President Bill Clinton, Arby's Roast Beef, and Norwest Bank have in common? They've all profited from the market insights provided by geographic information systems (GISs), a sophisticated type of graphics software that presents the answers to database queries as color-coded maps.

Originally developed in the 1960s to help scientists and government planning departments, GISs required the brute power of mainframes until the late 1980s. That's when two trends converged to make GISs popular with today's savvy marketers. One trend was the emergence of high-powered PCs with the add-in boards needed to operate high-resolution color monitors and high-capacity secondary storage devices—systems that offer the power of a mainframe for a fraction of the cost. The second trend was the increasing availability of computer databases containing demographic and market data with geographic components, such as zip codes and street addresses, which could be plotted on a map showing political or marketing boundaries. The U.S. Census Bureau, for example, sells the TIGER database—an $11,000 collection of 44 CD-ROM disks containing street maps showing economic and population data for the entire United States.

Although the databases and GIS software can be expensive, they're worth it to marketers, because the maps let them *see* and *analyze* patterns in mountains of data—patterns that help them spend their marketing dollars wisely and take advantage of market opportunities.

President Clinton's campaign for the presidency is a good example of a success story in which GIS software played an important role. Janet Handal, a technology strategist at the Clinton campaign headquarters, reported that Atlas Pro (a GIS program selling for around $600) let her team create maps with overlays showing political data. These maps helped the team chart trends in public opinion, recruit volunteers, decide where to send the candidates, and determine the number of television ads to buy in certain markets.

GISs are also great tools for selecting new restaurant sites, reports Hal Reid, Vice President for Development Research at Arby's Inc. With the help of their GIS, he says, his staff can create color-coded maps that let them compare potential locations on the basis of population characteristics (median age, income, and expenditures for fast food); traffic patterns; and the proximity of competitors.

The GIS's power to identify market niches was especially useful to Norwest Bank when it set about remodeling two branches in west St. Paul, Minnesota. With the help of the GIS, Senior Research Manager John Blissenbach saw that many young professionals lived near one branch. To cater to these customers' needs for speed and convenience, the bank installed an automatic teller machine in the vestibule and set up an express counter where clerks can process deposits or loan payments in less than a minute.

GISs can even help the sales reps who work on the front lines. Available for less than $100, a GIS called Automap can produce a detailed map showing the most efficient route between any set of locations in the United States, Canada, and Europe.

INFORMATION TECHNOLOGY IN PRACTICE

Small-Business Operators Need Never Be Out of Touch

Information technology goes a long way toward abolishing the limitations that make small businesses . . . small. An IT product that can greatly expand the horizons of a small business is the around-the-clock personal assistant for the traveler developed by Wildfire Communications, Inc., of Lexington, Massachusetts. The Wildfire Assistant incorporates speech recognition, audio output, and telephone communication into a system built around a Pentium-class desktop computer. It is connected to the telephone system, but it's much more than a telephone answering machine because it incorporates voice mail and electronic messaging.

Besides answering and placing calls, the Wildfire Assistant has processing capabilities that enable it to track down an individual who is traveling. Using call forwarding, the system can transfer an incoming call to the call-forwarded location of the intended recipient. (If the intended recipient is already on the phone, Wildfire Assistant will—if it has been told to

do so—discreetly *whisper* the name of the caller in his or her ear, and the person can decide whether to take the call!)

This system even has the ability to schedule appointments and then remind users of those appointments. An internal database stores schedule details that are perused to determine when events are scheduled as well as when new events can be planned.

The Wildfire Assistant understands voice commands, so when executives are traveling, they can call their office and verbally ask their assistant to look up and repeat telephone numbers and names, and Wildfire will incorporate them. They can even verbally ask Wildfire to place the call for them.

The Wildfire Assistant's capabilities can be tailored to companies of any size. Hence, a small company can easily gain the same features as a large business. Information technology in this case helps businesses overcome both distance and size limitations.

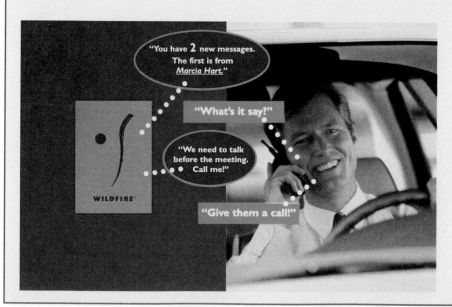

Wildfire is an Electronic Assistant that uses speech recognition to help busy people manage their daily telephone activities. The version of Wildfire now available through public telephone network carriers includes Intelligent Messaging™: Wildfire captures the caller's name and phone number, so the user can return the call by simply saying "give them a call"—nothing to write down and no number to dial.

The *Information Technology in Practice* feature entitled "Small-Business Operators Need Never Be Out of Touch" describes how high-speed processing, computer storage, and communication can be combined to aid small businesses (and large corporations, too).

Determining Processor Speed

What determines processor speed? In automobiles, greater speed comes from more engine power and greater fuel use. Aircraft engines produce higher speeds when they generate more thrust. But engine power, thrust, and fuel use have nothing to do with computers. A computer's speed is determined by its system clock, bus width, and word size.

SYSTEM CLOCK.   Because computers work at high speeds, synchronization of tasks is essential to ensure that actions will take place in an orderly and precise fashion. All computers have a **system clock,** a circuit that generates electronic pulses at a fixed rate to synchronize processing activities. Each time a pulse is generated, a new instruction cycle begins.

Clock cycles are measured in **megahertz (MHz),** or millions of electric pulses per second. One megahertz means that one million pulses are generated every second. The megahertz speed built into computers varies. Personal computers typically operate in the range of 66 to more than 200 megahertz.[4] The higher the megahertz, the faster the computer (see Table 4.1).

BUS WIDTH.   For a computer to process information, the details must be moved internally—that is, within the computer. Data are moved from input devices to memory, from memory to the processor, from the processor to memory, from memory to storage, and from memory to output devices. The path over which data are moved is a *bus,* an electronic circuit.

There are two types of bus. An **input/output (I/O) bus** moves data into and out of the processor—that is, between peripheral units (such as input devices) and the central processor. A **data bus** moves data between the central processor and memory (Figure 4.17).

The width of the bus determines the amount of data that can be moved at one time. An 8-bit bus, for example, transmits 8 bits of data at a time. Greater bus width equals faster movement of data.

Most PCs have 16- or 32-bit buses, while midrange and mainframe systems typically use 32- or 64-bit buses. Three bus standards are in widespread use. The Enhanced Industry Standard Architecture (EISA) is used on many MS-DOS microcomputers and on some IBM PCs. During the late 1980s and early 1990s, IBM also used a proprietary microchannel architecture. The third standard, the NuBus architecture, is used on Apple Macintosh computers.

WORD SIZE.   A **word** is the number of bits a computer can process at one time. Word size is measured in bits. An 8-bit word, for example, consists of 8 bits (8 electronic circuits). Alternatively, words are sometimes expressed in bytes.

system clock
A circuit that generates electronic impulses at a fixed rate to synchronize processing activities.

megahertz (MHz)
Millions of electric pulses per second—a measure of a computer's speed.

input/output (I/O) bus
A bus (electronic circuit) that moves data into and out of the processor.

data bus
A bus that moves data between the central processor and memory.

word
The number of bits a computer can process at one time.

[4]All computer processing is controlled by the system clock's speed. However, on midrange and mainframe computers, the actual megahertz speeds are much less meaningful. On these systems many tasks are performed simultaneously, and multiple processors are often used. Hence, in business, speed capabilities are usually determined by running a set of processing jobs on different systems and then comparing the results.

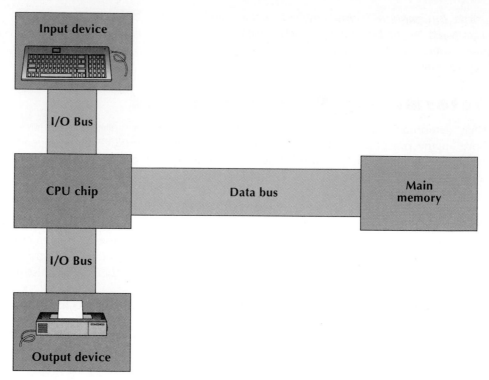

FIGURE 4.17
The Two Types of Bus
An input/output bus moves data into and out of the processor. A data bus moves data between units within the central processor

A 1-byte word contains 8 bits; a 2-byte word, 16 bits; and a 4-byte word, 32 bits. (Refer to Figure 4.4.)

The larger the word size, the faster the computer can process data and perform arithmetic and logic operations. Many micro and most midrange systems use 32-bit words; mainframes and supercomputers are built for 64-bit words. In contrast, most personal computers use 16-bit words (two 8-bit bytes), with the most powerful built around 32-bit word structures.

Increasing Computer Speed

The users of information technology are demanding more and more speed from computers. Processing and computer speed may be increased in six ways: through the use of cache memory, co-processors, accelerator boards, greater chip density, RISC computing, and parallel processing.

cache memory
A form of high-speed memory that acts as a temporary holding/processing cell.

CACHE MEMORY.   A special form of high-speed memory called **cache memory** eliminates the need to move data to and from main memory repeatedly. In systems without cache memory, the CPU sends data requests to main memory, where they are read and acted on. Main memory then sends the result back to the CPU. This process can be quite time-consuming if a large amount of information is stored in main memory.

Cache memory acts as a temporary holding/processing cell. As data requests pass between the CPU and main memory, they travel through cache memory and are copied there. Subsequent requests for the same data are recognized and captured by the cache memory cell, which fulfills the data request with the CPU. By decreasing the number of data requests to main memory, processing time is significantly reduced (Figure 4.18).

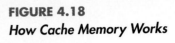

FIGURE 4.18
How Cache Memory Works

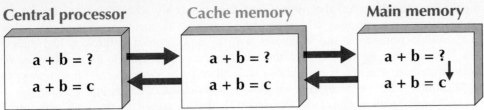

Central processor   Cache memory   Main memory

$a + b = ?$
$a + b = c$

a) The central processor sends a request to main memory, which accepts and acts on the request. When the data travel between the processor and memory, they travel through and are copied into cache memory.

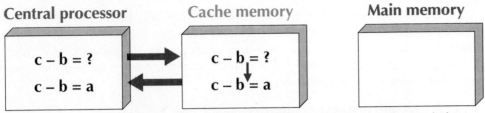

Central processor   Cache memory   Main memory

$c - b = ?$
$c - b = a$

b) Subsequent requests involving the original data are recognized by the cache memory and captured. The cache memory acts on the data requests and provides the response to the central processor. Because the data no longer travel on to the main memory unit, processing time is cut in half.

CO-PROCESSORS. When a certain task is performed again and again, special-purpose chips can be designed to handle it quickly and efficiently. These chips, called **co-processor chips,** are mounted on the processor board and function simultaneously with the primary processor chip. By taking processing work away from the main processor, they free the central processing unit to focus on general processing needs.

ACCELERATOR BOARDS. An **accelerator board** is an add-in circuit board that increases a computer's processing speed by (1) using a clock speed that is faster than the CPU's, (2) using a faster processor chip, or (3) using an arithmetic/logic unit that speeds up floating point calculations. Any combination of these three is possible.

An accelerator board's characteristics depend on the nature of the work the board was designed to help accomplish. For example, floating point arithmetic is important to engineering and scientific applications. Thus, a PC used in those areas may be outfitted with an accelerator board with a faster ALU. Or the computer may be outfitted with a specialized accelerator board, such as a graphics accelerator board. In most applications, accelerator boards yield speed increases of 200 to 400 percent.

INCREASED CHIP DENSITY AND INTEGRATION. Data and information move through the computer at faster than one-third the speed of light (which is 186,000 miles per second). Thus, reducing the distance traveled even by a little can make a tremendous difference in the computer's speed. This fundamental principle underlies the continual emphasis on miniaturization of circuits and greater chip density, or the number of circuits on a single chip.

Exactly how many circuits can be packed onto a chip? The Intel 80386 chip (usually called the "386"), introduced in 1985, holds .25 million transistors. The Intel

co-processor chip
A special-purpose chip mounted on a processor board; it is designed to handle common functions quickly and efficiently.

accelerator board
An add-in circuit board that increases a computer's processing speed.

80486 (commonly called the "486"), introduced in 1991, operates at speeds of 33 to 66 megahertz; executes at a speed of 54 million instructions per second; holds 1.25 million transistors; and integrates a CPU, input/output controller, high-speed graphics support, memory cache, and math co-processor—all on a chip the size of your fingernail. The 486 is compatible with all of its predecessors, so it can process applications software developed for earlier generations of chips and computers.

The Intel Pentium chip (see Figure 4.11), the successor to the 486, was introduced in early 1993. This chip, which many people expected to be called the "586," has more than 3 million transistors and operates at speeds exceeding 112 million instructions per second (see Table 4.1). An even more powerful Pentium II chip was introduced in 1997.

Experts predict that chips will hold 40 million transistors by the year 2000. Specialized chips will most likely operate at more than 250 MHz and provide a capability of 1 billion instructions per second, interacting with 1 gigabyte DRAM chips.

The photo essay at the end of this chapter shows the steps involved in creating these chips and microprocessors.

REDUCED INSTRUCTION SET COMPUTING (RISC).   The quest for greater speed has prompted computer designers to rethink how computers should process instructions. One type of processing, **complex instruction set computing (CISC),** has been used since the earliest days of computing. CISC moves data to and from main memory so often that it limits the use of registers to store temporary data values. Calling on the memory so frequently results in slower overall performance, since a portion of the processor must coordinate the execution of the movement instructions. (The instructions to do so are called the **microcode.**)

Recently, a second type of processing has become popular. **Reduced instruction set computing (RISC)** processes data more simply. With RISC, data for the execution of an instruction are taken only from registers. This simplifies—and accelerates—instruction processing greatly because the microcode is not needed. A separate set of instructions moves the data from memory to the registers.

At the University of New Hampshire's Institute for the Study of Earth, Oceans, and Space, scientists use RISC-based workstations to transform data into three-dimensional graphics and animation—an imaging process called *visualization*. Since the speed of the RISC-system computers is much greater than that of the other computers used in the laboratory, the scientists can turn mountains of data into animated pictures relatively quickly. Visualization makes it possible to see how the ocean's tidal forces interact with the underwater landscape of the eastern coast of the United States and Canada and to simulate tides. These spectacular images are useful for managing fishing and sea life as well as regulating shipping and commercial fishing activities in the area.

PARALLEL PROCESSING.   Sometimes we do things in sequence, one step after another. For example, we assemble model cars and airplanes one careful step at a time. Other times, we do things simultaneously. For example, we walk, talk, and gesture as we share information with a colleague. Computers, too, can be designed to do things sequentially or simultaneously.

Traditionally, computers have been designed for **sequential processing**—that is, processing in which the execution of one instruction is followed by the execution of another. But in recent years, computer designers have been developing **parallel processing**—that is, processing in which computers handle different parts of a problem by executing instructions simultaneously. In the end, the results of each parallel process are combined to produce a result.

complex instruction set computing (CISC)

A computing instruction set that moves data to and from main memory so often that it limits the use of registers.

microcode

The instructions that coordinate the execution of the instructions to move data to and from memory.

reduced instruction set computing (RISC)

A computing instruction set that takes data for the execution of an instruction only from registers.

sequential processing

Processing in which the execution of one instruction is followed by the execution of another.

parallel processing

Processing in which a computer handles different parts of a problem by executing instructions simultaneously.

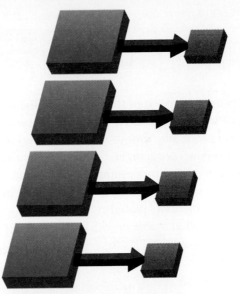

FIGURE 4.19
The Two Types of Parallel Processing

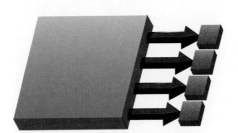

a) Single instruction/multiple data (SIMD) methods. In a SIMD computer, many data items are processed simultaneously by one instruction or by identical instructions on different processors.

b) Multiple instruction/multiple data (MIMD) methods. In a MIMD computer, multiple processors act independently on different data items.

Two types of parallel processing have emerged (Figure 4.19). **Single instruction/multiple data (SIMD) methods** execute the same instruction on many data values simultaneously. **Multiple instruction/multiple data (MIMD) methods** connect a number of processors that run different programs or parts of a program on different sets of data. Communication between the processors is essential to MIMD methods.

In New Haven, Connecticut, a team of scientists and physicians at Yale University is working to incorporate parallel processing into a computer that can monitor the condition of seriously ill patients. Currently, after a patient has surgery, nurses and physicians monitor the patient every few minutes, checking for changes in such vital signs as blood pressure, heart rate, and breathing rate. However, even the most dedicated medical personnel may not be able to detect subtle changes in the patient's condition.

Using parallel processing techniques, separate processors within a computer will be assigned responsibility for monitoring vital signs. Still other processors will be interconnected with medical databases and with the patient's medical history in order to compare data from all these sources and translate them into meaningful information for the physicians and the medical support staff. Because both medicine and the human body are complex, the system is necessarily very complex, but parallel processing promises to make this complexity manageable by turning over difficult coordination and analysis tasks to the computer.

Today, parallel processing is still the exception rather than the rule. In the future, computer systems of all sizes, from the smallest to the largest, will likely have parallel-processing capabilities. In fact, massively parallel computers are now beginning to appear. These computers contain hundreds of thousands—even millions—of microprocessors, and will be used in ways that were undreamed of only a few years ago.

single instruction/ multiple data (SIMD) method
A parallel-processing method that executes the same instruction on many data values simultaneously.

multiple instruction/ multiple data (MIMD) method
A parallel-processing method that connects a number of processors that run different programs or parts of a program on different sets of data.

SUMMARY OF LEARNING OBJECTIVES

1 **Describe the components and purpose of the central processing unit (CPU).** At the heart of every computer is the *central processing unit (CPU),* or *processor,* which executes program instructions and performs the computer's processing actions. The CPU is a collection of electronic circuits made up of thousands of *transistors* placed onto an *integrated circuit* (also called a *chip* or *microchip*). The two components of the CPU are the *control unit* and the *arithmetic/logic unit (ALU).*

2 **Distinguish between primary and secondary storage and between RAM and ROM.** *Primary storage* is the storage within the computer itself; it holds data only temporarily, as the computer executes instructions. *Secondary storage,* external storage that augments primary memory, is used to store data over the long term.

    Random-access memory (RAM) is memory that permits data or information to be written into or read from any memory address at any time. RAM stores data and information only as long as the computer is turned on. *Read-only memory (ROM)* also offers random access to data, but it can hold data and information after the electric current to the computer has been turned off.

3 **Describe the chips and boards that can be used to augment the CPU and main memory.** Both chips and boards are used to augment the CPU and main memory. *Processor chips* contain all of the processing capabilities of the control unit and ALU on one chip. *Memory chips* are used to augment primary storage. *Add-in boards* allow users to customize their computers' features and capabilities.

4 **Explain the process by which computers use registers to process data.** The processing sequence is a four-step process called the *machine cycle.* These four steps, all of which are directed by the control unit, are as follows: (1) *fetch,* or obtain the next instruction from memory; (2) *decode,* or translate the instruction into individual commands that the computer can process; (3) *execute,* or perform the actions called for in the instructions; and (4) *store,* or write the results of processing to memory. To execute the machine cycle, the control unit depends on *registers,* temporary storage areas in the processor.

5 **List and explain the three determinants of processor speed.** Three elements determine processor speed: the system clock, bus width, and word size. All computers have a *system clock,* a circuit that generates electronic pulses at a fixed rate to synchronize processing activities. Clock cycles are measured in *megahertz;* the higher the megahertz, the faster the computer. A *bus* is the path over which data are moved. The width of the bus determines the amount of data that can be moved at one time. Word size is measured in bits. A *word* is the number of bits a computer can process simultaneously. The larger the word size, the faster a computer can process data.

6 **Describe six ways of increasing processing and computer speed.** Processing and computer speed may be increased in six ways: through the use of cache memory, co-processors, accelerator boards, greater chip density, RISC computing, and parallel processing.

    Cache memory is a form of high-speed memory that acts as a temporary holding/processing cell and eliminates the need to move data to and from the main memory repeatedly.

    Co-processors are special chips designed to handle tasks that are performed often. By taking over this processing work from the main processor, they free the CPU to focus on general processing needs.

    Accelerator boards are add-in circuit boards that increase a computer's processing speed. Packing more transistors on a chip—that is, creating greater chip density—results in greater computing speed.

    Reduced instruction set computing (RISC) processes data more simply than complex instruction set computing (CISC). With RISC, data for the execution of an instruction are taken only from registers. This both simplifies and accelerates instruction processing.

With *parallel processing,* computers handle different parts of a problem by executing instructions simultaneously. In the end, the results of each parallel process are combined to produce a result.

KEY TERMS

CRITICAL CONNECTIONS

1   Rockwell Fashions PC for Trekkers

Rockwell   Rockwell International is developing additional models of its Trekker PC. One will include a connection to the Internet, enabling Trekker-equipped technicians to retrieve multimedia information. They will, for example, be able to watch an audio-video clip on the Trekker's "heads-up" display that shows, step-by-step, how to inspect or repair a mechanical system or an electronic connection.

Other options on future versions of the Trekker are in the speculative stage. For instance, imagine the possibilities if a wireless television camera could be mounted on the headband or integrated into the computer's display. The Trekker would then become a two-way device that would allow people at other locations to view the technician's repair activities in progress and offer helpful suggestions.

Questions for Discussion

1. What are the benefits to technicians of being able to use a computer in tight spaces?

2. Do you think the Trekker will lead to increased specialization by technicians? Or will the fact that it enables technicians to view training manuals, even step-by-step videos, as they are working reduce the skill levels required for these jobs?

3. What other uses can you think of for "wearable" computers and monitors?

2   Add-in Boards and CADD: The Trump Cards for BSW International

BSW International   BSW's managers point to at least two savings from using CADD. First, the powerful software lets the architects spend their time where it counts—on the differences, not the similarities, between stores. Design elements that don't change from store to store, such as distinctive windows or a standard plumbing or electrical layout, are simply copied from one computer file to another. The architects concentrate on the modifications required by the site, which may have an unusual shape. The second savings realized through CADD is that computer-created documents are easy to read and modify, which reduces mistakes and saves time at the construction site (where workers are paid by the hour).

Questions for Discussion

1. Many of the add-in boards for architects' computers allow the attachment of input/output devices of greater precision than those found on an office worker's computer. Why is this precision so important to an architect? Is the computer a good tool, in general, for architects? Why or why not?

2. Is it an advantage for a national chain to use basically the same design for all its retail stores? Why or why not? What advantage does CADD contribute to chains that choose to go with uniformity of design?

3. CADD facilitates continual improvements in the quality of BSW's drawings because, for example, the drawings for Wal-Mart Store 305 incorporate all the "corrections" made to the drawings for Wal-Mart Stores 1 through 304. Is this an important competitive advantage for BSW? If so, why?

3   Comdisco Helps Clients Guard Against Memory Loss

Comdisco   Comdisco sells its backup services by stressing that victims of chip theft often don't realize they've been hit because thieves frequently remove only a portion of the memory from desktop computers. Until a user-operated application fails because of insufficient memory, the theft will probably go unnoticed.

There's no way to estimate the monetary value of losses due to chip theft. Some losses are unnoticed; others go unreported because companies want to avoid the embarrassment of acknowledging that their security system has been breached.

Questions for Discussion

1. What steps might companies take to (a) detect and (b) prevent the loss of chips from their desktop computers?

2. What steps might manufacturers and suppliers take to (a) discourage the theft of chips and (b) make it possible to identify stolen chips?

3. Do you believe the problem of chip theft will grow?

Net Work

Engines on the Web

The Internet's resources are so vast that you'll want to use search engines to find information you may not be aware of. Search engines (discussed in Chapter 3) are programs, available on the Web, that were designed to help people find information through keyword searches. Among the principal search engines are

- *Yahoo!*   (http://www.yahoo.com)
- *Lycos*   (http://www.lycos.com)
- *Infoseek*   (http://www2.infoseek.com)
- *WebCrawler*   (http://www.webcrawler.com)
- *Galaxy*   (http://www.galaxy.einet.net)

Let's try a search using *Yahoo!*

1. Click the [icon] and enter *Yahoo!*'s URL, http://www.yahoo.com. Alternatively, you can enter the address on the browser's location line.
2. Notice that the browser gives you a visual sign that information is being loaded from the URL: A moving icon appears on the upper right side of the screen. In the lower right corner, a horizontal bar grows longer, reaching full length when all of the new page's information is loaded.

3. When the loading is complete, *Yahoo!*'s home page will appear on the screen. The page includes space to enter the topic or

keyword you want *Yahoo!* to search. On the bottom portion of the page, you'll find a list of topics that are indexed by *Yahoo!* (You can use the vertical scroll bar to bring other topics onto the screen.)

Now enter the keywords: Broadway Theater.

After a few moments, you'll see a screenful of entries related to the keywords, each entry accompanied by a brief description. You can click on each or any entry (it's a hyperlink), or you can scroll to the next page, where more responses are displayed. *Yahoo!* shows the results of each search in the same manner. It displays the responses that it believes most accurately fit the search key first. Later entries, although still meeting the search criteria, are those *Yahoo!* judges to be less useful.

4. Click on the first entry in the list. Then, using the [icon], return to the search results and try another entry.

5. Any topic can be searched in this manner. Try some other searches. You can make up your own topics, or you can try these:

General Topics
London museums
Airline tickets

On-line bookshops
Cruise ships
Jewelry

Specific Topics
Madonna
Apple Computer
Prentice Hall Publishers
CNN (or Cable News Network)
ESPN

6. Try one of the other search engines, using the same keywords you used with *Yahoo!* Compare their performances and search results with those of *Yahoo!*

7. When you're finished, remember to Exit from the browser and the Internet.

GROUP PROJECTS AND APPLICATIONS

Project 1

Suppose that your group wants to go into business for itself, and that after actively investigating local business conditions, you have decided to enter one of the following lines of business:

TYPE OF BUSINESS	MAIN BUSINESS ACTIVITIES
Desktop publishing services	• Creation of résumés for people in the job market. • Design of both color and black-and-white flyers and newsletters for local organizations. • Typing/keyboarding services for publishing houses and local writers. • Preparation of multimedia-based Web pages for small businesses.
Tax preparation and accounting services	• Preparation of income tax returns for individuals and small businesses in the area. • Assistance with accounts payable and payroll for local companies.
Marketing support services	• Preparation and maintenance of mailing lists composed of the current customers of local department stores. • Preparation and maintenance of a database of customers' purchases and likes and dislikes to use as the basis for a "relationship marketing" campaign for mail-order catalog companies.

After choosing one of these businesses, visit a local electronics or computer store (e.g., Computer Universe, PC Warehouse, or Radio Shack) and talk to the staff about the information technology needed to support your business. What software will you need? How much memory do these programs require? How fast a processor does your PC need? Will you require any add-in boards? Do you plan on networking your computer to other computers within your company or to any outside computers? If so, what kinds of equipment will you need?

Project 2

Information technology advances so quickly that it is sometimes hard to keep up with it. With the members of your group, prepare a time line showing the development of information technology over the last decade. Answer the following questions:

- How does the speed of the average desktop PC compare with that of one year ago? Two years ago? Five years ago? Ten years ago?
- How have the prices of PCs changed over the past 10 years?

- What can you now do on a PC that you couldn't do just two years ago?
- Read the "Information Technology" section in a set of recent issues of *Business Week*. What are the latest developments in IT? Add these to your time line.
- What sorts of IT developments seem probable over the next five years? Add a category titled "The Next Five Years" to your time line, and list your predictions there.

REVIEW QUESTIONS

1. What is the purpose of the central processing unit?
2. What is the difference between data and instructions?
3. Describe the role of the control unit and the two types of activities performed by the arithmetic/logic unit.
4. What is the role of primary memory in computing? What is the relationship between primary memory and the central processor? How does primary memory differ from secondary storage?
5. In what five ways is memory space used?
6. What is a memory address?
7. What is the difference between RAM and ROM?
8. How are DRAM and static RAM alike? How are they different?
9. What is a system board? What does the system board of a PC contain?
10. Distinguish between a microcomputer, a microprocessor, and a microprocessor chip.
11. What is SIMM memory?
12. Describe the characteristic of flash memory. How is flash memory similar to or different from RAM or ROM?

13. What is a port? An expansion slot? An add-in board?
14. Describe the purpose of PCMCIA cards. What advantages do these cards give to PC owners?
15. What is meant by "plug and play"? What advantages does plug and play provide to PC users?
16. What is the difference between a closed and an open architecture?
17. What are the four steps of information processing? How are these divided into the machine, instruction, and execution cycles of computing?
18. What is the role of registers in computing? Where are registers found?
19. Describe the purpose of each of the four types of registers.
20. What are MIPS? Megaflops?
21. What three features of a computer determine its processing speed?
22. Distinguish between an input/output bus and a data bus.
23. How do primary memory and cache memory differ?
24. What is a co-processor?

25. How do accelerator boards increase processing speed?

26. How many transistors are found on Intel's Pentium chip? How many instructions can the Pentium execute per second?

27. What does RISC stand for?

28. What is parallel processing? What are its potential benefits? What are the two types of parallel processing?

DISCUSSION QUESTIONS

1. One of the most notable trends in IT today is the availability of affordable micros with powerful processors, large amounts of memory, and the capacity to add boards that control sophisticated input/output devices. What potential business opportunities might this trend create? What difficulties might it create for businesses?

2. The availability of affordable high-power micros has spurred a trend toward downsizing, or moving business applications from mainframes to mini/midrange computers or PCs. Some companies, such as UPS and BankAmerica Corp., still maintain large data centers built around mainframes. Why do you think this is so?

3. Advertisements for microcomputers often list two amounts of RAM—the amount that comes with the computer and the maximum amount of memory that can be added. Why is this second figure important to a manager who is shopping for a computer?

4. A recent survey compiled by *Computerworld* estimates that graphical user interfaces (GUIs) were used on 1.4 million PCs in 1990; this figure is expected to swell to 25.3 million by the end of the decade. What does this trend mean for processor speed? For businesses that want to use popular productivity software?

SUGGESTED READINGS

Corcoran, Elizabeth. "Calculating Reality." *Scientific American 264* (January 1991): 100–109. A lucid discussion of the next generation of high-speed computers and how they will be used to model reality more closely than ever.

Drexler, K. Eric. *Engines of Creating: The Coming Era of Nanotechnology.* New York: Anchor Press, 1986. An enormously fascinating and innovative book about the consequences of advances in information technology. The author is a pioneering researcher who tells how the "nanotechnology revolution" can be used to achieve social goals like better health, a higher standard of living, and world peace.

Gilder, George. *Microcosm.* New York: Simon & Schuster, 1989. Provides an up-close look at the technological revolution that is creating unprecedented opportunities for businesses and for people. Also includes revealing portraits of some leading scientists, engineers, and entrepreneurs, as well as a comparison of the level of IT usage in different countries.

Pancake, C.M. "Software Support for Parallel Computing: Where Are We Headed?" *Communications of the ACM 34* (November 1991): 52–66. Examines the issues involved in parallel computing and the directions the field is taking.

Pountain, Dick, and John Bryan. "All Systems Go." *Byte 17* (August 1992): 112–116. A very readable evaluation of the advantages of parallel processing and cache memory.

Stix, Gary. "Toward 'Point One.'" *Scientific American 272* (February 1995): 90–95. Explores the continued miniaturization of computer chips and microprocessors, with an analysis of expected developments in the future.

Ullah, Nasr, and Philip K. Brownfield. "The Making of the PowerPC." *Communications of the ACM 37* (June 1994). This special issue is devoted entirely to the new design and manufacturing techniques that led to the creation of the PowerPC. It includes eight articles by industry experts.

CASE
STUDY

DigiCash Makes Money Electronic

DigiCash

The growing conduct of business over communications networks, including the Internet, is creating a trend toward payment for purchases with electronic money. Electronic money presents both challenges and opportunities for payment collection. Amsterdam-based DigiCash is one of the leaders in the exploding world of electronic money. E-cash, the company's patented payment method, devised by the company's founder, David Chaum, has been in operation since 1995.

Electronic money is augmenting—in many cases, replacing—traditional paper money and coins. This digital currency is not controlled by central banks or government agencies, such as the U.S. Treasury. Instead, it is "minted" by private companies. If the trend takes on enough momentum, companies, instead of governments, will one day have the responsibility for creating money and keeping it secure, valuable, and useful.

DigiCash soon realized that creating electronic cash entailed meeting certain challenges. One is security, or ensuring that the value of digital cash cannot be stolen when payment details are transmitted over networks. Another challenge is ensuring authenticity, so that both bank and recipient know the electronic money is not forged. Finally, there is the need to ensure anonymity, so that the spender cannot be identified by either the bank or the transaction processor.

Here's how DigiCash provides security. Its digital cash consists of a token that you can authenticate independently of the issuer. You can withdraw digital currency from your bank account on the Internet and store it as E-cash on your computer's hard drive or on smart cards the size of credit cards. E-cash uses digital "coins," each having a fixed monetary value. These coins are self-authenticating through a complex built-in software algorithm that is comparable to a digital signature.

Anonymity and authenticity can be conflicting values. DigiCash has cleverly gotten around the conflict in the following manner. Today, virtually every country prints serial numbers on its paper money, but these serial numbers are not used to track consumer spending habits. With electronic money, in contrast, serial numbers take on new value because they can be stored in a database together with records of who spent the money and what it purchased. Anticipating that consumers would not want such records of their spending activities maintained by third parties, DigiCash devised a *blind signature* method. When consumers make an E-cash withdrawal from their bank accounts, the PC assigns a random serial number to each digital coin. It also specifies a blinding factor—a random number that it uses in validating the coin serial numbers. Using its own secret key, a bank encodes the blinded numbers and debits the consumer's account. The bank then sends the authenticated coins back to the consumer, who removes the blinding factor. The consumer can then spend the bank-validated coins, but the bank will not have a record nor will it be able to trace how or where the coins are spent.

The growing use of communications networks to conduct business necessitates the development of new payment forms. Will DigiCash's E-cash become the principal means of paying with electronic money? It's too soon to tell. However, international banks have begun to adopt DigiCash's E-cash, a necessary step toward success.

Questions for Discussion

1. Why do you think electronic money has emerged as a means for making purchases over the Internet? What benefits does electronic money offer to buyer and seller?

2. Since banks ultimately manage the movement of money, and are, of necessity, the vehicle for converting electronic money into traditional money, do you think they, rather than information technology companies like DigiCash, will eventually create and control all electronic money?

3. If it becomes easy, cheap, and safe to move electronic money through personal computers and computer networks, do you think electronic money will replace ATMs?

THE MAKING OF A
Microprocessor

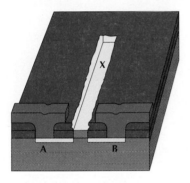

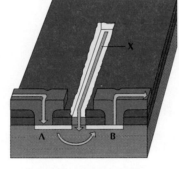

(a) Transistor off   (b) Transistor on

Microprocessors are built from sand and are constructed in layers consisting of circuits and pathways, doped silicon substrate, and silicon dioxide. ("Doping" the silicon allows it to conduct electricity well or not at all. This is important because computing is at heart an electrical process.) This photo essay describes the steps in creating the silicon wafer on which the circuits are created.

KEY:

- Positively doped silicon substrate
- Silicon dioxide
- Negatively doped silicon
- Pathway X
- Circuit pathway
- ⇒ Direction of electrical charge along pathway X
- ⇒ Direction of electrical charge along circuit pathway

Step One: Designing the microprocessor chip

1 A microprocessor's design is created using a powerful desktop computer equipped with a design program. Each component of the microprocessor is drawn and positioned using a digitizing tablet that allows the designer to translate images on paper into an electronic format, with the resulting image appearing on a display screen. Today's microprocessors contain millions of transistors and circuits, each microscopic in size.

2 The microprocessor's design is transformed into a series of photo masks, one for each layer of the chip. A typical microprocessor design includes 20 or more different photo masks.

Step Two: Manufacturing the chip

3 The entire process of manufacturing and testing the microprocessor takes place in a *clean room,* a work room that is virtually free of dust—more than 100 times more sterile than a hospital operating room. To avoid contaminating the atmosphere, all engineers and workers are required to don special gowns (called "bunny suits") before they enter the room.

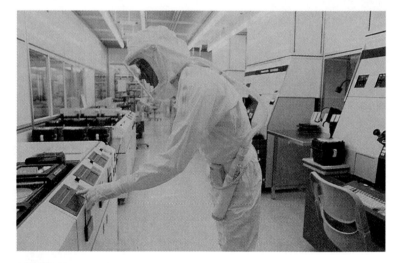

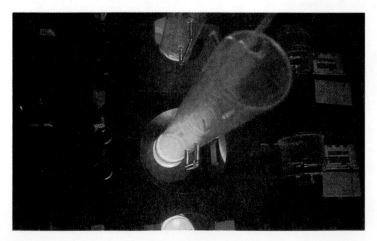

4 The first step in manufacturing is creating cylindrical silicon ingots. Silicon sand (hence the name *silicon* chip) is heated until it melts. The molten silicon, which contains almost no impurities or contaminants, is then grown into a cylindrical crystal that looks like a metal rod.

5 A diamond-tipped saw slices the silicon rod into very thin (3/1000 inch) discs, called wafers. The wafer, which may be 5" to 8" (13 cm to 20 cm) in diameter, is the base from which the microprocessor chips are built.

6 Wafers are sterilized and their surfaces polished to a shiny, mirrorlike finish.

7 During *photolithography*, a gelatinlike substance called *photoresist*, similar to the film used in ordinary photography, is deposited on the wafer's surface. A glass photo mask containing circuit patterns is held over the wafer and ultraviolet light is passed through the glass regions of the photo mask that do not contain the circuit pattern. A portion of the electronic circuit will subsequently be placed everywhere that the light exposes the photoresist on top of the wafer.

8 Wafers are taken into a "yellow room," so called because of the special yellow light used to illuminate the room. Here, after the resist is exposed, it is placed in chemicals to develop it. The exposed resist will remain on the wafer; the unexposed resist will be removed by the chemicals.

Next comes *oxidization*. Silicon heated and exposed to steam or dry oxygen (that is, oxidized silicon) will form silicon dioxide, more commonly known as glass. (An analogy: iron exposed to oxygen forms rust. Silicon "rust" is glass.) Unexposed regions of the wafer can be oxidized to separate the electronic circuits.

Following oxidization, special materials are diffused or implanted into the wafer. These materials change the electrical properties of the silicon so that the electronic circuits (or switches) can be made.

After implantation comes *deposition,* in which liquid metal or other films are "sprayed" on the wafer. These films will later be selectively patterned, following the photolithography steps described in number 7 above. In the final manufacturing step, called *etching,* chemicals that selectively remove one type of material or another are used to etch away patterned regions on the wafer, leaving only the required circuit patterns.

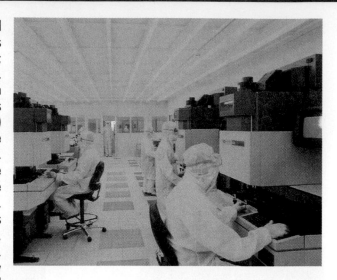

10 A wafer contains hundreds of identical chips. The rectangles near the center of the wafer are test circuits for monitoring the quality of the fabrication process.

9 The preceding five-step process is repeated to "build" images and electrical circuits into the wafer. Metals deposited on the wafer are selectively etched to provide thin wires interconnecting the circuits.

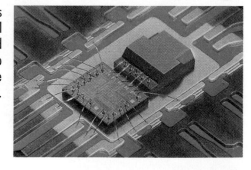

11 Each wafer contains millions of transistors. The color-enhanced close-up photo shown here shows the sections of the chip and the bonding pads along the edges of the chip.

Step Three: Testing the microprocessor

12 A wafer's *yield* is the number of good chips that result. Testing determines chip quality. During testing, large computer-controlled electronic testers determine whether a chip functions as it was designed. The chips that do function as designed are diced out of the wafers using diamond-tipped saws. Defective wafers are discarded.

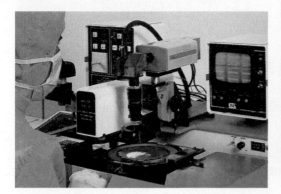

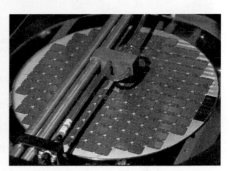

Step Four:
Packaging the microprocessor

13 By itself, the microprocessor chip is too fragile to be handled or used. Hence, it is mounted in a protective package. Each chip is bonded to a plastic base and the chip's wire leads are in turn wired to the electrical gold or aluminum leads on the package. The wire leads of the chip are thinner than a human hair. The microprocessor package is generally shaped in a square as a result of the dicing process.

14 During assembly of system (mother) boards, the leads of the microprocessor package are inserted into holes in the circuit board. Each lead contacts an electrical lead on the board, which is used to transmit to and receive electrical signals from other components mounted on the board.

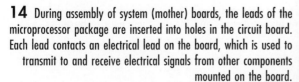

CHAPTER 5

Secondary Storage and Input/Output Devices

CHAPTER OUTLINE

When Staying in Touch Is Not an Option

Secondary Storage

Magnetic Storage • Optical Storage

Interaction with Computers: Input Devices

Keyboards • Terminals • Scanners • Digitizers • Digital Cameras • Voice and Sound Input Devices • Multimedia Audiovisual Devices • Audio Response Units • Multimedia PCs

Interaction with Computers: Output and Information Distribution Devices

Visual Displays (Monitors) • Printers • Plotters • Film Recorders

Case Study: Talbott Ties the Sales Knot with Information Technology

LEARNING OBJECTIVES

When you have completed this chapter, you should be able to

1. Discuss why people use secondary storage, not just the computer's main memory, to store information.

2. Distinguish between the two main types of magnetic storage and identify five newer magnetic storage alternatives.

3. Explain why optical storage is of growing importance in computing and describe the most commonly used forms of optical storage.

4. Identify the six most widely used input devices and describe how they are employed in computing.

5. Discuss the future of voice input and audio output devices as components of information technology.

6. Describe the four types of output devices and identify their uses in business.

When Staying in Touch Is Not an Option

Blip. Blip. Blip. This regular pulsing sound is part of the background noise for a medical attendant on duty at Suburban Medical Center. He is responsible for monitoring patients via the constant display of information on a desktop computer. Suddenly the pattern of sounds changes, instantly grabbing the attendant's attention. The condition of a middle-aged patient under treatment for a heart attack is changing right in front of him. Her electrocardiogram (ECG)—a graphic waveform corresponding to heartbeats—suggests an unacceptable irregularity in her heartbeat. Instinctively, the attendant contacts the patient's physician by telephone: "Doctor, the rhythm of your patient's heartbeat is unstable. You'd better take a look. I'm going to transmit the ECG."

Working quickly and calculatedly from his desktop computer, the attendant freezes a 15-second ECG snapshot on the screen. This graphic information, along with other vital signs (including temperature, pulse rate, and blood pressure), is transmitted electronically to the physician's palmtop computer.

Several miles away from Suburban Medical Center, a palmtop computer receives the attendant's information. When his computer emits an audible tone, the physician knows the message has arrived, complete with the patient's name, the date, time of day, the hospital's name, the care unit, and the patient's vital signs and ECG waveform, as well as the medical assistant's name and phone number. (Error detection prevents the display of invalid data.) The physician immediately views the information. As he quickly studies the 15-second waveform showing on the palmtop's display screen, he zooms in on a segment of the ECG that appears to be abnormal. Picking up his cellular phone, he calls the attendant, relaying his diagnosis and instructions: "Administer an injection of . . . Prepare the patient for . . . I'm on my way to the hospital. I'll be there in less than five minutes."

We sometimes forget that there is more to a computer system than a keyboard and a display monitor. All of the processing work is done "behind the scenes." Computers do use data to generate information, but very often the information enters the computer from outside sources and is processed there for use. In the opening vignette, for instance, the patient's ECG was processed only after it was input to the palmtop computer. Processing also uses data stored within the computer.

This chapter continues the detailed tour of the hardware components of a computer that we began in Chapter 4. We start with a discussion of secondary storage and its importance to business and personal computing. Then, in the second half of the chapter, we cover the many different input and output devices commonly used with computers. As you will see, getting data and information into and out of a computer, whether from primary or secondary storage, depends on having the right equipment.

The same caveat with which we began Chapter 4 applies to this material as well. The purpose of this chapter is not to make you an expert on equipment technology, but rather to familiarize you with the many technological options available to businesspeople today. Knowing which technology to use can make you both more productive and more successful.

Secondary Storage

Recall that *primary storage* is the section within the computer's central processing unit that holds data and information and instructions before and after processing. In contrast, **secondary storage,** sometimes called **auxiliary storage,** is a way of storing data and information outside the computer. Secondary storage is any external storage medium that can be read by a computer.

Secondary storage is an integral part of information technology for three reasons:

**secondary storage/
auxiliary storage**

A storage medium that is external to the computer, but that can be read by the computer; a way of storing data and information outside the computer itself.

1. *The contents of primary memory reside in the computer only temporarily* (see Chapter 4). Primary memory itself is used by many different applications, and between applications, the memory is, in effect, cleared and reassigned to the next application. Hence, any information or results obtained from an application must be stored outside of primary memory—that is, in secondary storage.
2. *Primary memory holds data only while the computer is turned on.* When the computer is turned off, the contents of primary memory are lost (if ordinary DRAM is used, and it usually is).
3. *Primary memory is seldom large enough to hold the large volumes of data and information associated with typical business applications.* For instance, it would be impossible to hold the transcripts of all the students at a large college or university in primary memory.

By doing what primary memory cannot, secondary storage helps the computer process and store large amounts of information. At the same time, it is economical, reliable, and convenient.

There are two main types of secondary storage: magnetic and optical.

The Federal Aviation Administration's "Black Box" Captures Aircraft Flight Information

The Federal Aviation Administration (FAA), which is responsible for enforcing air safety rules in the United States, requires every U.S. passenger aircraft that soars into the skies to carry two "black boxes": a flight data recorder and a cockpit voice recorder. (Actually, these "black boxes" are usually bright orange today to make them easy to spot in wreckage.)

The flight data recorder (FDR), required since 1958, captures details of the plane's flight—including airspeed, direction, and altitude—that are useful for determining the aircraft's performance in the event of any type of failure. Initially, FDR information was recorded on 400-foot rolls of metal foil. Today, Mylar magnetic recording tape is used because it can record several hours of flight information in much less space.

The cockpit voice recorder (CVR) captures sound in the aircraft's cockpit, including conversations between the pilot and co-pilot, transmissions over the intercom, and background noise. CVR information is captured on separate channels and recorded on magnetic tape that automatically overwrites itself every half hour, so in the event of a disaster, only the last half hour of sound recorded in the cockpit will be retained.

Both devices are housed in durable steel cases that are able to withstand high temperature, sudden impact, and catastrophic explosions in order to protect the recorded information inside. After a catastrophic incident, a search is made for the cases and the tapes from the "black boxes" are removed for computer processing by the National Transportation Safety Board. Details from the recordings are used to reconstruct the situation that led up to the incident.

Magnetic Storage

Since the earliest days of computing, magnetism has played a central role in storing data and information. The earliest form of secondary storage was magnetic tape. Magnetic disks followed later.

How exactly does magnetism store information? Data are stored on the magnetic medium by a **read/write head,** a device that records data by magnetically

read/write head
A device that records data by magnetically aligning metallic particles on the medium. The write head records data and the read head retrieves them.

aligning metallic particles (iron oxide mixed with a binding agent) of the medium. These particles correspond to binary digits (alignment represents a binary one, nonalignment represents a zero). The *write head* records data and the *read head* retrieves them.

Writing, or *recording,* converts the contents of electronic circuits in primary memory into spots on the recording surface of the storage medium. Each spot, or pattern of spots, stores one piece of data. *Reading,* or *retrieving,* is not the reverse of this process in the sense that it does not change or move what is stored. Rather, it leaves what is stored intact. The read process senses the coded spots and interprets them as data.

magnetic tape

A magnetic storage medium in which data are stored on large reels of tape.

MAGNETIC TAPE.   On large computers, **magnetic tape** often comes in large reels; on microcomputers, tape cartridges, slightly larger than audiocassettes, are common (see Figure 2.12d). Data are stored, or written, to the magnetic tape by a read/write head on the *tape drive,* a peripheral device that holds and processes the tape. The read/write head alters the magnetic direction of the metallic particles coating the tape. The *transport mechanism* moves the tape from one reel to the other. Reading and writing occur as the tape passes over the heads (Figure 5.1).

track

The area in which data and information are stored on magnetic tape or disk.

Two recording schemes are common, one using seven-bit bytes per character and the other using nine-bit bytes. This means that the magnetic tape surface is divided into seven or nine **tracks,** narrow areas in which each spot (invisible to the human eye) is being magnetized or demagnetized (Figure 5.2). (*Note:* The seven- or nine-bit structure is determined by the manufacturer of the tape drive; it is not something that the person using the drive can decide.)

record

A grouping of data items that consists of a set of data or information that describes an entity's specific occurrence.

To read the data, the head reads the magnetic patterns and translates them into electric pulses. These pulses become the 0's and 1's that the computer processes.

block

The writing of one or more records onto a section of magnetic tape.

The tape drive records onto the magnetic tape in groups or **records,** which are sets of data about a single transaction (e.g., the registration for a course or the payment of an invoice). One or more records may be written as a **block.** Because reading and writing occur only while the tape is moving, a space called

FIGURE 5.1

Transport Mechanism for Magnetic Tape Drive Unit

Reading and writing occur as the oxide side of the magnetic tape passes over the unit's read/write heads.

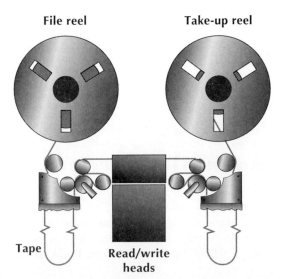

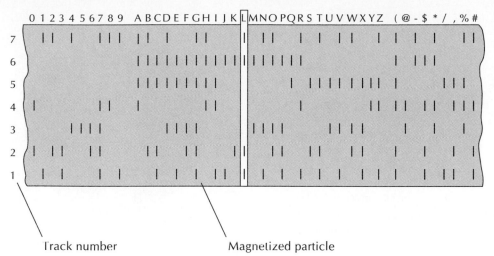

0 1 2 3 4 5 6 7 8 9 A B C D E F G H I J K L M N O P Q R S T U V W X Y Z (@ - $ * / , % #

Track number

Magnetized particle

FIGURE 5.2

Data Representation on Seven-Track Magnetic Tape

Representing data on seven-track tape entails magnetizing certain tracks and demagnetizing others. For example, the letter "L" is represented by magnetizing tracks 1, 2, 6, and 7 and demagnetizing tracks 3, 4, and 5. To read the data, the read head translates the magnetic pattern into electric pulses, which the computer then processes as "L."

a **gap** is left before and after the block so that the tape drive can stop without skipping over any data. The drive's **recording density** is the number of characters per inch at which it writes the data. A recording density of 6,250 characters or bytes per inch is most common (6,250 characters is comparable to the contents of 5 to 6 pages of printed information).

Compared with other forms of secondary storage, reading from and writing to magnetic tape can be very slow. If a large number of records is stored, a relatively long section of tape will be required to record the data. When you want to recall a particular record, the search for it must begin at the beginning of the tape and proceed record by record—that is, *sequentially*. The computer may, therefore, need to scan hundreds of feet of tape to find the record you want.

Despite these disadvantages, magnetic tape storage continues to be used in computers of all sizes because it is relatively inexpensive (approximately $25 for a blank reel) and reliable. Also, users can store a reel of tape for a long time without worrying about data loss.

MAGNETIC DISK. There are two types of **magnetic disk: flexible disks** (also known as **floppy disks**), which are made of flexible plastic; and **hard disks,** which are made of rigid aluminum. Data on a magnetic disk are stored in the same way they are stored on magnetic tape: spots are magnetized or nonmagnetized in a coding scheme that corresponds to the on and off states of circuits (bits) in the processor.

The decision to use aluminum in manufacturing hard disks came about only after a great deal of research. Researchers at IBM (where magnetic disks were invented) first tested glass, plastic, brass, and magnesium, but discovered that disks made of these substances wobbled when run at high speeds, causing serious data loss and errors. Today, hard disks are made of aluminum laminates clamped together and heated in ovens, a highly reliable storage medium. ■

gap

In magnetic storage, a space left before and after a block so that the tape drive can stop without skipping over any data.

recording density

The number of characters per inch at which a drive writes data.

magnetic disk

A general term referring to two types of storage disk: the flexible/floppy disk and the hard disk.

floppy disk/flexible disk

A type of magnetic disk made of flexible plastic.

hard disk

A type of secondary storage that uses nonflexible, nonremovable magnetic disks mounted inside the computer to store data or information.

FIGURE 5.3

Tracks and Sectors on a Magnetic Disk

On a magnetic disk, data are usually stored in all tracks except the outermost, which is reserved for a directory that lists the names of the files stored and a label that identifies the disk and the format used for recording. Data are written to or read from a specific track as the disk drive rotates the disk. As the disk drive spins, it positions the read/write heads over the proper track. When the correct sector has been found, the data are read or written over.

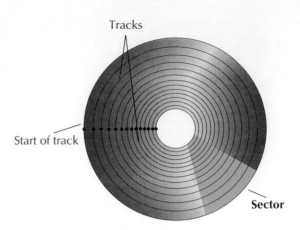

sector

A subdivision of a track on a magnetic disk; used to improve access to data or information.

head crash

The situation that occurs when the read/write heads that normally float close to a magnetic disk's surface actually touch the surface.

Winchester disk drive

A disk drive that contains a read/write head, an access arm, and a disk in one sealed unit.

disk pack

A stack of disks, enclosed in a protective plastic cover, that can be lifted onto or off a disk drive.

Like the storage area on magnetic tape, the storage area of a magnetic disk is divided into tracks. However, the tracks on disks are concentric circles rather than linear (Figure 5.3). These tracks are often divided into **sectors** for easier access during reading and writing. The tracks have a specified recording density. Data are read from or written to a specific track as the disk is rotated by the disk drive at a constant speed of several hundred revolutions per second. (This speed is controlled by the disk drive built into the computer or attached to the computer by cable.) As the disk drive spins the disk continually, it positions the read/write heads over the proper track. Some disk drives on large mainframes and super-computers position a read/write head over every track. This extra expense and complexity are justified because data can be retrieved much more quickly this way since there is no delay while the heads move from position to position.

It is important to note that the read/write heads are supposed to "float" very close to the disk surface, but never actually touch it. If the read/write heads do touch the disk, the result is a **head crash:** the data stored at the point where the head touched the disk will be lost and the head itself could be damaged.

Some disk drives, called **Winchester disk drives,** contain a read/write head, an access arm (which positions the read/write head over the appropriate track), and the disk(s) in one sealed unit. These drives, typical of hard drive units on microcomputers, are not removable from the computer. Other disk units feature a **disk pack,** a stack of disks enclosed in a protective plastic cover that can be

FIGURE 5.4

Disk Pack

A disk pack may contain as many as 12 disks stacked around a hollow core. After the protective plastic cover is removed, the stack slips onto a shaft in the disk drive.

lifted onto or off the disk drive (Figure 5.4). Disk packs allow the user to remove and store disks easily. They are useful for making backup copies of information or programs, for separating databases onto different disk packs, and for storing very large databases when all the data will not fit on a single disk pack. Many mainframes and supercomputers use disk pack–based storage.

Magnetic disk storage is often called **random access storage** or **direct access storage** to signify that a particular record of information can be retrieved from any track directly. The processor does not have to instruct the drive to start at the beginning of the disk and read each record sequentially. However, systems designers can create a sequential file and perform sequential storage and processing if they desire.

random access storage/direct access storage
The process of retrieving a particular record of information from any track directly.

THE FABULOUS FLEXIBLE DISKETTE. For the first decade of their existence, all magnetic disks were hard disks. In the early 1970s, as transistor chips became the dominant component of computer memories, engineers began seeking a way to preserve data even when the computer's power supply was turned off. (Recall from Chapter 4 that RAM chips are volatile, which means that their contents are lost when the computer's electrical current ceases.) Even the computer's operating system had to be reloaded if the computer was powered down for just a moment.

Early attempts to store the operating system permanently in the computer's memory met with no success. Researchers tested all known storage devices, including hard disks, magnetic tape, and even phonograph records, all to no avail.

The breakthrough came when an engineer on IBM's research team suggested using a very thin flexible disk—a disk so thin, in fact, that it would almost bend in half when held by one edge (hence the term "floppy disk"). Thinness was extremely important, for the researcher wanted to create a high-storage density on a 6-inch disk (the standard at the time was 14 inches) and to have the disk sit right next to the read/write head without causing damage to disk, data, or head.

The rest is history. Not only did the idea work, it also revolutionized the way data are stored on computers. Today's flexible disks, which are known as *diskettes,* are inexpensive (less than $1 each) and reusable. Data can be written to and erased from them quickly and easily. They are commonly found in 8-, 5¼-, 3½-, and 2-inch sizes, with the 3½-inch size (Figure 5.5) the most popular in business. In all likelihood, diskettes are here to stay.

FIGURE 5.5
The Fabulous Flexible Diskette
Like most other businesses, today's technology companies realize that the packaging is often as important as the product itself. One result: The once-standard black plastic coating for flexible diskettes has been replaced by all the colors of the rainbow.

The key to the success of the flexible diskette *isn't the disk.* Rather it's the holder.

The first disks produced by IBM's research team were so flimsy that they needed to be held in a foam-padded stiffener an eighth of an inch (3.18 millimeters) thick—thicker than the disk itself. After the flexible disk (stiffener and all) proved itself in tests, the question became how to pack the disk in marketable form. The answer was a custom-designed flexible plastic jacket. Today's flexible disks spin inside their own plastic sleeves. The inside of these sleeves is lined with a special nonwoven fabric that protects the diskette from abrasion and wipes it clean with each revolution. A small rectangular opening allows the read/write heads to write data or to retrieve data from the disk's surface.

The disk and packaging together are what we know as the *flexible diskette,* though "flexible" pertains only to the disk inside. Figure 5.6 illustrates additional features of the flexible diskette. ◼

OTHER MAGNETIC DISK STORAGE SYSTEMS.   Several variations on the disks— removable Zip disks, disk cartridges, hardcards, RAM disks, and disk caching— have emerged recently.

▪ **Zip drives** (Figure 5.7) use hard-shelled removable Zip disks that are approximately 4 inches square and slightly larger than the conventional diskette. Each Zip disk can store up to 100 megabytes of information, making them a useful device for storing backup copies of files and fast enough to run applications and multimedia. The Zip drive brings a new dimension of flexibility to today's powerful MMX, Pentium, and Pentium Pro-based personal computers. When

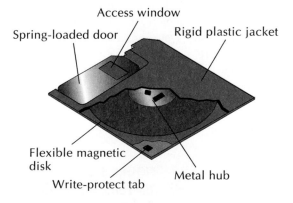

FIGURE 5.6   *Inside the Flexible Diskette*

A rigid plastic jacket protects the flexible magnetic disk. A spring-loaded door (open in this illustration) covers the jacket's access window. The door remains closed until the floppy disk is inserted into a disk drive, thus protecting the disk from dust and fingerprints. A metal hub, bonded to the underside of the disk, has one hole that serves to center the disk and another that spins it. Sliding the write/protect tab to open a hole in the corner of the jacket protects the disk from unintentional writing or erasure.

FIGURE 5.7
Zip Drive and Disks
The Zip disk is larger than a conventional diskette and holds as much as 100 MB of information.

loaded into the special Zip drive, information can quickly be transferred between the disk and computer memory. Iomega's Zip disks provide 70 times the capacity of traditional floppy disks at 20 times the speed, giving consumers unlimited capacity in 100 MB increments, increased flexibility, and a built-in backup system. Zip disks cannot be used with conventional floppy disk drives. Although the cost of a Zip disk is as low as $15 in contrast to less than $1 for a conventional floppy disk, their convenience and storage capacity make Zip disks a popular secondary removable storage device.

▪ **Disk cartridges** (Figure 5.8) offer most of the features of hard disks. Unlike Winchester disks, disk cartridges are removable. The cartridge—that is, the hard disk sealed in a protective package—is inserted into the disk drive for reading and writing data. When one cartridge is full, you replace it with another. Cartridges are a good way of making backup copies of files and databases stored on hard disk.

FIGURE 5.8
Disk Cartridge
The cartridge is removable; when one cartridge is full, it can be replaced with another.

- **Hardcards** are magnetic disks attached to a circuit board that can be mounted in a microcomputer's expansion slot. The hardcard allows users to upgrade older microcomputers by increasing their storage capacities. Hardcards offer the advantages of easy installation (you just slip the card into an expansion slot), affordability (several hundred dollars), and fast data retrieval. They do not take up desktop space and do not use a drive slot—a benefit because the drive slot may be needed to add a CD-ROM or magnetic tape drive to the computer.

- The continuing decline in the price of DRAM (dynamic RAM) has made the **RAM disk** a viable alternative to magnetic storage devices. Recall from Chapter 4 that DRAMs are memory chips that offer instant direct access to the data stored on them. The equivalent of a hard disk can be created in primary memory using DRAM chips, and the information stored on this RAM disk will be rapidly retrievable. The RAM disk acts like any other disk. Information can be written to and retrieved from it just as if it were a hard disk. However, when the computer's power is turned off, the contents of this disk will be lost. Any information that is to be retained, therefore, must be written to a hard disk before the power is turned off. RAM disks are often used in industrial settings to store the production data used by manufacturing equipment.

- **Disk caching** allows the system to store information that is frequently read from a disk in RAM. This process speeds up retrieval because it takes much less time to retrieve data from a disk cache than from a disk. Disk caching is used to manage large amounts of data. It improves retrieval time when used to prepare large documents with desktop publishing software or to perform calculations with spreadsheet software.

RAM disk
A disk created in primary memory that offers instant direct access to the data stored on it.

There is a trade-off between storage/retrieval speed and storage capacity. RAM disks offer more speed than hard disks, but not as much capacity. Optical storage methods, which we discuss next, offer large storage capacity, but slower retrieval times.

Optical Storage

The technology that made vinyl LPs obsolete by bringing us compact disks (CDs) for recorded music is bringing about a similar revolution in information technology. While it does not make magnetic disk storage obsolete, optical storage does provide a storage option for high-density data and information. Optical storage has been one of the factors in the emergence of multimedia applications.

optical storage device
A device that uses a beam of light produced by a laser to read and write data and information.

Optical storage devices use light rather than magnetism to store information. A beam of light produced by a laser is directed through a series of lenses until it is focused on the surface of a metal or plastic spinning disk. The disk's pattern of reflectivity, which corresponds to the data it carries, is an essential aspect of reading and writing data and information.

Optical disks use the same binary recording scheme used in all areas of information technology. During recording, a powerful laser beam makes a pit in the surface of the disk. The presence or absence of these laser pits corresponds to the 1's and 0's of binary code. To read the stored information, a weaker laser beam scans the disk's surface, sensing the pattern of pits. The pattern is reflected back to a reader that interprets and sends the data to the central processor. Figures 5.9 and 5.10 illustrate how data are read from an optical disk.

As with magnetic disks, information on optical disks is stored in circular tracks. Because a laser beam can be positioned extremely accurately, the tracks of data on an optical disk can be packed densely enough to provide immense storage

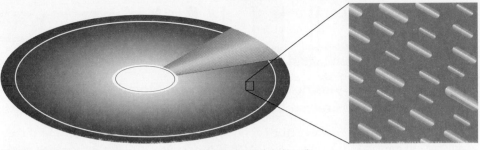

FIGURE 5.9
Reading Data from an Optical Disk

Topography of a disk. The pits on a prerecorded optical disk (detail) resemble parallel lines of regularly spaced ridges. Each of these pits is about .6 micron (.6 millionth of a meter) wide. If 3,000 pits were lined up side by side, they would be about as wide as this letter *o*.

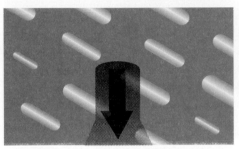
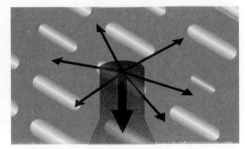

FIGURE 5.10
The Land and the Pit

The land. When a focused laser beam hits a flat space between pits—a *land*—much of its light is reflected straight back toward the detector. At the point where the laser strikes the disk, it has been focused to a spot about a micron in diameter. This diameter is only a little larger than the wavelength of the laser light. As a result, the beam, which was originally cone-shaped, assumes a cylindrical shape near its point of focus.

The pit. When the focused laser beam strikes the pit, much of the light is scattered sideways, so that very little is reflected back to the detector. Each time the beam moves from a land to a pit, the reflected light changes in intensity, generating a signal that can be decoded to reproduce the data written on the disk.

capacities. A floppy disk will have from 25 to 100 tracks per inch and a hard disk several hundred, but a prerecorded optical disk will contain more than 15,000 tracks per inch. Yet any individual track can be identified and read easily.

The most commonly used types of optical storage today are CD-ROM and videodisks, but several newer forms that offer distinct advantages have been developed.

CD-ROM. The **CD-ROM** (compact disk—read only memory) **disk** was originally adapted from audio disk technology. CD-ROM offers several advantages:

- It is the least expensive way to store large amounts of data and information.
- CD-ROM disks are durable and easy to handle.
- Information can be stored on CD-ROM for many years. And, because information cannot be erased from a CD-ROM disk, critical material is safe from being destroyed either accidentally or intentionally.
- Finally, CD-ROM disks can hold motion, video, audio, and high-resolution image information—essential features for multimedia applications.

CD-ROM disk
Short for "compact disk—read only memory," an optical storage medium that permits storage of large amounts of information. CD-ROM disks can only be written to and cannot be erased.

CRITICAL CONNECTION 2

American Express

American Express's Optical Storage Created Country Club Billing

If you've ever felt overwhelmed by a flood of monthly bills, consider the three million charge slips that pour into American Express Co. for processing and storage every day. With this kind of volume, it's easy to understand why American Express has turned to an image-processing computer system that uses optical storage.

At AmEx, the "images" are digital images of charge slips, which are created when the originals are scanned into the system at regional operations centers in Phoenix and Ft. Lauderdale. The digital images—complete with cardholder signatures—are stored on 12-inch optical disks; the flimsy paper originals are shredded. When cardholders' bills are prepared, the images are sorted by account number, and reduced facsimiles are printed eight to a page and enclosed with monthly statements prepared for billing via conventional data processing. The resulting service, called Enhanced Country Club Billing (ECCB), is unique in the industry and is very popular with AmEx's 5.1 million corporate cardholders, who often need help in documenting their expense accounts.

The system also helps American Express. Paper handling is cut by a factor of 10, improving productivity and reducing the number of lost or mishandled charge slips, and the optical disks take less storage space than paper records. Moreover, the system both shortens the billing cycle and minimizes disputes about charges—so AmEx gets paid sooner.

FIGURE 5.11
CD-ROM Package

Compton's *Jazz* CD-ROM package is a complete multimedia history of jazz in America.

CD-ROM also has its disadvantages:

- You cannot edit what is already written on the disk. Thus, what is an advantage when you want to ensure that material cannot be changed is a disadvantage when you do want to make changes.
- CD-ROM disks retrieve data and information noticeably more slowly than magnetic disks do.

CD-ROM is often used to store large volumes of reference information, such as dictionaries, encyclopedias, and financial reports (see Figure 5.11). Interior designers and illustrators use CD-ROM storage as a source of predrawn art and prepared photographs. They read drawings stored on CD-ROM into their computer's main memory and then embed them in the documents they are preparing. Similarly, engineers retrieve detailed blueprints from CD-ROM and copy them to main memory for their applications.

See the *Rethinking Business Practices* feature entitled "Rethinking the Business of Roadside Service in England" for an example of how CD-ROM can change the manner and place where information is displayed.

The use of CD-ROM is growing in all sectors of society. The Department of Defense, for example, has created a program called Computer-aided Acquisition and Logistics Support (CALS) to replace some of the massive printed documentation needed to operate and maintain complex aircraft systems. The department's goal is to put all its aircraft manuals—many of which run to a thousand pages— on CD-ROM eventually. The great virtue of CALS is that it allows pilots to view the documentation onscreen in the cockpit of an aircraft.

Boeing Aircraft, the largest aircraft builder in the world, has instituted a similar CD-ROM system to replace all operation and maintenance manuals for its civilian and military aircraft. Today, when an aircraft is delivered, Boeing must deliver thousands of pounds of paper documentation with it. Then it must keep this documentation updated as enhancements and changes are made to the aircraft. Replacing this material with CD-ROM versions will result in faster and easier access to information for the operators of the aircraft.

The demand for CD-ROM storage is growing rapidly. Fortunately, CD-ROM disks can be duplicated in a factory by methods similar to those used to duplicate compact discs. First, a master is made with a laser beam, and then copies of that master are stamped out in a press. (Magnetic tapes and disks cannot be duplicated through mass production stamping. They must be copied individually by recording— a more time-consuming and costly process.) Mass production techniques are both a cause and an effect of the trend toward making CD-ROM drives a standard component on many computer systems, particularly microcomputers. ■

VIDEODISKS. Like CD-ROM disks, **videodisks** are an optical read-only storage medium. Videodisks (Figure 5.12a) store images and sound, which when sequenced together produce full-motion animated information. Because videodisk players can be attached to computers, they are often a component of multimedia systems. Organizations use videodisks to deliver marketing information, product demonstrations, and training programs.

videodisk
An optical read-only storage medium.

RETHINKING BUSINESS PRACTICES

Rethinking the Business of Roadside Service in England

Traveling to a location by high-speed motorway saves time compared to traveling there on city roads and streets. It also means that when a breakdown occurs, the driver is likely to be some distance from a service center. For this reason, many government agencies responsible for motorways have special crews traveling the roads, on the lookout for stranded drivers. If the problem is a lack of fuel, the crew will supply it. If the problem is a mechanical breakdown, the crew will either call for a tow vehicle or give the driver a lift to the nearest service center.

The work of these special crews in Great Britain has changed drastically since the Royal Automobile Club (RAC), which patrols Britain's highways, often by motorcycle, set out to find a better way to help motorists whose vehicles had stalled. After rethinking its provision of roadside service, the RAC decided to equip its patrol force with notebook computers outfitted with CD-ROM players. Now when patrol members stop to aid a stranded motorist, they turn to their notebook computers to help fix the problem.

The CD-ROMs they use contain thousands of pages of diagrams illustrating the different parts of various motor vehicles—much more information than could possibly be included in a paper repair book. Using browsing and searching software running on the notebook computer, the person on patrol can find the necessary information with just a few keystrokes. The CDs also hold audio tracks containing tips and tricks provided by mechanics throughout Great Britain. Each month, the CD-ROM information is updated and new CDs are distributed to the patrol force.

With all this information, RAC staffers can usually diagnose the problem, and often they can perform the necessary repairs as well. Information displayed on the notebook computer enables them to do more complex repairs than would otherwise be possible. Even so, the average RAC repair stop takes less than 30 minutes.

Better service in less time—the result of rethinking the roadside troubleshooting process at the Royal Automobile Club.

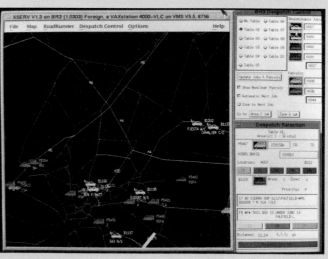

FIGURE 5.12
Videodisks and Multimedia
Like CD-ROM disks, videodisks are a read-only medium. Because videodisk players can be attached to computers, they are often an important component of multimedia systems.

a) The use of videodisks in the classroom is increasing. Here, a grammar school teacher uses the *Windows in Science* videodisk package to teach her students about the solar system.

b) A screen from IBM's comprehensive 180-hour *Columbus* Ultimedia multimedia package. Each of the program's ten segments is delivered through a combination of CD-ROM disks and two-sided videodisks.

For the 500th anniversary of Columbus's discovery of the "New World," IBM created a comprehensive multimedia program delivered on videodisk. Developed by Hollywood filmmaker and graphic artist Bob Abel, *Columbus* (Figure 5.12b) has 180 hours of interactive instruction, including a rich video collection of manuscripts, artworks, and interviews with 60 of the world's leading authorities on Columbus and his times. The series contains segments on Columbus and his vision, the world in 1492, money and power in fifteenth-century Europe, and changing views of the world and of humankind in the Renaissance. Each segment is delivered through a combination of CD-ROM disks and two-sided videodisks. The series is designed to run on an IBM personal computer with a CD-ROM drive, videodisk player, and high-resolution monitor.

IBM used multimedia technology for *Columbus* (and for several of its other educational titles) because the company believes that "to make learning fun, you have to make the student not just an observer of the discovery of America, but a participant, a discoverer him or herself."

NEWER OPTICAL DISK FORMATS.   CD-ROM disks and videodisks, which will only read data, were the first commercial applications of the optical disk. Two new types of optical disks—WORM and EOS—permit computer users also to *record* data.

- **Write once, read many (WORM) optical disks** allow users to write information to a disk only once, but to read it many times (Figure 5.13). People can use WORM disks to store and retrieve archival information or historical data. Because WORM systems do not allow the alteration of data once they are entered, WORM is used where the security of data is essential—in financial and legal documents, for example.
- **Erasable optical storage (EOS) disks** combine the erasability and editing options of magnetic storage devices with the permanence, capacity, and reliability of optical storage. Erasable optical disks tend to be even more reliable than their magnetic counterparts (which are highly reliable). Unlike magnetic disks, EOS disks are immune to the harmful effects of stray magnetic fields that can erase data and information stored on magnetic storage media. And

FIGURE 5.13
WORM Optical Disk
The "write once, read many"
technology is useful in storing
and retrieving archival
information or historical data.

because they rely on light beams instead of mechanical heads to read and write information, they are immune to head crashes.

If anything is more important to a bank than accuracy, it's the ability to pass an audit. A bank must be able to show the details of its transactions, when they occurred, and the sequence in which they occurred. The *audit trail*—as the series of documents describing a transaction is called—is a permanent record that can serve as a legal document should the need ever arise. Countless banks now use WORM optical disks to preserve their auditing activities. Transaction documents are imaged and recorded on WORM disks. Once recorded, this audit trail cannot be altered in any way. Yet all the details are readily accessible to the bank's personnel and can be retrieved easily through a computer network. WORM technology helps banks fulfill their legal obligations to provide audit trails and good customer service and to maintain records efficiently.

Computer-driven optical recording technology is advancing rapidly. As costs drop and read/write times become speedier, we are certain to see widespread use of read/write optical disks in business.

The *Information Technology in Practice* feature entitled "CD-ROM Publishing Puts Information at Your Fingertips" suggests how widespread optical disk usage will become.

input/output controller
A data controller with its own
memory and processor that
regulate the flow of data to
and from peripheral devices.

COMPUTER INTERFACES.   To use secondary storage devices, such as magnetic disk and tape, a computer must have a data controller with its own memory and processor to regulate the flow of data to and from peripherals. This **input/output controller,** which usually resides on a circuit board, reads data serially from the storage device and translates it into parallel format for input into the central processor or processor chip through the I/O bus. The board is mounted in a slot inside the main computer unit.

Interaction with Computers: Input Devices

Secondary storage and peripheral devices interact with computers through interfaces and ports. People use input and output devices connected to the ports to interact with the computer. Recall that input is the data or information entered into a computer, while output is the result of inputting and processing returned by the computer, either directly to a person using the system or to secondary

INFORMATION TECHNOLOGY IN PRACTICE

CD-ROM Publishing Puts Information at Your Fingertips

If you've ever wasted hours thumbing through a book in search of an elusive fact or statistic, you're going to love CD-ROM publishing—the distribution of databases, catalogs, manuals, reference works, and even games on CD-ROM disks that can be searched from beginning to end in minutes. Now that CD-ROM drives are becoming more affordable, this relatively new form of publishing is really taking off. There's already a catalog of *CD-ROMs in Print* (available in paper and on CD-ROM) and a top-10 bestseller list compiled by *Fortune* magazine:

1. *Monarch Notes* (Bureau Development). Study guides for 200 literary classics, combined with excerpts read by professional actors, period music, and high-resolution illustrations. (1)*

2. *Microsoft Bookshelf* (Microsoft). The full text of several highly integrated, fully searchable reference works (including the *Concise Columbia Encyclopedia*), complete with illustrations, animations, and audio; updated yearly. (2)

3. *Mammals: A Multimedia Encyclopedia* (National Geographic Society and IBM). A complete mammal encyclopedia that combines animated sequences, full-color photos, and video with sound clips for every known animal from the aardvark to the zebra. Based on National Geographic's acclaimed two-volume work. (1)

4. *Wild Places* (Aris Entertainment). One part of the "Media Clips" series. A combination of North American

nature photography and 50 original New Age music compositions that can be used, royalty free, to dress up multimedia sales and training presentations. (2)

5. *Great Literature* (Bureau Development). The full text of 1,896 literary classics combined with illustrations, narration, music, and a search-and-browse feature. (1)

6. *The New Grolier Multimedia Encyclopedia* (Grolier Electronic Publishing). The complete text of the print version's 33,000 articles, supplemented with pictures, maps, sound, and video. (2)

7. *Reference Library* (The Software Toolworks). The full text of the seven works contained in the legendary *New York Library Desk Reference*, including *Webster's New World Thesaurus*. (1)

8. *Sherlock Holmes, Consulting Detective* (Icom Simulations). Ninety minutes of video that let users test their powers of deductive reasoning. (2)

9. *The Oxford English Dictionary, Second Edition* (Oxford University Press). The authoritative 21-volume dictionary offered on a single CD-ROM disk for one-third the price of the printed version. (1)

10. *Street Atlas USA* (DeLorme Mapping). A map containing every street in the United States; valuable for planning business trips and vacations. (1)

With National Geographic's *Mammals Multimedia Encyclopedia,* viewers can see full-color photos of animals in their habitats, hear their distinctive sounds, and watch brief educational videos.

Note: (1) = IBM PC or IBM-compatible only. (2) = IBM PC or Apple Macintosh.
SOURCE: Fortune, ©1992 Time Inc. All rights reserved.

input device
A device by which input is fed into a computer's central processor.

output device
A device that makes the results of processing available outside of the computer.

storage. **Input devices** are the means by which input is fed into the central processor. **Output devices** make the results of processing available outside of the computer.

The six most commonly used input devices are keyboards, terminals, scanners, digitizers, digital cameras, and voice and sound input devices. Multimedia audio-visual devices are likely to be used more frequently in the future.

Keyboards

keyboard
The most common computer input device.

The most visible and common input device is the computer **keyboard** (see Figure 2.3). All keyboards are used to enter data and text information into a computer, but computer keyboards differ in four ways:

1. **Characters.** Both alphabetic and symbolic keyboards are available; the choice depends on the country in which the computer is used. In Japan, a symbolic keyboard containing the characters of the Kanji language is the norm. In most other countries, an English-language keyboard is the norm, with U.S. and international versions available.
2. **Key arrangement.** The arrangement of the keyboard's keys varies. The *QWERTY keyboard* (Figure 5.14) is the most common in English-speaking countries. This keyboard uses the conventional typewriter layout, in which the top row of alphabetic keys begins with the letters *Q, W, E, R, T,* and *Y*

FIGURE 5.14 *The QWERTY Keyboard*

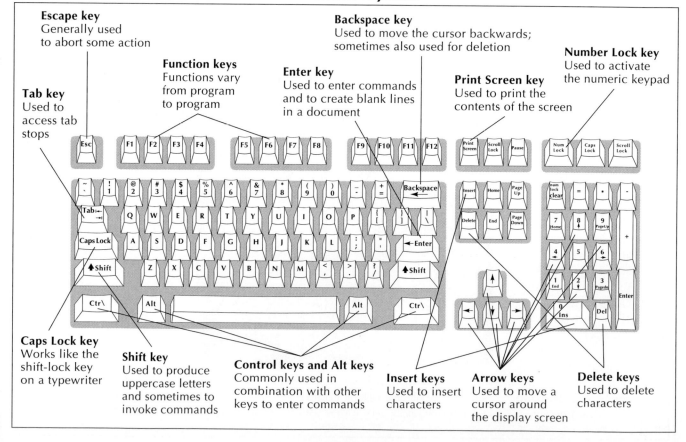

Escape key
Generally used to abort some action

Backspace key
Used to move the cursor backwards; sometimes also used for deletion

Number Lock key
Used to activate the numeric keypad

Function keys
Functions vary from program to program

Enter key
Used to enter commands and to create blank lines in a document

Print Screen key
Used to print the contents of the screen

Tab key
Used to access tab stops

Caps Lock key
Works like the shift-lock key on a typewriter

Shift key
Used to produce uppercase letters and sometimes to invoke commands

Control keys and Alt keys
Commonly used in combination with other keys to enter commands

Insert keys
Used to insert characters

Arrow keys
Used to move a cursor around the display screen

Delete keys
Used to delete characters

(reading from left to right). A newer design, called the *Dvorak keyboard,* uses an arrangement whereby the most used letters are placed in the most accessible places. Thus, the five English-language vowels (*A, E, I, O, U*) are the home keys of the left hand, while the five most often used consonants (*D, H, N, S, T*) are the home keys of the right hand. The next most frequently used letters are on the keys one row up, the next easiest position to reach.

Many countries' languages contain special characters that are not used in English words—for example, *à, á, â, ã, ä, å, æ, ç, ñ, ø, ¿,* and *¡.* Others have different alphabets. Keyboards used in these countries contain those characters and alphabets.

3. **Special-purpose keys.** Certain keys are designed to assist the user to enter data or information (e.g., the numeric keypad found to the right of the alphabetic keyboard section on many keyboards, as in Figure 5.14) or to control processing (the *Ctrl* and *Alt* keys). The uses of these special **function keys** vary from program to program. For example, the F7 key is used in one software package to search a document for specified words or phrases, in another to turn text from bold to italics, and in another to print a report.

4. **Detachability.** Most desktop computers have keyboards that can be detached from the rest of the computer system. However, built-in keyboards, the norm for early microcomputers, are still popular and are the norm for notebook and laptop computers.

> **function key**
> A key designed to assist the computer's user to enter data and information or to control processing.

Choosing a keyboard is often a very personal matter. The touch, the placement of keys, and the presence or absence of a click when keys are depressed are factors that can affect a user's level of comfort with a computer. Proper placement of the keyboard is also a factor in personal health.

Frequent computer use sometimes leads to such physical problems as carpal tunnel syndrome and tendinitis (muscle stiffness in the wrists). To prevent these problems, several manufacturers have devised a new style of keyboard for both Apple Macintosh and IBM-compatible computers (Figure 5.15). In contrast to the conventional fixed straight keyboard, these ergonomic keyboards split in the middle so that the portion designed to be used by each hand can be positioned at an angle that corresponds to the natural position of that hand. Since the two sections of the keyboard are movable, they can be adjusted by the individual to a position that feels most comfortable.

The *Information Technology in Practice* feature entitled "What You Need to Know About Ergonomics" explains more about the importance of having the right physical setup when using information technology.

FIGURE 5.15
Ergonomic Keyboards
These adjustable keyboards help reduce physical problems.

INFORMATION TECHNOLOGY IN PRACTICE

What You Need to Know About Ergonomics

Many computer-dependent workers have been disabled by carpal tunnel syndrome, an extremely painful condition due to damage in the nerves and tendons of the wrists. You can protect yourself (and the people you'll be managing) against this condition

through *ergonomics,* the study of how human bodies interact with equipment in the workplace. The table below lists a few of the problems to watch for—and some solutions, should you encounter them.

THE ERGONOMIC WORKSTATION

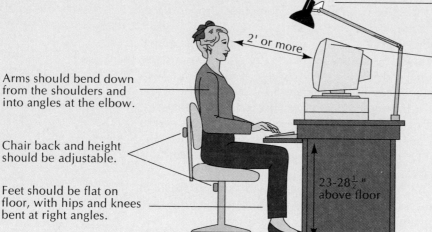

Use a reading lamp for close work, indirect light for general illumination.

2' or more

Top of screen should be no higher than eye level.

Arms should bend down from the shoulders and into angles at the elbow.

Monitor should allow tilt/swivel adjustment.

Chair back and height should be adjustable.

Feet should be flat on floor, with hips and knees bent at right angles.

$23\text{-}28\frac{1}{2}''$ above floor

Terminals

terminal
A combination of keyboard and video screen that accepts input and displays it on the screen.

A **terminal** is a combination keyboard and video screen that accepts input, displays it on the video screen, and displays the output sent by the computer to which it is attached. There are three common types of terminals (Figure 5.16).

1. **Dumb terminals** do not contain processing capability. (That is, they do not have control units or arithmetic/logic units. When they do, they are called *intelligent terminals.*) Therefore, they can only accept input from the key-

THE PROBLEM	THE HIGH-TECH SOLUTION	THE LOW-TECH SOLUTION
Repetitive stress injuries (RSIs). Painful nerve and tissue damage to the wrists and back caused by long hours at poorly designed computer workstations. Accounts for about half of all occupational illnesses; costs employers an estimated $7 billion in lost productivity and medical expenses.	Hire an ergonomics expert to recommend an ergonomically correct chair and computer desk with an adjustable keyboard insert. The chair should allow you to sit with your feet flat on the floor and provide good support for your lower back. The chair cushion should slope down in front, to avoid putting pressure on the backs of your legs. When the chair is properly adjusted, the keyboard should be raised or lowered so that you can type with your wrists and hands parallel to the floor.	Be sure you've adjusted your present chair for optimum support and conformity to your body, using a footrest or cushion if necessary. If the keyboard is too low, prop it up on books; if too high, either adjust the chair height or shorten the table legs. Buy a foam rubber wrist rest and use it during frequent short breaks. Better yet, stop work every 30 minutes and walk around the room for a minute or so.
Electromagnetic emissions from computer monitors. There is concern that prolonged exposure to these emissions can cause miscarriages, cancer, and other health problems. Research is ongoing.	If your monitor doesn't conform to the stringent Swedish MPR2 guidelines for electromagnetic emissions, buy one that does or switch to a laptop using an LCD (liquid crystal display) screen. As an interim measure, invest in an "antiradiation" screen. It won't block emissions, but some brands claim to cut 99% of electric radiation, and all reduce overhead glare.	Keep your screen at least at arm's length, where emissions are only one-sixth to one-eighth the strength they are when you work closer than four feet to the back or sides of a monitor (electromagnetic emissions are two times stronger there than in front). Turn the monitor off when you aren't using the computer.
Eyestrain and related vision problems. Vision difficulties caused by staring at the glare and flicker of a monitor for long periods affect an estimated 10 million Americans.	If your monitor produces noticeable flicker, replace it or your graphics board with one that creates a more stable image. To help prevent vision-related problems install an antiradiation or glare screen, and avoid staring at it. Replace overhead fluorescent lighting with indirect and table-top task lighting that uses incandescent bulbs.	Minimize glare by positioning the monitor at a right angle to the window and wear an eyeshade to block too-bright overhead lights. To keep eyes from drying out and to reduce neck strain, adjust the monitor so that the top of the screen is even with your eyes and you're looking down slightly. Take frequent work breaks.
Sick building syndrome. Flulike symptoms that show up in people when ozone emissions from laser printers and photocopiers, as well as indoor pollutants, accumulate in their work areas.	Hire a consulting engineer to evaluate the ventilation system and make recommendations for reconfiguring work areas to obtain better air flow. Buy an air purifier for your work area.	Don't work near printers and photocopiers, which give off electromagnetic emissions as well as ozone emissions. Keep lots of live plants around—they're great at soaking up indoor pollutants.

board and display information from the remote computer to which they are attached. Dumb terminals send whatever is entered through the keyboard to the main computer and display whatever they receive from the main computer without doing any processing (not even simple arithmetic).

2. **Automated teller machines (ATMs)** are limited-function intelligent terminals that usually contain a small video display, a keyboard consisting of only a few keys, and perhaps a sound speaker. Banks have long used ATMs to dispense cash, accept deposits, and transfer funds between accounts. But the

FIGURE 5.16
*The Three Types
of Terminals*

The three most common types of terminals are dumb terminals, automatic teller machines, and point-of-sale terminals.

a) The PC attached to IBM's AS/400 is used as a dumb terminal. It only accepts input from the keyboard and displays information from the remote computer (not shown here) to which it is attached.

b) ATMs have revolutionized banking around the world and are now being used in the airline and entertainment industries also.

c) POS terminals are most frequently used in restaurants and in retail, department, and grocery stores.

use of ATMs is growing in other areas as well. Airlines are now employing them to dispense tickets, state motor vehicle offices to issue drivers' licenses, and entertainment promoters to sell concert and theater tickets.

3. **Point-of-sale (POS) terminals** are widely used in department, retail, and grocery stores. Designed to assist salespersons in conducting transactions, POS terminals feature special keys (such as Sale, Void, and Credit) and a numeric keypad similar to the one found on a calculator. They are usually connected to a computer that processes data entered by an employee, perhaps accepting a product or stock number and providing a price in return. Frequently, the data entered by employees into the system are also used to update product inventory information maintained on the computer to which the POS is connected.

Scanners

Keying numeric and text data and information into a computer takes time and always includes the possibility of error. As anyone who has ever done any typing knows, it is easy to strike the wrong key. To avoid errors, many companies use **source data automation,** a method of data entry in which data enter computers directly from their written or printed forms without the intermediate step of keying. **Scanning,** which was discussed in Chapter 1, transforms written or printed data or information into a digital form that is entered directly into the computer.

Scanners are used in many industries, including the pharmaceutical industry, where it is extremely important to maintain adequate supplies. Patients expect a pharmacy to have the medicine they need when they take their prescription to be filled. On the other hand, pharmacies don't want to hold too large a supply of any medicine, not only because excess inventories take up room, but also because many drugs have a brief shelf life.

To help druggists maintain the proper inventory balance, San Francisco–based McKesson Corp. has developed a scanner system. (See Critical Connection 3 in Chapter 2.) To place an order, the druggist passes a laser scanner over a shelf ticket in front of the item to be ordered. This single swipe of the scanner cap-

source data automation
A method of data entry in which details enter computers directly from their written or printed forms without the intermediate step of keying.

scanning
The process of transforming written or printed data or information into a digital form that is entered directly into the computer.

CRITICAL CONNECTION 3

Lufthansa Airlines' Chip-in Cards Eliminate Tickets

Desiring to make it more convenient for its frequent fliers to travel, Lufthansa Airlines, the German national airline, combined computer chip technology with credit card thinking to create its Chip-in chip card system, which is used at airports throughout Germany. When cardholders make reservations with their travel agent or with Lufthansa directly, they give the reservations agent only their personal chip card number, and a reservation for them is entered into Lufthansa's system.

When cardholding travelers arrive at the airport, they simply wave their card in front of a Lufthansa ATM-style terminal. A radio signal from the terminal activates the card, transferring information about the traveler from it into the system. Then the terminal issues a printout listing departure gate, boarding time, seat assignment, and frequent flier mileage credit.

At the boarding gate, the Chip-in card provides an additional convenience: the traveler need only wave it in front of a small computer terminal in order to board the aircraft. Chip-in cards eliminate the need for a gate check-in, while providing added security that benefits both passenger and airline.

tures the product's name and the amount of it the pharmacist usually orders. These data are captured in a handheld computer that is later connected to a telephone line to McKesson's order department.

When the order arrives at McKesson, it is electronically transferred into the company's order-processing system. Because entries like this do not have to be keyed, mistakes are rare. When McKesson's employees fill the order, IT again plays a pivotal role. Strapped to the wrist of each employee is a combination portable computer, laser scanner, and two-way radio (Figure 5.17). Details of the order are transmitted by radio from the central computer to the wrist computer, telling the employee which item is needed and where it is located in the ware-

FIGURE 5.17

Source Data Automation at McKesson

Order fillers at McKesson Corp. use AcuMax wrist computers to locate inventory and bill customers' accounts directly.

house. When the order filler reaches the stock location, a quick point of the laser scanner at the shelf ticket confirms that the item is correct. When the worker pulls the stock, McKesson's inventory records are adjusted and the pulled item is added to the customer's bill.

Clearly, both parties benefit from this system. The customer gets fast service, often receiving the item within 24 to 48 hours of placing the order. McKesson avoids costly errors (a mistake costs five to seven times more than a correctly filled order) and ensures accurate inventory and billing information—not to mention satisfied, repeat customers.

There are two types of scanning: optical character recognition and image scanning.

OPTICAL CHARACTER RECOGNITION.   The term **optical character recognition (OCR)** refers to devices that can read information printed on paper and convert it into computer-processable form. There are three types of OCR: optical mark readers, optical character readers, and optical code readers.

Optical mark readers recognize the presence and location of dark marks on a special form (Figure 5.18) as the form is scanned. Many standardized tests, such as the SAT, use this format. In answering questions, students blacken designated spots on the scannable test form. The completed form is read by an OCR scanner, which sends the student's responses to a processor that determines the number of right and wrong answers and computes the student's final score. Government and medical offices also use optical mark readers to take large surveys (e.g.,

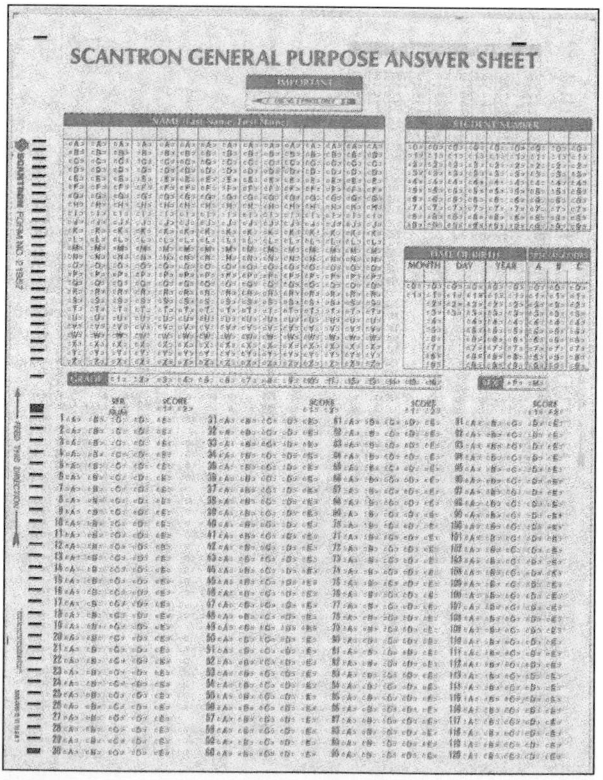

optical character recognition (OCR)
A technology by which devices read information on paper and convert it into computer-processable form.

optical mark reader
An OCR device that recognizes the location of dark marks on a special form as the form is scanned.

FIGURE 5.18
Sample Optical Mark Test Form
Many standardized tests use optical mark readers to determine scores. In answering questions, the test taker blackens a designated spot on the test form, which is then read and graded by an OCR scanner.
Courtesy Scan-Tron Corporation

marketing research surveys and the U.S. Census). The efficiency and reliability of optical mark readers allow these organizations to capture a large volume of information in a consistent format.

If you took the SAT or a similar college entrance exam, you probably sat in a large room with hundreds of other sweating students. You got a test booklet and an answer sheet on which you blackened the letter *a, b, c,* or *d* using a No. 2 pencil. This process may soon be obsolete.

Students can now take certain standardized multiple-choice exams on a computer. The main advantage of this is convenience. (The tests are not any easier.) Instead of adhering to the traditional Saturday test schedule, SAT takers can now call some test centers and make an appointment to take the test on any weekday. And instead of waiting six to eight weeks to find out their results, test takers (with enough courage) can ask the computer to flash the score as soon as they complete the exam. ■

Optical character readers recognize printed information rather than just dark marks. Optical character readers are often used by retail stores to read the product number of store merchandise, by libraries to read the call number of a library book, and by mail-order companies to read merchandise order numbers (Figure 5.19). Bank checks are processed by a special form of optical character reading

optical character reader
An OCR device that recognizes printed information rather than just dark marks.

FIGURE 5.19
Optical Character Reading
The Doubleday Book Club, headquartered in Garden City, N.Y., uses optical character reading on its new member enrollment forms. Members then order books on a different form, which is also read with OCR technology.

N762-3
YES! Send me 5 Books for 99¢ when I join
Please enroll me in *Doubleday Book Club* according to the risk-free membership plan described in the accompanying magazine. Send me the 5 BOOKS I've indicated, and my FREE GIFT. Bill me just 99¢, plus shipping and handling. I agree to purchase 4 more books in the next 2 years.

Choose your FREE GIFT here:
☐ Free Umbrella Tote Set #9159
or
☐ Free Book

Please initial here_____

0123456789

If you select a book that counts as 2 choices, write the first 4 digits of the book number in one row of boxes and 9999 in the next.

DOUBLEDAY
BOOK CLUB

85/86

MONEY-SAVING OPPORTUNITY
Send me the book indicated here. Bill me just $2.99, plus shipping and handling (books that count as two choices not eligible)

93286 85 86 9159 45

FALL 93

magnetic ink character recognition

A form of optical character reading in which preprinted information written in magnetic ink is read optically or sensed magnetically.

optical code reader

An OCR device used to read bar codes.

Universal Product Code (UPC)

A bar code that identifies a product by a series of vertical lines of varying widths representing a unique product number.

called **magnetic ink character recognition.** The check, bank number, and customer account number—all of which are preprinted in magnetic ink on the check—are read optically or sensed magnetically (Figure 5.20).

Optical code readers are used by supermarkets and other large retail stores. When customers check out at the cash register, the items they selected for purchase are usually passed over a piece of glass covering an optical scanner, which reads the **Universal Product Code (UPC)** printed on the package. The UPC is a bar code that identifies the product by a series of vertical lines of varying width representing a unique product number. This number is sent to a store computer, which contains pricing and inventory information. The price is rung up at the register, and in many systems the inventory information is updated at the same time. Alternatively, the checkout cashier may pass a handheld scanner (a *wand* or *gun*) over the UPC code (see Figure 2.7b).

Catalina Marketing of Anaheim, California, has converted the supermarket checkout scanner into an effective marketing tool. The company connects a personal computer to each checkout scanner to capture information on a purchase as the customer is making it. Using quick processing, the computer can then issue the customer a coupon to promote additional purchases. Suppose, for example, the customer is buying cat litter. The computer, thus informed that the customer probably has a cat, will print out a coupon for a cat food the store (or manufacturer) wishes to promote. Say, instead, the purchase is a six-pack of Pepsi. The Coca-Cola Company, Pepsi's biggest competitor, may have arranged for Catalina's backroom computer to print out for the Pepsi customer a two-for-one coupon for a six-pack of Coke. Or Pepsi may have arranged for a "half-off" coupon for Frito-Lay potato chips to be printed out with a purchase of Pepsi (Frito-Lay is owned by Pepsi).

image scanning

Examining an image and translating lines, dots, and marks into digital form.

IMAGE SCANNING. To scan drawings, entire documents, or photographic images, **image scanning** must be used. The scanner examines the images and translates its lines, dots, and marks into digital form.

FIGURE 5.20

Magnetic Ink Character Recognition

Magnetic ink characters are located on the bottom line of a check. On the left side are the bank identification number and the customer's account number. On the right side is the check amount, which is imprinted on the check after it has been cashed.

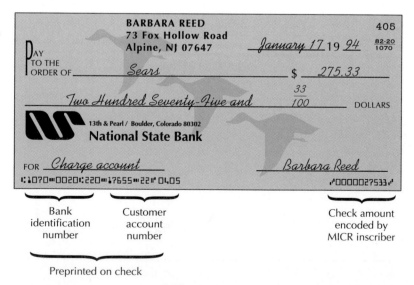

Flatbed scanners (Figure 2.6a) work like office photocopiers. The flatbed scanner is attached by cable to an input/output port on the computer. The person doing the scanning places the photograph, drawing, or page of text face down on a glass plate on top of the scanner. As a bar of light, controlled by software, passes beneath the glass, the light is reflected off the printed image onto a grid of photosensitive cells. The number of light sensors in the scanner determines the quality of the scanner's optical **resolution**—that is, the clarity or sharpness of the image. A scanner with a resolution of 300 dots per inch (DPI), for example, contains 300 sensors in each inch of the scanning mechanism. The more dots per inch, the higher the resolution (the sharper the image). The flatbed scanners used with most personal computers have resolutions ranging from 300 to 600 DPI. Scanners used by commercial printers have resolutions of up to 2,400 DPI, providing much sharper images.

As the flatbed scanner's light bar moves down the page, the image data are collected dot by dot. Depending on the type of scanner, the data may be sensed as shades of gray or in 256 or more colors. When the image is transmitted from the scanner to the central processor, color information is included so that the image can be properly recreated for processing, display, or storage.

Handheld scanners (Figure 2.6b) offer an inexpensive alternative to flatbed scanners, which typically cost $1,000 or more. Although they are not as powerful or as easy to use as flatbeds, handhelds often sell for less than one-third the price of flatbeds. Like flatbeds, they are attached by a cable to an input/output port on the computer. The user must place the document, drawing, or photograph to be scanned on a flat surface. As the scanner is dragged slowly from one end of the document to the other, the details under it are translated into dot patterns that can be processed by the computer. Handheld scanners are usually only several inches wide and thus, unlike flatbed scanners, cannot scan the entire width of a page at once.

The benefits of image scanning are well known to Consolidated Freightways, a nationwide freight carrier. It used to take the company as long as three weeks to respond to a customer's inquiry about an invoice, a damage claim, or a complaint. All this time was needed to locate and assemble the documents required to answer the inquiry. Then, in the early 1990s, the company invested $10 million in an imaging system. All documents and correspondence related to a shipment are now scanned and stored in the company's computer system. Up to three years' worth of shipping and billing documents—nearly 60 million pieces of paper—are accessible through the centralized system. Now, when a customer makes an inquiry, whether in writing or over the telephone, a customer service rep can get copies of all pertinent documents in approximately 10 minutes.

Digitizers

A **digitizer** is an input device that translates measured distances into digital values that the computer can process. As the digitizing device moves, electric pulses inform the computer of the change in position. The computer responds by shifting an indicator, such as an arrow (↖) or cross-hair cursor (✛), to the same position as the digitizer.

There are six types of digitizers, all of which must be connected to the computer by a communications cable.

- The **mouse** (see Figure 2.5) is a familiar input device found with many desktop computers. As the ball on the underside of the mouse moves, the horizontal

flatbed scanner
A large image scanner that works like an office photocopier.

resolution
The clarity or sharpness of an image.

handheld scanner
An inexpensive hand-held alternative to the flatbed image scanner.

digitizer
An input device that translates measured distances into digital values that the computer can process.

mouse
An input device with a small ball underneath that rotates, causing a corresponding movement of a pointer on a display screen.

and vertical coordinates of the corresponding mouse cursor change. By checking these coordinates, the computer knows where the cursor is and displays the indicator in the appropriate place on the display screen.

pointing stick

A device that positions the cursor on the computer screen.

- The **pointing stick** (Figure 5.21), an alternative to the mouse often used with notebook computers, directs the cursor across the computer screen. The growing use of notebook computers necessitated the development of a device more compact that the mouse. The pointing stick, embedded in the notebook's keyboard above the *b* key, is used to position the cursor on the display screen. The motion of the cursor on the screen is controlled by the amount of pressure applied to the point stick (it does not actually move, but rather senses finger pressure). The speed at which the cursor moves corresponds to the amount of pressure on the stick.

  When a computer is equipped with a point stick, the click buttons normally found on a mouse are located below the keys. As with a conventional mouse, the function of these click buttons is determined by the application program in use.

  The pointing stick offers two advantages. First, it does not take any extra space, so you can use the notebook computer in tight spaces (such as on the serving tray of an airline seat) where you would not have room to move a mouse to position a cursor. Second, you do not have to move your fingers from their typing position in order to use the pointing stick. Because of these advantages, a growing number of notebook manufacturers are adding the pointing stick, originated by IBM, to their computers.

light pen

An input device that uses a light-sensitive cell to draw images and to select options from a menu of choices displayed on a computer screen.

- The **light pen** (Figure 5.22) looks like a ballpoint pen, except that its ball is actually a light-sensitive cell. When the tip of the light pen touches a computer's display screen, the computer senses the pen's location on the screen and transmits this information to the processor. Movement by the light pen in any direction is sensed by the processor, which determines the meaning of the movement according to the application program in use. Light pens are used both to draw images and to select options from a menu of choices displayed on the screen.

FIGURE 5.21

Pointing Stick

The pointing stick is often used instead of a mouse with notebook computers to direct the cursor across the screen.

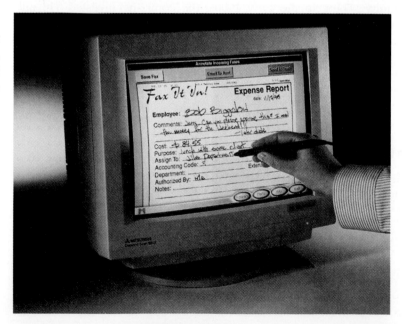

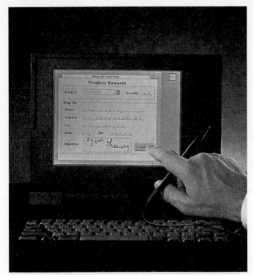

FIGURE 5.22
MicroTouch Light Pen
The MicroTouch light pen works in concert with shipping/billing software and a touch screen developed by Microsoft. After the requisitioner has signed his name with the light pen, he simply touches the "Send" button on the screen to send the order to company headquarters.

FIGURE 5.23
Logitech Joystick
Although joysticks are often associated with computer games, they are also used in training programs for pilots and astronauts.

- Often used to control computer games or simulations, the **joystick** (Figure 5.23) extends vertically from a pivot connected mechanically and electronically to a control box. As the joystick is moved up, down, right, left, or diagonally, it sends a signal to the computer's processor, which senses the distance and direction of the movement. These are incorporated as input data into the program, which then determines action status and steps to take. A visual display of the movement appears on the computer screen.

Want to fly a jet fighter without spending hours and hours of time training? Get the Falcon or the Microsoft Flight Simulator. Each of these computer games provides the operator with a realistic simulation of the inside of a fighter cockpit, complete with moving dials and gauges. Grab the joystick, pull back on it, and you will feel yourself gaining altitude quickly. Look to the right or left on the screen and you'll see a terrain with trees, buildings, and other objects getting smaller and smaller as you climb higher. Push the joystick to the right and you will begin a turn. Push it too far to the right, and you'll be flying upside down.

joystick
An input device used to control the actions in computer games or simulations. The joystick extends vertically from a control box.

FIGURE 5.24   *Logitech Trackball*

The trackball is gaining in popularity as an input device. Some notebook and laptop computers are now incorporating trackballs directly into their keyboards.

trackball

An input device that consists of a ball mounted on rollers. As the user rotates the ball in any direction, the computer senses the movement and moves the cursor in the corresponding direction.

digitizing tablet

A device by which an image on paper can be translated into electronic form.

- A **trackball** (Figure 5.24) is a ball mounted on rollers. As the user rotates the ball in any direction, the computer senses the movement in much the same way that it does with a joystick. Roll the ball to the left, and the cursor will move to the left. Roll the ball to the right, and the cursor will move with it. Many notebook computers use a trackball instead of a mouse. The click buttons, as on a mouse, are located next to the trackball.

- Images on paper can be translated into electronic form by tracing the image with a **digitizing tablet** (Figure 5.25). As a penlike stylus or cross-hair pointer is passed over the features of the drawing, the computer senses the dots and lines that compose the drawing and creates an electronic version in memory while displaying the information visually on the screen. Once the drawing is complete, the digitized form can be stored or modified.

Note that mice, joysticks, and trackballs all recognize movement and position, while light pens and digitizing tablets recognize the presence of absence of infor-

FIGURE 5.25
A Digitizing Tablet in Action

Digitizing tablets are often used in combination with graphic design programs. Here a clothing designer creates a sweater design. Once the original design is created, it can be stored in the computer's memory and modified later.

mation as they move. Digitizing devices are in widespread use on computers of all sizes.

Digital Cameras

Digital cameras are quickly gaining a foothold in photography. A **digital camera** (Figure 5.26) captures a photographic image as a collection of tightly grouped dots. Each digital image is captured on light-sensitive memory chips that can store approximately 20 to 75 images, depending on the make of the camera and size of its memory.

After digital images are captured, they can be copied into computer memory or stored on disk. These images can be printed or processed to change the size or alter the color of the dots, or even to remove them entirely. In addition, images captured by digital cameras can be transmitted over a communications link in the same way an c-mail image is.

A growing number of news photographers are relying on the digital camera because of the good quality of its photographs and the convenience of the digital form. Is a digital camera in your future? Perhaps not for taking family snapshots. But if you need to capture images for computer processing, there's a good chance that you will be using a digital camera soon.

digital camera
A device that captures a photographic image as a collection of tightly grouped dots that can be stored on disk or in memory.

Voice and Sound Input Devices

Digitizing the spoken word is being done more and more to take advantage of the multimedia capability of computers. Spoken words are captured in digital form by **voice input devices** connected to the computer. A microphone is attached either to a voice expansion board that fits within an internal slot in the computer or to a special microphone jack on the computer (see Figure 2.8). Special software controls the process of capturing and digitizing the human voice or any other sounds sensed by the microphone. Figure 5.27 explains how this process works.

The U.S. Transportation Command is considering using voice input devices to change the way it handles the movement of its aircraft around the world. When the organization's aircraft dispatchers are notified of bad weather or that an aircraft is running low on fuel, they must divert the plane to the airport that is closest to its current location. But since there are so many different airports, with varying capabilities for handling large and small aircraft, it is sometimes impossible for the dispatchers to recall instantly all of the information they need to direct the pilot.

voice input device
An input device that can be attached to a computer to capture the spoken word in digital form.

FIGURE 5.26 *Digital Cameras*
Digital cameras capture photographic images as a collection of tightly grouped dots, captured on light sensitive memory chips.

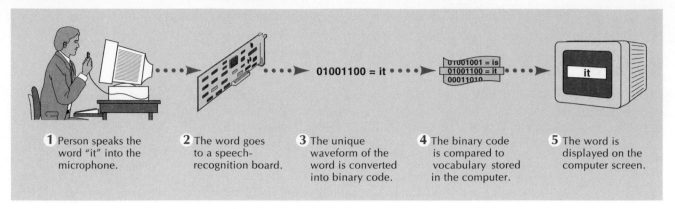

1 Person speaks the word "it" into the microphone.

2 The word goes to a speech-recognition board.

3 The unique waveform of the word is converted into binary code.

4 The binary code is compared to vocabulary stored in the computer.

5 The word is displayed on the computer screen.

FIGURE 5.27   *Capturing and Digitizing Sounds*

For this reason, the organization is thinking of creating a voice input system to assist dispatchers. Then, when a fog rolls in, making it impossible for an incoming aircraft to land at its intended destination in, say, Frankfurt, the dispatcher will be able to speak into a microphone built into the control tower computer: "Give me a list of all airports within one hour of Frankfurt, Germany." Instantly, a list will appear on the screen. The dispatcher then can query the computer by voice again: "Which airport is closest and not closed because of weather?"

Until recently, research in voice, sound, and speech input advanced slowly because of technological limitations. Most English speakers have a vocabulary of approximately 20,000 words, but the earliest voice input boards could usually recognize fewer than 100. One problem was that a huge amount of storage was needed to hold a decent vocabulary list. Another was the length of time needed to search the list of words.

Massive leaps in storage technology (both for primary memory and for secondary storage) and more powerful (i.e., faster) processors are solving these problems. Boards that have a vocabulary capacity of over 1,000 words are already in use on microcomputers. Actually, some of the newer systems have voice units with vocabularies that exceed 10,000 words. It is safe to assume that the technical barriers to voice input will eventually disappear.

But how and where would voice input be used? Certainly there are many situations where voice commands would be helpful—for example, in heavy manufacturing. Would people want to give dictation to their computer and have the system transform their rambling speech into a polished document with correct spelling and good grammar? Would they like their automobiles to have a voice-controlled guidance system that replaced the dashboard and stick-shift levers? And what about video arcade games? Could voice control create a new dimension of entertainment?

It is not too early for you to start thinking about these possibilities. Recognized experts have yet to emerge in this area; perhaps you can be one of the first. ■

Multimedia Audiovisual Devices

As microprocessor chips become more sophisticated and memory capacity expands, the line between computer input devices and devices currently used only for entertainment will blur. In fact, three common multimedia consumer electronic products are already being used as sources of input and output for computer processing (Figure 5.28a):

1. **Television.** Partitions (or "windows") of computer display screens can show several television programs simultaneously (Figure 5.28b). Whether the latest news, business reports, or even closed-circuit TV, these programs can be shown, captured, and stored for later viewing. The *Information Technology in Practice* feature entitled "Multimedia Lends a Helping Hand to Immigrant Workers" explores the benefits of a successful multimedia system that uses television.
2. **VCRs.** Whatever can be captured on video can be entered into a computer. After an image from a videotape is transferred into the memory of a computer through a video interface port, the digital form can be displayed, processed, and stored like any other data.
3. **Video cameras.** Both handheld and larger video cameras can be connected to a computer port directly. Anything the camera's lens sees can be input for display, processing, and storage.

More consumer-oriented input devices will surely follow these, as we discuss in Chapter 15.

Texaco uses several multimedia devices in its everyday operations. A good part of the company's profitability depends on getting information that managers need to determine when to buy and sell crude oil on the world market. Missing a breaking news item by just a few minutes can mean millions of dollars in lost opportunities. Texaco's trading room is equipped with high-speed computers that brokers use to create contracts electronically via a worldwide network. In one corner of the display screen is a window showing Cable News Network (CNN) in color, with full sound—the same live broadcast available on an ordinary color television. This use of IT and multimedia capability to obtain up-to-date news constantly gives Texaco's traders a solid advantage over competitors who still rely on delayed news broadcasts.

FIGURE 5.28
Multimedia Audiovisual Devices
The line between computer input devices and devices used for entertainment only is blurring.

a) The three most common consumer products used as sources of input and output for computer processing are television, VCRs, and video cameras.

b) "Windows" of TV screens can show several programs simultaneously. This feature can be adapted to multimedia uses.

INFORMATION TECHNOLOGY IN PRACTICE

Multimedia Lends a Helping Hand to Immigrant Workers

In their rush toward the global economy, Americans sometimes forget the valuable contributions made by recent immigrants, especially the migrant workers who labor in the fields and orchards of the United States. Many of these people know little or no English and therefore have trouble communicating with the government workers responsible for deciding whether they qualify for government assistance, such as food stamps and Medicare. The situation has been looking a little brighter in Tulare County, California, though, since the county government created a multimedia system called "The Tulare Touch" that lets the workers prequalify themselves for aid.

The system is extremely easy to use. Each multimedia station presents a video of a host or hostess who uses one of six languages—English, Spanish, and four Southeast Asian languages—to introduce the system, ask questions, and explain how to answer by pressing a blinking word or animated graphic on the touch screen (there is no keyboard). It is this combination of visual and audio cues, stored on a laser disk, that allows even illiterate workers to use the system. At the end of the interview, the system prints out a completed application form, which is then reviewed and approved by an eligibility worker.

Immigrants particularly like the system's hosts and hostesses—the Latina hostess, for example, is a popular television personality. The eligibility workers like the system, too, because it cuts back on paperwork, giving them more time to spend with applicants. And Tulare County likes the system most of all—in return for a $3 million investment, the county expects to save $20 million a year in welfare administration costs and to reduce overpayments to welfare applicants as well. Small wonder that government officials from around the country are trekking to Tulare County to study The Tulare Touch.

The ground-breaking Tulare Touch system offers multimedia instruction in six languages. A combination of audio and visual cues, stored on a laser disk, allows even illiterate workers to use the system.

SOURCES: Based on "The Emerging World of Multimedia," *I/S Analyzer,* March 1991, pp. 1–12; and John W. Verity et al., "Multimedia Computing: PCs That Do Everything but Walk the Dog," *Business Week,* August 12, 1991, pp. 62–63.

Audio Response Units

In the world of information technology, the spoken word is increasingly being thought of as a form of output. Data or information is transformed into sound by an **audio response unit** (also called a **speech synthesizer**) in the following manner. Upon receiving instructions from the central processor, the audio response unit retrieves the prerecorded voice messages and sounds stored in the *voice unit,* wherein they are assembled and sent to a speaker.

Audio response units are at work today in all types of business settings. Many supermarkets have them attached to their bar code scanners. As products are scanned, the response unit says the name of the product and its price aloud. Because they hear the price of an item, customers are assured that they are not being overcharged. The directory assistance services of public telephone companies and stock quotation services regularly use audio response units to give callers phone numbers, stock quotes, and trading volumes. Both the firm and the individual caller benefit from this speedier and cheaper service. Many newer airports around the world are using audio response systems to assist passengers. For instance, when you move between the concourses connecting the approximately 200 gates at Atlanta's Hartsfield International Airport, you do so on an easily accessible, complimentary shuttle train. A computer-controlled response unit announces the arrival of the vehicle at each gate and gives the traveler instructions on how to proceed from there. (It also controls the display of the same information in six different languages.)

audio response unit/ speech synthesizer

An output device that transforms data or information into sound.

Multimedia PCs

A great number of the desktop computers now purchased for use at work or at home are best described as **multimedia PCs** because they contain all the features of a PC (keyboard, mouse, disk storage, and a display unit) plus components that provide a capability for audio, video, animation, and graphics as well as text and data (Figure 5.29a). A multimedia PC has an audio board, stereo speakers connected to the audio board, and a CD-ROM drive. Above-average RAM storage and a high-resolution video card may be included as well. Many notebook computers are also equipped with some or all of these multimedia components (Figure 5.29b).

Multimedia PCs have become the norm as it has become more popular to present information and data using multimedia capabilities.

multimedia PC

A system that contains standard PC features but also has the capability to handle audio, video, animation, and graphics.

a)

b)

FIGURE 5.29
Multimedia PCs
a) Many desktop computers include components for audio, video, animation, and graphics.
b) This notebook computer includes a CD-ROM drive.

Interaction with Computers: Output and Information Distribution Devices

Five types of devices are used to display and distribute computer output: monitors, printers, plotters, film recorders, and digital cameras. Digital cameras were discussed in the previous section, on input devices. Here we describe the other four devices.

Visual Displays (Monitors)

A computer's visual display is its most visible component. Visual displays, usually called **video display terminals (VDTs)** or **monitors,** differ in size, color, resolution, bit mapping, and graphics standard.

video display terminal (VDT)/monitor

A computer's visual display.

RGB display

A video screen display with the ability to create 256 colors and several thousand variations on these colors by blending shades of red, green, and blue.

monochrome display

A video screen display that shows information using a single foreground color on a contrasting background color (e.g., black on white).

pixels

The dots used to create an image; the higher the number of dots, the better the resolution of the image.

- **Size.** Monitors come in many different sizes, from the small screen built into palmtops and laptops to the extra-large monitors used for special purposes. The standard monitor for personal computers is 13 to 16 inches (32 to 40 cm), measured diagonally, corner to corner. Large-screen monitors have been developed for use by engineers and illustrators, who need to examine fine details closely. These are commonly 16 and 17 inches (40 to 42 cm) wide and provide 45 to 60 percent more viewing area than standard monitors do.
- **Color.** Many monitors display color (Figure 5.30). These **RGB displays** can create 256 colors and several thousand variations on them by blending shades of red, green, and blue (hence the term *RGB display*). **Monochrome displays** show information using a single foreground color on a contrasting background color (e.g., white on black, black on white, amber on black, green on black).
- **Resolution.** Since all characters and images on a monitor are made up of dot patterns, the number of dots, or **pixels,** per inch determines resolution, or the sharpness of the image. A higher number of pixels means a sharper image. Common resolutions are as follows:

    640 columns × 480 rows of dots (640 × 480 = 307,200 pixels on the screen)
    800 columns × 600 rows (480,000 pixels)
    1,024 columns × 768 rows (786,432 pixels).

FIGURE 5.30

Color Computer Monitors

Until fairly recently, monochrome displays were the norm in computer monitors. With the explosion of computer graphics programs and capabilities, RGB displays have become much more common.

a) The Macintosh Quadra 800

b) MultiSync E1100

- **Bit mapping.** A monitor may or may not have bit-mapping capabilities. With **bit mapping,** each dot on the monitor can be controlled individually. Graphics created through bit mapping are sharp and crisp, without unseemly jagged edges. Prior to the introduction of bit mapping, **character addressing** was the norm. Character addressing permitted only letters, numbers, and other preformed letters and symbols—no lines or curved images—to be sent to and displayed on the display screen.
- **Graphics standard.** A graphics standard is one that combines resolution and use of color. A monitor's resolution and use of color are determined by a **graphics adapter card,** an interface board between computer and monitor that performs according to one of several widely used IBM-compatible standards: *color graphics adapter* (CGA—the oldest and lowest-resolution standard); *enhanced graphics adapter* (EGA); *video graphics array* (VGA); and *super VGA* (SVGA), which has the best resolution of all. Similar standards exist for Macintosh and other computers.

    Multisync/multiscan monitors are designed to work with a wide variety of graphics standards, automatically adjusting to provide the best possible resolution for the adapter card and computer configuration in use.

Resolution, color clarity, and graphics capabilities are steadily improving, making more sophisticated applications possible. Color and graphic displays on high-resolution monitors are changing the business of publishing (this entire book was designed and laid out using a color monitor), just as they are influencing the business of commerce and government.

bit mapping
A feature of some monitors that allows each dot on the monitor to be addressed or controlled individually. Graphics created through bit mapping are sharp and crisp.

character addressing
The precursor to bit mapping that allowed only full characters to be sent to and displayed on a VDT.

graphics adapter card
An interface board between a computer and monitor that is used to determine the monitor's resolution and use of color.

multisync/multiscan monitors
Monitors designed to work with a variety of graphics standards.

CRITICAL CONNECTION 4

IT: A New Ally in the War Against Disease

Scientists who battle cancer, heart disease, AIDS, and other life-threatening diseases have a powerful new ally in computer systems with large high-resolution color monitors that let them see their opponents "up close and personal."

Enlisting computers in the fight against disease is part of a new research technique called *rational drug design*. Instead of screening thousands of chemicals in the hope of finding one that might work, rational drug designers work backwards. Using what they know about how the body's immune system "locks" onto invaders, they search for chemicals that mimic or amplify the immune reaction. To do this, they create 3-D computer models of chemical molecules and body cells that can be displayed and manipulated on a computer screen. If a potential cure is found, the computer can perform a preliminary evaluation of the drug's impact in just minutes, instead of months or years.

Rational drug design was touched off in the late 1970s, when Squibb (a large international pharmaceutical manufacturer) used it to create a drug to treat high blood pressure. Since then, dozens of start-up companies devoted to rational drug design have sprung up. Agouron Pharmaceuticals, for example, now has an anticancer drug in testing. Within a decade, some experts predict, all drug companies will use these tools.

Printers

hard copy

The paper output from a printer.

impact printing

A printing process in which the paper and the character being printed come into contact with each other.

nonimpact printing

A printing process in which no physical contact occurs between the paper and the print device; the characters are produced on the paper through a heat, chemical, or spraying process.

laser printer

A nonimpact printer that uses laser beams to print an entire page at once.

A printer is an output device that produces **hard copy**—paper output. Two general categories of printers are impact and nonimpact printers (Figure 5.31).

In **impact printing,** the paper and the device printing the character come into contact with each other. In **nonimpact printing,** there is no physical contact between the paper and the print device. Instead, the characters are produced on the paper through a heat, chemical, or spraying process.

NONIMPACT PRINTERS. Laser, ink-jet, and thermal printing are the most frequently used kinds of nonimpact printers (see Figure 5.32).

- Because of their speed and capabilities, **laser printers** are the fastest-growing segment of the printer market. As the laser printer receives information from the central processor, it converts it into a laser beam (a narrow beam of light) that, in turn, encodes a photoconductor with the information. This process forms the character or image to be printed. The photoconductor attracts particles of *toner,* a black granular dust similar to that used in many photocopiers, which, when transferred to the paper, produce the full image. Finally, the image is fused to the paper by heat and pressure. The laser printer prints an entire page at once.

  The process is fast (from four to eight pages per minute on the slowest laser printers) and can print both text and images. Black-and-white laser printers are in widespread use now, and color laser printers are increasingly found in business and educational settings where multicolor documents (including visual transparencies) are needed to present data and information effectively. As prices continue to drop, color laser printers will be more attractive for use everywhere.

- **Ink-jet printers** spray tiny streams of ink from holes in the print mechanism onto the paper. The spray makes up a dot pattern that represents the character or image to be printed. Because ink-jet printers create characters and images by spraying ink rather than by striking preformed characters against paper, they are often used to create charts and graphs. The application software controls the information to be printed, and a controller within the printer oversees the actual printing process.

  Both color and black-and-white ink-jet printers are in widespread use. Versions are available for microcomputers as well as for larger computer systems.

- **Thermal printers** heat a wax-based colored ink contained in the printer ribbon and transfer it to a special paper. Three or four colored inks—usually yellow, magenta, cyan (blue), and black—are laid out in a repeating sequence of page-size panels along a length of the ribbon. Rollers sandwich the ribbon between the paper and a print head containing many small heating elements. These elements switch on and off, in correspondence to the characters and bits of information sent to the printer by the computer software. The paper must make four passes by the ribbon and heating element—one for each of the colors (Figure 5.33).

  Thermal printing is slower than single-pass black-and-white printing, but faster than ink-jet printing for color. It is also much cheaper than color laser processes.

a) IMPACT/DOT MATRIX PRINTING

Pin Patterns
The pins strike an inked ribbon that marks the paper with dots. The head signals fire the pins in different combinations so that each character is made up of several vertical dot patterns.

Ribbon

Pins

Paper

Dot Matrix Head
The printer head of a dot matrix printer contains a column of pins. The pins are driven by electromagnets responding to the head signals. These are binary signals that turn the electromagnets on or off.

Quality Printing
Seven pins are shown here for simplicity; good quality printers have 24 pins. To improve quality, the head may pass over the paper again and print dots that overlap with those printed on the first pass.

Head signal

Electromagnet drives hammer

Hammer strikes pin

Printer Control
All letters, numbers, and other characters have standard codes that the computer sends to the printer. A chip in the printer converts these codes into signals that drive the printer head as it moves across the paper and prints the characters. The power drive board amplifies the chip signals. Special motors move the head and paper to the right positions.

Printer chip

Power driver board

Head signal

b) NONIMPACT/LASER PRINTING

Like a dot-matrix printer, a laser printer builds characters up with dots, but the dots are so small that the printing is very detailed. A laser fires a beam of light at a spinning mirror. Another mirror and lenses then focus the moving beam onto a drum like that in a photocopier. Signals from the computer turn the beam on and off as it scans across the drum, building up an electrical image. The image is transferred onto the paper as in a photocopier.

Mirror

Lenses

Rotating Drum

Laser

Light beam

Paper

Spinning mirror

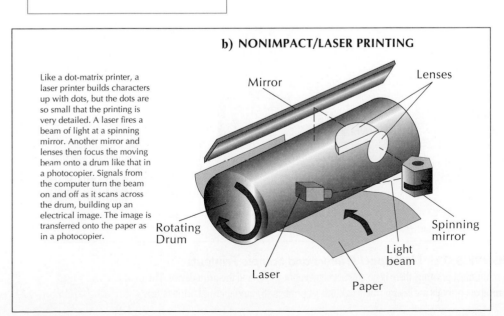

FIGURE 5.31
Printing Processes
(a) Impact and (b) nonimpact printers.

a) Tektronix Phaser 200e laser printer with sample printout.

b) Color toner for Hewlett Packard 1200C ink-jet printer and sample printout.

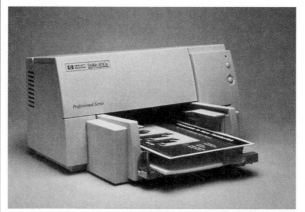

c) Hewlett-Packard color inkjet printer and sample printout.

FIGURE 5.32 *Nonimpact Printers and Sample Printouts*
In nonimpact printing, there is no contact between the paper and the print device. The most frequently used nonimpact printers are laser printers (a), ink-jet printers (b), and thermal printers (c).

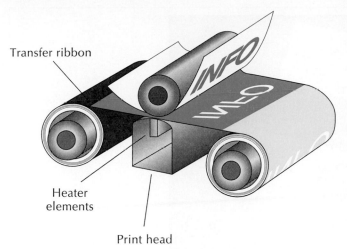

FIGURE 5.33
The Thermal Printing Process
All thermal-wax-transfer printers work by heating four colored waxes and fusing them to a special paper. The print head melts tiny dots of color from a ribbon onto the paper. The paper must pass the ribbon and heating element four times—one pass for each of the four colors: cyan (blue), magenta, yellow, and black.

IMPACT PRINTERS. Impact printers have existed for many years and have historically been very common in large and small computer configurations. Although they are being displaced by nonimpact printers, many are still used. Three important types of impact printers are dot matrix, line, and character printers (Figure 5.34).

- In **dot matrix printing,** the characters and images are formed by wire rods pushed against a ribbon and paper. A careful examination of the characters shows that each is actually a collection of small dots. Dot matrix printers have been used on systems of all sizes because of their speed, low cost, and simplicity.

- **Character printers** print one character at a time. In contrast to dot matrix and line printers, whose speed is rated at lines per minute, character printers are evaluated at the number of characters they print per second. (The slowest ones print approximately 30 characters per second, the fastest approximately 200.) Because the characters on a character printer are preformed on the ends of hammers or the petals of a wheel, character printers are not good for printing images. However, they have been widely used in the preparation of manuscripts and correspondence.

- High-speed **line printers** have enjoyed widespread usage on large computers. They print a full line (up to 144 characters) at one time on continuous-form paper that can be up to 14 inches wide. Because of their high speed, which ranges up to several thousand lines per minute, they have been used in computer centers that routinely print large volumes of documents or very long reports. Since they are character oriented, they are not suitable for printing images.

The *Information Technology in Practice* feature entitled "Lufthansa German Airlines Enhances Frequent Flier Perks" shows how a simple computer printer can become a tool for service in business.

a) Epson LQ-1070+ dot matrix printer and sample printout.

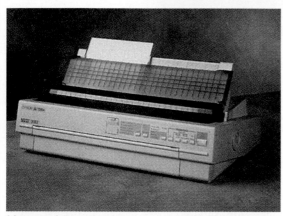

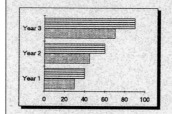

b) Lexmark 2391 Plus character printer and sample printout.

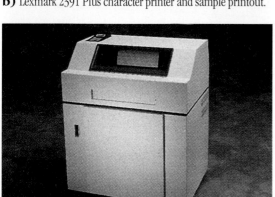

c) Dataproducts FP 2000 line printer and sample printout.

FIGURE 5.34 *Impact Printers and Sample Printouts*

In impact printing, the paper and the character being printed come into contact with each other. Although nonimpact printers are becoming the standard, many businesses still use impact printers. The three most common types are dot matrix printers (a), character printers (b), and line printers (c).

INFORMATION TECHNOLOGY IN PRACTICE

Lufthansa German Airlines Enhances Frequent Flier Perks

⊖ Lufthansa

During the 1980s, competition in the international airline industry intensified, partly because of the deregulation of U.S. airlines, and partly because of advances in information technology that made possible new marketing programs and services designed to attract the business traveler. Business travelers are particularly important to airlines because they often need to travel "at the last minute," and thus are willing to pay higher fares than the vacationing tourist, who plans months ahead in order to get "rock-bottom" air fares.

Many airlines developed frequent flier programs to entice business travelers into flying on their planes regularly. (Chapter 12 discusses the development of the American Airlines AAdvantage frequent flier program.) The airline gives frequent fliers mileage credit for each flight, and when these customers accumulate enough mileage credits, they can exchange them for free tickets to any destination to which the airline flies. Each month, the airline mails printed statements to program members informing them of the number of miles they accrued during the most recent month, any miles they have already used to gain free ticket awards, and the balance in the mileage account. Frequent flier programs have become a valued feature of air travel all over the world.

Seeking to provide better service to its valued frequent fliers, Lufthansa German Airlines created a self-service program that would enable customers to get, on demand, the balance of miles in their frequent flier account instead of waiting for the monthly statement. Customers enrolled in the "Lufthansa Miles and More" program would be able to feed their membership cards into self-service printers and receive a printed statement with this information. Before it went ahead with a full-scale version of the program, the airline needed to find out if frequent travelers wanted to know their mileage accumulations more than once a month.

In a test version of the program, Lufthansa installed self-service printers in the airports in Frankfurt and Munich, linking them to the airline's central computer in Frankfurt. As soon as the printers were installed, frequent fliers began requesting an average of several hundred statements daily. As a result of this test, Lufthansa decided to install the self-service printers in every airport in Germany. Giving up-to-date frequent flier information on demand through effective use of IT is likely to become standard practice at other international airlines.

HERTZ WIRELESS HANDHELD POINT OF SALE.   When you rent a car, you want to receive a new car at a good price. Most people also want to return the automobile quickly and without hassle. Hertz Rent-A-Car, like many rental car agencies, uses wireless point of sale terminals, called Instant Return, for their credit card customers at their airport locations so drivers can return their cars quickly. When the driver pulls into the return lot, Hertz attendants read the vehicle's identification number from the sticker on the windshield, keying the number, and a few other details, into a handheld terminal (Figure 5.35). The vehicle number is transmitted to the Hertz computer inside the rental office, where information about the rental contract is retrieved from the computer.

In seconds, the computer displays the renter's name on the handheld terminal, calculates total rental charges, and sends a wireless message to the attendant's portable electronic printer. A few more seconds pass while the driver's receipt is printed. In less than a minute from the time drivers arrive, they are on the way to the airport gate with a receipt in hand from settling the entire rental transaction.

Plotters

plotter
An output device that draws image information (such as charts, graphs, and blueprints) stroke by stroke.

Plotters (Figure 5.36) literally draw image information, such as charts and graphs, line drawings, and blueprints of buildings. Just as if it were drawing by hand, a plotter creates every line and character, including shadows and patterns, stroke by stroke.

FIGURE 5.35
Handheld Terminals in Use at Hertz
The attendant keys the identification number from the windshield sticker into a handheld terminal. Information is transmitted to a computer, which displays the renter's name on the handheld unit and prints a receipt.

The process is fascinating to watch. The plotter arm takes a felt-tip pen from a holder containing one or more pens and, under direction from the computer, it transforms electronic signals into marks on the page. The page may be of any size, from the common 8½ by 11 inches or A4 (210 by 297 millimeters) to the very large commercial blueprints used in architecture, engineering, and construction.

Film Recorders

Color (35mm) slides, transparencies, and other types of film output are produced on **film recorders** (Figure 5.37). Virtually anything that can be shown on a computer screen can be copied onto a film recorder. Under the control of a computer

film recorder
An output device that transforms an electronic image on a computer screen into a film image.

FIGURE 5.36
Hewlett Packard DeskJet 350c Plotter
Architects and other design professionals frequently use plotters to create detailed schematics of buildings, rooms, and floor plans.

FIGURE 5.37
Mirus Film Printer Turbo PC
Virtually anything that can be shown on a computer screen can be copied onto a film recorder. Under the control of a computer program, the film recorder transforms the electronic image on the screen into a film image, which can then be used to prepare slide presentations.

program, the film recorder transforms the electronic image on the screen into a film image. You might think of the film recorder as an electronic camera, setting the exposure and controlling the shutter to capture the electronic image on the computer screen on film.

Film recorders are being used by many businesses to prepare slide presentations in-house. (In days past, such presentations were developed almost exclusively by professional graphic artists using specialized tools.) Presentation software programs, used to create the shapes and images, enter the text, and control the color schemes, are widely available for under $500. If a company does not have its own film processor, it can store a copy of the presentation on disk and send it out to a slide-processing firm that will produce the color slides. The cost: $5 to $10 per slide.

Genigraphics, a world leader in computer-generated slides, transparencies, and color graphics, provides exactly this service. Using any of a number of imaging packages that run on Macintosh and IBM-compatible computers, anyone can create the text, image, and color specifications of a professional-looking presentation right on his or her desktop. When finished, the individual can either copy the file to a diskette and mail it to Genigraphics, or transmit the file to Genigraphics electronically over an ordinary telephone line. When Genigraphics receives the file, it transforms it into colorful output using film recorders, color laser printers, or other output devices. Within 24 hours (or sooner if necessary), the results are back on the originator's desk.

The technology for capturing digital images and for producing color slides and transparencies for presentations is readily available. It is important to keep in mind, however, that the most important element of information technology is know-how. The most valuable resources of graphic artists are not the tools they use but rather their professional experiences and skills.

When you begin your career, you will probably see many poorly conceived slides and graphic presentations assembled by people who have the necessary tools—the PC and the presentation software package—to do the job. What they lack is the know-how that makes the difference between a good and a poor presentation. No amount of IT can conceal that their ideas are poorly conceived and their message ineffective. The same is true with respect to IT. Know-how makes the difference between poor and effective use. ■

SUMMARY OF LEARNING OBJECTIVES

1 Discuss why people and businesses use secondary storage, not just the computer's main memory, to store information. People and businesses use *secondary storage* because (1) the contents of primary memory remain there only temporarily, (2) data vanish from primary memory as soon as the computer is turned off, and (3) primary memory is not large enough to contain the large volume of data and information associated with business applications.

2 Distinguish between the two main types of magnetic storage and identify five newer magnetic storage alternatives. The two main types of magnetic storage are magnetic tape and magnetic disk. *Magnetic tape,* the earliest form of magnetic storage, comes on large reels or cartridges. *Magnetic disks* come in two formats: hard disks and flexible (floppy) disks.

Five newer types of magnetic storage are (1) *zip diskettes,* removable hard-shelled diskettes that can store more than 100 megabytes of data; (2) *disk cartridges,* removable hard disks sealed in protective packages; (3) *hardcards,* magnetic disks attached to a circuit board that can be mounted in a microcomputer's expansion slot; (4) *RAM disks,* the equivalent of a hard disk created in primary memory; and (5) *disk caching,* which allows a computer system to store information that is read frequently from a disk in RAM.

3 Explain why optical storage is of growing importance in computing and describe the most commonly used forms of optical storage. *Optical storage* is of growing importance in computing because it can store high-density data and information. The most common types of optical storage are *CD-ROM,* the least expensive way to store large amounts of information, and *videodisks,* a medium that can store both images and sound. Neither CD-ROM disks nor videodisks can be written to. Two new types of optical disks, WORM and EOS, permit computer users to write data or information onto the disks.

4 Identify the six most widely used input devices and describe how they are employed in computing. The six most widely used input devices are (1) *keyboards;* (2) *terminals,* which are combination keyboard and video displays that accept input, display it on a video screen, and display the output sent by the computer to which they are attached; (3) *scanners,* which transform written or printed information (optical character recognition scanners) or photographic images, drawings, or entire documents (image scanners) into a digital form that is entered directly into the computer; (4) *digitizers,* which translate measured distances into digital values that the computer can process; (5) *digital cameras,* which capture photographic images on light-sensitive computer memory chips; and (6) *voice and sound input devices,* which are attached to the computer to capture spoken words and other sounds in digital form.

5 Discuss the future of voice input and audio output devices as components of information technology. *Voice input devices* capture the spoken word in digital form. Research in voice, sound, and speech input advanced slowly until recently, because of technological limitations, but with the development of new storage technologies and faster processors, this situation is changing. *Audio response units,* which transform data or information into sound output, are now in widespread use. The directory assistance services of public telephone companies regularly use audio response units to give callers phone numbers.

6 Describe the four types of output devices and identify their uses in business. The four types of output devices are (1) *video displays* or *monitors;* (2) *printers,* which produce paper output (hard copy); (3) *plotters,* which draw image information, such as charts and graphs, line drawings, and building blueprints; and (4) *film recorders,* which transform the electronic image on the computer screen into a film image. The uses of these devices vary greatly from business to business, but all businesses use output devices in their computer systems.

242 PART 2 *Tech Talk*

KEY TERMS

CRITICAL CONNECTIONS

1 The Federal Aviation Administration's "Black Box" Captures Aircraft Flight Information

At the urging of the National Transportation Safety Board, the FAA now requires the recording of many more details (over 100 different flight parameters) on the FDRs. Digital signals are recorded once every second.

The newest "black boxes" use nonvolatile memory chips instead of Mylar tape. Lockheed Martin, which employs this form of information technology in both its FDRs and its CVRs, says these solid-state systems, which use no moving parts, are more likely to stay intact in the event of a catastrophic incident than the old systems were.

Questions for Discussion

1. What benefits does *nonvolatility* in memory chips provide for FDR and CVR use?
2. What other benefits do memory chips provide in contrast to Mylar magnetic tape?
3. Which alternative do you believe is cheaper: a sense-and-record mechanism that uses magnetic tape or one that records on digital memory chips?

2 American Express's Optical Storage Created Country Club Billing

American Express American Express isn't the only company that is looking to image-processing systems to help it control a tidal wave of paper. Banks, too, are counting on image processing to stem the flood of 55 million checks that pass through their "back rooms" for processing and sorting every year. In fact, some banks are already charging higher fees to customers who insist on getting back the originals of their canceled checks—as opposed to image-processed facsimiles—with their monthly statements.

Questions for Discussion

1. Courts have ruled that reproductions of documents are admissible as evidence as long as they "accurately reproduce the original." Would this knowledge make you comfortable with a checking account statement that includes only image-processed facsimiles? What does your reaction and the reaction of your classmates imply for the future of a "checkless" society?

2. American Express, one of the first companies to adopt image processing and optical storage, likes to present itself as a leader in technology. How might this image help the company's marketing strategies?

3. In recent years, AmEx has been hurt because merchants and customers are turning to bank credit cards with lower interest rates, lower annual fees, and lower charges than those offered by American Express. How can ECCB help AmEx fight back?

3   Lufthansa Airlines' Chip-in Cards Eliminate Tickets

 The Chip-in card is part of Lufthansa's rollout of a paperless ticketing system. Eliminating traditional paper tickets for travel not only streamlines passenger check-ins, it also cuts operating costs. The traveler's card number both identifies the individual and provides security so that no other person can claim the ticket.

Whenever a reservation is made, the details of date and flight number, departure and destination cities, and ticket cost are entered into Lufthansa's automated system. Upon arriving at the airport, passengers with a Chip-in card need only wave their card in front of the terminal to confirm their reservation. No paper need change hands.

Questions for Discussion

1. How does the Chip-in card reduce the airline's costs of managing reservations?

2. What conveniences does the Chip-in card offer to passengers?

3. Why do you suppose more airlines do not use chip cards or offer paperless tickets?

4. Do you think it is possible for an airline to eliminate the printed listing passengers obtain when they check in at the airport ATM? Why or why not?

4   IT: A New Ally in the War Against Disease

Rational drug design will never entirely replace the traditional quest for miracle cures in places like the rain forests. Such compounds as the cancer drug taxol, derived from the Pacific yew tree, are simply too complex to create by computer. But the computer extends the power and scope of the researcher's reach. At the University of California at San Francisco, for example, a team of scientists used a computer to search a database containing 3-D models of 60,000 existing drugs. The team was looking for molecules that might lock onto the AIDS virus. Their research showed that haloperidol, a powerful antipsychotic drug, could block the AIDS virus, but only at dosage levels that would kill the patient. Nevertheless, the team hopes that pharmaceutical companies that make variants of haloperidol will build on its research by screening their products to see if they can be modified to fight AIDS.

Questions for Discussion

1. Recently, Merck & Co., a major force in the pharmaceutical industry, spent $230 million on information technology, including a new supercomputer for "computational chemistry"—the computerized manipulation of 3-D models used in rational drug design. What sort of input and output devices would you suggest that Merck purchase for its new computer?

2. Because drug patents last for only a few years, a pharmaceutical company's fortunes rise and fall with the introduction of new drugs to the market—a process that takes, on average, 12 years and an investment of $250 million. How can IT help these companies increase their profitability?

5   IT + You = Directed Mail

Information technology not only helps direct-mail marketers target their messages, it also helps them save money on postage. That's because the U.S. Postal Service offers discounts to bulk mailers who do some of the Postal Service's work for it. Sorting a mass mailing on the basis of carrier route, which is a simple task for database software, is a good example of this kind of work. Another is the printing of a bar code on a mailing piece where it can be read by one of the Postal Service's new wide-array optical scanners.

Questions for Discussion

1. How might the use of IT in direct-mail marketing create a win-win situation for both direct-mail marketers and environmentalists, who currently claim that direct mail wastes valuable corporate and environmental resources?

2. To further its goal of complete automation, the U.S. Postal Service wants Congress to give it permission to offer additional discounts to companies that print bar codes on their mail. As a future business manager, do you think this discount is justifiable? As a taxpayer, do you think it is fair?

3. Art Rushing, president of the Art Rushing Group, Inc., in Memphis, Tennessee, has created a device that can read a nine-digit ZIP code and print the appropriate bar code at a rate of 10,000 pieces of mail an hour. Can you think of other business opportunities created by direct-mail marketing?

Net Work

When News Is On-line

A growing number of newspapers are publishing on-line, taking advantage of the global reach of the Internet and World Wide Web as well as their unique capabilities for displaying information. Some newspapers make their pages available without charge, while others either require a monthly or annual subscription fee or charge for each viewing.

1. Search the Web and prepare a list of newspapers you find appealing. Note the URL for each one. Also indicate for each newspaper whether it requires a subscription fee or other charge for on-line viewing.

2. Peruse the pages of each on-line newspaper you chose to see the nature of the news it covers and how it is presented. Then consider the similarities and differences between each page you've viewed:

- How do the contents vary between newspapers?

- What characteristics of on-line newspapers do you find most appealing?

- What information is better obtained from the print version of the paper?

3. The Web's pages are not just for viewing. You can also print them. Choose a newspaper page and by clicking on the [Prt], print a paper copy of it.

4. Do you think on-line newspapers will ever replace the printed version?

5. What are the advantages of publishing newspapers over the Web?

GROUP PROJECTS AND APPLICATIONS

Project 1

Refer to Group Project 1 in Chapter 4. With your group, answer the following questions for the business you chose for that project:

- What type(s) of secondary storage media will you need?
- Which type(s) of input devices will you use? Will your business have any need for hand-held, palmtop, or laptop computers?
- Keeping in mind that high-resolution monitors are quite expensive, what type of monitor will your business use? What type of printer?
- How might your business use voice and sound input and output devices to increase customer satisfaction?

After completing Project 1 in Chapters 4 and 5, you should have a complete "IT Plan" for your new business. Present this plan to the class.

Project 2— Group Research Project

Several companies offer specially designed ergonomic devices to help prevent repetitive stress disorders (such as carpal tunnel syndrome). Others provide special "adaptive devices" for people with a wide range of disabilities so they can work comfortably with information technology.

With your group, investigate one of the following topics:

- Ergonomic workstations and equipment
- Input devices for people with disabilities
- Output devices for people with disabilities

Two good places to begin an investigation into adaptive technologies are the Americans with Disabilities Act Document Center (on the Internet at http://janweb.icdi.wvu.edu/kinder/) and the Apple Computer Disabilities Solutions Store (at http://www.apple.com/disability).

Each group should present one or two "enabling technologies" to the class, explaining the technology and how it works. The presentations should discuss the price of these adaptive technologies and whether the price is a barrier to use.

REVIEW QUESTIONS

1. How are primary and secondary storage alike? How are they different?

2. What advantages does secondary storage offer over main memory storage? Why is secondary storage needed in computing?

3. What are the two main magnetic storage media?

4. What is a track on magnetic tape? How does it differ from a track on magnetic disk?

5. What does recording density mean?

6. When does a head crash occur and why is it undesirable?

7. How do disk packs and diskettes differ?

8. Distinguish between sequential processing and random-access processing.

9. What is the origin of the term *floppy disk?*

10. Name and describe five magnetic storage alternatives to magnetic tape and magnetic disk.

11. How do optical storage devices work? How do they differ from magnetic storage devices?

12. How do CD-ROM, WORM, and EOS disks differ?

13. What are the five most frequently used input devices?

14. Why are scanners used in processing data and information? What are the two types of scanning?

15. What is a digitizer? Name six common types of digitizers.

16. What are the characteristics of digital cameras? How do digital cameras capture images and what advantages does this method offer?

17. Describe the purpose of voice input and multimedia audiovisual input devices.

18. Describe the characteristics of a multimedia PC. Do these characteristics vary between desktop PCs and notebook computers?

19. What is an audio response unit? When is such a device used?

20. What features distinguish one computer monitor from another?

21. What is the difference between impact printing and nonimpact printing?

22. Are laser printers impact or nonimpact printers? Explain your answer.

23. What is the purpose of a plotter? A film recorder?

DISCUSSION QUESTIONS

1. When a user of the computer system at the Amoco Research Center accidentally deleted 940 files relating to the remodeling of Amoco's building, an administrator was able to restore the files in about half an hour, using the magnetic tape backup created every night at 1 A.M. Why do you think the administrator chose magnetic tape over magnetic disks for the backups?

2. As part of its effort to organize a mega-auction of real estate and other items to secure $800 million worth of loans from 136 failed savings and loan associations, the Resolution Trust Corp. (RTC) hired a consulting company to create a computer system that would let bidders review copies or images of the relevant legal documents, photographs, and surveys. What type of secondary storage would you recommend for such a system? Why? What input and output devices would you recommend?

3. The Travelers Corp., an insurance firm based in Hartford, Connecticut, provides a toll-free number for consumers who want to learn the name of Travelers-approved doctors in their area or get a status report on their claims. Callers have the option of using a voice response system that extracts information from the computer files or speaking to a live operator who has access to the same files.

Why do you think that many experts in the field are convinced that customers are coming to expect these options?

4. Industrial Light & Magic, Pacific Data Images, and Pixar are just a few of the companies using computer graphics to create special effects for big-budget motion pictures. How might these companies use each of the output devices discussed in this chapter?

SUGGESTED READINGS

Brand, Stewart. *The Media Lab: Inventing the Future at M.I.T.* New York, Viking Penguin, 1987. Digital ears? Personal newspapers? Interactive television? These and many more innovative products and services are in development at the Massachusetts Institute of Technology's Media Laboratory. This book describes some of the fascinating ways in which input, output, and storage technologies will be combined to improve our lives. The discussions go well beyond pop technology and corporate fads to examine the possibilities for people, cities, and communities.

Hoffert, Eric M., and Greg Gretsch. "The Digital News System at EDUCOM: A Convergence of Interactive Computing, Newspapers, Television, and High-Speed Networks." *Communications of the ACM 34* (April 1991). This article is part of a special issue dealing with digital multimedia systems. The 11 articles it contains offer information on a broad spectrum of information technologies and their uses.

Kryder, Mark H. "Data-Storage Technologies for Advanced Computing." *Scientific American 257* (October 1987): 116–125. This article is part of a special issue on the revolution in computing. It examines the state of the art in the 1980s as well as expectations for the coming decades. It will be useful for many years to come.

Markus, Aaron, and Andries van Dam. "User-Interface Developments for the Nineties." *Computer 24* (September 1992): 49–57. Part of a special issue on information technology in the next decade, this article explains why people must be at the center of design when new computer applications are developed. It describes how dramatic advances in input and output methods are helping people become more successful.

CASE STUDY

Talbott Ties the Sales Knot with Information Technology

ROBERT TALBOTT

A walk down the steep hills of the quaint village of Carmel, a legendary place on northern California's Monterey Peninsula, will bring you to the waters of the blue Pacific and its trademark white sand beaches. On the way you'll see another well-known Carmel trademark: Robert Talbott, Inc., tie shops. From its Carmel home, Talbott competes in the North American "rag trade"—specifically, in the necktie segment of the men's clothing business.

Talbott's quality neckties, regarded as among the best in the world, are sold today in leading men's shops and top department stores such as Nordstrom's, Parisian, Bloomingdale's, and Dillard's. The Talbott tradition dates back to 1950, when Audrey Talbott, the original and current lead designer, founded the company with her husband on the encouragement of friends who treasured the ties she made as gifts each Christmas.

Audrey Talbott and her staff have always been careful to preserve the company's tradition of stylish design, good quality, and personable service. For many years, they shunned newer approaches to selling, even though their larger competitors thrived on them. Information technology was frequently discussed at Talbott, but it was not adopted until the sales reps were confident that it would aid rather than harm their personal service to buyers and improve their sales performance.

Today, when sales representatives visit buyers in stores carrying the Talbott brand, they bring their sample case of fabrics, as always. They also bring along a pen-based laptop computer equipped with wireless communications modems and portable printers. The computer has streamlined the sales process for both buyer and rep, but without loss of service. Here's how.

After arriving at a customer's office, the Talbott sales rep can bring up an order form on the screen and,

touching the special pen to the screen, indicate details of color, pattern, and style to order just a handful or perhaps thousands of ties. Even complex orders, such as those that are split into several deliveries, can be handled this way. (In the past, separate order forms would have to be completed for each delivery, which took more of the rep's time and inflicted a mound of paperwork on everyone.) As the details are entered into the laptop, the order-entry application checks the order for errors or incomplete information. If desired, a copy of the order can be printed right in front of the customer.

After the order is complete, the rep can transmit it from the laptop to Talbott's computer in Carmel, which records it and verifies that the desired inventory is on hand. If a color or pattern ordered by the customer is sold out, the salesperson is notified so that adjustments can be made without delay. Without this system, several days would pass before the sales rep would learn of the need to change the order, causing the customer inconvenience and loss of valuable time.

Talbott's pen-based system has cut the rep's order-handling time by several hours each day by eliminating the need to do a lot of paper shuffling in a hotel room at night. But there's more.

Talbott's designers are constantly creating new patterns, colors, and styles, and sales reps must be given this information to update the information on their computers. The company's system makes it unnecessary for the reps to key this new-product information into their laptop computers. Instead, throughout the year, the company's headquarters in Carmel creates CD-ROMs containing information on the new styles and sends them to the reps, who at the touch of a button load the information onto their computer's hard disk. Timely and accurate information, entered in an efficient manner . . . Talbott's way of supporting the sales rep.

Questions for Discussion

1. What features of Talbott's sales system do you think are most important to the sales reps?

2. How would you justify the cost of the Talbott system?

3. Do you think that the computer's ability to display high-resolution images of colorful ties will eventually make it unnecessary for reps to carry fabric samples to show customers?

Opportunities for New IT Products

Who Wants a Network Computer?

Faster, cheaper, smaller . . . hallmarks of the revolution in computers. Add to that high speed, widely accessible communications networks, and the availability of powerful off-the-shelf software, and it's easy to see why the information revolution evolved into the information technology revolution.

Yet, some see these very same characteristics as the basis for moving people *away* from personal computers. Promoters of the Network Computer think they have a better alternative.

The Network Computer

What is the Network Computer? Although it is described by various names including WebPC, Internet access device, and Net-top box, all refer to a low-cost personal

computer designed for use through interconnection to a network, not as a stand-alone computer. The target price for this fledgling product is $500.

To make the Network Computer economically feasible, manufacturers knew it had to consist of a microprocessor, an operating system, communications capability, a keyboard, and a mouse. The operating system had to be stripped down—so that it is much smaller than the conventional Windows or Macintosh systems—and to include only essential features. Thus,

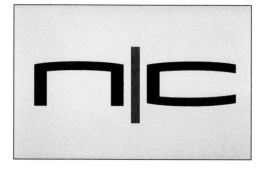

the Network Computer uses a very small amount of storage. Applications software resides only on the computer network to which the Network Computer interconnects.

Those promoting the Network Computer say it can do anything an ordinary PC can do, since it draws on software from the network.

Network Computer Users

Who will want the Network Computer? Three groups may popularize its use:

- **Business Groups.** Corporations, with high-speed networks already in place, are seeking ways to provide information technology capabilities to people throughout the company, but at a lower cost. The Gartner Group, an IT industry research firm, has shown that owning and supporting an ordinary PC running Microsoft Windows over a five-year period costs a business approximately $40,000. They estimate that moving the software to the network will make it possible to use the Network Computer, while dramatically reducing the cost of software and support for each user. The frequency of computer upgrades may be reduced as well, since the power will be in the network, not on the desktop.

- **Education Groups.** Although information technology is increasingly used in elementary and secondary schools, there are still not enough computers to go around in most schools. U.S. schools (grades K–12) now have one PC for every seven students, and often the computers are not in the classroom, but in a resource center that students can visit only on occasion. Computer and software costs remain significant barriers. It is hoped that the Network Computer, with its target price of $500, will prove to be the bargain that breaks through the economic barrier to greater IT use in education.

- **Home Users.** It's possible that the Network Computer will eventually become popular for home use, but at present, this is not a prime target market for the companies developing these computers. Still, the potential market for a $500 computer that can be used at home to gain access to the Internet and other communications networks could be high, so you can expect companies to pay greater attention to this group in the future.

Network Computer Success

Making a Network Computer with a $500 price tag has proved feasible, but skeptics say that at that price, too many features and capabilities that users are now accustomed to had to be eliminated. People are used to having their own software, tailored to their individual needs and quirks, right on their PC, and they are also accustomed to using a PC on a stand-alone basis. For these reasons, skeptics say, the Network Computer will never replace the ordinary personal computer, but at best will be a supplement for selected uses.

The Network Computer is already available in retail stores. Will it be successful? The answer will depend on who really wants it and whether manufacturers will offer systems with the features consumers demand. What do you think?

Questions for Discussion

1. Do you think a $500 Network Computer is a good product for business, education, or home use? Give some examples to demonstrate the reasoning behind your answer.

2. Public telephones are today an essential communication link. Do you think public Network Computers could serve a similar role by allowing people to interconnect with networks to send messages, check their e-mail, contact their bank, and so on?

3. Investigate the cost of components in an ordinary PC (e.g., a microprocessor, computer case, keyboard, power supply, and system board). Based on your investigation, determine whether you believe a $500 PC is economically feasible.

CHAPTER 6

Electronic Spreadsheets: Powerful Problem-Solving Tools

CHAPTER OUTLINE

The Spreadsheet of Visible Innovation

An Overview of Spreadsheets

The Functions of Spreadsheet Programs

Problem Solving Using Spreadsheets

Creating Business Graphics

Developing a Personal Spreadsheet Application

A Final Word

Case Study: Start-up Ad Agency Works by the Numbers

LEARNING OBJECTIVES

When you have completed this chapter, you should be able to

1 Describe the principal functions of spreadsheets and why they are used in business.

2 Identify the elements found on an electronic spreadsheet display.

3 Describe the four types of data created and stored in spreadsheet programs and differentiate between functions and formulas, explaining the benefits of each in creating worksheets for problem solving.

4 Summarize the capabilities offered by spreadsheet programs for changing and refining worksheets after data have been entered.

5 Discuss the uses of spreadsheet programs in sensitivity analysis and problem solving.

6 Explain the types of business graphics usually included with spreadsheet programs, when each is used, and how worksheet contents are transformed into business graphics.

7 Discuss the four steps involved in developing a personal spreadsheet application.

The Spreadsheet of
Visible Innovation

An *entrepreneur* is someone who knows where to scratch before there's an itch. An *innovator* seeks a better way to scratch that itch. Both types of people are essential to progress, for they are creating the future by experimenting today with technology that will become commonplace tomorrow. But how exactly do innovations and advances come about?

Consider the case of Dan Bricklin, a student at the Harvard Business School in 1977. Dan spent most of his evenings working on a seemingly endless series of business cases requiring analysis, decision making, and problem-solving skills. For each case, he needed to create a worksheet to map out the expenses and other financial concerns of the business he was studying. Each case also required him to consider several alternatives and different assumptions. This meant doing repeated calculations on the calculator and constructing worksheet after worksheet to show revenues, expenses, and the effects of competitors' activities. When an arithmetic error occurred—and such errors are a normal part of learning—that entire worksheet had to be redone.

What bothered Dan was not the time and the effort he spent analyzing each case, because he knew extensive analysis is a critical part of educating oneself and developing expertise. But Dan felt the time he spent keying numbers into the calculator and transferring them to the worksheet was neither exciting nor productive. In fact, it seemed to get in the way of the learning process because it left him less time to focus on important things: analysis and gaining insight into the case solutions.

Dan knew there had to be a better way. During the early months of 1978—when it's cold and snowy in New England—he and a friend, Robert Frankston, stayed indoors, working together to develop a new type of calculator that would ease their "number crunching." They wondered if they could find a way to use their new Apple II computer as a problem-solving tool.

In a few months, Dan and Robert had developed a computer program they called a *visible calculator* that performed spreadsheet arithmetic so that the user could change the data on a worksheet and see—immediately—how those changes affected the final outcome. No longer did Dan

Before the electronic spreadsheet…   …and after.

need to perform a seemingly endless set of calculations by hand every time he had to analyze a new case.

After the program was streamlined and the kinks were ironed out, Dan's entrepreneurial spirit kicked in. The visible calculator had helped him raise his personal productivity significantly. Surely it could also be of use to other people in similar situations. But what about the name: Who would buy a computer program called a "visible calculator"? The solution: Give it a snappier name.

VisiCalc, as the program came to be called, ran on the Apple II computer and became a runaway success. In fact, the program is often credited with selling more Apple computers than any other software product of the day. It literally changed the way people analyze and solve problems throughout the world.

VisiCalc was followed by a long line of products that improved on its basic concept. When the IBM PC was introduced in 1981, another entrepreneur/innovator who was also an expert in computer software, Mitch Kapor, developed a spreadsheet program that ran only on the IBM PC. As businesses began acquiring more and more PCs, they also purchased thousands of copies of Kapor's spreadsheet program, which became a success as quickly as 1-2-3. In fact, the program was called Lotus 1-2-3, and Kapor's company was known as Lotus Development Co.

VisiCalc and Lotus 1-2-3 are two historic successes created by people out to solve a problem—to scratch an itch—in an innovative way.

These simple, yet powerful, inventions are not magical solutions to unsolvable problems. Rather, the benefits of spreadsheet programs come from a sound understanding of what they can do and how to use them effectively. Using spreadsheets for problem solving often requires creating multiple worksheets, each focusing on a different part of the problem.

In the first part of this chapter, you'll see how spreadsheets can solve problems and increase your productivity. Then you'll learn how the details entered into a spreadsheet can be used to create a wide variety of business graphics, transforming numeric information into visual form and depicting graphically the relationships among different components of a problem. In the last part of the chapter, you'll create and develop a personal spreadsheet application.

When you have completed this chapter, you will have a good understanding of the components of an electronic spreadsheet package and of the principles of effective use. You will also be prepared to design and create a personal spreadsheet application.

An Overview of Spreadsheets

Spreadsheets, commonly called **worksheets,** have been used in manual form for decades by bookkeepers, accountants, financial analysts, and project planners—people who plan events and keep track of revenues, expenses, profits, and losses. You've undoubtedly seen spreadsheets, with their rows and columns of tabular data. But what exactly is a spreadsheet and what is it used for?

spreadsheet/worksheet
A table of columns and rows used by people responsible for tracking revenues, expenses, profits, and losses.

What Is a Spreadsheet?

Spreadsheets done by hand with pencil and paper—manual spreadsheets—have served planners and analysts well, helping them organize a project's work and structure its numeric details. They are easy to use: you simply read across the horizontal **rows** to see the data for individual categories or items of interest, and then read down the vertical **columns** to see the data for each time period. Totals are shown at the bottom of each column and sometimes in the far right column as well.

An **electronic spreadsheet**—an automated version of the manual type—is created and maintained using a software package called an electronic **spreadsheet program.** Because spreadsheets are usually personal applications rather than multiuser applications, they are typically run on PCs. Table 6.1 lists popular spreadsheet packages for both IBM-compatible and Macintosh computers. Versions for some mainframes and midrange computers are also available.

rows
The horizontal elements in a spreadsheet.

columns
The vertical elements in a spreadsheet.

electronic spreadsheet
An automated version of the manual spreadsheet, created and maintained by a spreadsheet program.

Why Use Spreadsheets in Business?

The electronic spreadsheet is often called a "killer app," a type of applications software that offers so many benefits that it even persuades people who don't own a computer to buy one. (Before Bricklin developed the electronic spreadsheet, the business community viewed the PC as a "toy" for hobbyists and game players, not a tool for serious business use.) To see why businesspeople have embraced the electronic spreadsheet so enthusiastically, let's consider a few of the ways in which spreadsheets support traditional business functions.

spreadsheet program
A software package used to create electronic spreadsheets.

THEY AUTOMATE RECORD KEEPING. Managers without good business records are operating in the dark and may eventually find themselves unable to meet financial obligations, collect payments, or plan for the future. A business is illuminated by clear, precise electronic spreadsheets in three ways. First, electronic

TABLE 6.1 *Leading Spreadsheet Packages*		
SOFTWARE PACKAGE	MANUFACTURER	COMPUTER VERSIONS AVAILABLE
1-2-3	Lotus Development	Apple Macintosh and IBM-compatible microcomputers, IBM midrange and mainframes
Excel	Microsoft	Apple Macintosh and IBM-compatibles
Improv	Lotus Development	IBM-compatibles
Quattro Pro	Borland	IBM-compatibles

CRITICAL
CONNECTION 1

Psion

Psion Organizes Business—and You

Spreadsheet programs are an essential part of business, so much so that people want to be able to use them anywhere and anytime. Today, you don't have to be at your desk or even lugging around a notebook computer in order to use a spreadsheet. Instead, you can take advantage of the popular spreadsheet programs built into the leading electronic personal organizers sold around the world.

Psion, PLC, of London, has combined spreadsheet processing capability with a personal organizer, all running on a palmtop computer that weighs less than 10 ounces and sells for a few hundred dollars. The personal organizer includes a database for names, addresses, and telephone numbers as well as an hourly, daily, monthly, and yearly calendar on which you can book events several years into the future. Both the database and agenda are searchable, so you can specify a name, event, or date and Psion will quickly find the information and present it to you on the display screen. You make additions or changes by entering details through the keyboard.

Need to do a quick analysis or prepare a cost projection (or maybe just balance your checkbook)? Enter the details through the keyboard and let Psion's spreadsheet capability do the work for you. Better yet, recall a template you've stored in Psion's memory (this tool has several meg of main memory) and enter the new data. Prestored formulas will be used automatically. And if you want to display a graphic of the information—perhaps to see a trend—just press a few keys and the trend line or bar chart will appear on the computer's screen.

Psion is a fully functional computer that's fast, windows-driven, and convenient. It organizes your life and provides a spreadsheet capability you can carry along with you anywhere you go.

spreadsheets let users record and store business data in a clear, legible format reminiscent of the old accountant's ledger. Second, the electronic spreadsheet's "Search/Find" and "Sort" functions let users find and reorganize specific data— for example, an alphabetical list of all customers with overdue accounts. Third, electronic spreadsheets let users embed mathematical formulas within them so that the computer will perform both simple and complex calculations automatically and without error. The savings in both time and labor are substantial.

THEY SUMMARIZE RAW DATA AND PRODUCE INFORMATION. The electronic spreadsheet's ability to swiftly add long rows or columns of data is essential to producing the organized, summarized information managers need to understand and analyze their organization's performance. Did the department meet its sales goals? Is the new marketing plan working? What does the latest customer survey say about our service? Often, the best answers to these questions are found in the analyses and summaries produced by an electronic spreadsheet package. And if the answers aren't clear enough in summary data form, managers can use the spreadsheet software to convert them into *business graphics*—charts and graphs that permit them to make comparisons and discern trends in the data (Figure 6.1).

Ray's Lobster Shack- Fourth Quarter Summary

	1	2	3	4
	OCT.	NOV.	DEC.	TOTAL
SALES				
Hackensack	12,000	8,500	14,750	35,250
New York	22,000	18,900	26,950	67,850
Philadelphia	16,500	12,000	18,800	47,300
TOTAL SALES	50,500	39,400	60,500	150,400
EXPENSES				
Rent	4,000	4,000	4,000	12,000
Salaries	20,000	20,000	20,000	60,000
Supplies	3,000	2,000	2,000	7,000
Utilities	1,250	1,300	1,400	3,950
TOTAL EXPENSES	28,250	27,300	27,400	82,950
NET BEFORE TAXES	22,250	12,100	33,100	67,450

FIGURE 6.1

The Benefits of Electronic Spreadsheets

In addition to saving time by recalculating data automatically, electronic spreadsheets allow users to create graphics from the data included on the spreadsheet.

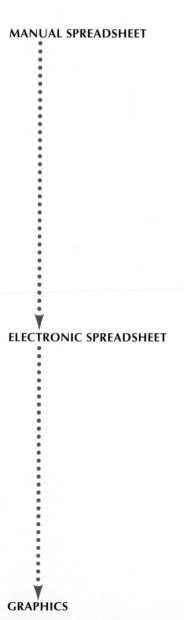

MANUAL SPREADSHEET

ELECTRONIC SPREADSHEET

GRAPHICS

File Edit Formula Format Data Options Macro Window

Normal

H31

	A	B	C	D	E	F	G
1			Ray's Lobster Shack				
2			Fourth Quarter Summary				
3							
4							
5		OCT.	NOV.	DEC.	TOTAL		
6	SALES						
7							
8	Hackensack	12000	8500	14750	35250		
9	New York	22000	18900	26950	67850		
10	Philadelphia	16500	12000	18800	47300		
11							
12	TOTAL SALES	50500	39400	60500	150400		
13							
14	EXPENSES						
15							
16	Rent	4000	4000	4000	12000		
17	Salaries	20000	20000	20000	60000		
18	Supplies	3000	2000	2000	7000		
19	Utilities	1250	1300	1400	3950		
20							
21	TOTAL EXPENSES	28250	27300	27400	82950		
22							
23							
24	NET BEFORE TAXES	22250	12100	33100	67450		
25							

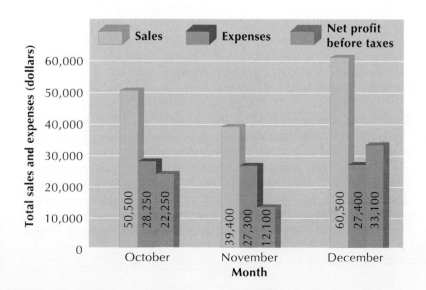

THEY PERFORM ANALYSIS AND IMPROVE PLANNING.   The summary information displayed on a spreadsheet or business graphic is a valuable resource for crafting management goals and plans. In addition, the electronic spreadsheet lets managers go beyond simple summaries to construct the sort of "what if" analyses Dan Bricklin struggled with as a student. Electronic spreadsheets aid managers in conducting three types of analyses. In the first, and simplest, form of analysis, *recalculating data,* the user changes one value within the spreadsheet and then lets the computer calculate how that change affects all the other elements within the spreadsheet. Thus, the user can experiment with different alternatives and get instant feedback. Suppose you want to know what will happen to profits if you cut costs by 5 percent. Change the appropriate data in the spreadsheet and you'll have the answer in less than a second.

The second type of analysis incorporates the mathematical tools of management science. A good example is using an analytical program for "back-solving" or "goal-seeking." Here, the user starts with a desired goal or output ("increase profits by 5 percent") and lets the software work backward, using the spreadsheet data and mathematical formulas to calculate the values for the various inputs (such as materials, labor, and price) that will achieve the goal. The most sophisticated of these analytical tools, called *optimizers,* let managers seek an optimal balance between minimizing costs and maximizing profits, given certain constraints (such as limited supplies of labor).

model
A plan that simulates the relationships between events or variables.

The third type of analysis, *scenario planning,* lets the user construct and compare a number of business plans, or **models,** that simulate the relationship between events or variables in the business world. Scenario planning is especially useful when the future holds a great deal of uncertainty. For example, Southern California Edison's managers used scenario planning to create 12 alternative models of the future, ranging from a Mideast oil crisis to an economic boom, for the electrical utility business. The resulting calculations helped then fine-tune their long-range capacity planning, which governs the number and size of California Edison's generating plants.

These three analytical approaches let managers incorporate many types of data into precise but flexible plans, created with little or no help from the IT staff or financial analysis.

THEY SIMPLIFY THE CONTROL PROCESS.   Businesspeople around the world are judged by the results they produce. Did the organization reach the goals specified in its plans? If not, what went wrong?

The data in a spreadsheet can help answer these questions, which are central to the business control process. Spreadsheets can even be constructed so that the numbers that indicate "exceptions" or potential problems show up in a different color on the computer screen, alerting employees to the need for corrective action.

THEY IMPROVE COMMUNICATION AND MOTIVATION.   Color-coding data is just one way a spreadsheet helps businesspeople improve communication and motivation. Summarizing spreadsheet data on a business graphic is another. In fact, many experts suggest that managers begin their reports with a summary graphic, and then supplement it later in the report with a detailed table of supporting data. Business graphics that summarize company data (e.g., a chart summarizing sales performance) can also help a manager lead and motivate employees. Many spreadsheet packages let users add an annotation to a report, such as "Great work, team!"

RETHINKING BUSINESS PRACTICES

Maxis Spreadsheets for Maximum Success

In business, three all-important facts influence a firm's performance: (1) Even though a company produces top-notch products, it can't be successful unless someone wants them. (2) The best way to be successful is to help your customer to be successful. (3) You can use reports to count sales . . . or to generate them. Such thinking is what led Sam Poole, CEO of Maxis, producer of such well-known software products as SimCity (a fun-to-use urban planning game) to capitalize on the power of electronic spreadsheets to change the way the company's sales process is managed.

When Poole joined Maxis as vice president of sales, the company, based in Oxnard, California, was in the midst of a transition in product distribution. Rather than relying on the distribution services of another company, it had decided to take responsibility for its retail sales and distribution system. If Maxis was to be successful in the future, Poole knew he would have to answer several important questions about the company's products and customers:

- How much of each product will we sell?
- What kind of information will I need to create forecasts?
- How can I get information on competitors?
- Which computer platforms are generating the most sales and profit?
- Which sales channels are most important to the company's success?
- Where is each product in its life cycle (growing, stable, or declining sales)?

To answer these questions, Poole used Microsoft Excel to create a spreadsheet into which he entered sales by customer, month, and product. Based on past experience, he decided that the analysis and projection capabilities of his spreadsheets would give him more useful information than he could obtain from ordinary monthly computer printouts that provided some facts about past sales, but few indications of future possibilities.

In an industry where success depends on the willingness of distributors to buy and promote your product, it's essential to have good information illustrating how your product will help make them successful. Using the spreadsheet, Poole and the Maxis sales force could not only answer the all-important product and customer questions but were also able to influence future sales: "By proving how well our products are selling and by demonstrating how fast the market is growing, we can persuade distributors to buy our products."

Today, Maxis' salespeople create their own reports using Excel. In addition to Maxis' own sales information, they integrate other industry information into their spreadsheet analysis. The spreadsheets developed by Poole and Maxis staff members do more than predict the future . . . they help create it.

Based on J. deJong and R. L. Scheier, "Virtual Selling," *Inc. Technology 16* (1994): 66.

THEY HELP MANAGERS MAKE DECISIONS. Although electronic spreadsheets are a powerful aid to business problem solving and decision making, the numbers they produce are no substitute for human judgment and common sense. In fact, managers should view the numbers on an unfamiliar spreadsheet with skepticism, since a faulty assumption or formula can destroy the usefulness of many calculations. This is why experienced spreadsheet users follow a clear sequence in setting up and documenting their spreadsheets. We discuss this sequence later in the chapter, after we describe exactly what spreadsheets do and how they do it.

The *Rethinking Business Practices* feature entitled "Maxis Spreadsheets for Maximum Success" illustrates how electronic spreadsheets helped a company successfully make the transition from using outside distribution services to handling its own retail sales and distribution.

Good problem-solving tools are those that fit the situation, are simple to use, and make you better at what you do. They seem natural to use when there is a problem to be solved or a solution to be found.

When you what to pound a nail into a wall, you probably use a hammer. It suits the situation and gets the job done. You can use other things besides a hammer to pound in a nail, of course. But why would you want to? No other tool would get the job done as efficiently as a hammer.

CRITICAL CONNECTION 2

Grill 23 — **The Grill 23 Spread**

Boston's Back Bay is full of history. There you'll find rustic old taverns and warehouses and the harbor that was the scene of the famous defiant act that helped start the American Revolution. Back Bay is also where you'll find Grill 23, a restaurant known for serving superb food and drink, carefully prepared from the best ingredients by caring chefs. Several hundred diners daily attest to the feast offered by Grill 23.

Though the building in which Grill 23 serves its patrons is historic, its business practices are not. The restaurant relies on the latest point-of-sale systems—interconnected PCs that capture the details of every meal served and prepare summary reports for management.

A look behind the scenes reveals that the PC is only the start of good management. Grill 23's staff electronically transfer the point-of-sale details to a Lotus 1-2-3 spreadsheet to which other ingredients are added: information from invoices, purchase orders, and vendor deliveries. These supplements to the point-of-sale information enable the restaurant's managers to evaluate day-to-day operations, spotting difficulties before they become problems and recognizing opportunities for building additional business. At Grill 23, putting on a good spread in front depends on having a reliable spreadsheet in back.

Like a hammer, a spreadsheet will help you get the job done more efficiently. And just as it's more comfortable to use a hammer when you know how to hold it, it's more comfortable to use a spreadsheet when you know how to handle it properly. ■

The Functions of Spreadsheet Programs

Spreadsheet programs carry out four principal activities:

1. Entering data.
2. Editing data.
3. Storing worksheets.
4. Printing worksheets.

Each of these activities includes many options that make it easy to enter and organize data.

Entering Data

Before you can enter data, you need to learn your way around the electronic worksheet and some basic spreadsheet terminology.

DIMENSIONS OF THE WORKSHEET. The worksheet is composed of cells, the number of which is determined by the user. A **cell** is the intersection of a row and a column. The **cell address,** or **cell reference,** is the intersection of a particular row and column. Much like a memory address, it distinguishes one location from another. For example, the Microsoft Excel spreadsheet software assigns letters to columns (from *A* to *Z, AA* through *AZ, BA* through *BZ,* and so on to *IV*) and numbers to rows (from 1 to 16,384). The address of the cell in column 8, row 6, will thus be cell H6.

As we discuss later, multiple worksheets can be created and linked together. Microsoft Excel supports up to 255 worksheets, each capable of containing as many as 256 columns and 16,384 rows.

The cell in which the user is currently working is called the **current cell** or **active cell.** It is highlighted with a **cell pointer** to show that data or information can be entered (or is being entered) into the cell. The active cell is also identified at the top left corner of the screen (Figure 6.2).

SCREEN LAYOUT. The spreadsheet display contains two distinct areas: the window and the control panel.

- **Window.** The largest section of the spreadsheet screen, the window, contains the **worksheet area**—the rectangular grid of rows and columns that compose the worksheet. Along the left side of the window are the row numbers. The column letters or numbers are shown across the top of the worksheet area.

    Because worksheets are often larger than the display screen on which they are viewed, the spreadsheet software will scroll the rows and columns onto the screen. On the right side and bottom of the window in Figure 6.2 are the vertical and horizontal **scroll bars,** which allow the user to move around the window (up and down, or to the right or left). As a row or column moves onto the screen on one side, another instantly moves out of view on the opposite side.

cell
In an electronic spreadsheet, the intersection of a row and a column.

cell address/cell reference
The intersection of a particular row and column in an electronic spreadsheet.

current cell/active cell
In an electronic spreadsheet, the cell in which the user is currently working.

cell pointer
The cursor in an electronic spreadsheet.

worksheet area
In an electronic spreadsheet, the rectangular grid of rows and columns that make up the worksheet.

scroll bar
A bar located at the right or bottom of the computer screen that allows the user to move around the screen—up, down, left, or right.

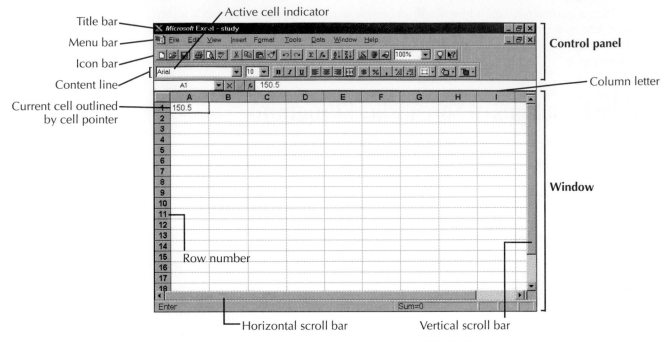

FIGURE 6.2   *The Components of an Electronic Worksheet*
An electronic spreadsheet display contains two main components: the control panel and
the window. In this illustration, the current cell is A1.

title bar
The line of an electronic
spreadsheet's control panel
that contains the program
name and sometimes the
name of the file in use.

menu bar
The line of an electronic
spreadsheet's control panel
that contains the commands
for working with worksheets,
creating graphics, and
invoking special data-
processing actions.

content line/edit line
The line of an electronic
spreadsheet's control panel
indicating the data or
information being keyed into
the active cell of the
spreadsheet.

icon bar
The line of an electronic
spreadsheet's control panel
that shows the icons (pictures)
used to invoke frequently used
commands.

- **Control Panel.** At the top of the spreadsheet screen, above the worksheet area, is the control panel. Its contents vary depending on the particular spreadsheet package used. Figure 6.2 shows the control panel for Microsoft Excel for Windows.

The first line of the Excel control panel, the **title bar,** contains the program name and sometimes the name of the file in use. The second line, the **menu bar,** contains the spreadsheet commands for creating, storing, retrieving, and editing files and worksheets; creating graphs; invoking special data-processing actions; and using other tools that change the appearance of the spreadsheet. Most Windows, OS/2, and Macintosh-based spreadsheet systems also include a "Help" function that provides assistance. The "Help" system is context sensitive, meaning that it provides information about the command you are seeking to use at the time you click on "Help." However, the menu also includes an index of capabilities (a "Help" index) so that you can obtain information on any feature of the spreadsheet at any time. Each command includes subcommands that can be invoked by pointing and clicking at the appropriate spot on the command menu.

The third line of Excel, the **content line,** also called the **edit line,** displays the data or information keyed into the active cell of the spreadsheet. The fourth line, the **icon bar,** contains small pictures—icons—representing frequently used commands. To invoke a command, the user simply points and clicks on an icon. Some common spreadsheet commands are listed in Table 6.2, and the icons used in the leading spreadsheet packages are shown in Figure 6.3.

CELL CONTENTS.   A cell can hold any of four different pieces of information: values, labels, formulas, or functions.

TABLE 6.2 *Spreadsheet Commands*

COMMAND	EXPLANATION
Sort	Arranges specified data into ascending or descending order.
Column width	Sets the width of one or more columns in the worksheet.
Delete	Removes one or more columns, rows, or worksheets and closes the space left by the deletion.
Exit	Ends the spreadsheet session and returns to the computer's operating system.
Graph	Opens a graph window within the worksheet and displays specified graphs.
Insert	Inserts blank columns, rows, or worksheets.
Move	Transfers data from one section of the worksheet to another.
New	Creates a new blank worksheet.
Open	Reads a previously created worksheet from secondary storage into main memory, where it can be processed.
Print	Prints all or a portion of the worksheet, as specified by the user.
Range	Enables user to perform processing on a portion of the worksheet.
Save	Saves the worksheet as a file in secondary storage.

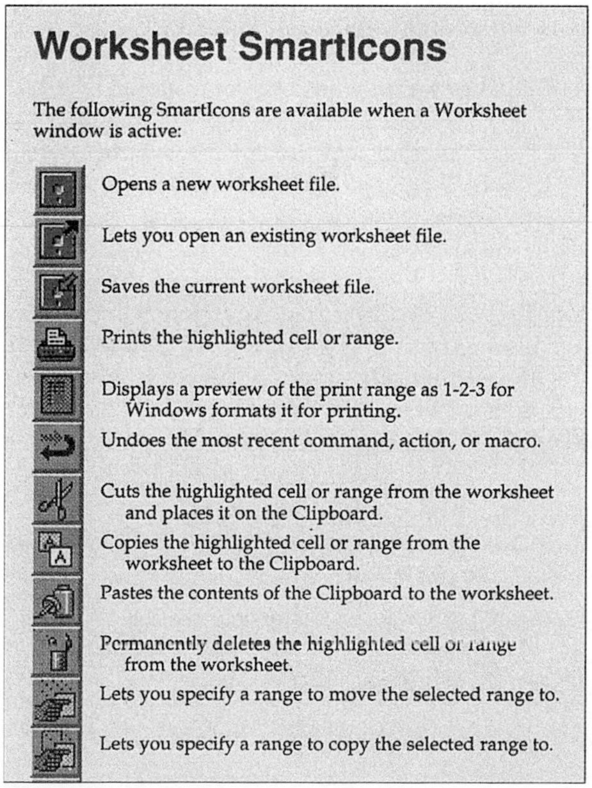

Worksheet SmartIcons

The following SmartIcons are available when a Worksheet window is active:

Opens a new worksheet file.

Lets you open an existing worksheet file.

Saves the current worksheet file.

Prints the highlighted cell or range.

Displays a preview of the print range as 1-2-3 for Windows formats it for printing.

Undoes the most recent command, action, or macro.

Cuts the highlighted cell or range from the worksheet and places it on the Clipboard.

Copies the highlighted cell or range from the worksheet to the Clipboard.

Pastes the contents of the Clipboard to the worksheet.

Permanently deletes the highlighted cell or range from the worksheet.

Lets you specify a range to move the selected range to.

Lets you specify a range to copy the selected range to.

a)

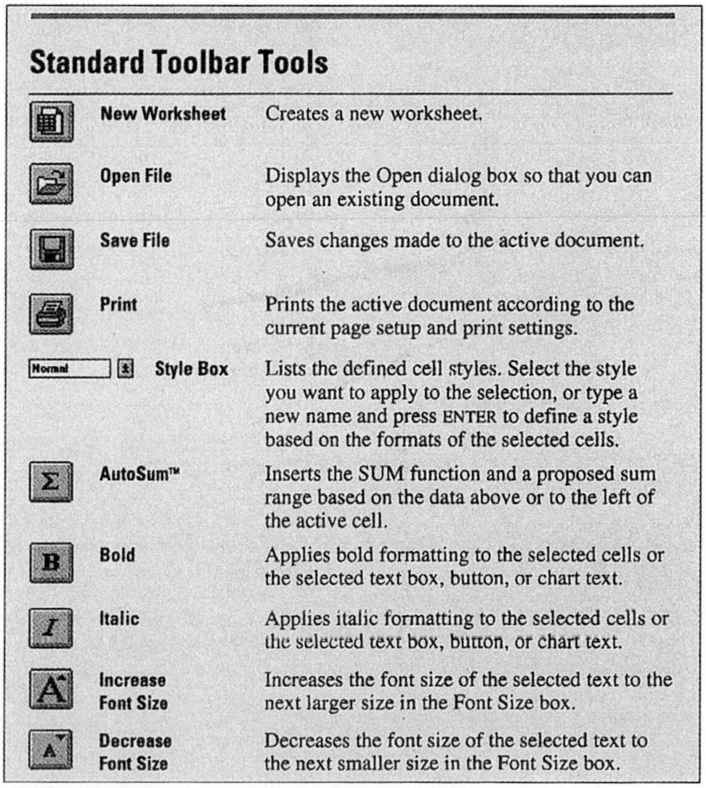

Standard Toolbar Tools

	New Worksheet	Creates a new worksheet.
	Open File	Displays the Open dialog box so that you can open an existing document.
	Save File	Saves changes made to the active document.
	Print	Prints the active document according to the current page setup and print settings.
Normal	Style Box	Lists the defined cell styles. Select the style you want to apply to the selection, or type a new name and press ENTER to define a style based on the formats of the selected cells.
Σ	AutoSum™	Inserts the SUM function and a proposed sum range based on the data above or to the left of the active cell.
B	Bold	Applies bold formatting to the selected cells or the selected text box, button, or chart text.
I	Italic	Applies italic formatting to the selected cells or the selected text box, button, or chart text.
A	Increase Font Size	Increases the font size of the selected text to the next larger size in the Font Size box.
A	Decrease Font Size	Decreases the font size of the selected text to the next smaller size in the Font Size box.

b)

FIGURE 6.3 *Icons Used in Popular Spreadsheet Packages*
Lotus User's Guide (a); Excel User's Manual (b).

value

A number that is entered into a cell of an electronic spreadsheet. It may be an integer, a decimal number, or a number in scientific format.

label

A piece of descriptive information pertaining to a row or column of an electronic spreadsheet.

formula

An electronic spreadsheet instruction describing how a specific computation should be performed.

- A **value** is a number entered into a cell. This may be an integer (500), a decimal number (500.12), or a number in scientific format (5.00 E+2, where "E+2" indicates the number of zeroes to add before the decimal point). All values can be used in computation. In Figure 6.4, the contents of cells B4 through E4 and B5 through E5 and cell E6 are values.

- A **label** is brief descriptive information pertaining to a row or column. Generally, labels are used as column and row headings or titles. They are not used in computation. In Figure 6.4, the contents of cells A1 and B3 through E3 are labels.

- A **formula** is an instruction describing a specific computation to be performed. The arithmetic symbols used in formulas include a plus sign (+) for addition, a minus sign (−) for subtraction, an asterisk (*) for multiplication, a slash (/) for division, and a caret (∧) for exponentiation. If the values in any cells are changed, formulas automatically recalculate results.

  In Figure 6.4, the formula (E4–E5) embedded in cell E6 tells the software to subtract total revenue from total expense to determine profit. Table 6.3 lists examples of formulas frequently used in spreadsheet programs.

  Formulas begin with a special symbol that distinguishes them from values. This symbol varies, depending on the spreadsheet software used. In Excel, the symbol is a mandatory = (equal sign); in Lotus 1-2-3, it's an optional + (plus sign). For example, the formula 3+2 in an Excel spreadsheet program would be represented by =3+2; in Lotus 1-2-3, it would be represented by +3+2. The *Information Technology in Practice* feature entitled "Electronic Spreadsheets: A Secret Weapon for the Small-Business Owner" lists some of the questions that small-business owners can answer with spreadsheet formulas.

function

A formula built into electronic spreadsheet software that will automatically perform certain types of calculation.

- A **function** is a formula built into the spreadsheet software that will automatically perform certain types of calculation. A single function takes the place of several entries that the user would otherwise have to make. (*Note:* Do not confuse *functions* with the *function keys* on computer keyboards.) The symbol @ identifies a command as a predefined function. Among the most com-

FIGURE 6.4
Cell Contents
A spreadsheet cell can hold four types of information: values, labels, formulas, and functions.

Function

Label

Value

Formula
(E4 - E5)
in this cell
produces
the result
shown

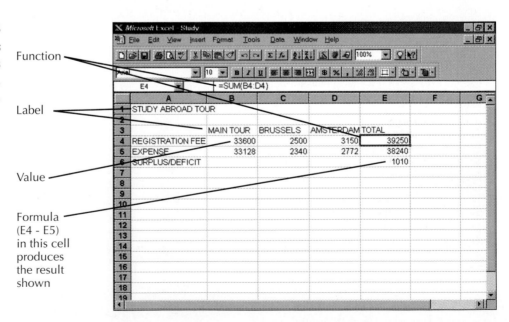

monly used functions are @SUM, which adds the value of a set of cells; @AVG, which calculates the average value of a list of numbers, and @MIN and @MAX, which determine the minimum and maximum values in a set of cells. Table 6.4 lists some other often-used functions.

TABLE 6.3 *Examples of Formulas Used in Spreadsheet Packages*

FORMULA	EXPLANATION
3+2	Add the numbers 3 + 2 and place the result in the current cell.
3−A1	Subtract the contents of cell A1 from the number 3 and place the result in the current cell.
22*(A1/A2)	Divide the contents of cell A1 by the contents of cell A2. Multiply the number 22 by the result of the division and place the result in the current cell.

TABLE 6.4 *Functions Commonly Used in Spreadsheet Packages*

STATISTICAL FUNCTIONS

@AVG	Averages a list of values.
@COUNT	Counts the nonblank cells in a list of ranges.
@MAX	Finds the maximum value in a list of values.
@MIN	Finds the minimum value in a list of values.
@STD	Calculates the population standard deviation of a list of values.
@STDS	Calculates the sample standard deviation of a list of values.

DATE AND TIME FUNCTIONS

@NOW	Calculates the value that corresponds to the current date and time on the computer's clock.
@TODAY	Calculates the data number that corresponds to the current date on the computer's clock.

FINANCIAL FUNCTIONS

@IRR	Calculates the internal rate of return for a series of cash flows.
@NPV	Calculates the net present value of a series of cash flows.
@DDB	Calculates the double-declining balance depreciation allowance of an asset.
@SLN	Calculates the straight-line depreciation allowance of an asset for one period.
@SYD	Calculates the sum-of-the-years'-digits depreciation allowance of an asset.
@FV	Calculates the future value of a series of equal payments.
@PMT	Calculates the amount of the periodic payment needed to pay off a loan.
@PV	Calculates the present value of a series of equal payments.
@TERM	Calculates the number of payment periods of an investment.

INFORMATION TECHNOLOGY IN PRACTICE

Electronic Spreadsheets: A Secret Weapon for the Small-Business Owner

Electronic spreadsheets are one of the most popular types of personal productivity software, mainly because they let even people who are uncomfortable with math manipulate complex formulas. These formulas hold the answers to financial questions that are of vital interest to both individuals and businesses. Some of these questions can be answered by using the spreadsheet's built-in functions. Answering others requires entering some of the formulas shown in the many handbooks and magazine articles designed to help end-users develop their spreadsheet skills.

To understand why a small-business owner might prize electronic spreadsheets, consider some of the basic business questions these tools can help model and answer:

- What's my break-even point? How much income do I need to produce each month just to cover my costs?
- Am I over or under budget this month?
- What's my predicted cash flow for the month? Will I have enough cash on hand to pay my bills?
- When should I reorder inventory and supplies and how much should I order?
- My goal is to increase sales by 3 percent next year. If my costs stay the same, what will happen to profits?
- A lot of businesses seem to increase sales when they discount prices. Would following their example help or hurt my bottom line?

- My business seems to be growing by leaps and bounds. Can I keep growing at this rate without taking out a loan?
- I need to take out a loan for my business. Will my bank approve the loan?
- The bank's advertised interest rate sounds too good to be true. What's the actual annual percentage rate, the one that reflects hidden financing costs like loan fees?
- If I get the loan, what will my monthly payments be?
- I've been making loan payments for a year. How much do I still owe?
- I'm doing some midyear tax planning. How much can I deduct for interest payments on my business loan?
- I'd like to save some interest charges by paying off the loan a year early. How much more should I pay the bank each month?
- I need a new delivery van for the business. Would it be cheaper to buy or lease?
- I'm already setting aside some money for retirement. Can I afford to sell the business and take early retirement when I hit 45?
- I will have accumulated almost $1 million by the age at which I want to retire. Will I be rich, or will inflation force me to go on working?

In Figure 6.4, the function =SUM(B4:D4) tells the computer to add the values in cells B4 through D4 and to place the result in cell E4.

Figure 6.4 shows the labels, values, formulas, and functions used by the Study Abroad Tour in its registration fees/expense/surplus spreadsheet. The Study Abroad Tour consists of a faculty-led student tour of London and Paris, with optional add-on visits to Brussels and Amsterdam. The Study Abroad Tour example will be used in the pages that follow.

The functions that accompany a spreadsheet package can be overwhelming if you attempt to commit every one to memory immediately. A better approach to learning how to put software to work for you is to first familiarize yourself with the software's general capabilities, and then use its more specialized capabilities.

Some frequently used functions, such as those for summation, determining averages, and identifying minimum and maximum values, are general and apply to many different areas. Learn how to use these first. Then bone up on the specific functions that are most applicable to your career field or job responsibilities. After you use these functions regularly for a while, you will find they become second nature to you, and you'll reach for them automatically when you need to apply them to your work. Use, not memorization, is the most effective means of learning. ■

CELL RANGE. A single cell by itself is not of much use in solving a problem or analyzing a situation. For this reason, most problem analysts use information from a range of cells. A *range* is a group of adjacent cells. It may be composed of a row, a column, or several rows and columns of adjacent cells. As we saw in the preceding example, formulas and functions frequently specify ranges for computation. In Figure 6.4, the function used for the Study Abroad Tour to sum revenues makes use of the cell range B4–D4. Figure 6.5 shows some other cell ranges.

As another example, consider a sales manager who is trying to assess who are the best, average, and worst performers on her sales team. To determine this information, she would first specify the range of cells in her spreadsheets that contain sales information, and then use the MAX, AVG, and MIN functions in that specified range of cells to get the information she is looking for.

IMPORTING DATA. Instead of entering data into a spreadsheet from the keyboard, the user may decide to import data from a file on disk. *Importing* means reading text or numbers into a spreadsheet file from a different spreadsheet file

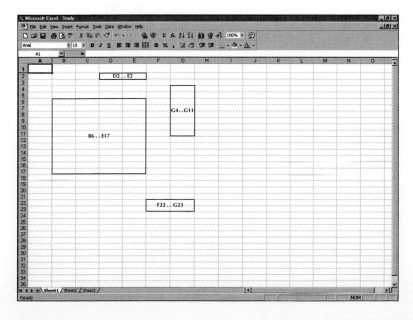

FIGURE 6.5

Cell Ranges

Different spreadsheet programs use different notations for ranges. Some use two periods (D2..E2); others use one period (D2.E2); others use a colon (D2:E2).

or from a file created by a database program, word-processing system, or other type of program. Importing not only saves time but also allows data to be shared across several programs.

FORMATTING VALUES.   Spreadsheet software uses a built-in, prespecified default format for data. For example, values are displayed without separators (such as commas) or currency signs (e.g., $, ¥, or £). But spreadsheet programs' formatting capabilities allow the user to change the appearance of characters both on the screen and when printed. Among the format adjustments that can be made are the following:

- Adding characters to the displayed contents of a cell (such as $, ¥, £, %, or decimal positions).
- Changing the width of columns.
- Specifying the alignment of the contents of a cell so that characters are centered, aligned on the left side of the cell, aligned on the right side of the cell, or aligned over a decimal point.
- Changing the style and size of the characters.
- Adding emphasis by making the characters bold, italic, or underlined.
- Changing the characters from lowercase to UPPERCASE.

Figure 6.6 shows the spreadsheet in Figure 6.4 reformatted to call attention to certain items. The objectives of formatting are to make the information easy to read and to ensure that the most important details of the spreadsheet stand out.

Editing Data

The details you entered into an electronic spreadsheet when you started to study a problem may change as you study it further. You can analyze the effects

FIGURE 6.6   *Reformatting a Worksheet*
Electronic spreadsheets offer many options to customize and reformat the standard worksheet.

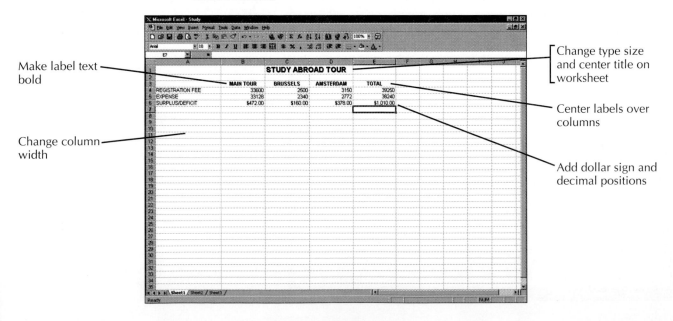

Make label text bold

Change column width

Change type size and center title on worksheet

Center labels over columns

Add dollar sign and decimal positions

of such changes in detail by using any of the spreadsheet's following editing capabilities:

- **Change, add, and delete data.** Spreadsheet programs allow you to correct or change the contents of a cell quickly and easily. They also let you add new data and delete the contents of cells whenever necessary.
- **Insert and delete rows and columns.** As your worksheet grows larger and more complex, you may want to add rows and columns to it. Spreadsheet programs allow you to do so with the click of a button. It is also easy to delete rows and columns when the material they contain is no longer necessary or relevant.
- **Copy, move, find, and sort data and formulas.** Using special commands, you can get a spreadsheet program to copy cells from one part of a spreadsheet to another, and even from spreadsheet to spreadsheet. You can also transfer data and formulas from one part of the spreadsheet to another. "Find" or "Search" commands allow you to locate particular entries quickly, and "Sort" commands allow you to order data numerically or alphabetically.
- **Freeze row and column headings.** When worksheets are large, column and row labels will scroll off the screen as you move around the worksheet. To avoid this inconvenience, you can instruct the software to keep the labels in a fixed location on the display screen.
- **Adjust column width.** All the cells in a worksheet are prespecified at the same width. When data are longer than the width of the column into which they will be entered, it is a simple matter to enlarge the columns to fit the data. By the same token, if columns are too wide, it is easy to decrease the column width. Most spreadsheet programs will spill over data from one column to the next when data values and labels exceed column width—provided the adjacent cells are not already in use. This feature is useful for the occasional item that is longer than normal. However, when most items exceed the current column width, the width of that column should be adjusted.
- **Undo actions.** If you change your mind after deleting a row of data, removing the contents of a worksheet, or moving data to a different part of the worksheet, all is not lost. Most spreadsheets allow you to reverse your action. The "Undo" command restores the affected area to the way it was before you took the action. But "Undo" must be performed immediately after an action, before any other step is taken. "Undo" does not allow you to reverse printing, storing, or importation activities.

Storing Worksheets

Before ending an electronic spreadsheet session, you must save the worksheet as a file if you want to keep it. To do so, you give the worksheet a unique file name, according to the rules of the computer's operating system, and the computer will store the worksheet under that name. Then, whenever you want to recall the worksheet, all you have to do is provide the file name and the computer will retrieve the file from storage and display the worksheet on the display screen.

Worksheet templates can also be created as files. A **template** is a worksheet containing row and column labels, and perhaps formulas, but not necessarily any values. The template is distributed to people as a guide for analyzing problems or providing data.

The Georgia Research Alliance (GRA), in Atlanta, helps government offices and universities obtain grants and funds to support public-interest programs and to

template
A worksheet containing row and column labels, and perhaps formulas, but not necessarily any values. It is distributed to people as a guide for analyzing problems or providing data.

Study Abroad Tour

	MAIN TOUR	BRUSSELS	AMSTERDAM	TOTAL
REGISTRATION FEES	33600	2500	3150	39250
EXPENSE	33128	2340	2772	38240
SURPLUS/DEFICIT	$472.00	$160.00	$378.00	$1,010.00

conduct research. One of GRA's goals is to develop cross-organization efforts in which as many as a dozen different program directors join forces to prepare proposals for submission to funding agencies. To help coordinate the various directors' submissions, GRA prepares spreadsheet templates—for budgets, staffing needs, and equipment and space requirements—and distributes them to all the people responsible for preparing proposals. By having all parties work from the same templates, GRA ensures that the final proposals will have a common appearance and contain all the essential information. The templates make it easier for funding agencies to evaluate the proposals.

macro
A time-saving miniprogram, identified by a name and a series of keystrokes, that is used to perform commonly repeated actions.

Another timesaving capability offered by spreadsheet programs is the **macro,** which allows the user to write programs within the worksheet. Each macro is actually a miniprogram identified by a name and a series of keystrokes. (Some programs also include a built-in macro editor that performs many of the functions of a software command language.) Creating a macro to perform commonly repeated actions (such as boldfacing certain entries, which would normally require three or four steps) can save the user a great deal of time and annoyance.

The *Information Technology in Practice* feature entitled "Templates Provide Spreadsheet Power" illustrates how all of these features are used in a financial analysis application.

Printing Worksheets

When a worksheet is printed, the contents of the entire worksheet or a selected range of cells are transferred to an output medium, usually paper or transparencies. Printing preserves the format of the worksheet's values and labels. If special type styles or formats were selected for the worksheet, they will appear on the printed output. Figure 6.7 shows a printout of the spreadsheet in Figure 6.6.

Problem Solving Using Spreadsheets

Two integral parts of problem solving are testing alternative solutions and breaking down problems into their component parts. Spreadsheet systems are an enormous support to the user in both these parts of problem solving. (We discuss the problem-solving cycle in detail in Chapter 8.)

Recalculation and Sensitivity Analysis

sensitivity analysis
The analytical process by which a computer determines what would happen if certain data change.

The benefits of using worksheets with formulas become evident when data change, as they often do. Perhaps the most valuable feature of electronic spreadsheets is their ability to perform **sensitivity analysis,** an analytical process by

INFORMATION TECHNOLOGY IN PRACTICE

Templates Provide Spreadsheet Power

Success with a spreadsheet application depends on getting the spreadsheet right to begin with, and then knowing how to use it. This entails setting up the most appropriate format and structure; using program features, such as macros, most efficiently; avoiding errors in formulas and elsewhere; determining extreme conditions and planning how to handle them (e.g., blanks in fields where data items are expected); and using enhancements effectively (e.g., application of color and protecting cells against inadvertent change).

To derive maximum benefits from their electronic spreadsheets, users can purchase a growing array of templates, which are spreadsheets predesigned to handle specific types of information processing and analysis, at a computer retail store. With a template, users can avoid such chores as designing the spreadsheet's layout, entering formulas, and developing reporting formats—all time-consuming activities. Of course, adopters must ensure that the template uses formulas and procedures in a way that accurately fits their business methods.

Let's look at how a set of templates for a typical financial analysis spreadsheet would be used. This set would comprise three-dimensional templates for preparing monthly, quarterly, and annually forecasted financial statements. After loading the templates onto a PC, the user enters information about the type of company and its financial management methods, including balance sheet account numbers, names, and balances; methods for calculating depreciation; and long- and short-term interest

rates. Once these details are entered, the application is ready to go. It's that simple.

Unprotected cells in the worksheet, where data are entered in using the system, are shown in one color. Those containing formulas or other information that cannot be altered are shown in a different color.

To print reports and analyses, the user chooses from formats built into the templates. (More than a dozen predesigned formats are available, including conventional financial statements and supporting schedules.) Another set of templates prints key ratios. Good layouts, effective use of color, and the incorporation of three-dimensional graphics add to the professional appearance of the printed information.

Because templates provide the power of spreadsheets without the cost of having to develop them from scratch, their use in large and small businesses will continue to grow.

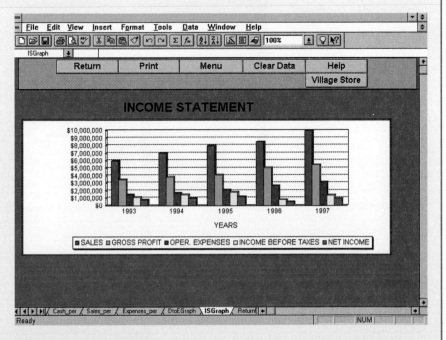

which the computer determines what would happen if certain data change. To continue the example we've been using, any adjustment in the revenue and expense categories of the Study Abroad Tour will result automatically in a recalculation of all totals on the spreadsheet. One of the greatest virtues of spreadsheets is that they make it possible to test the relationship between revenue and cost easily and quickly using many different figures.

Suppose that the main tour expenses are 10 percent higher than the original estimate (given in Figure 6.4)—owing, perhaps, to both fluctuations in international currency values and greater than anticipated expenses. Figure 6.8 shows the changes in all values in the SURPLUS/DEFICIT row. Instead of the original estimated surplus of $1,010, the tour will incur a deficit of $2,814.

In studying human behavior in business and everyday life, Nobel Prize winner Herbert Simon found that when people have difficulty finding a solution to a problem, they tend to settle for the first answer that meets their objectives. That is, they accept a solution that is "good enough," even if better solutions are available. Simon coined the term *satisficing* to describe this tendency. In contrast, when people can easily identify a solution to a problem they are facing, they are likely to continue to seek even better answers, often finding alternative solutions that surpass their original objectives by a substantial margin.

FIGURE 6.8
Recalculation to Test Sensitivity

One of the most important features of electronic spreadsheets is their ability to recalculate mountains of data automatically when one piece (or many pieces) of data changes.

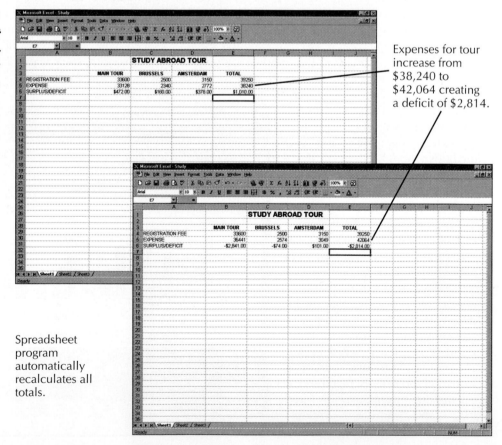

Expenses for tour increase from $38,240 to $42,064 creating a deficit of $2,814.

Spreadsheet program automatically recalculates all totals.

Interacting with a spreadsheet system to perform sensitivity analysis will help overcome the satisficing tendency. The spreadsheet software's ability to evaluate alternative "what if" ideas quickly and easily will encourage you to evaluate a greater number of options. ■

Linking Spreadsheets

In solving a problem comprising multiple parts, you need to identify and analyze each part independently to assemble information, evaluate strategies, and identify solutions. You then reassemble the parts and what you have learned about how they affect the whole so that you can manage the problem solution in its entirety.

All spreadsheet packages give users the option of creating individual worksheets to deal with each part of a problem. Most provide in addition a *linkage* capability that permits the interconnection of the separate worksheets and even the transfer of information among them. Many packages also provide a summary worksheet designed to accumulate the totals and results of all the other worksheets.

The Study Abroad Tour worksheet we're using as an example in this chapter reports the total registration fees and expenses for travel to the main tour cities, London and Paris, and the add-on cities, Brussels and Amsterdam. Earlier, we were concerned solely with the accumulated totals of each category. Here, we see that each category actually consists of several separate categories.

Another way of handling the Study Abroad Tour information is to establish a separate worksheet for each category, as shown in Figure 6.9. The London Expenses category includes individual expenses and costs for lodging, various types of transportation, meals, photocopies, and host gifts. Excel's linkage capability interrelates all the worksheets and accumulates the appropriate summary information on the summary worksheet in Figure 6.9.

Individual worksheets are prepared and the contents are used to compile a summary worksheet.

FIGURE 6.9 *Linking Multiple Worksheets*
Linking worksheets electronically increases productivity by facilitating the exchange of information between people, departments, and businesses.

The financial results shown on each individual worksheet are interrelated. The expenses incurred for the students in London, Paris, and the add-on cities of Brussels and Amsterdam (totaling $19,040) are determined on a separate worksheet and linked to the expense category on the main worksheet. Similarly, program expenses (totaling $19,200) are calculated on a separate worksheet that is linked to the main worksheet (i.e., total expenses of $38,240). The linkage feature of spreadsheet software allows a problem solver to evaluate these interrelationships and the effects of changing expenses on the entire tour surplus or deficit.

The *systems concept* states that components of a system interact with one another to produce a certain result. This concept underlies many business practices and explains why organizations create departments and units to deal with specific activities. Depending on the extent to which information flows among the different units, employees may work independently or they may coordinate their activities to ensure the best possible results.

Spreadsheet packages, which provide the capability for multiple worksheets that are independently created and used, yet linked with one another, embody the systems concept. The separate worksheets are the individual components of analysis, while the entire set of worksheets is the entire system of analysis. Because of the linkage feature, information can flow easily among the worksheets.

The Study Abroad Tour program is an example of a system. Its components are the program's principal activity centers: the main tour, the Brussels option, and the Amsterdam option. Each center consists of such components as transportation, lodging, meals, photocopies, and host gifts. Each center also has revenue components—the registration fees shown in Figure 6.4.

These centers are so linked that a change in one will affect the overall outcome. Thus, if transportation to London costs more than expected, the overall cost of the tour program will be higher, possibly requiring a higher registration charge for everyone participating in the program. The higher cost for transportation to London also changes the earlier-anticipated surplus or shortfall for the program. As our example illustrates, in a system of any type, the components are so interrelated that a change in any one of them affects the overall performance and outcome of the system. ■

Creating Business Graphics

The numeric information that is created and analyzed through a spreadsheet program provides powerful support to problem solvers. When translated into high-quality graphic form, this information can be even more useful.

The Benefits of Business Graphics

Business graphics present information visually through charts, graphics, and symbols. Generally, graphics are used to illustrate the relationships between spreadsheet elements (e.g., revenue and expenses). Being visual, they convey information about these relationships more quickly than numbers in tabular form can. They are also more exciting to look at.

Graphics do not relieve you of the responsibility to obtain accurate and reliable information. Nor do they substitute for tabular presentation of numeric detail. Rather, they are a supplement, useful for illustrating trends, proportions, highs and lows, and relationships. Figure 6.10 shows several popular forms of business graphics.

Spreadsheets and Business Graphics

Five types of business graphics are usually included in spreadsheet software:

1. **Bar charts** consist of a series of bars, each representing a particular element in the worksheet. Bar length indicates the value of the data: the longer the

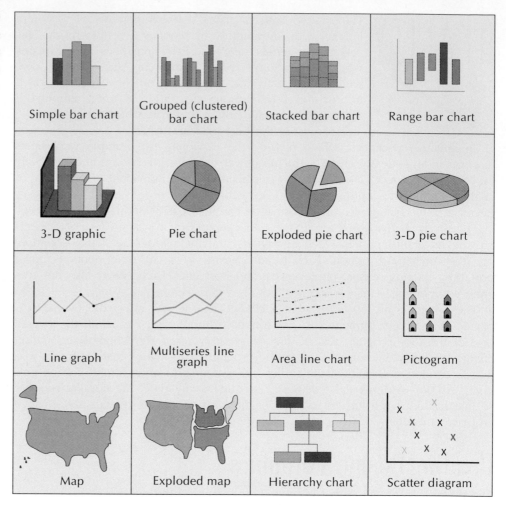

bar, the higher the value of the data it represents. Bars can be "stacked" to show different values of an element at different times.

2. **Pictograms** depict data as icons or symbols that represent the magnitude of the data values. Usually the image is symbolic of the element it stands for. For example, a pictogram showing real estate sales might use houses as icons, with one icon representing 100 houses sold.

3. **Pie charts** demonstrate the proportion or percentage of the whole that is represented by each element. The proportions are shown as a part of a circular graphic—that is, like slices of a pie.

4. **Line charts** plot changes in data values over time and connect these points by a line. Each line in the graph represents the fluctuation of a single element.

5. **Area line charts** use lines that are "stacked" or combined to show the total in each category. Each line's values are added to those of the line below.

Figure 6.11 offers some tips for choosing the best type of graphic to use in different business situations.

Always keep in mind that even well-prepared graphics do not automatically improve the effectiveness of your data presentation. You have to use them at the right time and in the proper manner. Business graphics are most effective for

FIGURE 6.11 *Choosing the Best Type of Business Graphic*

Choosing the right type of business graphic can help you summarize your data and grab your readers' interest, motivating them to look for the detailed information contained in a spreadsheet like this one for The Runner's Foot chain of shoe stores.

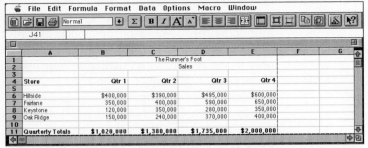

Store	Qtr 1	Qtr 2	Qtr 3	Qtr 4
		The Runner's Foot Sales		
Hillside	$400,000	$390,000	$495,000	$600,000
Fairlane	350,000	400,000	590,000	650,000
Keystone	120,000	350,000	280,000	350,000
Oak Ridge	150,000	240,000	370,000	400,000
Quarterly Totals	$1,020,000	$1,380,000	$1,735,000	$2,000,000

When You Need to...	Choose a...	Description
Compare data values associated with a specific time period, such as regional sales per quarter.	**Bar Chart**	Transforms each row or column of spreadsheet numbers into a set of bars with the same pattern or color; resulting bars are then grouped by time and/or location.
Compare the change in totals at specific time periods or compare several groups of data in a clear, concise way.	**Stacked Bar Chart**	Same as a bar chart except the colored or shaded bars are stacked on top of each other, showing a total for each time and/or location.
Show the magnitude and significance of data totals and/or increase corporate identity or motivation.	**Pictogram**	Replaces bars of bar chart with a number of icons or symbols; each icon or symbol represents a specific unit of measurement.
Provide a quick overview of budgets, market share, or any other data that can be divided into a limited number of categories.	**Pie Chart**	Shows the relationship between a total and its components, usually expressed as percentages. Each "slice" represents a data value within a spreadsheet row or column.
Show trends or changes over time.	**Line Chart**	Uses a line (or "curve") to link data points that represent the numbers within a spreadsheet row or column.
Emphasize general trends, rather than differences between regions or product lines.	**Area Line Chart**	Uses the sum of two adjacent cells to create a "stacked" line chart; the area beneath the uppermost curve represents a total for all divisions or product lines.

- Detecting patterns in data.
- Detecting trends or changes in trends.
- Identifying relationships.

They are least effective for

- Determining the values of specific data points.
- Determining the absolute change in numeric values represented in trends.
- Representing a small amount of data (i.e., a few data values).

Another point to keep in mind when choosing a graphic is that it should be appropriate to the data you are illustrating. An unfamiliar form will only confuse and irritate your audience. For example, a business income statement, an income tax statement (in the United States), or a value-added tax statement (in Europe) in graphic form would be unfamiliar and probably unacceptable.

A picture (or a graph) is worth a thousand words, as the saying goes—but only if the picture is recognizable and used in a way that readily makes sense. Lotus Corp. found this out the hard way when it introduced a program with only moderate graphics capabilities in Japan. For details, see the *Information Technology in Practice* feature entitled "Lotus 1-2-3: Meeting the Japanese Challenge."

Generating Graphic Information with Spreadsheets

Users can generate graphic information with spreadsheet software quickly and easily because the software uses the values in the worksheet's rows and columns to generate the graphs. To create a graph, the user follows six steps:

1. Select the values to be graphed from the worksheet.
2. Activate the spreadsheet's graphing commands.
3. Select the type of graph desired.
4. Generate the graph.
5. Add descriptive information to the graph.
6. Store or print the graph.

Suppose a faculty coordinator of the Study Abroad Tour wants to prepare a graphic showing the proportion of revenues relative to expenses for each destination category. A bar chart comparing fees and expenses for London and Paris, Brussels, and Amsterdam seems appropriate. To create the graphics, the manager first highlights the revenue and expense rows and the column headings for each category. Next she selects a side-by-side bar chart from the list of graphics options. Finally, she adds the headings and annotations after the computer has drawn the graph. The result is shown in Figure 6.12.

FIGURE 6.12

Bar Chart Generated from Worksheet Data

The spreadsheet program created this bar chart automatically from the data in Figure 6.4.

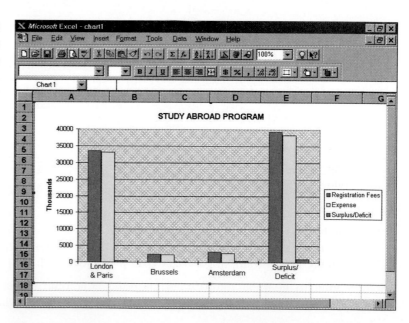

INFORMATION TECHNOLOGY IN PRACTICE

Lotus 1-2-3: Meeting the Japanese Challenge

Shortly after being introduced in the early 1980s, Lotus 1-2-3 became the most popular spreadsheet for IBM-compatible PCs in the United States. So it's not surprising that by 1984 Lotus Development Corp. was looking to conquer the rest of the world. Gaining a foothold in Europe was relatively easy, but Lotus encountered both technical and cultural barriers in Japan. The challenges it faced—and the solutions it found—offer valuable lessons for any business that wants to be a player in the global economy.

Challenge: Understanding the Japanese business market and its expectations for software.
Solution: Form a lasting relationship with local experts. Lotus realized fairly early that it needed some insight into the Japanese software market. One of the company's advantages here was that its president, Jim Manzi, had spent two years in Japan as a management consultant. Another advantage was the two years the Lotus development team spent working with SoftBank, Japan's largest software distributor. SoftBank taught Lotus that it had to make 1-2-3 much easier to use and improve the program's business graphics dramatically if it wanted to succeed in Japan.

Challenge: Making Lotus user-friendly when your users aren't accustomed to a keyboard. The standard QWERTY keyboard is a fixture in U.S. offices, and most high-school graduates have

mastered it. Not so in Japan. The main problem there was how to accommodate almost 2,000 Japanese *kanji* and *kana* characters—as well as Latin, Greek, and Cyrillic characters—on a keyboard with a limited number of keys.
Solution: Delegate the challenge to local experts. Lotus formed a technical partnership with Kanri Kogaku Kenkyusho (K3), a Japanese software house. K3 wrote a pop-up program that can transform phonetic phrases typed in the Latin alphabet into the proper *kanji-kana* characters onscreen. K3 also helped create Japanese-language menus, help screens, and manuals; a Japanese learn mode; an electronic tutorial in Japanese; and built-in formulas and chart types customized to Japanese needs.

Challenge: Meeting Japanese standards for graphics. Japanese consumers, accustomed to the sophisticated graphics of Japanese computer games, were decidedly unimpressed by the crude graphics that characterized early versions of Lotus 1-2-3.
Solution: Meet standards abroad, and jump-start your product development at home. The Japanese version of Lotus impresses potential customers by offering eight types of grid lines in its graphs, user-selectable on-screen colors, and other high-quality graphing functions. Many of these same features were incorporated into the next update of Lotus 1-2-3 for the United States.

Challenge: Winning acceptance in a market that is attuned to buying Japanese products.

Solution: Ask consumers and local experts how buying decisions are made. When the Lotus team inquired about the consumer decision-making process, it learned that Japanese consumers often base their software buying decisions on the number of how-to books that are available for a particular package. Lotus responded by hiring eight authors to write Japanese-language books on Lotus 1-2-3. The books were in the bookstores before Lotus began shipping the software.

Lotus also mounted an advertising campaign on Japan's crowded subways, a tactic no other software company had tried. The result: Millions of consumers were exposed to the Lotus name. The happy ending: Within a month of its release, the Japanese version of 1-2-3 was at the top of the sales chart and stayed there for the rest of the year. At year's end, it received the Software of the Year award from *Nikkei PC* magazine. To celebrate its success, Lotus bought a full-page advertisement in *Nihon Keizai Shimbun,* the Japanese equivalent of *The Wall Street Journal.* Its subject? A very humble and Japanese thank-you and salute to the consumers who had made Lotus 1-2-3 Japan's favorite spreadsheet software.

Source: Carol Ellison, "Why Japan Can't Write Software" and "Selling 1-2-3 in Japan," *PC Computing,* December 1988, pp. 110–122. Copyright © 1988, Ziff-Davis Publishing Company, L.P.

FIGURE 6.13

Pie Chart Generated from Worksheet Data

The spreadsheet program created this summary pie chart automatically from the data in Figure 6.4.

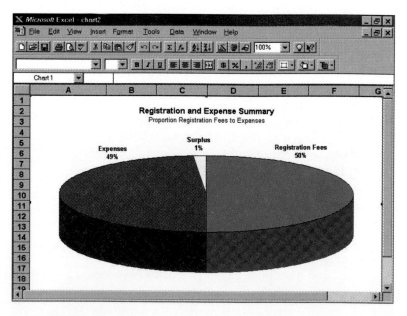

A pie chart could also be a useful graphic for illustrating the proportion of profit to expense. The values in column E, rows 5 and 6, of Figure 6.4 describe total expenses and the surplus/deficit, respectively. The pie chart based on these data is shown in Figure 6.13.

Figure 6.14 offers some tips for preparing a spreadsheet report with business graphics.

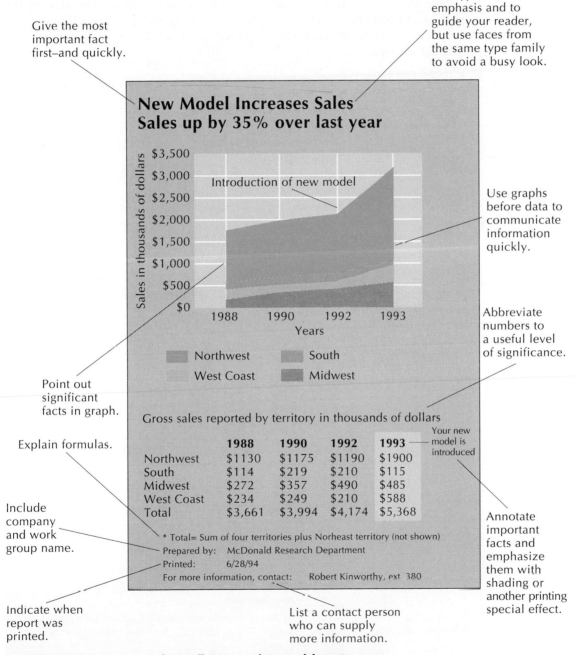

FIGURE 6.14 *Anatomy of a Well-Designed Spreadsheet Report*
A well-designed spreadsheet report should be informative and easy to read.
SOURCE: Daniel Gasteiger, "The Outs of Spreadsheet Power," *PC/Computing*, June 1990, p. 110. Copyright © 1990, Ziff-Davis Publishing Company, L.P.

Developing a Personal Spreadsheet Application

If you're setting up a spreadsheet to do just a few quick calculations or some preliminary planning, you can be fairly casual in the way you label rows and columns and enter formulas. But the value of spreadsheet software is that it helps you solve recurring problems. That's why the businesspeople who build, use, and share spreadsheets on a daily basis follow a more formal process when they set up and document their spreadsheets. This formal problem-solving process has several advantages.

- It helps you think through a problem and identify the inputs, outputs, assumptions, and formulas needed to devise a solution.
- It helps you remember the assumptions and formulas you used in building the spreadsheet.
- It helps you find your way around a large spreadsheet with many rows, columns, and links to other spreadsheets.
- It lets you create instructions and documentation that will help others use your spreadsheet for their own work.
- It gives you—and others—an opportunity to evaluate your logic and to test your spreadsheet with simple data before you begin to use it yourself or share it with others.
- It creates a more flexible spreadsheet that is easy to revise and adapt to different circumstances.

Developing a spreadsheet for a business application involves the following four steps (Figure 6.15):

1. Define the problem.
2. Plan the spreadsheet's layout.
3. Enter the spreadsheet into your computer.
4. Test and use the spreadsheet.

FIGURE 6.15
Developing a Spreadsheet Application, Step by Step
Each phase of spreadsheet application development requires the designer to answer several key questions.

STEP	KEY QUESTIONS TO ANSWER
1. Define the problem.	What is the spreadsheet's purpose? What are the desired outputs? What inputs can be changed? What assumptions will be used in your calculations? What formulas will be used to calculate the desired outputs?
2. Plan the spreadsheet's layout.	How will you organize labels, data, formulas, and other instructions for maximum efficiency, clarity, and flexibility?
3. Enter the spreadsheet layout into your computer.	What commands are needed to enter, edit, and store values, labels, formulas, and functions in the desired layout?
4. Test and use the spreadsheet.	Does the spreadsheet produce accurate results when sample data are entered?

To see how this process works, let's look at how you might use it to solve a problem in your own business, The ShirtWorks.

The ShirtWorks Problem

You created The ShirtWorks almost by accident, after some volunteer committee work made you an expert on working with the wholesalers, artists, and printers needed to produce T-shirts imprinted with the names and slogans of campus groups. Now, after reading that the average American buys about eight printed T-shirts a year,[1] you've decided to widen the scope of your business.

After speaking to a potential customer about his group's T-shirt needs, you draw up an estimate that reflects the cost of the blank shirts, shipping, and printing; a markup (or profit); and, in some cases, the cost of artwork you've commissioned from a graphic artist. If the customer likes your ideas and your price, you ask for a 50 percent deposit, which gives you the money to order the T-shirts and begin the manufacturing process. You work directly with the suppliers and the printer. Finally, you collect the balance due when you deliver the finished shirts to your customer.

Like many small-business owners, you've been running the business out of a spare bedroom on a part-time basis, figuring your prices by using a calculator and handwritten notes on a scratchpad. You think you are doing fairly well, especially since you are receiving a growing number of inquiries from local businesses, sports teams, and theater and music groups who are considering using your custom-printed T-shirts for their promotions and advertising.

Clearly, it is time to take The ShirtWorks more seriously. You attend a seminar on price-setting, and come away with a sinking feeling. It turns out that your prices are the lowest around—too low, in fact, to cover your expenses and leave an adequate profit. Your worries are confirmed when you go to the library and find an article titled "Starting a T-Shirt Business" by Spider, who, together with his wife, runs a T-shirt business called Spider & Co. from their home in Mesa, Arizona.[2] An artist, printer, lecturer, and consultant with 35 years' experience in the T-shirt business, Spider warns that "improper pricing can drive newcomers out of business before they really get going." You decide to use your Macintosh computer and Microsoft Excel software to develop a spreadsheet application that will incorporate all the professional advice you've been gathering. Before you turn on your computer, though, you need to do some preliminary planning.

Step 1: Define the Problem

Before you can set up a spreadsheet, you need to define the problem you are trying to solve and your solution requirements. To do this, you have to decide on the spreadsheet's purpose, its desired outputs, and the inputs, assumptions, and formulas needed to produce these outputs. (If you were developing a spreadsheet for other people, you would have to spend some time talking to them, helping them to specify all these things for their problem.)

Because you have lived with The ShirtWorks' pricing problem for a while, you find it easy to define the problem and the spreadsheet's purpose. The problem: Your prices are too low and you are not making a sufficient profit.

[1]Eric Zorn, "Just What We All Need: A New T-Shirt," *Chicago Tribune,* June 8, 1993.
[2]Spider, "Running a T-Shirt Business," *Home Office Computing,* November 1992, pp. 46-47.

THE SPREADSHEET'S PURPOSE.   The spreadsheet's purpose, you decide, is to automate the process of setting customer prices, calculate the deposit required with an order, and prepare an order form.

THE DESIRED OUTPUTS.   You want the spreadsheet to produce four outputs:

1. A wholesale cost that reflects your cost of goods (the price you pay for blank T-shirts, shipping, and printing) and a markup (representing your profit).
2. A wholesale price that reflects your wholesale cost plus overhead costs (the money you spend on business-related rent, utilities, telephone, and automobile expenses).
3. A total order price that includes the wholesale price of the printed T-shirts plus any charges and commissions on original artwork.
4. The deposit required before you will accept an order.

THE NECESSARY INPUTS.   The inputs into the spreadsheet are the values that can vary from time to time and affect any of the outputs produced by the spreadsheet:

1. The cost of the blank T-shirts.
2. The shipping cost charged by the blank T-shirt supplier.
3. The cost for printing.
4. The markup, expressed as a percentage of the T-shirt's wholesale cost.
5. Monthly overhead costs.
6. The fee charged by a graphic artist.
7. The commission you charge on artwork, expressed as a percentage of the price of the artwork.

THE BASIC ASSUMPTIONS.   A few basic assumptions will simplify your calculations and affect the figures you show your customers.

1. The minimum order size allowed by both T-shirt suppliers and printers is one gross (12 dozen, or 144) shirts; orders must be placed in multiples of one gross. You will pass on this requirement on to your customers.
2. To simplify your calculations and presentations to customers, printed T-shirt prices will be expressed per unit, or shirt.
3. The cost of blank T-shirts and shipping costs will come from the supplier's latest catalog.
4. Overhead costs per shirt will be based on the assumption that only one order of 144 shirts will be processed per week.
5. The cost of original artwork will vary; it will be billed, along with your commission, directly to the customer.

THE FORMULAS USED.   The formulas you embed in your spreadsheet will determine the accuracy of all the spreadsheet's calculations. That's why you need to state them, using business terms like *markup,* in a mathematical format that you will convert into spreadsheet formulas. These statements will allow you to evaluate your reasoning and to find any errors in your logic. As you think through the problem, you realize you'll need a number of formulas for your spreadsheet. The key formulas for the ShirtWorks' spreadsheet are listed in Table 6.5.

   This kind of painstaking analysis may seem unnecessary for such a relatively simple problem. But you will appreciate it six months from now, when you need to consider the effect of a rent increase on your overhead costs or reexamine the assumptions you used to set a minimum order size.

TABLE 6.5 *Formulas Used in The ShirtWorks Pricing Worksheet*

Unit Cost	=	Cost per Gross of Blank Shirts
Unit Cost of Goods	=	Unit Cost of Shirt + Unit Cost of Shipping + Unit Cost of Printing
Markup per Unit	=	Unit Cost of Goods × Markup Percentage
Wholesale Unit Cost	=	Unit Cost of Goods + Markup
Wholesale Unit Price	=	Unit Cost of Goods + Unit Cost of Overhead
Monthly Overhead Costs	=	(One Year's Business-Related Rent + Business-Related Utilities + Business-Related Telephone Expenses + Business-Related Car Expenses) ÷ 12
Artwork	=	Artist's Fees × (1 + Your Commission)
Total Order Price	=	(Wholesale Unit Price × Quantity Ordered) + Artwork
Deposit Required	=	Total Order Price × .5

Important: All formulas to be used in the spreadsheet should be checked for accuracy before they are embedded in the spreadsheet. The formulas here use × for multiplication and ÷ for division; these signs will need to be converted to "*" and "/" when the formulas are embedded in the worksheet.

Think, too, about the number of assumptions and input values you needed to solve this relatively simple problem. Then imagine the number of assumptions, data values, and formulas you would need to handle a larger, more complex spreadsheet. Could you or your co-workers remember them from week to week without some sort of memory aid?

Step 2: Plan the Spreadsheet's Layout

Once you've defined the problem, you need to plan your spreadsheet's layout in a way that will be clear to you and others. Although there is no right or wrong way to lay out your spreadsheet, it is helpful to follow some general guidelines. One guideline mandated by all the experts: Don't be afraid to underestimate your own memory or the knowledge of others who will be using your spreadsheet. Another guideline: Divide your spreadsheet into six sections: a title page, user instructions, the input information area, the calculations area, a scratch area, and a summary. These can be either six sections of a large spreadsheet or six linked spreadsheets (Figure 6.16).

THE TITLE PAGE. Like the title page of a book, the title page of a spreadsheet contains important introductory information. This information, shown in Figure 6.16, is as follows:

- *The computer file name and an expanded spreadsheet name.* If you were working on an IBM-compatible PC, your file would be limited to 8 characters—a restriction that sometimes leads to creative but cryptic file names. You are working on the Macintosh, though, and the Macintosh operating system lets file names be as long as 32 characters. As a result, there is no difference between your Macintosh file name and the application name, so the title page shows only the file name.

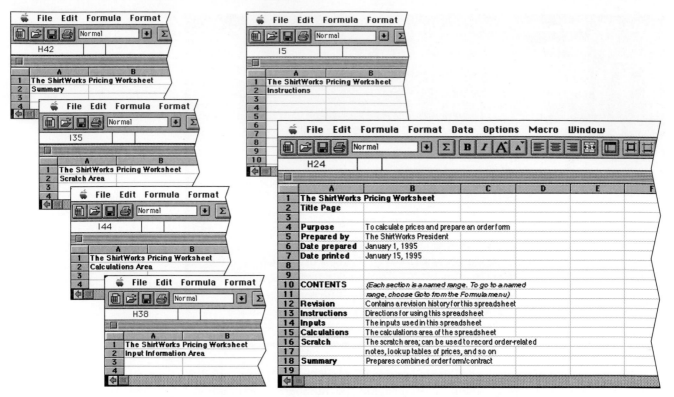

FIGURE 6.16   *A Guide to the Well-Designed Spreadsheet*
Well-designed spreadsheet applications have six distinct areas: a title page, user instructions, an input information area, a calculation area, a scratch area, and a summary.

- *A statement of the spreadsheet's purpose.* (You can pick this up from the problem definition.)
- *The name, title, and affiliation of the person preparing the spreadsheet.* This may seem like overkill for a one-person business like The ShirtWorks, but it is vital in larger businesses, where people routinely share spreadsheet applications developed by others. Entering the application developer's name here lets other users know whom to call with questions or comments.
- *The date this application is developed.*
- *The date this report is printed.*
- *A table of contents, or map, showing the file's major divisions.* This feature helps readers move around the spreadsheet quickly and easily. You can key the map to specific ranges of cells (e.g., B22:H22), or you can assign the range a descriptive and easy-to-remember name, such as January Sales. The map shown on the title page in Figure 6.16 uses range names. To move around the spreadsheet, users simply call up the "Goto" command and type in the range name.

Note that the first entry in the map refers the user to a revision history—a table of who revised the spreadsheet, what was revised, and when. As The Shirt-Works grows, for example, you might decide to hire salespeople to work on commission. This decision would force you to revise the spreadsheet to include this cost in your calculations.

USER INSTRUCTIONS. This section of the spreadsheet includes step-by-step guidelines for entering data and using the results of calculations. Often, the instructions section will end with directions for using a macro to print the instructions on paper. Having the instructions on paper is a comfort to inexperienced users. It also saves time for users who have moved on to other sections of the spreadsheet but need to review the instructions from time to time.

THE INPUT INFORMATION AREA. This section incorporates the input information you generated in Step 1 into your spreadsheet file. Including this information here has one major benefit: it identifies the inputs that will be used in the formulas in the calculations area. The data values for these inputs can be changed at will, allowing you to perform "what if" analyses (e.g., "What happens if I increase markup to 50 percent?"). If your spreadsheet uses a number of macros, you should group an explanation of them somewhere within the spreadsheet, showing the keystrokes used to activate each. Depending on the number and type of macros used, you can place this explanation in the input information area or at the top of the calculations section. Both locations will make the macros easy to find and revise.

THE CALCULATIONS AREA. This section of the spreadsheet is reserved for the table of formulas designed to produce the answers you need. You'll want to use care in the way you enter your formulas. A common mistake made by beginning spreadsheet users is encoding specific input values into the formulas contained in the calculations area. This shortcut hides some of your input values—for example, the size of your commission—when the spreadsheet is printed. It also defeats one of the main benefits of using an electronic spreadsheet—the power to change one number and let the spreadsheet calculate the effect of that change on the rest of the spreadsheet numbers. To see the drawbacks of this shortcut, look at Figure 6.17, where the markup is entered as 50 percent. What happens if you want to change the markup? You will need to go into the spreadsheet and change several formulas by hand—a time-consuming and potentially error-producing task.

FIGURE 6.17 *Improper Calculations Area Design*

⌘ File Edit Formula Format Data Options Macro Window					
H82					

	A	B	C	D	E	F
56	The ShirtWorks Pricing Worksheet					
57	Calculations					
58						
59	Wholesale Cost	Price/Gross	Unit Price	Markup	Item Total	
60						
61	Shirt	468	=B61/144	=C61*50%	=C61+D61	
62	Shipping	30	=B62/144	=C62*50%	=C62+D62	
63	Printing	12	=B63/144	=C63*50%	=C63+D63	
64						
65	Total				=SUM(E61:E63)	

SCRATCH AREA. Just as you use scratch paper when you are working with paper and pencil, you can use the spreadsheet's scratch area for any intermediate calculations or notes you might want to make. For example, you might use this area to record details of orders (color, size, and quantities ordered, say). Or you might calculate your estimated profit on the order as part of a quick tax-planning session. Or you might create a table of shirt or shipping costs so that you don't have to stop your work at the computer to search through a paper catalog.

You can also use the scratch area to create summary tables that group selected rows or columns from the calculations area. This capability is useful for spreadsheet packages that can create spreadsheet graphics only from rows and columns that are next to each other.

SUMMARY. The summary section of the spreadsheet is generally used to create a summary table or business graphic illustrating the solution created by the spreadsheet. But you can also use this section to create an entirely different table, form, or report for your business. Consider your problem at The ShirtWorks. Calculating a price for your shirts is just one issue. You also need to summarize the price estimate and present it to your customers, along with the details of their order and the deposit they need to give you before you accept their order. Figure 6.18 shows how you could use the summary section to create an order form summarizing the order, the price, and the terms of a contract you will ask your customers to sign. Data from your spreadsheets can be automatically entered into this form.

Step 3: Enter the Spreadsheet into Your Computer

It may seem natural to plan some of the spreadsheet's layout as you sit at the computer. After all, it is often hard to estimate how much you can fit on a computer screen when you are working with paper and pencil. If you haven't entered your layout or if you've begun the process but need to finish it, now is when you need to do so. When you have completed entering the spreadsheet layout, you should save it as a template or blank form ready for the entry of data values.

Step 4: Test and Use the Spreadsheet

The final step in developing a spreadsheet for any application is creating or collecting test data, then loading the data into your spreadsheet to see if it calculates the correct answers. You might draw your data from examples given in the pricing seminar or the magazine article written by the T-shirt expert, or you might collect simple representative data from your own files. At the minimum, you should construct three sets of data. Because you will be trusting this spreadsheet with your business's lifeblood—its prices—you may want to test more than three samples, looking for formulas that produce inaccurate answers.

As you complete each test, print a copy of the spreadsheet that shows the input values and results. These results will become an important part of your records. Having paper-based proof that the spreadsheet worked at one time will help you find errors introduced during future revisions.

THE

SHIRT WORKS

ORDER FORM

Date	

Customer Name	Address	Telephone
Organization	Street	Day
Contact	City/State/Zip	Evening

Description of Order

Shirt Type	Size	Quantity (Dozens) (Minimum Total Order: 12 Dozen)
Color 1	Small Medium Large X-Large	
Color 2	Small Medium Large X-Large	
Color 3	Small Medium Large X-Large	
Printing color(s) and location		
Source of artwork (attach sketch)		

Pricing Summary

Quantity Shirts Ordered x Unit Price (Minimum Order: 12 dozen or 144 shirts)	Customer Pays
Artwork	
TOTAL	
DEPOSIT REQUIRED (Balance due on delivery)	

Customer Signature _____ Date _____

FIGURE 6.18
Order Form Created for Summary Area
The summary area of the spreadsheet may contain a special form designed to summarize the details of a transaction.

When you have completed testing to your satisfaction, you may begin entering real data into the spreadsheet.

A Final Word

A cautionary note: The integration of calculating, charting, and editing features in spreadsheet software has changed the way people solve problems. The spreadsheet's potential for improving people's productivity and effectiveness is substantial. However, like all aspects of information technology, the benefits provided by this tool are only as good as the people who use it. Productivity tools will never replace people—they can only help make them better at what they do.

SUMMARY OF LEARNING OBJECTIVES

1 **Describe the principal functions of spreadsheets and why they are used in business.** Spreadsheets help planners and analysts organize their work and structure the numeric details of their projects. Spreadsheets are used in business to automate record keeping, to summarize raw data and to perform analysis and improve planning, to simplify the control process, to improve communication and motivation, and to help managers make decisions.

2 **Identify the elements found on an electronic spreadsheet display.** The spreadsheet display contains two distinct areas: the *window* and the *control panel*.

The window contains the *worksheet area*—the rectangular grid of *rows* and *columns* that make up the worksheet. The intersection of a row and a column is called a *cell*.

The control panel, located at the top section of the spreadsheet screen, consists of the *title bar,* which includes the program name and sometimes the file name; the *menu bar,* which contains spreadsheet commands for creating, storing, retrieving, and editing files and worksheets; the *content line,* which contains the cell address and data or information entered into the active cell; and the *icon bar,* which contains small pictures (icons) used to represent frequently used commands in the menu bar.

3 **Describe the four types of data created and stored in spreadsheet programs and differentiate between functions and formulas, explaining the benefits of each in creating worksheets for problem solving.** A spreadsheet cell can hold any of four different pieces of information: values, labels, formulas, or functions. A *value* is a number that is entered into a cell. It may be an integer, a decimal number, or a number in scientific format. A *label* is a piece of descriptive information pertaining to a row or column. A *formula* is an instruction describing how a specific computation should be performed. A *function* is a formula

built into the spreadsheet software that will automatically perform certain types of calculation. Formulas and functions are often used to create worksheets to solve problems.

4 **Summarize the capabilities offered by spreadsheet programs for changing and refining worksheets after data have been entered.** A spreadsheet's editing capabilities allow the user to change, add, and delete data; insert and delete rows and columns; copy, move, find, and sort data; freeze row and column headings; adjust column width; and undo actions. The spreadsheet program will automatically recalculate or adjust all data that have been affected by these changes.

5 **Discuss the uses of spreadsheet programs in sensitivity analysis and problem solving.** Perhaps the most valuable feature of electronic spreadsheets is their ability to perform *sensitivity analysis,* in which the computer determines what would happen if certain data change. All spreadsheet packages allow users to create individuals worksheets to deal with each part of a problem. Most also provide a linkage capability that allows the user to interconnect the separate worksheets and even to transfer information among them. This linkage feature allows the problem solver to evaluate relationships and the effects of changing data.

6 **Explain the types of business graphics usually included with spreadsheet programs, when each is used, and how worksheet contents are transformed into business graphics.** *Business graphics* present information visually through charts, graphics, and symbols. They are an effective supplement for tables of numeric details. Five types of business graphics are usually included in spreadsheet software. *Bar charts* consist of a series of bars, each representing a particular element in the worksheet. The length of a bar indicates the value of the data. *Pie charts* show the proportion or percentage of the whole represented by each element. *Area line charts* use lines that are "stacked" or combined to show the total in each category. *Line charts* plot changes in data values over time and connect these points by a line. *Pictograms* depict data using icons or symbols that represent the magnitude of the data values.

Six steps are involved in creating business graphics from a spreadsheet program: (1) select the value to be graphed from the worksheet; (2) activate the spreadsheet's graphing commands; (3) select the type of graph desired; (4) generate the graph; (5) add descriptive information; and (6) store or print the graph.

Discuss the four steps involved in developing a personal spreadsheet application. The four steps involved in developing a spreadsheet are (1) define the problem; (2) plan the spreadsheet layout; (3) enter the spreadsheet into the computer; and (4) test and use the spreadsheet.

KEY TERMS

cell 261
cell address/cell reference 261
cell pointer 261
columns 255
content line/ edit line 262
current cell/active cell 261
electronic spreadsheet 255
formula 264

function 264
icon bar 262
label 264
macro 270
menu bar 262
model 258
rows 255
scroll bar 261

sensitivity analysis 270
spreadsheet/worksheet 255
spreadsheet program 255
template 269
title bar 262
value 264
worksheet area 261

CRITICAL CONNECTIONS

1 Psion Organizes Business—and You

Psion

Psion's spreadsheet power is compatible with both Microsoft Excel and Lotus 1-2-3. You can also add application modules that will assist you to track expenses or keep a record of your personal and business contacts—with name, phone number, and more. Hook up a printer, including any widely used laser printer, and you can prepare a printed report complete with graphics.

Psion's communication capabilities (both telephonic and wireless transmissions are possible) let you transfer spreadsheet details to and from your desktop PC. The compatibility with the most widely used spreadsheet programs means no conversion of data is needed.

Portable, powerful, personal information handling is the reason the Psion palmtop computer is so widely used. It puts spreadsheet data and information in the palm of your hand.

Questions for Discussion

1. What business or personal situations can you think of that would be made easier if you had a portable spreadsheet program at your fingertips?

2. What benefits are provided by Psion's ability to transfer spreadsheet details to and from a desktop computer?

2 The Grill 23 Spread

Grill 23

The Lotus spreadsheet is the foundation of Grill 23's inventory and control program. It charts the number of meals served at each sitting and the size of the average check—essential information for knowing whether business is up or down on a particular day of the week or month of the year.

Good restaurant management is not just about using tasty recipes, delighting the customer, and increasing sales. It's also about catching fluctuations in cost, however subtle they may be. For instance, food suppliers seldom highlight price increases, so Grill 23's back office routinely monitors the costs of ingredients using its spreadsheet tools. All unannounced price increases are highlighted by the program in time for the restaurant's managers to react appropriately before profit margins on the dish that uses the newly more expensive ingredient shrink.

Good restaurants get business by delivering the right food and service in front. They stay in business by using the right tools in back.

Questions for Discussion

1. What advantages does a spreadsheet model of business performance offer Grill 23 over purchased point-of-sale software that reports only on food and beverage sales?

2. What spreadsheet methods are most useful for highlighting fluctuations in the number of patrons the restaurant serves daily and weekly?

3. What is your reaction to Grill 23's practice of taking data and information from one automated system and electronically transferring it into another system?

3   Kraft & Associates Create Spreadsheet Magic

Kraft & Associates On a typical project, Donald Kraft begins by meeting with clients and asking them many, many questions. What do they need to do? How much do the end-users already know about spreadsheets? What is their deadline? "Often, I don't know what I don't know about a job until I am alone in front of my computer and I start designing a spreadsheet," says Kraft. "I usually make another list of the questions and go back to the client a second time."

Once the project's goal and scope are clear, Kraft starts to work. Drawing on his 23 years' experience with IBM, he uses professional programming techniques to plan and structure the project. Then he begins to write macros to perform certain procedures or tasks. On one of his projects, a data analysis worksheet for a major pharmaceutical company, Kraft says it took exactly 999 lines to record the macros.

To make the macros easy to find and use, Kraft may show them as new entries on the standard pull-down menus of Lotus 1-2-3 for Windows. Or he may create an entirely new menu that groups all the macros in one place. He can even replace the standard menu bar with one that has been customized for his client. Kraft can also create customized dialog boxes, information boxes, and on-screen color-coded annotations to guide users. As a finishing touch, he uses his flatbed scanner to capture the client's logo, displaying it on the opening screen and on printed reports. Once he has tested and debugged the spreadsheet using sample data, he finalizes the documentation and provides training and ongoing support as needed.

"Most of the people I've worked with have been incredibly sharp," says Kraft. "But in almost every case I found that they were doing too many tasks by hand, instead of letting the spreadsheet work for them."

Questions for Discussion

1. Why do you think Kraft spends so much time talking to his clients before he begins to create a spreadsheet?

2. It's Kraft's business to construct spreadsheets that let people perform complex tasks easily and quickly. Nevertheless, he feels that even casual end-users need to understand spreadsheet software and how it works. Why do you think he believes this?

3. Kraft says that his most challenging assignments occur when he is hired to revise a spreadsheet application that has been created and modified by individuals who are not familiar with the practices of IT professionals. What types of challenges do you think he means?

SOURCE: Personal interview with Donald H. Kraft.

Net Work

When Companies Use the Web

Many companies around the world have established home pages on the Web, using the Internet's resources to share information about their products and services. Some widely publicize their Web presence, including the company's URL on its brochures and in its television and radio promotions. Some update their Web pages frequently, while others do so only on rare occasions spanning several months.

Anyone in business, large or small, should not only be aware of the Web but should also recognize its possible uses and, equally important, its limitations for business. The best way to decide? Go Net_Work.

Using the Web's search capabilities, search out a set of companies that have Web sites. Focus on companies that have something in common—chose Fortune 500 companies, consulting firms, multinational companies, non-U.S. companies, manufacturing companies, or high-technology businesses—and then search according to that category.

To evaluate the uses and features of each company's site, complete the table below. Each site will have strengths and weaknesses—characteristics you'll want to take into consideration when developing your own Web site for personal or business use.

1. What is the apparent purpose of the Web site? Perhaps it's marketing, dissemination of company news, recruiting new employees, building public relations, accepting customer orders (i.e., sales).
2. How current is the information? Is there an indication of when the information was last updated?
3. What types of information does the company tend to use? Text, audio or video segments, drawings?
4. How effective is the company's use of graphical information? Does the page include graphics of any type? If so, are they useful or simply ornamental?

CHARACTERISTIC	COMPANY 1	COMPANY 2	COMPANY 3	COMPANY 4	COMPANY 5
Company name					
URL					
Principal purposes of company's Web pages					
Currency of information					
Form of information					
Use of graphical information					
Ease of navigation between pages					
Use of hyperlinks					
Other factors of importance					
Strengths of the Web site					
Weaknesses of the Web site					
Overall assessment of company's Web site on a scale of 1 (low) to 10 (high)					

5. How easy is it to navigate the pages? How does a reader move around the pages of the Web site?
6. Does the page include hyperlinks? Are hyperlinks used and are they easy to find and follow? Can you get back to the starting point easily?
7. What other factors are important? What makes the company's pages attractive? What detracts from the pages' attractiveness?
8. What are the strengths and weaknesses of the Web site? Critique any other features or characteristics not included in the above categories.
9. What is your overall assessment of each company's Web site? Based on the information you've assembled, how do you rate this site on a 1 (low) to 10 (high) scale?

GROUP PROJECTS AND APPLICATIONS

Project 1

Consider the following situation:

Ellen Todd has started a business, Todd's Pen Place, that specializes in selling upscale writing implements (mostly fountain pens) and accessories. She is running the business out of her home. Her stock is composed of the following:

1. Cross Pens—Models 107, 205, 316, and 445.
2. MontBlanc fountain pens—Models XJ6, XJ8, MX5, and MX11.
3. Waterman fountain pens—Models A119, B325, and C688.
4. Osmiroid inks in bottles of 8 ounces each—blue, black, brown, red, and lavender.
5. Samothrace parchment paper, in pads of 20, 50, and 100 sheets.

Todd purchases her entire stock at wholesale prices, then marks up each item by 200 percent. She offers no discounts and does not accept orders under $50. Her main expenses are advertising in *Pen World* magazine, business stationery and supplies, postage, insurance, and telephone.

Todd has called in an advisory group to help her run her business more profitably. The advisors have recommended that she set up and maintain a spreadsheet that will help her relate costs, inventory, and sales revenue. Role-play the consultant team and answer the following questions for Ellen Todd.

- What are the desired outputs of the spreadsheet?
- What are the necessary inputs?
- What types of formulas should be used?
- What should appear on the spreadsheet's title page?

Project 2

Assume your team owns a chain of Mexican restaurants called Casa Mia. The chain consists of ten individual restaurants (or "stores," as they are known in the business) in New York, New Jersey, and Pennsylvania. Recently, you have been considering taking the chain national—expanding first into the Midwest, then the South, next the Southwest, then New England, and finally the West Coast.

Before you make a final decision, however, you need to analyze all the data you've compiled in your research. You want to convert these data into easy-to-read business graphics in order to entice stockholders.

For each of the following data groupings, suggest which type of business graphic would be most effective in conveying the information. (For a review of the different types of business graphics, see Figure 6.10.)

a. Your data show that Mexican food has become increasingly popular in the United States over the last 10 years. Each year for the last decade, people have increased their consumption of Mexican food. In your existing restaurants, sales have more than doubled over the past 5 years.

b. Your restaurants in New York and New Jersey are slightly more successful than those in Pennsylvania. You want to show how revenues from the three regions compare, which region contributes the most to the total income of the business, and which region contributes the least.

c. Sales in your New York stores have climbed each quarter for the past three years. You want a visual way of showing how these sales have taken off.

d. You want to color-code the six regions in which you hope to operate. (You've decided to group your current stores into one region called "Middle Atlantic.")

e. For some reason, you sell the most burritos in your New Jersey stores, the most chimichangas in your New York stores, and the most enchiladas in your Pennsylvania stores. You want to compare sales of these three items in each of your current regions.

REVIEW QUESTIONS

1. Describe the purpose of a spreadsheet. Does the purpose differ depending on whether the spreadsheet is created manually or through computer software?

2. What is an electronic spreadsheet program?

3. For what reasons do people use electronic spreadsheets in business?

4. What is the difference between a row, a column, and a cell?

5. What two areas make up an electronic spreadsheet display?

6. Describe the contents of each line of the control panel.

7. What four types of information can a worksheet cell contain? Explain each type.

8. What does "data importing" mean?

9. Describe six data-editing activities.

10. Describe the characteristics of a template. What benefits do templates provide to their users?

11. What is sensitivity analysis? What benefits does it offer?

12. Why is the capability to link spreadsheets useful in problem solving?

13. What benefits do business graphics offer?

14. What five types of business graphics are usually included with spreadsheet packages?

15. What four steps are involved in developing a spreadsheet application?

16. Define "model."

17. What six sections should a spreadsheet include?

18. What is the value of testing a spreadsheet before entering "real data" into it?

DISCUSSION QUESTIONS

1. Because their contracts call for payments that are tied to specific milestones, contractors who handle highway and other heavy construction often need help forecasting cash flow. How might such contractors use spreadsheets in their business?

2. In his book *The Education of David Stockman,* William Greider describes the way David Stockman, the director of President Ronald Reagan's Office of Management and Budget, used a spreadsheet to analyze the effects of the president's tax cuts in the early 1980s. When the first analysis showed that the cuts would produce huge budget deficits (a politically undesirable answer), Stockman worked with the spreadsheet until it showed the "right" answer—a manipulation that probably contributed to the large budget deficits of the late

1980s. What ethical question does this example raise about the use of spreadsheets in business and government?

3. Leading financial consultants suggest that small-business owners who want to computerize their finances use either a spreadsheet or a personal finance manager. (Personal finance manager software packages, such as Quicken or Managing Your Money, are designed to handle routine financial matters, like balancing a checkbook or tracking expenses for software.) Under what circumstances could a spreadsheet package be the better choice?

4. A leading consultant suggests that the "perfect" spreadsheet report begins with a business graphic. Why do you think he makes this recommendation? Do you agree or disagree?

SUGGESTED READINGS

Paller, A.T. "Improving Management Productivity with Computer Graphics." *IEEE Computer Graphics and Applications 1* (October 1981): 9–16. This article discusses the impact of graphics presentations on individual performance and emphasizes how good business graphics can boost individual productivity.

Person, Ron. *Using Excel 4.* Indianapolis, IN: Que, 1992. This how-to book teaches the beginner the ins and outs of Microsoft's Excel spreadsheet package.

Robinson, Phillip. "Variations on a Screen." *Byte 14,* (April

1989): 249–288. This article is one of a series in a special supplement on computer graphics that emphasizes the impact of computer hardware and software on the display of graphic information.

Using Lotus 1-2-3. Indianapolis, IN: Que, 1993. A good introduction to both the basic and advanced features of the Lotus 1-2-3 program. The book includes excellent illustrations of personal and business uses of spreadsheet programs.

Start-up Ad Agency Works by the Numbers

Horton Ahern Bousquet

It sounds like an American fairy tale come true: Horton Ahern Bousquet, a small start-up ad agency in Providence, Rhode Island, brings in almost a quarter of a million dollars in its first year. Add the fact that the three founding partners (and only employees) fled the corporate world, though, and the tale takes on a decidedly modern twist. Another modern twist is the central role played by Macintosh computers and spreadsheet software in the firm's success. To understand the role of IT at HAB, let's go back to the agency's beginning.

First, there was John Horton, who left another ad agency shortly before it went bankrupt. Despite his 15 years in marketing, public relations, and client management, Horton rejected the idea of going it alone as a consultant. "I knew my own strengths and knew I needed two other legs on the stool," says Horton, who founded HAB in 1990.

He found the other two legs in Tom Ahern and Lisa Bousquet, both of whom had strong backgrounds—and numerous contacts—in the health, education, and high-tech fields. An award-winning expert with a personal computer and Pagemaker desktop publishing software, Ahern had extensive experience in advertising and marketing. (In his most recent staff position, he had been manager of marketing promotion at GTECH, a company that runs state lotteries.) "I was in business for myself," he says, "but had reached my limit. I didn't know how to make a business grow." Ahern became the agency's creative director. Bousquet, meanwhile, had worked in both sales (for a pharmaceutical firm) and marketing (for a health assessment facility) before leaving to have her first child. She became HAB's operations manager.

The agency's success is even more impressive when you realize how close it came to failing. After just two months, the partners got a rude surprise: they were all caught up on their work and didn't have any new business coming in. That's when the agency began to work by the rules on numbers.

- **Remember the 80/20 rule.** A common rule in sales holds that 20 percent of a business's customers will bring in 80 percent of its income. HAB used this rule to work backward from its basic goal: If it wanted to make $300,000 its first year, 20 percent of its clients would have to provide $240,000, while the other 80 percent brought in $60,000.

  Using price estimates based on their previous work experience, the partners translated this rule into new-business requirements. On average, they needed to develop one major new client every 1.5 months and pick up 2.6 minor new clients every month.

- **Spend 40 to 60 percent of your time looking for new business.** "At the basic level, getting new business is a numbers game. Everyone told us that and now we know it," says Ahern. Horton shoulders the heaviest burden here; he has a goal of making 40 sales calls each week. However, each partner is responsible for making five new contacts each week, and the agency has a goal of sending out at least one sales letter or promotional piece per day.

  To help them meet these quotas, the partners loaded spreadsheet software onto their personal computers. Horton uses Excel to print out daily action lists, while Bousquet uses FileMaker Pro (a database package that is discussed in the next

When John Horton, Tom Ahern, and Lisa Bousquet started HAB, they thought of their agency as a fairly traditional one that would create and place ads. Now, because the market they've entered is made up primarily of companies that don't use traditional ad agencies, they think of themselves as problem solvers with a specialty in direct mail. "We solve problems with communications," says Ahern. "And direct response is the communications product of the moment."

chapter) and Excel to create time management sheets summarizing the amount of time each partner spends on getting new business (as opposed to client service or administrative tasks). Just one month after the new system was in place, new-business efforts averaged 31 percent. The next month, the agency hit its goal of 40 percent.

- **Focus your marketing energies on high-profit jobs.** The partners also used spreadsheet software to perform a monthly billing analysis for each job that showed the amount billed for marketing, public relations, and production services, as well as the direct costs billed to clients for printing and mailing direct-mail pieces and newsletters. Because these direct costs don't contribute to agency profits, the partners decided to focus on jobs with higher creative charges—and bigger profit margins.

Of course, making contacts would not help the agency win and keep clients if HAB didn't offer outstanding service. Just like the big ad agencies, HAB focuses on "relationship marketing," ensuring its staff listens to clients' problems and presents clear but powerful solutions. A case in point: The first issue of the agency's promotional newsletter, *2nd Thoughts (300 seconds of reading to help you market better [Really!])*, netted them a new client who wanted "a newsletter just like that for myself." In fact, the agency uses everything from its stationery to follow-up sales letters to emphasize the benefits it offers. As one promotional piece reads, "Because our overhead is low, since we use computers for much of our work, our rates are lower than those of comparable agencies—at least a third lower. Our standards are unreasonably lofty—our prices are not."

The partners also maintain and upgrade their skills continually. The agency budgets $100 a month for business-related books, and the partners routinely attend small-business conferences and workshops on sales, marketing, and management. Ahern, the chief copywriter (and a professor of marketing and public relations at Brown University and the Rhode Island School of Design), even uses Grammatik, a grammar-checking program, to analyze his copy. If it has too many sentences compared to prize-winning direct-mail pieces, he sits down at the computer and goes over the copy again—until the analysis produces acceptable results.

Questions for Discussion

1. Discuss the ways the partners at HAB are using spreadsheet software to manage their business.

2. How might the information provided by spreadsheets improve the services HAB offers?

SOURCE: Based on Nick Sullivan, "From $0 to $200,000 in One Year Flat," *Home Office Computing,* February 1992, pp. 62–66.

CHAPTER
7
Database Applications for Personal Productivity

CHAPTER OUTLINE

LEARNING OBJECTIVES

When you have completed this chapter, you should be able to

1 Explain why businesses use databases.

2 Describe the main components of a database.

3 List and describe five objectives of database management systems.

4 Identify when a business should use a spreadsheet and when it should use a database.

5 Identify the seven-step sequence for developing database applications.

IT in Private Practice
Is Making the Rounds

D r. Hagelyn Wilson has been practicing medicine for more than 30 years in her hometown of Montgomery, Alabama. In 1957, when she decided to become a physician, many of the residents of Montgomery who knew her thought the idea laughable. What made the daughter of a southern black preacher think she could successfully pursue a career in medicine? It's evident the answer was her personal determination and a supportive family.

When she is asked what she thought about the steep odds against her getting into medical school and ultimately becoming a physician—and the odds against a young black woman in the 1950s were indeed formidable—Dr. Wilson doesn't hesitate. "I never really thought about it," she says. "There were a lot of people who gave me a hard time, but I never let them get me down. I believe you can do almost anything with enough faith and discipline."

Her practice centers around patients and personal attention. Six mornings a week are reserved for seeing patients in the office. The afternoons are reserved for *home* visits. (Dr. Wilson is the only physician in Montgomery who regularly sees patients in their homes.)

When Dr. Wilson began her practice, a computer in a doctor's office was unheard of. Even as late as 1990, she was still without a computer. Then a patient gave her one as payment for treatment. Neither Dr. Wilson nor her staff had any notion of how to use a computer, but they were determined to learn. Every Sunday afternoon they came into the office to practice, initially with word processing and spreadsheets. Soon Dr. Wilson learned how to create computer procedures and passed her knowledge along to her staff. Within a month or so, information on all of her regular patients had been incorporated into a spreadsheet: names, addresses, medical history, and billing information.

Recently, Dr. Wilson upgraded to a new computer and began using software she obtained from health insurance providers Medicaid, Medicare, and Blue Shield, which made it possible to submit insurance claims electronically. This reduced the insurers' payment time substantially, from 6 weeks to less than 30 days.

Today, Dr. Wilson's practice relies on database applications written by her son, who is an IT professional. The on-line patient databases he has developed have the capability to monitor the treatment of her patients. These records are linked to an accounting database that is used with other office procedures. Dr. Wilson also encourages her staff to familiarize themselves with the capabilities of IT, including paying the cost of seminars and workshops to develop their skills.

The use of IT has enhanced not only her practice, but the well-being of her patients who receive quality medical care at an affordable cost. IT enables Dr. Wilson to contain the cost of maintaining records—a savings she passes along to her patients in the form of lower fees. She also stays on top of medical developments through her computer. She uses it to stay in touch with other physicians. She particularly enjoys the discussions of recent medical advances that go on over the Net, since attending medical conferences is too expensive for a doctor with her kind of practice.

Information technology and databases are no substitute for a good doctor making the rounds and visiting patients at home when they need her. But they can certainly make a caring physician even better at her profession.

An Overview of Personal Database Systems

A *database,* as you learned in Chapter 2, is a collection of data and information describing items of interest. Traditionally, its contents have included text and numbers—hence the name *data*base. Increasingly, though, people and organizations are broadening their view of databases to include image, graphic, and voice information. For example:

- California's Division of Motor Vehicles maintains a computerized driver's license database that includes drivers' names, addresses, and personal attributes (height, weight, birth date, and so forth), along with their photographs and an image of their signatures.
- Many hospitals and medical centers, including Massachusetts General Hospital, the Mayo Clinic, and the Harvard Community Health Plan, have begun to maintain patient records in databases that include personal information, insurance and financial data, medical history, and medical images (such as X-rays and electrocardiograms).
- Manufacturing and service companies like IBM, Wal-Mart, and General Motors are installing multimedia training systems that feature databases containing video clips, color slides, narrative (text) screens of information and instructions, self-tests, and voice narrations. These training systems use all of the trainee's senses (with the possible exception of smell, and they're working on that).

The point is clear. People collect data and information because they expect it to be useful later—whether to identify drivers, to diagnose and treat medical problems, or to train employees. In other words, the all-important assumption underlying database creation is that data and information should be stored when they are expected to be useful in problem solving.

At one time, people focused primarily on storing data—numbers and text. However, with the advances in computers' storage capabilities over the last decade or so, the contents of personal and organizational databases have broadened. As a result, the terminology is gradually changing, too. The term **information repository,** or simply **repository,** may soon replace *database* as the name of this information resource. (We'll stick with *database* in this chapter because it is still the most widely used term, but *repository* is almost certainly the term of the future.)

information repository/ repository
A synonym for database.

The Benefits of Databases in Business

Many of the databases you'll encounter in organizations will be large multiuser systems developed and maintained by IT professionals. But a growing number of managers and staff members, as well as small-business owners, are turning to smaller personal database systems to boost their productivity. To help you to understand this trend—and to get an idea of how a personal database might help you in business—we'll consider some of the benefits of a personal system.

IDENTIFYING AND STRUCTURING DATA NEEDED TO SOLVE BUSINESS PROBLEMS.

Marketers need to analyze customer likes and dislikes; salespeople need to track sales calls and their results; and accountants need to record key details about all the business transactions of their clients. To meet these needs, managers must be familiar with the relationship between business events and their own business goals and be able to identify the resources they require to effectively and efficiently reach those goals.

After people, a business's most important resources are data and information. Creating a database system will help a business collect and structure these data. As you'll see later in this chapter, studying a business problem and identifying the users' data and information requirements are the first two steps in developing any database.

During these steps, managers may even identify better ways to solve business problems. Perhaps certain procedures can be improved through IT, saving time and effort. Some process steps may be eliminated entirely. Many large corporations are overhauling their business procedures to weed out unnecessary steps. (We discuss this process, called *reengineering,* further in Chapters 11 and 12.)

COLLECTING, STORING, EDITING, AND UPDATING DATA.

Data and information are useless unless there is an effective system in place for collecting, storing, and retrieving them. These capabilities are especially important for businesses, which may need to manage a huge database of their customers and suppliers or a mailing list for a quarterly catalog.

Database systems can help here in a number of ways. First, the database software employed to create and maintain databases can be used to display a blank form on the computer screen so that when users fill in all the blanks, they will have collected the "right" data. And if users follow good procedures for saving and backing up their data, they can be reasonably sure that the data will be stored safely. Second, database software is especially designed to help users *manage* data. As you'll see a little later in this chapter, database software functions include routines for editing, updating, and integrating databases; for ensuring their accuracy; and for protecting them from unauthorized users.

RETRIEVING AND SHARING DATA.

One of the most important advantages of a database is that it allows users to both retrieve and share data. Data collected on sales, for example, can be organized and summarized into information useful for planning a marketing campaign or for determining inventory levels, and then shared with the relevant company departments and personnel.

In some cases, users or IT professionals will work with the database software to create **database applications,** routines for collecting, retrieving, or manipulating data to meet recurring needs. A quarterly sales report, broken down by

database application
A computerized database routine for collecting, retrieving, or manipulating data to meet recurring needs.

INFORMATION TECHNOLOGY IN PRACTICE

Database Processing Plus Personal Productivity Builds Good Bagels

Large companies have been using databases to assist them in marketing their products and services for a long time. But don't think this valuable business-building capability is only for big firms. The power of information technology, including database processing, is available to companies of virtually any size.

Personal productivity means more than the number of bagels baked in a day at Finagle-A-Bagel. This Boston-based company bakes some 50,000 bagels a day. Larry Smith, the company's founder and president, knows a lot about bagels. He also understands a great deal about servicing customers and building up a business. IT has played an important role in satisfying the company's college, restaurant, and institutional customers, as well as in identifying new business opportunities. Smith uses IT to

track orders, plan and monitor sales, and manage the making of bagels. But more important to the company's success is the way Finagle-A-Bagel uses IT to manage its customer relations.

When customers call—usually on the company's toll-free telephone line—marketing manager Heather Robertson sees to it that their names and questions are entered into a database running on a personal computer: "How many calories in an onion bagel?" "Can you make the salt bagels saltier?" "Why don't you open a store in the Beacon Hill area?" Robertson sends every caller a coupon for a free half-dozen bagels—an important gesture. Sometimes Larry Smith will call a customer himself to learn more about his or her inquiry. That's important, too.

Like many small companies, Finagle-A-Bagel used

---

division or salesperson, is a typical result of a database application. Collecting new visitor information at a hotel or inn is another. The *Information Technology in Practice* feature entitled "Database Processing Plus Personal Productivity Builds Good Bagels" illustrates the value of database software in the successful operation of a big-city business where competition is tough.

In other cases, individuals satisfy short-term or pressing needs by posing **queries,** questions to be answered by accessing the data in a database. There are three general techniques for querying a database system:

query
A question to be answered by accessing the data in a database.

query by example (QBE)
A query format in which the user fills in the blanks with simple commands or conditions.

1. **Menus.** This is the simplest, but least flexible, technique. Bars of commands, or menus, guide the user through the query process.
2. **QBE.** QBE (short for **query by example**) shows a blank table that reflects the database's underlying structure. To form a query, the user fills in the appro-

to keep track of customer inquiries on Post-it Notes. But, recognizing that the information coming from customers was invaluable to building the business, it did not want to lose any ideas, suggestions, or complaints through this fragile paper system. It also realized that as the company grew, so would customer inquiries—to the point where any paper system of managing customer relations would be cumbersome. The solution: a powerful, but easy-to-use PC database system.

Now whenever a customer calls, name, phone number, and other information are entered directly into the marketing database along with the caller's comments. Repeat callers are common, so when Robertson (or anyone else) takes a call, she asks the customer's name and tells the database software to check for prior calls by that customer. Every detail of every previous request or complaint made by that customer is quickly displayed on the computer screen. You can imagine the impression it makes on customers when Robertson or another responder is able to discuss their past history with the company. Such a capability not only makes it possible to follow up on inquiries but also builds unbeatable customer loyalty.

Sorting the database periodically allows Smith, Robertson, and others at Finagle-A-Bagel to detect new product ideas ("Do you have any berry bagels besides blueberry?"), ideas for enhancing product features ("Can you make a low-fat cinnamon-raisin bagel?"), and areas that need improvement ("Why is it that the _____ restaurant never has your pumpernickel bagels?").

The simple expedient of setting up a personal computer customer database has turned out to be a highly effective business builder at Finagle-A-Bagel.

priate blanks with either simple commands or conditions. (Look ahead to Figure 7.13 if you'd like to see an example.) QBE is easy to learn and use.

3. **Query Languages.** A **query language** is a specialized computer language that forms database queries from a limited number of words (such as "Select," "From," and "Where") that are combined according to specific rules. The languages themselves are fairly simple, but they can be used to create flexible and powerful queries. The most widely used query language is *SQL*, short for *structured query language*.

query language
A computer language that forms database queries from a limited number of words.

EMPOWERING KNOWLEDGE WORKERS.

If you read business magazines and journals, you're probably familiar with the "empowered" knowledge worker who has the information, skills, and authority to make effective decisions and act independently. A database system empowers workers in three ways. First, it lets

EMI Music

EMI Music's Database Tracks Careers

EMI Music is no stranger to hits or to identifying talent. This international record company has recorded many world-famous and talented rock stars on its prestigious label. But it knows that fame comes and goes, and with it the monetary value of an entertainer's records. Thus, EMI carefully tracks the careers and popularity of its entertainers.

Behind the scenes, EMI also tracks the careers of its other talent—some 300 senior and fast-track junior executives scattered across the 35 countries of the world where EMI has business interests. For a while, EMI used a system of paper reports and memos describing the skills and development of its executives. However, it discovered that collecting and analyzing the reports centrally was cumbersome at best.

Determined to find a better alternative, EMI sought computer assistance that would eliminate all these paper documents. It needed a system that could be used across countries to rate the present performance and the potential of its key employees. The search for a package that would meet its business needs internationally took EMI into England, France, the Netherlands, and elsewhere.

SOURCE: Ann Field, "Precision Marketing," *Inc. Technology,* No. 2 (June 18, 1996): 56–57.

users collect, store, and retrieve the company data and information they need to act, without having to call upon a supervisor or a file clerk. Second, experience with one database system generally gives people the skills and confidence to work with other database systems, such as the growing number of databases that can be accessed by modem. By tapping into these on-line databases, users can retrieve timely data and information that can help them make key decisions. Third, experience with database systems is a great benefit when a staff member, manager, or small-business owner has to interact with an IT professional in developing a particular database system.

Database Terminology

Users rely on a precise terminology to describe the structure and details of a database. This terminology makes it possible to generalize across many different situations without getting bogged down in the jargon of a particular industry, company, or problem setting. Five of the most commonly used database terms are *entity, attribute, data item, record,* and *relation.*

entity
A person, place, thing, event, or condition about which data and information are collected.

ENTITIES AND ATTRIBUTES. An **entity** is a person, place, thing, event, or condition about which data and information are collected. For example, universities and colleges collect information about several entities, including students, faculty members, courses, and degree programs. Information in a hospital database typically focuses on such entities as patients, physicians, nurses, and rooms. In business, entities include customers, suppliers, and orders.

Choosing entities is an important step toward understanding a problem and devising its solution, for the right entity must be agreed upon before a problem can be addressed effectively. For instance, to institute a new security system, a university needs the following data and information about each of its students:

Entity	*Data and Information (Attributes)*
Student	Name
	Street address
	City
	State
	Postal code
	Student ID number
	Telephone
	Date of birth
	Residency status
	Person to contact in case of emergency
	Fingerprint
	Picture

Each category of data or information describing the entity is called an **attribute.** An attribute is a *fact* about a student. The last two attributes of the student entity—fingerprint and picture—may surprise you because they are a different form of information from the other items, all of which can be recorded in text or numeric format. But remember that information can be composed of several different components, including data, text, graphics, sound, and images (Figure 7.1). In the future, other details may be added: voice prints, spoken phrases, and video segments.

DATA ITEMS AND RECORDS. Once the specific facts of an individual entity are stored in a database, they are known as **data items.** Hence, the university's name data items may include such entries as Thomas O'Rafferty and François La Fleur. A **record** is a grouping of data items. It consists of the set of data and information

attribute
A category of data or information that describes an entity. Each attribute is a fact about the entity.

data item
A specific detail of an individual entity that is stored in a database.

record
A grouping of data items that consists of a set of data or information that describes an entity's specific occurrence.

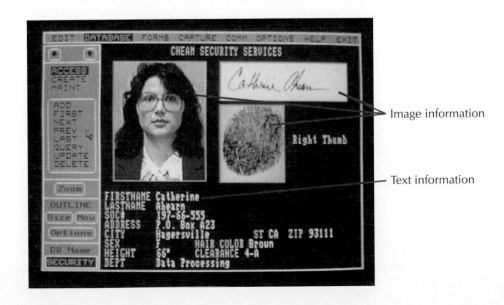

Image information

Text information

FIGURE 7.1

The Components of Information in a Database

In addition to data and text information, a database can contain graphic, sound, and image information.

(data, text, sound, or image) that describes an entity's specific occurrence (or instance). Each record in a database describes one specific occurrence of an entity. For example, as Figure 7.2 shows, the record for the student Thomas O'Rafferty includes the data items describing one occurrence of this "student" entity.

The *Rethinking Business Practices* feature entitled "TOPAZ INTERNATIONAL, Ltd. Capitalizes on Databases for Lowest-Cost Airline Tickets" shows how the everyday practice of purchasing an airline ticket can be improved when databases of comparative information are used.

Knowledge entails more than collecting facts and details. Indeed, collecting data is not nearly so important as arranging those data in a useful way. A good database organizes all the data relevant to an entity and gives its users the ability to assess a situation and determine what course of action to take.

For example, a university's database will contain data on students, including their name, their date of birth, where they live, the courses they have taken, their grade point average, and when they plan to graduate. *Knowledge* comes from assembling and synthesizing these details in a way that allows you to answer questions like the following:

- Is this individual someone you would recommend to a prospective employer?
- Do you think this person will graduate on time?
- Is this person highly creative and innovative?

The answers to these questions are not contained as facts in the database. Rather, they are derived from an analysis of the facts contained in the database. Knowledge comes from making use of data and information when they are relevant to the situation at hand. ■

Records hold the information about an instance—one record per instance. If the university used a paper-based system, it would probably create a paper record: a form or an index card for each student. Records stored in a computer database are usually maintained on magnetic storage.

FIGURE 7.2
Database Terminology
Each record in a database specifies one instance of an entity. Here, the specific instance of the student entity is Thomas O'Rafferty.

ENTITY: STUDENTS AT NEW YORK UNIVERSITY

General record structure for student entity

Attributes/fields {

| Student Name |
| Street Address |
| City |
| State |
| Postal Code |
| Student ID |
| Telephone |
| Date of Birth |
| Residency |
| Contact |

Specific record

| Thomas O'Rafferty |
| 1201 Sixth Avenue |
| New York |
| New York |
| 10020-3021 |
| 102347654 |
| 212-555-6760 |
| 01-17-69 |
| Commuter |
| Deborah O'Rafferty |

} Data items

FIGURE 7.3   *The Elements of a Relation*

STUDENT RELATION

Name	Student ID Number	Street Address	City	State	Postal Code
Gorzynski, John	253054720	71 West Washington	Chicago	Illinois	60602-1634
Markus, Lewis	762027721	22 Ocean Blvd	Atlantic City	New Jersey	08103
Martin, Carol	934841834	33 Hightower Lane	Montgomery	Alabama	36116
O'Rafferty, Thomas	102347654	1201 Sixth Avenue	New York	New York	10020-3021
Patterson, Jane	376358722	440 Holcomb Lane	Atlanta	Georgia	30338-1538

Attributes or Fields → columns; Records or Tuples → rows

RELATIONS. The most common type of database is a **relational database.**[1] This type of database structures information in a table format consisting of horizontal rows and vertical columns.

The table itself, called a **relation** or **file,** describes an entity. The rows of the relation are its records, or **tuples,** representing instances of interest. The relation's columns are its attributes, or **fields.**

Relations have four general characteristics:

1. Each column contains a single value about the same attribute.
2. The order of columns in the relation does not matter.
3. The order of rows in the relation does not matter.
4. Each row is unique—one row cannot duplicate another.

As Figure 7.3 shows, all the records in a relation contain the same number of data items. However, there can be any number of records in the relation and they can be entered in any order. (Processing will retrieve information in a particular sequence if the application requires that.)

A word of advice: Don't let the different terms confuse you. People often alternate between these formal and common names for database components:

Formal Name	Common Name
Attribute	Field
Tuple	Record
Relation	Database or file

We'll use the more common names throughout this book. However, you should be familiar with the formal terms, particularly if you interact with systems analysts or other information technology professionals.

relational database
A database in which the data are structured in a table format consisting of rows and columns.

relation/file
The table in a database that describes an entity.

tuples
The rows of a relation. Also called *records.*

fields
The columns of a relation. Also called *attributes.*

[1]Other types of databases were common in the past, notably hierarchical and network database structures (see Chapter 11), which are still sometimes found in mainframe and midrange computer applications. However, because relational databases are currently the predominant type across all classes of computers, large and small, we will not discuss the other types here.

RETHINKING BUSINESS PRACTICES

TOPAZ INTERNATIONAL, Ltd. Capitalizes on Databases for Lowest-Cost Airline Tickets

In many industries, *business* and *travel* are synonymous. In the United States alone, several billion dollars are spent each year on business travel, much of it on airfares. Managers are under constant pressure to reduce travel costs.

Business executives usually rely on either outside travel agents or a company department that acts like an internal travel agency to make the flight reservations that will get them to the right city at the right time, with the least delay and for the lowest cost. Travel agents obtain information on the times and costs of flights through the airline computer reservation system (CRS) of an airline. A travel agent will, by contractual arrangement, use a specific CRS. In the United States, there are four principal CRSs: SABRE (American Airlines), Apollo (United Airlines), WorldSpan (Delta Airlines, Northwest Airlines, and TWA), and System One (Continental Airlines). European airlines operate two CRSs: Amadeus and Galileo. Each computer airline reservation system lists flights of all carriers operating in the region, not just their own. Hence, by agreeing to use one airline's CRS, travel agents do not lose access to the schedules and fares of other airlines. (It would be prohibitively expensive for travel agents or travel departments to belong to all CRSs.)

Business customers have long relied on travel agents to book reservations that meet their need to be in a certain place at a designated time. They have assumed that, if instructed to do so, the agent will obtain the lowest fare possible. But how do business customers know that they are, in fact, getting the best ticket price time after time? This question is of interest to a growing number of companies in these cost-conscious times.

Some ways are obvious. A company could hire staff to constantly check ticket prices—in essence, they would be auditing the travel agents' bookings. But that alternative would probably add more costs, and it would certainly complicate the process. Another possibility is to have the company's travel department or its outside travel agent subscribe to multiple CRSs in order to do comparison shopping. An even better alternative is to work with an outside auditor.

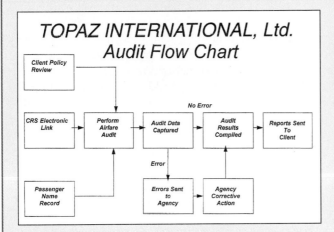

TOPAZ INTERNATIONAL, Ltd.
Audit Flow Chart

A growing number of businesses are doing just that, turning to companies that are expert at finding the lowest fares by using databases to do comparison shopping. TOPAZ INTERNATIONAL, Ltd. of Portland, Oregon, has been providing this type of service since 1978. Its international base of customers includes both corporations and travel agencies.

The TOPAZ process works as follows. Travel agents who are being audited by TOPAZ make a plane reservation in the normal way, except for one additional step: the agency places an electronic copy of the reservation (containing passenger name, flight number and date, and ticket cost) into a queue on its computer. TOPAZ auditors access the queue, look at the reservation, and immediately search through all the CRSs to determine whether the reservation repre-sents the lowest possible fare to that destination at that time. TOPAZ then checks its own database of information describing the customer's travel policies (e.g., will accept nonstop flights, desires to rely on a single airline, is amenable to booking reservations for nonrefundable tickets).

If TOPAZ finds a lower-cost ticket alternative that meets its customer's policies, it sends an electronic message containing the details back to the customer. The customer can then decide whether it wants to change the original reservation to the lower-cost alternative found by TOPAZ. Since time is of the essence in business travel, TOPAZ completes the process within a few hours after the original reservation was placed in the database. Even complex international comparisons are done on the same day, within at most 8 to 10 hours of making the original reservation. Each month, TOPAZ processes its own database to prepare a summary report that shows reservation and ticket price comparisons over time.

Since the cost of TOPAZ service is reasonable (approximately $2 for each reservation check), it's unsurprising that both companies and travel agencies are rethinking their reservation processes. Adding a same-day TOPAZ audit step to the process has saved companies millions of dollars yearly on their travel costs. Personal databases and information technology are the means to business success for TOPAZ INTERNATIONAL, Ltd. and its large group of international customers.

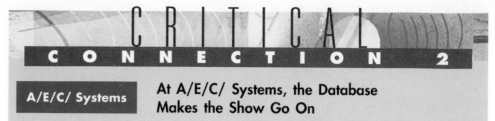

At A/E/C/ Systems, the Database Makes the Show Go On

Since 1980, A/E/C/ Systems, headquartered in Exton, Pennsylvania, has relied on database management and marketing to drive its business activities. This well-known company specializes in organizing and producing computer trade shows for the design and construction industries. Architects and engineers attend these shows to view the latest computer hardware and software products for their industry.

A/E/C/ Systems recognized from the beginning that attracting large numbers of the right attendees would be crucial to the company's success. Even if the company managed to get the industry's best exhibitors to demonstrate their products and services at a show, the operation would be a failure unless the show attracted a large number of architects and engineers interested in the exhibitions.

When the company was started in 1980, Michael Hough, A/E/C/ Systems' owner, contracted with a mailing house to handle the distribution of all promotional literature about A/E/C/'s trade shows. Targeted mailings were sent to engineers and architects whom the company thought were potential attendees based on 13 separate attributes, including prior attendance at trade shows.

It didn't take Hough long to realize that the database and promotional mailings could be handled in-house if a system relying on a personal computer database and desktop computers was created. The company set up such a system, and was able to double the number of names and attributes it maintained in the database while improving the overall effectiveness and efficiency of its efforts to reach exhibitors and attendees.

The Objectives of Database Management Systems

database management system (DBMS)

A program that makes it possible for users to manage the data in a database in order to increase productivity.

Obviously, it is much better to *manage* data and information than to allow them to just accumulate. Managing data is precisely the objective of the various personal **database management system (DBMS)** packages now on the market. The most popular of these packages are listed in Table 7.1.

TABLE 7.1 *Popular Personal Database Management Systems*		
SOFTWARE PACKAGE	**MANUFACTURER**	**COMPUTER VERSIONS AVAILABLE**
Access	Microsoft	IBM-compatible
dBASE V	Borland	IBM-compatible
FileMaker Pro	Claris	Apple Macintosh
Foxpro	Microsoft	IBM-compatible
Paradox	Borland	IBM-compatible

Database management systems provide users with three tools: (1) a **data definition language (DDL),** which allows users to define the database; (2) a **data manipulation language (DML),** which lets users store, retrieve, and edit data in the database (a query language is a type of data manipulation language); (3) a variety of other capabilities (discussed later in this chapter) that help users increase their productivity.

Managing data means taking deliberate actions guided by specific objectives. Database management systems are designed to achieve the following five objectives:

1. Integrating databases.
2. Reducing redundancy.
3. Sharing information.
4. Maintaining integrity.
5. Enabling database evolution.

You might think of these as both problem-*solving* and problem-*avoiding* objectives.

INTEGRATING DATABASES. Because the data and information needed to solve a particular problem often reside in several databases, problem solvers must be able to integrate databases. Database management systems allow the merger of separate files, created at varying times or by different people.

Integration is often done to process an inquiry or to create a report. Suppose that the university we discussed earlier wants to generate a report listing all courses, instructors, and the office numbers and office hours of each instructor. As Figure 7.4 shows, the DBMS prepares this report by integrating information retrieved from separate databases. In integrating databases, specialized databases (e.g., a course database and an instructor database) are maintained. Yet the benefits of processing them together are achieved.

REDUCING REDUNDANCY. Duplication of information between databases is termed *redundancy.* When files are developed independently, some data and information may be repeated in the databases, and unfortunately, these multiple copies sometimes become inconsistent. Because the data and information in databases are updated or changed at varying times, often by people who are not aware of the existence of other databases with the same information, only one copy may be altered. The others will be out-of-date and therefore inaccurate.

In well-managed databases, most data items are not duplicated. Rather, the DBMS extracts copies of the information from the appropriate databases to produce the necessary report.

Not all redundancy is bad, however. Information that is common to different databases makes possible the integration of descriptions and the preparation of reports. In the student/course/instructor example, for instance, several data items are included in all the databases (see again Figure 7.4). Figure 7.5 identifies those areas where redundancy is and is not necessary.

SHARING INFORMATION. An important advantage of databases is that they allow the sharing of information among many people in various locations. The *information-sharing* capabilities of database management software mean that information can be stored once and then retrieved any number of times by any authorized user of the database. This capability both reduces overall storage needs and helps to ensure consistency in the information obtained by people working in different areas of the same organization.

data definition language (DDL)
A tool that allows users to define a database.

data manipulation language (DML)
A tool that allows users to store, retrieve, and edit data in a database.

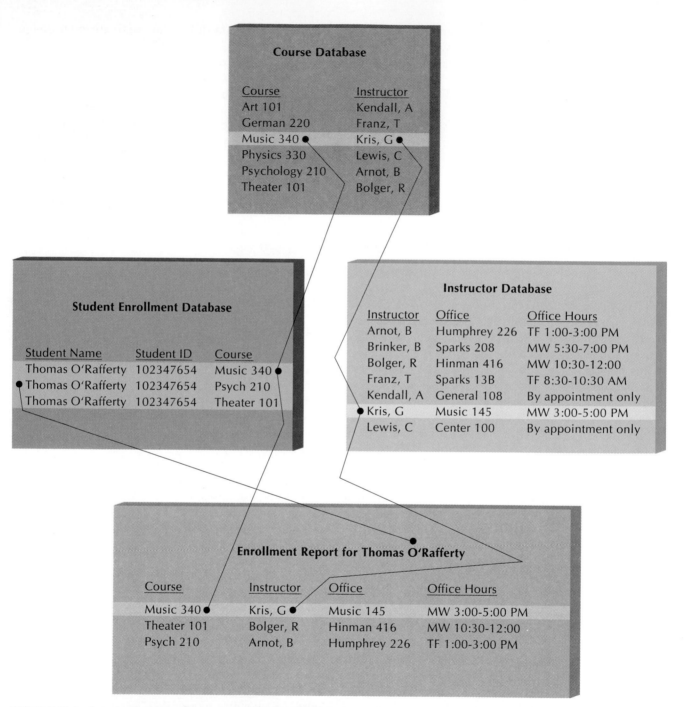

FIGURE 7.4 *Integrating Databases to Produce a Report*
Database management systems frequently integrate information from separate databases into a special report.

Information sharing also means that the same information can be shared by different applications. The alternative, having a different set of information for each application, would lead to redundancy and, most likely, inconsistency between the different sets.

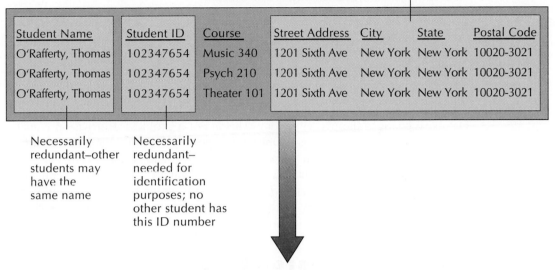

FIGURE 7.5 *Database Redundancy—Necessary and Unnecessary*
The student's street address, city, state, and postal code are not needed in the student enrollment database. Since each student's ID number is unique, that is enough to ensure that two students with the same name will not be confused.

MAINTAINING INTEGRITY.   Database management systems play an important role in database security. When a database is *secure,* access to its information is controlled so that only authorized people can retrieve or process it. Security is important, especially when personal information (such as salary history and telephone numbers) is involved.

A DBMS also helps to ensure database *reliability,* meaning that the information in the database is accurate and available when needed. A DBMS forces people to take precautions to ensure that the information they are entering into the database is correct. It also makes them maintain backup copies of the database in case of loss or damage.

A database that is both secure and reliable is said to have *integrity.*

ENABLING DATABASE EVOLUTION.   Databases are not stagnant. They evolve because the environment in which they are used—home, campus, or office—is constantly changing.

Databases change in two ways:

- **Content.** The data items in current records change, new records are added, and existing records are deleted.
- **Structure.** The data items that make up a record change the database's logical structure, either because fields are added or deleted, because data items' characteristics change (e.g., more space is needed for a data item than is currently allocated), or because the way the database is stored physically changes.

Database changes happen every day. This is not a problem if provision is made for the evolution of the database. Only when people find that they cannot adjust the database to fit new circumstances is there a problem. Database management systems give users the capability to modify the database and to avoid inflexibility. The *Information Technology in Practice* feature entitled "Databases Support a Global Alliance" describes how a husband-and-wife team uses database software to manage their businesses on two continents.

Database or Spreadsheet—What's the Difference?

Lotus 1-2-3, the spreadsheet that swept the business world in the early 1980s, actually integrated three basic functions: an electronic spreadsheet, database management, and business graphics. Since then, many people have tried to use Lotus 1-2-3 and similar spreadsheet packages to build personal databases, only to find that what they really need is a database management system.

THREE BASIC QUESTIONS.   How do you decide whether you should use a spreadsheet or a database management system in your work? Simply ask yourself these three questions:

1. **What do I need to do with the data?** Much of a spreadsheet's power comes from its embedded formulas, which let you explore the numerical relationships between business variables such as costs, price, and profit. The spreadsheet is therefore an ideal tool for performing "what if" financial analyses and forecasts. The database, in contrast, is designed to collect, store, and retrieve data items that are structured in a particular way. Although database management systems can perform mathematical functions (such as sums and averages), their main strength is their ability to maintain the *relationships* among data items.
2. **How much data do I need to store?** Spreadsheets do have "Find" and "Search" functions that help users retrieve specific records, but the process can be slow and cumbersome if the spreadsheet is very large. (And some spreadsheets can become very large.) So a small-store owner might find it practical to record accounts payable in a spreadsheet, while a major credit card company would find it more practical to use a database.
3. **How important are the data?** Data and information are often described as the lifeblood of the modern organization. With them, managers can carefully monitor the organization's performance and plan for the future. In some situations, data and information have life-and-death consequences; a record of patient drug allergies is one such situation. Other data, such as sales forecasts and employee salaries, are so sensitive and confidential that if they get

INFORMATION TECHNOLOGY IN PRACTICE

Databases Support a Global Alliance

Brian Wood and Odile Rousseau are living a global alliance. During the winter, they and their young daughter, Sophie, share a loft in New York City's Chelsea neighborhood, where Wood creates the paintings he sells to fashionable art galleries. Come spring, the family jets off to France's Loire Valley, where Wood paints and Rousseau runs an exclusive guest house built into the ruins of a medieval abbey. An enviable life—and they owe it all to shared goals and personal databases.

Wood's database contains all the records he needs to treat his art as a business: a mailing list of collectors, galleries, and museums, as well as a schedule of his exhibitions. Rousseau's database contains a list of past and potential clients, as well as reservation records for the abbey guest house—maintained with the help of an assistant in France, who stays in touch with Rousseau when she is in New York by phone and fax.

Although Rousseau mails out brochures and advertises in *The New York Times,* much of her business comes through word-of-mouth. Wood says, "It's a wonderful place, people love it, and she's a great hostess." Rousseau agrees: "What makes this business a success is my welcome, of course," she says. "But the technology makes it so much easier to run the whole thing. It's perfect." As for the future, Wood says, "I'll always do business in New York—that's where the art world is." But he's also looking into more sophisticated computers that will make it easier for him to "shift the global balance" anytime he wants to.

Odile Rousseau, shown here with her daughter Sophie, spends her summers running a guest house in the ruins of a medieval French abbey (background). Rousseau's husband, Brian Wood, is a New York City–based painter. Information technology allows the couple to lead a seasonal lifestyle—New York in the winter, France in the summer.

SOURCE: Based on Michael Rubner, "Dear Abbey," *Home Office Computing,* December 1992, pp. 60–62. Used by permission of Scholastic, Inc.

into the wrong hands, the organization or individuals could be harmed. Hence, it is important that data be both accurate and protected from unauthorized users.

A spreadsheet does not offer much help here, for anyone who can access the spreadsheet file can also read—or change—the data it contains. A database management system, in contrast, contains many functions a spreadsheet cannot perform, including (but not limited to) those that are designed to eliminate common data entry errors and protect the data from unauthorized users. (You'll read more about these functions a little later in this chapter.)

SPREADSHEETS AND DBMSs: A TEAM FOR THE FUTURE. Spreadsheets and databases both have a valuable role to play in the modern organization. At many firms, for example, corporate data are warehoused in a multiuser database system and safeguarded by a database management system. Authorized users, however, can use queries to download a copy of specific data into their desktop computers, where they can use a spreadsheet to perform "what if" analyses. Or, alternatively, they can use a PC and a spreadsheet to collect raw data, which are then transferred into the multiuser database system. (Au Bon Pain, an international chain of French-style cafés, uses this arrangement.) Clearly, knowledge workers of the future will need to know how to use both spreadsheet and database software.

Developing Database Applications

Like the process of developing a spreadsheet application, the process of developing a database application is a form of problem solving. It proceeds in a deliberate fashion, with one action leading to the next in the most efficient and effective manner possible. Database application development can be viewed as a seven-step sequence (Figure 7.6):

1. Study the problem.
2. Determine the requirements.
3. Design the database.
4. Create the database.
5. Design the application.
6. Create the application.
7. Test the application

FIGURE 7.6

Database Application Development Sequence

The seven steps in database application development are common to all database development projects, whether large or small.

STEP	DESCRIPTION
Study the problem.	Describe the system's data entry (input) requirements, inquiry requirements, and output requirements.
Determine the requirements.	Determine the problem's characteristics and how database creation and processing can assist in solving the problem.
Design the database.	Identify entities of interest, determine the data or information that describes them, and determine which data items will be used to distinguish one entity from another.
Create the database.	Name the database; establish the database structure (field names, types, widths, and decimal positions; field indexation).
Design the application.	Develop data entry, report generation, and query-processing methods.
Create the application.	Write the programs to perform data-processing tasks.
Test the application.	Evaluate the application's processes and procedures to ensure they are performing as expected.

In the sections that follow, we will use a problem commonly faced by student association offices on university campuses to illustrate each phase of the database development process.

Study the Problem

Studying a problem involves determining its characteristics and how database creation and processing can assist you to solve it.

The problem is as follows: The Student Association Office (SAO) at the University of Wyckoff is responsible for keeping all members of all student clubs informed of membership requirements and special events. At present, the director's office maintains a file of index cards on which names, addresses, telephone numbers, and other personal information are recorded. But there are now nearly 50 organizations on campus, each with 25 to 50 members, and the director wants to develop a better system.

After studying the problem, the director and his staff decide to develop a database for the SAO. Using the student database in the university's student records office would make their job much easier, but university policy dictates that this database can be used only for official university business. It is not available to social and service organizations.

Because the director's office already uses personal computers, the director and staff decide the database should be created and maintained on a PC. Before they plunge into the development tasks, they check to ensure that two essential conditions are met:

- The designated PC on which the database will be established has adequate storage capacity for the database and for the computer-based procedures that will be needed to use the database.
- The database management software they seek to use will run on the designated IBM computer and the system's main memory and disk storage capacity are sufficient.

They find that these conditions are met, so they can set out to determine the application's requirements.

Determine the Requirements

The database's *requirements* are the capabilities the system must have for capturing, storing, processing, and generating data and information. These include input/data entry requirements, query requirements, and output requirements. Determining requirements begins with the formation of a project committee to oversee the effort. This committee includes managers, informed staff members, and students. Bringing these three groups together should ensure that all meaningful ideas will be considered.

The project committee sits down to evaluate the manual system of index cards currently in use with the objective of determining which features work well and which are inefficient. Because database applications have a way of generating additional uses after they are developed, committee members also try to identify possible future uses of the data and information that will be included in the database. For example, the committee may decide that a likely new use of the database will be to keep track of the location of student club members after they graduate.

Contact Manager Helps Farmland Boost Sales

When most people think of a farm in the United States, they picture a solitary tractor tilling the earth from dawn to dusk. But the modern U.S. farmer is also a major consumer, one who spends thousands of dollars on feed, fuel, and chemicals at the local farm cooperative. The co-op, in turn, buys its wares from distributors, such as Farmland Industries, which has thousands of salespeople crisscrossing the Midwest.

Because Farmland's salespeople tend to specialize in certain product lines, several might visit the same co-op—with mixed results. One problem, the company found, was that this was a duplication of effort. Another, more serious, problem was that Farmland's salespeople didn't know what their colleagues had or had not already sold and therefore often missed opportunities to sell farm supplies related to the products they specialized in.

The firm decided to turn to IT for help. Most of the company's salespeople already had laptop computers with modems, which meant they could easily access a database of products and prices. The next logical step was to install a contact manager—a data management system designed to help salespeople manage their work—on the network.

Thanks to the recently installed network-based contact manager, Farmland's salespeople now use their modems to tap into a centralized database and extract a complete account history for each customer, including a record of what colleagues sold that customer on their last sales calls.

After much discussion, the committee formulates the following requirements. People using the new system must be able to

- Enter and maintain records in the database.
- Prepare reports listing all members of student clubs
  —in alphabetical order.
  —in postal code order.
  —in alphabetical order by name of student club.
- Prepare mailing labels.
- Process queries to display or print information about a particular club member who is identified either by name or by student ID number.
- Make copies of the database for backup purposes.
- Protect the database from unauthorized use.

The committee members believe that they can design a new application that meets all of these requirements.

Design the Database

With the requirements set, the project leader can turn to the design process. Database design consists of three activities:

- Identifying the entities of interest.
- Determining the attributes that describe the entity of interest.
- Determining which data items will be used to distinguish one entity from another (for retrieval purposes).

For the student club database, the primary entity is the student member. The most important attributes describing the members are

- Name.
    - Last name
    - First name
    - Middle initial
- Student ID number.
- Student club/society name.
- Room number (in student club facilities).
- Year of graduation.
- Office held in student club (if any).

Office staff members want to be able to retrieve information from the database using the individual's name (last name, then first name), but they expect that in some instances it will be necessary to rely on the individual's student ID number. As in Figure 7.5, each student will have a unique ID number to ensure that students with the same last and first names are not confused. These three data items—last name, first name, and student ID number—are all used as **index keys** or **search keys.** When the user specifies a search key, the database management software searches through the database to locate the record containing the specified data item.

index key/search key
A data item used by database management software to locate a specific record.

Create the Database

Creation of a database entails naming the database and defining its structure, which consists of five elements (Figure 7.7):

1. Names of the individual fields (attributes).
2. Type of information stored in each field.
3. Maximum width of information stored in each field.
4. Number of decimal positions allowed in each field (when appropriate).
5. Whether or not each field will be indexed.

FIELD NAMES. Field names distinguish one field from another. The guidelines for naming the fields are contingent on the data management software used. For example, in the popular data management systems running under Microsoft Windows 3.1, field names can be no longer than 10 characters. The first character must be a letter; the other characters may be letters, numbers, or the underline (_). Blank spaces within a field name are not permissible. (For example, the 9-character field name DAY OF WK ["day of week"] is not permissible because it contains blank spaces. However, DAY_OF_WK is allowed because the underlines are not considered blanks.) Data management systems designed for later versions of Microsoft Windows, as well as those used on Apple Macintosh computers, can use long field names—they are not constrained by the 10-character limitation.

The project committee decides to use Microsoft Access to create the SAO's database. The database will contain eight fields with the following names: LastName, FirstName, Initial, StudentID, Society, RoomNumber, Officer, and YearOfGraduation.

FIGURE 7.7

Database Structure for Student Club Database (Using Microsoft Access)

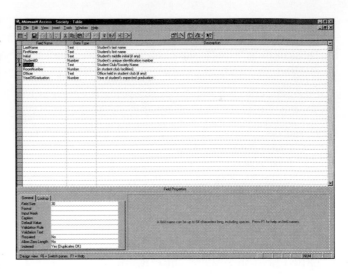

FIELD TYPES. In addition to naming each field, database creators must specify the *type* of data the field will hold. The most popular database systems permit six different types of data (Figure 7.8):

1. **Character**—the letters *A–Z*, the numbers 0–9, and any other characters on the keyboard (such as & and #). Most fields contain character, or alphanumeric, information. (The terms *character* and *alphanumeric* are used interchangeably.) Numbers treated as character data cannot be used in arithmetic or computation, but are for identification purposes only (e.g., student ID numbers).
2. **Numeric**—any integer (i.e., any whole number, such as 1, 2, 50, or 100) or any number with a decimal point or a minus sign (−). Unlike alphanumeric data, numeric data can be used in arithmetic processes.
3. **Floating point**—decimal numbers (e.g., 1.5, 2.33, 50.84, and 100.992). Floating point numbers are used when greater precision is needed. They can speed arithmetic processing when the numbers are very large.
4. **Logical**—only a single character—Y or y (yes), T or t (true), N or n (no), or F or f (false). Some systems allow entry of yes-or-no values and convert them to true-or-false values when storing the data in the database.
5. **Memo**—text information consisting of alphanumeric characters. Memo fields are designed to hold long blocks of text, often several thousand characters in length.
6. **Date**—in the form mm/dd/yyyy (month/day/year). For example, January 3, 1999, can be described as 01/03/1999. The data management system inserts the slash (/) character.

In the not-too-distant future, database management systems will include image and graphic data types as well.

FIELD WIDTH. The width of the field specified in the database structure determines how long, in characters, each field can be. For some fields, like the logical, date, and memo fields, length is predetermined by the database management system. Other field lengths are specified by the database designer. For instance, the chosen length of the StudentID field will depend on the number of characters the university includes in all student identification numbers. Wyckoff University uses Social Security numbers as student ID numbers, so the width of the StudentID field is 9 characters.

FIELD TYPE	DESCRIPTION	EXAMPLE
Character or alphanumeric	Alphabetic or special characters and numbers (cannot be used in arithmetic processes).	O'Rafferty 12001 Sixth Avenue
Numeric	Any integer or any number with a decimal point or minus sign (can be used in arithmetic processes).	540 -12 4.7
Floating point	Decimal numbers (typically used in applications involving frequent multiplication and division).	128.6
Logical	One space used to indicate True or False, or Yes or No.	Tt Ff Yy Nn
Memo	Text data used to explain or annotate other details contained in the record, frequently at length.	"Details captured by Jerri Olenburg during interview with student on April 14."
Date	Calendar date in the format mm/dd/yyyy (month, day, year)	07/15/1999

FIGURE 7.8
Field Types
The six most common field types are listed here. A growing number of database management systems can also include *image* and *graphic field types.*

DECIMAL POSITIONS. When decimal data will be included in the database, the designer specifies the number of positions to allow after the decimal point. If a field will describe money, two decimal positions is customary (c.g., the monetary figure $34.78 has two decimal positions). The SAO at Wyckoff University does not need to use decimal numbers in its database, so the relevant fields have decimal positions of zero.

INDEXATION. **Indexing** is the structural element that permits the database system to find fields and records in the database. The designer must specify which fields will be used for retrieval so the database management system can create an index of key fields and storage locations. Once the designer chooses the respective fields, the database management system does all the work. Figure 7.7 shows that the project committee has chosen to index LastName, StudentID, and Society. The "Yes" at the bottom of the screen means that the field will be indexed. A "No" would mean that it will not.

indexing
A database system's capability to find fields and records in the database.

Design the Application

Database processing includes many features that make data and information accessible to people and that help safeguard the existence of the database. It is during the application design step of the development process that these features are determined. The most important of them are the methods for data entry, report generation, and query processing.

DATA ENTRY. Database creation, as we just saw, is the process of establishing the database's structure by defining the database's different fields and their characteristics. **Data entry** is the process of *populating* the database with data and information. During data entry, new records are added to the database by providing the details for each field in the record. At the University of Wyckoff, data entry methods will determine how all the student club details, such as LastName, FirstName, and StudentID, will be entered into the database.

data entry
The process of populating a database with data and information.

data entry form
Custom-developed video display used to enter and change data in a database.

Data entry forms are custom-developed video displays used to enter and change data in a database. Forms can be very basic, or they can be designed to look like the paper forms and reports that the database will generate. Figure 7.9 shows two different data entry forms. The form at the top asks the user to enter data directly, using field names as a prompt. The form at the bottom has been specially designed and formatted for ease of use and aesthetic appeal.

The data entry portion of application design involves determining the method and sequence in which the data are entered. Typically, data are still entered through the keyboard, but scanners, microphones, and light pens are being used more frequently.

REPORT GENERATION.   A *report* is a printed or onscreen display of data or information in the database. Some reports are simply a list of the records in the database, one record after the other; others contain only certain elements of the database (Figure 7.10). Most of the time, however, a report is more than just a list. A good report organizes data into a form that is meaningful and helpful.

Reports are most useful when they

- Contain the records that meet the recipients' needs.
- Contain only the information that is needed from the records.
- Present information arranged in a sequence that fits the users' needs (perhaps in alphabetical order or grouped by category according to the contents of particular fields).
- Have the date of preparation, titles that identify the purpose of the report, and headings that identify the contents of the rows and columns of information.
- Have numbered pages, with the title repeated on each page when reports are lengthy.

In a well-designed report, such as that shown in Figure 7.11, information appears where users expect it and headings and titles are clear and useful. In other words, the focus is on the information rather than on the design itself, which is hardly noticed.

Database systems also can generate output in the form of labels. At the University of Wyckoff, items from the database are printed on mailing labels or on labels for file folders and reports (Figure 7.12).

FIGURE 7.9
Two Data Entry Forms

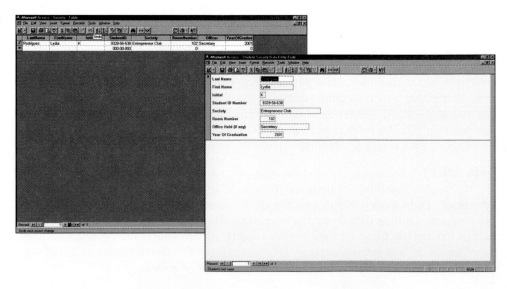

LASTNAME	FIRSTNAME	INITIAL	STUDENT_ID	SOCIETY
JAMISON	JULIETTE	R	535460299	ENTREPRENEUR
HUNT	MARTHA	L	325937742	ENTREPRENEUR
RODRIGUEZ	LYDIA	K	932856638	ENTREPRENEUR
LING	MAI	T	535257812	ENTREPRENEUR
GONZALEZ	RAMON		285339934	STUDY ABROAD
MARKS	DAVID	M	883226077	STUDY ABROAD
CHO	JOHN	D	488249931	STUDY ABROAD

FIGURE 7.10   *Unformatted Database Printout*

This report is simply a printout of certain elements of the student club database. It contains information from the database, but is not organized usefully.

QUERY PROCESSING.   Recall that a *query* (also called an *inquiry*) is a question that guides the retrieval of specific records in a database. In solving problems, it is common to pose "who are" or "how many" queries. In the student club example, for instance, the SAO may ask

Who are the members of the Entrepreneur Club?
How many students expect to graduate this year?
Who are the members of the Entrepreneur Club who expect to graduate this year?

An important part of designing a database application entails establishing the form of the queries. Figure 7.13 shows how a database management system

FIGURE 7.11   *Formatted Database Report*

This report contains the same data as the printout in Figure 7.10, but is organized alphabetically by club and by student's last name.

Page No. 1				
08/08/94				
SOCIETY	**LASTNAME**	**FIRSTNAME**	**INITIAL**	**STUDENT_ID**
ENTREPRENEUR	HUNT	MARTHA	L	325937742
ENTREPRENEUR	JAMISON	JULIETTE	R	535460299
ENTREPRENEUR	LING	MAI	T	535257812
ENTREPRENEUR	RODRIGUEZ	LYDIA	K	932856638
STUDY ABROAD	CHO	JOHN	D	488249931
STUDY ABROAD	GONZALEZ	RAMON		285339934
STUDY ABROAD	MARKS	DAVID	M	883226077

FIGURE 7.12

Mailing Labels Generated as Database Output

Database management systems allow users to custom-design mailing labels with data items from the database.

HUNT MARTHA L
325937742 ENTREPRENEUR

JAMISON JULIETTE R
535460299 ENTREPRENEUR

LING MAI T
535257812 ENTREPRENEUR

RODRIGUEZ LYDIA K
932856638 ENTREPRENEUR

CHO JOHN D
488249931 STUDY ABROAD

GONZALEZ RAMON
285339934 STUDY ABROAD

MARKS DAVID M
883226077 STUDY ABROAD

processes the query "Who are the club members who graduate after 2000?" The fields at the bottom of the screen in Figure 7.13 are the *view,* the fields that the database will use to retrieve the necessary data. The ">" symbol in the YearOf-Graduation field is called a **relational operator.** Relational operators tell the database system to make a comparison to call up the requested data. The most commonly used relational operators are listed in Table 7.2.

relational operator
A symbol that tells a database system to make a comparison to call up the requested data.

Of course, you could review each record in the database, one by one. But this would not be an efficient use of your time. Well-designed database systems, like the Everlink system designed for the entertainment industry, allow users to search them quickly and accurately. For more details on Everlink, see the *Information Technology in Practice* feature entitled "Database Plays Matchmaker for Showbiz Professionals."

Create the Application

Most microcomputer-based database systems contain a set of commands that can be combined to carry out the desired processing activities. Database applications contain procedures for the following processing actions:

- Add records.
- Delete records.

FIGURE 7.13

Query for Retrieval of Selected Data

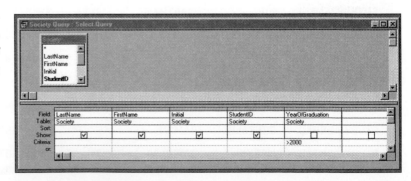

TABLE 7.2 *Commonly Used Relational Operators*

RELATIONAL OPERATOR	COMPARISON
<	Less than
>	Greater than
=	Equal to
< > or #	Not equal to
<=	Less than or equal to
>=	Greater than or equal to

- Edit records.
- Process queries.
- Prepare reports.
- Make copies of the database (for backup purposes).
- Process information: carry out calculations.
- Process information: sort information into a particular sequence.

Figure 7.14 shows the processing menu on the SAO's student club database.

During application creation, the actual programs to perform these database-processing tasks are created.[2] There are two common methods for creating database-processing applications on microcomputers. In **custom programming,** programmers write detailed procedures using the commands and functions built into the database management software. Every step of each application must be specified in detail. In **application generation,** programmers use menus and simple commands to describe the components, or objects, that constitute the application to an *application generator*—a system program that creates the set of detailed commands to perform the procedures as they have been defined.

custom programming

In a database system, the writing of detailed procedures using the commands and functions built into the database management software.

application generation

In a database system, the use of menus and simple commands to describe the application to a system program that creates the set of detailed commands.

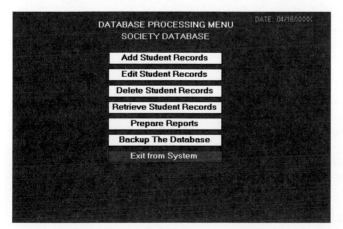

FIGURE 7.14

Database Menu for Selection of Processing Actions

Using the main menu of the student club database system, the user can add, edit, delete, or retrieve student records; prepare reports; back up the database; or exit from the system.

[2]Database processing on mainframe and midrange computer applications often uses general-purpose processing languages and has for many years relied on the COBOL language. More recently, easier-to-use languages such as Natural and Focus have been employed for database processing.

INFORMATION TECHNOLOGY IN PRACTICE

Database Plays Matchmaker for Showbiz Professionals

As a former producer of *Saturday Night Live*, John Kelly knows that a producer's life is not always a bed of roses. Like all business managers, producers face financing, budgeting, and scheduling challenges. They also spend countless hours in preproduction— a grueling treasure hunt for the locations, actors, and behind-the-scenes artisans needed to create magic on the screen. Worldwide, about 145,000 commercial productions, ranging from television commercials to industrial films, go through preproduction every year. Sensing a major problem (and an appealing business opportunity), Kelly teamed up with Howard Gollomp to create Everlink, an on-line multimedia database network designed for the entertainment industry.

For a small fee, actors and behind-the-scenes specialists can list their résumés and credits in the database. Meanwhile, anyone who pays a one-time fee of about $200 can access the database for $1 a minute, using either an IBM-compatible or a Macintosh computer. The system features a simple query language that lets producers search for specific needs, such as

blond actors who speak French or a list of all sound stages in Arizona. Everlink also offers a graphic user interface that lets users call up actors' photos and even manipulate their hair color on-screen.

The database made its debut in late 1992, following testing by some of Hollywood's hottest production companies—Ron Howard's Imagine, Francis Ford Coppola's American Zoetrope, and Rob Reiner's Castle Rock. Within months, it seemed, the entire industry was talking about how Everlink's database helped producers save time and money. "Everlink seems to save so much lost time in tracking down people such as cinematographers by just giving you their phone numbers," says Clarisse Perritte of Sharona Productions, a smaller, independent production firm.

SOURCES: Based on Matthew Mandell, "Network Makes Movie Debut," *Computerworld,* April 19, 1993, p. 45; and Steve Morgenstern, "The Best Software for Tracking Contacts," *Home Office Computing,* May 1992, pp. 66–72.

The trend is toward developing increasingly powerful application generators so that users can concentrate on the problem to be solved rather than on the detailed programming procedures needed to produce the information. The steps taken in designing the Student Association Office database, such as creating the processing menu and input form, resulted in the creation of a set of detailed commands. These commands were not visible because they were developed and managed by the Microsoft Access software.

Test the Application

No application design is complete until it is tested. Testing entails using sample data to verify that the results come out as expected. Almost certainly, testing will reveal mistaken assumptions, incorrect procedures, or errors in completing a particular stage of design and development. Obviously, then, failure to test an application can lead to serious problems.

A Final Word

The example we used in this chapter to illustrate the development of a database system involved a fairly simple database. But whether the application is a student club directory or a business database intended to manage day-to-day contacts with customers and suppliers or the processing of important transactions, the steps for creating the database are the same. The capabilities of database management systems can make people much more effective—but only if the appropriate steps are followed in creating and using the database.

SUMMARY OF LEARNING OBJECTIVES

1 Explain why businesses use databases. After people, a business's most important resources are data and information. Databases can help businesses identify, structure, collect, store, edit, and update data. They are also useful because of their ability to retrieve and share data and to empower knowledge workers.

2 Describe the main components of a database. The five most common terms used to identify the components of a database are entities, attributes, data items, records, and relations. An *entity* is a person, place, thing, event, or condition about which data and information are collected. Each category of interest in an entity is an *attribute* of that entity. A *data item* is a specific piece of data or information about an entity's attributes that is entered into the database. A *record* is a grouping of data items. A *relation* is the table (consisting of rows and columns) in a database that describes an entity.

3 List and describe the five objectives of database management systems. Database manage-

ment systems have these five objectives: (1) integrating databases, (2) reducing redundancy, (3) sharing information, (4) maintaining integrity, and (5) enabling database evolution.

4 Identify when a business should use a spreadsheet and when it should use a database. If a business has only a small number of variables to record or needs an application that will examine the numerical relationships between business variables, such as costs and profits, it should use a spreadsheet. If a business has many records structured in a particular way or needs to put security measures in place to protect the data, it should use a database.

5 Identify the seven-step sequence for developing database applications. There are seven steps to developing a database application: (1) study the problem, (2) determine the requirements, (3) design the database, (4) create the database, (5) design the application, (6) create the application, and (7) test the application.

KEY TERMS

CRITICAL CONNECTIONS

1   EMI Music's Database Tracks Careers

EMI Music   The consolidated database EMI Music finally settled on is now a vital ingredient in the company's long-term plans. The system, maintained at EMI's New York offices, runs on desktop computers and uses database software that is available around the world.

EMI's chairman, its chief executive, and the heads of its key business divisions use the career database at the headquarters to keep tabs on senior and fast-track junior executives in the company's 50 separate businesses. Alternate-language versions and customization to suit the needs of executives in the 35 countries where EMI does business are further aiding the company to keep track of its managerial talent.

Questions for Discussion

1. What questions do you think must be raised about database and software when an application is going to be used internationally?

2. EMI wanted a centralized database that could be used around the world, yet the company also wanted local customization in individual countries. Are these contradictory requirements?

3. What data and information would you capture and store in a database if you were responsible for

tracking the career accomplishments of EMI's executives? How does a database accommodate storage of this data and information?

2   At A/E/C/ Systems, the Database Makes the Show Go On

A/E/C/ Systems   Using large databases to contact potential exhibitors and attendees increases attendance at trade shows. However, good attendance can be achieved with fewer mailings and, therefore, lower cost when information in a database is carefully culled. At A/E/C/ Systems, Hough decided to use this more focused strategy. The database was scanned more carefully to identify potential attendees, and over the course of a year, Hough was able to reduce the number of mailings to 25 carefully focused promotional pieces. This was one-third fewer mailings than had been sent out the previous year. Promotional costs had been reduced by one third. The strategy paid off: conference revenues from attendee registration increased by some 30 percent.

Applying insights gained from this experience, Hough and the A/E/C/ Systems staff sharpened their database information even more, tracking 39 different exhibitor and attendee attributes. The gains were gratifying: more focused mailings to fewer prospects resulted in a doubling of conference revenues. As Hough's experience demonstrates, the power of database marketing pays its highest dividends when the information is used to beam in on the right prospects.

SOURCE: Ann Field, "Precision Marketing," *Inc. Technology,* No. 2 (June 18, 1996): 56–57.

Questions for Discussion

1. What features of database systems support the development of targeted marketing strategies?

2. Using the A/E/C/ Systems example as a basis, what factors do you believe determine whether the preparation of mailing lists and the distribution of promotional material should be maintained within a company or contracted out to a specialist?

3. What factors determine the optimal size of databases created and maintained on desktop computers? Are such databases typically constrained to be small in size or to contain few attributes?

3 Contact Manager Helps Farmland Boost Sales

Farmland In addition to allowing Farmland's salespeople to share valuable account histories, the contact manager helps them maintain a customer address book, schedule sales calls, create to-do lists, track expenses, and set up a special "tickler" file to remind them of important dates and appointments. The contact manager also lets salespeople create extra displays of demographic information to support their sales presentations. Says the firm's network manager, "Our goal is to turn our salespeople into consultants. If a salesperson can have the account's information, then the salesperson can know the needs of the co-op rather than just selling one product."

When a new edition of the contact manager software was released, with additional tracking and analysis features, Farmland's salespeople capitalized on the new capabilities. Now they can use the built-in scheduling feature to record the time they spend with each customer and to make comments about the sales call. At the end of the week, they send in summary reports to regional managers, who track their performance and then work closely with those salespeople who are not top performers.

Questions for Discussion

1. How can Farmland's sales staff use the contact manager to meet its needs for up-to-date pricing data?

2. How can the contact manager make Farmland's sales staff more efficient? How can the contact manager make the staff more responsive to the needs of Farmland's customers?

Net Work

Journey into Cybercruiting

In the scramble to snare top-notch talent, a growing number of companies are using the Internet to recruit employees. While companies have not dropped the conventional methods of recruitment, many are finding that *cybercruiting*—posting jobs on World Wide Web sites and in news groups—extends their reach into different geographic areas. It also allows them to make a good deal of information available to a prospective candidate instantly, via on-line access, saving them the cost of preparing and distributing printed materials. The drawback is that designing an effective Web page takes time and resources.

The best way to assess the benefits and drawbacks of cybercruiting is to visit Web sites designed for this purpose. Among the most active and best-known sites are

- **Careerpath** (http://www.careerpath.com). Contains recruitment advertisements from major metropolitan daily newspapers (e.g., *Boston Globe, Chicago Tribune, New York Times, Washington Post*).
- **CareerMosaic** (http://www.careermosaic.com). Provides job listings, a résumé database, and tips on

career development. Focuses on West Coast companies.

- **Computerworld**
  (http://www.careers.computerworld.com). Run by *Computerworld,* a weekly newspaper for the information technology industry. Focuses on IT careers.
- **Online Career Center**
  (http://www.occ.com). One of the oldest career databases.
- **The Monsterboard**
  (http://www.monster.com). Provides job listings, a résumé database, and career

counseling. Focuses on East Coast.

1. What information is typically found on an organization's recruiting home page?
2. What assistance is offered to candidates regarding their résumés?
3. What assistance do Web sites provide for companies seeking to recruit candidates?
4. Based on your review of Web sites, would you say cybercruiting tends to attract a certain type of job candidate, or do you think it is an effective means to reach all types of candidates? Explain the reasons for your answer.

GROUP PROJECTS AND APPLICATIONS

Project 1

Your marketing company, Concepts Unlimited, has just landed a major new account. The Barnes & Noble Bookstore chain has embarked on a massive new marketing program and has asked your company to create a database of all its customers and what they purchase. It plans to do the following:

1. Keep track of all credit card purchases. Because Barnes & Noble uses scanners, it can keep a record of the titles sold to each credit card number. From the credit card company, Barnes & Noble can get the following customer information: name, street address, town, state, zip code, sex, age, types of pets, type of computer, yearly annual income, number of children, and ages of children.
2. Determine what types of books sell best in individual areas. For cash sales, cashiers will ask customers for their zip code, which they will then enter before each transaction. For credit purchases, Barnes & Noble can get the zip code from the credit card company.
3. Embark on a direct-mail campaign offering volume discounts. People who spend over a certain amount each month will receive a

gift certificate equal to 10 percent of their purchases.

Your group is in charge of database design at Concepts Unlimited. Brainstorm the possibilities and answer the following questions:

- What types of information/reports should the database be able to generate?
- What entity(ies) will be used in the database?
- Which attributes will be used to describe the entity(ies)? Which of these fields will use characters? Which will be numeric? Which will be logical?
- How might a spreadsheet be integrated with the database package?
- Suppose Barnes & Noble wishes to sell more children's books through mail order. Which attribute(s) will it want to extract from the database to create a mailing list?
- Now suppose Barnes & Noble is thinking about offering a discount on computer-oriented titles. In which attribute(s) will the company be most interested?

Project 2

Some detractors claim that database marketing is an invasion of privacy. Whenever you purchase anything on a credit card, whenever you shop through a catalog, whenever you subscribe to a magazine, your name (along with other personal information) gets entered into a database. Other companies then buy or rent portions of this database with the goal of getting advertisements into your mailbox. Some even call your home to annoy you with offers while you are eating dinner or sleeping on Saturday morning.

In this project, two groups of four persons each should debate the benefits and drawbacks of database marketing, taking privacy issues into account. After the first person from each side has spoken, the second individual questions the opponent's arguments, looking for holes and inconsistencies. The third person attempts to answer these arguments. The fourth person presents a summary of each side's arguments. Finally, the class votes on which team has offered the more compelling argument.

REVIEW QUESTIONS

1. What is a database?
2. Discuss the meaning of the term *information repository* as it relates to a database.
3. Name four benefits of using databases in business.
4. What is a query? What purpose does it serve?
5. Describe entities, data items, records, and relations.
6. What are the formal terms for fields, records, and databases?
7. Describe the three tools included with a database management system.
8. Identify and describe the five objectives of database management systems.
9. Why is the ability to integrate databases valuable in problem solving?
10. Why should redundancy in databases be managed? Should redundancy be altogether eliminated from databases?
11. What two components constitute database integrity?
12. In what two ways can databases change?
13. In deciding whether to use a spreadsheet or a database, what three questions should you ask yourself?
14. What seven steps are involved in developing a database application?
15. What three activities take place during database design?
16. List the five elements of a database structure.
17. What six types of data can a database field hold?
18. What is the difference between database creation and data entry?
19. What data or information must a database report contain to be useful?
20. Distinguish between custom programming and application generation.

DISCUSSION QUESTIONS

1. When Mary Ann Morley was hired as a human resources assistant at the American Pharmaceutical Association in Washington, D.C., one of her first assignments was to collect the data managers needed to reschedule all salary reviews for January and prorate each employee's new salary. (At the time, salaries were reviewed at 75 different dates throughout the year, based on each employee's starting date.) Morley accomplished the task with a relational database for human resources departments. What data items or fields do you think she included in each row or tuple of her database? Explain your answer.

2. How does Morley's use of the database illustrate the benefits of using a database in business?

3. Levi Strauss & Co. maintains a PC-based interactive computer network called OLIVER (On-Line Interactive Visual Employee Resource) that allows employees to tap into a mainframe database in order to review their total compensation packages. Which function of a DBMS do you think would be most important in creating this type of application?

4. OLIVER uses a series of easy-to-use menus to help employees learn about their benefits, including health care, disability, and pension earnings. Why do you think the system's designers chose this access method?

SUGGESTED READINGS

Grauer, Robert T, and Maryann Barber. *Exploring Microsoft Access for Windows*. Upper Saddle River, NJ: Prentice Hall, 1997. An easy-to-follow, well-illustrated introduction to the use of Microsoft Access in a variety of applications. Includes an appendix discussing how to get the most value and performance out of Microsoft Access.

Grehen, Rick, Ben Smith, and Jon Udell. "Database Building Blocks," *Byte 17* (January 1992): 204–224. Part of a special section on databases and microcomputers, this article explores the development of database applications, with special emphasis on assembling libraries of procedures to avoid having to develop applications from scratch. Other articles evaluate different personal databases, feature by feature.

Halverson, Michael, and Michael Young. *Running Microsoft Office 97*. San Francisco, CA: Microsoft Press, 1997. An in-depth reference book for using the family of Microsoft programs—Access, Powerpoint, Word, and Excel—together. This well-illustrated source provides design guidelines and usage tips for transferring data and information among the programs, thus providing a comprehensive system of applications.

Litwin, Paul, Ken Getz, and Mike Gilbert. *Access 97 Developer's Handbook*. Berkeley, CA: Sybex, 1997. This 1,500-page book provides broad coverage of the many characteristics of the Access database system, with emphasis on its use for creation of personal database systems.

Townsend, James J. *Introduction to Databases*. Indianapolis, IN: Que, 1992. An excellent discussion of the characteristics of personal database systems that describes features and uses in a variety of different application settings.

CASE STUDY

Haven Corporation:
Do-It-Yourself Attitude
Spawns a Million-Dollar Business

Bruce Holmes has given a new meaning to the phrase "do-it-yourself." When this former fitness guru couldn't find a good, affordable software package to help him manage his mail-order business, he wrote his own. Today, almost a decade later, the mail-order business is but a memory and Holmes is the CEO and president of Haven Corp., a software company based in Evanston, Illinois.

The company's leading product is Mail Order Wizard, the program Holmes created for his mail-order business in the mid-1980s. The cost of a single-user version runs from $695 to $995; multiuser versions range from $2,995 to $6,995. But the program's users think Mail Order Wizard is well worth the money.

Peggy Glenn, for example, uses it to manage a mailing list of more than 10,000 names for the *Firefighters Bookstore,* the catalog through which she sells special-interest books by mail and by phone. She has learned that she might have been able to duplicate the Wizard's features with a less expensive, general-purpose relational DBMS, but she admits that she didn't (and still doesn't) have the know-how for that undertaking. Moreover, Holmes's package includes many useful features she might not have thought of. "I'm convinced that it's because of the program that I've been able to grow so effortlessly so quickly. I'm not working any more hours than when I first started, I'm just able to get a whole lot more done—and make a lot more money—in the same amount of time."

Glenn especially likes the software's conversational on-screen messages that have helped her learn the system. But the software's user-friendly style hides a number of sophisticated and powerful database features:

- *The ability to recognize names.* Enter a name and the software will search the database. If it finds a match, it will display a message asking if this is the same customer who lives at such-and-such an address.
- *The ability to fill in customer information.* If the database has found the right record, the user taps a function key and the software fills in the address and billing information, as well as such comments as "slow pay; accept only COD orders."
- *The ability to track inventory.* If an item is out of stock, the software beeps and initiates a back order transaction. (A back order is an item that is shipped to the customer after the stock has been replenished.) The software also prints an inventory list, sorted by supplier, to simplify the restocking process.
- *The ability to track customer buying habits and analyze ad responses.* The software lets users enter special codes that help them analyze the cost effectiveness of ads and special promotional pieces.
- *The ability to create and print invoices, mailing labels, charge card slips, bank deposit forms, past due notices, packing slips, and so on.* This feature saves entrepreneurs like Peggy Glenn countless hours. In addition, the software can create reports showing overdue accounts, quarterly revenues, and the amount of sales tax owed to the government.

But even the most sophisticated features can't ensure the kind of customer loyalty enjoyed by Haven Corp. Bruce Holmes traces that to customer service, his

Haven Corp.'s founder Bruce Holmes is seen here coaching a local school's chess team in Evanston, Illinois.

Peggy Glenn uses the Mail Order Wizard package created by Holmes to manage a mailing list of more than 10,000 names for the Firefighters Bookstore and the catalog she uses to sell books for firefighters. Glenn says, "I'm convinced that it's because of the program that I've been able to grow so effortlessly and so quickly. I'm not working any more hours than when I first started, I'm able to get a lot more done—and make a lot more money—in the same amount of time."

obsession. This service includes a year of toll-free technical support, a quarterly newsletter, regular customer satisfaction surveys, and annual get-togethers for the Holmes family of software users in party towns like New Orleans. Every new featu7re suggested by a user goes on an electronic wish list; if enough customers request it, Holmes will try to include it in the Wizard's next upgrade. As one user wrote, "We really bought more than software. We got a support team we feel is on our side."

Although referrals accounted for about 20 percent of Haven Corp.'s business in 1992, the company recently launched a direct-mail campaign using specially designed postcards and brochures and an ad campaign in computer and direct-marketing magazines. In 1993, after 1992 revenues approached $1 million, Holmes finally had to move his business out of his three-story Victorian home to a more formal office building. "Progress caught up with us," he admitted. "I never looked far enough into the future to imagine 18 people working out of my home."

Questions for Discussion

1. Describe the database functions contained in Mail Order Wizard.

2. In addition to Mail Order Wizard, Haven Corp. sells a variety of other mail and list management programs, including WizKid, a scaled-down Wizard program for smaller, start-up businesses. Looking to the future, Holmes plans to expand into software for retail, contact management, telemarketing, and shipping. Do you think this expansion will prove to be a smart marketing move? Explain your answer.

SOURCES: Lisa Kleinholz, "How One Mail-Order Company Makes Business Grow," *Home Office Computing,* April 1991, pp. 32-33; and Rosalind Resnik, "Best Businesses Contest Winners: Creating a Customer Haven," *Home Office Computing,* July 1993, pp. 42-43.

CHAPTER 8

Multimedia Presentations

CHAPTER OUTLINE

LEARNING OBJECTIVES

When you have completed this chapter, you should be able to

1 Describe the characteristics of multimedia presentations.

2 Discuss five effective uses of multimedia presentations.

3 Describe why multimedia technology is actually a collection of technologies.

4 Distinguish between authoring and viewer software.

5 Identify the four types of digital information used in multimedia presentations.

6 Discuss the importance of sampling in creating multimedia information forms.

7 Explain the principal differences between multimedia slide presentations and interactive multimedia presentations.

Olympic Fly-Over

The Atlanta Committee for the Olympic Games told its convincing story about the city's commitment to the Centennial Olympic Games through creative use of sight, sound, and animation. The International Olympic Organizing Committee (IOC) was able to visit each venue for the games, even though some had not yet been constructed, via a multimedia system—the first ever used in an Olympic bid. This system, which ran on an ordinary desktop microcomputer, offered viewers the opportunity to fly over the city, seeing virtually every building, road, and tree from a vantage point several thousand feet in the air. Rotating the trackball pointing device to the right turned the viewer's line of sight to the right; rotating it further permitted the viewer to see the sights just passed.

This presentation of Atlanta from the air began with a crew filming the city from an aircraft. Segments of the video footage were edited to include many different views of the city's downtown and midtown areas, as well as its villages and landmarks. Multimedia technology supplied the venues that had not been constructed. After capturing architects' drawings and models in computer storage and animating them, the creators of Atlanta's Olympic presentation superimposed these images on the areas of the city where they would be constructed. The city's Olympic appearance was real—and altogether visible on a viewer-controlled fly-over.

The visual fly-over was only the beginning of the Atlanta Committee's multimedia campaign. The technology gave viewers the capability to zoom in on a specific sporting venue to check out the exterior of the site and the surrounding areas. A click of the button put the viewer inside the venue, in a position to scan the stadium and zoom in on a particular seat or visit a certain concession. To complete the illusion, the roar of the crowd and the waving of national flags accompanied the running, jumping, diving, and swinging of the athletes—all enjoyed on a desktop computer.

The Atlanta Committee gambled that drawing heavily on multimedia technology to communicate the city's commitment and capability to the world and to the International Olympic Committee would pay off. And it did. This innovative presentation was highly instrumental in the IOC's decision to award the Centennial Games to Atlanta.

Multimedia also played a special part in running the Centennial Olympic Games. Point-of-service systems around the city dispensed tickets, provided narrated maps of the area, and showed highlights of events with complete audio and visual information captured during the games. A network inter-connecting all multimedia kiosks—more than 2,000 were stationed around the Olympic festival area—ensured that each service point would provide the most up-to-data and complete information ever assembled for attendees at the Games.

Such reliable and innovative communication for the athletes, the media, and the host city's many visitors made the Centennial Olympics memorable. Of course, the Games' real thrill was supplied by the athletes who assembled in Atlanta.

Good content is essential to any presentation. That's as true in business as it is in athletics. But it often is not enough. The *way* information is presented affects how that information is received, be it journalism, packaging, adver-tising, or financial reporting.

We tend to think of written or printed *visual* information whenever anyone mentions *presentation*. However, good presentation of *audio* information is just as important. When either is poorly done, the message gets lost and an oppor-tunity to communicate is missed.

This chapter explores how information technology augments effective com-munication by enabling you to add image, sound, and motion to a message. As you will see, *multimedia presentations* change the content of information as well as its presentation. In the first section of the chapter, we explore the nature of multimedia, highlighting its distinguishing characteristics and describing the ways in which it can be applied. Then we discuss the two major types of multimedia presentations: multimedia slide shows and interactive media presentations. Finally, we take a look at how information becomes digital.

The Nature of Multimedia Presentations

multimedia presentation
The seamless integration, through information technology, of different forms of information, including text, sound, still and animated images, and motion video.

A **multimedia presentation** is the seamless integration, through information technology, of any or all of the following forms of information: text, sound, still images, animated images, and motion video. The information may originate from and be presented by different media. Compared to other forms of communica-tion, such as broadcasting and publishing, which are one-way means of com-munication, multimedia invites participation by the receiver of the information, typically by way of a graphical interface.

Origin of Multimedia

Multimedia presentations have three different points of origin (Figure 8.1):

1. The combining of 35mm slide shows with the simultaneous playing of voice or music from prerecorded audiotapes.
2. The invention of motion pictures, in which every motion, sound, and light-ing pattern is carefully crafted to accompany scripted words.
3. The introduction of television, with its combination of sound and images broadcast to viewers within reach of the transmitted signal.

a) Thirty-five millimeter slide presentation.   **b)** Seventy millimeter motion picture film.   **c)** Color television.

FIGURE 8.1 *The Origin of Multimedia Information Presentation*

Each of these developments created new opportunities for communicating and sharing information. Information Age multimedia has excited people and organizations by enhancing the capabilities of earlier forms of multimedia and by adding innovative capabilities that offer new possibilities. The most important advance in multimedia stemming from information technology is the capability for *dynamic, interactive presentation of information.* Today, recipients of a multimedia presentation can *interact* with the presentation—that is, they have the option of making the communication two-way. It has also made it possible for developers of multimedia presentations to *change* the content or sequence of the presentation quickly. Contemporary multimedia presentations are not limited to the static sequences of the past, but rather can unfold in *multiple different sequences.*

Multimedia Technology

Multimedia technology is not a single technology, but rather a collection of technologies. Thus, you can't walk into a computer store and purchase a multimedia program in the same way you can buy a word-processing, database, or spreadsheet program. Instead, you must purchase a combination of programs and devices, the components of which depend on what multimedia information you wish to present and the manner in which you wish to present it.

The principal types of programs involved in multimedia presentations are the following (Figure 8.2):

- **Capture software.** Used to capture audio, video, and motion sequences.
- **Editing software.** Used to edit captured multimedia information.
- **Authoring software.** Used to create multimedia presentations and insert instructions that control and synchronize the presentation of information, including the playing of audio, video, and motion sequences. Authoring software is the multimedia equivalent of a film director, who combines and orchestrates the different elements of a movie. This software also has a viewing capability, so the presentation can be examined as it will appear when played through a viewer program.
- **Viewer software.** Used to play presentations. Viewer programs do not permit changes to authored presentations.

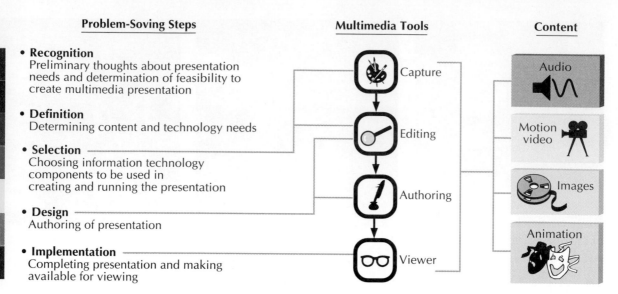

Problem-Soving Steps

Violet
Blue-Violet
Blue
Green
Yellow
Orange
Red

- **Recognition**
  Preliminary thoughts about presentation
  needs and determination of feasibility to
  create multimedia presentation

- **Definition**
  Determining content and technology needs

- **Selection**
  Choosing information technology
  components to be used in
  creating and running the presentation

- **Design**
  Authoring of presentation

- **Implementation**
  Completing presentation and making
  available for viewing

Multimedia Tools

Capture

Editing

Authoring

Viewer

Content

Audio

Motion video

Images

Animation

FIGURE 8.2   *Tools Used in Multimedia Presentations*

The term *multimedia* recognizes that this technology represents a convergence of several information forms (Figure 8.3):

- **Text**—narrative descriptions, including words, descriptions, and symbols.
- **Still images**—photographs, drawings, and figures, whether in black and white, shades of gray, or full color.
- **Audio sequences**—sounds of human voices, music, special effects.
- **Motion video sequences**—integration of sound and full motion pictures (movies).
- **Animation sequences**—succession of discrete still images that, when played under computer control, are interpreted by the human mind as a smooth-flowing moving picture.

Effective Multimedia Uses

Producing effective multimedia presentations is a creative process in the same sense that writing, composing, and painting are. Knowing *when* multimedia can yield benefits in the communication of ideas, impressions, and information is the first step in this process.

Five areas stand out as particularly suitable to multimedia presentations: sales and merchandising, learning systems, operations support systems, multimedia products, and electronic slide presentations.

SALES AND MERCHANDISING.   The first and foremost requirement in sales and merchandising is to meet customers' needs. In some cases, this means illustrating the products or services available to customers. In other cases, it means being prepared to provide personalized services when salespeople are unavailable, perhaps because there are too many customers at one time. These are natural settings in which to capitalize on the power of multimedia to convey just the right message, quickly, through colorful images, sound, and animation.

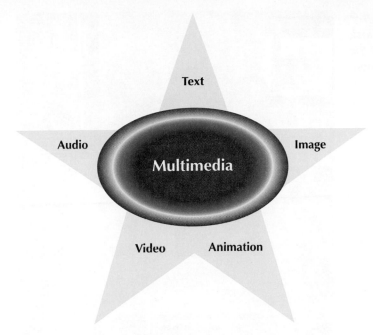

FIGURE 8.3 *Multimedia: A Convergence of Information Forms*

- San Francisco–based Emporium Department Stores recently turned to multi-media kiosks to cope with the Christmas rush. The system replicates the inter-action that occurs between salespersons and customers. To start the sales consultation, customers tell a cartoon figure of Emporium's mascot—Jimmin'E—what type of gift they are looking for by touching an icon on the screen corresponding to " 'Tis the Season," "Stocking Stuffers," or "Leisurely Pursuits." Uncertain customers tell the system to prompt them further, in which case another display screen appears with selections such as "Romantic," "Tra-ditional/Classic," "Has Everything," and "Business Associate."

  Then customers are asked to identify the person for whom they are shop-ping by gender and age, and to indicate the price range they are seeking for the gift. The multimedia system responds with high-resolution photographs of gift suggestions (Figure 8.4). Sound and color graphics add to the presenta-tion. In the end, the customer can request a printed description of the gift sug-gestions, complete with price and location in the store. Customers have responded enthusiastically to Emporium Department Stores' multimedia sales and merchandising.

  Sometimes it's good business to use multimedia to show customers what their alternatives are when it's impossible to show them the actual product. An exam-ple is a vacation or business meeting package that will actually occur thousands of miles away.

- Delta Airlines designed its DeltaStar system to help travelers select tours and accommodations. Color graphics and powerful desktop workstations give DeltaStar the capability to display images of hotel rooms and pool or beach areas, complete with the sounds of splashing water and frolicking children. The multimedia information may be captured on the agent's video cameras and

FIGURE 8.4
A Multimedia Kiosk Helps Shoppers at the Emporium Department Store

transferred to the system; the images may be downloaded from the airline's database, or they may be played from a prerecorded CD-ROM. Systems are emerging that will signal the travel agent's office printer to generate a brochure-quality photo (e.g., the shipboard cabin, banquet facilities, or golf courses). This process uses the agent's and the prospective traveler's time productively, and it is effective in increasing sales (with less time needed to close).

Good communication and accurate information are essential ingredients in every sales process. Multimedia offers these plus additional capabilities in sales and merchandising—all aimed at guiding prospective customers in their selection and decision-making process. Multimedia presentations go beyond written descriptions and static photographs to illustrate more fully the nature of the product or service offered, which is especially important when customers cannot inspect the product or service in person. Through the power of sound, video, and animation, multimedia can also demonstrate how to use a product or service, including those that must be customized to the particular needs of the buyer prior to delivery. The *Rethinking Business Practices* feature entitled "Attina's Point-of-Sale Manufacturing Creates a New Tune" relates how multimedia's capabilities changed merchandising in a local music shop.

LEARNING SYSTEMS.   Since medieval times, scholarship and education at universities have rested on the written and printed word. Today, educational institutions at all levels are reexamining that tradition as they experiment with multimedia systems designed to assist students to learn. Corporations are also using multimedia systems so innovatively that they are revolutionizing employee training programs and producing high payoffs.

RETHINKING BUSINESS PRACTICES

Attina's Point-of-Sale Manufacturing Creates a New Tune

There's no doubt about it, it's impossible to make a sale if you don't have the item in stock. Yet, if you're the owner of a music shop with limited space, it's difficult to know what sheet music to carry.

At Attina's Music Shop in Atlanta, ingenuity has solved this problem. Here, service and custom manufacturing come together in point-of-sale manufacturing through a system called NoteStation.

Customers can browse the approximately 5,000 titles of sheet music available at the store through this system, scanning by artist's name, composer, or song title. They can tell the system to play a piece and hear it performed in stereo through the system's built-in speaker. They can even "jam" with the system using their own instruments.

Right song, but wrong key? Use NoteStation's keyboard to instruct the system to transpose the selection up or down the scale. Then play it back again, this time in the new key.

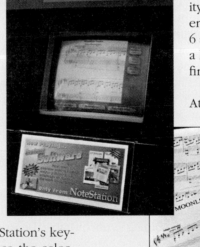

When you're satisfied the song is right, press another key and NoteStation will print the sheet music, complete with all annotations and credits. Should you choose to do so, you can even print the music on a diskette.

What's the limit for this system? NoteStation's CD-ROM has a capacity of approximately 20,000 different selections. You can add up to 6 additional CD-ROMs and have a huge library of music at your fingertips.

Out of stock? Not likely at Attina's.

Multimedia learning systems are particularly effective when applied in fields where personal knowledge depends on accumulated experience. One such field is medicine.

The medical student is confronted by an elderly patient complaining of shortness of breath. The student can listen to a computerized stethoscope and hear the heart murmur that indicates aortic stenosis, a partial blockage of the aorta. (This is valuable learning since often no actual patient with aortic stenosis may be on the ward at the time the topic is discussed in class.) Then, by pressing a key, the student can compare the pathological murmur to the sound of a normal heartbeat.

Perhaps the student hears a snap sound in the second part of the heartbeat. 'What disease might cause that?' the student ponders. On request, the computer brings up a list to consider. Using the hypothetical diagnosis of aortic stenosis, the student can then ask what other findings one might expect and order tests, such as an X-ray, which shows that the patient has a large ventricle. The student zooms in on the picture to examine calcification of the aortic valve. The system retrieves and displays in another window the medical textbook discussion of the diagnosis in question, including characteristic symptoms and possible treatments of the disease.

Then the student requests a cardiac angiogram, and a motion video sequence shows the heart beating as iodine contrast dye flows through it. The results of any test can be explored aurally or visually. Furthermore, the individual must first post a diagnostic hypothesis before the system will allow the test to be performed.[1]

Traditional corporate training programs often provide essential information in downright boring ways, deluging trainees with facts and figures, policies and techniques. Unimaginative training generally produces unimaginative employees.

- At General Accident, Plc, Britain's largest insurance group, the training of underwriters and claims handlers has taken a new direction through the creative use of multimedia technology. Appealing to the *imagination,* General Accident's programs stimulate trainees to think of themselves as detectives on the prowl for important policy-related information. To drive home this way of approaching their jobs, the multimedia system has brought to life the legendary private eye Philip Marlowe, hero-investigator of Raymond Chandler's detective novels.

  For example, it takes a great deal of investigation to determine the validity of an insurance claim. Instead of having trainees read a long narrative section in a manual describing in mind-boggling detail how to investigate such claims, General Accident's multimedia system has Marlowe enact a scenario that relates the job of claims investigation to a detective's work (Figure 8.5). On the display screen, the image of an actor dressed as a private eye, coupled with an audio in a distinctly American accent, presents a series of points trainees will need to consider in seeking the "clues" about the policyholder's claim. This kind of training is memorable because it stimulates the imagination.

Unlike training programs, which focus on teaching people how to respond in specific situations, education seeks to convey broad knowledge to students that they can use in many different types of situations. Yet both types of learning systems can profitably use multimedia. Simulations of actual situations enable students and trainees to intervene and apply their knowledge and skills to influence outcomes. Multimedia is a more practical and cost-effective teaching method than field trips and on-the-scene investigations (although good multimedia learning systems are neither easy to create nor inexpensive). Both students and trainees also benefit from multimedia's ability to present a rich array of information in ways that stimulate them to consider all kinds of possible problems and events. The *Information Technology in Practice* feature entitled "Blackstock's Smart School: How It Got That Way" describes how the creative use of multimedia produced a dramatic turnaround in education at a junior high school in California.

---

[1]C. Lambert, "The Electronic Tutor," *Harvard Magazine,* November–December 1990: 56.

FIGURE 8.5
General Accident Insurance, Plc, features Detective "Philip Marlowe" in its interactive multimedia training system.

OPERATIONS SUPPORT SYSTEMS.   The area of multimedia use most often overlooked is that supporting day-to-day business operations. Yet the effectiveness of its operations often determines the longevity of an enterprise. Poorly managed operations lose money, lead to poor-quality products and services, and alienate customers.

The multimedia capability that serves so well in training and education applications—the ability to transfer knowledge and know-how interactively—can also boost operations effectiveness by making the information needed for completing operations easily accessible. Graphic illustrations can be designed to describe how to conduct a specified activity or what actions to take when a troublesome problem arises. Step-by-step instructions are much more understandable when shown on a display screen or monitor to the person charged with carrying out the activity, who can then duplicate them on-the-spot. A narrated video or animation demonstrating how to conduct a specific operation in the setting where such operations actually occur is more helpful than the most carefully worded narrative, as this example illustrates:

- American Airlines, headquartered at the Dallas–Fort Worth airport, operates more than 2,000 flights worldwide every day. Among the many preparations for each flight that we take for granted are the maintenance procedures, the preparation of the flight plan, the completion of the passenger manifest—and the preparation of passenger meals. At American Airlines, approximately 175,000 meals are prepared daily. Each must have the right items, be prepared on time, and be attractively presented to passengers.

  For many years, American spent over $200,000 annually to print paper cookbooks to be used in its flight kitchens. Seeking a better way to run this culinary

INFORMATION TECHNOLOGY IN PRACTICE

Blackstock's Smart School: How It Got That Way

Blackstock Junior High School in Oxnard, California, is racially and ethnically diverse, with white students the fourth-largest ethnic group. Some 45 percent of Blackstock's students are in English-as-a-second-language programs. Many are poor. Just a few years ago, the school's students were ranked only at the 56th percentile in the California Assessment Program, a scholastic evaluation program that encompasses the entire state. Blackstock's faculty and administrative staff regarded this disappointing standing as a challenge instead of an irremediable problem.

Today, the school's students rank at the 94th percentile, and educators from around the world visit Blackstock to learn the secret behind this dramatic improvement. *Custom education* in what administrators call the "smart school" seems to be responsible for the turnaround. Here's how Blackstock customized.

The school's new paradigm builds on self-paced learning rather than on memorization and recall of facts. It recognizes that children learn more effec-

tively by *doing* than by *hearing* how to do something. And it keeps children in the same grade in the same room instead of segmenting them by ability or language facility, as so many other schools do.

Every student has access to, on a *one-to-one basis,* a multimedia computer, with CD-ROMs, video clips, and laser discs. The computer is an integral tool in Blackstock's customized learning program. Multimedia applications span basic math and science, as well as the social sciences, drawing on full-motion video, colorful graphic images, and sound to teach students in ways that mesh with the way they learn things in their everyday lives outside of school. The system is designed so that it adjusts to accommodate the individual student's learning ability and learning objectives. Because each multimedia module is bilingual, non–English-speaking students can work at the same level as their classmates who are fluent in English. At the appropriate time, non-English speakers make the transition to learning in English.

The students participate in class, small-group, and individual activities, all aimed at moving them toward fulfillment of their learning objectives. The instructor's role has changed from that of content provider

operation, American decided to create the first multimedia cookbook in the airline industry.

To American, the preparation of attractive airline meals means more than just getting the right ingredients. An important part of the meal preparation operation is providing the detailed information caterers need to know in order to perform each task—from the slicing of vegetables to make them visually appealing, to the complicated steps required to make American Airlines' signature lobster fajitas (served in the first-class cabin of selected flights), to the elegant arrangement of china, silverware, and condiments on trays destined for first-class passengers.

American Airlines' multimedia cookbook was created in two segments, each with video, color photographs, and audio explanations. The first segment includes scheduling information for each flight, including the specific items

to that of facilitator who orchestrates the experiences of each student. Now that they are motivators, coaches, and tutors, instructors need good skills, shrewd insight, and a sincere commitment to the students, as well as healthy doses of information, to achieve and sustain exceptional levels of improvement.

The Blackstock school's approach has proved to be a smart investment. One wonders why more schools haven't switched to this approach. After all, the payoffs are exceptional—both for students and for the society they will live and work in.

each caterer must prepare for that flight (Figure 8.6). The second segment gives cooking instructions and illustrates how each meal should be prepared (Figure 8.7).

Management was so proud of this innovative system for flight kitchen operations that it entered it in the prestigious Mercury awards competition conducted by the International Flight Catering Association in Glasgow, Scotland. American Airlines' multimedia operations system captured first prize.

Other types of operations that can benefit from multimedia presentations are manufacturing (e.g., a step-by-step demonstration of how to attach the door to an automobile on an assembly line), hotel management (e.g., the proper procedure for registering an incoming guest at the front desk), and safety inspections (e.g., certifying the condition of a home or office building).

FIGURE 8.6
American Airlines Relies on a Multimedia Cookbook to Guide the Preparation of Meals

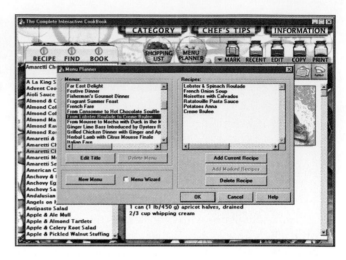

MULTIMEDIA PRODUCTS.   The rich information capabilities of multimedia have stimulated the creation of a wide array of new products. The video games of Nintendo, Sega, and 3DO, not to mention the countless versions of golf, road racing, and travel adventures (Figure 8.8), are multimedia products by Sony Computer Entertainment America. Each consists of sound, images, animation, and video that are either delivered on a CD-ROM or a diskette or built into a ROM chip that is inserted into an arcade game. These video products have dramatically changed the way we entertain ourselves.

Art and music are emerging as multimedia products, to such enthusiastic acceptance that multimedia publishers are scrambling to create working arrangements with museums, art galleries, film studios, and record companies to distribute their vast collections in multimedia form (Figure 8.9). These multimedia products offer more than an alternate delivery system for content. For instance, Microsoft's *Musical Instruments* is an interactive journey into the world of musical instruments (Figure 8.10). In addition to describing and illustrating each instrument and its origin, it gives users the option to play the instrument (through their computers) and to include its sounds in various musical arrangements. So, besides delivering descriptive content, *Musical Instruments* provides its users with the means of exploring and experimenting with different musical traditions.

FIGURE 8.7
Multimedia Cookbook Illustrates the Presentation of Meals

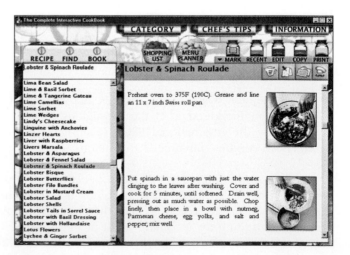

Multimedia Macintosh Plays Angel of Mercy

Dr. Edna Durbach had a problem. As special advisor for patient and family education at Children's Hospital in Vancouver, British Columbia, she wrote pamphlets and maintained a small but well-stocked resource library. On top of that, the clinical staff of this 242-bed hospital spent almost 30 percent of their time answering anxious parents' questions. Nevertheless, the parents weren't getting the information they needed about their sick and injured children.

Part of the problem, Dr. Durbach realized, was that parents simply didn't know the right questions to ask. What they required, she decided, was an angel of mercy who was a fount of information—a knowledgeable presence that was always calm, cheerful, and collected, and ready to help them find out what they needed to know.

Where could Children's Hospital find such an angel? The answer turned out to be a Macintosh, a microcomputer that houses a powerful CPU in a plastic case not much bigger than a child's teddy bear. Twenty-four hours a day, the Mac, along with a variety of specially developed multimedia applications, sits in the resource library, ready to answer the questions of worried parents. This angel of mercy dispenses its wealth of information at the click of a computer mouse.

FIGURE 8.8
Popular Multimedia Games from Nintendo, Sega, and 3DO by Sony Computer Entertainment America

FIGURE 8.9
*Some Examples of
Multimedia Publishing*

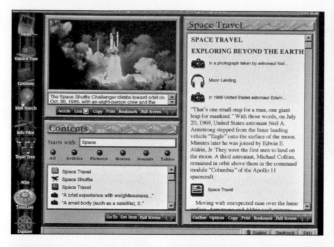

On-line books are a totally different multimedia product. Reference books (including encyclopedias), cookbooks, medical anthologies, and investment guides, are delivered on CD-ROM. These narrative texts are accompanied by colorful graphics and movie clips—all accessible through keywords or sequential review.

It's unlikely that multimedia technology will replace traditional book publishing because few people would be willing to give up the convenience of a printed book that can be marked up, highlighted, and stuffed into a briefcase or purse. However, multimedia accompaniments to published books are growing in importance. Certainly, more and more reference and nonfiction books will include a CD-ROM within their binding. Will the same happen with fiction? The possibilities are intriguing.

ELECTRONIC SLIDE PRESENTATIONS.   Whether in the lecture hall, the seminar room, or at a conference workshop, communicating information today often involves showing the audience a series of transparencies or color slides. Fortunately, the era of barely legible handwritten transparencies is fading fast because word processors have made it simple to create word slides in type that is large and clear. Moreover, color slides can be an invaluable aid in presentations if their content is carefully designed.

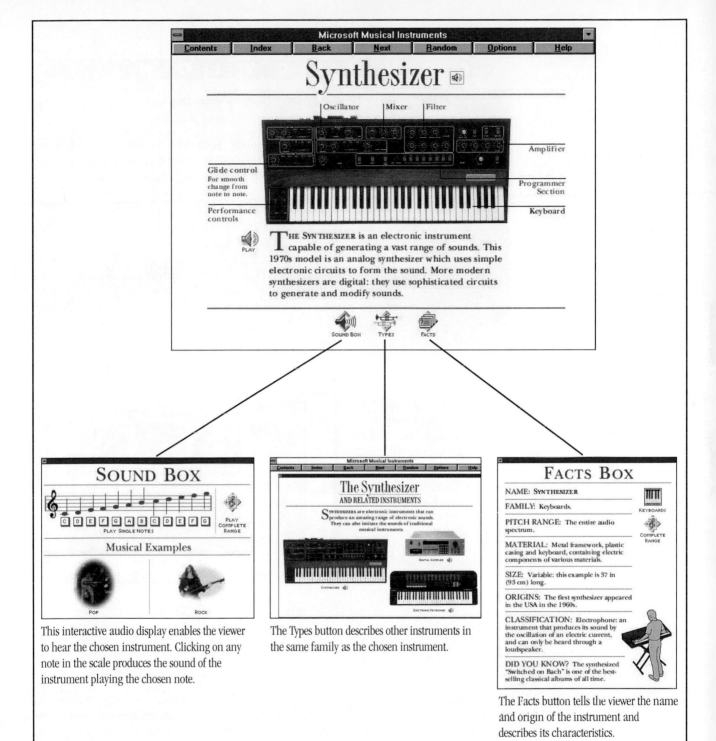

FIGURE 8.10 *A Multimedia Production Featuring Musical Instruments*

Clicking on the Sound button at the bottom of the screen provides additional information on the chosen instrument.

CRITICAL CONNECTION 2

Time

Time's Digital Library and the Breaking Story

Ever wonder how *Time,* the weekly news magazine, can capture stories that broke just yesterday and report the details, complete with color photographs, in the issue that hit the stands today? Good reporters and efficient production capabilities are principal reasons for *Time*'s timeliness. So is the magazine's digital photo library.

A master library of some 20 million different photographs has been prepared in digital form. Each photo was scanned, using a high-quality digitizer, and then stored in computer-readable form. Thus, writers and editors are able to search the library and retrieve photos instantly from either

their Windows-based or Macintosh personal computers. Under the old system of storing paper photos, it could take hours for a researcher to locate and retrieve a requested photo. Now needed photos can be located in seconds, often by the writer preparing the story.

Once identified, photos can be downloaded to the writer's desktop computer, where they can be

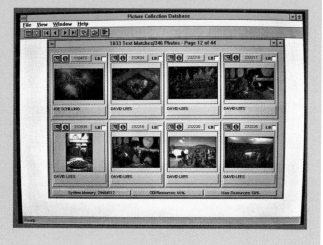

pasted into the text of the story. When text and illustrations are complete, the writer can transmit the entire story electronically to editors overseeing the final preparation and printing of the magazine.

Countless business, government, and educational institutions are discovering the power of multimedia in the form of slide presentations. Electronic slides created through such widely used programs as Microsoft Powerpoint and Lotus Freelance give users the ability to present sharply focused text and graphic information in full color. Moreover, each slide, when played electronically on a computer or projected onto a viewing screen, can include full-motion video and animation. By connecting the slide to a sound system, the user can make audio (music and/or voices) a component of the presentation.

The power of multimedia can produce payoffs in a wide range of situations. It can also produce confusion and annoyance when applied ineptly or in the wrong situation. Manipulating multimedia effectively is a skill that can be acquired only with study and practice.

The remainder of this chapter will show you how to transform an array of boring facts and figures into an exciting and illuminating multimedia presentation of ideas and insights.

Authoring Multimedia Presentations

Some multimedia presentations are designed to present information in a predetermined linear sequence. Others are dynamic, which means they depend on cues from the presenter to determine what to do next. We call the first type *multimedia slide shows,* and the second *interactive multimedia presentations.*

Multimedia Slide Shows

Presenting multimedia information in a predetermined sequence is an effective style when presenters know what information they wish to communicate and the order in which it should be shown. In a **multimedia slide show,** one screen of information is displayed at a time. The effect is comparable to what you would see if the presentation were made using 35mm color slides or overhead transparency slides. Since each screen of information is comparable to a slide, the presentation consists of telling the computer to move from one slide to the next in sequence. Slide shows are the easiest multimedia form to author but are powerful nonetheless.

AUTHORING MULTIMEDIA SLIDE SHOWS. **Authoring** is the sequence of activities used to create a multimedia production, including deciding on the presentation's purpose, determining its contents, selecting the components, and incorporating them into a presentation. An **authoring system** is the set of software tools used to create a multimedia presentation.

For a multimedia slide show, each slide's contents are separately authored. The authoring system provides the slide format and the tools needed to create the contents of each slide. The most common authoring systems for the slide format are shown in Figure 8.11. Each consists of text and drawing tools, a menu bar that contains commands for creating slide components, and a work surface or drawing board.

Each component—like the title of the slide in Figure 8.12, "Creating Multimedia Presentations," as well as the subtitle, "Photo, Sound, & Video"—is a stand-alone object. These objects are stand-alone in the sense that each one can be added, deleted, altered, or moved without affecting the other objects on the slide. (For that matter, each *slide* is also an object, consisting of other objects, that can be changed or removed without affecting the other slides.) The colors of the background as well as of each text object are selected by the developer, and can be any of several thousand different shades and hues.

To enhance the title slide in Figure 8.12, the text can be repositioned from its center location simply by instructing the authoring system to do so. Highlighting the title text followed by a single click of the Left Justify button will move the title

multimedia slide show
A multimedia presentation in which information is displayed in a predetermined sequence, one slide at a time.

authoring
The sequence of activities used to create a multimedia production: deciding on purpose, content, and components, and incorporating them into a presentation.

authoring system
The set of software tools used to create a multimedia presentation.

FIGURE 8.11
*Desktops for Widely
Used Slide Show
Authoring Systems*

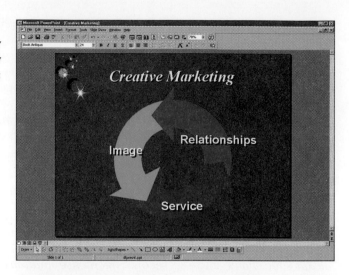

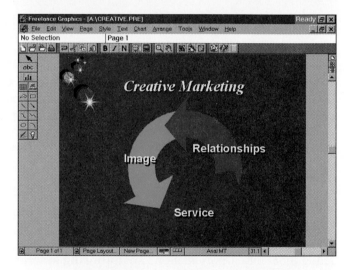

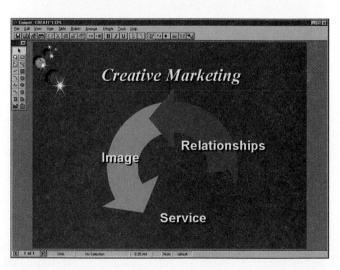

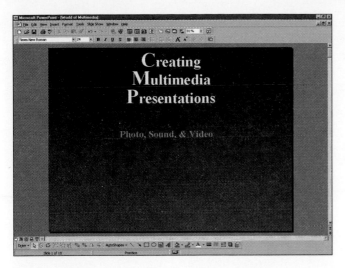

FIGURE 8.12

Adding Text Blocks to a Slide

Authoring systems allow a slide presentation's creator to enter text on the work surface.

text to the left. The same applies to the subtitle. Any object can be moved on the screen. For instance, the subtitle object can be moved closer to the title object.

Further enhancement is possible by importing a digital image to serve as the slide's background. The authoring system does this when the Insert command is selected, the picture option chosen (Figure 8.13), and the name of the picture object entered. Figure 8.14 shows the results of moving the title and subtitle objects and adding a digital image object to the background.

A new slide is added to the presentation simply by telling the authoring system to do so. This slide is created much the same way: the title information is added first, then other text information. Colored bullets are placed in front of the lines of text automatically by the authoring system if the designer has chosen this option. The clip-art images of the CD-ROMs are imported as objects in the same manner as the background photograph (see the menu choices in Figure 8.13). Figure 8.15 shows the result.

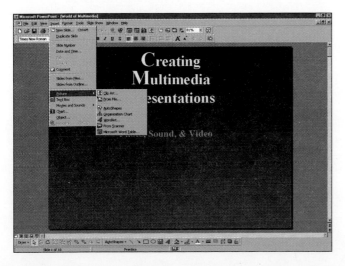

FIGURE 8.13

Inserting Images on Authoring System Desktop

Authoring systems allow slide developers to insert photographs and other graphic images.

The third slide in our example is intended to emphasize the powerful combination of digital image, video, and sound, so it will include both a photograph and a motion video clip. The title is entered ("Image & Sound Bring Information To Life") first, followed by a digital image used as background (a panorama photograph of a red sunset over the city). Finally, the motion video object is added:

1. The authoring system is told to insert an object.
2. The authoring system is told to import a motion video object by selecting movies and sound (Figure 8.16a).
3. Using the mouse, the developer selects the media clip by its name, DOWN-TOWN.AVI (Figure 8.16b), and the authoring software automatically inserts it into the slide; a frame from the media clip is shown on the screen to indicate the clip has been "pasted in" to the slide (Figure 8.16c). The designation AVI indicates that the object contains both audio and visual information. When the presentation is given, this motion video clip will play the video and sound in its entirety.

FIGURE 8.15

Slide Containing Clip-Art and Bullets

Selective use of clip-art and bullets improves communication and sets off important information.

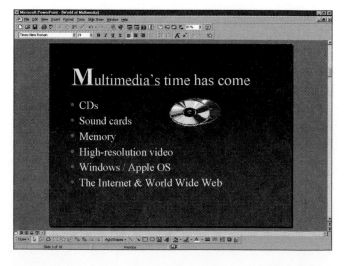

FIGURE 8.16

Inserting Movie Clip on Authoring System Desktop

a) Authoring systems allow slide developers to insert movies and sound in a presentation.

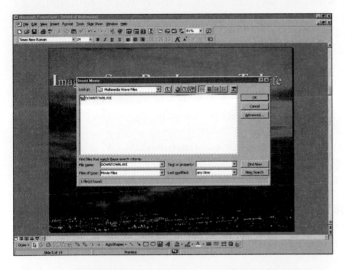

b) Instructing the authoring system which clip to insert into a slide.

c) Inserting a movie reveals an image that will begin moving when the slide is played during a presentation.

That completes the slide. Note its multimedia nature: it has text, image, and motion video (i.e., audio/visual) objects.

The fourth slide in the presentation will contain both a drawing and animation, which visually moves information into place one line at a time. First a new slide is added and the title "Multimedia Alternatives" is entered. Since this slide will deal with the power of text and graphics, we want to include a drawing here. Adding a drawing—or, in the language of multimedia, *line art*—requires following the same procedure as when adding a digital image: the authoring system is told to insert a picture object followed by the name of the picture object (the computer system and authoring system both treat drawings and photographs in the same way, although the amount of storage needed by each varies significantly). Once the drawing is inserted on the screen, it can be moved into position and adjusted in size using the mouse (Figure 8.17).

Next the text is entered, a line at a time. Colors, using the color button, are chosen to distinguish headings from subpoints.

build

The animation technique that displays text one line at a time in a multimedia slide presentation.

Now, the animation. For this slide, the developer decided to have the text displayed one line at a time when the presentation is actually given. In multimedia terminology, this is called a **build** (as in *build* the contents of the slide one line at a time when the presentation is played). To create a build, the developer pulls down the Slide Show menu, selects the animation option, and chooses the desired alternative (Figure 8.18). Instructions to carry out this process are inserted into the slide and will be executed when the presentation is given.

Building the rest of the presentation continues in the same fashion. Each of the alternatives for inserting multimedia objects remains the same regardless of the information they contain.

thumbnail

The display of miniature images of each slide in a multimedia slide presentation so the designer can check them for sequence.

To check the sequence of each of the slides, **thumbnails,** which are miniature images of each slide, can be displayed (Figure 8.19). In this way, the designer can view a series of slides at one time.

VIEWING THE PRESENTATION. When a multimedia presentation is viewed or played, the slides are displayed one at a time, under the control of the presenter. They remain on the screen as long as desired, since the presenter determines when to display the next slide.

When a slide is played, the authoring system's menus and toolbars are no longer visible (Figure 8.20). Only the slide's information is visible. When build slides are played, they are unfolded step by step, beginning with the title and background information, and continuing with each line (Figure 8.20a–i). During presentation, the presenter interacts with the computer only to tell it to display the next slide, often done by clicking the mouse or depressing a key on the keyboard.

Interactive Multimedia

The multimedia slide show is a powerful means of communication. Yet, in many instances, it is inconvenient to present information in a prespecified sequence. Rather, the situation demands a dynamic presentation of information. Here are three examples:

- *When the order of the presentation of information will depend on questions received from viewers of the presentation.* If a customer viewing a salesperson's multimedia presentation about a product's capabilities asks about optional

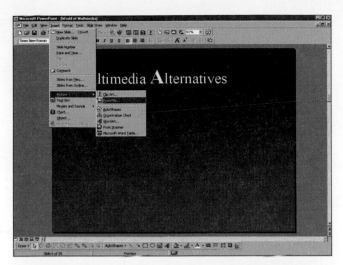

FIGURE 8.17
Inserting Drawing on Authoring System Desktop
a) Authoring tools enable developers to insert drawings and other art into a slide.

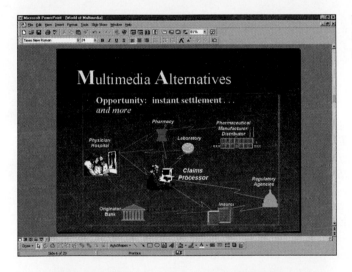

b) When a drawing is inserted by the authoring system, it is visible on the work surface.

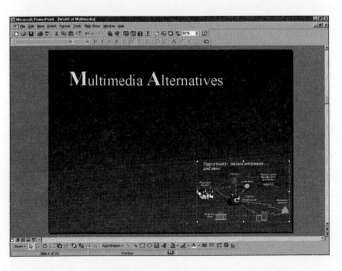

c) Once inserted into a slide, drawings can be adjusted for size, and positioned anywhere in a slide.

FIGURE 8.18
*Instructing the Authoring
System to Create
a Build Slide*
Authoring systems provide the
capability to add animation to a
multimedia presentation.

features, the salesperson wants to be able to jump to that portion of the presentation that illustrates the product's options.

- *When the order of the presentation of information depends on responses entered by the user to questions posed by the system.* A multimedia training program is designed so that if the individual using the system responds properly to an evaluation question, the system will move on to the next topic. An erroneous response, on the other hand, will elicit additional text, audio, and video information on the current topic.

- *When the person giving or viewing the multimedia presentation wants to explore any of a number of different topics or alternatives.* A student studying art history, for example, may become interested in the work of a particular artist while viewing information on all the important artists of sixteenth-century Florence. To learn more about that artist, the student tells the system to present more information on him. After viewing that information, the student decides to explore the artist's techniques, and so instructs the multimedia system.

Each of these alternatives requires an interactive multimedia authoring system.

FIGURE 8.19
Thumbnails of Slides
Thumbnail copies of each slide
allow viewers to view sections of a
presentation.

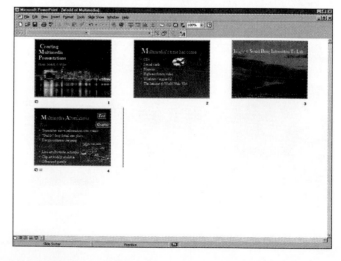

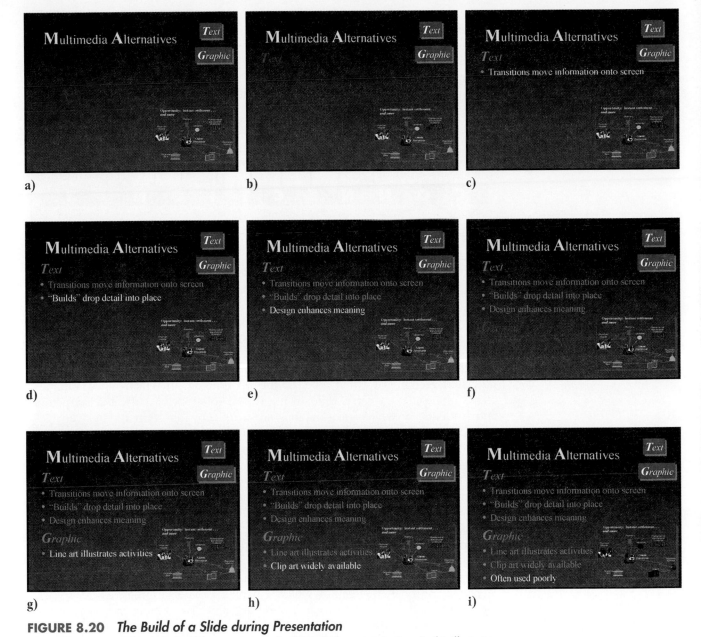

FIGURE 8.20 *The Build of a Slide during Presentation*
When slides are animated with the build feature, sections of a slide unfold one step at a time. In this illustration, the slide's information is presented in nine separate steps. As each new line is presented, prior lines are dimmed.

INTERACTIVE MULTIMEDIA AUTHORING SYSTEMS. Authoring **interactive multimedia presentations** requires all the procedures described for authoring slide presentations. The alternatives for text, graphics, images, audio, and video are the same. Capture and editing of these objects takes place in the same manner and is done with the same tools. Inserting the objects into the presentation also occurs in a similar fashion.

The principal differences between the two kinds of authoring is that the developer of interactive multimedia presentations provides the viewer with the capabilities to quickly determine:

interactive multimedia presentation
A multimedia presentation in which information is presented dynamically—that is, it can be shown in many different sequences, depending on the viewer's instructions.

1. How to move from one display screen to another (the next screen or the previous screen).
2. How to exit the presentation.
3. How to enter or change information.
4. How to retrieve information.
5. How to receive assistance in viewing the presentation (a Help feature).

At Zurich's Union Bank of Switzerland, You Can Bank on Interactive Multimedia

Banking ranks as Switzerland's most important industry. Indeed, the world associates banking with the Swiss. Yet, Swiss bankers face the same challenge that confronts other bankers around the world: How do you train new employees in the intricacies of good customer service, including how to sell the bank's products, complete the many forms that accompany varying transactions, and know when to hand out a particular brochure?

In banking and other industries, there are pretty much four ways to orient new staff members to their jobs: on-the-job training, in which the newcomer works alongside a veteran to learn the ropes; role-playing between instructors and students, in which job situations are acted out; question-and-answer testing, sometimes augmented by computer-assisted drills; and, most recently, training through multimedia.

Union Bank of Switzerland's interactive multimedia training system, known as Vista, makes all the other training methods obsolete. With its combination of text, graphics, video, animation, sound, and database capabilities in a desktop computer system equipped with a CD-ROM drive, sound card, and speakers, Vista is capable of simulating a work environment in a realistic manner. New employees who train with this interactive multimedia system are well prepared to handle their job responsibilities.

A trainee customer service representative, for example, will see a video segment playing on her screen in which a bank customer approaches her to ask for information on how to open a new account. The trainee not only hears the customer's words and tone of voice, she also observes the customer's facial expressions and gestures. Another window on the screen allows her to refer to service manuals, copies of bank forms, and tips from experienced service reps. It provides a scratch pad for taking notes as well. The representative can pull up information to help the customer in an instant.

Questions and answers can be exchanged to aid the representative in providing the proper service. If she takes too long, asks the same question twice, or overlooks an important option, the customer's expression will visibly change to register the mistake. At any time, the representative can interrupt the session to review her actions or obtain additional aid in handling the transaction.

Vista monitors the spoken dialog between customer and representative and monitors the rep's actions and advice for their suitability. A "client satisfaction" meter in the corner of the screen keeps the trainee representative informed about her performance.

Hence, in addition to the presentation information included in multimedia slide shows, interactive multimedia requires **navigation** information—that is, details on how to move around within the presentation. The authoring systems provide this capability. Sometimes developers of interactive media choose to write the application in programming languages, such as the C or Visual Basic languages, rather than authoring systems.

The authoring systems used to develop interactive multimedia presentations need to have more capabilities than the systems used to develop multimedia slide shows. The toolbars have more tools, the windows have means for both displaying and accepting information (Figure 8.21), and differing methods for showing alternative paths through the presentation are essential.

navigation

A capability of interactive multimedia presentations that allows the viewer to move around within the presentation.

NAVIGATION WITH INTERACTIVE MULTIMEDIA. When viewers see a multimedia interactive presentation on a display screen, they should easily understand what actions they can take. Menu items and buttons are used for this purpose. The multimedia display screen shown in Figure 8.22 ("Historical Atlas") gives viewers 40 different choices. As the instructions in the lower left portion of the text indicate, viewers can choose to examine artwork from any of 27 different European locales or 8 different time periods, or they can select any of the 5 navigation buttons at the bottom of the screen. The only action they need take is to click on the desired alternative. Hence, selecting the alternative *Paris* leads to the display of the screen shown in Figure 8.23.

Hypertext. **Hypertext,** an important feature of many interactive presentations, is a multimedia text display system in which specific words or phrases are highlighted to signal the viewer that clicking on them will reveal additional information. Hypertext (sometimes called *hyperlinks*) creates a web- or treelike navigation pattern (Figure 8.24) in which the viewer can examine a series of display screens interconnected by topic rather than a predetermined linear sequence.

The display screen in Figure 8.23 contains four hypertext links signaled by bold print: Cardinal Richelieu, Simon Vouet, Lubin Baugin, and Le Nain. The viewer can select, or choose to ignore, any of them. If *Cardinal Richelieu* is selected by

hypertext

A multimedia text display system in which words or phrases are highlighted to signal that clicking on them will reveal additional information. Also called *hyperlinks*.

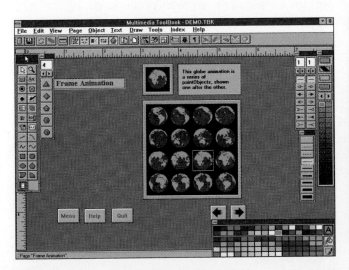
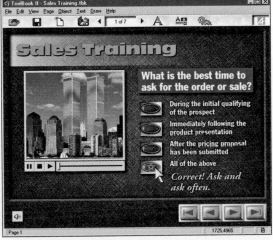

FIGURE 8.21 *Example of Desktop for Interactive Multimedia Authoring System*
Authoring systems used for presentations in which the viewer will interact to choose options require more additional design features and have more tools on their work surface.

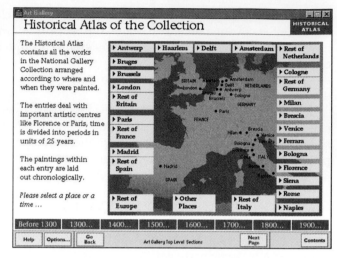

FIGURE 8.22

An Interactive Map Providing Quick Access to Art History

Interactive multimedia presentations allow viewers to choose the information they will see. This Historical Atlas, included in the Multimedia Collection of the National Gallery, London, gives the viewer 40 choices.

clicking on the text, a small display screen of information will be overlaid on the screen (Figure 8.25).

Linear Sequence. Linear sequencing plays some part in interactive presentations because there are many instances in which the viewer will want to go from the current display screen to the next one in sequence, or back to the preceding screenful of information. Designers frequently use forward and backward arrows, Next and Last buttons, or similar designs to allow viewers to do this. In Figure 8.25, the directions are Go Back and Next Page.

Methods of navigation in many familiar nonelectronic settings are practically second nature to us. For instance, when reading a book, we know that when we come to the bottom of a page, the next thing to do is to move ahead to the next page. And we don't need to be told it is necessary to turn a right-hand page in order to get to the next page—we just grasp the page automatically and move it

FIGURE 8.23

Interactive Display of Information with Hypertext

When the Paris button is clicked on the Historical Atlas, a colorful map of the City of Paris is presented on the viewer's screen.

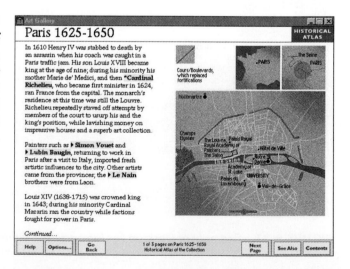

from one side of the book to the other in order to reveal the next page in the sequence of reading. Similarly, when we have completed or want to put away a book, we simply close it and set it down. This, like page turning, is an established convention that needs no explanation.

Interactive multimedia presentations have no equivalent conventions. Getting from one page to the next and closing a presentation so it can be put away are not automatic actions, since there are no universally accepted methods for doing these things. So designers have to include either buttons or text information that tells viewers how to accomplish these actions.

Users hardly notice such features when they are properly designed. It is when they are poorly designed—or missing—that users become irritated and confused. ■

Jumps.   Still another way to move around in an interactive multimedia presentation is to jump directly from one screen to another, regardless of how far apart the two screens are in the presentation. This is known as *direct navigation*. **Jumps** suspend the display of the current screen and immediately display a new one containing the information requested or a requested location in a particular sequence.

jump
To suspend the display of the current screen and immediately display a new screen; direct navigation.

FIGURE 8.24 *Structure of Hypertext Design*

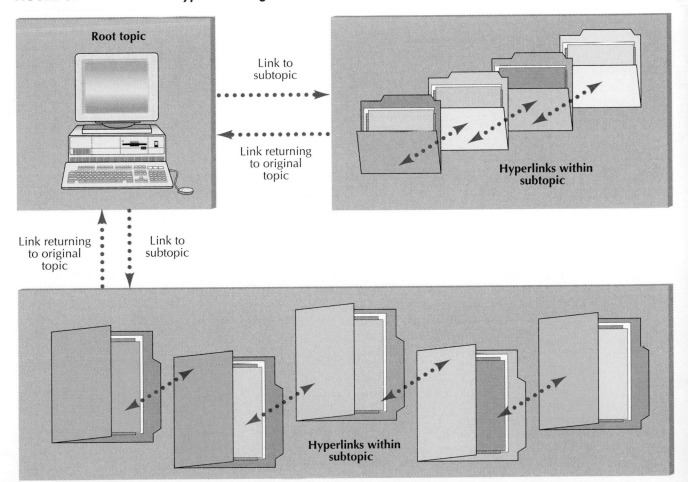

Clicking on the hyperlink for Cardinal Richelieu in the Paris map produces a description of the famous patron of French art in the 17th century.

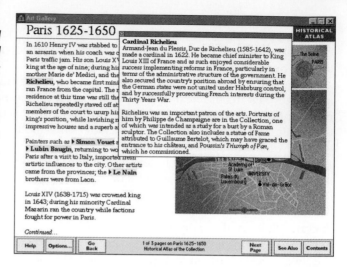

Direct navigation is commonly used when viewers have a question for which they need explanation. Clicking on a Help button allows the viewer to jump directly to a section of the program aimed at providing assistance in viewing the presentation. A Contents or Main Menu button is often included so viewers can get directly to the main list of alternatives for using the system. Often an Exit button is included so viewers can jump from their current location to the termination point of the program.

We've just seen how the manner in which a multimedia presentation is created—choice of content, position of information, means of presentation, and methods of navigation—determines its usefulness. Now let's take a look at how the components themselves come to be in digital format.

How Information Becomes Digital

All the components of a multimedia presentation—text, audio, images, full-motion video, and animation—must be in digital format, since that is the only form computers can process. When text information is entered through a computer keyboard, it is automatically captured and stored as digital information. No extra steps are needed. However, other types of multimedia information must either be captured in digital form or translated from their original form through digitizing.

Digital Audio

Audio refers to sound. The normal form in which we hear sounds—a human voice, piano music, radio and television programs—is **analog audio.** Computers, on the other hand, can only process discrete binary pulses, or **digital audio.** Two widely used forms of digital audio are examined in this section: WAVE and MIDI.

CAPTURING WAVE AUDIO. **WAVE audio** formats capture sound through **sampling** (Figure 8.26). The sound board and its accompanying software *samples*

---

audio
Sound. The two forms of audio are analog and digital.

analog audio
Sound transmitted by acoustic, mechanical, or electrical frequencies or waves; the normal version of sound.

digital audio
Sound transmitted by discrete binary pulses; the computerized version of sound.

WAVE audio
A form of digital audio that captures sound through sampling.

sampling
The process of capturing and converting audio sound waves into digital signals that are then stored as a digital file ready for playback.

Audio source produces analog sound waves

Capture board converts analog sounds to digital signals

Digital signal is analyzed at a specified number of times per second (i.e., at the sampling rate)

Sampled digital signal is stored as a digital file, ready for playback

Microphone

```
00100101
01011011
01001010
10101010
10100010
```

FIGURE 8.26   *WAVE: A Standard for Capturing Audio Information*

sound at close enough intervals (typically at some 44,000 times per second) that the human ear cannot tell the sound is not continuous. Each discrete sound sample is, in turn, translated into a set of digits that, when processed by the computer through a sound board, will recreate a very close approximation of the original sound—so close that the human ear may not be able to tell the difference between it and the original. For example, you can sample the sound of a telephone ringing, a barking dog, or the toot of a whistle. Then you can adjust it by shifting it up or down in pitch or frequency, perhaps to create a special effect.

WAVE audio files containing sound in digital form are like any other file (e.g., those containing text or data) in computer memory, on disk, or on CD-ROM. The WAVE file[2] can be read and played at any time to reproduce the audio sound.

CAPTURING MIDI AUDIO.   **MIDI (musical instrument digital interface) audio** is the second form of digital audio. MIDI objects contain sound created by musical instruments and stored in computer-processable form. MIDI provides a communication path between musical instruments, synthesizers, computers, and playback equipment. Hence, a musical instrument can be connected to the computer via MIDI, and as the instrument is played, the individual sounds of music are captured by sampling and stored in digital form.

MIDI can also be used to produce musical output. In this case, an instrument is attached to a computer and "played" by instructions sent to it as part of a multimedia program (Figure 8.27).

To play any audio, speakers must be attached to a sound board in the computer (discussed in Chapter 4). (The computer's small built-in speaker is not suitable for multimedia because it does not have the capabilities for realistic sound reproduction.)

MIDI (musical instrument digital interface) audio
A form of digital audio in which objects containing sound created by musical instruments are stored in computer-processable form.

[2]The name *WAVE file* comes from the widely understood notion of *sound waves*. Typically, sound files are called WAVE (in abbreviated form, WAV) files to distinguish them from other types of data and multimedia files stored in computer systems.

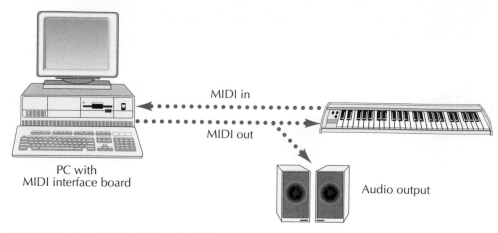

FIGURE 8.27   *MIDI: A Standard for Capturing and Playing Musical Instruments*

EDITING AUDIO FILES.   Once captured, audio files are easily edited. If multimedia designers want to play a portion of the file, they can designate where the playback should begin and where it should stop. Alternatively, they can attach more than one audio file in sequence so that when the playing of one segment stops, the next begins.

mixing
An editing process in which two or more audio files are integrated during playback.

Editing also includes the capability of **mixing,** integrating more than one audio file during playback (Figure 8.28). For example, if a human voice reading a script seems too bland an accompaniment for a video display of information, you can add a musical background by mixing the voice and music files. When played, both voice and music will be heard together.

Individual sound tracks are played simultaneously and captured as a single sound (WAVE) file

(fireworks in background)

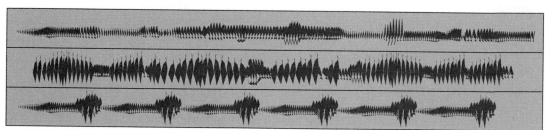

Mixed (WAVE) file

FIGURE 8.28   *Mixing Digital Signals*

Most desktop computers sold today, and many notebook computers, are equipped with the capabilities to both capture and play sound. A sound board (often called a *sound card* by computer retailers), complete with jacks for connecting microphones, tape recorders, and CD-players, has become standard equipment. Included with the sound board is the necessary software to capture, store, edit, and play the sounds.

Older computers can be equipped with a sound board for fairly low cost. The board and software can often be added for less than $100. ■

Digital Images

Still images—photographs—also play an important role in multimedia presentations. They can be used either to communicate the principal message of a presentation (Figure 8.29) or to provide an attractive background or setting for the message.

CAPTURING DIGITAL IMAGES. Digital images are created when ordinary paper photographs, which are analog, are turned into **bitmapped images.** As a digital bitmapped image, a photograph is represented in computer memory or storage as a series of tightly spaced dots such that the color of each can be carefully controlled (bitmapping is discussed in Chapter 4).

still image
A paper photograph; an analog image.

bitmapped image
A paper photograph that has been digitized.

FIGURE 8.29
Capturing Information Digitally
Digital capture methods mean still images play an important role in multimedia.

Digital bitmapped images can be acquired in three ways. The first method uses a digital image scanner to digitize an image from its hard copy form (Figure 8.30). The photograph is placed on the glass of a digitizing scanner. As the reading heads of the scanner pass over it, thousands of sections of the photograph are captured through a process similar to audio sampling and converted into bits—hence the name *bitmapping*. Once in digital form, the photograph is a collection of bits that can be processed or stored by the computer. Adapter boards can be added to computers to make it possible to capture in a similar way the analog images from VCRs or video cameras.

The second method uses devices manufactured to capture images in digital form, thus eliminating the need for scanning. For example, cameras are now available that take digital, rather than analog, photographs. These images can be transferred directly to a computer by connecting the camera to the computer with a cable and instructing the computer to read the images from the camera's memory (digital cameras do not use the traditional photographic film).

The third method of acquiring digital images is to purchase them. A vast array of digital images are available on CD-ROMs for very low cost. Alternatively, digital images can be downloaded from the Internet or from computer bulletin boards (see the discussion of bulletin boards in Chapter 10).

High-quality digital images demand high resolution. To get this degree of sharpness, a large number of bits, or pixels, must be used. These take up a great deal of storage, which means more time is required for loading the images into a presentation. To avoid this delay, **image compression,** a technique for reducing stored image size, is frequently used. A compressed bitmapped image takes only a fraction of the space of an uncompressed bitmapped image, yet will provide good image quality when viewed in a presentation. To be viewed, the image is uncompressed, a process in which the individual pixels are regenerated to recreate the image (Figure 8.31).

image compression
A technique for reducing the size of stored images.

FIGURE 8.30
Digital Camera and Photography
Digital photography means images can be captured and presented without use of film or paper.

**Uncompressed
Video Segment**

**Compressed
Video Segment**

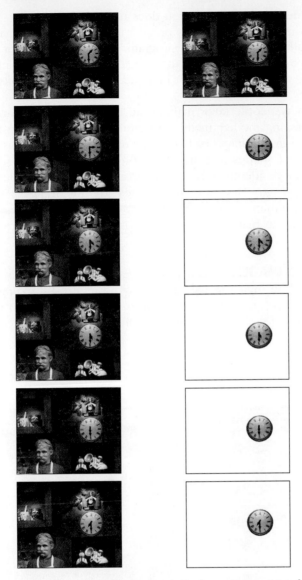

FIGURE 8.31   *Compression of Digital Images Reduces Space Needs*

Although many image compression methods have been introduced into the field of computer images, there is widespread interest in making one type, the **JPEG (Joint Photographic Expert Group) format,** the standard.[3] When JPEG is specified, the image capture program arranges the digital image information in pixel blocks so that the amount of storage needed is reduced. This method includes with the compressed image a set of embedded information that enables another program using the JPEG standard to regenerate the image in its original form.

**JPEG (Joint
Photographic Expert
Group) format**

An image compression method that stores images in pixel blocks embedded with information that makes possible the regeneration of the image.

[3]The Joint Photographic Expert Group is the body within the International Standardization Organization (ISO) that is advocating this standard. A similar standard, the MPEG (named for the Motion Picture Expert Group of the ISO), is being advocated for digital video. MPEG capitalizes on the fact that digital image data are compressible because changes in pixel intensity from one frame to another tend to be gradual and so concentrated at low frequencies that high frequencies can be discarded.

Creating a multimedia presentation does not require knowing how to produce JPEG format compression since this process is carried out automatically when the capability is built into a multimedia program. Anyone authoring a multimedia program does have to know whether the images are compressed into the JPEG format, and if so, whether the chosen multimedia presentation software will accept JPEG images.

fractal method

An image compression method that stores images in pixel blocks and matches those blocks with fractal shapes whose identifying numbers constitute a mathematical formula that is used to regenerate the image.

Although many people favor making the JPEG format the standard method of image compression, another method is gaining popularity. The **fractal method** also divides the image into pixel blocks, but then matches those blocks against a library of fractal shapes that are based on circles, squares, and other geometric forms that can be identified by a mathematical formula that identifies the stored decompressed image. Decompression times are much faster than with JPEG because the information need not be regenerated by processing the coding scheme. Instead, the mathematical formula is processed to recreate the shape.

EDITING DIGITAL IMAGES.   Once reproduced through any compression/decompression methods, a digital image can be altered in size by *scaling* it up or down to make it larger or smaller. An image may also be *cropped* to eliminate a portion that the designer does not want to include (Figure 8.32).

FIGURE 8.32   *Cropping and Scaling Images Produces the Desired Result*

Digital Video

Our attraction to movies and television is due largely to our fascination with moving images. Those authoring multimedia presentations can capitalize on this fascination by attaching VCRs, laser disk players, or even video cameras to computers (Figure 8.33). The moving images are transmitted from these devices to the computer, which, in turn, projects them onto the visual display screen.

This is not a new capability of computers—it has actually been used for many years in computer-based training programs (e.g., a computer will signal a laser disk player to show a specific segment of motion video in response to a keyboard entry from a trainee user). What is new is that the data and information making up motion video for desktop multimedia presentations are digital, not analog, and are in computer storage. **Digital video** (sometimes also called **digital motion video**) can therefore be processed by computer or transmitted over communications networks. Computer processing makes it possible to insert digital video into multiple presentations. As a result, the digital video can be supplemented with titles, headings, explanations, and illustrations—all in high-resolution color.

digital video/digital motion video

The presentation of data and information as moving images that can be processed by computer or transmitted over communications networks.

VIDEO CAPTURE.   Video comprises a series of individual frames of information that vary slightly one from another. When the frames are played in rapid succession, the changes between frames give the illusion of motion. This is the principal behind all motion pictures, whether on 70mm film (used in movie theaters) or on videotape.

To capture digital video, the analog video source is played and the images are communicated over a cable connecting the player to the computer video capture board. Capture software samples the stream of incoming video information to create a digital file. Video quality is largely determined by the number of frames per

FIGURE 8.33 *Digital Video Capture*

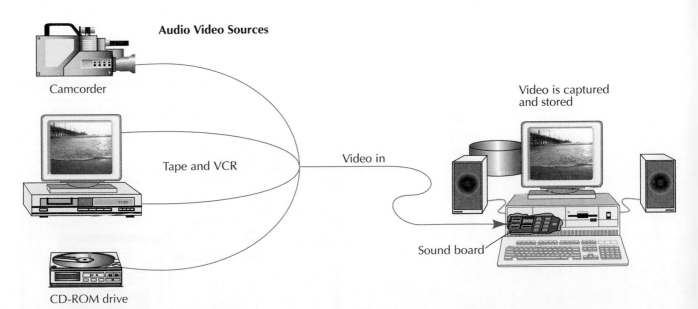

second sampled. Full-motion video uses sampling of 30 frames per second. However, this level of sampling produces a very large file that may exceed the storage capacity of a particular computer system. Therefore, sampling rates of 5, 10, or 15 frames per second are frequently used instead. The difference is noticeable when the video is played back: videos with lower sampling rates have a somewhat jerky appearance (the motion of people looks like a series of rapid starts and stops rather than like the continuous flow we are accustomed to from movies and television).

The video capture software performs both the capture process and the compression of images into a computer file. The file can be stored, copied, and transmitted, just like any other computer file.

VIDEO EDITING.   Digital video can be edited so that, if desired, only a portion of the segment is included in the presentation. (The original full segment remains on disk, untouched.) Special effects can be added to the beginning and end of the video clip as well (Figure 8.34).

A video segment can be mixed with a different sound track. It can also be cropped to remove information.

Digital video is not yet as widely used as digital audio. Thus, the systems sold through computer retailers seldom include the capability to *capture* digital video, although they typically can *play* video files. Equipping a desktop computer to capture digital video requires adding a video capture board. Such boards, including the necessary software, retail for approximately $500. The *Information Technology in Practice* feature entitled "The Artist's Electronic Studio" tells how Joni Carter makes creative use of multimedia to show the artistry of athletes.

Strictly speaking, the term *digital video* implies only motion, not sound. In reality, the videos used in multimedia presentations frequently include both audio *and* video. Hence, sound and video information are captured and integrated into a single computer file. When multimedia software plays a video file, then, it is actually playing both audio and video (the video through the computer display and the audio through the computer's sound board and speakers). ■

FIGURE 8.34
Editing Video Clip to Add Special Effects
Desktop editing systems allow multimedia developers to add special effects to video segments.

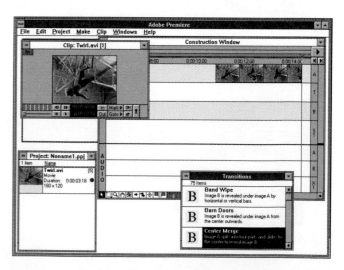

INFORMATION TECHNOLOGY IN PRACTICE

The Artist's Electronic Studio

Michelangelo expressed his greatest art on the ceiling of the Sistine chapel. Picasso, Monet, and countless other artists poured out their creativity on canvas. Joni Carter expresses her creativity through the multimedia art she creates in her studio overlooking Sunset Boulevard and the Pacific Ocean in Los Angeles.

Carter is a sports artist who has made sports art videos for the Indianapolis 500, the Superbowl, the Winter and the Summer Olympic Games, and many of sporting's other important events. She is as intent on catching athletes' intensity and emotion as she is on capturing their grace and speed.

How does she work? Carter attends sporting events to see and feel the action live. She also interviews athletes, taking photographs in the process. With that information in hand, and an idea of what feeling she wishes to express, Carter sits down in her studio, "an electronic canvas" at her fingertips. Using a video graphics board, she electronically paints a series of pictures, stroke by stroke, and edits them to tell a story. Next, she scores the audio components—adding music and other sound to give the images more life and underscore their powerful message. The result is a dynamic, vividly colored, moving rendering of an important sports event.

To Joni Carter, the skillful use of information technology is not a substitute for artistic creativity. Rather, she feels IT expands her creativity. "This technology expands the horizons," as she puts it.

INFORMATION TECHNOLOGY IN PRACTICE

Sail Sweden's Seventeenth-Century Warship

For centuries, the harbor at Stockholm, Sweden, held a treasure, but not until 1961 did the sea give up its prize: a seventeenth-century royal warship. To this day, the *Vasa* is the only fully preserved warship of that period that has been salvaged.

The *Vasa's* distinction is twofold. It was one of the first ships in the Swedish armada to have two gun decks. Its other distinction? Its maiden voyage ended in disaster when the warship sank on August 10, 1628, within 15 minutes of setting out from Stockholm. The numerous cannons on the ship's gun deck, which had been placed there against the shipbuilder's better judgment, made the vessel unstable. Unable to maneuver through Stockholm harbor's winds and currents, the *Vasa* capsized.

After the vessel was raised, dried, and restored in 1961, the curators at the Vasa Museum in Stockholm faced a dilemma that confronts museum curators all over the world: how to preserve a valuable artifact without storing it away, out of sight of the general public. The solution devised by the Vasa Museum was to make clever use of multimedia to fulfill the public's right to view the *Vasa* while preserving the ship from the harm it would suffer if subjected to hordes of visitors on its decks.

The museum put the *Vasa* on display, but also developed two multimedia presentations to satisfy public curiosity about the ship without having them trample through it. The first, *Close-Up Vasa,* is a narrated encyclopedia of information about the warship and the period in which it was constructed. It includes video clips depicting the *Vasa* and its crew. The viewer gets to see what life aboard a seventeenth-century ship was like. Through this video, you sail the seas and witness sea battles. A wealth of historical information is accessible; you choose top-

ics that interest you, thus creating your own personal tour of the ship.

Sail the Vasa is an interactive multimedia simulation program that allows you to rebuild the warship, altering specifications such as the shape of the hull, the placement of the cannons, and the type of riggings. After construction is complete, your design is tested as the ship sails through the winds blowing over Stockholm harbor. If it proves unseaworthy, the King lets you know of his displeasure, expressing his furor by firing you or in other unpleasant ways. Multimedia can overcome a centuries-old disaster by making the *Vasa* ride the waves again, but it can't overcome a bad design.

Digital Animation

Digital animation is a method for making an object appear to move across a computer display screen. For example, in a multimedia presentation intended to demonstrate how to use an automated teller machine, you might want to have an individual's plastic ATM card move from his or her hand to the read slot on the ATM.

To construct this animation, the presentation author captures a digital image of the ATM card and another of the ATM machine. Both images are then stored in digital form. To create the illusion of movement, the author tells the software to show the ATM card image at different points, using horizontal and vertical coordinates, along a predetermined path to the image of the ATM machine's reader (see Figure 8.32). When the presentation is run, the software rapidly shows the card's image at a location's coordinates, while erasing the image at the previous coordinates, to give the viewer the illusion of movement. When this sequence takes place in front of an appropriate background (perhaps an image of the bank with people standing nearby) and is accompanied by sound, the animation can be quite realistic.

Compared to full-motion video, which relies on thousands of unique images, each slightly different from the other, digital animation demands far less computer storage and processing power. It uses a single image, which is reshown as many times as specified by the author. However, presentations using animation are more difficult to create than those using full-motion video because each movement of the image must be scripted using animation software.

When simple movement of one image will create the desired message and it's necessary to manage the amount of storage used for the motion segment of a presentation, animation may be an effective solution. The *Information Technology in Practice* feature entitled "Sail Sweden's Seventeenth-Century Warship" describes how the power of multimedia has brought an old sailing ship back to life.

digital animation
A method for making an object appear to move across a computer screen.

A Final Word

The power of multimedia presentations is within the grasp of anyone who can use a computer. However, as with all information technology, the value is not in the technology itself, but in how it is used. Good content and the right design are necessary to create the desired impact with multimedia.

SUMMARY OF LEARNING OBJECTIVES

1 Describe the characteristics of multimedia presentations. *Multimedia* refers to the seamless integration of text, sound, still and full-motion images, and animation, under computer control. It includes both linear and interactive presentations of information.

2 Discuss five effective uses of multimedia presentations. When employed effectively in *sales and merchandising,* multimedia not only provides personalized assistance, but also illustrates products and services with high-resolution images accompanied by sound and motion. When applied in *learning systems,* multimedia can enhance the effectiveness of both education and training by creating highly realistic situations that would otherwise be difficult for the student or trainee to experience. Multimedia *operations systems* illustrate and describe how to take specified actions when unusual conditions occur. A natural outgrowth of multimedia's capabilities for packaging complex action and information in an easy-to-use format are electronic *products,* such as video games, collections of art and music, and books. *Multimedia slide presentations* can transform static facts and figures into exciting and memorable ideas and insights.

3 Describe why multimedia technology is actually a collection of technologies. Multimedia uses a combination of devices and programs. Important hardware elements include sound boards, high-resolution monitors, and devices for interacting with the system. The principal types of programs used in multimedia are *capturing software,* for capturing audio, video, and motion sequences; *editing software,* for editing multimedia information; *authoring software,* essential for designing and developing a presentation; and *viewer software,* enabling an individual to play, but not alter, a presentation.

4 Distinguish between authoring and viewer software. *Authoring software* consists of a set of tools that enables the designer to create and position objects on a display screen and to integrate all forms of text and digital information. *Viewer software* enables the user of multimedia to play a completed multimedia presentation in which builds of information, including audio and motion clips, unfold at the appropriate time. It also allows viewers to manage the presentation to determine which actions come next.

5 Identify the four types of digital information used in multimedia presentations. *Digital audio* includes the human voice, music, and other sounds that can be captured, stored, edited, and played under computer control. WAVE and MIDI are the two important digital audio formats. *Digital images* are paper photographs that were digitized by being turned into a bitmapped form and compressed. *Digital video,* also known as *digital motion video,* is a series of unique images that when played in rapid succession give the viewer the illusion of motion. The moving images may be provided with sound accompaniment or otherwise edited to create the desired effect. *Digital animation,* in contrast, uses a single image and instructs the computer software to rapidly show that image at different coordinates to give the illusion that an object is moving on the display screen. These four types of digital information can be used together to transform text into a dynamic presentation.

6 Discuss the importance of sampling in creating multimedia information forms. A combination of hardware (the sound board) and software captures and samples (converts into digital form) incoming sound information at intervals close enough so that the human ear cannot hear that the sound is not continuous when the digital audio is replayed. Once sampled, the information can be digitally adjusted to create a desired effect. The sampling principle can also be applied to video information.

7 Explain the principal differences between multimedia slide presentations and interactive multimedia presentations. *Multimedia slide presentations* are collections of information displays, called *electronic slides,* that are placed one after the other in a predetermined linear sequence.

Interactive multimedia presentations, in contrast, can be shown in many different sequences. Depending on the viewer's instructions, the presentation may involve *linear* sequences, *hypertext*, or *jumps.*

KEY TERMS

analog audio 368
audio 368
authoring 355
authoring system 355
bitmapped image 371
build 360
digital animation 379
digital audio 368
digital video/digital motion video 375

fractal method 374
hypertext 365
image compression 372
interactive multimedia presentation 363
JPEG (Joint Photographic Expert Group) format 373
jump 367
MIDI (musical instrument digital interface) audio 369

mixing 370
multimedia presentation 340
multimedia slide show 355
navigation 365
sampling 368
still image 371
thumbnail 360
WAVE audio 368

CRITICAL CONNECTIONS

1 Multimedia Macintosh Plays Angel of Mercy

By clicking a mouse on any of a number of colorful computer graphics, parents at Children's Hospital can call up a variety of multimedia applications. *Click!* The screen displays a guided tour of the hospital, complete with live-action video introducing hospital staff and explaining what they do. *Click!* The computer takes parents to a hospital "floor" where computer animation and digitized sound recordings explain certain disorders. *Click!* The Macintosh prints out a reading list of other materials in the resource library. *Click!* The computer asks parents about their concerns and prints out a list of questions they might want to ask the doctor. The Macintosh can go as fast—or as slow—as the user wants it to.

Even though the system is still under development, Dr. Durbach reports that parents are already raving about the computer and its marvelous bedside manner.

Questions for Discussion

1. One of the truisms of information technology is that the more powerful the computer's CPU, the more patient and "friendly" it can seem to inexperienced users. Why do you think this is true?

2. One of Dr. Durbach's goals for the hospital's multimedia system is to educate parents by leading them through the same steps doctors follow when they make a diagnosis and weigh alternative treatments.

Do you think a computer is well suited to this use? Why or why not?

3. Although the hospital's managers know that their primary goal is to help sick and injured children, they are aware of the need to compete with other hospitals for patients. How might the new multimedia system help Children's Hospital compete successfully?

SOURCE: Donna Barron, "Multimedia in the Hospital," *The World of Macintosh Multimedia* (Vero Beach, FL: Redgate Communications Corp., 1992), p. 30.

2   *Time's* Digital Library and the Breaking Story

Time   Photos are stored in *Time's* digital library in two ways. Low- and medium-resolution photos, which take little space (less than 100 KB), are stored, along with accompanying text, on a computer hard drive. The hard drive library is connected to the magazine's local area network.

High-resolution photos, which can take as much as 5 M, are stored digitally on magnetic tape. The tapes, which are more economical than hard disk storage, are housed in a tape library maintained at the magazine's editorial offices. Backup copies are stored at off-site facilities.

Both forms of storage provide the kind of rapid access writers need when they're seeking to get a breaking story into the next issue of the magazine. So, whenever you marvel at the speed with which the magazine captures up-to-the-minute news in well-illustrated stories, you can be sure *Time's* digital library played a key role.

Questions for Discussion

1. What benefits does having the library in digital form provide to *Time* and its editors?

2. Does a digital photo library offer greater or lesser protection than a print photo library against loss or damage of images?

3. In what ways would you index/search a digital library so that desired photos can be found quickly?

3   At Zurich's Union Bank of Switzerland, You Can Bank on Interactive Multimedia

 The Bank of Switzerland's interactive multimedia system not only creates training situations but also evaluates trainees' actions and responses. Vista remembers the responses of the customer and judges resulting actions accordingly.

The multimedia system is so effective that many Union Bank representatives don't like to leave it after they have completed their training sessions. Often, they stay afterward, trying out alternate situations, evaluating their methods of dealing with customers, and reviewing tips and service procedures for unusual situations.

Bank officials have noticed that representatives trained by Vista are more confident in their jobs and have more extensive knowledge of the bank's products and services. Their higher skill levels and good customer service ratings bode well for their careers . . . and for Union Bank of Switzerland.

Questions for Discussion

1. What capabilities possessed by the interactive multimedia system developed by the Union Bank of Switzerland could not be easily duplicated with the other training methods?

2. What features must an interactive multimedia training system have to keep trainees tuned into the training?

Net Work

Web browsers like Netscape Navigator and Microsoft Explorer are your window onto the Web, giving you the means to visit a site and to jump from one site to another. Web browsers also provide you with the means of viewing information, regardless of its multimedia form—print, audio, video, animation.

Browsers have a series of built-in capabilities, one of which is the ability to continually expand the available features as new technologies and innovations are developed. The term *plug-ins* refers to applications that can be added to—or plugged into—a browser. Thus, when a software development company creates a new multimedia capability, it prepares an application in a form that can be plugged into popular browsers. Typically, demo versions are made available to Web users without charge so they can test the features of the application.

When a Web site developer decides to use a particular technology to enhance the way the site provides information to visitors, it will usu-ally choose one of the most effective applications available and then inform the visitor, via a message on the Web site, which plug-in they should use to view the information in its fullest form.

The range of plug-ins is constantly evolving. Fortunately, it is relatively easy to keep track of the most popular ones. All the most popular Web browser providers maintain a list of plug-ins at their own Web site. Most are available in demonstration versions for downloading from the Web browser company's site.

To review the most popular plug-ins available, visit the Web site of either Netscape Navigator (http://www.netscape.com *or* http://netscape.com/comprod/mirror/navcomponents_download.html) or Microsoft (http://www.microsoft.com *or* http://www.microsoft.com/sbnmember/download/download.asp). After reading the descriptions of each plug-in, summarize its capabilities in the following table.

NAME OF PLUG-IN	PRINCIPAL CAPABILITIES PROVIDED (E.G., AUDIO, SOUND, 3-D)	NAME OF COMPANY	COMPANY'S URL	NO-COST DEMO VERSION AVAILABLE? (YES OR NO)

GROUP PROJECTS AND APPLICATIONS

Project 1

With a team of four classmates, choose one of the businesses listed in Project 1 in Chapter 4 (page 184) and plan the design of a multimedia CD-ROM that will serve as an advertising piece for your company. To grow your business, you will send this CD-ROM to a wide variety of potential clients across the country.

Brainstorm the possibilities for your CD-ROM. You will want to take advantage of the full range of multimedia's capabilities, so be sure to specify what items your CD-ROM will include in the following categories:

- Text
- Still images
- Audio sequences
- Motion video sequences
- Animation sequences

If time allows, contact a CD-ROM/multimedia developer and ask for a quote on how much it would cost to produce your multimedia presentation. Is this amount higher or lower than you expected?

Present your plan to the class. Other class members should feel free to critique it and to present ideas that would make your multimedia presentation more effective.

Project 2

Groups of four or five students each should choose one chapter from this book, each group taking a different chapter.

Formulate a plan for turning your chapter into an interactive presentation. What text would you use? What images? What kinds of new material would you create? What would you delete?

In addition, consider the following questions:

- What are the pros of using multimedia in education?
- What are the cons of using multimedia in education?
- Do you think some disciplines lend themselves better to a multimedia format than others do? If so, which would benefit the most from a multimedia presentation? Which would benefit the least?
- Do you think a multimedia presentation would be a good substitute for a teacher? If so, why? If not, why not?

Present your ideas to the class.

REVIEW QUESTIONS

1. What is multimedia? Why is it not a single technology?
2. What are the principal types of programs used in creating a multimedia presentation?
3. Describe the different information forms included in multimedia presentations.
4. Identify five general uses for multimedia presentations in business. For each, describe the role played by multimedia technology.
5. How do digital and analog information differ? What benefits does digital information offer in multimedia presentations?
6. Describe the characteristics of digital audio.
7. What is sampling and what role does it play in the creation of digital multimedia information?
8. How do WAVE and MIDI audio forms differ? When is each form used?

9. How does mixing change the content of a multimedia presentation? What benefits does mixing provide to a multimedia designer?

10. What are bitmapped images? What benefits do they offer over traditional images?

11. In what ways are bitmapped images created?

12. Why is image compression used in the handling of multimedia images? How are bitmapped images viewed in a presentation?

13. How do fractal images differ from bitmapped images? What benefits does the fractal image method offer compared to the bitmapped image method?

14. What are scaling and cropping and what benefits do they provide in the multimedia use of images?

15. Describe the characteristics of digital video. What advantages does digital video offer over conventional video from VCR and video cameras?

16. How is digital video created?

17. What determines video quality? What digital video performance levels offer the highest quality?

18. How does full-motion video differ from animation?

19. When do designers tend to choose animation over full-motion video?

20. Describe the two general forms of multimedia presentations, indicating the factors that distinguish each. Is one form preferable to the other? Why or why not?

21. What is an authoring system and what role does it play in the creation of multimedia presentations?

22. How do authoring and viewer software differ? Who are the principal users of each?

23. What are objects in multimedia presentations? What benefits does object use provide to the multimedia designer?

24. Why do designers use builds in multimedia presentations?

25. What are thumbnails and when do designers use them?

26. Describe the advantages of interactive multimedia presentations. What additional challenges do designers face when they decide to create interactive multimedia presentations rather than slide presentations?

27. What is hypertext and why is it used in interactive multimedia presentations?

DISCUSSION QUESTIONS

1. The storage capacity on devices such as magnetic and optical disk is increasing dramatically each year, along with the memory capacity and processing speeds of computers. What implications do these trends have for the quality of the audio, video, image, and animation that are used in multimedia presentations?

2. The storage density of CD-ROMs makes it practical to deliver entire books—fiction, nonfiction, reference books, and textbooks—on a single CD-ROM that can also include audio, image, motion video, and animation clips. Since these capabilities are both economical and widely available, do you desire to see books take a different form—a *multimedia* form? How do you think the comfortable paper form of books will change in the future?

3. The typical desktop computer delivered by a computer manufacturer through a retailer is fully equipped with multimedia components. Software for playing multimedia presentations is also widely available, and is usually included with newly purchased computers. Do you think computer hardware and software manufacturers, educational institutions, and businesses should take steps to help buyers capitalize on the capabilities of multimedia technology? Or would it be better to let the use of multimedia evolve at its own pace?

4. In what ways can multimedia technology be poorly used or abused? Describe some situations in which multimedia would not improve a presentation or would actually hinder it.

5. Does the use of multimedia technology stimulate or inhibit personal creativity?

SUGGESTED READINGS

Bieber, Michael, and Tomás Isakowitz. "Designing Hypermedia Applications." *Communications of the ACM 38* (August 1995): 26–29. This is the lead article in a special issue devoted to the user of hypertext in a wide variety of multimedia applications. The seven articles in this issue span educational and business uses of hypertext and include colorful illustrations of hypertext in products.

Luther, Arch C. *Authoring Interactive Multimedia*. San Diego, CA: Academic Press (1994). A concise and useful discussion of the principal concerns of developers of interactive multimedia presentations. Spans the gamut from linear to highly interactive presentations, and highlights the distinguishing features of a variety of different authoring systems.

Sanchez, Julio, and Maria P. Canter. *Computer Animation Programming Methods and Techniques*. New York: McGraw-Hill, 1995. A comprehensive treatment of the principles, methods, and problem-solving techniques associated with computer animation. Includes many examples and code segments.

Shank, Roger C. "Active Learning Through Multimedia." *IEEE Multimedia 1* (Spring 1994): 69–78. Describes how properly designed multimedia systems encourage the active participation of students and discusses the need for a suitable learning architecture. This illustrated article identifies 10 principles underlying the effective use of multimedia in learning situations.

Wolf, Beverly Park. "Intelligent Multimedia Tutoring Systems." *Communications of the ACM 39* (April 1996): 30–31. Describes the power of multimedia technologies in learning, using examples from the fields of medicine and engineering. This article is one of a set of 11 articles in this issue on the topic of learner-centered systems designs.

ESPN SportsZone: Multimedia Coverage of Men's and Women's Events On-line

To real sports enthusiasts, attending sporting events, watching broadcasts of games, and following the scores of teams around the country are not enough. The multibillion-dollar worldwide industry of established broadcasters, publishers, and ticket sellers cannot satisfy all the desires of sports fanatics. That is why the cable network ESPN and its networking partner, Starwave, did not regard the well-ensconced sports print and broadcast businesses as posing a competitive barrier when they decided to undertake their on-line venture, ESPNet SportsZone.

ESPNet SportsZone was launched in April 1995 by Starwave*, a developer of Internet sites headquartered in Bellevue, Washington. From the beginning, it was designed to cover a wide variety of men's and women's sports around the world. More than 40 sports are now included in its pages, each showcased by a range of multimedia information that is accessible over the Internet.

ESPNet SportsZone quickly became one of the most popular places on the Internet. Its success can be traced to the breadth and depth of its sports news, analysis, and statistics, as well as to its cutting-edge graphics. These graphics, not available anywhere else, include live-game flowcharts, showing the ebb and flow of a sporting event and how leads and momentum change; basketball shot charts illustrating, quarter by quarter, the

shots attempted and completed; football drive charts illustrating, quarter by quarter, how every NFL game unfolded and the plays each team ran when it had the ball.

But ESPNet SportsZone offers much more than charts and statistics to entertain sports enthusiasts. With a click

of their mouse, fans can see video clips of the highlights of their favorite game—the key plays, the controversial calls, the record-breaking actions.

The first live broadcast of a sporting event over the Internet—a baseball game—took place on ESPNet SportsZone in September of 1995. That set the precedent for further on-line broadcasts. Today, for instance, the entire season's schedule of all games of every team in the National Basketball Association are broadcast over ESPNet SportsZone. And fans no longer need worry about being within broadcast range of a local radio or TV station—ESPNet SportsZone makes it possible to hear every call of every game, regardless of where you are. A fan who misses a game can see it rebroadcast, at any time he or she chooses, by calling upon ESPNet SportsZone's archive.

Among the network's most interesting innovations are fantasy games viewers participate in by choosing a team and then playing against another team. Information on drafts, player performances, and bulletin board messages from the various sports league offices are all available to help the user pick the best team.

Other forms of on-line participation are offered to fans. They can conduct live interviews with leading sports luminaries. They can also join chat rooms and discussion groups and get into vigorous exchanges about events, players, drafts, and trades. If they want, they can print copies of these dialogues for later review.

ESPNet SportsZone has all the makings of a publication, too, with its syndicated columnists, in-depth coverage of all professional sports, and up-to-the-minute news. More than 100 local correspondents are assigned to cover professional and major college teams; they dig out the news and gossip on teams in fans' neighborhoods and regions.

It's no wonder that advertisers are clamoring to have a presence on ESPNet SportsZone; they get to use all the power of information technology to display their messages to a prequalified audience. And that audience is likely to grow, for ESPNet SportsZone's monthly subscription fee is about the same as the price of a single issue of the typical sports magazine. Industry watchers expect the subscription base of ESPNet SportsZone to soon exceed that of the most widely sold sports magazine.

Questions for Discussion

1. What are the most attractive features of ESPNet SportsZone?

2. Compared to broadcasts of men's and women's sporting events over television and radio, what advantages and disadvantages does ESPNet SportsZone provide viewers of important games?

3. What additional features and capabilities do you think ESPNet SportsZone should consider offering? Consider all the capabilities of multimedia technologies and how they can be combined with network communications and the Internet.

---

*Starwave's Internet capabilities are devoted to such wide-ranging topics as sports, entertainment, outdoor activities, and parenting. The company is the brainchild of Paul Allen, co-founder of Microsoft.

PHOTO ESSAY
MULTIMEDIA
CREATING LIVING IDEAS

Walt & Roy Disney opened Disney Brothers Studio in Burbank, California in 1923, the first step in bringing their ideas to life. In 1928, the studios released the beginning of many Walt Disney firsts: a feature film starring Steamboat Willie. With it, Mickey Mouse, the firm's central character, was born in the industry's first full-length feature cartoon and as the start of a string of colorful Disney characters. Generations have grown up enjoying the fruits of Walt Disney's imagination and the characters he created. Then and now, Disney often has a special place in the memories of many youngsters, dating back to the first film they recall. Possibly it's a feature length cartoon with Snow White and a band of seven dwarfs—Bashful, Doc, Dopey, Grumpy, Happy, Sleepy, and Sneezy—romping across the screen. Or perhaps their recollection is of such other Disney classics as 101 Dalmatians, Beauty and the Beast, or Winnie the Pooh. For others, the name Walt Disney means a vacation trip to Disneyland entertainment parks (in California, France, or Japan), or to Florida's Disney World. Here the famous Disney characters come to life in entertaining rides, in the park's movie theaters, and on stage.

Another Disney dream came to life in 1955 when the original Disneyland in Anaheim, California, opened its gates. Here the Disney characters were the focal point for novel rides that thrilled fans, both young and old. A few years later, another Disney first was introduced at the park: the multimedia technology known as audio-animatronics (or simply animatronics). Pirates of the Caribbean, still running today, was an entertaining theatrical ride like no other form of amusement. The ride—the first to use animatronics—featured a rowdy band of hooligans who looted, plundered, chased, ransacked, and burned in the night.

Lifelike and full of mischievous energy, these pirates still repeat their antics every few moments, to the accompaniment of stereo music and special sound effects, as an audience gazes at the spectacle from open boats moving slowly past the scenes. Each move of every animated character is carefully synchronized electronically to create the right effect in this special indoor ride-through theater.

Disney Studios continued to advance animatronics as it opened Disney World's Magic Kingdom and Epcot Center parks, near Orlando, Florida. An entire industry has grown out of the early Disney innovations. Other companies, such as Sally Corporation in Jacksonville, Florida, developed animatronics further, aiding in the widespread introduction of a new form of theme and amusement parks where people, animals, and monsters come to life right on front of the eyes of visitors. Whether the focus is on a Caribbean pirate, a former president like those found in Disney's Hall of Presidents, or an alligator at Florida's Universal Studios, animatronics makes them lifelike. Here's how.

Animatronics uses mechanical and electronic systems to simulate the movement of creatures. To create an animatronic character, an armature providing the character's basic structure is first designed. Pneumatic devices are added to the armature to control the movement and position of the character's limbs.

For humanlike animatronic characters, a separate head mechanism is constructed. Getting the position of lifelike moveable eyes just right is essential so that the character can pass for the real thing. Then other components are added in proportion to the eyes. Finally, the head mechanism is ready for its skull.

A novel visual effect can be created by leaving the character's structure exposed. Sally Corp. found this technique especially entertaining when it created Victor, a very avant-garde rendering of a French Legionnaire, for La Ronde Park in Montreal, Canada.

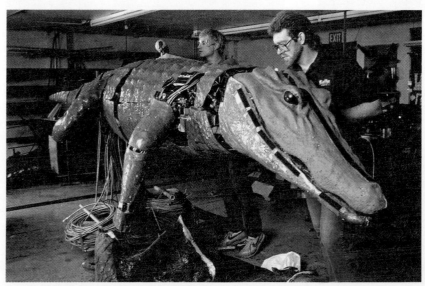

Animatronic creatures, such as alligators and dinosaurs, are also created by first creating an overall structural skeleton that will hold the wires and electronic devices. The "muscle" behind many animatronic movements consists of circuit boards, sensors, and motors. An electronic signal from an input device or processor "sends" the output arm, head, leg, or other part to the desired position.

With the electronic components in place on the armature, the skull and skeleton are covered to hide the electronics and create the character's familiar appearance. The surface of each character is carefully smoothed and painted. An alligator like the ones used at Universal Studios must have the right skin texture and color, as viewers will instantly spot a defect.

Furry animals are covered and then trimmed to take on a lifelike appearance.

When creating a human character, animatronic designers often spread a soft wax over the image's exposed areas. Next, the wax is smoothed and shaped to create the expected texture for the character's skin. Finally, the character is dressed in an appropriate costume and placed in the right theatrical scene, creating the lifelike character needed to entertain viewers. These steps are behind the evolution of the animatronic Charles Darwin in the Living World at the St. Louis Zoo.

Behind the scenes, computers and microprocessors oversee the production, controlling lighting, sound, and movement of each animatronic character. Using the combination of multimedia technologies, scenes can be designed where everything is lifelike. In the Craftsman's Workshop, created by Sally Corp. for Cardi Furniture Co., the craftsman, toolbox, paint cans, cuckoo, and slide-out miniature band are all animated.

The multimedia power of animatronics has brought about a form of entertainment that promises to grow more sophisticated and entertaining. Animated musical groups featuring cartoon-style characters have been extremely popular ever since Disney introduced *Country Bear Jamboree* years ago, first at Disneyland and then at Disney World. To meet its customers' requests, Sally has developed a variety of musical groups that play all forms of music: bluegrass, country music, Dixieland jazz, and even German-style Oktoberfest-type "oompah" music.

Using animatronics to create living ideas means the only real limit may be one's imagination.

CHAPTER 9

Developing Single-User Systems

CHAPTER OUTLINE

LEARNING OBJECTIVES

When you have completed this chapter, you should be able to

1 Describe the origin of single-user systems in business and understand why they have become so prominent.

2 Identify the distinguishing characteristics of a single-user system.

3 Explain the benefits of single-user systems in business.

4 Define the problem-solving cycle and state how it relates to the development of a single-user system.

5 Discuss the five steps involved in developing a single-user system.

6 Distinguish between choosing a single-user system and creating single-user applications.

7 Explain the importance of continual evaluation and evolution in single-user systems development.

HOK Sports Awards: Design Excellence Meeting Client Needs

H OK (Hellmuth, Obata & Kassabaum, Inc.), with its 1,800 architects, designers, and support personnel, plays a very important role in the success of professional sports teams in the United States, United Kingdom, continental Europe, and the Pacific Rim. HOK doesn't recruit or train athletes. Rather, it provides a place for them to play.

The Kansas City–based HOK Sports Facilities Group, whose staff of 240 is dedicated solely to sports architecture, has been a dominant force in the creation of professional, college, and sports facilities for well over a decade. It counts among its achievements Hong Kong Stadium, the National Cycling Center in Manchester, England, and the Toulouse Stadium renovation in Toulouse, France. In the United States, HOK has worked with 29 of the 30 National Football League franchises and 24 of the 28 Major League Baseball clubs. Its many sports facility accomplishments include Redskins Stadium, Joe Robbie Stadium, Oriole Park at Camden Yards, and Jacobs Field.

The countless awards HOK has won for its outstanding architecture, both in sports and in general building design, and construction (including the No. 1 ranking by *Building Design and Construction* magazine) are a tribute to the architects and designers who make up the firm. These achievements owe a good deal to the tools HOK's professionals use to create the award-winning designs. If you think of architecture and design as tedious fields where people work hunched over a drawing board, pen in hand, think again. HOK began using computer-assisted design software more than a decade ago. While this software has certainly proved more efficient than the labor-intensive process of producing paper and film drawings—that is, in *presenting designs*—that's not its only role. Even more important is the role software is playing in *creating designs*.

Sketching by hand is a quick way for an architect to try out a design idea for a project to determine whether the concept will work. So is a three-dimensional building model constructed of clay, wood, or cardboard. Both sketches and models can be scanned into the computer. Once in digital form, they can be rotated for viewing from the top, the bottom, and other angles. After getting a good look at the model in this fashion, the architect can make any modifications that seem desirable and generate new images that can also be viewed on-screen. In addition, the architect's design software can determine angles, material strength requirements, and costs of the project.

The firm's in-house CADD, Computer-Aided Design and Drafting system, gives the architects the ability to produce computer-generated drawings in either the HOK drawVision or the popular AutoCAD system used throughout the industry. CADD production offers accurate drawings and assists in working between offices by providing quality control and interdiscipline coordination. With this capability, HOK Sport can produce complete plans and details for architectural, structural, civil, plumbing, heating, ventilation, air conditioning, power, and lighting construction documents.

HOK Sport's computer capabilities can provide

- *Sight Lines.* There cannot be a bad seat in the house; every spectator must have an unimpeded view of the events.
- *Geometric Layouts.* Because the requirements for different sporting and entertainment events differ, a geometry must be developed to work in conjunction with a particular sport or, in some cases, multiple functions. These are analyzed quickly on CADD.
- *Seat Count.* Upon establishing the cross sections and facility geometry, quantities of spectator seating can be established quickly.
- *3-D Studies.* Many times, marketing or financing considerations will require sports facilities to be made "real" prior to design finalization. CADD enables three-dimensional models to be generated and placed within site context to examine its acceptability.
- *Computer Animation.* HOK Sport uses its CADD capabilities to develop video presentations. After the facility design and the surrounding site data have been input into the system, the computer can generate 3-D images necessary to create a visual "fly-over" or fly-through of the facility.

IT, of course, will never replace the architect. Nor will it convert a poor architect into Frank Lloyd Wright. But it can make architects who have mastered their profession a lot faster and more effective—provided they know the principles of single-user IT systems and how to apply them to the task at hand.

In this chapter, we discuss the development of single-user systems and explore the capabilities of these personal systems in general. (The terms *personal system* and *single-user system* are used interchangeably.) Because people have different information technology needs, depending on their personal situations, we will also help you identify your personal IT needs. In the first section of the chapter, we describe the characteristics of single-user systems. Then, we look at the impact these systems can have on personal productivity, effectiveness, and creativity. In the last section, we examine the process of developing a single-user system. We discuss the process of developing multiuser systems in Chapter 12.

What Is a Single-User System?

A **single-user system** is an IT system used by only one person. Usually composed of a PC or workstation, various input and output devices, and programs, it is tailored to the specific needs and wants of one individual. Single-user systems, frequently called **personal systems,** free their users from time-consuming routines and procedures so they can focus on the creative aspects of their work. Because personal systems are so cost-effective, they are now an important tool in both personal and business activities. The *Information Technology in Practice* feature entitled "IT Produces Net Gain: Tools and Strategy in Action" describes how information technology aids a successful tennis pro off the court.

single-user system or personal system
An IT system used by only one person. A system that stands alone and is not interconnected with other companies or shared by other people.

The Origin of Single-User Systems

In the early days of data processing—the 1950s through the 1970s—when information technology was synonymous with large computers and vast communications networks, single-user systems were unheard of. At that time, computing meant spending large sums of money (often millions of dollars) to set up an IT system, hiring specialists to run it, and keeping support personnel nearby (or at least on call) to clean, adjust, and repair the system's components. In acquiring an IT system, an organization knew it was making a substantial financial commitment.

Technological progress and innovation in the 1980s and 1990s changed many aspects of computing. Large computers are still in widespread use, and will be for years to come, but personal computers, designed for individual users, are now the norm. Because of advances in electronics and engineering over the last two decades, PCs have powerful capabilities, and as a result of strong competition in the computer industry, they are widely available at affordable prices. Today, they are the dominant source of IT capability in many organizations. In fact, many universities, colleges, and training centers around the world now assume that students either own or have ready access to personal systems—that is, PCs and software.

Today, there are millions and millions more personal computers installed worldwide than mainframe and midrange systems combined. The number of PCs in use (the *installed base*) continues to grow annually.

Many organizations have a goal of placing PCs on the desks of all their knowledge workers. The intention is often to interconnect these PCs with communications networks. But the main objective is to assist workers to become better at their job—to be more productive, effective, and creative.

Although some companies suggest a standard **configuration** (a specific combination of hardware and software in a system) for each type of worker in the firm, standards are very limiting. Most people will add their own software, adjust the system's features to suit themselves, and perhaps add hardware attachments that accommodate their needs. This is as it should be, for a single-user system is a personal tool, not a vehicle for making everyone alike. ■

configuration
The specific combination of hardware and software in a system.

INFORMATION TECHNOLOGY IN PRACTICE

IT Produces Net Gain: Tools and Strategy in Action

There is a striking similarity between a net serve and a net gain. *Net serve* forces you to do it over again, while *net gain* inspires you to want to do it again. At least that's the way Atlanta tennis professional Edward Balch views things. Balch is relying on his own insights, aided by information technology, to create a comfortable retirement for himself and his wife, Linda. Three decades of investing experience have made him knowledgeable about what he wants from his personal investment support system.

Balch's investing strategy focuses on mutual funds, which are portfolios of stocks, bonds, and other securities in which investors purchase shares. These diversified portfolios offer investors the opportunity to participate in big gains during periods of financial growth while protecting them against wrong stock picks. Depending on their financial goals, age, and temperament, in-

vestors can choose riskier mutual funds that pursue aggressive gains in value, or they can pick lower-risk funds that seek more moderate and predictable rates of growth.

For market analysis, Balch relies on a system of purchased mutual fund software packages and on-line reporting services. These convenient software packages create and use a database containing information describing your investment strategy (e.g., high growth, moderate growth, high investment security). Formulas embedded in the software (you don't have to be a math whiz to use mutual fund software) translate your personal preferences, along with your current financial status, into a recipe for investing. Finally, the program recommends specific mutual funds and the amount of money to invest in each.

The Characteristics of Single-User Systems

hands-on system
A system in which a user enters data and information, directs processing, and determines the types of output to be generated.

Three characteristics distinguish single-user systems (Figure 9.1). They are designed for hands-on usage, are tailored to an individual's requirements and preferences, and are used to improve personal performance.

DESIGNED FOR HANDS-ON USAGE. Single-user systems are **hands-on systems**—meaning the user actually operates the system, entering data and infor-

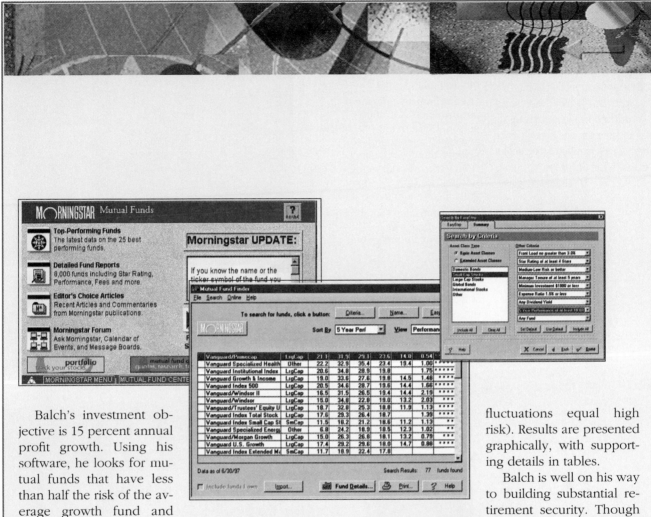

Balch's investment objective is 15 percent annual profit growth. Using his software, he looks for mutual funds that have less than half the risk of the average growth fund and twice the return. He also utilizes an investment database available by dialing into America Online. The on-line service provides additional investment analysis, filtering out those mutual funds that do not meet Balch's targets by processing the daily price quotes of each fund and then calculating the fluctuations over days and weeks in comparison to other funds (wider fluctuations equal high risk). Results are presented graphically, with supporting details in tables.

Balch is well on his way to building substantial retirement security. Though he is years away from retirement, his nest egg already exceeds $500,000. In the investment game, as in tennis, he feels that the most important thing is to develop a strategy and then follow it. Commitment means staying with the strategy and doing things that support it—using the right tools in the right way . . . and doing so regularly.

mation, directing the processing, and determining which types of output will be generated. Because the user directs the processing, he or she can watch, control, and adjust the activities as they occur, and can even stop processing if a change must be made. In contrast, large-scale shared systems are usually running at a remote location, often a great distance away from the individuals using the system.

The artist who draws an illustration on-screen using a mouse or other pointing device is a hands-on user. So is the writer who enters text using a keyboard and then prints the text on a laser printer. The trainer who creates a multimedia

FIGURE 9.1

The Characteristics of Single-User Systems

Frank Serafine of Serafine FX uses a single-user system to concoct sound effects for major motion pictures. To capture noises, Sarafine has jammed microphones in Jacuzzis, up air conditioners, and through sewer drains, then transferred the samples to a keyboard linked to a Macintosh II personal computer.

Tailored to personal preferences—To help synchronize the sound effects to the movie, Serafine has tailored his work studio to include not only keyboards and computers but also a large movie screen.

Used to improve personal performance—Serafine's personal system lets him quickly and easily alter sounds to achieve the desired effect. "Once the music is in the system," he says, "it's like Silly Putty. I can bend every sound."

Hands-on usage—Serafine operates the various components of the system himself.

sequence of text, voice, sound, and animation on a PC by assembling a combination of keyboard entries, prestored music and art, and scanned images is also a hands-on user.

The information generated by a single-user system is usually stored within the system or on an attached secondary storage device. In large multiuser systems, the information may reside at remote locations, not under direct user control.

The National Institutes of Health Use IT to Help the Blind to See

More than 12 million people in the United States must cope every day with severe visual impairment. A U.S. National Institutes of Health's (NIH) prototype system is aimed at enabling a blind person to read a newspaper, view a computer display, or catch a bus—activities that sighted people do every day without giving them a second thought.

The user of the NIH IT-based system wears a visual prosthesis consisting of eyeglasses fitted with a thumb-size video camera mounted on one lens. The camera "sees" and transmits images to a hand-held box of microprocessors, which translate visual images into patterns of light. The patterns are, in turn, transmitted to a tiny microelectrode (a fraction of the diameter of a human hair) implanted in the brain's visual cortex. A weak electronic signal from the chip stimulates the brain to produce pinpoint-sized dots of light. When organized into a meaningful pattern, the dots reproduce the image captured by the camera lens.

NIH tests have indicated that the simplified patterns of light are recognizable to those with severe visual impairment. New hope is being offered even to the people whose blindness was caused by birth defects.

TAILORED TO PERSONAL REQUIREMENTS AND PREFERENCES. Single-user systems are tailored to the needs of their users.

- The hardware configuration chosen determines the system's speed, power, and capacity. For example, special effects designers may configure their personal systems to feature high-resolution color graphics, high-speed "flicker-free" animation, and stereo sound generation.
- The programs installed on the system create its "personality." Load one combination of programs and the system fulfills the requirements of a professional copywriter or novelist. Load a different set and it is ready to assist a medical researcher.

Personal preference plays an important role in personal systems, too. Some people like to rely on a keyboard, while others prefer to use pointing devices for entering instructions and invoking processing activities. The choice of how to tailor a single-user system is, of course, personal.

USED TO IMPROVE PERSONAL PERFORMANCE. Ultimately, the value of a personal system is that it makes the user better at what he or she does. Whether that person works at home, in an office, or as part of a team, the purpose of the single-user system is the same: to assist that person in carrying out his or her activities. We'll be looking at many examples of how personal systems can improve performance in the pages ahead.

The Impact of Single-User Systems

When properly designed, single-user systems have three main effects: improved productivity, greater effectiveness, and increased creativity.

IMPROVED PRODUCTIVITY. We've spoken of productivity often in this book. As we saw in Chapter 1, **productivity** is a measure of accomplishment—the amount of work that can be accomplished with a given level of effort. So, if you want to accomplish more work in general in a period of time, or to complete a specific task or project more quickly, you're concerned about productivity.

Formally defined, productivity is the relationship between the results (output) of an activity, a work process, or an organization and the resources (inputs) used to create those results. Productivity can be measured by dividing the outputs by the inputs (Figure 9.2). A higher ratio means a higher level of productivity.

Productivity can be increased in three ways.

1. **Activities are completed more quickly.** Person A is more productive than Person B if A can complete a task in less time than B.
2. **More activities are completed in a particular period of time.** Person X is more productive than Person Y if X can complete more work than Y in the same amount of time.
3. **Activities are completed with fewer resources.** If Company Z can conduct manufacturing, inventory management, and other business processes with fewer resources (people, space, financing, vehicles, and so forth), Company Z has increased its productivity.

Personal systems are designed to raise personal productivity—that is, to permit activities to be completed more quickly, allow more activities to be completed in a particular period of time, or allow a task to be completed with fewer resources. Single-user software packages for creating spreadsheets (Chapter 6),

productivity
The relationship between the results of an activity and the resources used to create those results. Equal to outputs/inputs.

FIGURE 9.2
*Productivity: A Measure of
Accomplishment*

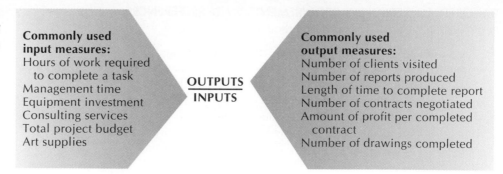

Commonly used
input measures:
Hours of work required
    to complete a task
Management time
Equipment investment
Consulting services
Total project budget
Art supplies

OUTPUTS
INPUTS

Commonly used
output measures:
Number of clients visited
Number of reports produced
Length of time to complete report
Number of contracts negotiated
Amount of profit per completed
    contract
Number of drawings completed

**personal productivity
software**
Software packages that permit
activities to be completed
more quickly, allow more
activities to be completed in a
particular period of time, or
allow a task to be completed
with fewer resources.

personal database systems (the second half of this chapter), and multimedia documents and presentations (Chapter 8), are all designed to increase productivity. For this reason, they are often called **personal productivity software.** To aid the user, personal productivity software is making more and more use of artificial intelligence tools, as the *Information Technology in Practice* feature entitled "Artificial Intelligence Moves into Personal Productivity Software" discusses in detail.

Two warnings are in order here. First, productivity gains from working faster should not come at the expense of quality. If working faster causes mistakes, those mistakes will have to be corrected and the time used to do that may cancel out the gains from working faster. Moreover, when quality suffers, an organization's reputation can be quickly damaged. Second, an organization's productivity gains should not come at the personal expense of workers. If an organization chooses to use PCs simply to force more work out of its employees, any apparent gains are likely to be short-lived. People will tire of the pressure and will seek ways to cut corners in order to meet production goals. The results may be product defects, shoddy service, careless mistakes—lower quality.

When the consulting firm Gestion y Control de Calidad (GCC) conducted a study of quality in Spain at the beginning of the 1990s, it found that the cost of defective products and services in the average Spanish company was equivalent to 20 percent of sales.[1] This was four times higher than the level in Japan and West Germany, two countries known for their high-quality products and services. The Spanish have invented the word *chapuza* to describe mistakes made through carelessness and neglect.

Proud of both their heritage and their country, the Spanish resolved to fix the quality problem. They started with their biggest national industry, tourism, which was in a state of crisis. For decades, Spain had been an international holiday playground for all of Europe, hosting visitors seeking to relax, play, and enjoy sports. But in the early 1990s, tourism was falling off. Spain's chief tourism official, Ignacio Fuejo, examined the problem and decided that "The main reason for the current crisis is the poor price-quality ratio." Recognizing that prices were not going to fall, Fuejo declared, "The only solution is to improve quality." Quality programs, workshops, and training programs were launched with wide participation throughout the tourism industry.

Fuejo's initiatives have been paying off. Barcelona hosted the Summer Olympics and Seville held the World Expo in 1992 (Figure 9.3). Visitors from around the world enjoyed the hospitality of these and other Spanish cities, while millions

[1]Marina Specht and James McCarthy, "A Step in the Right Direction: Quality in Spain," *Financial Times,* October 29, 1990, p. 13.

FIGURE 9.3
Increasing Quality in Spain's Tourism Industry
Spain's quality initiative has made it a more popular vacation spot than ever before.

more learned about Spain through television programs and discussions with returning visitors. Today, Spain's reputation as a place to visit is better than ever. And *quality,* not quantity, remains the watchword for the tourism industry: the Spanish know that if the quality is there, the quantity (of visitors) will follow.

Spanish banks, auto manufacturers, and companies in many other industries have picked up the initiative, developing their own programs to enhance quality while maintaining productivity levels.

GREATER EFFECTIVENESS. Some people are described as "effective workers," "effective managers," or "effective speakers." Some security procedures are considered "really effective." What exactly do we mean by *effectiveness?*

Effectiveness, which we first defined in Chapter 1, entails doing the right things to accomplish a task. It is the extent to which desirable results are achieved. People are effective when they take actions that produce desirable results. An effective speaker presents ideas, stories, and illustrations in a manner that not only captures and holds the attention of an audience but also makes a point memorably. The speaker seems to say the right things in just the right way.

Single-use systems improve individual effectiveness when they help people do the right things. Perhaps a spreadsheet package helps an analyst perform a more extensive analysis of alternatives to produce a high-impact result, or a graphics package helps an artist create magazine illustrations that have more realistic characters and scenery. Both people have used their personal systems to increase their effectiveness.

effectiveness
The extent to which desirable results are achieved.

REALITY CHECK

Productivity and effectiveness are both important in business, but the terms are not interchangeable. *Productivity* is concerned with *quantity* of work, the time or effort needed to produce a result, and the resources used in producing an output. *Effectiveness,* in contrast is concerned with the *quality* of results.

A single-user system gives you a personal advantage only if you learn to use the system to your benefit. The key concept here is leverage—doing what you do best, while using IT to

INFORMATION TECHNOLOGY IN PRACTICE

Artificial Intelligence Moves into Personal Productivity Software

If you use today's powerful personal productivity software, you've probably encountered *artificial intelligence (AI),* a complex field with two main branches. The first branch continues the quest, begun in the late 1950s, to unravel the mysteries of human thought, speech, vision, and hearing. The second, sometimes called *applied intelligence,* looks for ways to build these human capabilities into computer programs, including some of the software that runs on today's personal computers. There are three AI tools:

1. The **algorithm** is a collection of rules and step-by-step procedures used to identify patterns and perform tasks ranging from playing chess to spell-checking and approving credit applications.
2. The **neural network** tries to simulate the way the web of neurons in a living brain processes, learns, and remembers information. Instead of passively following rules and algorithms, neural networks observe patterns, form associations, and learn by example and by trial-and-error. In one lab, for example, a robot taught itself to swing, arm over arm, from the ceiling like a gibbon—but only after it fell several times. In the

business world, corporations are now using neural networks to detect credit card fraud, predict the performance of stocks, and schedule airplane maintenance.
3. **Fuzzy logic** got its name from its ability to solve problems involving ambiguous data and inexact instructions that don't fit the true-false patterns of traditional computer logic. Fuzzy logic is most often used today in controllers embedded in computers, automobile components, consumer electronics, and home appliances, but it is also being used in decision support systems in business, finance, and medicine (see Chapter 13).

Together, these tools promise to create an exciting new generation of silicon servants.

They're already making computers easier to use. Here are just a few examples:

- **Handwriting recognition.** People who can't or don't want to use computer keyboards have been intrigued by the idea of pen-based computing. This is part of the appeal of the personal digital assistant (PDA), introduced in 1993. To make it work, designers had to develop handwriting recognition software, another type of pattern

compensate for your weaknesses. This idea draws on the principles of productivity and effectiveness.

For example, if you are a financial analyst, your single-user system should be configured to help you become a better financial analyst. That is the primary goal. But if you are weak at writing reports, your system should also have the tools—the software—to help you become a better writer. Prestored report formats, appendixes, and illustrations that can be used repeatedly, along with the other writing support features of a word-processing program, can help you compensate for your writing weaknesses.

Do not think of "single-user system" as just another name for "computer." Think of it, rather, as a package of tools specifically designed to help *you* be the best at what you are or want to be. ∎

recognition. The first generation of this software used algorithms, with mixed success. The next generation will use neural networks.

- **Speech recognition.** Another type of pattern recognition, speech recognition can use algorithms, neural networks, fuzzy logic, or a combination of all three AI tools.

- **Expert or knowledge-based systems.** These systems use a large database of rules and algorithms to analyze problems and make decisions. Although expert systems are common in corporations and hospitals (see Chapter 13), they're also found in desktop software. One example is the grammar checker. Another is a system called Mavis Beacon Teaches Typing, which covers both the conventional and Dvorak keyboards. This software uses an expert system to assess the user's skill level and progress. (If "Mavis" senses you're getting frustrated or tired, she'll even suggest a break or a typing-related game.)

- **Software agents.** A software agent goes beyond providing on-line help to offer interactive advice or instructions. Microsoft pioneered this technique. Its *Wizards* software agent leads users, step by step, through complex procedures, such as adding a chart to an Excel spreadsheet. A related Excel feature, *Tip Wizards,* analyzes the way users work and suggests more efficient techniques. Agents are also available in such products as Quattro Pro (a spreadsheet), Microsoft PowerPoint (presentation graphics), Microsoft Word, and WordPerfect for Windows.

In the future, experts predict, software agents will play a bigger role in computing, anticipating their users' needs, sensing when they require help, and taking over routine or often-repeated tasks. As neural networks and fuzzy logic become more common, users may be able to tell their computers to "do what I mean" (DWIM) instead of "do what I say" (DWIS).

Already, General Magic in Mountain View, California, has created Telescript, a software language that can be used to create and dispatch software agents to the electronic marketplace of on-line information services and interactive television. Given relatively vague instructions ("Find the best price for a two-week cruise to Alaska, leaving the first week of June"), the agent will do your shopping and report back, letting you make the final decision.

INCREASED CREATIVITY. Creativity is hard to define, but most people agree that it entails a high degree of artistic or intellectual inventiveness. Some people are born with creative ability; others have to work at it.

Actually, everyone is creative in his or her own way. The challenge is to identify your creative areas and then find a way to unlock the inventiveness inside you. Single-user systems can help here by providing tools that do routine work while you focus on the creative aspects of the activity. For example:

- A particular artist's strongest skills are design, layout, and use of color. Drawing images is not her strong point. A combination of clip art and scanned images can help her overcome this weakness so that she can focus on deciding what to illustrate and how to create the desired image and message.

- A musician likes to compose music sitting at his keyboard. He finds it distracting to have to stop to write down the notes as he is composing. Using special software, he can compose music by playing it on an electronic instrument, and the software will take care of printing the notes or displaying them on a screen. The composer is free to work at creating music without pause because the PC is capturing the information and performing the appropriate processing.

- A journalist has a much greater flair for describing natural disasters than for spelling and grammar. A personal system equipped with word-processing software allows her to enter her ideas and observations almost as quickly as she thinks of them, and then go back and make revisions—repeatedly if necessary. She can use automatic checking and correction software to ensure that her creative flair is correct to the word, letter, and period.

We seldom think of financial analysts and other businesspeople as creative in the same way that artists and writers are. Yet assembling investment packages, arranging financing for investments, and suggesting financial portfolios is creative

CRITICAL CONNECTION 2

AMERICAN GREETINGS

Personalize Your Thoughts with American Greetings' CreataCard*

Custom calls for recognizing special occasions—birthdays, holidays, and important achievements—with a greeting card. Each year retailers stock and sell millions of carefully designed greeting cards that send just the right message. That's the way it's been for decades: visit a store and choose from the array of cards on hand the one that best expresses your sentiment.

American Greetings, headquartered in Cleveland, Ohio, recently has made it possible to send personalized cards using the capabilities provided by today's information technology. If you have a personal computer and access to the Internet, you can download a sample version of American Greetings Creata-Card software, or you can purchase the complete program at a computer retailer. This software will enable you to personalize cards, as well as stationery, certificates, and invitations. You can craft thoughtful personal messages and print them at home on a color inkjet printer. American Greetings makes available a wide array of high-quality, electronic card designs that have colorful photographs and illustrations on the front and space for personal messages inside. They're personal because you can add your own special touch to them. You can change not only the text but can also select alternate artwork.

Using the software, which includes a variety of electronic card designs, and their PC, customers can create a unique message for that special person whenever the need arises. The available sets span nearly every topic you might want, including A Little Romance; Oh, Baby! Birthday Fun; For Cat Lovers; Over the Hill; Hot Stuff for Him; Hot Stuff for Her; and Thoughts to Live By. (New electronic card designs are always available for ordering through the Internet.)

*The following are trademarks of American Greetings Corporation and its subsidiaries: American Greetings with rose design and CreataCard.®

work when done well. Creative financial analysts don't want to be bothered with calculating returns on investment, payback periods, or payment and interest rates while working on ideas for new products or packages, so they use PC software to handle the calculations for them.

Developing a Single-User System

Developing single-user systems is an exercise in problem solving. In this section, we briefly review the nature of problems and the problem-solving process (which we first discussed in Chapter 1), and then apply this process to the development of a single-user system.

Problems and the Problem-Solving Cycle

A **problem** is a perceived difference between events and conditions as they are and as you would like them to be. Problems touch every aspect of our business and personal lives. For example:

problem
A perceived difference between a particular condition and desired conditions.

- You find out that the cost of repairing your car is higher than its current value.
- The time of a business meeting is changed on short notice and now conflicts with another important meeting that you must attend. You cannot be in two places at once.
- You are offered a job at a rapidly growing company. The new job is riskier than your present position because the company is newer, but the salary is 50 percent higher than your current salary. You have also been offered a generous bonus plan that will make you part owner of the company in a few years. Yet you know that if you stay in your current position for two more years, you will exceed the new salary and face virtually no risk. You have to decide on the job offer by tomorrow.
- The course you were planning to register for this term, your last before graduation, is closed and no additional registrations are allowed. The course is required for graduation.
- The stocks in which you invested have decreased in value by 25 percent, and their value is expected to go even lower in the next few months. However, one year from now the market price of your stocks is expected to exceed your original purchase price by an attractive percentage. Selling the stock now provides tax advantages. Waiting will not produce any tax advantages this year, but may lead to long-term benefits.

Undoubtedly, you could add to this list. The point is clear, though: Problems are an everyday occurrence. They are not the exception, but the expectation. They remain problems only if you cannot solve them or turn them to your advantage.

Single-user systems are problem-solving tools when they make you more productive and more effective in recognizing problems, defining them, selecting strategies to deal with them, designing solutions to them, and implementing those solutions. These five activities constitute the **problem-solving cycle** (Figure 9.4). The problem-solving cycle is a structure that helps you address problems in a structured way. This approach is much more effective than lashing out at a problem in an effort to eliminate it or hoping that it will just go away. When problem solving is effective, each step toward a solution narrows the distance between the condition as it is and the condition as it is desired to be. The *Rethinking*

problem solving cycle
The five-step sequence of activities designed to address and solve problems in a structured way.

RETHINKING BUSINESS PRACTICES

Caere Turns a Problem into a Product: OmniForm Eliminates Paper and Creates Impact

Caere, headquartered in Los Gatos, California, built its success on providing people with easy-to-use software that tackles tough problems and makes them seem to disappear. For Caere, problems become products. Early in the company's young life, its designers recognized how frequently people want to transform a printed document into a computer-readable version. So they developed OmniScan, a software program that works with a desktop scanner to read printed documents, line by line, and enter each letter, symbol, and image into computer memory and, in turn, into a word processing program. Scanning with OmniScan accomplishes the same results as keying the entire document, but in about 1 percent of the time.

Caere specializes in software that enables people to create single-user systems and rethink their business practices at the same time. One rule for rethinking business practices is: Eliminate paper whenever possible. Yet the information recorded on paper, such as business forms, is essential for the orderly conduct of business. To resolve this apparent conflict, the designers at Caere created OmniForm.

OmniForm replaces paper with electronic forms that can be displayed, stored and retrieved, or printed. Since the forms are electronic, they can also be sent to another location by e-mail or by fax. Best of all, no computer languages are needed to do any of this.

How does it work? OmniForm will scan an existing paper form into a PC or allow you to create your own form from scratch. When scanned, text and lines on paper are recreated in digital form in the PC. They can be stored or handled in the same way as any form created from scratch.

OmniForm uses two modes to create electronic

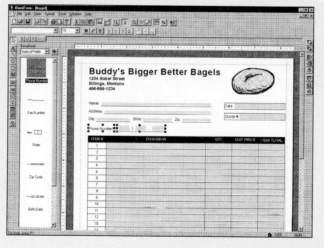

Business Practices feature entitled "Caere Turns a Problem into a Product" illustrates how careful analysis can convert a problem into a business opportunity.

As we saw in Chapters 6 and 7, effective problem solving proceeds through the five steps of the problem-solving cycle. That is, it begins with recognizing the existence of a problem, defining the problem, and evaluating possible solutions from which a desired solution is selected. The solution is then designed and implemented. The entire process may take moments, hours, days, weeks, or longer, depending on the nature of the problem and the characteristics of the

forms. In *design mode,* you can create a template of the form, using a mouse to specify where information should appear and where details will be provided by the user. Drawing tools let you add circles, rectangles, and lines. Checkboxes, shading, and even watermarks (which place a faint image in the background of the form) can be included to give the form just the desired look. You can also add colorful photos or logos.

Form fill mode displays the electronic form on the computer screen so you can enter details directly into each of its areas. Hitting the <Tab> key permits skipping between areas of the form. If requested, OmniForm will also handle any arithmetic you need it to, automatically calculating costs, multiplying quantities, and determining taxes.

OmniForms works with database systems, too. As each electronic form is completed, it is stored in a database, ready for retrieval at a moment's notice. Suppose a customer calls to inquire about the status of a particular order. Using the PC, the receptionist can enter a search field—in this case, the customer's name—and OmniForm will quickly locate the desired record. With just a few clicks of the mouse, the electronic record is displayed on the screen. (Changes can even be made while the record is on the screen if the designer provided this capability.)

The increasing use of information technology by individuals, both at home and at work, is creating a rising demand for easy-to-use, yet powerful, tools. Companies that can see ways to eliminate the challenges of creating applications—that is, that can turn problems into products—are making a new future for us and for themselves.

solution. Evaluation of the problem solver's current understanding of the problem and the desired result is continual throughout the process.

In the pages that follow, we describe how one individual developed a single-user system to aid in her career. The process, outlined in Figure 9.5, can serve as a model for developing many different types of single-user systems. (The PC Buyer's Guide at the end of this chapter offers some simplified guidelines for first-time PC buyers.) We begin with problem recognition and the preliminary investigation.

FIGURE 9.4
The Problem-Solving Cycle
When problem solving is effective, each step narrows the distance between the existing and the desired condition.

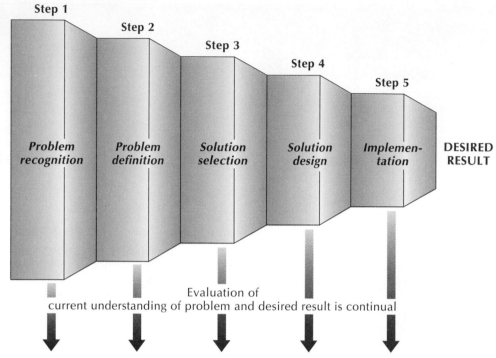

CURRENT
SITUATION

| Step 1 | Step 2 | Step 3 | Step 4 | Step 5 |

Problem recognition · *Problem definition* · *Solution selection* · *Solution design* · *Implementation*

DESIRED
RESULT

Evaluation of current understanding of problem and desired result is continual

Step 1. Problem Recognition: Conduct a Preliminary Investigation

Throughout her years of study at the Sorbonne in Paris, Monique had capitalized on her writing, research, and people skills by working as a free-lance writer. She found this work exciting and rewarding. In addition to preparing and selling articles for publication in magazines, she wrote sections of corporate annual reports and drafted portions of newsletters. After graduating from the Sorbonne, Monique decided that she could turn her part-time work into a successful career.

outsourcing
A business practice in which firms use freelancers and consultants, rather than in-house staff, for selected activities.

What led her to this decision? She had read about (and been part of) a 1990s business trend called **outsourcing,** in which firms contract out single jobs—or even a range of jobs—to specialists and experts, sometimes for years at a time. Outsourcing avoids the need for permanent in-house staff while allowing the firm to hire top-notch talent on a contract basis. Monique believed her track record as a professional writer, her recognized writing skills, and her ability to learn about new areas quickly would serve her well in her chosen career as a freelance writer.

She quickly realized that embarking on this career required her to invest in a personal IT system. But what kind? She took stock of her current tools and resources. With assistance from her family, Monique had acquired an Apple Mac-

FIGURE 9.5

Developing a Single-User System

Step 1. Problem Recognition: Conduct a Preliminary Investigation
  Organize Preliminary Thoughts
  Define the Problem
  Assess Feasibility
    Cost Feasibility
    Operational Feasibility
    Technical Feasibility
Step 2. Problem Definition: Determine the Requirements
  Operational Requirements
  Program Requirements
  Storage Requirements
Step 3. Solution Selection: Choose the New System
  Choose the Computing Platform
  Buy the System
Step 4. Solution Design: Create the New Applications
  Install Application Programs
  Design Application Features
  Test Applications
  Document the System and Procedures
Step 5. Implementation: Convert to the New System
  Conversion
  Training
  Cutover
Evaluation and Evolution of the System

intosh computer when she began her studies at the Sorbonne. She had spent many hours at the Macintosh in her apartment in the Latin Quarter (only a few minutes' walk from the university) and was well versed in its capabilities.

The Macintosh computer had served her well in college, but she knew that her career needs would require more capability than her current system was providing. She thought of simply buying a more powerful Macintosh and transferring her word-processing program to the new computer. But a great deal was at stake (her career!), so she decided to seek out new options—even if that meant purchasing a different brand of computer and another word-processing program.

ORGANIZE PRELIMINARY THOUGHTS. As the first part of her preliminary investigation, Monique organized her thoughts. In order to select the right IT combination, she believed she needed to

- Determine her budget and visit computer stores to become acquainted with equipment and prices.
- Contact publishers and editors and ask what kind of IT combination they require of their freelancers.
- Contact other freelance writers to see what IT they use and obtain their suggestions.

Monique wanted a system that did more than provide good technical performance. She also expected it to fit her needs and desires. With this thought in mind, she began to clarify her needs and wants with respect to IT capabilities. She found that to do so, she needed to define her problem more concretely.

DEFINE THE PROBLEM.   In attempting to define her problem in concrete terms, Monique identified the three challenges she was facing:

Challenge 1: Need to acquire the IT resources required to support a career as a freelance writer.
Challenge 2: Current system does not have the necessary speed, capacity, or flexibility.
Challenge 3: Need to increase both productivity and personal effectiveness ("I can't waste time preparing a unique invoice for each client; I need one that I can generate quickly and easily").

She also identified two constraints she faced:

Constraint 1: A maximum of 50,000 French francs (FF) or $10,000 (from various sources) to invest on information technology.
Constraint 2: Regardless of personal preferences, need to acquire a system compatible with those of editors and publishers.

Monique decided not to let her current hardware, software, and know-how be a constraint. If she had to learn the characteristics of new IT, she would do so because she wanted the best all-around system to support her career.

ASSESS FEASIBILITY.   After defining her IT needs, Monique set out to determine the feasibility of setting up a new system. Specifically, she considered three types of feasibility:

- **Cost feasibility:** "Can I pay the cost of a new system?"
- **Operational feasibility:** "Can I assemble and learn to use new hardware and software quickly?"
- **Technical feasibility:** "Are suitable hardware and packaged software generally available?"

If it turned out that her project was not feasible, she was going to have to find a different path toward her career.

Cost Feasibility.   "Can I get a complete system within my cost constraints?" Monique asked herself. Visiting several computer stores provided her with preliminary cost estimates for a range of different brands of computers and peripheral equipment. At the end of her preliminary survey, Monique listed the following estimates:

Computer and monitor (including main memory, storage space, and disk drives)	FF 10,000 to FF 22,500	($2,000 to $4,500)
Printer	FF 5,000 to FF 10,000	($1,000 to $2,000)
Software	FF 10,000 to FF 20,000	($2,000 to $4,000)
Scanner	FF 5,000 to FF 7,500	($1,000 to $1,500)
Fax/data modem	FF 500 to FF 2500	($100 to $500)
Total	**FF 30,500 to FF 62,500**	**($6,100 to $12,500)**

Monique felt that her overall estimate of FF 30,500 to FF 62,500 ($6,100 to $12,500) indicated the feasibility of acquiring a powerful system with the necessary computer and communications capabilities while remaining within her financial constraint. She also reminded herself that supplies, such as additional disks and printer paper, would be paid for out of her normal operating/supplies budget, so she did not need to consider them as part of the system's acquisition cost.

Operational Feasibility. Could Monique set up and learn how to use a new system? Long use of the Macintosh had given her a wealth of know-how and experience. In fact, that was why she had been able to assemble cost estimates on the various equipment alternatives so quickly. She also believed that her Macintosh experience would serve her well in moving to new hardware and software; she had no doubt that she could learn the components of the new system quickly.

Technical Feasibility. Was the technology that Monique needed available, and could it be acquired in a timely fashion? The information she received from computer retailers gave her confidence that she could meet her needs with brand-name computers, printers, and off-the-shelf (prepackaged) programs. Speaking to experienced users of those products also convinced her that the different components would work together to meet her needs effectively.

Now that Monique had completed her general preliminary investigation and determined that purchasing a new system was feasible, she was ready to take the next step in the process of developing a single-user system: determining precisely what her new system would have to do.

Database Gives Composer More Time to Play Around

If you watch network TV, you have probably heard Jonathan Wolff's work. Wolff is a composer, and his company, Music Consultants Group, Inc. (MCG), of Burbank, California, provides the music that smooths transitions and sets moods in a number of television shows.

For years, Wolff kept his compositions on tape, relying on paper lists to help him find a suitable piece of music. Many times, he found it faster to write something new than to hunt through the files. "It meant less time that I had to do music that absolutely had to be done," he says.

Finally, Wolff asked system developer Steven Lack to create a personal database for MCG. Lack created a menu-driven application that lets users cross-reference the database's five parts, browse easily, and create a sheet of music cues for each show. As an added bonus, Wolff has loaded the database on a notebook computer he carries to studio dubbing sessions. The great virtue of this new system is that Wolff now spends more time being creative and less time flipping through paper files.

SOURCE: Based on Christopher Lindquist, "Alpha Database Is Music to Composer's Ears," *Computerworld*, November 9, 1992, p. 35.

Step 2. Problem Definition: Determine the Requirements

To think through her new system's requirements, Monique took a stroll down the Champs Elysées, making a mental note of the professional activities for which she was most often hired: drafting and editing text (magazine articles, newsletters, advertising brochures, and the like); designing document layouts and arranging text alongside photographs and clip art; and taking notes written by staff members and expanding those notes into a polished article.

She also took note of the business trends and IT advances influencing her work. First, she thought about the growing number of editors who were asking her to transmit manuscript copy electronically, over a telephone link, to the publisher's offices. Many were also requesting a follow-up disk copy and hard copy via courier or overnight mail. Monique was also receiving more requests to send documents by fax. "The publishing world revolves around facts and fax," she thought to herself. In the past, she had used the communications capabilities of a friend's computer and had relied on the fax service at a local copy center. But she knew these options would be inconvenient for the volume of work she would be sending and receiving in the future.

Second, she had noticed that more and more publications were making back issues available on CD-ROM. Monique knew this trend could be an asset in conducting research for magazine articles and corporate annual reports. Maintaining CD-ROMs of important publications would reduce the space she needed to store copies of old articles and shorten the time she spent retrieving information as well. In addition, developers of computer clip art were now distributing the art on optical disk.

Finally, she remembered the number of inquiries she had received over the last few months asking whether she was willing and experienced enough in multimedia to apply her journalistic skills to the production of multimedia presentations. She recalled the requests of certain clients who wanted to develop multimedia training programs and sales information. Monique saw multimedia presentations as an exciting opportunity. Unfortunately, her current system had neither an optical drive nor multimedia capabilities—and adding them would be both difficult and expensive, if possible at all.

Because of the many demands made on her time throughout college, Monique had been careful to keep a record of her editorial contacts: editors, marketing directors, graphic designers, and publishers. She recalled how often she had told herself, "All of my business world is contained in my card file." Her clients were scattered, not only throughout her own country, but also throughout other nations and regions of the world. (Her knowledge of several languages and cultures, augmented by her study abroad, had been an important factor in landing this international clientele.)

She also maintained a separate set of records for information sources: personal contacts, including executives, politicians, business staff members, and public relations directors. This file contained a separate card for each individual, nearly 500 entries in all. She wanted to put all these data and information into a database format that she could search quickly and expand to meet her changing needs.

From this soul-searching session, Monique formulated three types of **requirements,** or features that had to be included in her system. These were operational, program, and storage requirements.

requirement
A feature that must be included in a system.

OPERATIONAL REQUIREMENTS. A system's operational requirements are those characteristics necessary to support a particular set of professional activities. Monique's list of operational requirements was as follows:

- A set of IT tools for writing, editing, designing, and laying out documents.
- The capability to send and receive documents electronically over telephone links.
- The capability to send and receive documents by fax.
- Ample storage capacity.
- The capability to print black-and-white documents.
- The capability to scan color documents.
- The capability for color display of documents and information.
- The capability to run two to three applications at a time and to display multiple documents simultaneously.

To guide her in appraising different solutions, Monique created the personal system checklist in Figure 9.6.

PROGRAM REQUIREMENTS. Monique recognized that her computer hardware needs would be heavily influenced by her software requirements. Hence, she focused hard on identifying the software packages she would need. She was certain that she could meet all of her program requirements with prepackaged software. Some adaptation of her working habits and tailoring of the software's setup might be necessary, but she did not foresee any serious difficulties in that area.

Many of the programs Monique examined were available for both Macintosh and IBM-compatible computers. When this was not the case, she found functionally comparable packages.

Program requirements influence both the amount of main memory and the amount of disk storage needed within a system. Monique's review of many different software packages (during her store visits and her discussions of program characteristics with friends and colleagues) provided her with ample information. Figure 9.7 shows her summary of internal program memory requirements and the price she could expect to pay for software.

STORAGE REQUIREMENTS. To estimate her secondary storage requirements, Monique identified the files and databases she intended to store on disk, calculating the space needed to store each one. Files and databases often grow with use, so she also estimated annual increases for each file. Her estimates are summarized in Figure 9.8.

After completing her estimates, Monique determined that she wanted a minimum of five times her current estimate. She decided to purchase 170 MB of disk space, a size that fit easily within the storage ranges supported on the systems she had examined. Expansion space for new programs and additional files also did not seem to be a constraint because of the excess capacity on systems she was evaluating and because additional storage capacity could be added later if necessary.

FIGURE 9.6
*Monique's Personal
System Checklist*

PERSONAL SYSTEM CHECKLIST

Computer:

Microprocessor	_____	(e.g., Intel "386," "486," or Pentium; Motorola 68030 or 68040)
Memory included	_____	RAM
Memory capacity	_____	RAM
Cache memory	_____	
Number of expansion slots	_____	
Other upgrade features	_____	
	_____	
Number of ports	_____	
Warranty	_____	Years

Additional for Laptop/Notebook Computers:

Battery type	_____	
Estimated use on full charge	_____	Hours
Computer weight	_____	With battery
Charger included?	_____	(yes/no)

Disk Storage:

Hard Disk Drives	_____	Manufacturer
	_____	Model
	_____	MB capacity
	_____	Data access speed
Warranty	_____	Months/years
Flexible Disk Drives	_____	Number included
	_____	Sizes (3-1/2",5-1/4")
	_____	Capacity (720K, 1.44MB, 2.88 MB; other)
Warranty	_____	Months/years
Optical Disk Drive	_____	(yes/no)
	_____	Manufacturer
	_____	Model
	_____	Data transfer rate
Warranty	_____	Months/years

Software Bundled with Computer:

Name	Type	Disk included?	Documentation included?	Software preloaded?
_____	_____	_____	_____	_____
_____	_____	_____	_____	_____
_____	_____	_____	_____	_____
_____	_____	_____	_____	_____
_____	_____	_____	_____	_____
_____	_____	_____	_____	_____
_____	_____	_____	_____	_____

FIGURE 9.6
(continued)

Monitor:

Color _____ (yes/no)
Capability _____ (CGA, VGA, EGA, SVGA)
Size _____ (13/14/15/17/20 inch; 330, 355,
381, 431, 508 mm)
Multisync _____ (yes/no)
Warranty _____ Years

Printer:

Manufacturer _____
Type _____ Laser/dot matrix/other
Speed _____ Pages per minute/lines per minute
Communication _____ Serial/parallel
Port to be used _____
Warranty _____ Years

Communication Modem:
(alternatively fax/modem)

Manufacturer _____
Modem speeds _____
Fax speeds _____
Fax resolution _____ (100 DPI; 200 DPI; other)
Installation _____ Internal board/external via
communications port
Port to be used _____
Warranty _____ Years
Software included? _____ (yes/no)

Mouse:

Included _____ (yes/no)
Type _____ (serial/bus)
Software included? _____ (yes/no)

Scanner:

Manufacturer _____
Resolution _____
Warranty _____ Years
Software included? _____ (yes/no)

Cables:

Printer _____ Included/purchase _____ Length
Monitor _____ Included/purchase _____ Length
Modem (fax/modem)* _____ Included/purchase _____ Length

* Cable not needed for internal modem, fax, or fax/modem

FIGURE 9.7

Monique's Program Requirements (with Main Memory Requirements) and Approximate Cost of Software

SOFTWARE TYPE	IBM REQUIREMENTS	APPROXIMATE COST	MACINTOSH REQUIREMENTS	APPROXIMATE COST
Word processing	6 MB memory 16 MB disk space	FF 1995/$399	8 MB memory 25 MB disk space	FF 1595/$319
Spreadsheet	4 MB memory 11 MB disk space	FF 1595/$319	4 MB memory 6 MB disk space	FF 1545/$309
Database	12 MB memory 20 MB disk space	FF 1995/$399	8 MB memory 8 MB disk space	FF 2145/$429
Drawing (includes clip art imaging library)	8 MB memory 24 MB disk space	FF 1995/$399	5 MB memory 8 MB disk space	FF 2045/$409
Desktop publishing	8 MB memory 24 MB disk space	FF 2895/$579	5 MB memory 25 MB disk space	FF 2995/$599
Data communications	8 MB memory 20 MB disk space	FF 445/$89	4 MB memory 8 MB disk space	FF 445/$89
Scanning	Included with scanner purchase		Included with scanner purchase	
Approximate Total Software Cost		**FF 13,915/$2,783**		**FF 13,765/$2,753**

Step 3. Solution Selection: Choose the New System

platform

The computer foundation on which applications are built. The two most common platforms for PCs are IBM-compatibles and Apple Macintosh.

Everyone Monique spoke to had a favorite computer **platform**, the computer foundation on which applications are built. Many publishers, editors, and illustrators told her that they use Macintosh platforms in their business, while many people in other industries preferred an IBM-compatible platform. There were exceptions in both groups, however, so Monique's final choice would depend on which computer platform she herself preferred.

She was at the point of taking the plunge and purchasing her new system.

CHOOSING THE COMPUTING PLATFORM.   In the end, Monique knew that whether she chose the Macintosh or IBM-compatible computing platform, she had to be able to communicate with and transfer data and information to the other platform.

After much thought, she narrowed down her alternatives (Figure 9.9). She selected the software applications first, determining that they should drive her

choice of computers, printers, and scanners. After considering price, performance, and the features she needed, she chose an IBM-compatible PC (but planned to keep her Apple Macintosh computer). The hardware cost slightly more than she had originally estimated, but she was pleased with her choice.

BUY THE SYSTEM.   Monique purchased all of her hardware and software from a single dealer. Hence, she was able to pick up the computer, printer, scanner, and all the software in a single trip to the store. Prior to Monique's arrival, the computer dealer assembled and tested the computer and communications hardware. He also installed the fax/modem that Monique bought.

FIGURE 9.8
Monique's Data Storage Requirements

Initial Data Storage Requirements
    Name and address file
        500 individuals @ 280 bytes each = 140,000 bytes (.14 MB of storage)
    Editorial development tools
        Dictionaries, thesaurus, and grammar tools @ .5 MB each: 1.5 MB
    Clip art (size requirements taken from documentation in package)
        Photo art   7 MB of storage
        Line art   3.5 MB of storage
    Active manuscript space
        5,000 pages: 250 words per page @ 5 bytes per word   6.25 MB
    Total: 17.39 MB
Data Expansion (Update) Requirements (Annual)
    Name and address file expansion
        500 individuals @ 280 bytes each = .14 MB of storage
    Editorial development tools
        25% expansion   .375 MB
    Clip art
        25% expansion   2.6 MB
    Active manuscript space
    (presumes migration of older manuscripts to diskettes for off-line storage)
        7,500 pages: 9.375 MB
    Total 12.49 MB

Grand Total: **29.88 MB**

Step 4. Solution Design: Create the New Applications

After bringing her new system home, Monique needed to create its new applications. In her situation, this process consisted of installing the application software, designing the application features, testing the applications' specific capabilities, and documenting the system and procedures.

INSTALL APPLICATION PROGRAMS. Both the operating system and Windows software were installed on the PC when Monique brought it home. All she had to do was unpack the printer and scanner, and then plug them into the ports on the back of the computer. The computer dealer had included the cables needed to do this.

Each of Monique's application programs was packed separately. As Monique opened each box, she did two things right away:

- Completed the registration card, which she would mail to the manufacturer on her next trip to the post office. When the manufacturer received the card, it would add her name to a mailing list for future announcements of enhancements and new versions.
- Made backup copies of each program disk to protect the master disks from accidental damage.

She then installed each of the programs, using the backup copies, onto the computer's internal hard disk according to the manufacturer's step-by-step installation instructions. The install routine built into each software package prompted

FIGURE 9.9

Monique's Computing Platform Alternatives

ALTERNATIVE 1

Software: Word processing (with dictionaries and related writing tools), electronic spreadsheet, desktop publishing, drawing, imaging, clip art, database management, and data communication programs (with Internet access capability).

   System 7 operating system (current version).

   Software Cost: FF 13,765/$2,753

Hardware: 133 megahertz, Apple Macintosh (PowerPC RISC processor) with 16 MB main memory, 1.2 GB hard disk, high-resolution color monitor, fax/data modem, keyboard and mouse; laser printer (adapter card included); high-resolution scanner (software and adapter included).

   Hardware Cost: FF 33,625/$6,725   **TOTAL COST:** FF 47,390/$9,478

ALTERNATIVE 2

Software: Word processing (with dictionaries and related writing tools), electronic spreadsheet, desktop publishing, drawing, imaging, clip art, database management, and data communication programs (with Internet access capability).

   Windows 95 operating system.

   Software Cost: FF 13,915/$2,783

Hardware: 200 megahertz, IBM-compatible computer (Pentium microprocessor) with 32 MB main memory, 3.0 GB hard disk, SVGA display adapter and color monitor, internal fax/data modem, keyboard and mouse; laser printer (adapter card included); high-resolution scanner (software and adapter card included).

   Hardware Cost: FF 31,335/$6,267   **TOTAL COST:** FF 44,250/$9,050

CRITICAL CONNECTION 4

| Dell |

Dell Looks to Service and Support for Competitive Edge

It's four o'clock and you're racing to finish a proposal that's due at five o'clock sharp. *Zap!* Your computer dies. What do you do?

   It's sad but true: desktop computers sometimes fail. In fact, *PC World* has reported that a significant percentage of all PC buyers encounter some hardware failure, ranging from minor to serious, within two years of purchasing their PCs. No wonder that many personal computer satisfaction surveys have found that service and support are customers' top concerns when purchasing personal systems.

   Direct marketer Dell Computer Corp. has received consistently high marks for service and reliability, largely because the "Dell Vision" holds that customers must be "pleased, not just satisfied." CEO Michael Dell sees superb support and service as one way to gain a competitive edge in the price wars raging in the computer industry.

Monique with a few questions: On which disk drive do you want this system installed? What printer will be used with this program? To which port is the printer connected?

Had Monique run into any difficulty, she could have called the free technical support telephone numbers listed in the program manuals or used the software's Help features. Fortunately, microcomputer software generally installs quickly and easily, so there is usually no need to call technical support specialists. So even though Monique kept the phone numbers handy as she installed the programs, it turned out she didn't need to use them.

Installing each program took from one to two hours, depending on the number of disks in the package. After she had installed each package, Monique started the program to ensure that it would run. Because she had decided to install all the programs at once, it took her nearly a full day to load them.

DESIGN APPLICATION FEATURES. Before buying the system, Monique had determined that her needs for managing records would evolve. Hence, she had decided to use a database package rather than a prewritten name-and-address program that includes a predesigned database format. She knew from experience that many of the prewritten name-and-address programs presume a domestic address and telephone number—which were not appropriate for her purpose, because she worked with editors and publishers in many different countries. She also judged most name-and-address programs to be designed either for generating mailing lists and labels or for use in sales management. Her needs were much broader, so she chose a powerful but easy-to-use database program.

Once she had loaded the database management software onto her computer, Monique had to define the features of her database application. She did so by entering the database descriptions shown in Figure 9.10.

TEST APPLICATIONS. Monique tested each personal productivity package—word processing, electronic spreadsheet, database management, drawing, and imaging—after installation. The testing process for each consisted of

- Creating a test document.
- Storing the document.

DATA ITEM	SIZE	TYPE
Name	30	Alphanumeric
Building/floor	48	Alphanumeric
Street address	48	Alphanumeric
City	24	Alphanumeric
State	16	Alphanumeric
Country	16	Alphanumeric
Postal code	10	Alphanumeric
Telephone	16*	Numeric
Fax	16	Numeric
E-mail	24	Alphanumeric
Assistant	16	Alphanumeric
Assistant's telephone	16	Alphanumeric

*Provides space for international dialing codes

FIGURE 9.10
Monique's Database Application Design

- Retrieving the document from storage.
- Editing and storing the changed document.
- Retrieving the edited document and inspecting the changes.
- Printing the document.

The testing process was as much an evaluation of Monique's understanding of the program's essential features as it was a test of the software packages. Of course, learning each program's advanced features would require more time. Rather than sitting down to master every advanced feature described in the program manuals, Monique decided to learn these features a little at a time by using the package in her work.

Because of writers', editors', and publishers' growing reliance on electronic transmission of manuscripts. Monique also conducted communications tests with several different publishers. Within a week, she found she could use two communications standards to communicate with everyone. Hence she adjusted her communications software so that she could choose either standard at a click of the mouse. (We discuss communications in detail in Chapter 10.)

Monique also tested her PC's built-in fax by transmitting and receiving several documents. The tests went well, and within a single morning the fax was ready to use.

DOCUMENT THE SYSTEM AND PROCEDURES.   After loading the software, entering the database specifications, and testing the applications, Monique gathered up all the documentation for the system. She placed the manuals accompanying the programs on her bookshelf for easy reference. In a clearly marked ring binder, she put a list of the serial numbers of all her equipment. She also recorded the serial number and version number of all her software and kept copies of every software licensing agreement and product warranty.

In a separate binder, she placed the information describing her first database's definition. She planned to use the same binder to keep copies of all her DTP layouts, worksheets created with spreadsheet software, and word-processing formats. She also included procedures for using the different applications (including source documents, transmission of documents and output, and fax phone numbers) in a special procedure section of the binder.

Developing these procedures made Monique realize that she needed additional information in certain areas (e.g., regarding fax transmission and client telephone billing procedures) and that she had to keep track of version numbers of her manuscript drafts. It also prompted her to establish a schedule for making periodic backup copies of software, data, and documents. To secure her documents, she decided to store copies of important manuscripts in a safe deposit box at her bank.

Step 5. Implementation: Convert to the New System

Now that all the software was loaded, Monique had to make a transition to the new system. Implementation of a single-user system involves conversion of existing records, training, and cutover. Here's what Monique did in these key areas.

CONVERSION.   After entering the database description into the database management software, Monique began converting her existing handwritten name-and-address lists into an electronic format. Entering and visually proofing each name and address took approximately 30 seconds. It took Monique half a day to enter the entire contents of her database. Once entered, the name-and-address file became a ready reference.

TRAINING. Each software package Monique purchased was accompanied by an on-screen tutorial designed to familiarize new users with the program. Monique had used these during the solution design phase to get acquainted with each program's basic characteristics. During the implementation phase, she used advanced tutorials to learn about the packages' special features and ways of adjusting the system's characteristics to suit her needs.

Because of its many powerful features, the desktop publishing software required a different approach. Although Monique had good knowledge of document design and layouts, she did not know how to prepare these with her new DTP software package. To overcome this weakness, she decided to attend a three-day workshop to learn the package's capabilities. She also subscribed to a user's magazine that includes instructions, tips, and case studies in every issue.

Monique's ongoing training included keeping abreast of developments in the IT and publishing industries. Periodicals, magazines, and industry newspapers are useful for doing so because of the articles and the many advertisements contained in each issue. Figure 9.11 lists some of the most popular IT publications.

CUTOVER. Because of her experience with similar packages running on her Macintosh, Monique was already familiar with the characteristics of the word processing and database systems. Thus, she was able to put these to use right

---

MAGAZINES

Aldus	*Macworld*
ASAP	*MacWeek*
Business Week	*MacUser*
Byte	*Multimedia*
Compute	*Multimedia Solutions*
DBMS	*01 Informatique*
Décision Micro	*PC Computing*
Dr. Dobb's Journal	*PC Magazine*
Fortune	*PC World*
Forbes	*Portable Office*
Home Office Computing	*Presentation Products*
HomePC	*Publish*
Information Week	*Télécoms*
Internet World	*Windows*
LAN Technology	*WordPerfect*

NEWSPAPERS

Computerworld Japan*	*Network World*
Computer Shopper	*PC Week*
InfoWorld	*Web Week*
Le Monde Informatique	

*Computerworld is published in a variety of national editions, including *Computerworld Argentina, Computerworld France, Computerwoche* (Germany), and *China Computerworld.*

FIGURE 9.11

A Sampling of Personal Systems–Oriented Periodicals and Magazines

away. She began working with other applications more gradually. She did not discard her card file, choosing to hold onto it until she became comfortable with the new database software. She did not use her spreadsheet system until she had to prepare a project proposal for a major editorial project. After than, she used it constantly for many different aspects of projects, including the preparation of project proposals, budget creation, and cost management.

Evaluation and Evolution of the System

Monique's system is personal—it is a collection of carefully selected IT tools adapted to her needs (both now and in the future) and designed to augment her know-how as a writer and journalist. As her career evolves, her IT needs will undoubtedly change. Hence, continual evaluation of her system—which includes keeping up with new ideas and advances in software and hardware—is in her professional interest. Simple activities, such as subscribing to magazines and making contact with other people in your field, can be as important as IT in building careers.

Or as Monique said, *"Magnifique! Ce n'est que le début."* [2]

[2] Magnificent! This is only the beginning.

SUMMARY OF LEARNING OBJECTIVES

1 **Describe the origin of single-user systems in business and understand why they have become so prominent.** In the early days of data processing, large computers and vast communications networks were the norm. Although these large systems are still in widespread use, technological progress in the 1980s and 1990s, coupled with increased affordability, has made personal systems the dominant source of IT capability in many organizations.

2 **Identify the distinguishing characteristics of a single-user system.** Single-user systems are designed for hands-on usage, are tailored to an individual's requirements and preferences, and are used to improve personal performance.

3 **Explain the benefits of single-user systems in business.** When properly designed, single-user systems have three main effects: improved productivity, greater effectiveness, and increased creativity.

4 **Define the problem-solving cycle and state how it relates to the development of a single-user system.** The problem-solving cycle is composed of five activities: recognizing problems, defining them, selecting strategies to deal with them, designing solutions, and implementing those solutions. The process of developing a single-user system begins with problem recognition and is ongoing through system evaluation and evolution.

5 Discuss the five steps involved in developing a single-user system. The five steps involved in developing a single-user system are (1) problem recognition—conduct a preliminary investigation; (2) problem definition—determine the system's requirements; (3) solution selection—choose the new system; (4) solution design—create the new applications; and (5) implementation—convert to the new system.

6 Distinguish between choosing a single-user system and creating single-user applications. Choosing a single-user system entails finding the right platform and tailoring it to personal require-ments and preferences. Creating single-user applications involves installing the application programs, designing the application features, testing the applications' specific capabilities, and documenting the system and procedures.

7 Explain the importance of continual evaluation and evolution in single-user systems development. Because an individual's needs change, a single-user system must evolve to meet those needs. To remain effective, the user must keep abreast of the latest advances in hardware and software.

KEY TERMS

configuration   397
effectiveness   403
hands-on system   398
outsourcing   410

personal productivity software   402
platform   418
problem   407
problem-solving cycle   407

productivity   401
requirement   415
single-user system/personal system   397

CRITICAL CONNECTIONS

1 The National Institutes of Health Use IT to Help the Blind to See

The visual prosthesis developed by the National Institutes of Health (NIH) does not draw an object in its entirety. Rather, it depends on the human ability to recognize patterns and fill in missing information—that is, the missing dots needed to form an object fully. The human mind is extremely powerful at providing missing information, and that ability is essential to the hoped-for success of the NIH's visual prosthesis.

This system is still in the early stages of development. If testing determines that it is functionally and commercially feasible, the NIH will seek private companies to conduct the clinical trials needed to obtain U.S. Food and Drug Administration approval for release of this innovative prosthesis to the public.

Questions for Discussion

1. What information technology capabilities and characteristics underlie the capabilities of the NIH's visual prosthesis?

2. Relatively few physicians and scientists are exploring ways to harness the power of information technology to aid people with disabilities. Considering that information technology is so pervasive in business and society, why do you suppose this is true? Do you feel that the use of IT for biological purposes (as illustrated in this example) should be pursued by medicine and science?

2 Personalize Your Thoughts with American Greetings' CreataCard*

The popularity of CreataCard has led American Greetings to introduce these alternatives:

- **Add-a-Photo**—Enables you to place the photo of your choice on the front of a card or put it on the inside of any of more than 1,000 cards. How? Drop your film off at any participating local developer or retailer, or mail it to a development center. The developer will place your photos on-line, protected by a password. You'll be notified when your photos are on-line and ready for use. Then, when visiting the American Greetings Web site, you can link to the photos, view thumbnails (small copies of the full-size images), and choose the one(s) you want inserted into a greeting card. The software product also allows you to add photos to card designs using a scanner, CD-ROM photo disk, or digital camera.
- **Send cards electronically**—You can visit the American Greetings Web site (URL: http://www. americangreetings.com) to prepare animated greetings that are sent by e-mail via the Internet.
- **Mail delivery**—At the Web site, you can personalize a card using your PC and have American Greetings print and mail it for you.

Questions for Discussion

1. Would you use the American Greetings CreataCard program? Why or why not?
2. What characteristics of the CreataCard make it attractive for individual users?
3. What are the apparent limitations and drawbacks of the Add-a-Photo and e-mail alternatives?

*The following are trademarks of American Greetings Corporation and its subsidiaries: American Greetings with rose design and CreataCard.®

3 Database Gives Composer More Time to Play Around

Loading the database onto his notebook computer has proved a real help to Jonathan Wolff at dubbing sessions. When a producer wants to make a last-minute change, Wolff can quickly search the database for a suitable replacement.

When he started using the music database, Wolff was still storing his actual music on audiotape. This caused a slight delay while he searched for the right tape and loaded it onto a tape deck. Now that he knows something about multimedia, he is planning to build a link between the database and a Macintosh computer that will let him store, retrieve, and play his music through the computer itself.

Questions for Discussion

1. Describe how Wolff's personal system has increased his productivity and effectiveness.
2. How might Wolff's personal system give his company a competitive advantage?
3. What provisions has Wolff made for the continuing evaluation and evolution of his personal system?

4 Dell Looks to Service and Support for Competitive Edge

Dell

By the early 1990s, desktop computers were being sold by many companies in many ways. Packard Bell, for instance, began selling them through warehouse buying clubs. Name-brand companies like IBM, Compaq, Dell, Gateway 2000, and AST Research saw their share of the PC market shrink.

To fight this trend, Compaq recently announced a series of sharp price cuts. Consumers were delighted by the price war that followed. Soon industry observers were speculating that only the strongest companies would survive.

Dell was one of the companies that cut its prices for desktops. In addition, Dell announced an expanded range of support and service options for its more expensive models. Along with its standard service plan—one year of on-site service and lifetime telephone support—Dell offered the SelectCare plan to large corporate accounts. Under this new plan, customers could buy extended warranties that provided as much—or as little—service and support as they wanted. The options ranged from parts-only coverage for up to four years to on-site Critical Care Service and a Self-Maintainer Program designed to train the company's technical support staff. Within weeks, several other name-brand companies had followed Dell's lead, announcing their own extended support and service programs.

Questions for Discussion

1. Local computer dealers once justified their slightly higher prices by offering more direct support, such as setting up and testing a desktop system prior to delivery. How do you think these dealers have been affected by recent developments in computer marketing?

2. By the early 1990s, many IT professionals who were used to dealing with mainframes and minicomputers found themselves linking PCs together in networks. How do you think this trend has affected the demand for support and service? Can you think of other trends that have affected the demand for support?

3. Some computer makers now offer three-year warranties with two years of on-site service. Why do you think on-site service is an important consideration in purchasing and setting up a personal system?

Net Work

A growing number of computer buyers are finding it easy and worthwhile to shop for a computer on the Web. Companies such as Dell, Gateway 2000, and Micron have built a substantial business by selling direct to company and private purchasers.

Since Web-based computer sales do not involve face-to-face discussions with retail salespersons, a company's Web site must anticipate and address customer questions. At the same time, it must make it easy for potential buyers to shop for computers and configure their system properly. Buyers must also be able to place the order, receive confirmation, and arrange payment over the Web, or call the company and complete the order verbally over the phone. In either case, good design of the sales site is essential to business success.

To see the way in which Dell, Gateway 2000, and Micron have chosen to develop their Web sites, you can visit each company at its respective URL:

Dell Computers: http://www.dell.com
Gateway 2000: http://www.gateway2000.com
Micron: http://www.micron.com

In comparing these companies' methods, consider the following questions:

1. What assistance does each company provide in selecting the features of a personal computer?

2. How do the companies vary in the way they inform you of the price of a specific computer?

3. With which companies can you place an order for a computer over the company's Web site? What is the procedure for placing the order?

GROUP PROJECTS AND APPLICATIONS

Project 1

With a group, visit a small- or medium-sized business in your area. Different members of the group should interview someone in each of the company's different departments—accounting management, marketing, finance, production, and so forth—regarding the personal system on their desks. Ask the following questions:

- How is your system designed for hands-on usage?
- How have you tailored the system to your personal requirements and preferences?
- How does your system differ from that of a colleague who does essentially the same job that you do?
- Has your system helped you improve your personal performance? Has it increased your productivity, effectiveness, and creativity? If so, how?
- What suggestions would you make for setting up a personal system? Any "must-haves"? Any pitfalls to avoid?

Present the results of your interview to the class. Be sure to write a thank-you note to the people you've interviewed.

Project 2

In groups of five, brainstorm a business that you'd like to establish in your area. For example, you might decide that you could open and operate a CD/tape store profitably near your campus, or you might think of starting a babysitting service for the professionals in your area. To run your business effectively, you will want to set up a personalized computer system.

The Small Business Administration (SBA), a branch of the U.S. government, was set up to assist small-business owners. The SBA's advisors can help you develop a marketing plan, put you in touch with other local businesspeople, and assist you in securing bank loans and other financing. They can also help you determine what types of IT will be most helpful to you.

After deciding on the type of business you'd like to open, contact an SBA representative in your area and ask him or her to assist you in setting up your personal productivity system. You can visit the SBA's home page on the World Wide Web (http://www.sba.gov) to find the office nearest you.

Share the advice you've received with the class.

Project 3

Write up a plan for developing a single-user system suited to the business you chose to start in Project 2. Follow the outline in this chapter (pages 410–422), and be sure to specify

- The problem(s) you are trying to solve.
- The feasibility of your proposed solutions.
- The operational, program, and storage requirements your system will need (use the checklist in Figure 9.6).
- The way you will test your system before using it.

REVIEW QUESTIONS

1. What is a single-user system?
2. How did single-user systems originate? Why are mainframe systems not considered single-user systems?
3. What are the three characteristics of single-user systems?
4. What is a "hands-on user"?

5. What is productivity? List three ways in which productivity can be increased.

6. How can single-user systems aid productivity?

7. What is personal productivity software?

8. Describe the importance of effectiveness and the role of single-user systems in improving effectiveness.

9. How are productivity and effectiveness different?

10. Define the concept of leverage.

11. What is a problem? What five activities constitute the problem-solving cycle? How do these activities relate to the process of developing a single-user system?

12. What is outsourcing?

13. What three steps are involved in conducting a preliminary investigation into a problem?

14. What three types of feasibility must be considered in developing a single-user system? Describe each briefly.

15. Explain the three types of requirements that a single-user system must fulfill.

16. In choosing a new system, are needs or desires more important? Explain your answer.

17. What four activities are involved in the solution design step of developing a single-user system?

18. Describe the three components of implementing a single-user system.

19. What role does evaluation play in the development of a single-user system?

DISCUSSION QUESTIONS

1. If Monique's budget for her single-user system were to be cut in half, how could she set priorities in deciding what hardware and software to purchase? Can you identify an area in which she should *not* economize?

2. Corporate Fact Finders, DataSearch, and InfoQuest are all "information brokers," companies that do library and on-line database searches to meet their clients' research needs. For their services, information brokers are paid $40 to $300 an hour. If you were a freelance information broker, what requirements would your single-user system have to meet?

3. CompUSA and a number of other national computer chains offer regular training classes. Why are these training classes important to current and potential customers? Why might you take a training class during the preliminary investigation stage rather than waiting until you actually buy and install a single-user system?

SUGGESTED READINGS

De Bono, Edward. *Lateral Thinking*. New York: Harper & Row, 1970. Describes a series of approaches to increasing your creativity in identifying and solving problems. Can be applied to many aspects of IT use in business.

Edwards, Paul, and Sarah Edwards. *Working from Home*. New York: Putnam, 1990. A practical discussion of the steps needed to set up and market a personal business. Includes effective ways to analyze the characteristics of the personal support systems required for the business.

Eyler, David R. *Starting a Home-Based Business*. New York: Wiley, 1990. Presents a complete "nuts-and-bolts" discus-

sion of the requirements for starting an independent business. Also describes the steps and considerations in selecting a cost-effective personal IT system.

Simon, Herbert A. *Administrative Behavior* (2d ed). Englewood Cliffs, NJ: The Free Press, 1957. A classic treatise on problem solving that examines the process and pitfalls of creating solutions to problems across a variety of business and personal settings.

C A S E
S T U D Y

Freightliner Corp. Couples the Power of Information Technology with Sheer Horsepower to Create King-Size Success

The developed nations of the world move huge quantities of freight—food, building materials, automobiles, clothing, and more—by truck. In countries where the trucking industry has been deregulated so that competition, rather than government rulings, determines the cost of moving freight, truckers continually seek ways to improve their productivity. Likewise, the companies that build king-size over-the-road trucks to pull giant cargo trailers across the nation's motorways are striving to ensure that the performance of their trucks meets their customers' needs.

Freightliner Corporation of Portland, Oregon, is a unit of Daimler-Benz AG, headquartered in Stuttgart, Germany. Freightliner is the largest manufacturer of huge over-the-road trucks in the United States, accounting for nearly one out of every three trucks sold here. Freightliner trucks are priced from $75,000 to over $100,000, depending on their features. Known as an innovator since its origin during the 1930s (Freightliner

was the first company to use aluminum components in its trucks, beginning in the 1940s), the company is today a leader in the use of information technology in both its trucks and its manufacturing process. Freightliner believes that the power of information technology is just as important as the horsepower in the engines of its trucks.

Freightliner's trucks depend on IT for achieving efficient engine performance and for ensuring safety. For instance, microprocessors govern braking, speed control, and collision-warning systems. These systems are so well integrated into the truck's operation that drivers are seldom aware that they are using information technology.

On-Board Driver's Computer

Another Freightliner innovation—optional today, but soon to be required equipment in all the company's

trucks—is an on-board computer, priced at $5,000 to $7,000, that monitors the truck's performance. The computer routinely captures and processes some 50 different types of diagnostic information. When the truck is running properly, drivers are unaware they have a computer on board. However, when the computer detects a problem—from high engine temperature to low air pressure—drivers are alerted by a message displayed on the computer monitor built into the dashboard control panel. The computer automatically records data about the problem; drivers need take no action with the computer.

When the driver pulls into an authorized Freightliner service center, the on-board computer can be asked to suggest causes of the problem. It is also interconnected with the mechanic's computer, so the diagnostic details can be downloaded for analysis. Since mechanics have both the data and the computer analysis, they are usually able to speedily and accurately resolve the problem.

Companies that opt for the on-board driver's computer justify its cost in several ways. It lets them know quickly when a mechanical or operational problem occurs so they can get the truck into repair, avoiding further problems or damage to expensive parts. The time savings means more on-time deliveries, which maintains present clientele and builds future business. Actually, the safety factor alone justifies the equipment's price for many companies: the computer system is thought to help avoid accidents and dangerous roadside breakdowns.

Evolution of On-Board IT

Freightliner designers are considering expanding the use of IT in the driver's cab. They are well aware that many drivers travel with cellular phones. Moreover, companies operating large fleets of trucks often have satellite links with their trucks that they use to communicate with drivers regarding changes in routes and loading assignments. By integrating these capabilities with the on-board computer, Freightliner will be able to offer customers the capability to wirelessly transmit diagnostic information from the truck's on-board computer while the truck is still on the road to a nearby repair center, where the problem can be diagnosed. When necessary, mechanics will be able to question the driver, and then, based on their understanding of the situation, transmit appropriate instructions back to the driver to

ensure safety and avoid damage to the vehicle. The parts needed to correct the problem can even be arranged at the service station so they are ready when the driver arrives there.

Questions for Discussion

1. What benefits does the information technology in Freightliner trucks provide to the seller, the buyer, and the driver?

2. How should a company buying Freightliner trucks determine whether the cost of the on-board computer is justified in its case? What factors should it consider?

3. What other possibilities should be considered for linking Freightliner trucks with remote locations by way of wireless communications methods?

THE
PC BUYER'S
GUIDE

Over the past few years, buying a microcomputer system has emerged as the third most significant purchase most people will ever make—right behind buying a house and a car. Buying and setting up a single-user system is a thrilling and fulfilling experience—if you go about it systematically. The 10-step process that follows will help you bring a little method to the madness.

Step 1. Prepare yourself for the Information Age.

You wouldn't buy a car before you learn how to drive, and you shouldn't buy a PC before you understand its capabilities and what you can do with it. A course like the one you're taking now should help here, as would a general course or lab course geared toward microcomputer applications. If you're interested in a specific area, such as desktop publishing, look for a course that will give you a good overview.

Step 2. Determine your information and computing needs.

Take some time to think about both your current and future needs. If you think you might want to work with computer graphics or multimedia applications, check the minimum hardware requirements listed on various software packages and factor them into your research.

Think, too, about your work habits. Do plan to work in one location, or do you need the portability of a laptop or notebook computer? Will you be the only person using the computer, or will you be sharing it with others? And will you want to exchange computer files with friends and colleagues? If so, you need to be sure your systems are compatible.

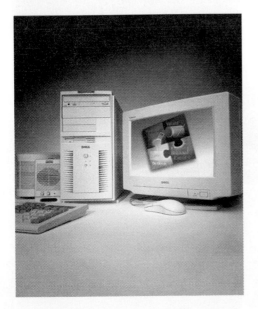

Step 3. Assess the availability and quality of software and IT services.

Determine what software and information services are available to meet your needs. Good sources of this type of information are periodicals, salespeople at computer stores, and acquaintances who have IT experience. Other good sources of information are the IT courses you take and your instructors.

Step 4. Select a platform and investigate specific software packages for that platform.

Because most software is written to run on an IBM-compatible or an Apple Macintosh platform, your choice of a platform will narrow your software options.

Once you've chosen a platform, you're ready to take a closer look at specific software packages. Software packages with essentially the same capabilities may have price differences of several hundred dollars. Some graphics software creates displays of graphs in seconds, while others take minutes. Some software packages are easy to learn; others are more difficult. This and other software-rating information can be found in product reviews and IT journals and via word-of-mouth. Considering the amount of time you will spend using software, any extra time you devote to evaluating your software options will be well spent.

Step 5. Decide how much you are willing to spend.

Microcomputer systems can cost as little as a few hundred dollars or as much as $40,000. Assess your finances and decide how much you are willing to commit to the purchase of a personal system at this time. Don't make the mistake of thinking, "I'll wait until the price goes down a little more." If you adopt this strategy, you may be able to buy a more powerful computer for less money. But what about the lost opportunity to increase your productivity? Even a moderately priced system can make you more efficient and more effective.

Step 6. Choose a microprocessor.

One measure of state-of-the-art technology is the computer's processor. Most experts recommend a 20 MHz 386SX microprocessor at minimum. But if you want to explore more challenging applications, you may need a more powerful microprocessor, such as the Intel 486 or Pentium chip (see Figure 3.9). Desktop publishing and other graphics-based applications function best with a powerful microprocessor, a large-capacity hard drive, and a high-resolution monitor.

Step 7. Compare micro configurations.

A keyboard and mouse are standard on most personal systems today. You will also want to scan advertisements and identify your needs with respect to memory capacity, secondary storage drives, monitor characteristics, and expansion slots.

Also important are warranty and service agreements. Many manufacturers offer a one-year warranty with free on-site service. *Technical support hotlines* are also common, but the service varies widely. Some companies provide users a toll-free 24-hour hotline; others charge as much as $50 per hour or limit the period of time support is available. Retailers, too, usually service what they sell, sometimes on a carry-in basis. Another option is a maintenance contract. Many shoppers forgo such contracts, though. They elect to treat their PCs like a television or car: once the repair costs exceed a certain sum, they simply shop for a replacement.

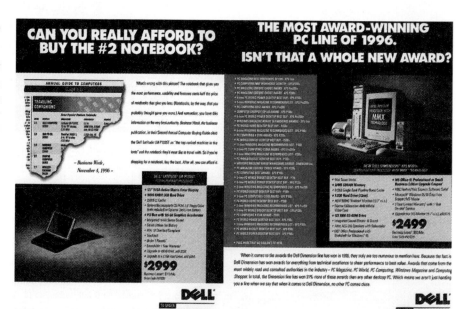

Step 8. Determine the additional peripheral devices, software, and accessories you'll need.

Your main consideration here will probably be selecting a printer, although you may also want to add other peripherals. You should also look at your software want list and budget for furniture and other accessories. If you have a spending limit, the following cost ranges are useful for first-time buyers: a printer ($200–$1,000); software ($100–$1,500); maintenance ($0–$500 a year); diskettes and tape cassettes ($50–$200); furniture ($0–$350); insurance ($0–$40); and printer ribbons or cartridges, paper, and other supplies ($40–$400).

The main challenge here is setting your priorities. If you need a high-quality laser printer, for example, you may decide to delay the purchase of a fax-modem board.

Step 9. "Test-drive" several alternatives.

Once you have selected several software and hardware alternatives, spend enough time to gain some familiarity with them. Does one keyboard have a better touch than others? Does one monitor seem sharper than others? Given the amount of time you will spend at your computer, these are important considerations. If one system seems superior in all aspects *except* for its keyboard or monitor, can you negotiate for a replacement?

Many software packages offer demonstration and/or tutorial disks, which walk you through a simulation of the key features. Salespeople at most retail stores are also happy to give you a "test drive"—just ask. Some stores will even let you bring in your own files and see how a system performs the applications that interest you.

This is a good time, too, to begin shopping for price. To get a good idea of the going prices for various hardware and software components, check the mail-order advertisements in computer magazines.

The worksheet in Figure 9.6 should help you compare configurations, prices, and your comments about the various systems you test.

Step 10. Select and purchase your system.

PCs and related hardware and software can be purchased through several channels. The most traditional are local retailers and outlets of nationwide chains, such as ComputerLand, ENTRE, and MicroAge. Another, newer channel is the computer superstore, which offers supermarket displays and steeply discounted prices. PCs are also sold in the electronics departments of most department stores and by electronics retailers.

Another alternative is the mail-order house. If you know what you want, you can call a toll-free number, give the operator a credit card number, and your system will be delivered to your doorstep.

Another source is your employer. In cooperation with vendors, companies make volume purchases of PCs at discount rates, then offer them to employees at substantial savings. Many colleges sponsor similar programs to benefit students and professors.

Once you've made your purchase, the only tasks left are to open up the boxes, follow the instructions, and start enjoying your new system.

Opportunities for Personal Technology

Capitalizing on the Power of Virtual Reality

Information technology is altering the very meaning of information. At one time in business, "information" usually meant words and numbers, possibly a few graphics—pretty dry stuff. Information technology has expanded the meaning of information in business to include sound, animated movement, and video clips. Multimedia technologies have brought these forms of information to business life.

IT has created another type of information—virtual reality (VR). VR enables people to interact with three-dimensional computer-generated environments that incorporate sight, sound, touch (and perhaps one day taste and smell). Long a staple of science fiction, virtual realizing has moved out of the realm of the imagination and into our everyday world. Medicine, education, business, and law are making use of VR. Some predict that VR will become the "ultimate computer interface," an unobtrusive way to interact with data and information. And because it lets

users share their virtual experiences, many see VR as an entirely new tool of communication.

Virtual Reality's "Unlocking" Power

The power of virtual reality unlocks previously unattainable opportunities

- **To experience.** Virtual reality experiences are more real than you can imagine if you haven't tried them.

Consider newspaper columnist Dale Dauten's first encounter with VR. Even though he knew he was walking across a solid floor, he couldn't make himself step onto a virtual plank suspended high above a virtual chasm. (Could you?) That was one experience, virtual or not, Dauten decided to forgo.

- **To explore.** A growing number of architects and structural engineers are relying on virtual reality as they design new buildings. VR enables them to electronically "walk through" an informational representation of a building, exploring and feeling room size and ceiling height, the location of doors and walls, the position of lighting fixtures, the impact of a certain color scheme. Before VR, they had to construct the building before they could *see* these things.

- **To test and visualize.** After a long illness or a period of healing following an injury, people need to test their strength before they go back to work, especially when there is a risk of reinjury if they return to the job too quickly. With a treadmill equipped with a steering device and cables that hook it into a VR system, these people can test their strength, balance, and vision, as well as the direction, speed, and distance they've "traveled."

- **To practice.** When weather prohibits getting out on the golf course, fans of the game can still get in their rounds. Through VR, they can not only practice their drives, chips, and putts but can also do so on a course of their choosing, for virtual reality can recreate the championship courses of the world. Using clubs tethered to the computer, golfers can see whether their swing on a downhill or uphill lie will get their ball on the green or cause it to hook out of bounds. After testing their virtual game, these "rainy day" golfers may long for the more forgiving feel of real grass. But then again, which "reality" is more accurate?

Virtual reality frequently involves peripheral devices. Those most commonly used are a head-mounted dis-

high-resolution video display units are also bringing VR onto the screen.

In addition to all these peripherals (and their cables), VR explorers need a powerful computer with huge amounts of secondary storage to store and manipulate an extensive database of graphical, acoustical, and tactile data at a speed that will seem "real." (If the speed is too slow, or falls in what VR experts term the *barf zone,* users will either be baffled or become nauseated.) Some VR systems can run on desktop computers equipped with powerful graphics cards, but most are built around large processors or graphics workstations. In fact, some VR systems use a network of computers to control and coordinate the various devices. One system, for example, uses two workstations to control the display unit alone—one for each eye.

Questions for Discussion

1. What VR capabilities and uses would benefit you if you were shopping in a retail clothing store or new-car showroom? What about studying in a biology classroom?

2. What disadvantages does VR offer to disabled people seeking to overcome their disabilities?

3. Do you agree that VR will become the "ultimate user interface"? Why or why not?

4. Japan's NEC Corp. has designed a prototype VR system that will let up to five people share the same virtual world, even if they are scattered around the globe. Why would a multinational corporation or research institute be interested in buying such a system? How would such a system benefit engineers, executives, or scientific researchers?

play and audio units, control devices (such as a joystick, keyboard, or mouse) tracking devices (frequently mounted inside helmets worn by users), and navigation devices (which sense movement). Improvements in

CHAPTER 10

Multiuser and Network Computing

CHAPTER OUTLINE

LEARNING OBJECTIVES

When you have completed this chapter, you should be able to

1 Identify the reasons that multiuser systems are used in business.

2 Describe eight network service applications used in business.

3 Discuss the three types of communications networks and the advantages offered by each.

4 Discuss the two types of communications channels used in networks and the ways that computers interconnect with them.

5 Explain the role of a network operating system.

6 Discuss the activities involved in network administration.

7 Explain the three types of multiuser architectures and the advantages offered by each.

Minitel: Another French Revolution

France. A country of 47 million people. The year ... 1974. For those 47 million people ... 7 million telephone lines. In the midst of the Information Age, French people had to wait four years to have a telephone line installed by the Direction Générale des Télécommunications, the government telephone directorate. Rural areas of the country were still equipped with manual switches.

France's newly elected president, Valéry Giscard d'Estaing, looked at the situation, and decided to make over-hauling the nation's weak telecommunications infrastructure a top priority. *Le téléphone pour tous* (a telephone for all) became the theme for the program that was designed to help thrust the nation into a new era of information and knowledge. Another French revolution was in the offing, this time in telecommunications.

As a result of the French government's program, 7 million new phone lines were added between 1974 and 1979. But even as one problem was being solved, another was being created: France Télécom (the new name for the government telephone directorate) could not keep its telephone directories up to date. As quickly as they were printed—twice a year—it seemed directory assistance was overloaded with calls from customers wanting to know the telephone number of friends and businesses. And with an *additional* 7 million lines to be added over the next five years, the number of telephone operators needed in 1979—4,500—was expected to double by 1984. The paper and printing costs associated with directories were sky-rocketing. There just had to be another way ... a French solution.

France Télécom, in consultation with government officials, decided the solution was to create an electronic videotex telephone directory that would be accessible to all French citizens through a computer terminal. Testing began, and by 1984, under President François Mitterand, the distribution of terminals to all those citizens who wanted one was underway. The terminals were free, courtesy of the government-run PTT.

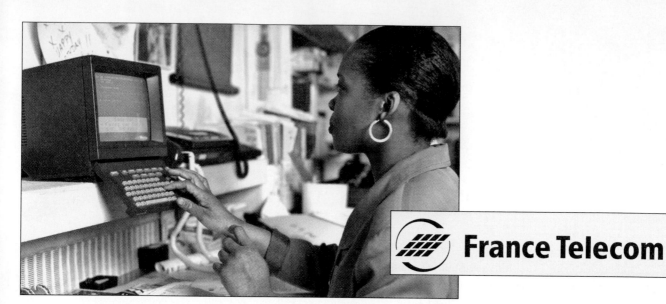

The videotex system, known as Minitel, had the capability to provide other services, including electronic advertisements and business services. Both were controversial, especially with newspaper publishers, who saw a potential loss of advertising revenue. But another capability proved universally popular: the communications capability that connected people to *electronic chat services,* as they came to be called.

Minitel steadily grew in usage, particularly with people in the age range of 25 to 49. By the mid-1990s, it was considered the most successful videotex system in the world. Today, approximately 14.2 million users benefit from some 25,000 different services provided by Minitel (more than use the well-known Prodigy and Compuserve network services), including home and grocery shopping, travel planning and ticket purchases, entertainment reservations, games, home banking—and, of course, telephone directory services. In addition, as of January 1997, there are more than 7.4 Minitel on-line terminals and modem-connected terminals in use. France Télécom and the French telephone system are considered to be world class in every respect. Indeed, France Télécom "exports" Minitel around the world, including to the rest of Europe and to North America.

France went from worst to first in telecommunications in just a few short years because the nation's leaders recognized that communications and IT are not luxuries but essentials in the Information Age.

Information technology's communications capability provides the means for overcoming two important business barriers: distance and time. Geographic distance hinders business when it prohibits firms from delivering a product or service, providing the desired level of service, monitoring activities of competitors, maintaining information flow between the organization and its employees, or having a physical presence in an area. Time barriers cause delays in meeting customer or business requirements.

A business's communications capabilities take on special importance when they are employed to overcome these barriers and gain a business benefit. Network communications add value to the firm when they are used to conduct business in ways and at locations that would be otherwise impossible (or undesirable).

Principles of Multiuser Systems

A hallmark of the Information Age is the astonishing advances in **communication,** which involves the sending and receiving of data and information over a communications network. Communications networks are the foundations of **multiuser systems,** which we defined in Chapter 2 as systems in which more than one user share hardware, programs, information, people, and procedures. IT professionals often refer to using a network as *resource sharing.* Here we take a close look at the purposes of multiuser systems and the role communications networks play in their creation and use.

The Purposes of Multiuser Systems

Business communication is relying on multiuser systems at an increasing rate. As Figure 10.1 shows, a multiuser system has three business purposes:

- To increase the productivity and effectiveness of the people using the system.
- To increase the productivity and effectiveness of the organization in which the system is used.
- To improve the services provided to those who rely on others using multiuser systems.

Note that the emphasis here is on *people.* In business, solving a problem or capitalizing on an opportunity almost always involves you with other people. Perhaps they tackle a part of the problem, carrying out actions to overcome a challenge or remove an obstacle for you. Perhaps they have access to essential information or to someone else who can provide valuable insights or assistance. Or perhaps people at field locations render extra services to your customers—services that depend on quick support from headquarters. The *Rethinking Business Practices* feature entitled "In a Tight Squeeze for a Good Fit . . . It's Levi Strauss & Co.'s Personal-Fit Jeans" describes a system in which people working in different areas of the Levi Strauss organization must coordinate their activities to be successful. This example demonstrates why effective communication among people is an essential element of business success.

communication
The sending and receiving of data over a communications network.

multiuser system
A communications system in which more than one user share hardware, programs, information, people, and procedures.

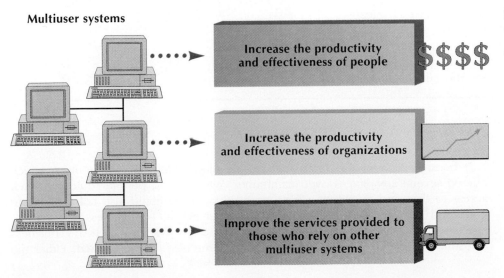

Multiuser systems

Increase the productivity and effectiveness of people

Increase the productivity and effectiveness of organizations

Improve the services provided to those who rely on other multiuser systems

FIGURE 10.1

The Purposes of Multiuser Systems in Business

RETHINKING BUSINESS PRACTICES

In a Tight Squeeze for a Good Fit . . . It's Levi Strauss & Co.'s Personal-Fit Jeans

In retailing, the worst possible conditions are too much inventory, which forces price markdowns that translate into lost revenue at the end of the selling season, and the wrong inventory, which translates into lost sales as customers go elsewhere for what they want. Every year in the U.S. apparel industry, more than $25 billion of goods either go unsold or get marked down dramatically. And there is a 30 percent chance that a store will not have the item customers want when they come in to make a purchase.

Levi Strauss's *Levi Link* has changed the way the company's dealers manage their stores. This network, which captures all sales transactions in Levi's stores for analysis at company headquarters to determine what items must be made and shipped to replenish stock, has helped ensure that Levi's popular jeans will be on the shelves in the styles and quantities demanded by customers. Capitalizing on the insight and knowledge they gained through developing and using Levi Link, Levi Strauss's managers recently launched a merchandising service that makes innovative use of information technology.

The new service, called *Levi's Personal Pair* jeans, offers personal-fit jeans at reasonable prices. Using a computer equipped with easy-to-use touch-screen software, the sales clerk at an Original Levi's® Store enters four measurements for the customer: waist,

hips, inseam, and rise. Then the customer tries on a prototype pair of jeans closest to the measurements entered into the computer. As the customer suggests where the fit should be a little different ("need the legs a little longer"; "a little tighter across the back end"; "pinch in the waist a tad more"), the sales clerk enters the adjustments into the PC. When the cus-

It became clear in the 1980s that people liked using microcomputers, which offered several advantages over mainframes. With micros, people could get quick access to data and information from their desks. They could also tailor the computer and software they used to their personal needs. Nonetheless, some managers—even some IT professionals—questioned the wisdom of heavy business investment in PCs. Microcomputers were underutilized, it was argued. Either the

ing line and be shipped to the store or directly to the customer.

The personal fit is achieved in a fraction of the time associated with the normal order/manufacturing/delivery process and without guesswork. By capitalizing on communications links and information technology to rethink its business processes in this fashion, Levi Strauss & Co. is participating in an emerging manufacturing revolution known as *mass customization*—or the customization of mass-produced goods.

tomer is satisfied that the fit will be just right, the remainder of the order details are entered, including color and prewash choices.

An ordinary telephone link enables the store to connect the PC to a Levi Strauss & Co. processing center, which routes them to a Levi Strauss processing center. Details of the order are transmitted over a phone link, which in turn routes the measurements and order information to a Levi Strauss & Co. manufacturing center, where the details are fed into a computer-driven cutting machine. As soon as the material is cut, the pieces enter the sewing and finishing portions of the manufacturing process. A special bar code on the jeans identifies the order so it can be detected when it comes off the end of the manufactur-

PC merely emulated the dumb terminal it replaced (meaning that the built-in processing capabilities of the PC went largely unused), or it was used for a limited number of activities and for just a few minutes a day.

That was then. Now, as we approach the twenty-first century, microcomputers are being used in ways undreamed of only 10 years ago. Many people work at them all day long, every day. Computers are constantly increasing in speed,

TABLE 10.1 *Trends Driving Business in the 1990s*

- A growing awareness of the **international nature of business** and the emergence of global commerce.

- A heightened awareness of the importance of **speed** in responding to the needs and desires of consumers, customers, and suppliers, regardless of their location. It is imperative today to ensure that products and services are available when needed.

- A new awareness that **business alliances**—partnerships among businesses—can be created so that all parties to the alliance benefit from mutual cooperation.

- An awareness that people have to know what is happening in other areas of their firm, not just in their own department. Instead of being concerned solely with their assigned departmental tasks, businesspeople are increasingly thinking about **cross-function business processes.** Entire business processes have been redesigned so that individuals focus on the complete set of tasks making up the process from beginning to end rather than on just the activities that fall within their work area.

- A new **emphasis on the roles of those companies with which the firm interacts,** either as customers or suppliers. Suppliers are now recognized as an integral part of a company's success or failure and the satisfaction of its customers.

storage capacity, and reliability while shrinking in size and cost. This "PC revolution" was brought about by several major trends in the business world, the most important of which are listed in Table 10.1.

Driven by the need to compete effectively in a global market, companies have dispersed their executives and other employees throughout the world, at both company facilities and customer locations. And they have turned to IT professionals for help in answering these pressing questions:

- How can we get our products to market more quickly?
- How can we more effectively share information, both internally and with other companies?

Better coordination was the answer, which meant finding ways to overcome time and distance barriers between people within organizations and between organizations themselves. Communications networks, the key elements in multiuser systems, provide those capabilities.

The Role of Communications Networks

communications network
A set of locations, or nodes, consisting of hardware, programs, and information linked together as a system that transmits and receives data and information.

node
A communication station within a network.

A **communications network** is a set of locations, or **nodes,** consisting of hardware, programs, and information that are linked together as a system that transmits and receives data and information. When a computer is connected to another computer, both are part of a network. Networks may link people across relatively short distances, or they may span wide areas. (The different types of networks are discussed in detail later in this chapter.)

It has become much easier to connect computers for multiuser activities. For this reason, communications networks are common today in both large and small organizations. These networks enable people and organizations to share and transmit important data and information, in the process overcoming the barriers created by geographic distances.

Communications networks can be used in any or all of these four roles (Table 10.2):

TABLE 10.2 *The Role of Communications Networks*

ROLE OF COMMUNICATIONS NETWORKS	NETWORK APPLICATION
• Send and receive messages or documents electronically.	Electronic mail (e-mail) Voice mail Electronic document exchange Electronic commerce Electronic funds transfer Internet/WWW Videotex
• Hold meetings involving participants who are at different locations.	Videoconferencing Work group conferencing Internet/WWW
• Share and distribute documents or information from a repository.	Electronic bulletin boards Internet/WWW
• Establish an electronic presence.	Videotex Internet/WWW

- Sending and receiving messages or documents electronically.
- Holding meetings involving participants who are at different locations.
- Sharing and distributing documents or information from a repository.
- Establishing an electronic presence.

These roles are fulfilled through *network services,* those applications that businesses can choose to provide on their communications networks.

The Internet and World Wide Web (WWW) applications, discussed in detail in Chapter 3, illustrate each of the roles of a communications network. Recall that an individual linked to the Internet—and its most frequently used feature, the World Wide Web—can send and receive documents of all types, including those containing sound, animation, video, and colorful graphics. Hence, you'll find the Internet playing a growing role in company communications. Already it is being used at a growing rate to communicate within a company (a network application known as an *intranet*) and between companies and organizations.

Network Service Applications

The applications available on a communications network are called **network services.** This section discusses the eight most frequently used network applications in business: electronic mail, voice mail, videoconferencing, work group conferencing, electronic bulletin boards, electronic funds transfer, electronic data interchange, and videotex.

network services
The applications available on a communications network.

Electronic Mail

You probably know the game of "telephone tag." You call someone, only to find that he or she is not in. So you leave a message. The person returns your call just when you have stepped out to run an errand, attend a meeting, or get a cup of coffee—and leaves a message for you. When this sequence is repeated constantly, both parties can become very frustrated.

Electronic mail, sometimes called *e-mail,* and voice mail (which we discuss in the next section) are designed to avoid telephone tag and to overcome the communication barriers created by time and distance. E-mail is a service that transports text messages from a sender to one or more receivers. It ensures that your message is delivered, not lost in a mailroom or message center. When you send a message from your computer, the network transmits it to the proper destination and inserts it into the recipient's **electronic mailbox,** an area of space on magnetic disk in the server or host computer that is allocated for storing an individual's messages.

The recipient need not be at the computer when e-mail arrives. When the intended recipient of the message returns to the computer, he or she will be alerted, often by a flashing note, that a message is waiting in the electronic mailbox. The recipient can then display the message on the screen and decide whether to print it, send a response, store it for later review, or pass it along to another individual on the network.

E-mail messages that are stored on the network can be replayed at a later date. They can also be *broadcast*—that is, sent to a number of individuals simultaneously. The sender need only type the message into the system, enter the identification names of the intended recipients, and instruct the network to send the information. The e-mail system does the rest (Figure 10.2).

electronic mailbox

An area of space on magnetic disk in a server or host computer that is allocated for storing an individual's e-mail.

FIGURE 10.2 *E-mail Network and Mailboxes*

Electronic mail sent via a network can be stored, replayed, and broadcast to other nodes on the network.

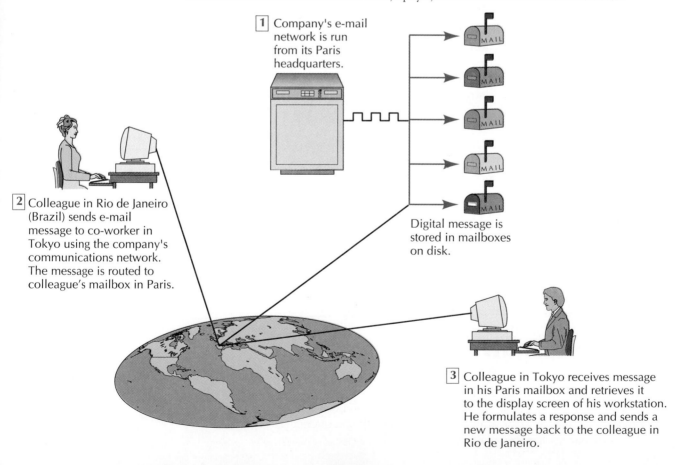

1 Company's e-mail network is run from its Paris headquarters.

Digital message is stored in mailboxes on disk.

2 Colleague in Rio de Janeiro (Brazil) sends e-mail message to co-worker in Tokyo using the company's communications network. The message is routed to colleague's mailbox in Paris.

3 Colleague in Tokyo receives message in his Paris mailbox and retrieves it to the display screen of his workstation. He formulates a response and sends a new message back to the colleague in Rio de Janeiro.

 The broadcast capability of e-mail is a feature included in the software that manages many networks. Broadcasting is not unique to communications networks, however. You are already familiar with this capability from two other communications media—radio and television. The terms *radio broadcast* and *television broadcast* mean that the same transmission (music, news, or multimedia information) is sent to all receiving nodes that are turned on at the time. E-mail has one advantage over radio and television broadcasting, though. An e-mail transmission can be sent to many different nodes simultaneously *or* it can be directed to a specific location. ▧

People can acquire e-mail capabilities in three ways: by purchasing an e-mail package, by subscribing to a public information service, and by using a university network.

- *E-mail software packages can be purchased and loaded onto a network.* Some of the packages available for the different types of networks are listed in Table 10.3. These software packages are purchased for a one-time fee. A copy is needed for each workstation that will send and receive messages.
- *E-mail capabilities are also available through commercial public data services.* For a monthly subscriber fee, plus a variable charge based on usage, you can have a mailbox established on the network. Using your identification name, others connected to the public network can send messages to you.

  The most widely used public data services offering e-mail are America Online, CompuServe, MCI Mail, Prodigy, and The Source. These services, sometimes called *information utilities,* are based in the United States but are accessible around the world.
- *Finally, university faculty and students involved in faculty support can interconnect with the university's computer network,* which, in turn, is connected to external communications networks such as the Internet (including the World Wide Web). From their desktop PCs, faculty members can exchange messages and documents with other faculty within the university and with faculty members at other institutions around the world. A growing number of businesses are also linking to the Internet to send and receive messages.

TABLE 10.3 *Widely Used E-Mail Software Packages*	
CC:Mail	A system designed to run on both Macintosh and IBM-compatible computer local area networks.
Eudora	A popular application used to interconnect desktop computers with the Internet.
Mail	A system created by Microsoft that runs on both Macintosh and IBM-compatible computers.
Pine	A shareware program, developed at the University of Washington, designed for use with the Internet.
Quick-Mail	A system created by the CE software company for Macintosh computers.
PROFS	An acronym for PRofessional OFfice Systems, an IBM software package used with host-based networks. White House staff members were among the first users of this package.
All-In-One	A system developed for Digital VAX computer systems.
VAX Notes	An alternate system developed for Digital VAX computer systems.

Andersen Consulting's e-mail system is representative of the e-mail systems used in large companies across the globe. Thousands of consultants and staff members throughout Europe, Asia, the South Pacific, and North and South America are connected to Andersen's e-mail system. A consultant needing to get in touch with someone can send an e-mail message to the person simply by typing in the individual's name or computer address and the message. The network locates the individual and transmits the message to the recipient's mailbox, where it is held until the recipient is ready to read it.

Andersen's e-mail system is used for much more than electronic conversation, however. It also drives business opportunities and new-product ideas. For example, when consultants, project managers, or members of Andersen's management team have questions about a problem they are wrestling with, they broadcast a message across the network. Say the following message is sent out: "An important Andersen customer wishes to interconnect its home office in Atlanta, Georgia, with a manufacturing site in Jakarta, Indonesia, but has not worked with any communications carriers servicing that region. What experience have Andersen partners and staff members had with any carriers providing service in the area, good or bad? What advice do you have about approaching the carriers?" In a few hours, the individual who transmitted the message will probably have a wide variety of detailed responses to the inquiry in his or her electronic mailbox—responses that will help the customer get accurate and timely advice from Andersen on how to capitalize on an important business opportunity. Moreover, the electronic conversation can continue between selected team members as additional questions are posed or more complex problems arise.

Voice Mail

voice mail
A system that captures, stores, and transmits spoken messages using an ordinary telephone connected to a computer network.

Messages created in *text* form are sent through a network via e-mail. But businesses also use **voice mail** systems, which capture, store, and transmit *spoken* messages. Voice mail systems use an ordinary telephone connected to a computer network. A sender enters a message by speaking into the telephone, and this message is transformed from analog to digital form (digitized) and then stored in the recipient's voice mailbox (Figure 10.3). Later, the recipient can use a phone to dial into the system and retrieve the stored message, which is reconverted to analog signals and played back over the telephone. As with e-mail, voice messages can be broadcast to others on the network, stored on the network, or replayed.

Voice mail systems are available worldwide, some from computer vendors, others from providers of telephone equipment, and still others from telephone companies or PTTs (Post, Telephone, and Telegraph companies—a general term for telephone companies outside the United States). Many of these systems run on a local or wide area network. But some organizations keep their voice mail system separate from their computer networks.

While voice mail is quite popular, some people are reluctant to use its capabilities because they do not like talking to a computer or a recording. Others find the process of retrieving or replaying messages too cumbersome. IT professionals will need to address these concerns if voice mail is to continue to expand.

Amway Corporation is known around the world for its global network of successful independent distributors. Staff members at its Ada, Michigan, headquarters strive not only to ensure that distributors have a vast array of high-quality, properly priced products, ranging from sporting goods to food to personal grooming products, but also to help them use information technology effectively. Among the most important tools is the AMVOX, a powerful network voice-messaging sys-

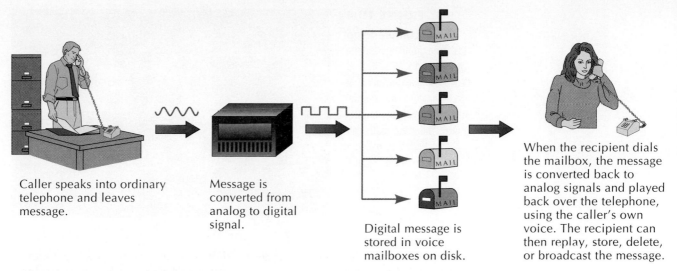

Caller speaks into ordinary telephone and leaves message.

Message is converted from analog to digital signal.

Digital message is stored in voice mailboxes on disk.

When the recipient dials the mailbox, the message is converted back to analog signals and played back over the telephone, using the caller's own voice. The recipient can then replay, store, delete, or broadcast the message.

FIGURE 10.3 *How Voice Mail Works*

tem. AMVOX provides all the expected features of voice mail, including the capability to make, receive, and answer voice messages and to give them to callers. In addition, it offers the following features:

- *Information updates.* Provides callers with messages about products, services, and important news and events.
- *Pager.* Alerts people about incoming messages by having the voice mail system automatically dial the telephone number of the distributor's personal pager.
- *Rebroadcasts.* Sends incoming messages to other mailboxes on the network.

Distributors often use AMVOX to send, as well as receive, messages. For instance, one distributor, responsible for 60 other representatives in a region spanning several states, keeps in touch with her salesforce regularly to give them pricing updates, product information, and meeting news. With AMVOX, she can send a message to one representative only, or she can send the same message to all of them by using a single distribution list. She can even mark a message "Urgent" so that it is the first one received and listened to by her sales representatives. The AMVOX voice mail system is making her more successful as it helps make her representatives more successful.

Videoconferencing

Audio and visual communications come together in **videoconferencing,** a type of conferencing in which video cameras and microphones capture sight and sound for transmission over a communications network (Figure 10.4). Videoconferencing makes it possible to conduct meetings with the full participation of group members who are hundreds, even thousands, of miles apart physically. People interconnected this way see one another "live" on large display screens.

Videoconferencing is more than a two-way audio and video system, though. Because computers can be linked to the videoconferencing network, documents and images stored on magnetic or optical devices are accessible to conference participants. Information retrieved from a central database or entered into a computer linked to the network can be transmitted to all conference locations simultaneously. And the parties to the videoconference do not have to use computers or terminals to participate in discussions. Rather, they can express their

videoconferencing
A type of conferencing in which video cameras and microphones capture the sight and sound of participants for transmission over a network.

FIGURE 10.4

Videoconferencing

Pediatric cardiologists at the University of Kansas Medical Center use videoconferencing equipment to monitor the heartbeat of a patient 300 miles away. The screen on the left shows the patient's electrocardiogram.

ideas verbally, with microphones capturing their comments and passing them to the network for transmission.

Air Products Europe, headquartered outside London, frequently conducts video-conferences with its home office in Allentown, Pennsylvania. A videoconference facility at each site uses satellite communications to put executives and managers separated by the Atlantic Ocean in touch with one another. The facilities, which cost less than $100,000 each, have not only eliminated many time-consuming cross-ocean trips but have also increased communication and information sharing among key executives. Air Products Europe's executives say they can no longer imagine running their business without videoconferencing.

Kmart, the large U.S. discount retailer with more than 2,300 stores nationwide, operates a videoconferencing system linking its store managers to its headquarters in Troy, Michigan. The company regularly broadcasts live satellite transmissions from Troy to all of its stores. Interactive presentations by senior executives enable store managers out in the field to pose questions by telephone and hear immediate responses over the network.

Work Group Conferencing

work group conferencing

A type of conferencing that uses a software package called groupware to interconnect participants' computers at their various locations. Participants interact through a microcomputer directly linked to a server and their comments are broadcast to all others taking part in the conference.

Work group conferencing uses a type of software package called *groupware* to organize an electronic meeting in which participants' computers are interconnected from their various locations. The participants may be in the same room, linked by a local area network, or geographically dispersed and interconnected over a wide area network. The electronic conference centers around the entry of ideas, comments, suggestions, and the retrieval and display of information. Typically, each participant interacts through a microcomputer directly linked to a computer acting as a server (servers are discussed later in this chapter). The individual's typed comments are then broadcast to all other participants in the conference and stored for later analysis (Figure 10.5).

Work group systems are ideal for bringing far-flung individuals together via the network to tackle a problem. The group gets the benefit of shared thinking and distribution of information without the costs and time involved in travel.

Groupware and videoconferencing capabilities will likely be merged into a single service in the not-too-distant future. Experts expect this type of conferencing to retain the name *groupware* or *group support systems*. (Group support systems are discussed in depth in Chapter 13. The benefits of one specific groupware package, Lotus Notes, are described in the Photo Essay at the end of this chapter.)

C R I T I C A L   C O N N E C T I O N   1

Mellon

Mellon Bank—Where Customers Can See and Talk with Experts Miles Away

Mellon Bank Corp., of Pittsburgh, adopted desktop videoconferencing several years ago to link its officers and staff members, thereby reducing the need for these two groups to travel back and forth between bank offices. This innovative capability has had some unexpected payoffs. Besides saving on travel costs, videoconferencing has allowed more of Mellon's employees to participate in key meetings, improved their decision making, and reduced the time it takes the bank to develop new products.

Mellon's internal success with videoconferencing led the bank to think of ways to use videoconferencing for the direct benefit of its customers. A new banking program enables Mellon customers at retail bank sites in four states to use a PC to link up with a banking expert for a two-way videoconference. By clicking on the PC screen with a mouse, customers gain video access to a banking expert prepared to advise them on loans, investments, insurance, mortgages, and private and business banking services. Since the videolink is two-way, each party to the exchange can observe the other's actions and facial expressions—which makes the conference more satisfying than a telephone call would be.

Mellon believes videoconferencing will not only improve its service but will help sell its services and gain it new customers as well.

Electronic Bulletin Boards

Electronic bulletin boards have come into widespread use along with desktop computers. The electronic version of a bulletin board is similar to the bulletin board at the supermarket where you post or read messages and announcements. To use an electronic bulletin board, you simply dial into the board over a communications link and leave a message, a file, or a program. Others dialing into the bulletin board can retrieve the information and copy it into their system.

Creating a bulletin board requires only four things: a computer, a telephone line, a bulletin board program, and a telephone modem. Callers can dial the telephone number of the bulletin board and interconnect with it through the modem. The bulletin board program monitors who is calling, connects the caller, inserts or copies information, and disconnects the caller at the end of the session. Many bulletin board programs also provide password screening to ensure that only approved individuals can gain access to the files and databases maintained within the system.

Electronic bulletin boards are commonly used to share information among members of clubs and organizations (Figure 10.6). However, many companies are finding them to be an excellent vehicle for distributing product and service information to actual or potential customers. Best of all, the cost of creating a bulletin board is low: good software is available at usually well under $100.

Before software giant Microsoft marketed its new-generation operating system for IBM-compatible computers, dubbed Windows 95 (a replacement for the

electronic bulletin board
A network service application that allows messages and announcements to be posted and read. It is accessed by dialing a telephone number and interconnecting with the bulletin board through a modem.

FIGURE 10.5
Work Group Conferencing
Team members and people from different functional areas of Seattle's Boeing Computer Services use groupware frequently to exchange ideas and discuss challenges. Meetings are generally conducted by a moderator, who stands at the front and center of the conference room.

combination of DOS and Windows), it tested the software for several years to ensure that both its features and its performance would be suitable for the intended users. Since changes were made continually throughout the months prior to the release of Windows 95 for public sale, Microsoft needed a quick and efficient way to keep software testers around the world informed as well as a way to distribute program changes.

Microsoft found this way in a private computer bulletin board it established on the CompuServe network. Testers dialing into CompuServe with the proper identification information could peruse any of the following messaging sections and libraries about the new system:

Messaging Sections

- Forum News—announcements and news posted by Microsoft.
- Open Discussion—technical support from Microsoft support engineers and peer-to-peer interaction among tester sites, regardless of international location.

Libraries

- Upload Bug Reports—tester submission of problem reports to Microsoft.
- Software Changes—updates and files posted by Microsoft that testers could download to their computers.

The beneficial freewheeling exchange of information and software that went on throughout the extensive testing period for the PC new software generation would not have been possible without this network application.

FIGURE 10.6
Electronic Bulletin Boards
Electronic bulletin boards are often used to share information among members of a community, club, or organization. Many companies also use them to facilitate communication among their employees and to distribute product and service information to their customers.

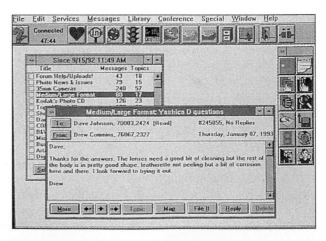

Electronic Funds Transfer

Within the world's banking community, information is transferred much more often than money is. Seldom do actual coins and paper currency move. But *information about money transfers* moves all the time—often instantaneously.

Electronic funds transfer (EFT) is the movement of money over a network. In banking, a clearinghouse accepts transfer transactions and settles accounts for both the sending bank and the receiving bank. The automated teller machines we discussed in Chapter 4 also make use of EFT.

EFT settles credit card transactions by transferring funds between the seller and the issuer of the credit card. It is also used to deposit payroll checks and government support checks directly into an individual's bank account. It is certain that there will be even less movement of actual cash in the future as more and more information about funds is transferred electronically.

The electronic movement of money (or, rather, information about money) depends on communications networks. Of particular importance here are networks of automated teller machines (ATMs), which provide customers with access to their money around the clock at thousands of locations away from the bank itself. An international automated teller network called the PLUS ATM network enables cardholders to obtain cash almost anytime and anywhere by using their credit or deposit access (i.e., debit) cards on any ATM machine.

Say you're getting ready for an evening out with friends: dinner and a bit of late-night entertainment. A quick look at your wallet tells you that you need more cash to make it through the evening. No problem. You simply stop by an ATM on your way to dinner. These machines seem to be everywhere today—made possible by reliable and efficient communications networks. When you stop at the ATM of your choosing, you insert your plastic credit or debit card (they're becoming virtually indistinguishable), enter your identification information, and specify the amount of money you want. The cash and a receipt of the transaction are dispensed immediately. And behind the machine, the details of the transaction are routed over an invisible communications network of processors back to your bank, where they are stored on magnetic disk and your account is adjusted to reflect the transaction. The ATM you used probably did not belong to the bank, but rather was part of a large network, such as the PLUS or CIRRUS networks, which offer similar services and capabilities.

The PLUS network is large. Some 250,000 PLUS ATMs are scattered through nearly 100 countries and territories of the world. More than 500 million cards can access the PLUS worldwide network.

A single connection to the PLUS network (Figure 10.7) allows the network's customers, which include banks and a vast array of merchants, to use their ATMs to service their customers. PLUS can capture Visa, Discover, American Express, Diners Club, the Armed Forces Financial Network, CIRRUS, and MasterCard transactions in the United States, plus a wide assortment of credit and debit cards from around the world.

For the individual consumer, PLUS provides convenience in the form of ready access to money anytime. For the banks and merchants who use the system, PLUS provides services that help them satisfy their customers. In addition, they get on-line processing and settlement of sales and credit transactions, along with management and statistical reporting, from PLUS.

All parties benefit from the rapid transfer of funds through such networks. Their usage around the world continues to grow (Figure 10.8).

electronic funds transfer (EFT)
The movement of money over a network.

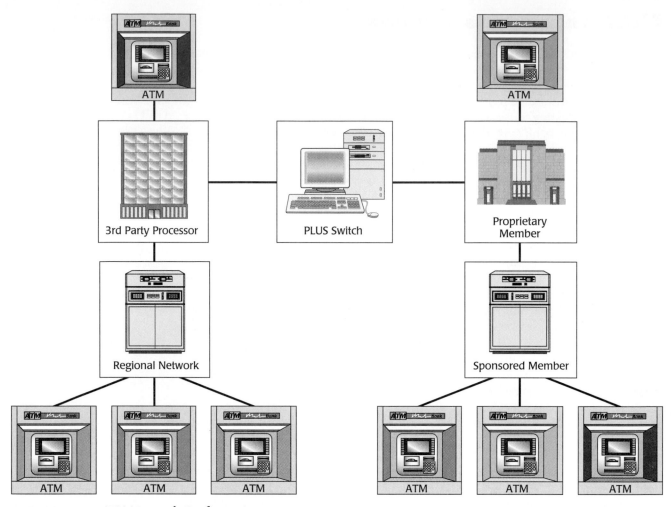

FIGURE 10.7   *ATM Network Configuration*

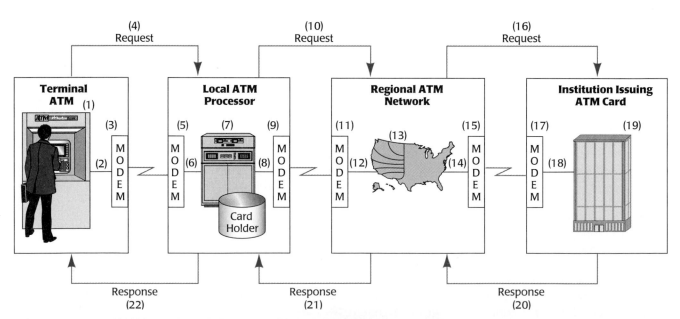

FIGURE 10.8   *ATM Networks Link Regional, National, and International Banks*

Debit cards, an alternative to the familiar credit cards, were designed to eliminate the need for people to carry money. When making a purchase, the cardholder inserts her debit card into an electronic reader (Figure 10.9) and keys in her personal authorization number, thereby directing her bank to transfer from her account to that of the merchant funds equal to the amount of purchase. In effect, she is sending a message to her bank indicating that she's just taken out a short-term loan against her line of credit. The transfer, which occurs immediately, is an information exchange: a message is sent over the network interconnecting the debit card reader, the cardholder's bank, and the merchant's bank telling each bank to change the information describing the amount of money in each account.

FIGURE 10.9
Debit Card and Reader
Use of a debit card in a retail store triggers the exchange of messages about money between the banks of the retailer and the cardholder.

Don't be surprised to see people using cash even less frequently in the future. Although the well-established credit card already substitutes for cash in many instances, and debit cards will become more and more common, another alternative is in the offing: *digital cash*. Every year, more than $1.8 trillion is spent worldwide on purchases of $10 or less. Many of these transactions involve a face-to-face exchange of coins and paper money. Digital cash is emerging as an alternative for those who neither want to pay by credit nor draw small amounts of money out of their account through debit cards. Here's how it works: You buy a card that contains a predetermined digitally recorded value. Then each time you purchase something, you pay for it by having the amount deducted from the balance on your cash card.

Digital cash began in the form of public telephone and transit cards, which are widely used in many European cities. For example, each time you make a phone call, you insert the cash card into the appropriate slot on the public telephone. At the end of the call, the digital reader inside the telephone deducts the cost of the telephone call from the balance on your card and writes a new balance—digitally, of course. Digital cash . . . it's on the way. ■

Electronic Data Interchange

E-mail is the transmission of text messages. **Electronic data interchange (EDI),** in contrast, is a form of electronic communication that allows trading partners to exchange business transaction data in structured formats that can be processed by applications software. In industries from transportation (railroad and trucking) to automobile manufacturing to retailing, companies are using EDI to reduce the time needed to transfer business information and to obtain products and services. Approximately one-third of all business documents, including purchase orders, invoices, and payments, are moved by EDI (Figure 10.10).

EDI often uses value-added carriers that provide communications services designed specifically for EDI. Translation software interacts with the computer to transform data from the format stored in a company's database into a form that can be transmitted. *Translation software* on the other end changes the received information into the form required by the receiving company.

In the pharmaceutical industry, California-based Bergen Brunswig Corp. (Figure 10.11) has launched its EDI-based Electronic Partnership Program to strengthen its links with its suppliers. The purchase orders and subsequent invoices and payments that Bergen Brunswig interchanges with its vendors account for nearly all of the merchandise distributed by the company. The

electronic data interchange (EDI)
A form of electronic communication that allows trading partners to exchange business transaction data in structured formats that can be processed by applications software.

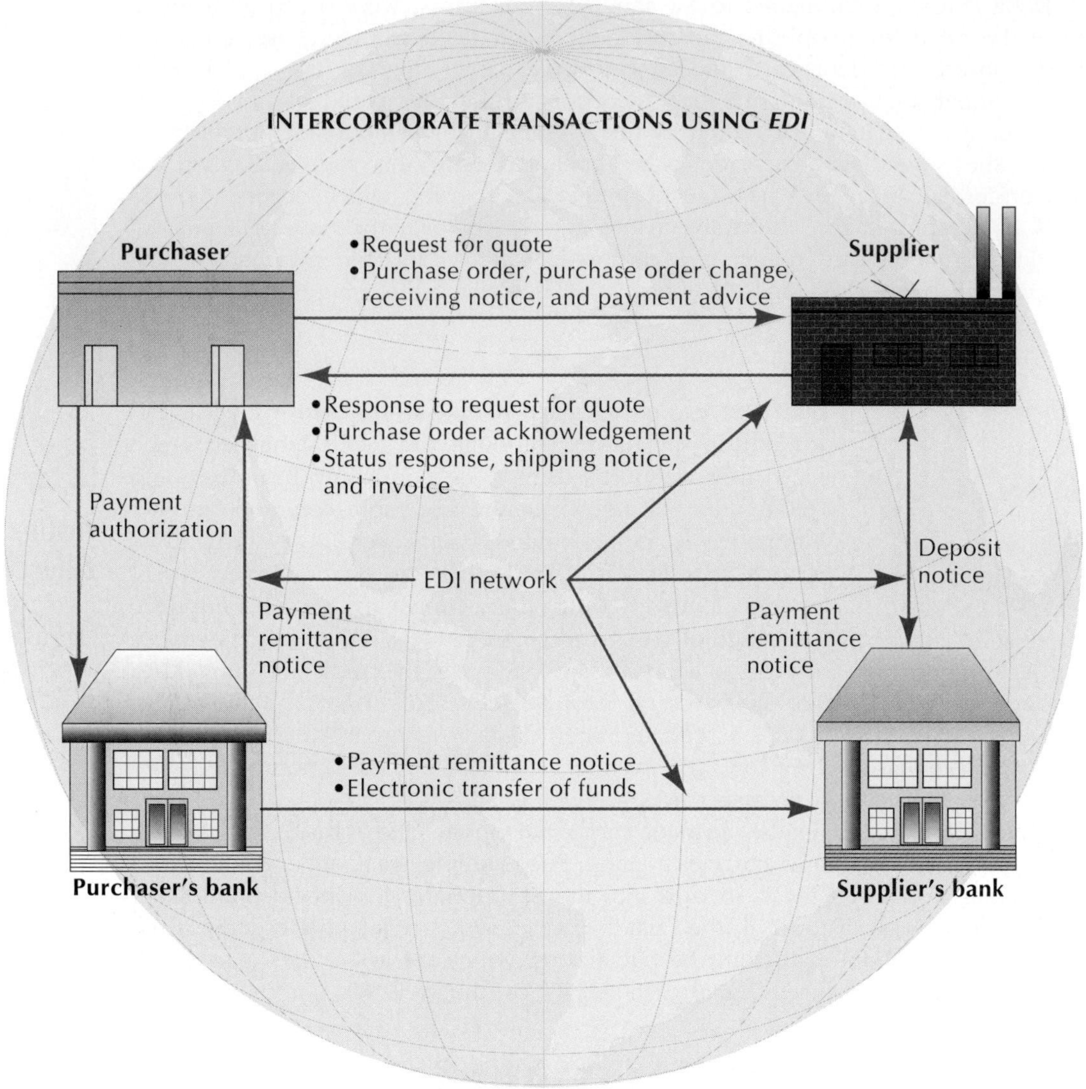

FIGURE 10.10   *Electronic Data Interchange (EDI)*
EDI greatly simplifies business transactions by allowing trading partners to exchange data in structured format.

company's business goal of dealing electronically with 100 percent of its suppliers is based on its desire to develop more accurate and timely ordering practices that will reduce inventory levels and improve cash management. In an industry in which the average after-tax profit is less than 1.5 percent, electronic opportunities can mean the difference between a profit and a loss. The time needed to process orders also diminishes when EDI is used: drug wholesalers using EDI have reduced the order/delivery cycle by over 50 percent.

The role of EDI is rapidly increasing in international commerce. Two obstacles dramatically affect the more than $2 trillion of international trade that takes place annually: the enormous flow of paperwork and delays in the transit of goods and information. Many firms dedicate sizable staffs to tracking orders, payments, or shipping papers, working against diverse time zones and business customs. Some estimates suggest that the flow of paperwork in international trade creates costs equal to 7 percent of the value of the product traded. In this area, then, the benefits of EDI can be enormous. When shippers, transporters, customs agents, and customers send documents electronically, they overcome the barriers posed by geographic distance—barriers that cost valuable time. Because EDI makes such a difference in international trade, some companies have told their suppliers to "link up or lose out"—that is, implement EDI or lose them as a customer.

Videotex

British Telecom gave birth to **videotex** in the early 1970s when it developed a two-way, interactive, text-only service operating on mainframe computers. The system quickly evolved to include two essential features:

- An easy-to-use interface that allows people to select options through successive menus providing choices and English-like commands.
- Medium-resolution graphics that present product and service information visually. On videotex, information is displayed one page at a time. People using videotex systems can both review and respond to information displayed on their computer or terminal.

The vignette that opened this chapter is an impressive example of one country's determination to create an effective infostructure that enables people to acquire a vast array of information and services through an easy-to-use network terminal. France's Minitel is just one example of the capabilities of videotex. This interactive system can be used to provide a variety of business services:

- Sony Corp. created a sales support videotex system that allows personnel to place orders, fill out expense accounts, and receive messages. Sales agents respond to information displayed on the screen by filling in an electronic form also on-screen or answering inquiries with short statements.
- The Motor Vehicle Department of British Columbia (Canada) uses videotex to test driver's license applicants. Multiple-choice questions regarding driving laws and practices are presented on the videotex screen at the testing center. As applicants respond to each question, the system checks their responses against the correct answers stored on the host computer. Would-be drivers must pass the videotex portion of the exam before they can proceed with a road test.
- In the 1980s, the Buick Motor Division of General Motors created a database of more than 2,000 videotex pages describing automobile specification and design options. Interacting through a computer terminal, a salesperson and customer can together select different options and determine the price and availability of the vehicle. The initial success of this Electronic Product Information Center (EPIC) led to an advanced version that allows people to see the automobile with chosen color, trim, and options displayed on the screen. When sales staff and customers are not using EPIC, the system automatically displays a series of videotex advertising pages.

Videotex is quickly growing into a data communications network for home shopping. Customers peruse video display catalogs of merchandise, complete with price and product specifications. If they wish to buy something, they enter their

videotex
A two-way, interactive, text-only service operating on mainframe computers that combines a video screen with easy-to-follow instructions.

FIGURE 10.11
Bergen Brunswig
Many firms dedicate sizable staffs to tracking orders, payments, or shipping papers, working against diverse time zones and business customs.

order and payment information directly into the videotex system, and the payment funds are transferred automatically from their bank account to the vendor. Today, cable television companies are providing most of the videotex shopping services available. It is likely that you will see these services in most airports, shopping malls, and sports arenas of the future.

The eight network application services discussed here are providing businesses and the people they serve with an effective means for overcoming time and distance barriers. In many cases, the network is the system, for it not only connects sites, but also directs the movement of information, routing it from one location to another. Without the network, there could not be a system for collaboration, exchanging messages, or moving other types of data and information.

But what exactly is a communications network and how do PCs, ATMs, and other devices work with a network? Just how do they interconnect devices and people across the hall or around the world? The next section examines these questions.

Types of Networks

topology
A network configuration, or the arrangement of the nodes or workstations of a network in relation to one another.

Networks come in three configurations, or **topologies,** as Figure 10.12 shows. The type of connection and the span of the network define the three types of networks: wide area, local area, and metropolitan area.

Wide Area Networks

wide area network (WAN)
A network that connects sites dispersed across states, countries, or continents.

When companies and governments must interconnect sites dispersed across states, countries, or continents, they develop **wide area networks (WANs).** The following companies make use of wide area networks:

- London-based British Petroleum runs a worldwide WAN linking its data centers in order to provide information about oil and exploration, energy distribution, and chemical research and development to employees around the globe (Figure 10.13). The network links hundreds of company sites in North and South America, Europe, and Asia. The company's main data center in Glasgow, Scotland, is linked by communications channels to major business centers in Aberdeen, Glasgow, London, and Stavanger (Norway); U.S. hubs in Houston, Cleveland, and Anchorage; and South American hubs in Caracas (Venezuela) and Bogotá (Colombia). Business centers in Moscow and Jakarta (Indonesia) can also communicate with the main data center in Glasgow through the firm's wide area network. The network is designed to enable individuals at any location to operate as if they were at the host computer site.
- Toys 'R' Us operates a WAN that links more than 750 U.S. Toys 'R' Us and Kids 'R' Us retail stores, as well as 170 other locations in Europe and Asia. The system is designed to allow 30,000 employees to share inventory and sales information and to send messages to one another via electronic mail. This multilevel network interconnects each store to one of 19 regional centers located around the world. Information is then routed from the center to company headquarters in Paramus, New Jersey. Toys 'R' Us is also building a special network that will eventually allow the direct broadcast of information to each store via satellite.
- Levi Strauss, the San Francisco–based clothing manufacturer and retailer, has a PC-based cash register in each of its stores. As discussed earlier in this chapter, a network known as Levi Link captures all sales transactions, and at the

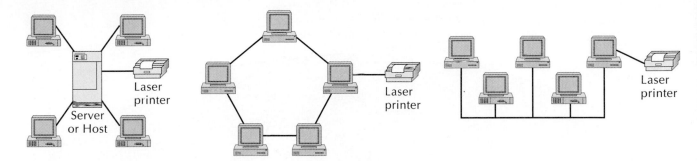

The *star topology* interconnects many different sites through a central computer system (a server). The central computer is typically a mainframe. Nodes may be other mainframes, midrange systems, or microcomputers. Sending a message from one node to another entails sending the message to the central server or host computer first, which receives and retransmits the message to the intended destination.

In the *ring topology,* each node is connected to an adjacent node. There is no central node. A message is sent from one node through the network. Each location examines the identification code in the message (which is inserted by network software) and accepts the message if it has the code. Otherwise, it transmits the message to the next node. The process continues until the message reaches its destination.

The *bus topology* is a linear network— a "data highway," so to speak. All nodes tap onto the bus. Data transmissions from one node are sent to every other node on the network. Each node examines the identification code, accepting those messages containing its code and ignoring the others.

FIGURE 10.12 *The Topology of Networks*

The topology of a network is its shape—the arrangement of the nodes or workstations of a network in relation to one another. In determining which structure to use, network designers consider the distance between nodes, the frequency and volume of transmissions, and processing capability at each node.

end of the day, it sends details of these sales to a computer at headquarters. There the information is analyzed to determine what has been sold, which items must be shipped to replenish inventory at the store, and what goods need to be manufactured. Levi Link helps to keep the stores fully stocked, thus giving them a sales advantage over competitors that use manual inventory methods.

In all of these examples, information must travel over distances that are far too long to be spanned by a single cable linking one location to another. For this reason, *teleprocessing* is frequently used in wide area networks. The telephone lines used to link different sites to a central computer are generally not owned by the company, but rather are leased from a telephone or communications company. In many other parts of the world, the telephone company is called the **Post, Telephone, and Telegraph,** or **PTT,** so this has become the general term used for all telephone companies outside the United States. We discuss another type of transmission link for wide area networks in the section on communications channels that comes later in this chapter.

A company furnishing public communications facilities for voice and data transmission is called a **common carrier.** The most visible common carriers in the United States are AT&T (the largest), MCI, and U.S. Sprint. Common carriers in the United Kingdom include BT (British Telecom) and Mercury Communications. France has France Télécom, Germany has Bundespost, and Japan has Nippon Telephone and Telegraph.

Post, Telephone, and Telegraph (PTT)
A general term used for the government-controlled telephone company in a country other than the United States.

common carrier
A company that furnishes public communications facilities for voice and data transmission.

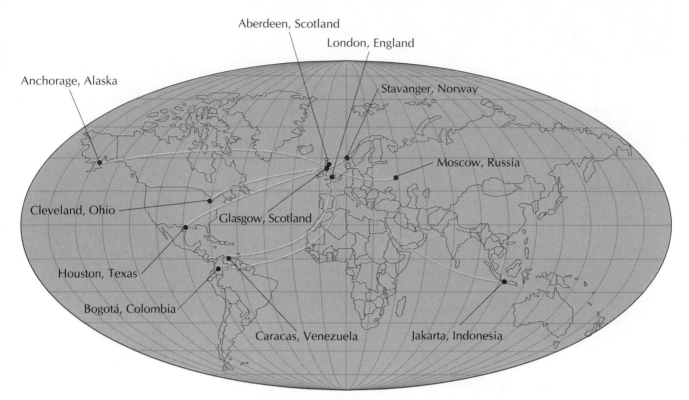

FIGURE 10.13 *British Petroleum's Global Wide Area Network*
London-based British Petroleum runs a worldwide WAN linking its data centers and providing information to employees around the globe. The network links hundreds of sites in North and South America, Europe, and Asia to the company's main data center in Glasgow, Scotland.

BANDWIDTH. The speed at which information is transmitted over a communications medium is determined by *bandwidth*. A greater bandwidth means that more information is sent through a medium in a given amount of time. The bandwidth of a network is measured (indirectly) by the bits of data transmitted per second:

- **Kilobits per second (Kbps)**—thousands of bits of information per second.
- **Megabits per second (Mbps)**—millions of bits per second.
- **Gigabits per second (Gbps)**—billions of bits per second.

Hence, a transmission at 2,400 bits per second, a common speed for transmitting data from a terminal to a mainframe over a wide area network, is said to be at 2.4 kilobits per second.

Corporations often develop high-speed WANs that transmit over networks using a **T-carrier,** a very-high-speed channel designed for use as the backbone of a network and for point-to-point connection of locations. A *backbone* is a high-speed transmission link that interconnects lower-speed networks or computers at different sites. Transmission rates for U.S. T-carriers are as follows: T-1 lines at 1.544 megabits per second; T-2 at 6.312 megabits per second; T-3 at 44.736 megabits per second; and T-4 lines at 274.176 megabits per second. Outside of the United States and Japan, T-carriers are known as *PCM carriers.*

T-carrier
A very-high-speed channel designed for use as the backbone of a network and for point-to-point connection of locations.

To put bandwidth in perspective, consider the following examples. A standard page of typed correspondence contains approximately 275 words—about 2,000 bytes or 16,000 bits (recall that a byte equals 8 bits) of information, including punctuation, spaces, and blank lines. Transmitting one page of correspondence over a standard modem takes approximately 6 seconds. Sending the page of correspondence at the faster voice transmission rate of 50 Kbps takes .28 seconds. Using a high-speed network transmitting at, say, 1.544 Mbps, would shorten transmittal time to 1/100 of a second.

Suppose you wanted to transmit 600 pages of this book over a wide area network. Assuming that each page contains 3,000 bytes (24,000 bits) of information, it would require

- At 2,400 Bps—7,000 seconds (116 minutes, or approximately 2 hours).
- At 56,000 Bps—300 seconds (5 minutes).
- At 1.544 Mbps—10.8 seconds. ■

Local Area Networks

Local area networks (LANs) interconnect computers and communications devices (printers, fax machines, and storage devices) within an office, series of offices in a building, or campus of buildings (Figure 10.14). They typically span a distance of a few hundred feet up to several miles. The network components (the LAN's nodes), including the cable linking the devices, are generally owned by the company using the network.

You would not expect to find mainframes on a LAN. LANs generally comprise desktop computers and the printers designed to work with them. A desktop computer connected to a network is usually called a **workstation** (alternatively, it may be called a *node* or a **client**). The computer that hosts the network and provides the resources that are shared on the network is called the **server.** The server provides services to each of the workstations attached to it. When workstations access a server, they can use ("execute") the software residing on the server or process data in a file or database on the server.

The server typically has more primary memory and storage capacity and a higher processing speed than the other computers on the network. Some networks have multiple servers, either to provide a backup in case one is not working or to distribute databases more quickly for faster access to information.

A **file server** is a computer containing files available to all users connected to a LAN. In some LANs, a microcomputer is designated as the file server. In others, a computer with a large disk drive and specialized software acts as the file server. We will examine client/server computing in detail in Chapter 11.

LAN transmission speeds generally range from 1 to over 100 megabits per second. This speed will increase as new transmission technologies are developed.

Metropolitan Area Networks

Metropolitan area networks (MANs), which have evolved from LAN designs, transmit data and information over longer distances than LANs can (approximately 30 miles, or 50 kilometers) and may do so at greater speeds (up to 200 megabits per second). Moreover, MANs are often designed to carry more diverse forms of

local area network (LAN)

A network that interconnects computers and communications devices within an office or series of offices; typically spans a distance of a few hundred feet to several miles.

workstation/client

A desktop computer connected to a network.

server

A computer that hosts a network and provides the resources that are shared on the network.

file server

A computer containing files available to users interconnected on a LAN.

metropolitan area network (MAN)

A network that transmits data and information over citywide distances and at greater speeds than a LAN.

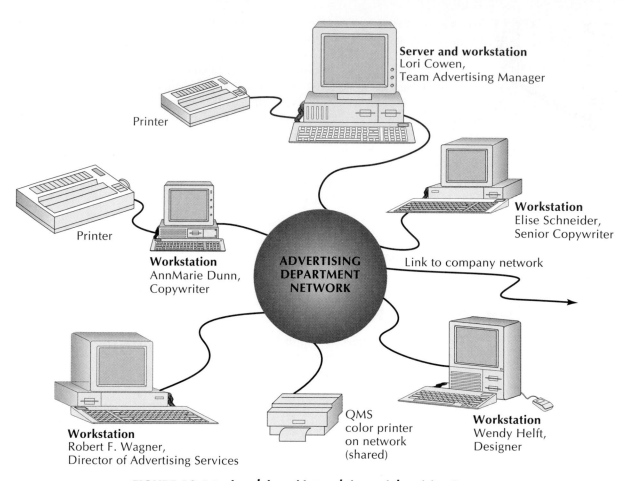

FIGURE 10.14 *Local Area Network in an Advertising Department*

information than LANs are, including combinations of voice, data, image, and video. MANs are usually optimized for voice and data transmission. Western Union's MAN in Atlanta is shown in Figure 10.15.

MANs do not operate over telephone lines. Rather, to obtain the combination of high-speed performance and citywide transmission (hence the name *metropolitan* area network), fiber-optic cables are generally used as the transmission medium. SONET (synchronous optical networking standard) is a high-speed (45 megabits per second to 1.5 gigabits per second) network specification using fiber-optic channels. It is often used to obtain both the high-speed performance and the multimedia transmission capabilities that people want in metropolitan networks.

With research support from the University of Western Australia, Telecom Australia, headquartered in Sydney, has developed a metropolitan area network service that it is installing in selected cities in the South Pacific and Europe. Companies can subscribe to the service to augment their other networking capabilities. For example, Novo Dordisk AS, a multinational pharmaceutical supplier, uses Telecom Australia's MAN to provide high-speed interconnection of its existing scientific and administrative networks. The MAN delivers faster performance times than the other alternatives available.

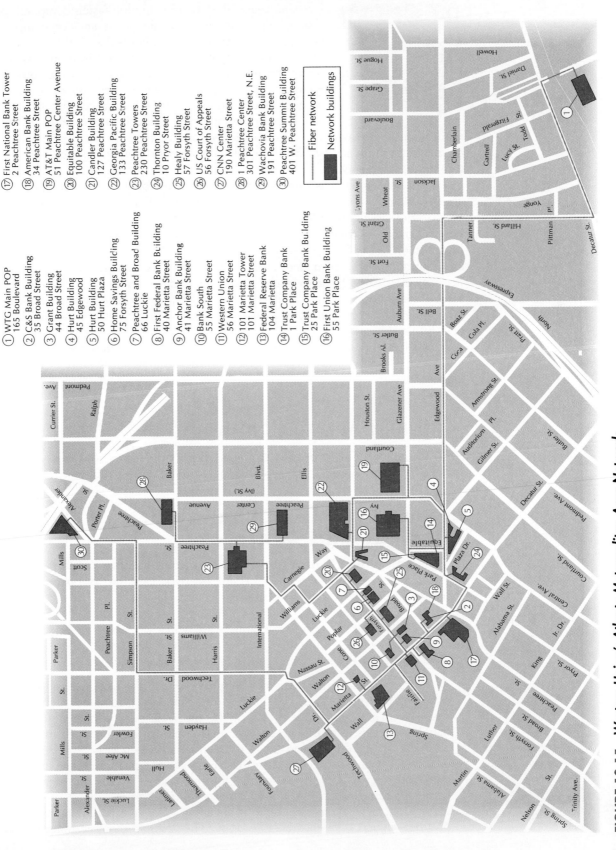

NETWORK LOCATIONS

1. WTG Main POP
   165 Boulevard
2. C&S Bank Building
   35 Broad Street
3. Grant Building
   44 Broad Street
4. Hurt Building
   45 Edgewood
5. Hurt Building
   50 Hurt Plaza
6. Home Savings Building
   75 Forsyth Street
7. Peachtree and Broad Building
   66 Luckie
8. First Federal Bank Building
   40 Marietta Street
9. Anchor Bank Building
   41 Marietta Street
10. Bank South
    55 Marietta Street
11. Western Union
    56 Marietta Street
12. 101 Marietta Tower
    101 Marietta Street
13. Federal Reserve Bank
    104 Marietta
14. Trust Company Bank
    1 Park Place
15. Trust Company Bank Building
    25 Park Place
16. First Union Bank Building
    55 Park Place
17. First National Bank Tower
    2 Peachtree Street
18. American Bank Building
    34 Peachtree Street
19. AT&T Main POP
    51 Peachtree Center Avenue
20. Equitable Building
    100 Peachtree Street
21. Candler Building
    127 Peachtree Street
22. Georgia Pacific Building
    133 Peachtree Street
23. Peachtree Towers
    230 Peachtree Street
24. Thornton Building
    10 Pryor Street
25. Healy Building
    57 Forsyth Street
26. US Court of Appeals
    56 Forsyth Street
27. CNN Center
    190 Marietta Street
28. 1 Peachtree Center, N.E.
    301 Peachtree Street
29. Wachovia Bank Building
    191 Peachtree Street
30. Peachtree Summit Building
    401 W. Peachtree Street

Fiber network
Network buildings

FIGURE 10.15 Western Union's Atlanta Metropolitan Area Network

Metropolitan area networks transmit data and information over longer distances than LANs and at greater speeds.

 In recent years, the combination of faster computer processing, larger storage capabilities on smaller computers, and high-speed computer networks has led to a distinct trend toward computer *downsizing*. Applications that were previously run on shared mainframes are being moved to midranges; applications that were once run on midranges are now often run on powerful microcomputers. Yet all these different computers can be linked together by communications networks. Thus, downsizing means more than moving applications to smaller computers; it also means interconnecting different computers in a distributed environment.

The appeal of downsizing is closely tied to costs: midrange computers are cheaper than mainframes, and micros are cheaper than midranges. But there's more to downsizing than lower costs. Companies that take advantage of the power now available in smaller computers while standardizing applications across the organization see application performance improve. The reason is that if they move an application to its own dedicated computer, people can use it whenever they need it; they don't have to wait for another application to finish running on a shared computer. Response time for data and information retrieval is noticeably faster—an important benefit in a time when speed to market is a critical element of a firm's success.

Downsizing is not a fad, it's a trend. It is fueled by the quest for greater speed in business and commerce and enabled by the continuing advances in information technology. ▪

Multiuser Network Hardware

How are networks put together? In this section, we describe the hardware components of networks and the devices used to interconnect different networks.

Communications Channels: Physical and Cableless

communications channel/communications medium

The physical or cableless media that link the different components of a network.

A **communications channel,** also called a **communications medium,** links the different components of a network. There are two categories of communications channels: physical channels and cableless channels.

PHYSICAL CHANNELS.   Physical channels are wires or cables along which data and information are transmitted. There are three types of physical channels: twisted pair, coaxial cable, and optical cable (Figure 10.16).

twisted pair

A physical communications channel that uses strands of copper wire twisted together in pairs to form a telephone wire.

- As we mentioned earlier, teleprocessing gave rise to the use of telephone wires as a popular medium for transmitting data and information between multiple user sites. They remain the most popular medium today, whether strung from telephone poles, run through underground conduits, or embedded in the walls of buildings. Often referred to as **twisted pair,** this telephone wire medium consists of strands of copper wire that are twisted in pairs. Because the twisted pair channel was developed for the transmission of voices and text, IT professionals refer to this medium as a *voice-grade channel.*

   Twisted pair channels transmit at a variety of speeds, from as slow as 110 bits per second to as fast as 100 Mbps. The *feasible speed* of transmission is

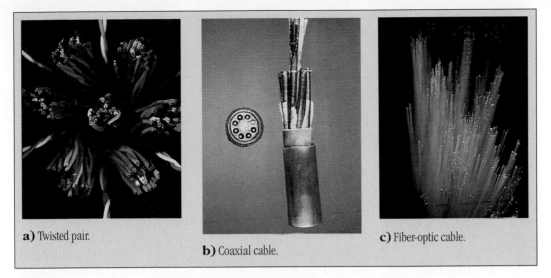

a) Twisted pair.

b) Coaxial cable.

c) Fiber-optic cable.

FIGURE 10.16 *Physical Communications Channels*
Physical communications channels transmit data and information along a wire or cable.

established by the carrier, independent of the data or information transported on the channel. The *actual speed* of transmission is determined by the hardware attached to the medium and the programs managing the communications process.

- **Coaxial cable,** sometimes called just **co-ax,** consists of one or more central wire conductors surrounded by an insulator and encased in either a wire mesh or metal sheathing. Co-ax offers higher transmission speeds than voice-grade lines and a capability for transmitting all types of information effectively (not just voice and text). If you have cable television, you are using coaxial cable to receive the broadcast programs without interference.

    Coaxial cable comes in two types. *Baseband* cable, which carries a single communication or message at very high megabit speeds, is often used in local area networks. *Broadband* cable carries multiple signals simultaneously; each signal can be a different speed. Cable television uses broadband cable. Both types of coaxial cable achieve bandwidths of more than 100-megabit speeds. These speeds will continue to increase through advances in networking technology.

- **Fiber-optic cable** is the newest type of physical communications channel. This high-bandwidth transmission medium uses light as a digital information carrier. Glass fibers, rather than wire, are the transmission medium. Because the glass fibers are much thinner than wire, many more fibers can be packed into a cable, with each transmitting at much higher speeds than twisted pairs or coaxial cable. And because laser (light) beams, rather than electricity, carry the data and information, fiber-optic cables are immune to electrical interference within buildings or when strung near electrical lines.

    The costs of manufacturing, installing, and maintaining fiber-optic cables are lower than those for wire channels. These advantages, combined with the benefits of high transmission speeds, make it easy to see why the use of fiber optics is growing at a rapid rate worldwide. Indeed, most telephone companies and PTTs are installing only fiber-optic cable when they lay new lines to expand their networks. Hence, if you make a telephone call or transmit data

coaxial cable/co-ax
A physical communications channel that uses one or more central wire conductors surrounded by an insulator and encased in either a wire mesh or metal sheathing.

fiber-optic cable
A physical communications channel that uses light and glass fibers.

over a telephone line, there is a good chance your message will be sent over fiber-optic cables, at least part of the way to its destination.

The term *line* is a carryover from the days when all data communications were carried by twisted-pair lines. IT professionals use the term today to refer to all communications media, both physical and wireless.

private branch exchange (PBX)/computer branch exchange (CBX)
A private telephone system designed to handle the needs of the organization in which it is installed.

Most office buildings have a communications network running through their offices. A **private branch exchange (PBX),** or **computer branch exchange (CBX),** is a private telephone system designed to handle the needs of the organization in which it is installed. Telephones—that is, *stations or extensions*—are interconnected with the network. Calls coming into the organization from outside lines are processed through the PBX, which switches the call to the appropriate internal extension. Calls originating inside the organization are routed by the PBX to an available outside line.

Since most PBX systems today are computer based—microprocessors manage the switching activities and keep track of the location of various extensions—PBX implicitly means CBX. ■

CABLELESS CHANNELS.   The four most common types of cableless transmission media are microwave, satellite, infrared, and radio waves. Depending on the company's needs, these media may be used alone or in conjunction with each other and the three types of physical channels. Wireless channels will be the predominant network medium for pen-based computers and personal digital assistants, both still in their infancy (see Chapter 1). Experts predict that they will also be used more frequently for other types of computers.

Microwave.   This form of transmission uses high-frequency radio signals to send data and information through the air, without wire or cable connections between sites, all in a fraction of a second. **Microwave** signals can be transmitted using terrestrial stations or communications satellites. With terrestrial stations, relay towers stationed approximately 30 miles apart receive and retransmit communications to link source and destination sites. The path between each tower must be unobstructed, though, because the signals are sent in a straight line (Figure 10.17a). For this reason, microwave stations are often located on the tops of buildings in metropolitan areas or at the peaks of mountains and hills in remote regions.

microwave
A cableless medium that uses high-frequency radio signals to send data or information through the air.

Satellites.   The preferred method of transmission of information between sites when large distances must be spanned or when obstructions are in the way is by **satellite.** With this type of cableless transmission, the significance of distance disappears. Each communication is beamed from a microwave station to a communications satellite in orbit 22,000 miles above the earth. Transmissions are relayed from one sending earth station to another or to multiple earth stations (Figure 10.17b).

satellite
A cableless medium in which communications are beamed from a microwave station to a communications satellite in orbit above the earth and relayed to other earth stations.

Of growing importance are **very small aperture terminals (VSATs),** which have been incorporated into corporate networking strategies at an increasing rate in recent years. A VSAT is a fairly inexpensive (it costs only a few hundred dollars) satellite earth station with an antenna diameter of under one meter (40

very small aperture terminal (VSAT)
A satellite earth station with an antenna diameter of under one meter.

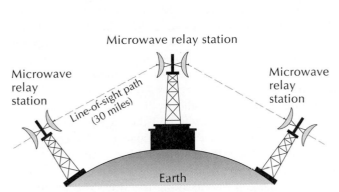

Microwave relay station

Microwave relay station

Line-of-sight path (30 miles)

Microwave relay station

Earth

a) Terrestrial Transmission. In terrestrial microwave transmission, dish-shaped antennas 30 miles apart relay signals from one to another. Paths between relay stations must be unobstructed.

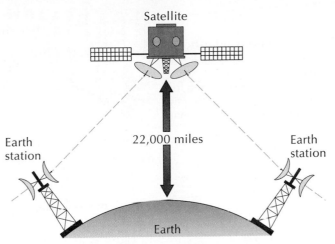

Satellite

Earth station

22,000 miles

Earth station

Earth

b) Satellite Transmission. In satellite microwave transmission, a satellite orbiting approximately 22,000 miles over the earth acts as a relay station that transmits a signal from one earth station to another.

FIGURE 10.17 *Terrestrial and Satellite Microwave Transmission*

inches). VSATs enable companies to use networks in creative and effective ways because the earth station can be installed just about anywhere and still maintain contact with the orbiting satellite.

In the United States, Schneider National, a large long-haul trucking company based in Green Bay, Wisconsin, was the first to equip its trucks with VSATs (Figure 10.18). Mounted on top of the driver's cab, these receivers allow the company and driver to communicate anywhere and at any time. The dispatcher at the company's office simply determines the location of a truck and sends the driver a message instructing him to make additional pickups, to change his delivery schedule, or to perform any other task that would make the company more effective. Schneider pays for access to an orbiting public communications satellite. Its transmissions are sent to the satellite and then beamed to the truck, all in a matter of seconds.

FIGURE 10.18

Very Small Aperture Terminal Communication at Schneider National

A receiver mounted on top of Schneider National's truck cabs (left) allows drivers and headquarters to communicate anywhere and at any time. Schneider pays for access to an orbiting public communications satellite, from which its messages are beamed to its drivers' trucks (right).

cellular telephone
A device used to send and receive voice communications and computer and fax transmissions while allowing users freedom of movement.

People's desire to enjoy greater freedom of movement while staying in touch with the office, customers, or colleagues has created tremendous growth in **cellular telephone** use (Figure 10.19). Using cell stations located throughout a geographic region, cellular phones send and receive voice conversations (and can be used for computer and fax transmissions as well). As long as the caller stays in the cell region, he or she can communicate over the mobile telephone. If the caller travels beyond the cell region, a cross-region service provides the necessary service and billing authorization.

The demand for extended calling capability has fueled the expansion of these cross-region services. In Europe, for example, a Pan-European cellular communications network has been developed by the telecommunications company Groupe Spéciale Mobile (GSM). Using the GSM network, it is possible to drive from Rome to Helsinki and make calls on the same cell phone along the way. The telephone registers on the cellular network of the country in which it is switched on, and the GSM network automatically updates its location throughout the journey. Incoming calls are automatically rerouted through the multicountry network. Similar capabilities are available for fax and data transmission. ■

infrared
A cableless medium that transmits data and information in coded form by means of an infrared light beamed from one transceiver to another.

transceiver
A combination transmitter and receiver that transmits and receives data and information.

Infrared. **Infrared** communications occur via a combined transmitter and receiver, or **transceiver;** data and information are transmitted in coded form by means of an infrared light beamed from one transceiver to another. Infrared systems are limited to a single area, such as an open retail store space or a large room, because the transmitter and receiver must be in sight of each other. Infrared communication between different areas or buildings can be achieved only if they are close to each other (no more than 220 yards or 200 meters apart) and only if the transceivers are in windows of the buildings, visible to each other.

Kroger Co., a large supermarket chain based in Cincinnati, Ohio, has installed a series of infrared transceivers on the ceilings of its stores and equipped shopping carts with flat screen display terminals. As shoppers wheel their carts through the store, the transceiver senses their presence and transmits advertising and pric-

FIGURE 10.19
Cellular Telephone on the Job
Cellular telephones send and receive voice communications, and sometimes fax transmissions, via cell stations located throughout a geographic region. In terms of convenience alone, cellular telephones have increased productivity greatly. But because cellular conversations are easily eavesdropped upon, many companies prohibit their employees from discussing confidential business matters on cellular telephones.

FIGURE 10.20
Infrared Marketing
VideOCart's supermarket system pioneered the use of infrared to sense the presence of shopping carts and transmit advertising and pricing information to a screen on the cart. The cart offers supermarkets the opportunity to call attention to new items, products on sale, and coupon specials. Shoppers can use the VideOCarts to locate hard-to-find items and favorite products.

ing information to the screen on the cart (Figure 10.20). In the produce department, the screen suggests innovative ways to cook seasonal fresh vegetables. As the consumer enters the frozen food section, the display shows information about special prices and this week's sales. In the snack food area, the consumer is reminded about upcoming televised sporting events and the need to stock up on extra snacks for the family to enjoy while watching them. The added expense of installing 30 to 40 transceivers in each store has been more than justified, Kroger managers say, by advertising revenues and the extra sales generated.

Radio Waves. **Radio wave transmissions,** sometimes called **radio frequency (RF) transmission,** use transmission frequencies rented from public radio networks in a region. The company or individual user pays a monthly fee for airtime and transmits information at the assigned frequency. A transmitter sends information to a receiver designed to accept the same frequency. Radio wave transmissions are not practical for transmitting large files or databases because of their relatively low transmission speeds (see Table 10.4).

Governments in different countries regulate radio frequencies in different ways and assign the frequency ranges for varying purposes. In general, governments have not reserved any RF transmission frequency for local area network use.

radio wave transmission/radio frequency (RF) transmission
A cableless medium that uses frequencies rented from public radio networks to transmit data and information.

TABLE 10.4 *Transmission Speeds of Communications Channels*	
CHANNELS	**TRANSMISSION SPEEDS**
Twisted pair	Over 100 Mbps
Coaxial cable	140 Mbps
Fiber-optic cable	Over 2 Gbps
CABLELESS CHANNELS	**TRANSMISSION SPEEDS**
Microwave	275 Mbps
Satellite	2 Mbps
Infrared	275 Mbps
Radio waves (RF transmission)	275 Mbps

There are two major players in the worldwide public radio network market. In the United States, Motorola and IBM have created as a joint venture the ARDIS Co. In Europe, RAM Mobile Data Co. uses a mobile data network system developed by the Swedish company Ericsson AB. Each of these companies provides a series of public radio channels in major metropolitan areas that are available to users for a monthly fee that covers rental of air time and transmission equipment. The network companies run and maintain the network.

Otis Elevator uses a public radio network to transmit information to its field service staff. Maintenance and service personnel can send and receive information about parts and procedures for servicing an elevator or diagnosing a problem. The company finds the network an effective way of routing personnel from one service call to the next (Figure 10.21).

In the United States, Otis's system has other benefits as well. Because the company can stay in touch with service employees throughout the day, it does not have to assign the day's service calls in the morning or rely on telephone calls to do so throughout the day. Instead, it is able to manage the entire service team in the most efficient way possible, responding to customer emergencies that arise during the day and accommodating a service call that takes a little longer than expected. Both customer and company benefit from this wireless network.

Communications Channels for WANs and MANs

Three different communications channels are widely used by companies creating wide area or metropolitan area networks. These are public access networks, private networks, and value-added networks.

- **Public access networks.** U.S. telephone companies and the world's PTTs— that is, the common carriers—maintain certain networks for use by the general public: hence the term **public access networks.** Specialized carriers also operate other focused services, such as making satellite communications links available to the public. All carriers interconnect their networks with other networks to give their customers a seamlessly integrated single network. The complete set of public access networks is often called the **switched network,** so named because the telephone company operates and maintains the switching centers that make it possible to transmit a call or information from its origin

public access network
A network maintained by common carriers for use by the general public.

switched network
The complete set of public access networks, so named because the telephone company operates and maintains the switching centers that make it possible to transmit data and information.

FIGURE 10.21
Otis Elevator's Service Network
Otis Elevator uses a public radio network to transmit information to its field service staff. Maintenance personnel can send and receive information about parts and procedures via a portable handheld computer.

through the nodes of the network to its destination. *Switched access* refers to communications access over a switched, nondedicated line. This means that the line is assigned to a different caller each time, and the completion of a call requires the carrier to switch between different lines to create a link between the caller and the desired destination of his or her call.

- **Private networks.** When organizations transmit large volumes of information regularly, it may be more economical and effective for them to lease lines from a common carrier than to use a public access network. When an organization agrees to lease a line for a period of time, the carrier will *dedicate* that line to the company, meaning it will reserve it for the exclusive use of that company. Hence, **leased lines** are sometimes called **dedicated lines.** Networks comprising dedicated lines are known as **private networks.**

- **Value-added networks.** A public data communications network that provides basic transmission facilities plus enhancements (such as temporary data storage, error detection and correction, conversion of information from one form to another, and electronic mail service) is called a **value-added network (VAN).** The VAN provider generally leases the transmission channels from a common carrier and then creates the "value added" to its customer by investing in and operating the network so that the customer doesn't need to do so.

leased line/dedicated line
A communications line reserved from a carrier by a company for its exclusive use.

private network
A network made up of leased (dedicated) communications lines.

value-added network (VAN)
A public data communications network that provides basic transmission facilities plus enhancements (e.g., temporary data storage and error detection).

Communications Channels for LANs

Local area networks seldom use public switched networks or satellite transmission channels because these do not provide much distance between nodes. Although wireless methods are increasingly popular, fiber-optic, coaxial cable, and twisted pair lines remain the most common methods of connecting the nodes of a LAN. In most cases, the company simply has the cables installed on its premises by a wiring contractor. When companies and institutions expect a large number of people to use their LAN, they often build either a high-speed transmission facility called a **backbone network** or an arrangement of such facilities. When developed as part of a wide area network, the channels are often T-carriers.

Georgia State University and the Georgia Institute of Technology (Georgia Tech), both in Atlanta, have developed backbone networks for their entire campuses. Communications cables buried in the ground run near all campus buildings and laboratories. Each backbone serves as a conduit that connects lower-speed communications lines or dispersed communications to computing devices. The lower-speed components move data onto the backbone, where they are transported to the intended destination at high speed. At the destination, the data move off the backbone to the lower-speed network and eventually to their intended recipient.

backbone network
A transmission facility designed to move data and information at high speeds.

Connecting to the Channel

A communications medium provides only the *capability* to transmit and receive information. It is entirely separate from the other hardware components of the computer system: computers, printers, or other devices that determine *what* and *when* to communicate. Different devices are used to connect computers to WANs and LANs.

In WANs using the public telephone network, special devices called **modems** connect computers to the communications medium and translate the data or information from the computer into a form that can be transmitted over the channel. The term *modem,* a contraction of *mo*dulation-*dem*odulation, describes the

modem
A device that connects a computer to a communications medium and translates the data or information from the computer into a form that can be transmitted over the channel. Used in WANs.

device's operations. Computers generate digital signals (combinations of the binary zero and one), but voice-grade lines transmit analog signals. The modem on the transmitting end translates the digital signal into analog form so it can be transmitted. On the receiving end, another modem transforms the analog signal back into a digital form that the computer can process (Figure 10.22).

Modems come in several different forms. *External modems* consist of circuit boards mounted inside a protective case and interconnected with the computer through a cable that plugs into a port on the computer (Figure 10.23, left). *Card* or *internal modems* are circuit boards that can be pushed into a slot in the computer (Figure 10.23, right). The communications line connects to both types through a plug on the modem. The speed of the modem determines how quickly data and information will be transmitted on the line.

multiplexer

A device that converts data from digital to analog form and vice versa in order to allow a single communications channel to carry simultaneous data transmissions from the many terminals that are sharing the channel.

Multiplexers that are used to connect terminals to an analog communications line also convert data from digital to analog signals and vice versa. These devices allow a single communications channel to carry simultaneous data transmissions from the many terminals that are sharing the channel.

In the most commonly used LANs, both the devices and the network channels transmit digital information. Thus, there is no need for a modem. A circuit board called a **network interface card** (Figure 10.24) plugs into the computer, printer, or other device, thus becoming part of the device itself. The network channel, in turn, connects to the interface card by way of a special plug spliced to the cable. If a wireless channel is used, the network interface card contains the transceiver for sending and receiving information.

network interface card

A circuit board used in LANs to transmit digital data or information.

The network card and the cable type used in the LAN must agree, so the choice of cable is affected by the network card (or vice versa). If an office area is wired for coaxial cable, the computer must be equipped with interface cards that will interconnect with coaxial cable.

FIGURE 10.22 *Converting Digital Signals to Analog Signals Using a Modem*

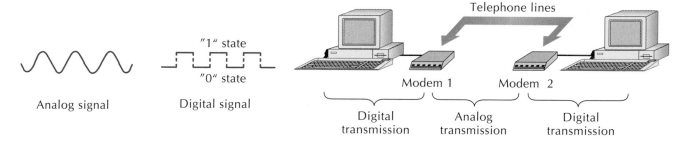

The signals sent along a communications medium can be digital or analog. The phone system carries **analog signals**—continuous waves—over a frequency range.

Most types of computing equipment use **digital signals**, which code data into blocks of zeroes and ones.

When a computer sends data to a modem for transmission at a specified speed, it represents the digital blocks of zeroes and ones electrically as −5 and +5 volts, respectively. The modem changes, or **modulates**, the electrical signals into two analog frequency tones. It converts zeroes into a frequency of 2025 cycles per second (2025 hertz) and ones into a frequency of 2225 cycles (2225 hertz) per second.

This process is reversed at the receiving end of the transmission, where a second modem converts the analog signals back into digital signals.

FIGURE 10.23 *Modems*

Modems come in several different forms. *External modems* consist of circuit boards mounted inside a protective case and interconnected with the computer through a cable that plugs into a port on the computer (left). *Card* or *internal modems* are circuit boards that can be pushed into a slot in the computer (right).

Interconnecting Networks

Because communications networks vary so widely in type and structure, it is common for companies to operate many different networks. Distributed processing presumes multiple networks, and it is likely that people will want to interconnect networks to share information and other resources. We've discussed how computer and communications devices are interconnected, but how do networks themselves interconnect? It all depends on whether the networks are the same or different types and whether they are managed by the same or different software.

Bridges and **routers** are devices that interconnect LANs, making it possible to send information from a device on one network to a device on another network. In essence, both take packets of information transmitted on one LAN and move them to another LAN. Hence, the two LANs can be treated essentially as one big LAN.

bridge
A device that interconnects compatible LANs.

router
A device that interconnects compatible LANs.

FIGURE 10.24
Network Interface Card
A circuit board called a *network interface card* plugs into the computer, printer, or other device, thus becoming part of the device itself. The network channel, in turn, connects to the interface card by way of a special plug spliced to the cable.

gateway
A device that connects two otherwise incompatible networks, network nodes, or devices.

Gateways interconnect two otherwise different and incompatible networks, network nodes, or devices. The gateway performs conversion operations so that information transmitted in one form on the first network can be transformed into the form required for transmission to its destination on the second network (Figure 10.25).

FIGURE 10.25 *Interconnecting Networks with Bridges and Gateways*

Bridges interconnect compatible LANs, making it possible to send information from a device on one network to a device on another network. *Gateways* connect otherwise different and incompatible networks.

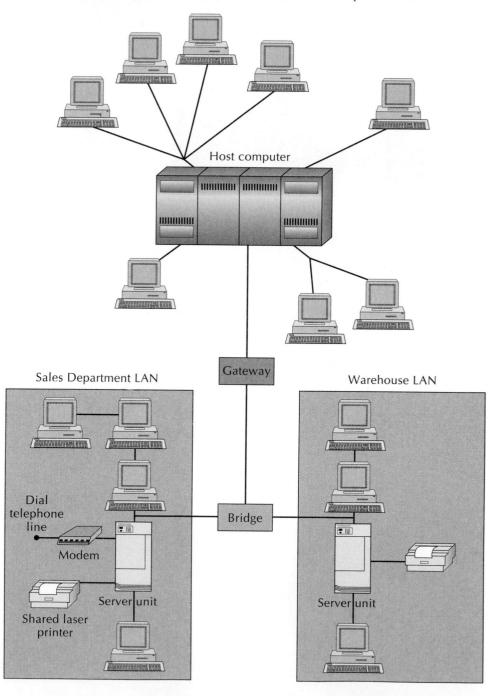

The Peapod Promise.
Friendly People. Superior Service.℠

Peapod Makes Grocery Shopping Easy

If you don't like grocery shopping but do have access to a computer with a modem, Andrew and Thomas Parkinson would like to help you out. The Parkinson brothers are the founders of Peapod, Inc., an Illinois-based company that combines 24-hour-a-day on-line grocery selection at major grocery stores with Peapod's own delivery service.

Peapod started small. In 1990, it signed an agreement to serve a single store for Jewel Food Stores, Inc. A few years later, Peapod membership starter kits were being offered in Jewel Food Stores in 13 Chicago suburbs as well as in the city's North Side. In 1993, Peapod signed an agreement with Safeway, the giant supermarket chain, to launch a pilot program in the San Francisco area.

How does the system work? Peapod's communications software taps into the supermarket's database and presents a series of menus that let members browse the aisles, shopping by item, brand name, and unit price, or create a personal shopping list of family favorites. In addition to specifying special instructions ("Only buy green bananas"), members can indicate they are using coupons for certain purchases and specify the day and time the groceries should be delivered. Peapod's trained shoppers fill the orders, pack the perishables in coolers, and whisk the completed orders to members, who hand over their coupons and pay Peapod. Many people have found that the savings in time and trouble more than offset the fees they pay to Peapod.

Network Operating Systems

Every computer that runs a network must have a **network operating system (NOS),** a software program that runs in conjunction with the computer's operating system and applications programs and manages the network. Like computers, networks cannot function without their operating system (Figure 10.26).

The NOS communicates with the LAN, WAN, or MAN hardware, accepting information transmitted from one device and directing it to another. It also manages the sharing of peripherals and storage devices, keeping track of the location of the devices and who is using them at a particular moment. Some widely used network operating systems are listed in Table 10.5.

network operating system (NOS)
A software program that runs in conjunction with the computer's operating system and applications programs and manages the network.

Protocol and Communications Control

Every conversation, whether interpersonal or electronic, needs to proceed in an orderly fashion. How do computers know when and how to talk to one another? The rules and conventions guiding data communications are embedded as coded instructions in the network software. This **protocol** performs the following tasks:

protocol
The rules and conventions guiding data communications, embedded as coded instructions in the network software.

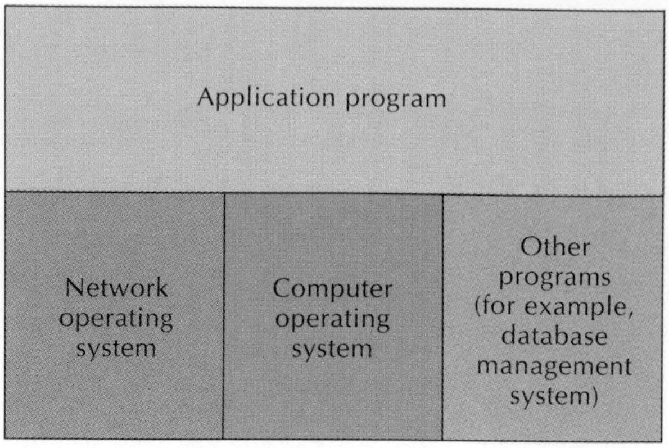

FIGURE 10.26

Network Operating System in Relation to Other Software

A network operating system runs in conjunction with a computer's operating system and applications programs and manages the network.

Application program		
Network operating system	Computer operating system	Other programs (for example, database management system)

- Signals the receiving computer that another computer wants to send a message.
- Identifies the sender.
- Transmits messages in blocks, if it detects that each block is received as it is sent.
- Retransmits a message, if it detects that the previous attempt was not successful.
- Determines when an error occurs and recovers from the error so that transmission can continue.
- Signals the receiver at the end of the transmission that no more messages will follow.
- Terminates the connection.

Many protocols have been established as standards in the use of information technology in wide area networks. The most common of these are Xmodem (developed for use between microcomputers), SNA (IBM's system network architecture), TCP/IP protocol suite (Transmission Control Protocol/Internet Protocol for large-scale, high-speed backbone networks), X.25 (for public data networks),

TABLE 10.5   *Widely Used Network Operating Systems*

System Network Architecture	The IBM network structure for linking applications on mainframes and midrange systems.
SNA Distribution Services (SNADS)	An IBM architecture for interchanging information through an SNA network. With SNADS, users can distribute information to other systems without worrying about the details of the other systems. SNADS can also link a variety of small processors into the network.
LAN Manager	Microsoft's operating system for local area networks running on IBM-compatible computers.
Apple Talk	Apple Computer's network operating system for Apple computers, Macintosh computers, and the Apple Newton personal digital assistant.
Novell NetWare	The most widely used network operating system for microcomputers.
DECNET	The most widely used network operating system on Digital Equipment Corp. (DEC) computers.

TABLE 10.6 *LAN Protocols*

Carrier Sense Multiple Access (CSMA)	The CSMA protocol follows the rule, "Don't begin transmitting without first listening on the network to see if anyone else is using it. If not, send the message." A variation on CSMA, called *carrier sense multiple access with collision detection (CSMA/CD)*, is designed to avoid the case where two microcomputers begin to transmit at the same time, each thinking it is the only network user. The CSMA/CD protocol says, in effect, "Listen before you transmit *and* while you transmit. If you detect someone else using the network (a collision), wait for the other transmission to stop and then start your message again." The CSMA and CSMA/CD protocols are built into the Ethernet network developed by Xerox Corporation for LANs and into the LANs used by Apple Computer, Digital Equipment Corp., and some IBM systems.
Token Ring	The token ring protocol, so named because it is used with a ring topology, is based on a simple rule often invoked at large meetings: "Don't speak unless you have the microphone." When implemented as a LAN protocol, a token (string of bits) rather than a microphone is sent around the network. If no one is transmitting, the token is available for a member of the network to take and begin transmitting. When the transmission is completed, the token is sent back to the network so that another computer can retrieve it. With only one token, there can't be any collisions, because protocol allows transmission only when a computer is holding the token. The token ring protocol is used often in IBM and Novell LANs.

and X.400 (for electronic mail between different types of computers). In local area networks, two protocols are in widespread use: carrier sense multiple access (CSMA) and token ring. Table 10.6 summarizes the differences between these protocols, and Table 10.7 explains some other terms used in communications control.

Since protocol is needed between different components in communication, network designers developing communications use a seven-layer *open system interconnection (OSI) model* (Figure 10.27). Computer applications programs, network operating systems, and transmission protocol are defined within the OSI model, constituting what network professionals refer to as the *system network architecture*. (People using communications networks need not worry about these layers since they are handled by the software and network personnel.)

TABLE 10.7 *Communications Control Terminology*

TYPES OF TRANSMISSION LINES		TYPES OF TRANSMISSION	
Simplex Lines	Transmit data in one direction only (either send or receive).	Asynchronous Protocol	Data are transmitted one character at a time. Transmission of data bits is preceded and followed by special start-stop sequences.
Half-Duplex Lines	Transmit data in either direction, but in only one direction at a time (alternate between send and receive).	Synchronous Protocol	Transmission is continuous. The transmitting and receiving terminals must be synchronized—that is, in phase with each other. A clock (usually in the modem) governs transmission by determining when each data bit is sent.
Full-Duplex Lines	Send and receive data simultaneously.		

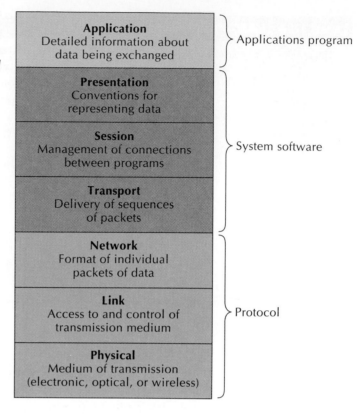

FIGURE 10.27
Open System Interconnection (OSI) Model

Application Detailed information about data being exchanged	} Applications program
Presentation Conventions for representing data	
Session Management of connections between programs	} System software
Transport Delivery of sequences of packets	
Network Format of individual packets of data	
Link Access to and control of transmission medium	} Protocol
Physical Medium of transmission (electronic, optical, or wireless)	

Network Administration

network administration/network management

The management of a network, consisting of those procedures and services that keep the network running properly.

The management of a network, usually called **network administration** or **network management,** consists of procedures and services that keep the network running properly. An important part of network management entails making sure that the network is available (or "up and running," as IT professionals say) when employees and managers need it. Other network administration activities are

- Monitoring the network's capacity to ensure that all transmission requirements can be met.
- Adding capacity to the network by increasing bandwidth, interconnecting additional nodes, or creating and interconnecting additional networks.
- Training people to use the network effectively.
- Assisting IT professionals in writing applications that will make good use of the network's capabilities.
- Backing up the network software and data regularly to protect against the failure of the network or any of its components.
- Putting security procedures in place to make certain that only authorized users have access to the network, and ensuring that all security procedures are followed.
- Making sure that network personnel can respond quickly and effectively in the event of a network operational or security failure.
- Diagnosing and troubleshooting problems on the network and determining the best course of action to take to solve them.

As in business in general, the success of a network depends on the people who design and manage it. Network specialists include *network designers,* who specify the necessary features of the network and oversee its construction and installation; *network administrators,* who manage the day-to-day operations of the network; and *network security personnel,* who develop and oversee the use of procedures designed to protect the integrity of the network and ensure that is used in the intended manner and by authorized persons only. In large organizations, these roles are usually filled by different people. In smaller firms, one person may have multiple responsibilities.

The network professional's job is far from easy. Connecting wildly different systems to each other poses many challenges, as the *Information Technology in Practice* feature entitled "The Challenge of Networking the European Union: A Test of Ingenuity" attests. How network professionals interact with the employees and managers of an organization—the users of the network—and with other IT professionals to accomplish their goals can have a dramatic effect on the perceived usefulness of the network and the extent to which it is used.

Multiuser Architectures

A communications **architecture** is the structure of a communications network; it determines how the various components of the communications network are structured, how they interact, and when cooperation between the system's components is needed. There are three types of multiuser system architectures: centralized architecture, distributed architecture, and architectures that combine elements of centralized and distributed systems.

Centralized Architecture

In a **centralized architecture,** all network hardware and software are found at a central site, usually in a computer center. Centralized computing is also called **host-based computing.** The central computer (or set of computers linked together at a single site) performs all processing and manages the network—that is, it hosts the network (Figure 10.28). It may retrieve information from a database, store new information, or accept and transmit information from one individual to another. All security protection works through the host computer, which validates individual passwords and restricts the activities that individual users are allowed to perform. IT staff members make backup copies of information and programs from the original versions, which reside on the host computer.

Throughout the 1960s, 1970s, and most of the 1980s, information technology was largely centralized. Organizations ran their applications on centralized mainframe or minicomputers located in data centers. Initially, dumb terminals—a display and keyboard without a processor (see Chapter 4)—were connected to the mainframe by a cable. For this reason, the terminals could not be too far away from the computer center. Users had to come to the computer center to use the computer, hauling their work with them.

A major advance in network technology came in the late 1960s, when computer manufacturers devised ways for people to connect with the centralized computer through telephone lines. This **teleprocessing** capability was an important advance in IT because the central computer's processing power and storage capacity could now be accessed and shared by many people from many locations simultaneously. People could remain at their work location and still use the host computer's processing capabilities. Figure 10.29 on page 482 explains in detail how telephone communication works.

architecture
The structure of a communications network, which determines how the various components of the network are structured, how they interact, and when cooperation between the system's components is needed.

centralized architecture
A communications architecture in which a computer at a central site hosts all of the network's hardware and software, performs all of the processing, and manages the network.

host-based computing
Centralized computing.

teleprocessing
The processing capability made possible by connecting desktop computers to a remote computer through telephone lines.

INFORMATION TECHNOLOGY IN PRACTICE

The Challenge of Networking the European Union: A Test of Ingenuity

Drawn by the vast commercial potential of the European Union (EU)—a common market that today encompasses more than 400 million consumers in Austria, Belgium, Denmark, Finland, France, Germany, Greece, Ireland, Italy, Luxembourg, the Netherlands, Portugal, Spain, Sweden, and the United Kingdom—thousands of companies around the world have poured money into European investments. But companies that decide to design and operate a WAN in Europe face some stiff challenges.

- *Varying levels of service and technical support.* The level and quality of service offered by public access networks varies from excellent (in London, Paris, and Frankfurt) to almost nonexistent (in Greece and Portugal).
- *Inconsistent standards.* Computing and communications standards backed by the EU still vary slightly from country to country, which makes linking countries electronically somewhat tricky.
- *Laws and regulations.* Although many nations are deregulating their PTTs, the pace has been neither consistent nor predictable. Laws regarding privacy and the use of information are another challenge. Generally speaking, European laws in these areas are stricter than U.S. laws, although they vary from country to country. French law, for example, forbids the transfer of employee information across national borders. Faced with this barrier, Sonoco Products Co., a South Carolina recycling and packaging company, abandoned its plans for a network and decided to process payroll data locally.

- *High networking costs.* Partly because of slower progress toward deregulation, communications costs in the United Kingdom are about four times higher than they are in the United States. For other European nations, experts suggest multiplying U.S. costs by a factor of 8 to get a reasonable estimate. The good news is that this situation is changing.

Nevertheless, a few brave U.S. companies are creating their own WANs in Europe. For example, Prudential Securities negotiated directly with Mercury and British Telecom, two of the UK's common carriers, to redesign a network linking its European offices to its headquarters in New York. Most U.S. companies that want to do business in the EU, however, are turning to third-party vendors—either consultants or firms that specialize in creating international value-added networks. Gilette Co., for example, signed an agreement with Syncordia, a subsidiary of a British common carrier, to handle its telecommunications in 180 countries. J. P. Morgan turned to an AT&T subsidiary, AT&T Istel, for help in creating a 14-city network. "There is no way we could have installed the system in the same time frame [five months] with in-house sources," says the vice president of global communications at J. P. Morgan. The vice president of MIS at Campbell Soup Co. agrees. "We're in the food business," he says. "I'm not interested in becoming an expert on pan-European telecommunications."

By the 1970s, minicomputers had enabled small and medium-sized companies to establish computer networks without having to invest in expensive mainframe computers. Minicomputers could serve as hosts, provided the volume of processing to be done was not so large as to overwhelm the processing and stor-

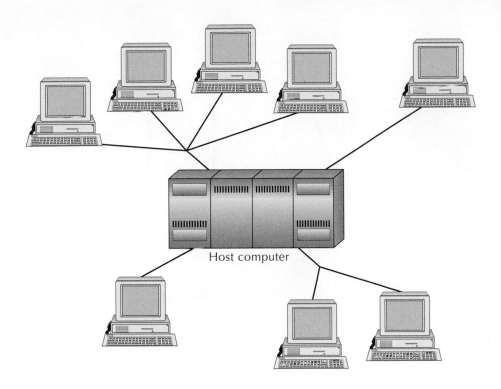

FIGURE 10.28
Centralized Architecture
In a centralized architecture, all network hardware and software are found at a central site, usually in a computer center. The central computer performs all the processing and hosts the network.

age capabilities of the computer. Some companies also began using **front-end computers,** minicomputers loaded with special programs to handle all incoming and outgoing communications traffic in a host-based centralized system (Figure 10.30). A front-end mini frees the host computer to carry out the processing, storage, and retrieval tasks for which it is best suited.

front-end computer
In a centralized system, a minicomputer loaded with special programs to handle all incoming and outgoing communications traffic.

Distributed Architecture

As these changes came about, business and government leaders began to challenge IT professionals, saying, in effect: Our people are distributed, so our information and our processing capabilities must be, too. Therefore, we'd like to find out

- How can we get more value from our current IT capabilities?
- How can we interconnect different systems to achieve maximum efficiency?
- How can we make different computer and communications systems work together?

The answer to all these questions was distributed architecture. In a **distributed architecture,** computers—supercomputers, mainframes, midrange systems, and microcomputers—reside at different locations, rather than in a single data center, and are interconnected by a communications network. The computer at each location primarily serves the needs of that location. The distributed computers work together through the network, retrieving information from some locations within it and acting as a source of information for other locations in the network.

distributed architecture
A communications architecture in which the computers reside at different locations and are interconnected by a communications network.

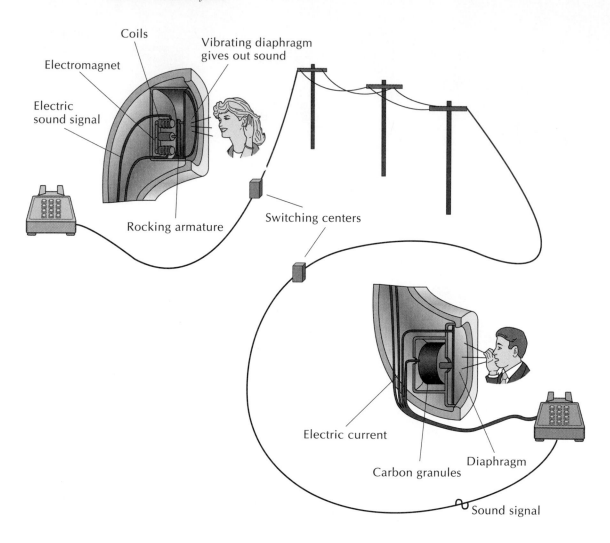

FIGURE 10.29 *How Telephone Communication Works*

When you speak into the telephone, a small microphone in the handset captures the sounds through a vibrating diaphragm, causing the electrical current flowing through the microphone to vary. From the handset, these electrical signals are sent over metal telephone wires. In the public telephone network, the electrical signals may be translated into light signals that are beamed over fiber-optic lines (see Figure 10.16). Alternatively, they may be converted into radio signals transmitted over radio networks or by microwave (see Figure 10.17).

How does a telephone call or data communication transmission get to the right place? How are so many conversations and messages sent over a communications network? Today's communications systems convert speech into digital form—the same digital codes used in computer systems. Using *multiplexing,* several messages can be packed together and sent simultaneously on the network. The messages are divided into blocks that are sent in very short intervals. Built into each block of data are identification and routing codes. When these are read by the digital switching components that are a part of the network, the message can be switched from one line to another, perhaps repeatedly, so that it reaches its intended destination. Because data move at the speed of electricity or at the speed of light (186,000 miles per second), a message reaches its destination in a fraction of one second.

The identification codes make it possible to keep one message distinct from another and to ensure that the right data are sent to the proper destination. At the destination, a *demultiplexor* unpacks the various streams of data and routes the message blocks back to the correct telephone.

These same principles apply in computer communications (see Figure 10.22).

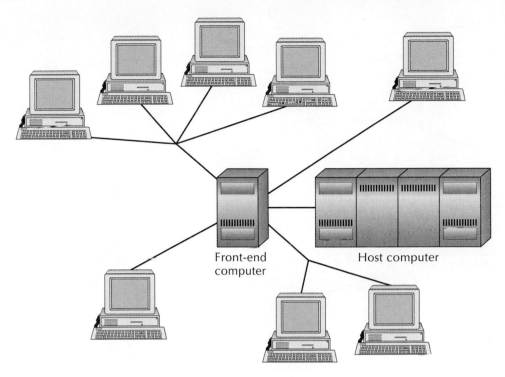

FIGURE 10.30
Centralized Architecture Using a Front-End Computer
A front-end minicomputer allows the host computer to carry out the processing, storage, and retrieval tasks for which it is best suited.

Front-end computer

Host computer

A distributed architecture supports **distributed processing,** in which an application runs on one or more locations of the network simultaneously (Figure 10.31). In a distributed processing system, the hardware, software, or information needed for the application may be physically located at a different location. **Distributed databases** (which we discuss in Chapter 11) are databases that reside on more than one computer system in a distributed network. Each component of the database can be retrieved, processed, or updated from any node in the network, rather than through a central host computer only.

Kmart utilizes a very large distributed architecture (Figure 10.32). All of its stores use point-of-sale bar code scanning on all items that pass through the checkout counter. By means of its satellite link, this purchase information is transmitted immediately to merchandise buyers at the company's Troy, Michigan, headquarters and to a large number of the company's suppliers. Credit authorization for customers paying by credit card is also obtained through this communications link, thus speeding the checkout process while ensuring that the card is valid.

Each Kmart store is interconnected with one of the company's 12 distribution centers nationwide, where inventory records are maintained. Sales information is transmitted continuously between the stores and the distribution centers' computers. In addition, Kmart's key suppliers, which have invested in their own computer systems that let them monitor inventories at Kmart's distribution centers electronically, automatically replenish the stock, without awaiting approval from Kmart, when supplies run low. Even small suppliers can take advantage of these distributed capabilities because the hardware and software needed to set up this type of system cost under $15,000 altogether.

distributed processing
Processing in which an application runs on one or more locations of the network simultaneously.

distributed database
A database that resides in more than one system in a distributed network. Each component of the database can be retrieved from any node in the network.

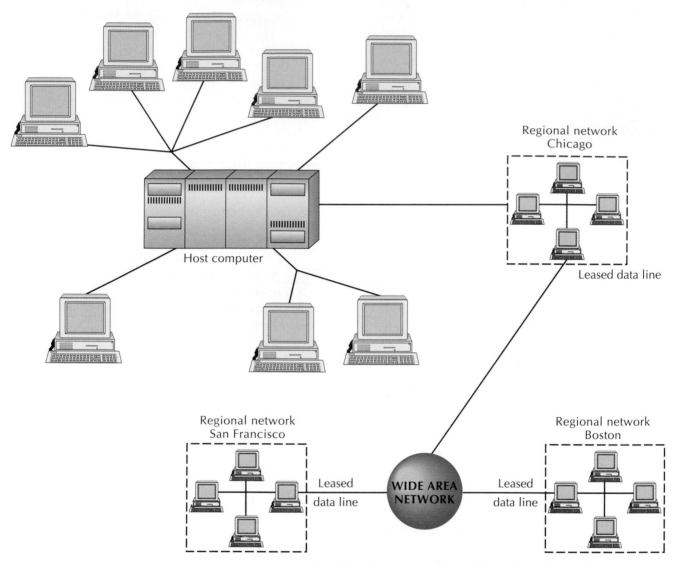

FIGURE 10.31 *Distributed Architecture with Distributed Processing*
In a distributed architecture, computers reside at different locations, rather than in a single data center, and are interconnected by a communications network.

Combining Architectures

One type of architecture is not always better than the other. Each has benefits and drawbacks. For example, centralized systems are easier to manage because of the central location. Distributed systems, though more difficult to manage, place information at the locations where it is used most often while ensuring that other nodes in the system have access to it.

hybrid network
A communications architecture that combines centralized and distributed architectures to take advantage of the strengths of both.

To take advantage of all the benefits of both configurations, companies sometimes combine architectures. In general, these **hybrid networks** mesh centralized teleprocessing and distributed features. In hybrid networks, the computer at the top of the system (usually a mainframe) controls interaction with all the devices attached directly to it. The host does not, however, directly control those computers interconnected at lower levels of the network (Figure 10.33).

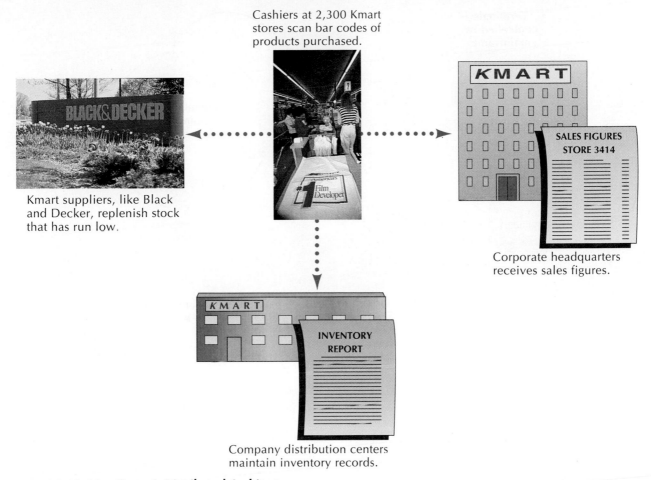

Cashiers at 2,300 Kmart stores scan bar codes of products purchased.

Kmart suppliers, like Black and Decker, replenish stock that has run low.

Corporate headquarters receives sales figures.

Company distribution centers maintain inventory records.

FIGURE 10.32 *Kmart's Distributed Architecture*

HYBRID NETWORKS IN THE AIRLINE INDUSTRY. Hybrid networks can take many forms. Some companies, for example, have combined networks that span vast geographic regions with others that link desktop computers within a single building. One such system now in widespread use in the airline industry evolved in the 1980s, when many European airlines suddenly confronted heightened competition from deregulated U.S. airlines. To stay in business, their managements concluded, these airlines would have to expand beyond their national borders. Doing so was a challenge, however, for two main reasons.

First, travel agents—independent businesspeople who receive a commission on every sale of a ticket for an airline—sell the majority of airline tickets. Travel agents can sell tickets for virtually all of the world's airlines, so they tend not to promote a single carrier. Second, no single European airline had the resources to develop its own network to interconnect the travel agents in the many countries to which it flies. The system development and operations costs were prohibitive. Nonetheless, each airline had to find a way to share information with travel agents about schedules, fares, and reservations.

Out of this necessity evolved an alliance among more than 20 airlines (including Air France, Iberia, Lufthansa, and SAS) and the network-based Amadeus system. Through this network, the airlines and a vast array of travel agents

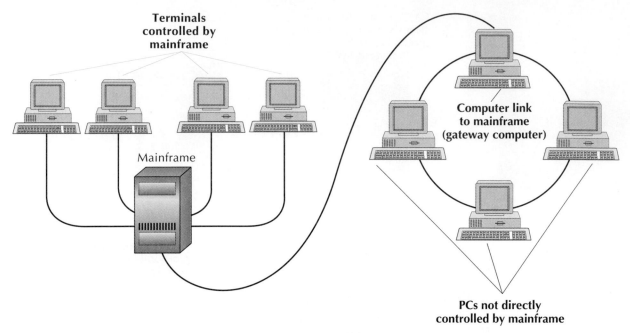

Terminals
controlled by
mainframe

Mainframe

Computer link
to mainframe
(gateway computer)

PCs not directly
controlled by mainframe

FIGURE 10.33   *Hybrid Architecture*

Hybrid architecture combines centralized and distributed features. The computer at the top of the network (here, the mainframe) controls interaction with all the devices attached directly to it. The host does not control the computers interconnected at lower levels of the network.

throughout the world share flight information. Development of the Amadeus network provided the foundation for other network-based travel services. For example, Amadeus is now used to book reservations for ferry and Hovercraft crossings, trains, and automobile rentals.

The strength of Amadeus lies in a hybrid network. Each airline, hotel, or other business enterprise connected to Amadeus continues to operate its own computer network. Some of these individual networks are centralized, while others are distributed; some span large areas, while others span small areas; all use different combinations of computers, programs, and screen displays. Amadeus links these individual networks.

The combination of business alliances with a hybrid network architecture has changed the way international airlines compete and the markets they serve. But multiuser computing and communications networks are also of great interest to societies. In fact, an industry-sponsored study conducted by the Iacocca Institute at Lehigh University in the early 1990s recommended the creation of a nationwide communications network to link factories across the United States, with the goal of boosting the global competitiveness of U.S. manufacturers.

Under plans developed as part of the Iacocca study, the Factory America Net will allow most companies to interconnect with the network. For example, a company developing a new product will be able to send a message across the network asking suppliers to provide information on their ability to manufacture a component or to provide a service needed for the new product. The creation of **virtual companies**—business enterprises that come together operationally, but not physically, to design and manufacture a product—is expected to be one result of this hybrid network.

virtual company
A company that joins with another company operationally, but not physically, to design and manufacture a product.

Delta Air Lines

Delta Air Lines: What's Your Preference— An Office or a Living Room in the Sky?

There's nothing thrilling about the inside of passenger aircraft to frequent business travelers. The planes of one airline look pretty much like those of another. So the choice of which one to fly on often comes down to how an airline and its crew fulfill passenger needs.

Delta Air Lines, headquartered in Atlanta, has realized high payoffs since it employed information technology to meet traveler needs *and* to make long flights more enjoyable by creating a "living room in the sky."

Recognizing that many business travelers need to be in touch with others while they're up in the air, Delta installed telephones in seatbacks or armrests throughout the cabins of its planes. To use the telephone, all you have to do is zip a credit card through the special slot on the phone and dial whatever number you want. You reach your party (or a busy signal!) without ever leaving your seat. You can also connect a modem to the telephone and send or receive data and information from someone on the ground.

For the laptop computer user, who never seems to have enough battery power for long transcontinental flights, Delta installed power jacks. Plug in your laptop, and no matter how long the flight, you won't have to worry about batteries conking out.

Now that power and connectivity are available at airline seats, can the World Wide Web be far behind?

The Factory America Net will undoubtedly evolve as the concept advances from idea to reality. It is long-term in scope, designed to be an integral component of U.S. manufacturing strategies in the twenty-first century.

A Final Word

As you leave this chapter, one thing should be clear: communications networks are an essential component of IT. If you can't link up, you can't communicate, and you will probably lose out. That is the reality of business today.

SUMMARY OF LEARNING OBJECTIVES

1 **Identify the reasons that multiuser systems are used in business.** Multiuser systems are used in business for the following reasons: (1) to increase the productivity and effectiveness of the people using the system; (2) to increase the productivity and effectiveness of the organizations in which the system is used; and (3) to improve the services provided to those who rely on others using multiuser systems.

2 **Describe eight network service applications used in business.** The eight network service applications most frequently used in business are electronic mail, voice mail, videoconferencing, work group conferencing, electronic bulletin boards, electronic funds transfer, electronic data interchange, and videotex.

Electronic mail, or *e-mail,* is a service that transports text messages from a sender to one or more receivers via computer. *Voice mail systems* capture, store, and transmit spoken messages. They do not use computer keyboards, but rather a telephone connected to a computer network. *Videoconferencing* is a type of conferencing in which video cameras and microphones capture sight and sound for transmission over networks. Large display screens show the other parties in the conference "live." *Work group conferencing* uses a type of software package called *groupware* to organize an electronic meeting in which participants' computers are interconnected from their various locations. Each participant interacts through a microcomputer directly linked to a main computer; comments are broadcast to all participants in the conference. *Electronic bulletin boards* are similar to the bulletin boards at the supermarket where messages and announcements are posted and read. Users of an electronic bulletin board dial into the board over a communications link and leave a message, file, or program. Others dialing into the bulletin board can retrieve the information and copy it to their system. *Electronic funds transfer (EFT)* is the movement of money over a network. *Electronic data interchange (EDI)* is a form of electronic communication that allows trading partners to exchange business transaction data in structured formats that can be processed by applications software. *Videotex* is a two-way, interactive, text-only service operating on mainframe computers that provides a video screen with easy-to-follow instructions.

3 **Discuss the three types of communications networks and the advantages offered by each.** The three types of networks are (1) *wide area networks* (WANs), designed to span large geographic regions; (2) *local area networks* (LANs), which interconnect desktop computers and communications devices within an office or series of offices; and (3) *metropolitan area networks* (MANs), which use fiber-optic cables to transmit various types of information around a city or metropolitan region.

4 **Discuss the two types of communications channels used in networks and the ways that computers interconnect with them.** Two types of communications channels are used in networks. The *physical channels* (twisted pair, coaxial cable, and optical cable) utilize a wire or cable along which data and information are transmitted. The *cableless channels* (microwave, satellite, infrared, and radio frequency transmission) are wireless transmission media.

In WANs, *modems* connect computers to the communications channel and translate the information from the computer into a form that can be transmitted over the channel. In LANs a *network interface card* is used.

5 **Explain the role of a network operating system.** Every computer that runs a network must have a *network operating system (NOS),* a software program that runs in conjunction with the computer's operating system and applications programs and manages the network.

6 Discuss the activities involved in network administration. Network administration, or management, consists of all the procedures and services that keep the network running properly. One important aspect of network administration entails making sure that the network is available when users need it. Other parts of the network administrator's job are monitoring the network's capacity to ensure that all transmission requirements can be met; adding capacity to the network when necessary; conducting training to prepare individuals to use the network; assisting IT professionals in writing applications; backing up the network software and data regularly; putting security procedures in place; ensuring that network personnel can respond quickly to an operational or security failure; and diagnosing and troubleshooting problems on the network when they occur.

7 Explain the three types of multiuser architectures and the advantages offered by each. In a *centralized architecture,* all network hardware and software are located at a central site where the central computer, or host, performs all of the processing and manages the network. Centralized systems are easy to manage. In a *distributed architecture,* computers reside at different locations and are interconnected by a communications network. Distributed architecture places information at the locations where it is used most often while ensuring that others in the system have access to it.

To take advantage of the benefits of both types of architecture, companies can choose to combine them in a *hybrid architecture*. Here, a mainframe controls interaction with all the devices attached directly to it. The host does not, however, directly control those computers interconnected at lower levels of the network.

 # KEY TERMS

CRITICAL CONNECTIONS

1 Mellon Bank—Where Customers Can See and Talk with Experts Miles Away

 Mellon   Thanks to videoconferencing's attractive costs and the widespread availability of transmission links, Mellon's experts need not always be at the same location to be available to customers for a live conference. Customer videoconference calls can be routed to them whether they are at headquarters, in a branch office, or even in their own home. The bank's experts can always have the customer's information handy as well, for databases and electronic records are accessible on-line and viewable on the display screen of their PCs.

Questions for Discussion

1. Do you think videoconferencing will change the work bankers must do for their customers? Will it change job descriptions?

2. Mellon wants to gain new banking customers through two-way videoconferencing. Would this service attract you to bank with Mellon (or retain you as a customer if you already do your banking with Mellon)?

3. Consider what *could* happen if banks combined widely used ATMs with videoconferencing. What new services would banks be able to offer to customers through "video ATM"?

2 Peapod Makes Grocery Shopping Easy

The Parkinson brothers are hoping that key demographic trends will help Peapod grow. These trends include the increasing number of people who have access to modem-equipped computers, either at home or at work, and the growth of the time-poor "sandwich generation"—dual-career couples in their 30s and 40s

torn between caring for their children and their aging parents. (Many adult children use Peapod to shop for their elderly parents.) Another boost may come from people with disabilities and the elderly, two groups who have limited mobility.

Questions for Discussion

1. Some experts estimate that half of all supermarket purchases are made on impulse. If you were a manager of a grocery store, would this estimate make you more or less eager to enter into an alliance with Peapod? If less, how could Peapod use your reaction to its advantage?

2. Some shoppers hesitate to let others pick out their produce. What other objections to Peapod's services can you think of? How could Peapod overcome these objections?

3. Peapod has signed up a fraction of all shoppers in its service area and, in order to prosper, would like to increase the percentage of the market it serves. What suggestions would you make to help Peapod increase its membership?

3 Delta Air Lines: What's Your Preference—An Office or a Living Room in the Sky?

Delta Air Lines   Delta sees other passenger-gratifying possibilities in information technology. The airline recently installed a satellite TV antenna on designated aircraft to capture the same digital signals that you can get with a satellite dish at home. As the plane travels from origin to destination, the antenna moves, keeping the aircraft in line with the satellite, to ensure uninterrupted communications. Live television pictures can be shown in the cabin, or passengers can tune in to the channel they wish. The biggest challenge may not be in deciding what to watch, but rather in keeping track of who has the "clicker."

Soon the airline will provide individual controls and separate viewing screens at each viewer seat so that passengers will be able to choose the program they want to watch regardless of what the passenger next to them is viewing.

Business or pleasure? An office or a living room? Those are the choices provided by on-board information technology.

Questions for Discussion

1. What makes it possible for the same Delta cellular telephone link to transmit both voice conversations and data and information via modem over the same communications link?

2. If you were an executive at Delta Air Lines, what justification would you advance for installing live television, via satellite, on aircraft used for long-distance flights?

3. Do you think passengers will be willing to pay an additional fee to see live television programs during long flights?

Net Work

Collaboration on the World Wide Web

Although the Web is widely used for e-mail and for the viewing of pages of information, it also provides a capability for collaboration between individuals and groups in different locations. CU-SeeMe (pronounced See You, See Me) is a free Internet software program (but copyrighted by Cornell University and its collaborators) that makes it possible to conduct desktop videoconferencing over the Web. Anyone with a Macintosh or Windows computer and a connection to the Internet can use CU-SeeMe to videoconference with another site located anywhere in the world. Multiple parties at different locations can participate in a CU-SeeMe conference, each from his or her own desktop computer.

With CU-SeeMe, launched directly from the Web browser on your desktop, you can participate in "Live over the Internet" conferences, broadcasts, or chats.

If you wish more information on Cornell's freeware version of CU-SeeMe, you can find it at URL http://cu-seeme.cornell.edu.

Consider the capabilities of CU-SeeMe and answer the following questions:

1. What characteristics of the Internet make it a powerful resource for videoconferencing?

2. What examples of business applications can you think of where having videoconferencing from your desktop would be useful?

3. What personal uses of CU-SeeMe would be beneficial to you?

GROUP PROJECTS AND APPLICATIONS

Project 1

With a partner, visit a company in one of the following industries, which all make use of large-scale computer networks:

- Transportation
- Retailing
- Manufacturing

Interview the network manager or someone in the IS department. What are the benefits of a wide area communications network to the company? What types of applications run on the network? What type of architecture is used? What functions does the network operating system perform? What business challenges does the company face, and how is the network helping to meet those challenges?

Prepare a two-page report summarizing your findings. Exchange reports with another group, then read and critique each other's report. Try to answer any questions that the other group may have.

Project 2

All parts of the United States have both local and long-distance telephone carriers. Contact a representative from one of these providers to discuss the company's position on developing additional communications capabilities for the nation's business and commerce infrastructure. What kinds of breakthroughs are expected over the next few years? What are the company's long-term plans? How will both businesses and private citizens benefit from these new technologies?

If possible, invite the representative to speak to your class. Before the lecture, the class should brainstorm a list of questions to ask the rep.

REVIEW QUESTIONS

1. Define a multiuser system and state the three business purposes of multiuser systems.

2. What is a communications network? What is a node?

3. Why do communications networks qualify as multiuser systems?

4. Discuss the nature of communications architecture and distinguish among the three types of communications architecture. What advantages and disadvantages does each type offer to business?

5. How do host computers and front-end computers differ? What purpose does each serve in a communications network? Is each a required component of a network?

6. Describe the distinguishing characteristics of a wide area network (WAN), local area network (LAN), and metropolitan area network (MAN). Under what circumstances do companies use each type of network?

7. What are the two types of communications channels?

8. Identify the three types of physical communications channels. Which has been in use for the longest period of time?

9. Describe the four types of cableless communications media.

10. Explain the differences among public access networks, private "leased line" networks, and value-

added networks. What advantages does each offer to business?

11. Do LANs use the same types of communications channels as WANs? Explain.

12. What is the purpose of a modem? A network interface card?

13. Why do businesses sometimes want to interconnect their communications networks? What are the two means for doing so? What determines which method of interconnection will be used?

14. Describe the role of a network operating system

in a communications network. How is it different from a computer operating system? Does using one eliminate the need for the other?

15. What responsibilities are entailed in network administration?

16. How are electronic mail and voice mail different? What advantages does each system offer?

17. How do videoconferencing and videotex differ? What purpose does each serve?

18. Describe electronic data interchange.

DISCUSSION QUESTIONS

1. The U.S. Congress recently enacted legislation aimed at building a nationwide high-speed communications network of optical fibers. Should the federal government take an active role in creating this network? How would the network benefit a company that operates a WAN spanning 10 states?

2. Matson Navigation Co., a 110-year-old company that operates ships carrying cargo between the West Coast of the United States and Hawaii, uses electronic mail, fax, and local area networks linked to a mainframe to track containers on its ships and on the 600 trucks that pass through its terminal gates daily. What type of network architecture is Matson using? What type of network is it using?

3. The Internet, today a maze of thousands of networks around the world, was originally created in the mid-1960s to facilitate the sharing of information between researchers at government agencies and universities. Now that thousands of private enterprise employees exchange electronic mail on the Internet every day, company officials often stress that none of these messages involve confidential data. Why would officials emphasize this point?

4. Managers typically spend between 30 and 70 percent of their time in meetings. Why might this fact be inspiring companies to use workgroup conferencing?

SUGGESTED READINGS

Cats-Baril, William L., and Tawfik Jelassi. "The French Videotex System Minitel: A Successful Implementation of a National Information Technology Infrastructure." *MIS Quarterly 18* (March 1994): 1–20. An interesting in-depth, yet candid, discussion of the revolution that occurred in the French telecommunications system from the mid-1970s to the mid-1980s. The article also describes the evolution of Minitel up into the mid-1990s.

Dertouzos, Michael L. "Communications, Computers, and Networks." *Scientific American 265* (September 1992). This special issue contains 11 articles dealing with different aspects of multiuser computer systems and communications networks. Each article, written by an expert in the field, focuses on the implications of advances in IT for people, business organizations, and government.

Gilder, George. "Into the Telecosm." *Harvard Business Review 69* (March–April 1992): 150–161. Gilder presents a fascinating view of the future of multiuser computer networks. Taking a business perspective, he examines what companies and individuals can already do with computer networks and what obstacles must be overcome if they are to do even more. His global outlook makes him argue that business leaders should develop national networks rather than "a tower of Babel" of private networks.

Hummel, Robert L. "Eight Ways to the Future." *Byte 21* (December 1996): 85–88. Eight technology leaders agree: change is the only sure thing about IT in the next decade. Leaders from communications and computing companies share their views on 10 key areas of information technology, pointing out areas of sharp disagreement.

Horton, Patrick R., and Michael D. Morris. "A Shared Network Spreadsheet." *Byte 12* (July 1987): 185ff. Horton and Morris explore the many ways in which personal applications software can be shared in a multiuser local area network. Their article emphasizes such practical issues as maintaining applications security and data integrity.

Kumar, Kuldeep, and Han G. van Dissel. "Sustainable Collaboration: Managing Conflict and Cooperation in Interorganization Systems." *MIS Quarterly 30* (September 1996): 279–300. The authors examine the challenges of creating and sustaining IT-enabled collaboration between organizations. Three types of interorganization systems prescribe the way companies exchange information and collaborate over networks.

Sprague, Ralph H., Jr. "Electronic Document Management." *MIS Quarterly 19* (December 1995): 29–50. This paper explores the ways and means of storing, retrieving, and caring for electronic documents that are transportable over communications networks. Examples span such areas as manufacturing, human resources, and customer service.

Stallings, William. *Local Networks* (3d ed.). New York: Macmillan, 1990. A standard textbook on the design, construction, and use of local area networks. Includes excellent comparative information regarding the trade-offs that must be made in moving from mainframe-based wide area networks to local area networks.

Wright, Karen. "The Road to the Global Village." *Scientific American 262* (March 1990): 83–94. Wright's article explains why and how, after more than a century of electronic technology, societies are finally extending themselves globally, transcending both space and time barriers. Among the topics discussed are cooperative work, "infotainment," "knowbots," and virtual reality.

C A S E
S T U D Y

Satellites Help CNN Span the Globe

Executives at the world's traditional television networks scoffed when Ted Turner announced plans for an all-news network in the late 1970s. What did Turner, head of an outdoor advertising business and small TV stations, know about journalism? At that time, Turner Broadcasting System (TBS) consisted of two independent television stations—one in Atlanta and one in Charlotte, North Carolina. Both aired a steady diet of old movies, sports, and reruns—usually opposite television network news. Turner's Atlanta station broadcast just 40 minutes of news daily—the minimum needed to meet U.S. licensing requirements—and then, usually in the middle of the night.

But the doomsayers didn't count on Ted Turner's three most important qualities. One was his drive and determination. Dubbed "Captain Outrageous" for the "winner-take-all" daring that helped him win the America's Cup in 1977, Turner recalls "I just love it when someone says I can't do something."

Turner's second strength was his vision, the ability to see the potential in these trends:

- The emergence of cable television as an alternative to the established and powerful television networks.
- The popularity of all-news radio, a concept pioneered by WINS in New York during the 1960s. WINS' slogan, "Give us 22 minutes and we'll give you the world," became the model for the basic "news wheel"—the continuous repeating and updating of news stories interspersed with expensive advertising spots.
- The growing number of commercial communications satellites carrying transponders, devices that can be tuned to receive a signal from one satellite dish and relay it to another.

When Home Box Office, Time, Inc.'s "premium" cable service, announced that it would begin using satellite transmission, Turner decided to follow suit. Unde-

terred by the fact that leasing a satellite transponder would cost $1 million a year, plus another $750,000 for the station's satellite dish, Turner plunged ahead and converted his Atlanta station into, in his own words, a "superstation" whose signal blanketed the United States. If one transponder could blanket the nation, Turner thought, why not lease a second and a third? Thus, he created a cable news network that covered the world.

Turner's third important quality was his ability to assemble a team of people who shared his vision and knew how to turn it into reality. One of the most important members of Turner's team in the early days was Reese Schonfeld, a dedicated journalist who was then struggling to create a video news service. When Turner asked him if an all-news network could be established, Schonfeld presented him with a vision of an all-electronic newsroom that would be linked by phone lines and satellite to newsrooms and reporters around the world. If Turner didn't have his own reporters on the scene, Schonfeld pointed out, he could buy coverage of major events from independent journalists or local television stations.

The rest is history. Today, the network envisioned by Schonfeld is a reality: Cable News Network (CNN) covers breaking news almost anywhere in the world. A good example is CNN's 1992 coverage of Operation Restore Hope in the African nation of Somalia, which has virtually no infrastructure. Reporters went to Somalia packing portable electricity generators, food, and water, in addition to the gear they needed to connect to CNN's news desk. This gear included laptop computers, collapsible satellite dishes that fit into oversize suitcases, and Inmarsats—portable telephones that incorporate tiny satellite dishes.

Since its debut in June 1980, CNN has garnered journalists' respect for its skill in using information technology to provide live, unedited coverage of historical events. CNN viewers watched firsthand the 1986 explosion of the space shuttle *Challenger,* the 1989 students' revolt in China's Tiananmen Square, and the 1991

Persian Gulf War. Today, CNN airs in more than 130 million homes in 200 countries, and it is a fixture at airports and hotels catering to diplomats and the international community. Foreign ministries, including U.S. State Department consular offices, routinely monitor CNN around the clock. In 1991, CNN received the cable industry's highest award for its Persian Gulf coverage—which had been followed closely by both U.S. and Iraqi leaders. *Time* magazine named Ted Turner its "Man of the Year" for 1991. It was a heady triumph for a man who started a network on a shoestring and a dream.

Along with his bold vision and his ability to see the "big picture," Turner is a manager with clear priorities for his network and the people who work for him. The top priority for Turner's IT professionals is the creation of "flyaway phone systems"—portable satellite links—that will give CNN reporters access to whomever or whatever they need to access anywhere in the world.

Turner's director of management information systems has made a guarantee to all end-users: "You need to talk to another department, another country even, and we'll get you there—without putting another box on your desk. . . . My job is not to disrupt user comfort."

Questions for Discussion

1. Describe the different types of networks in use at CNN. How do these networks illustrate the principles of multiuser systems?

2. Turner is so committed to the concept of the global economy that he chides workers who use the term *foreign* instead of *international*. How does CNN's success reflect the other business trends listed in Table 10.1?

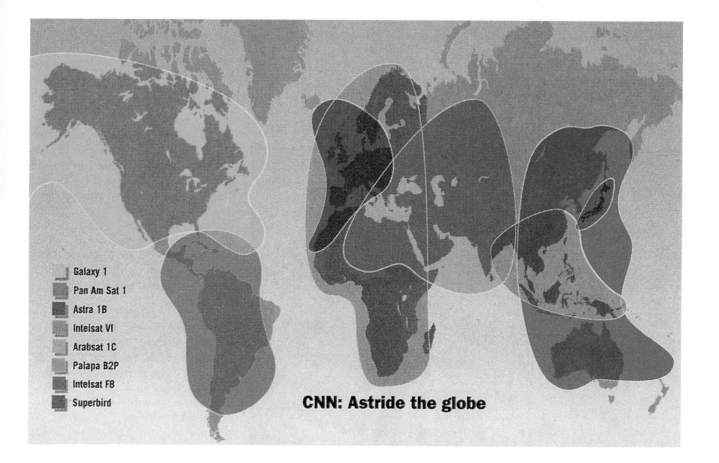

- Galaxy 1
- Pan Am Sat 1
- Astra 1B
- Intelsat VI
- Arabsat 1C
- Palapa B2P
- Intelsat F8
- Superbird

CNN: Astride the globe

USING Lotus Notes TO COLLABORATE

Collaboration software (also called *groupware*), such as Lotus Notes, can be used as a conferencing system for group problem solving, as a tracking tool for project management, and as a library for policies, documentation, or news. Collaboration systems are much more convenient and powerful than e-mail, for they let people use their own personal productivity tools, including spreadsheets, presentation programs, and drawing packages, to share knowledge in the form of documents and responses to documents anytime, anywhere.

A Lotus Notes database is a collection of related documents stored under a single name. It can be small—for example, a phone directory used collectively by a project team—or it can be a large group of customer, supplier, or personnel records. Unlike structured relational databases, a Lotus Notes database contains *documents*. A document can be as short or as long, as structured or as unstructured, as the person creating the document desires. In addition, Lotus Notes documents may contain graphics, tables, and a variety of type fonts, sizes, presentation styles, and attachments. Because all of a database's documents are stored on a server, all members of the collaborating team have shared access to the database.

Lotus Notes' principal work surface, or *desktop,* contains menus, tabbed pages, and database icons (which are stored on the tabbed pages). The program allows a network to include client systems that are either Apple Macintosh computers or IBM-compatible computers running Windows, OS/2, or UNIX. The menu bar across the top of the screen includes the familiar pull-down commands for opening, closing, and printing files (FILE), editing documents (EDIT), changing the view on the desktop (VIEW), and sending mail (MAIL). Six colored tabs at the top of the workspace represent pages. Clicking on the tabs allows the user to switch between pages.

Each icon in the workspace represents a different database. These databases may contain a variety of different types of information, including discussions about customer projects, tracking of service requests, and address books. To use a particular database, you add its icon to a tabbed page by dragging the icon to the tab. Users usually leave open on the desktop the databases they need most often during the day. When they want to open a particular database, they need only double-click on its identifying icon.

Here's how one company with offices in many different countries uses Lotus Notes to help manage projects.

The First Afternoon

1 Frank Bobson just received a request from an important customer who wishes to place a large order for a seemingly simple product, globes. However, because the world's regions have changed dramatically in recent years, the customer wants to be certain the globes reflect the latest changes in international political boundaries. Frank knows that getting the order depends on getting these globes to the customer fast. Realizing that accepting and delivering this order requires collaboration between team members, Frank wants to get a discussion going among all his team members, who work at various locations. For example, Thierry Bouchard is located in Neuilly, a city on the outskirts of Paris. Roberta Hughes is in San Francisco, and James Carlton and others are located in different parts of the building with Frank. Fortunately, all members of the team are interconnected through Lotus Notes.

To begin a discussion on this order, Frank clicks the Worldwide Discussion icon on his desktop. Once in Worldwide Discussion, he uses the word processing capabilities within Lotus Notes to pose a question to members of his team: "How fast can we turn the request around to save the sale to the customer, Education Resources, Inc.?" Frank needs this information in three days, but—being a good businessman—knows he has to convey a sense of urgency. He asks for a response by the same afternoon.

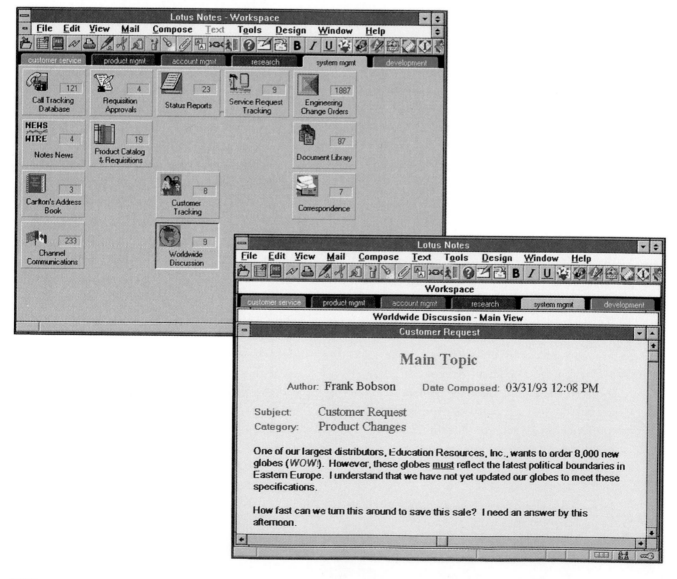

2 Frank decides to work through his lunch hour to assemble some background information on his request. He decides to check out the Customer Tracking database for any background information that might be useful to the group. After clicking on the Customer Tracking icon to open the database, he searches for the customer's name. Up comes the first document, a customer profile document created on January 21, 1993 by Hattie Henderson. The document provides the general information Frank's team needs to judge the importance of the customer and the necessity of carefully considering the request. The icon in the lower left corner of the screen indicates that more information is attached to the document. When Frank clicks on the icon, an additional window containing a table of sales data for 1991 and 1992 appears within the document.

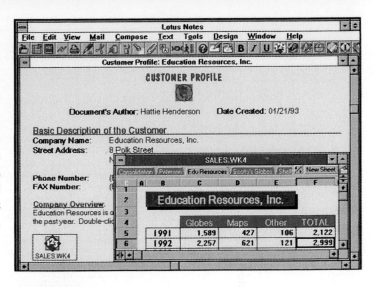

3 Frank also opens the News Wire database to get information on the political changes around the world affecting international boundaries. In News Wire, he finds a document titled *The Rapidly Changing Map of Europe*. By clicking on the document's title, he can instantly view the item's contents on his desktop. All of the information available to Frank on his Lotus Notes system is also available to other team members.

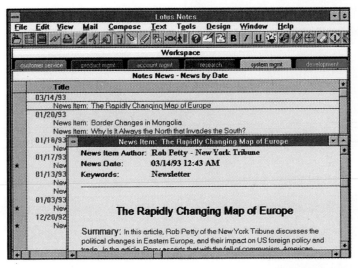

4 Thierry Bouchard, in the France office, receives Frank's message on his Apple Macintosh client system. His desktop contains the same features as other Notes users, except that he prefers to have the menu commands and other informative notes displayed in French. Upon receiving Frank's note, Bouchard immediately opens a set of documents from a recent rush job to review the handling of that order and whether that procedure might be useful now.

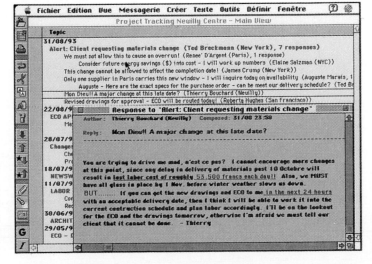

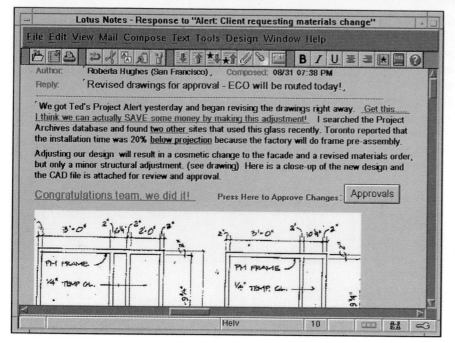

5 Roberta Hughes, in San Francisco, received Frank's document on her UNIX client system. Noting that Education Resources has requested a design change, she retrieves an electronic document prepared for an earlier project with a similar design change in the company's archives. The document includes a drawing of the design change. It also shows the button the document's author included at the time for approval of the drawing.[1]

[1] Lotus Notes facilitates committee approvals, without a face-to-face meeting, by making it possible for readers to signify their agreement by acting right on the document. Clicking the Approval button in this case signifies agreement. Notes transmits the concurrence to other team members.

The Next Morning

6 The next morning, Frank returns to his original message to find that two team members have submitted responses. He knows these documents have arrived because the comment "(2 Responses)" and a question mark icon have been added at the top of the document.

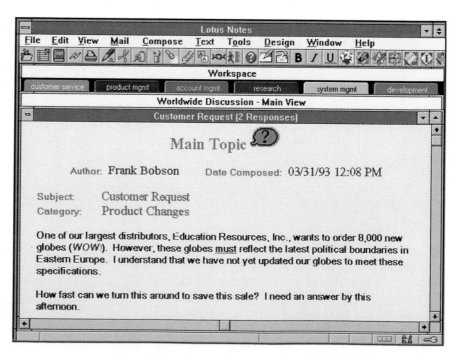

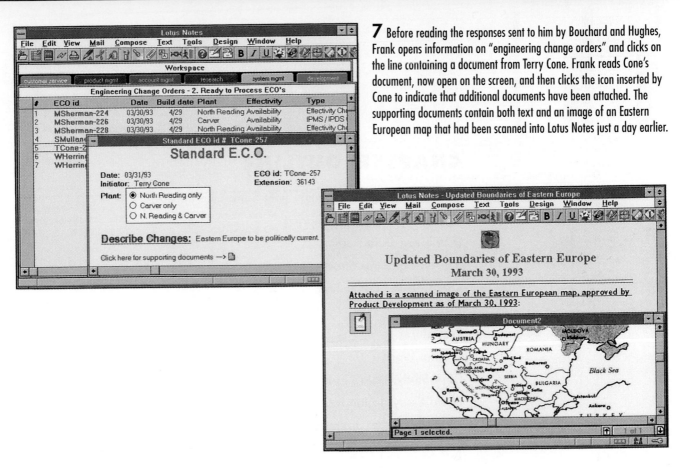

7 Before reading the responses sent to him by Bouchard and Hughes, Frank opens information on "engineering change orders" and clicks on the line containing a document from Terry Cone. Frank reads Cone's document, now open on the screen, and then clicks the icon inserted by Cone to indicate that additional documents have been attached. The supporting documents contain both text and an image of an Eastern European map that had been scanned into Lotus Notes just a day earlier.

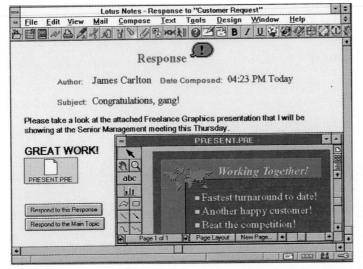

8 Even as Frank is reading Cone's document, James Carlton, another team member, is preparing to send Frank a message congratulating him on the order. Carlton's message will indicate that he sees no delay responding to the order because a new map of Eastern Europe's changed boundaries has already been prepared. To James's response is attached the new map that he prepared using Feelance Graphics (a presentation program running on his system) and copied into a Lotus Notes document. When Frank clicks on the icon labeled Present.Pre, the map is displayed on the screen. Carlton's document also includes buttons that readers can click either to comment on his response or to comment on the original topic created by Frank. When Carlton finished his response, Notes automatically forwarded it to everyone electronically linked into the discussion.

The team works back and forth throughout the morning to work out the details. By noon, Frank knows the job can be done. Lotus Notes allowed the group to collaborate electronically, sharing ideas, documents, and responses. No one was required to travel, send documents by courier, or even make lengthy telephone calls. In the end, the problem—and the opportunity—were managed quickly and with full participation.

CHAPTER 11

Shared and Distributed Data

CHAPTER OUTLINE

LEARNING OBJECTIVES

When you have completed this chapter, you should be able to

1 Identify the reasons organizations choose to share databases and the functions of a database management system.

2 Differentiate between shared and distributed databases.

3 Explain the difference between relational and object-oriented databases and their uses in business.

4 Describe the differences between schemas, views, and indexes.

5 Discuss the benefits of client/server computing.

6 Distinguish between a database administrator and a systems programmer.

7 Discuss database administration procedures and concurrency procedures and explain why these are an essential part of a shared database system.

Outsmarting the Competition with Sonic-Like Speed

Fast delivery used to mean a letter or package arrived at its destination in a couple of days. Then along came Federal Express,[1] and our expectations for fast delivery changed to *overnight* and "absolutely, positively" before 10:30 A.M. For some things, even overnight won't do, so fax machines have become a key tool in business. Fax is fine for letters and papers, but it can't transport a package. So what are you supposed to do if you need a package delivered the same day?

A Scottsdale, Arizona, company's clever use of IT may provide the answer for you. SonicAir, a subsidiary of United Parcel Service that received the Arthur Andersen Award for Distinguished Achievement in Fostering Innovation in 1996, provides *same day* delivery service. It specializes in

getting a package from one place to another—across town or across the country—in about four to six hours. Yet Sonic-Air doesn't own any planes, doesn't operate a fleet of speedy delivery trucks ... it doesn't even have neighborhood dropboxes. And chances are you've never even heard of SonicAir—unless, that is, you regularly need fast package delivery.

To meet its customers' needs, SonicAir relies on specialized databases, a sense of competitiveness, *commercial* aircraft, and independent drivers. There are several thousand drivers around the country who take care of SonicAir's pickup and delivery upon request. The company knows who's reliable because it keeps careful records in its database, including descriptions of the drivers, their hours of availability, their truck sizes, and their track records for on-time delivery. Those who don't meet the company's performance standards are quickly weeded out. SonicAir maintains a successful on-time delivery rate of better than 98%.

[1]The photo essay at the end of this chapter entitled "Inside Federal Express" describes the FedEx system.

Because commercial airlines are essential to SonicAir's business, the company keeps a computer-based database of some 50,000 commercial flights daily. It also tracks the performance of the 10 most important commercial airlines and the 10 key commuter airlines. The company's database contains details on how fast a particular carrier loads freight and baggage, its likelihood of canceling flights, and its on-time arrival record.

So if you need to get a package from here to there *fast*, SonicAir will take your call. It will check the airlines' schedules and evaluate their on-time record in going from your location to the specified destination for your package, and choose a carrier accordingly. Then it will select a driver from the database and contact that driver to pick up your package, get it to the airport, and check it onto the flight. When the plane lands, another SonicAir contract driver will be waiting to take the package to its destination.

SonicAir has vision, databases, and commitment. Oh, just one other thing: Is SonicAir a transportation firm . . . or a communication company? Or both?

A *multiuser system* is a system shared by more than one user. As we saw in Chapter 10, both hardware and programs can be shared. Multiple users in the same building can share computers, printers, and other hardware; people across the hall or in different cities, states, and countries can share a communications network. Different types of programs, including application programs, the network operating system, and the computer operating system, oversee the activities of different components in the multiuser system.

In addition to sharing hardware and programs, people can share data to make effective use of available resources and to become more productive. If, for example, a group of related businesses shares a set of data, each business will have the same view of a customer, supplier, resource level, or business transaction.

In this chapter, we examine the sharing and distributing of data among multiple persons. We begin by discussing the principles of data sharing and distribution and examining the structure of relational and object-oriented databases. Throughout the chapter, we will see how data can be organized and stored to meet the needs of database users. We also will see the opportunities that client/server computing offers and the importance of good procedures. Finally, we will see that the sustained usefulness of shared databases is dependent on the people who manage them.

The Principles of Data Sharing

database
A collection of data and information describing items of interest to an organization.

As you learned in Chapter 7, a **database** is a collection of data and information describing items of interest (sometimes called *entities*) to an organization. Data are collected on such entities as people, places, things, events, and conditions (Figure 11.1). Each *data item* in the database—whether numeric, text, image, graphic, or sound—describes an *attribute* of the entity.

Why Share Data?

Capturing, storing, and maintaining data in a database is an expensive process. In fact, managers who examine the human, physical, and financial resources they have invested in compiling their organization's data find that data collection and maintenance are very costly indeed. Thus, it makes sense to use this important

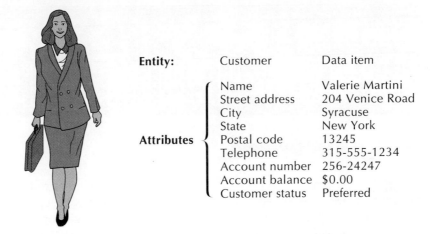

Entity:	Customer	Data item

	Name	Valerie Martini
	Street address	204 Venice Road
	City	Syracuse
	State	New York
Attributes	Postal code	13245
	Telephone	315-555-1234
	Account number	256-24247
	Account balance	$0.00
	Customer status	Preferred

Instance of entity as database record

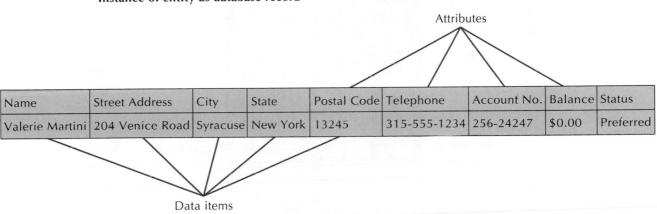

Attributes

Name	Street Address	City	State	Postal Code	Telephone	Account No.	Balance	Status
Valerie Martini	204 Venice Road	Syracuse	New York	13245	315-555-1234	256-24247	$0.00	Preferred

Data items

FIGURE 11.1   *Entity Description in a Database System*
The "customer" entity includes nine attributes and a data item for each attribute.

resource as often as possible and to manage it as effectively as possible. To do so entails making sure that all members of the organization who need the data will have access to them.

Sharing data means that all persons in the organization will work from the same set of data items for an entity. This consistency is important to the business's short-term and long-term success. Imagine the problem on a university campus if the campus bookstore used an enrollment figure from the registration database to order books for a course while the course instructor knew that many more students had been allowed to add the course to their semester's studies.

When databases are shared, two facts quickly become evident: (1) people need different data from the database; and (2) people often need the same data, but organized in different ways. We'll see later in this chapter how these needs can be met even if users and databases are at different locations. The *Rethinking Business Practices* feature entitled "Remaking Europcar" illustrates how effective use of databases transformed one company's operations throughout Europe.

RETHINKING BUSINESS PRACTICES

Remaking Europcar

Europcar ⬛ **Inter rent** When Belgian-born Freddy Dellis took over as chief executive of Europcar International SA, headquartered in Paris, he was immediately challenged by the need to make over the largest European car rental firm so that it would operate as a single enterprise. At the time, the separate branches of Europcar were highly nationalistic, a result of the company's growth over the years through the acquisition of independent auto rental companies in Switzerland, Germany, Italy, Austria, Portugal, and Scandinavia.

Understandably, country managers tended to buy and lease cars that carried their own national brands (e.g., the manager in the United Kingdom bought Rovers, the manager in France favored Peugeots) or that met their own personal preferences (the country

manager in Italy preferred German-made BMWs, and so they dominated Europcar's Italian fleet). As a result, Europcar paid more for all of its cars because it was not buying as a European company and negotiating lower prices based on the volume purchases in its pan-European market.

When Freddy Dellis and his staff looked closer, they found that the car makes were not the only important country differences: no rental rates were alike; every computer system was different; business practices varied dramatically; the language in contracts and for conducting business was inconsistent. Yet Europcar was supposed to be a *European* company, providing the same familiar "look and feel" to its customers in any country on the Continent or throughout the United Kingdom. Consistency was essen-

Database Management Systems

database management system (DBMS)

A program that makes it possible for users to manage the data in ways that increase accessibility and productivity.

Databases are used by different applications and for multiple purposes. **Database management systems (DBMS)** are programs that make it possible for users to manage the data and to increase productivity. Through the DBMS, the data are accessed, maintained, and processed.

The database management system program operates in conjunction with the other programs running in a computer system, including the application program, operating system, and network operating system (Figure 11.2). It maintains the structure of the data and interacts with the other programs to locate and retrieve the data needed for processing. It also accepts data from the application program and writes it into the appropriate storage location.

THE FUNCTIONS OF DATABASE MANAGEMENT.   As we saw in Chapter 7, database management is meant to accomplish five objectives. A brief review will be useful here.

tial if the company was to compete successfully with the large American rental companies then entering Europe: Hertz and Avis.

Dellis set out to rethink Europcar's ways, his principal objectives being to provide integrated business practices that would benefit both customer and company and to reduce business costs. Rethinking business practices implied restructuring. The nine-country structure was replaced by one of four regions, and the regional directors and 22 territory managers were told to concentrate on the customer side of the business. They were made responsible for development of marketing strategies, concentrating principally on sales and supporting reservation systems. Europcar headquarters also restructured the company's automobile purchases to capitalize on volume discounts. Thus, headquarters staff negotiated high-volume pan-European prices for the two styles of vehicles that would now make up its rental list: German cars (built for speed) and French cars (engineered for comfort and a smoother ride).

Overhauling the company's information systems was a very important part of strategy. The 55 different information systems Europcar had been running across the countries it served were scrapped and a centralized reservation system was implemented. Thanks to the new communications network and the powerful database capability at its center, up-to-the minute information was now available throughout Europcar's offices and at headquarters as well. With information on reservations and sales activities flowing quickly through the system, auto inventory and maintenance records were kept up-to-date and were used in running the business. (The system even enabled managers to tell whether or not rental offices were washing cars fast enough to meet customer demand.)

Dellis's international executive team (two Germans, one Frenchman, one Dutchman, and one Briton) has reworked Europcar's business practices and its information technology capabilities in order to capitalize on the international market and meet customer demand. Making the transition was challenging. But choosing *not* to restructure the company might have been devastating in the light of the sharp competition Europcar was facing.

1. **Integrating databases.** Through database management, individual databases, created at various times or by different people, can be joined, partly or entirely, to provide the information required to solve a problem or deal with a business issue.

2. **Reducing redundancy.** Unnecessary or undesirable duplication of data across databases can be eliminated through database management. Some redundancy, however, is desirable if it assists the people using the databases.

3. **Sharing information.** People at remote locations can share stored data that are made accessible to them.

4. **Maintaining integrity.** Good database management ensures the integrity of the database by allowing controlled access to information, providing security measures, and ensuring that data are available when needed.

5. **Enabling database evolution.** A database management system helps to ensure that the database will be able to evolve to meet the changing requirements of its users.

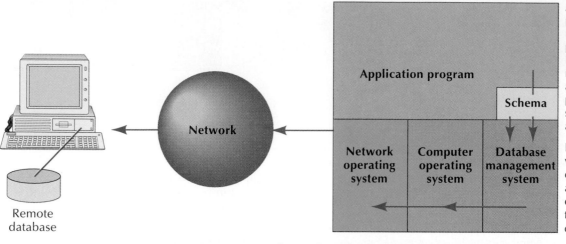

FIGURE 11.2 *Relationship of DBMS to Other Programs in Computer Memory*
A DBMS works in conjunction with the other programs running in a computer system.

The database management system achieves these objectives through database creation, database inquiry, database updating, and database administration (see Chapter 7 if you need to review these terms).

Distributed Databases

shared database
A database shared among many users and applications.

distributed database
A database that resides on more than one system in a distributed network. Each component of the database can be retrieved from any node in the network.

Databases are almost always shared among many users and applications. These **shared databases** can also be distributed. A **distributed database** is a database whose data reside on more than one system in a network. These data can be accessed, retrieved, or updated from any node in the network. Distributing data provides the needed data and information at a specific location, while allowing those same data to be used at other locations in the organization as well.

Anyone using distributed databases need not be aware of the location of the database because the application programs, communications software, and database management systems will automatically interact to identify, locate, and retrieve the data and information the user needs.

Partitioning and Replication

partitioning
A method of database distribution in which different portions of the database reside at different nodes in the network.

replication
A method of database distribution in which one database contains data that are included in another database.

Databases may be distributed in two ways: partitioning and replication. With **partitioning,** different portions of the database reside at different nodes in the network. To partition effectively, the database designer divides the database into the logical or meaningful subsets needed to support a specific type of application or business usage. The actual storage location of each database partition is known to the database management system but is not something the database user need be concerned about.

When a database contains data that are included in another database, it is said to be *replicated*. **Replication** is designed to speed the retrieval of data and, in turn, speed processing. It is particularly useful if certain parts of the database are required repeatedly for processing at different locations in a network. Avoiding continual transmission of information requests and the subsequent transmission

Electronic Expense Reporting Creates Advantage for American Express and Carlson Wagonlit

Making out a business expense report is a nuisance. The more one travels, the greater the nuisance. Until now. For a small annual fee, American Express and Carlson Wagonlit, both well-known worldwide travel agencies, will provide their business customers with software and support for low-hassle processing of business expenses.

The system is simple and convenient. Travelers use their American Express or Carlson Wagonlit credit card to pay vendors for airline tickets, hotel stays, and other expenses. The vendor then submits the bills to the credit card company for payment. After processing the payment, the credit card company electronically transmits a detailed record of the expenditures to a database at the traveler's company.

At the end of the trip, the traveler signs on to the system, reviews each expenditure, and adds account codes and explanations. A click of the mouse submits the report for approval and on to accounting for payment.

of the requested data minimizes delay and perhaps lowers network or communications costs.

PARTITIONING AND REPLICATION AT CRÉDIT LYONNAIS. A good example of partitioning and replication can be seen at Crédit Lyonnais, one of the 10 largest banks in the world. Headquartered in Paris, it has more than 1,700 branch offices serving customers throughout France. The heart of the bank's operation is a multilevel distributed system that includes a distributed customer database, interconnected local area networks, and multiple mainframe data centers that each run other banking databases.

Every Crédit Lyonnais branch office includes a LAN that links tellers, customer service representatives, loan officers, and the branch's managers. Each branch office, in turn, is linked to one of 18 regional centers, where midrange computers maintain a portion of a partitioned customer database (Figure 11.3). This relational database contains personal and financial profiles of the bank's customers in that region. Because the regional centers are linked to one another by multiple private digital communications lines, each center has access to database partitions at any of the other centers. (Prior to the creation of this system in 1992, each center maintained its own separate database. These databases were neither compatible with one another nor accessible to bank personnel outside the region.)

In addition, each regional center is linked by communications lines to data centers running mainframe computers in the cities of Lyons, Tours, and Paris. These three centers have access to all the regional database partitions, store account balance information, and handle the processing of customer loan applications.

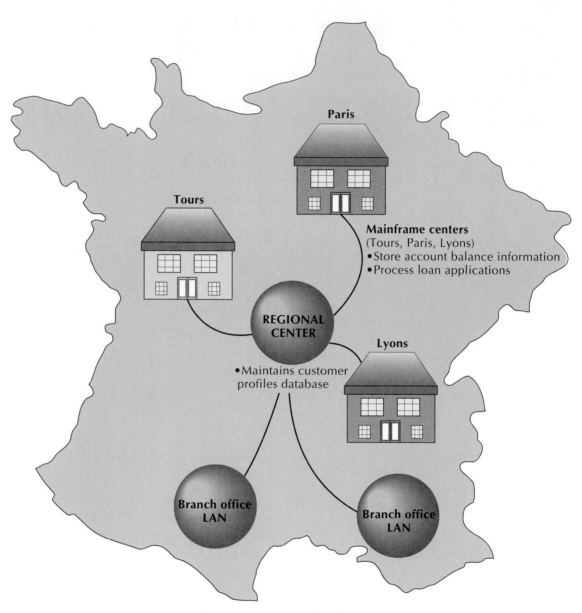

FIGURE 11.3 *Crédit Lyonnais's Distributed Database System*
Crédit Lyonnais's distributed database system spans 1,700 branch offices, 18 regional centers, and 3 mainframe centers.

This combination of a multilevel distributed system and partitioned databases has made data and information accessible to Crédit Lyonnais personnel when and where needed. The structure has an additional benefit: the potential to develop new business. For example, while tellers are assisting a customer to deposit a check or make a withdrawal from a savings account, they can retrieve the customer's profile from the regional center and have it right in front of them on-screen. This information enables tellers to determine whether the customer is a candidate for other bank services, which they can explain while serving the customer at the bank window.

All parties benefit from the system. Bank employees make more efficient use of their time because they do not have to deal with paper records and printed reports. Customers get better service; if they have a question about a past transaction while they are at the bank window, the teller will be able to answer it by looking at their customer profile on-screen. Managers benefit from the system because it lets them spend more time developing customer relations and new banking services and less time handling special cases or managing cases of missing information.

DISTRIBUTION STRATEGIES.   Database designers decide to partition or replicate by choosing the strategy that best fits the manner in which an organization conducts its business. The two most common distribution strategies are geographic and functional.

In a **geographic distribution strategy,** a database, or database partition, is located in a region where the data and information will be used most frequently. Crédit Lyonnais, with its databases partitioned across 18 regions, uses a geographic distribution strategy. Each partition is accessible to bank employees in all the regions.

A **functional distribution strategy** stresses processing functions over physical location. For example, it is common for business units to distribute databases according to business functions. Figure 11.4 illustrates how a company might use a computer network to distribute the various components of its database. The sales database includes the names and addresses of current and potential customers, the manufacturing database holds the schedules for the production and assembly of finished goods, the inventory control database holds inventory records of materials, parts, and finished goods, and the accounting database holds records of revenues due the company and monies to be paid out.

geographic distribution strategy
A database distribution strategy in which the database is located in a region where the data and information are used most frequently.

functional distribution strategy
A database distribution strategy in which the database is distributed according to business functions.

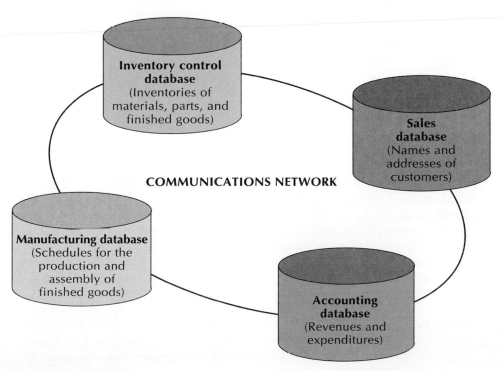

FIGURE 11.4
Functional Distribution of a Database
A functional distribution strategy stresses processing functions over physical location.

Functional distribution strategies are effective only when communications networks interconnect each database or partition. If, for example, salespersons do not know what products are scheduled for manufacturing (information in the manufacturing database) or which customers' accounts are overdue (information in the accounting database), they will not be able to function effectively. Throughout the business world, executives, managers, and staff members are increasingly recognizing the interdependence of business functions. Multiuser networks make communication among the various business functions faster and easier than once thought possible.

Designing a Distributed Database

In Chapter 1, we talked about the principle of high-tech/high-touch, which emphasizes the importance of considering the "people" side of information technology. In general, IT works best when it adjusts to people, not when people have to adjust to it. This simple principle applies just as much to the design of distributed databases as it does to the design of software packages for individual users.

The secret to making distributed databases effective is to keep their operational details invisible to their users. People using a database should be able to focus on the customer, supplier, or other business opportunity without having to worry about which database to use, how it is structured, or where it is located. The database management system should handle all the technical details behind the scenes so users don't have to think about how the DBMS works. For instance, a **database directory**—a requirement for shared databases—keeps track of the location of data and information so that users do not have to. This directory may be centralized, partitioned, or replicated.

database directory
The component of a shared database that keeps track of data and information.

The vast public telephone network does an excellent job of applying the principle of high-tech/high-touch (see Chapter 1). To make a telephone call, all you need to do is pick up the receiver and dial a few numbers. The telephone network does the rest. It translates the telephone number for processing by the network, retrieves routing information from the appropriate partition (the public phone system does not have a single centralized directory), and uses the routing to connect you. In short, it manages the entire process while all you have to do is wait for your party to pick up the receiver at the other end. The public phone system utilizes a distributed database to make your life easier.

OTHER DESIGN FACTORS.   Distributed database designers are influenced by six factors besides the need for ease of use:

1. **Storage costs.** Duplicating data in multiple partitions increases storage costs. Hence, designers must carefully monitor the volume of data in the distributed database and associated directories.
2. **Processing costs.** Because the cost of processing data and information rises as the extent of database distribution increases, designers must ensure that the database is distributed only to those who will use it.
3. **Communication costs.** The distribution of data increases the need for communication between nodes and, consequently, the costs of communication. The designer must ensure that these costs are justified by improvements in the business activities they support.
4. **Retrieval and processing.** The location of data, coupled with the architecture of the communications network, determines response time (i.e., elapsed time due to retrieval and processing). Database designers must be aware that

wider distribution will increase response time if data and information must be assembled from several remote locations. If, on the other hand, the data needed most often are located at or near the node requiring those data, retrieval and processing time may diminish substantially.

5. **Reliability.** Designers must safeguard both the existence of and access to important databases. Higher levels of reliability often mean higher costs because database partitions, which allow retrieval of duplicated information maintained at another node if one node breaks down, must be duplicated.

6. **Frequency of updates and queries.** Designers generally locate databases at those locations that update the databases most frequently. If processing requires retrieval of data and information in response to queries rather than just for updates, local storage of a database or directory at a node may not be justified.

Although cost-cutting is a recognized fact of business life in the 1990s, merely minimizing costs is not enough to guarantee success for a distributed database. For a distributed database to be truly useful, the IT professional who designs it must weigh storage costs, processing speed, and reliability against the frequency of use of the database and the manner in which it is used (entering or changing data as opposed to retrieving data). The more frequently the database is used, the more important it is to evaluate these criteria properly.

Shared Database Structures

All databases, whether shared or not, must be defined. An important part of definition entails describing the data items and records composing a database's structure.

Schema

The formal name for the definition of a database structure is its **schema.** The schema describes the names and attributes of each entity about which data are collected and stored. It provides a structure only; it does not include data items (e.g., the customer's name or address). You might think of the schema as the framework that outlines the structure of the database, with the database's entities and the relations between them fitting within that framework. Figure 11.2 shows the schema's relationship to other items in computer memory.

Each database has only one schema. Different databases use different schemas.

schema
The structure of a database.

SCHEMA FOR RELATIONAL DATABASES. Recall from Chapter 7 that **relational databases** are made up of data structured in a table format (a *relation*) consisting of rows and columns. The horizontal rows of the relation are called *records* or *tuples*. The vertical columns are the *attributes*, or *fields*, and contain *data items* of a record. The term *record* can also refer to a grouping of data items that describes one specific *occurrence* of an entity. For example, a student database includes records of all relevant data for each student. Throughout this chapter, we'll use this second definition of record.

The schema for a relational database identifies the database by a unique name and describes the relations contained within the database. A relation, in turn, is defined by its data items, each of which is identified by a name, type (such as numeric or text), and length specification. In this manner, the schema gives a distinct structure to the relational database.

relational database
A database in which the data are structured in a table format consisting of rows and columns.

SCHEMA FOR OBJECT-ORIENTED DATABASES.   A newer type of database that is emerging alongside relational databases is the **object-oriented database.** An **object** is a focal point about which data and information are collected. Hence, customers and orders—items we called "entities" when discussing relational databases—are also objects. Object-oriented database systems store data and information about these objects.

Data and information can be stored about both entities and objects. However, unlike relational databases, object-oriented databases store **actions,** instructions telling the database how to process the object to produce specific information.

The U.S. brokerage and investment firm Shearson Lehman Brothers has created an object-oriented database as the basis for many of its business activities. In this database are account objects (customers), contract objects (management agreements between Shearson Lehman and firms that have signed investment contracts), and security objects (the descriptive details of stocks, bonds, and stock options). Each object contains the descriptive data you would expect (names, addresses, prices, and so on). Each also contains information describing when and how to purchase an investment instrument. Thus, an individual account (the object) can buy a security, just as if a broker were initiating the action, but without human intervention.

Object-oriented databases offer the capability to store more sophisticated types of data and information than relational databases do. For example, such complex information as three-dimensional diagrams, animated video clips, and photographs do not fit easily within the row-and-column structure of relational databases. However, because both data and processing instructions are part of object descriptions, such information can be handled in an object-oriented database.

Both U.S.-based Boeing Aircraft Co. and England's British Aerospace Ltd. use object-oriented databases to maintain data about the design, components, and maintenance of their multimillion-dollar aircraft. These object databases store detailed schematic drawings of the planes' interiors, exteriors, and electronic components, including their extensive cable and wiring systems. Manufacturing and cost information is also included in the databases.

Before moving to object-oriented databases, both companies maintained their data on groups of separate databases. This system was costly and inefficient because it made it difficult for designers and engineers to get a complete picture of the repercussions of a particular action. For example, if the cost of a component changed, a project engineer would first have to search the component database to see where and in what quantity that component was being used. Then the engineer would have to search the order database to see if the component was being used in a specific aircraft configuration. Finally, the engineer would have to go to the manufacturing database to retrieve construction and assembly details related to the component. The process was both time-consuming and error-prone. Today, drawings, cost, manufacturing, and assembly details regarding a component are all combined in the object database. Data and information are available much more quickly, and the cost of managing data and information is lower.

OTHER DATABASE SCHEMAS.   Two other types of database schemas are worthy of mention here. *Hierarchical databases* store data in the form of a tree, where the relationship among data items is one-to-many (that is, one data item is linked to several other data items). In *network databases,* the relationship among the data items can be either one-to-many or many-to-many (i.e., several data items

---

object-oriented database
A database that stores data and information about objects.

object
A focal point about which data and information are collected. Used in object-oriented databases.

action
An instruction that tells a database how to process an object to produce specific information.

are linked to several other data items). Detailed explanations of these types of databases are beyond the scope of this discussion. It is enough to say here that hierarchical and network databases store data in a way that makes access to them faster for certain types of queries and slower for others.

 Object-oriented technology promises to be the basis for many types of applications in the future. The object-oriented concept of combining data and processing instructions is now being embedded in programs (object-oriented programs) and application development procedures (object-oriented design), as well as in databases.

We can draw an analogy between objects and Lego blocks, the plastic building blocks that snap together. Each Lego can be attached to any other Lego to build any type of structure—a house, a barn, a skyscraper, a car, or a medieval castle. Should the builder decide partway through the process to change the structure's design, she can either add more Lego blocks to the current design or reassemble the blocks in a different way. Objects can be used in a similar way. Although they are different on the inside, they are like Legos on the outside in that an assortment of objects can be assembled in many different ways. Therefore, applications can be created quickly and efficiently by connecting individual objects to create a desired result. ∎

Views

When a database is created, it is designed and stored according to a designer-determined structure of relations. As we noted earlier in this chapter, however, users of shared databases often want to organize the data differently from the way in which they are stored. Database management systems address this need.

Users who want to organize data and information differently from the way in which they are stored in the database can use views to do so. A **view** is a subset of one or more databases, created either by extracting copies of records from a database or by merging copies of records from multiple databases.[2] Like databases themselves, views have names and records composed of data items. As Figure 11.5 shows, multiple views of data can be extracted from the database and used in any application, including calculation, sorting, and generation of reports and other output.

In one sense, a view is simply a logical grouping of data. It gives the appearance that data have been moved or combined to meet processing requirements, although the database's physical structure (schema) has not been altered. Savvy marketers purchase large databases and create views to help them target advertising campaigns, as the *Information Technology in Practice* feature entitled "Database Marketing: The Personal Art of Persuasion" explores in detail.

Viewing capabilities provide many benefits to business users.

- Views allow users to examine data in different ways without changing the physical structure of the database.
- Users can make changes in the data in a view while leaving the data in the database in its original form.

view

A subset of one or more databases, created either by extracting copies of records from a database or by merging copies of records from multiple databases.

---

[2]In some organizations, views are called *subschemas*—or subsets of the schema. In effect, subschemas (views) partition the database among applications.

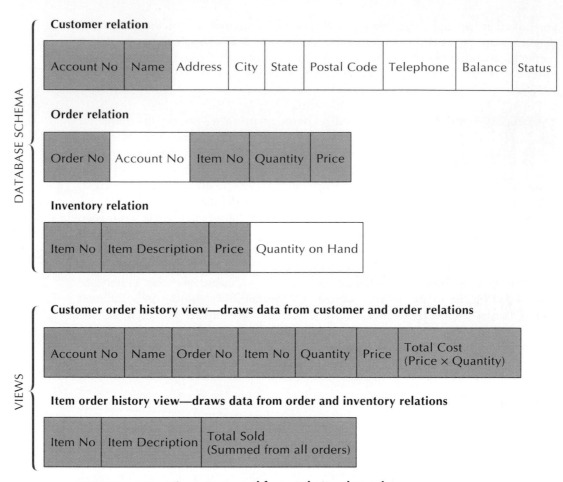

FIGURE 11.5   *Views Extracted from Relational Database*
Data from a relation can be extracted and used in many applications.

- Database security is maintained because individuals and applications can be kept away from sensitive data since they will process from the views rather than from the database itself. Sensitive or protected data are not included in a view.
- Views shield users from changes in the physical database (e.g., the restructuring of records so that they reside in a different location or a different sequence).

Views from multiple databases can be combined to meet business requirements. The State of Georgia Department of Revenue, for example, has linked several different databases in an effort to collect the state sales and withholding taxes owed by businesses. During the processing of income tax refund checks, department staff members use personal and business ID numbers to link records showing an individual's business income tax, the sales tax the state received from the business, and the withholding tax it received from the company's employees, even though each database is maintained by a separate system and a different agency (Figure 11.6 on page 520). When the Department of Revenue's computer determines that a refund is due to an individual, it checks with the other databases before cutting the check. If it finds a match with a record describing sales tax

INFORMATION TECHNOLOGY IN PRACTICE

Database Marketing: The Personal Art of Persuasion

Mass markets, mass merchandising, mass media. To many people, these phrases define marketing. They think of big companies seeking to appeal to massive groups of people through print or broadcast messages. For some companies, that image of marketing is true. But for a sizable number of others, it's inaccurate, and has been so for some time.

Many of the world's leading companies view their customers, current or potential, not as a large, anonymous group with uniform taste, but rather as individuals with unique needs and desires. For these companies, *database marketing* is a means for serving people even as the firms help themselves.

Database marketing combines the availability of databases of customer and consumer information with sophisticated new software capable of extracting valuable marketing information. Don't confuse database marketing with *direct-mail marketing,* in which large name and address lists are used to mail catalogs, brochures, applications, and announcements by the thousands (even millions). Database marketing focuses on the *individual,* not the addressee.

Sophisticated companies try continually to capitalize on their strengths in order to close the gap between themselves and their customers, to provide more tailored services, and to fill a niche where needs are not being met. Of course, they want to keep their existing customers—and perhaps woo more business from them—even as they win over new customers. But to do that, they must know the wants and needs, as well as the likes and dislikes, of individual buyers. They must *personalize* the art of persuasion. And that's where database marketing comes in.

A restaurant's software might extract from its customer database the information that your birthday is approaching and automatically address and mail a birthday card to you containing the gift of a "complimentary birthday dinner." Of course, the restaurant expects you to bring along some friends to help you celebrate your birthday—so it will have the chance to attract new customers even as it pleases an old one with a free meal.

Other examples abound. Take Goodyear Tire Co., which sends you a message offering free rotation of the tires you purchased from it several months back. Interestingly, the card arrives just when you've run up enough miles to need a rotation to get the best wear out of your tires. Is there a gimmick here? No. The rotation is free, but the company knows that if other things on your car need attention, you will probably have them done at the same time, giving more business to Goodyear.

And then there's Delta Airlines, which sends out announcements of special services being offered at its new Frankfurt, Germany, terminal. The message goes only to those frequent fliers who travel to Europe frequently.

There's also Brady's, a San Diego–based chain of men's clothing stores, which asks customers to complete a card noting their size and style preferences.

From these cards Brady's creates a database its sales-people use to identify which customers should be reminded about sales. The same database yields information ensuring that every Brady's shopper gets a birthday card containing a discount coupon worth $15. The result? Even though Brady's cut its advertising budget by 60 percent, its sales increased by 10 percent and the chain expanded from two to five stores in just two years.

Finally, there's the grocery chain that has designed a system to determine what products people purchase as they go by the checkout counter, and then offer coupons on the spot for complimentary store-brand products. The idea is that if the store can get people to sample a product they never thought of buying, they may like it enough to add it to their shopping list the next time they come to the store. (And besides, "freebies" usually stimulate customer loyalty.)

Companies are learning to take advantage of valuable databases they already own from recording a business transaction or the customer information supplied on warranty cards. With the help of the right software, marketers can analyze these details to identify opportunities for reinforcing customer loyalty or increasing sales.

Marketing indeed involves the art of persuasion, but the style of persuasion is changing. The trend is away from brute force selling to the masses toward meeting the real needs and wants of customers in a way that benefits both customer and company.

owed by the same person through his or her business, it automatically applies the refund to the sales tax debt. At the same time, it sends the individual a message saying, "We have determined that you still owe sales tax and have applied your income tax refund against that obligation." Before the state acquired this ability to interrelate databases, a large amount of sales taxes went uncollected.

Indexes

An important advantage offered by databases and a DBMS is flexibility of retrieval. Views provide users with a way to assemble data from different databases. Indexes make it possible to retrieve data in different sequences and on the basis of different data items.

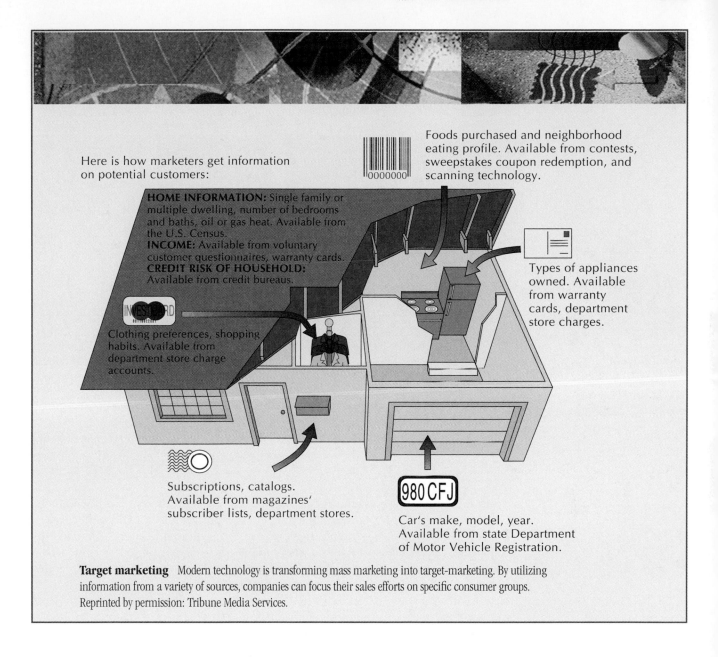

Here is how marketers get information on potential customers:

Foods purchased and neighborhood eating profile. Available from contests, sweepstakes coupon redemption, and scanning technology.

HOME INFORMATION: Single family or multiple dwelling, number of bedrooms and baths, oil or gas heat. Available from the U.S. Census.
INCOME: Available from voluntary customer questionnaires, warranty cards.
CREDIT RISK OF HOUSEHOLD: Available from credit bureaus.

Types of appliances owned. Available from warranty cards, department store charges.

Clothing preferences, shopping habits. Available from department store charge accounts.

Subscriptions, catalogs. Available from magazines' subscriber lists, department stores.

Car's make, model, year. Available from state Department of Motor Vehicle Registration.

Target marketing   Modern technology is transforming mass marketing into target-marketing. By utilizing information from a variety of sources, companies can focus their sales efforts on specific consumer groups. Reprinted by permission: Tribune Media Services.

An **index** is a data file that contains identifying information about each record (the record key) and its location in storage. The **record key** is a designated field used to distinguish one record from another. For example, the record key by which university students are typically identified is a unique student ID number. Each number is unique in that it is assigned to only one student.

A DBMS is able to automatically build and use indexes according to specifications prepared by the database administrator, whose role we will discuss later in this chapter. When an application, by providing the record key, requests the DBMS to retrieve a record, the DBMS quickly searches the index to find the right record key. It then accesses the database to locate and retrieve the record so that it can be processed by the application.

index
A data file that contains identifying information about each record and its location in storage.

record key
In a database, a designated field used to distinguish one record from another.

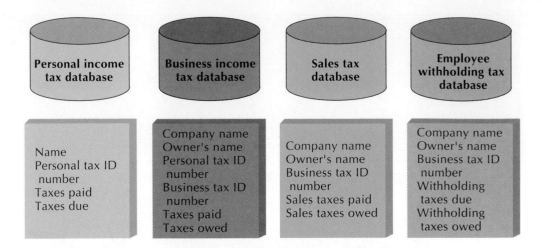

| Personal income tax database | Business income tax database | Sales tax database | Employee withholding tax database |

| Name
Personal tax ID number
Taxes paid
Taxes due | Company name
Owner's name
Personal tax ID number
Business tax ID number
Taxes paid
Taxes owed | Company name
Owner's name
Business tax ID number
Sales taxes paid
Sales taxes owed | Company name
Owner's name
Business tax ID number
Withholding taxes due
Withholding taxes owed |

Department of Revenue cross–database view, created by using common data fields of personal tax ID number and business tax ID number

Name	Personal tax ID number	Business tax ID number	Amount of refund*	Business tax due*	Sales tax due*	Withholding tax due*

* Value determined by calculation

FIGURE 11.6 *Using a View to Span Multiple Databases at the State of Georgia Department of Revenue*
By linking several databases, the State of Georgia Department of Revenue can collect taxes owed before it issues refund checks.

As Figure 11.7 shows, the index and search process takes place "behind the scenes" as part of processing. Therefore, neither the index nor the search is visible to an individual user. Information about the student can be obtained by requesting the database to locate and retrieve the record for the person with a specific ID number. To speed retrieval, the database system searches an index containing all student ID numbers and location information for each record associated with the student's ID, and then retrieves data and information directly from the specified location. Indexes eliminate the need to search all records in a database to find the one needed.

THE FEDEX INDEX. Federal Express Corp., the Memphis, Tennessee–based overnight shipping company, uses an index to keep track of the location of each package shipped through its system. The company's central database at corporate headquarters in Memphis is accessible to all FedEx drivers and telephone agents throughout the world. When a customer calls in to inquire about the location of a package, FedEx can provide a speedy response. Here's how it's done.

Each package is identified by a unique number (called a tracking number), by the name of the individual and company shipping the package, and by the recipient. Two million packages enter the system every day. For this reason, a huge database (60 billion bytes) must be searched whenever a customer calls to ask, "Has my package been delivered?"

FedEx creates multiple indexes for its tracking database, one each for the tracking number, sender's name, sender's company, recipient's name, and recipient's

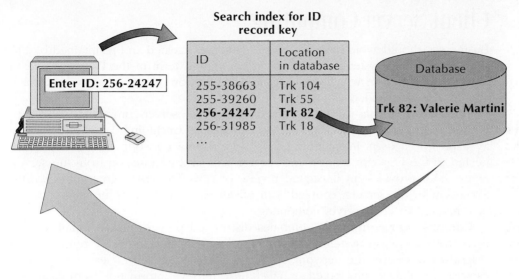

Retrieve copy of data from database
and place in main memory

FIGURE 11.7   *Using an Index to Retrieve Data*
An index uses a record key—in this case, a student ID number—to locate and retrieve a record for processing.

company. When a customer calls with an inquiry, a customer service rep asks for the tracking number. If the customer has this number handy, the rep can enter it into the computer and immediately display the shipment information on the video screen. If the caller does not have the tracking number, the rep will ask for shipper or recipient information and have the DBMS search through the appropriate index to obtain the desired information. The system also checks the name phonetically in case the correct spelling was not provided (e.g., Andersen, Anderson, and Andersson sound the same).

There is no question that DBMS capabilities help Federal Express give its customers the service they expect when, as the company's slogan says, "It's absolutely, positively gotta be there overnight."

Federal Express's tracking system uses neither an uncommon type of information technology nor custom-made hardware or software. Rather, the company relies on the same information technology that is available to any business or organization. Nonetheless, FedEx provides the combination of good service and reliable information that its customers want.

The point to be taken from this example is one that we've noted again and again. The benefits of information technology do not come from IT itself. Rather, they come from the manner in which the technology is used. Federal Express is so successful because it has been able to identify its customers' needs and then use IT effectively to meet them. Computers, communications, and know-how are all equally important to the company.

Of course, you have to keep moving ahead or competitors will catch up with you. Federal Express is at the moment receiving strong challenges from UPS and other competitors. In some areas, its competitors have even taken the lead in use of IT. ■

Client/Server Computing

Businesses should avoid having separate databases created and maintained by different application systems. *Islands of automation,* a term of the IT trade used to describe situations in which databases and applications cannot share related data, should also be avoided.

The sharing of data can be facilitated through file server computing (see Chapter 10). A **file server** is a computer containing files (including databases) that are available to all users interconnected on a local area network. Workstations connected to the LAN can request and receive data and information from the server. Figure 11.8 provides an illustrated review of how file server computing works. Success with file servers, coupled with advances in desktop computing capabilities, has led to client/server computing.

Client/server computing combines distributed processing and multiuser systems with database systems. All data and information retrieval requests and responses pass over the network. As Figure 11.9 shows, client/server computing can use a multilevel distributed architecture to retrieve information from databases outside of the user's immediate network.

Client/server computing differs from host-based computing (see Chapter 10) in several ways. In a host-based architecture, data and information are stored, and applications run, on a central computer. People log onto the computer using a dumb terminal (or a microcomputer functioning as a dumb terminal) and run

file server
A computer containing files that are available to all users interconnected on a local area network.

client/server computing
A type of computing in which all data and information retrieval requests and responses pass over a network. Much of the processing is performed on the server and the results of the processing are transmitted to the client.

FIGURE 11.8 *Data and Information Retrieval Using File Server Computing*

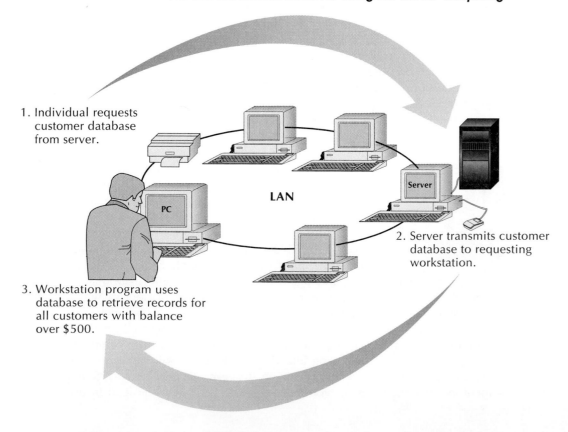

1. Individual requests customer database from server.

LAN

PC

Server

2. Server transmits customer database to requesting workstation.

3. Workstation program uses database to retrieve records for all customers with balance over $500.

applications by a teleprocessing link. The terminal itself adds nothing to the processing. In client/server computing, in contrast, individual desktop computers play a significant role in processing. In essence, the application is running on the user's desktop rather than on a remote computer. The **client**—that is, the desktop workstation—plays the lead role, initiating and driving the processing by requesting selected data and some processing from the main computer, or **server.** Once the server has performed the requested tasks, the requested data and information and the results of processing are transmitted back to the client.

CLIENT/SERVER COMPUTING AT BURLINGTON. Burlington Coat Factory, headquartered in Burlington, New Jersey, operates more than 200 retail outlets throughout the United States and Mexico. The company relies on a client/server computing architecture to link all its stores and distribution centers to headquarters. Point-of-sale cash registers are interconnected through a LAN to a powerful workstation that acts as a store processor (Figure 11.10). The store processor is a file server for the cash registers, providing product and pricing information while capturing each consumer's purchase for inventory information. Department managers who need inventory, sales, or other information interact with the system by means of PCs. Each store processor is also a communications gateway to the central host computer in New Jersey.

Burlington's headquarters system is composed of a battery of processors that receive information from stores via a satellite-based communications network. The headquarters system processes incoming transaction data, updates company databases, redirects transactions—such as Visa/MasterCard authorization requests—to destinations outside the company, and accepts responses.

client

In client/server computing, a desktop workstation.

server

In client/server computing, the main computer that responds to requests from a computer that hosts a network and provides the resources that are shared on the network to a client.

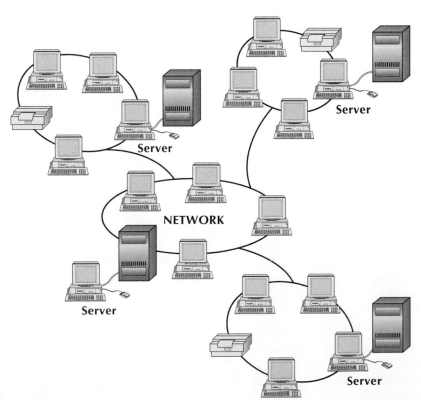

FIGURE 11.9
Multilevel Client/Server Architecture
Client/server company can use a multilevel distributed architecture to retrieve information from databases outside of the user's immediate network.

Burlington's client/server system provides rapid response to processing requests while linking different IT devices together, both within individual stores and across the country. The system has the added benefit of being extremely reliable: there are so many different components and links in the network that it is unlikely processing in the Burlington system as a whole will fail.

The Benefits of Client/Server Computing

Client/server computing offers several benefits to its users. Most important, the server computer processes database requests and the client computer takes the results and works with them. Since as much of the processing as possible is performed on the server before the requested data and information are transmitted to the client, the client receives only the specific information requested—not complete files or large sections of databases—and can begin processing that information immediately.

Figure 11.11 shows how this process works. When a bank employee at a client computer wants to send a personalized letter to all customers with balances over $500, the employee sends a request from her workstation program to the server asking the system to review the customer database. The server processes the database to identify all customers meeting the $500 criterion, then transmits only the records of those customers to the client workstation. The employee's program extracts name, address, and balance information from the data and inserts them into a customized letter prepared through the word-processing program on the client workstation. Without the shared processing between client and server, either entire databases would be copied from one system to another or repeated requests would be necessary to retrieve names and addresses.

FIGURE 11.10

Client/Server Computing at Burlington Coat Factory

Burlington Coat Factory relies on client/server computing to link more than 200 stores throughout the United States and Mexico.

a) Point-of-sale terminals at Burlington's stores are interconnected through a LAN to a workstation that acts as a store processor. Each store processor is also a gateway to the central host computer in New Jersey.

b) The host computer receives information from the individual stores and processes incoming data, updates company databases, and redirects transactions. The same information can then be used to automatically replenish stock at an individual store. The host computer even prints out the price tags and mailing labels.

In addition to saving time and money, client/server computing can make users more productive by ensuring their access to the information they need when they need it. Client/server computing allows many users to share common data resources, including files and databases as well as computer storage and printers. Sharing data and information eliminates the need for personal management of data and/or peripheral devices. Finally, client/server computing allows the integration of geographically distributed users and computing resources into a cohesive computer and communications environment. All of these advantages result in faster access to data and information for users, better service for customers, quicker responses to changes in the business environment, more efficient business processes, fewer errors, and, in general, higher levels of productivity.

For more information on the best-known client/server system, review Chapter 3, which discussed the Internet and the World Wide Web.

CLIENT/SERVER COMPUTING IN ACTION: AMR CORP. AND CSX CORP. When companies turn cargo over to a shipper for transport to a customer, they frequently lose contact with the goods. Unlike FedEx, most shipping companies do not have a computerized tracking system that allows them to retrieve shipping and delivery information on-line so they can know the exact location of the boat, plane, or railcar carrying their goods. AMR Corp.—the parent company of

FIGURE 11.11 *Data and Information Retrieval Using Client/Server Computing*

In client/server computing, specific information—not complete files or huge sections of databases—is transmitted from the server to the client.

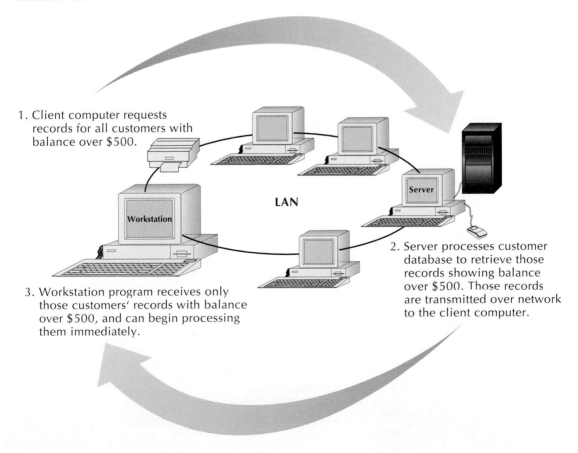

1. Client computer requests records for all customers with balance over $500.

LAN

Workstation

Server

2. Server processes customer database to retrieve those records showing balance over $500. Those records are transmitted over network to the client computer.

3. Workstation program receives only those customers' records with balance over $500, and can begin processing them immediately.

American Airlines—and CSX Corp.—one of the largest land, ocean, and rail cargo shippers in the world—have teamed up to remedy this problem by developing the Encompass system for tracking the movement of freight worldwide. With this system, the status of any shipment can be determined from the time the goods leave the shipper's freight dock until they arrive at their final destination.

Establishing the Encompass system required linking manufacturers, shippers, and third parties worldwide, each of which had its own computing and communications systems and its own databases. To link all these different systems, the designers of Encompass turned to client/server computing (Figure 11.12). AMR and CSX provide their customers (clients) with software that can be used on the clients' computers to request tracking information from servers in the Encompass network. Clients can book shipments, determine the route over which their freight will travel, manage their inventory in transit by determining its location and scheduled arrival dates, evaluate their own shipping activities through an operations analysis module, and even evaluate the performance of the transportation companies. They can also prepare essential shipping documents (air bills, shipment notices, purchase orders, shipping instructions, invoices, and the like). On-line databases, high-speed communications networks, and powerful servers make it possible for all these activities to occur in real time. (Review the definitions of real time and batch processing in Chapter 2, if necessary.)

The benefits of the Encompass system to AMR and CSX are enormous. Like FedEx, they are offering a capability that is attracting new customers, thus increasing their business. While other companies struggle to catch up, AMR and CSX plan to stay several steps ahead of competitors by constantly adding features and capabilities. Good people and know-how lead to the creation of systems like Encompass.

Workstations together with good database management practices can improve business practices in many ways. The *Information Technology in Practice* feature

FIGURE 11.12

The Encompass System

With the Encompass system, shippers and carriers can determine the status of their shipments from the time the goods leave the dock until they arrive at their final destination.

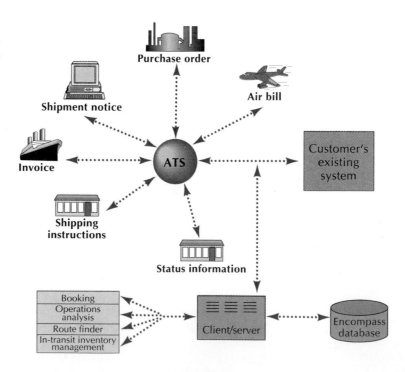

Pitney Bowes

Client/Server System Speeds Information Flow at Pitney Bowes

Pitney Bowes' old paper-based engineering system could be very frustrating. For instance, engineers in the Mail Systems unit often had to spend a lot of time tracking down design engineers to ask them urgent questions. (The engineers are scattered across five sites in Fairfield County, Connecticut.) Or the manufacturing department would find out in the middle of production that it was working with an outdated set of engineering drawings.

The resulting delays were cutting deeply into the company's bottom line, so Pitney Bowes decided to set up a *concurrent engineering system* that will let all its engineers work simultaneously on a project.

The heart of the system is a shared database that contains one consistent and current set of engineering drawings, specifications, and production schedule for each product. This database is maintained on "master servers" that are linked by fiber optics to "client" workstations on the engineers' desks. Now a design engineer can download preliminary specs directly to manufacturing and ask to have a prototype, or working model, created from those electronic specs. If a problem is discovered in the prototype, the manufacturing and design engineers can call up the same drawing on their respective screens and work out a solution together over the phone. With this new system, the design cycle for some products has dropped from five or six weeks to two or three days.

entitled "Estimating Databases Take the Guesswork Out of Fixing Dings and Dents" illustrates the power of desktop computers and network connections in what many people consider to be a low-tech industry.

People

The people who work with databases are the applications programmers, who embed database interaction instructions in application programs, and the end-users, who interact directly with the database, using applications that they have created or that were developed for them. In addition, two types of IT professionals are closely connected to database development and management: database administrators and systems programmers.

Database Administrator

The IT professional with the most extensive database management responsibilities is the **database administrator (DBA),** sometimes called the *data administrator.* The database administrator is responsible for managing all the activities and procedures related to an organization's database (we discuss these in the next section). In some organizations, the database administrator is one person. In others, a team fulfills this administration function, with each team member responsible for some aspect of the data administration procedures.

database administrator (DBA)

The IT professional responsible for managing all the activities and procedures related to an organization's database.

INFORMATION TECHNOLOGY IN PRACTICE

Estimating Databases Take the Guesswork Out of Fixing Dings and Dents

GLASS S
INFORMATION SERVICES

Selling cars is a big business around the world. So is fixing them. Wherever you go, it seems that body shops that do the repairs to remove dings and dents have backlogs of work. Preparing reliable estimates of the costs of repairs takes time, but also brings in repeat business. Yet it sometimes requires inspired guesswork to know just how something will need to be fixed—and thus how much a repair will cost. To eliminate much of this guesswork, a number of automobile dealerships in the United Kingdom, along with insurance companies (such as Royal Insurance and Guardian Insurance) and several car rental companies, use an estimating system called Glassmatix.

Glassmatix, a system developed by Glass's Information Services, features a database containing information on more than 500,000 car parts. The database incorporates repair time estimates provided by an insurance industry–sponsored research center in Thatcham, England, and part prices provided by the manufacturers. The parts and labor database is updated monthly. Glass provides the know-how to integrate the information in a database and computer

software so that quick and accurate estimates can be prepared.

The system works like this. An estimator in a body shop examines a banged-up vehicle to determine what damages must be repaired. Then the estimator looks up the car parts in the Glassmatix system's catalog. The estimator passes a handheld scanner, attached to a desktop computer, over the item, triggering the system to read its bar code and retrieve the related repair information. Say the damaged car needs a new door, replacement of several windows, a new side molding, and a new front fender. The estimator finds each item in the catalog and scans the bar code into the computer.

Next the desktop computer assembles the parts information and determines the cost of all repairs, including parts and labor. (Labor estimates are included in the Glassmatix database.) Once the full cost of repairing the damaged car has been estimated, the system determines whether the car is worth repairing and makes its recommendation to the estimator. (The system keeps track of the value of cars and knows that when repairs exceed a dealer-specified level—say, 35 percent or so of the value of

Systems Programmer

systems programmer
A software and hardware specialist who works with the physical details of a database and the computer's operating system.

Organizations that use large, complex databases may have a **systems programmer,** a software and hardware specialist who works with the physical details of the database and the computer's operating system. The systems programmer organizes the data on magnetic disk (or other storage medium) according to a structure determined by the database designer. The systems programmer also determines the optimal way to arrange records and objects in storage, and creates indexes and other devices for retrieval in conjunction with guidelines established by the database administrator.

the car—the repairs are probably not worthwhile.) Finally, Glassmatix suggests a preferred order in which to make the repairs to minimize labor costs.

Glass's Information Services has developed a related IT capability it calls Glassimage. Also designed to be used in preparing repair estimates, this system is portable, so it can be taken to an accident scene (or anywhere else the damaged vehicle is located). Glassimage can scan photographs or videotape images into computer memory, compress them, and transmit the images over a telephone link or radio network to the body shop, where the images are viewed by estimators.

The Glassmatix is a valuable resource that eliminates the need for estimators to spend time running down parts costs or haggling over labor estimates. Other systems of this nature are emerging throughout Europe and North America. Because dings and dents occur everywhere there are cars, and because the databases can be modified to incorporate details about cars used in a specific region, along with local labor costs, there is no limit to where in the world this system can be used.

Database administrators' primary responsibility is managing the database. This task occupies virtually all of their workday. Systems programmers spend only a portion of their time on database-related activities. The rest of their time is spent working with the operating system, managing the network, and handling other types of hardware and software matters.

Procedures

A *procedure* is a step-by-step process or set of instructions for accomplishing a specific result. The procedures associated with databases are grouped under the general heading of **database administration procedures.**

database administration procedures
The procedures associated with managing a database.

Database Administration Procedures

Database administration means managing the database. This entails doing what is necessary to develop and safeguard the database in the most beneficial way. Procedures for data administration include six areas of responsibility:

1. **Database planning.** Like any valuable resource, a database must be planned. Planning includes being aware of and understanding business needs and user requirements, selecting the DBMS, developing standards for usage, and outlining security strategies.
2. **Database design.** To be as useful as possible, the database must be carefully designed. Designers define the records and objects—including the schema, data names, and length specifications—that make up the database.
3. **Database creation.** The database design is only a framework. The database becomes a reality when data are entered into the design and saved on a storage device.
4. **Database maintenance.** As users' needs and demands change, the database may need adjustment. New records or objects may be added or changes may be made to the existing structures. Database maintenance pertains to the *structure* and *organization* of the database. Maintenance of the *contents* of individual records (the data items) is the responsibility of those using the database, not the database administrator.
5. **Analysis of usage.** Managing a database means monitoring how and when it is used. If data and information retrieval patterns change, the database administrator may decide that adjustments (maintenance) are needed to restructure the database to meet new user requests.
6. **Creation and monitoring of security procedures.** The existence and integrity of the database must be safeguarded at all times. Developing, implementing, and monitoring security procedures are important parts of database administration.

Much of a database's value comes from the procedures the database administrator uses to develop and maintain the database. These responsibilities are quite different from those of individual users or systems programmers.

Concurrency Procedures

Whenever more than one user has access to a database, there is a chance that several people will want to access the database simultaneously. With **concurrent data sharing,** users can do exactly that. With **nonconcurrent data sharing,** individuals can use the data in a database only when no other person or application is processing the data. The database is shared, but *not simultaneously,* by different people.

In developing a database or an application, the systems designer or database administrator must determine what type of sharing is to be permitted. With concurrent data sharing, if two or more people try to retrieve and change existing records simultaneously, the result can be chaos. To understand why this is so, consider the following example:

1. Travel Agent A retrieves from the database a copy of the inventory record for seats available on Flight 10 to London on November 28. The record shows him that five coach seats remain for sale.

Setting up a distributed database involves more than just collecting a pool of data. You may also need to "reengineer" your procedures after they've been instituted to be sure they reflect current goals and information needs. Just ask the American Red Cross, which provides more than half the U.S. blood supply and is in the midst of a massive reengineering project that has a budget of $120 million. The need for the project came to light in 1990, when the Food and Drug Administration (FDA) shut down two regional Red Cross blood centers and an investigation confirmed FDA charges that sloppy record keeping, computer errors, and poor communications were endangering the health and lives of blood recipients.

In its defense, the Red Cross described the new complexities of operating a blood bank. By 1990, it was testing every unit of blood for 10 different diseases. That meant that between 1985 and 1990, Red Cross labs had had to conduct 100 million more tests than were required in the previous five years. To complicate the situation, the 54 regional Red Cross centers weren't using the same procedures, the same blood-testing software application, or a network to facilitate communications among them. Clearly, changes were needed—fast.

2. At virtually the same instant, Travel Agent B retrieves a copy of the same record. Her goal is to book seats for her clients, who are traveling to London on November 28.
3. *Both* travel agents are proceeding based on the availability of five seats. Neither one knows that the other is using a copy of the record or preparing to book seats on the same flight.
4. Travel Agent B's customers give the go-ahead for the reservation first, so B books seats for her four customers. The database system writes the change into the database, noting the names of the customers and adjusting seat inventory to show one remaining seat.
5. Travel Agent A's screen still shows five seats available. A wishes to book a party of three for the flight to London. If the database allows him to do so, and then shows two remaining seats available (the original five minus the three he just sold), two passengers of the seven booked by A and B will be stranded without seats.

Systems developers can use several different strategies to avoid this type of situation. First, they can choose not to allow concurrent sharing. Second, they can decide to partition the database, with each partition assigned to one user or group of users. If different users access separate portions of the database independently, concurrent data sharing will be avoided. Third, they can partition database processing, a strategy that entails assigning the database to a particular user for a period of time (perhaps mornings rather than afternoons, or odd-numbered days rather than even-numbered days). But since travel agents need access to flight information 24 hours a day, none of these strategies would be right for them.

When concurrent data sharing is essential, the proper procedures must be developed to avoid the type of debacle described in our flight booking example. The most common of these concurrency procedures is **record locking.** When a record is being used by one person, it is locked and another user cannot access or alter it. The record is unlocked when the initial user finishes processing the record. Locking and unlocking occur automatically. Today's airline reservations systems use record locking to ensure that seats are not sold more than once. To revert to our example, Travel Agents A and B *cannot* sell the same seats on the same flight simultaneously because while one agent is assigning the seats, the other is prevented (locked out) from entering a sales transaction for those seats.

File locking is another common concurrency procedure. It is used in systems that store unstructured information and have file-level sharing. For example, in a word-processing or spreadsheet system, the principal document processed is a file. If file locking is specified by the designer, only one user or application will be able to use a specific document at a given moment.

Whenever record locking is used, there is a chance that two or more users will find themselves in a **deadlock,** a situation in which each user of the database is waiting for the others to free (unlock) the record. Although deadlocks are rare, the DBA must develop procedures for dealing with them. Typically, the solution is for the DBMS to detect the occurrence of the deadlock and issue a message to the users asking them to release the record or reenter the details of their transaction.

record locking
A concurrency procedure that prohibits another user from accessing or altering a record that is in use.

deadlock
A situation in which each user of a database is waiting for the others to unlock a record.

A Final Word

Shared and distributed data create many opportunities for businesses to serve customers and conduct day-to-day activities. However, as in all other areas of information technology, computers and communications systems provide only potential capabilities. It is up to the firm's people to determine how and when IT can be used to achieve the desired results.

SUMMARY OF LEARNING OBJECTIVES

1 Identify the reasons organizations choose to share databases and the functions of a database management system. Organizations choose to share databases because data collection and maintenance are very expensive. Managing these data effectively entails making sure all members of an organization who need them have access to a consistent set of data. The five functions of a database management system (DBMS) are integrating databases, reducing redundancy, sharing information, maintaining integrity, and enabling database evolution.

2 Differentiate between shared and distributed databases. A *shared database* is one that is shared among many users and applications. A *distributed database* is a shared database whose data reside on more than one system in a network. These data can be accessed, retrieved, or updated from any node in the network.

3 Explain the difference between relational and object-oriented databases and their uses in business. *Relational databases* consist of data structured in a table format consisting of rows and columns. *Object-oriented databases* store data and information about objects. Unlike relational databases, object-oriented databases can store *actions*—instructions telling the database how to process the object to produce specific information. Object-oriented databases offer the capability to store more sophisticated types of data and information than relational databases do.

4 **Describe the differences between schemas, views, and indexes.** A *schema* is the structure of a database. A *view* is a subset of one or more databases, created either by extracting copies of records from a database or by merging copies of records from multiple databases. An *index* is a data file that contains identifying information about each record and its location in storage.

5 **Discuss the benefits of client/server computing.** Client/server computing combines distributed processing and multiuser systems with database systems. All data and information retrieval requests and responses in client/server computing pass over the network. This offers several benefits to users. Because much of the processing is performed on the server, specific information—rather than complete files—is transmitted to the client. In addition to saving time and money, client/server computing makes users more productive

by ensuring their access to information when they need it.

6 **Distinguish between a database administrator and a systems programmer.** The IT professional with the most extensive database management responsibilities is the *database administrator (DBA)*, who is responsible for managing all the activities and procedures related to an organization's database. A *systems programmer* is a software and hardware specialist who works with the physical details of the database.

7 **Discuss database administration procedures and concurrency procedures and explain why these are an essential part of a shared database system.** Database administration procedures include six areas of responsibility: database planning, database design, database creation, database maintenance, analysis of usage, and creation and monitoring of security procedures. In addition, concurrency procedures allow more than one user to access a database simultaneously. All these procedures are an essential part of a shared database system because they provide for an efficient, well-managed database and increased worker productivity.

KEY TERMS

CRITICAL CONNECTIONS

1 Electronic Expense Reporting Creates Advantage for American Express and Carlson Wagonlit

American Express Carlson Wagonlit This electronic expense reporting system benefits travelers, their companies, and, of course, American Express and Carlson Wagonlit. Travelers are relieved of a lot of paper shuffling and can prepare their expense reports in a fraction of the time it used to take them. Their companies are freed from the need to process and file reams of paper. Both benefit from the fact that expense reports can be submitted from anywhere, which raises the likelihood that statements will be submitted and settled in a timely manner. Companies are also able to keep tighter tabs on what their employees are actually spending on business trips. (The software for this program will even flag expenditures that are beyond the company's normal spending limits.) Finally, by providing this service, the credit card companies enjoy extra revenues from the greater use of their cards as well as from the service itself.

Questions for Discussion

1. Based on your own travel experience, what would you say are the strengths and weaknesses of the electronic expense reporting system described in this Critical Connection?

2. How would you feel about all your travel expenses being reported automatically?

3. In addition to the revenue from the software and annual processing fees, how do American Express and Carlson Wagonlit benefit from the electronic reporting service?

2 Client/Server System Speeds Information Flow at Pitney Bowes

Pitney Bowes The concurrent engineering system under development at Pitney Bowes promises to do more than boost engineering productivity. The real payoff will come down the road, once the company finishes a project that will integrate its concurrent engineering system with the databases used by the marketing, sales, and accounting applications. The objective is a smooth, paperless flow of information from the field salesforce to the manufacturing execution systems and from marketing to engineering.

Salespeople will like the new system; they'll be using PCs to call up product prices, check inventory levels, and send orders directly to manufacturing—all without having to touch a single piece of paper. More important, the system will revolutionize the way Pitney Bowes creates and markets its products. In the old days, someone in charge of new-product development would decide what the market requirements were, then go to engineering, and on to manufacturing, and finally ring up a person in sales and say, "Guess what—we have a new product. Now sell it." Under the new system, every product will be assigned a core team consisting of representatives from all the company's marketing, engineering, manufacturing, sales, and information systems departments. With the help of IT, the team will work together from Day 1, using marketing data on changing customer requirements to speed the development of competitive new products.

Questions for Discussion

1. Engineers sometimes "reinvent the wheel"—that is, spend days or even weeks designing, say, a stamping mechanism that is similar to one on a product already in production. How might a concurrent engineering system prevent this waste of time?

2. How might its finished client/server system increase Pitney Bowes' ability to compete?

3. How does the company's system illustrate the principles of data sharing?

3 "Reengineering" Project Aims at Rebuilding Confidence in Blood Bank

American Red Cross Less than a year after the new Red Cross president announced the reengineering project, IT staffers were admitting that the initial two-year timetable may have been too optimistic. A more realistic estimate, it seemed, was three years, owing to the amount of time consultants from IBM, Andersen Consulting, and KPMG Peat Marwick were spending with representatives from the regional centers to analyze information needs.

A few moments' reflection will give you an idea of the challenges the experts faced in this situation. On one level, the Red Cross had a textbook inventory problem—how to match blood demand with blood supply at different locations, given that both tend to fluctuate throughout the year. Complicating the problem was the fact that blood has a "shelf life" of only about 40 days, after which it can't be used.

The experts decided the project entailed three basic requirements. First, a computer network linking the centers and national headquarters was needed to speed the task of electronically checking "inventory" at other centers, as well as to permit the monitoring of operating efficiency from national headquarters. Second, if the centers were going to exchange units of blood, the units would have to be as interchangeable as possible. Therefore, each unit of blood would have to be tested and cataloged using the same procedures and software. (The 54 regional centers were using 20 different systems; under the new system, testing will be consolidated at 10 labs using standardized procedures and custom-created software.) Third, the system had to provide a way to identify and track the location of every unit of blood so that if a test came back positive, the staff would be able to find the contaminated blood and make sure it was destroyed.

Setting up the distributed database system devised by the experts is but one of the challenges faced by the American Red Cross. The next challenge will come when it implements, or installs, the system. This process is expected to take about two years, as the regional centers are closed, one by one, to change equipment and train staff members.

Questions for Discussion

1. The Red Cross currently maintains a centralized Donor Deferral Registry at national headquarters in Washington, D.C. This database of donors who should *not* be allowed to give blood has serious data integrity problems, mainly because it relies on the manual entry of reports from the regional centers. How might this problem be avoided in the reengineered system?

2. Use what you have learned about computer software and hardware to suggest ways the reengineered system could help the Red Cross staff ensure that no contaminated blood is released for use. (*Hint:* Consider using input devices such as bar codes and bar code readers.)

Net_Work

The Internet is often thought of as a huge network that interconnects people and companies. However, it also provides access to a wide range of databases. Among the publicly accessible databases on the Internet are telephone directories from around the United States and other countries of the world.

Using any of the search engines available on the Internet (see Net_Work, Chapter 4), locate and provide the URL for any of the following databases:

Any directory of toll-free (800 or 888) telephone numbers.

Any airline flight schedule.

Any library on-line card catalog.

Any theater or sports team schedule of performances or games.

GROUP PROJECTS AND APPLICATIONS

Project 1

Once your name is entered into a database, it becomes part of a massive marketing and direct-sales system. To find how names are transferred from one company to another through databases, a group of students should perform the following experiment.

Each member of the group should request a free catalog or publication. When you make the request, vary the spelling of your name. For instance, if your name is Cathy Jones, make the request under Cathi Joans. If you are John Smith, temporarily become Jon Smyth. Over the next several weeks, watch your mailbox for unsolicited advertisements bearing your assumed name.

What kinds of marketing material are you receiving? How are these materials related to the original material you requested? For example, if you requested a catalog of children's toys, you may soon find yourself receiving offers from children's portrait studios and children's book clubs, as well as coupons from diaper and toy companies.

Each member of the group should report on his or her findings to the class at the end of the semester.

Project 2

In a group, visit a small or large company in the area. The group should then break up to individually interview various people involved with the company's database activities. One group member should interview the company's database administrator to learn more about the job. Specific questions you might ask are the following:

- What activities occupy the bulk of your time?
- How big is your database—that is, how many records does it contain?
- Is the database relational or object-oriented?
- In what ways is the database used?
- How long has the database existed? Is it fairly static, or is it expanding?
- How many workers do you support?
- What are the benefits of the distributed database to the company?
- Do you use client/server computing?
- What procedures do you follow daily, weekly, monthly?
- What are the biggest challenges of your job?

Other members of the group should interview people who *use* the database. Ask the following questions:

- What exactly is your job? What are your responsibilities?
- How do you use the database in the course of a day?
- How exactly do you access the data you need? Are some data classified as "confidential" or off-limits to you? If so, why?
- How does the database administrator support your efforts?
- Do you have a "wish list" for the database? Would you like the database to include views or indexes that do not currently exist? Why?

Prepare a two- to five-page summary of your interviews. Be sure to write thank-you notes to the people you've interviewed.

REVIEW QUESTIONS

1. What is a database? Why are databases shared?

2. What is the purpose of a database management system (DBMS)?

3. What is a distributed database? How is it related to or different from a shared database?

4. Define the two ways of distributing databases. How may a database be distributed between different locations?

5. What benefits do businesses gain from distributing databases?

6. Describe the difference between a functional distribution strategy and a geographic distribution strategy.

7. Discuss the factors that must be considered in designing a distributed database.

8. What is a database schema? How many schemas does each database have?

9. How are relational and object-oriented databases different? What is an object? An action?

10. What is the purpose of a database view?

11. What is the difference between a database schema and a database view?

12. What is the function of an index?

13. What is client/server computing? What are its benefits?

14. Describe the relation between client/server computing, communications networks, and shared databases.

15. Describe the responsibilities of a database administrator and a systems programmer.

16. Describe the six areas of responsibility in data administration.

17. What is the difference between concurrent and nonconcurrent data sharing?

18. What is record locking and why is it used in shared database processing? What is a deadlock and how does it occur?

DISCUSSION QUESTIONS

1. Allegheny Ludlum Corp., a Philadelphia-based manufacturer of special steel and metals, is using IT to achieve above-average growth rates. A network that links the firm's plants in six states provides a steady flow of data and information from the shop floor to the marketing department.

   One of the company's recent strategies has been to move to relational database management systems. Why might Allegheny Ludlum want to consider instead a move to object-oriented databases? What management tool might help the company evaluate the advantages of moving to an object-oriented structure?

2. Texas-based retailer Neiman Marcus recently equipped its 27 stores and two warehouses with a set of client/server systems that will record point-of-sale data on a server within each store as well as on a host computer at central headquarters. One goal is to automate the "client book" each

sales associate presently keeps on the tastes and preferences of long-standing customers. What measures can the IT staff take to protect this confidential client data from the snooping eyes of unscrupulous employees and still ensure that sales associates have the information they need to do their jobs? What benefits does the new client/server system offer to the retailer's upper-level managers and how might these offset the need to implement stringent security measures?

3. A team at Levi Strauss & Co. is overseeing a pilot project named Orion. Orion's goal is to determine whether client/server computing would offer significant advantages over the host-based computing the company now uses. What types of duties do you think this task force is performing? Why do you think no single person has been assigned to these duties?

4. Condé Nast Publications, Shearson Lehman Brothers, and Grumman Corp. are just a few of the companies that have instituted stringent portable computer protection policies. These policies are designed to thwart industrial spies who steal portable computers to get at their hard disks, which are full of sensitive company data, as well as modems set up to tap into the company's database. Should general managers or IT managers have the primary responsibility for designing security procedures to prevent this sort of theft? What does your answer indicate about the relationship between database administration professionals, IT professionals, and non–IT personnel in the age of distributed computing?

SUGGESTED READINGS

Bertino, Elisa, and Lorenzo Martino. "Object-Oriented Database Management Systems: Concepts and Issues," *Computer,* April 1991, pp. 33–47. In this article, Bertino and Martino explain how object-oriented database technology combines the power of a computer programming language with effective data management techniques. The discussion, which includes careful explanations of terminology, explores the processing of applications developed using object structures.

Brachman, Ronald J., Tom Khabaza, Willi Kloesgen, Gregory Piatetsky-Shapiro, and Evangelos Simoudis. "Mining Business Databases," *Communications of the ACM 39* (November 1996): 42–48. Describes the power of mining data—an aspect of data warehouses—to turn a business resource into a competitive advantage. This journal issue includes seven in-depth articles on data warehouses.

Cattel, R. G. G. "Next Generation Database Systems." *Communications of the ACM 34* (October 1991): 30–120. This special issue contains eight comprehensive articles describing recent developments and opportunities in shared database systems. All the articles presume a good understanding of the fundamentals of database management.

Jeffrey, Brian. "Enterprise Client/Server Computing." *Information Systems Management 13* (Fall 1996): 7–18. A highly readable discussion of client/server computing strategies that synthesizes centralized and distributed computing for delivery of organizationwide benefits.

Martin, James, and James J. Odell. *Object-Oriented Analysis and Design.* Englewood Cliffs, N. J.: Prentice Hall, 1992. An authoritative in-depth examination of object-oriented computing. The book introduces the basic terminology and concepts associated with objects, databases, and IT applications, and offers suggestions for turning concepts into reality.

Özsu, M. Tamer, Duane Szafron, Ghada El-Medani, and Chiradeep Vittal. "An Object-Oriented Multimedia Database System for a News-On-Demand Application." *Multimedia Systems 3* (1995): 182–203. With the meaning of databases expanding to encompass all forms of information, this article is a useful illustration, from both a research and a practical standpoint, of the issues that must be addressed when creating a working application.

Ram, Sudha. "Heterogeneous Distributed Database Systems." *Computer 24* (December 1991): 7–9. This article is one of eight in-depth articles in a special issue devoted entirely to distributed databases. The piece examines a variety of issues, including development of schemas, security and recovery procedures in multidatabase environments, and obstacles to the management of distributed databases.

Sinha, Alok. "Client-Server Computing: Current Technology Review." *Communications of the ACM 35* (July 1992): 77–98. This informative article looks at the evolution of client/server computing, from its origins with the emergence of powerful PCs to its future with new network operating systems and powerful databases. It includes both a description of the uses of client/server methods in business and a detailed examination of the underlying technology.

Weldon, Jay Louise, and Alan Joch. "Data Warehouse Building Blocks." *Byte 22* (January 1997): 82ff. This "state of the art" series explores the power of data warehouses and the manner in which they are created in practice. Liberal use of graphics illuminates virtually all aspects of data warehouses.

Data's in the Warehouse for France's TGV

Many people hold in their minds an image of railroads that can be traced back to childhood memories of the distant, lonesome whistle of a diesel engine heard across open farmland. Others—usually a bit older—associate railroads with a giant fire-breathing, smoke-belching "iron horse" chugging down the tracks, dragging a load of freight behind it. Although the golden age of railroads is the inspiration for many colorful memories, today's reality is very different.

For a contemporary railroad to be successful and profitable, its executives must be expert at more than running trains. They have to know how to manage the entire system effectively, know who is riding on their trains, and understand the usage patterns of their customers. And they have to recognize that there is no such thing as an average train.

One of France's most prized possessions is its national rail system. The French National Railroad—the Société Nationale des Chemins de Fer Français, or simply SNCF—operates some 1,600 trains daily, rolling from the northern coast, bordering on the English Channel, to the southern coast, where France spills into the Mediterranean Sea. The French are particularly proud of the SNCF's bullet trains, the *Train à Grande Vitesse (TGV)*. The 400 daily TGV trains are not only sleek in appearance—a far cry from the chugging steam-puffing iron locomotives that have historically been the train's image around the world—but also whip around the country at average speeds of 300 kilometers per hour. In fact, the TGV

holds a world speed record for a train (more than 515 kilometers per hour).

New designs and engineering advances are responsible for the high speeds and many traveler comforts enjoyed by people riding the TGV. But information technology and data warehousing are responsible for the

high passenger revenues and effective daily utilization of these trains.

Recognizing the necessity to plan better utilization of its trains, meet passenger demand, and fund continued expansion of the TGV, SNCF officials determined they had to analyze the details of their operations more effectively. Accordingly, they set up a data warehouse that runs on a special database computer to support strategic decision support analysis.

A data warehouse is a large data store that combines details of both current and historical operations, usually drawn from a number of sources. The business objective of data warehousing is to identify patterns, trends, and rules that are embedded in the business activities, products, or services of an enterprise. When properly identified and incorporated into management decision making, the resulting information can improve competitiveness, enhance revenues and profits, and transform business processes. Since data warehouses combine both current and historical operations details from a number of sources, they are much larger than ordinary operational databases.

How do data warehouses differ from application-oriented databases? Frequently, the databases associated with transaction-oriented systems focus on a single type of current business activity and are designed to support related transactions in the most efficient manner. To enable managers to deal with multiple business activities, and hence several databases, a data warehouse draws details from multiple databases that span weeks, months, and years of the business history.

Prior to creating its data warehouse, SNCF managers treated all TGV lines the same, using a rigid fare control system that had passengers paying comparable fares for trips of similar distances, regardless of whether the tickets were purchased well in advance or at the last minute. With data warehousing, SNCF officials can analyze data in new ways by regularly reviewing current and historical details on reservations, fleet management, marketing, and accounting systems for each train. For instance, its marketing analysts can tell when and where passengers on the train from Paris to the coastal city of Rennes purchased their tickets, how much they paid for them, and whether they ordered meals en route or booked rental cars at their destinations.

Data warehousing has also enabled SNCF to create a yield management system similar to that pioneered by U.S. airlines. Yield management enables officials to analyze the patterns and trends associated with each train and to understand customer behavior with more precision, avoiding the need to rely on averages.

Officials can now customize the prices and services for each train. Instead of assuming the average train has a certain percentage of no-shows and an average ticket price, the data warehouse system lets them more accurately anticipate how many people will request first-class and coach seats on a particular train on a given day, as well as the number of no-shows. With this information in hand, SNCF officials can determine whether to offer a certain number of discount seats on the train and what percentage of seats should be overbooked to counter the no-shows. The result: maximum revenue is collected for each trip.

SNCF's data warehouse has allowed French railroad officials to make better-informed decisions while creating an infrastructure for reusing data in numerous ways. Best of all, it has increased revenues and improved flex-ibility in meeting passenger needs. In France, there is no such thing as an average train.

Questions for Discussion

1. How does a data warehouse enable SNCF to make better decisions about running the railroad?

2. In addition to questions related to the impact of ticket prices and overbooking on passenger revenue and train utilization, what other questions do you think management can use its data warehouse to address?

3. It's often said that without data warehouses, even companies with well-designed database systems spend too much time locating data and not enough time analyzing it. How can data warehouses overcome this problem?

INSIDE Federal Express

Since its founding by Fred Smith, Federal Express has seen the value of time in helping its customers to distinguish their products and services. By helping its customers to be successful, the company has continually increased its success. Because of its innovative leadership, company-wide dedication to customer satisfaction, and effective use of information technology, Federal Express became the first U.S. service company to win the highest honor in American business, the Malcolm Baldrige National Quality Award.

Federal Express's information technology not only ensures its customers receive prompt, reliable service, but it is so unobtrusive you hardly ever see it. Here's a peek behind the scenes.

In the night skies above Memphis, Tennessee, the company's headquarters city, a string of Federal Express planes stretches beyond the horizon. One lands and another takes off every minute. Inside those hundreds of planes are thousands of containers. Every one of the more than two million packages that are carried on a typical day is urgently needed somewhere else.

Neither the sender nor the receiver can afford to worry about whether or not it will be delivered. FedEx's control system starts when a company calls to request pickup of an outgoing package or when a package is dropped off at a company location. The airbill attached to each package is more than just a shipping label, for it also contains billing information, an important identification number, and a bar code incorporating that identification number. You might even think of it as the package's unique fingerprint.

As soon as a driver accepts the package, the bar code is scanned using a handheld SuperTracker scanner developed especially for FedEx. From that moment on, the package is in the FedEx system, where its every move is tracked by effective use of information technology.

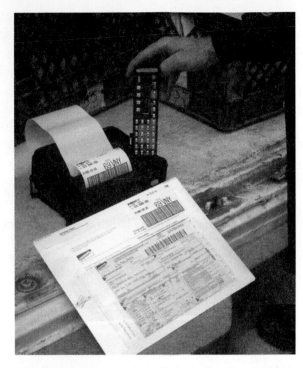

When the driver returns to the truck, he or she can print tracking labels or place the scanner into the Digitally Assisted Dispatch System (DADS). DADS uploads the data about the package over the satellite network to the company's tracking system. From its first stage of the journey through its final destination, the package will be scanned at least six times. Frequent scanning keeps both customer and company informed as to exactly where the package is in the system.

As soon as an aircraft lands at Memphis, FedEx staff members unload the aircraft, moving packages secured by huge nets and wheeling shipping containers holding thousands of packages from the aircraft to the sorting facility.

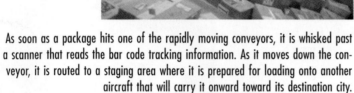

As soon as a package hits one of the rapidly moving conveyors, it is whisked past a scanner that reads the bar code tracking information. As it moves down the conveyor, it is routed to a staging area where it is prepared for loading onto another aircraft that will carry it onward toward its destination city.

When FedEx's aircraft arrive at the destination city, packages are unloaded and scanned in a regional sorting center. Then they are loaded on the vehicle best suited for ultimate delivery to the customer.

Any customer can check on the location of his or her package by calling a FedEx customer representative who with a few mouse-clicks can look at the customer record using an on-line workstation featuring large, graphically based windows. Or the customer can check FedEx's World Wide Web site on the Internet where, by entering the airbill number, complete information on the package is instantly available.
(You can also use the Web to schedule a pickup.)

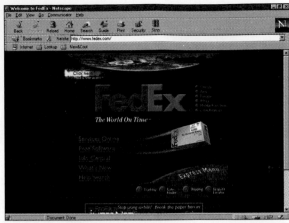

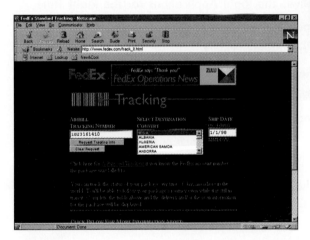

What can customers ship via FedEx? Letters, packages . . . even automobiles. Just about anything that "absolutely positively" needs to be at a destination overnight.

FedEx is successful because it helps its customers to be successful. But the company knows that it has competitors who are just as dedicated to their customers and equally committed to providing top-notch service. Hence, you can expect that additional innovations, and even more creative uses of information technology, are in the making.

CHAPTER
12

Developing Shared IT Applications

CHAPTER OUTLINE

Colgate-Palmolive: The Right Applications for the Right Time
Developing Open Shared Systems
The Origin of a Systems Project
The Systems Development Life Cycle
The Systems Analyst's Tools and Techniques
Computer-Aided Systems Engineering (CASE)
IT Development Personnel
A Final Word
Case Study: Shoot-Out Whets Sara Lee's Appetite for Client/Server
Computing

LEARNING OBJECTIVES

When you have completed this chapter, you should be able to

1 Describe the principal functions and roles of a systems analyst.

2 Identify the characteristics of shared systems.

3 Discuss the changing process for developing information systems applications.

4 Explain how a systems project begins and how its desirability is determined.

5 Describe the six phases of the systems development life cycle.

6 Describe the tools and techniques available to systems analysts for collecting data and developing IT applications.

7 Explain the roles of the four types of IT systems development professionals.

Colgate-Palmolive: The Right Applications for the Right Time

Colgate-Palmolive Co., the global consumer products giant headquartered in New York, was built on the principle of always having the right product for the consumer. Its successful track record, and its well-known brand names (including Ajax, Mennen, Softsoap, Hills, Colgate, and Palmolive), have pleased customers and shareholders for nearly 200 years.

Yet, in today's competitive business world, having the right product is no longer enough. Colgate's new mandate for success—having the right product in the right place at the right time—has changed the way the company conducts its business. Colgate would not be so successful today if it had not integrated information technology into its business processes, for IT plays a pivotal role in the company's relations with customers and in the management of its own manufacturing processes.

Colgate has designed essential new information technology applications characterized by electronic links to its major customers. These applications enable it to monitor constantly the sales of its products at such retail giants as Wal-Mart, Kmart, and Target. The systems are designed so that transaction details are transmitted from the store's point-of-sale terminals directly to Colgate. Similar IT applications link Colgate with its key suppliers.

Manufacturing schedules at Colgate factories are linked both to what is selling and to what is in the company's inventories. Even the raw materials mixed into a product are monitored as they are used. Whenever workers overseeing a manufacturing activity mix a batch of a product, they enter a few details describing the batch into a personal computer at their workstation. These details are then transmitted to the servers running the systems that make up Colgate's corporate nerve center. The systems immediately go to work, looking up the manufacturing recipe and then adjusting the

inventory levels of all the ingredients that were used in the batch mixture. Suppliers hundreds of miles away also receive the details for the ingredients they provide so they can keep Colgate's supply of those ingredients at just the right level (just as Colgate docs with its customers).

As Colgate knows, having good information technology is not enough to be successful in business today. Developing the right IT applications (in the right way!) to solve the right problems goes to the very heart of business success.

You will likely be involved at some point in your career in the development of IT applications. If you are pursuing a career as an IT professional, you may be part of a development team or even the project leader. If you are an IT user, you will be consulted by IT professionals who want to involve you in the development activities for applications you will later use.

In this chapter, we look inside the process of developing shared IT applications. The first part of the chapter emphasizes the importance of good systems development management and describes the origin of systems projects and the systems development life cycle. The second part discusses the tools available to systems analysts. Because just having the right tools is not enough, the chapter closes with a discussion of the skills that good systems analysts need to work effectively with businesspeople and to create effective applications.

The purpose of this chapter is not to teach you to be a systems analyst. Rather, it is designed to give you a good idea of what systems analysts do and how to work with them to develop effective shared IT applications.

Developing Open Shared Systems

shared system
A system in which two or more users share computers, communications technology, and applications.

Recall that a **shared system** is a system in which two or more users share computers, communications technology, and applications. The introduction of a shared system into a work group or organization affects everyone who interacts with the application or receives information generated by the system. For this reason, shared systems are usually not developed by individual staff members, but rather by the organization's information technology group. This group goes by various names, including the information systems department, the management information systems (MIS) department, and the information resources group.

Development Alternatives

The information technology group can take any of three approaches to developing an application:

1. **Build the application itself.** Assemble a team of analysts, designers, and programmers who formulate the specifications for an application and write the computer software needed to fulfill the specifications.
2. **Purchase a prewritten application.** Assign to a team of IT professionals the responsibility for searching out a prewritten software package that performs the specified functions and can be purchased from a commercial supplier or vendor. Many vendors specialize in the development, marketing, and support of applications designed to meet business needs.
3. **Contract out the application development.** Under this approach, the company hires a software development firm (large or small) that specializes in writing computer and communications software. Either a legal contract or an informal working agreement is constructed that specifies what the software should do along with the features it should contain. The firm may decide to hire a software development company to either formulate specifications for a

system and then prepare software to meet those specifications or write software that meets specifications provided by the company. A price for the services is agreed on, either a lump sum to be paid when the application is completed or a specified per-hour price.

Considering the importance of IT in business, it should not surprise you that many companies use all three approaches, although there is a growing emphasis on the purchase and contract options. We'll examine these three widely used alternatives in more detail later in the chapter.

Strictly speaking, a shared system is one in which two or more individuals use the same computer, interconnected to the system by communication links. They also share applications, data, and information. At a growing rate, shared systems are open systems.

The *Rethinking Business Practices* feature, "Xerox's IT of the Future: Not a Copy of Its Legacy," discusses how one well-known company has embarked on a new course to manage its information systems practices.

Open Systems for Sharing

Shared systems depend on being open to different hardware and software. **Open systems** are software systems that perform on different computer and communications hardware. They are built on *nonproprietary* operating systems—that is,

open system
A software system that performs on different computer and communications hardware.

Circuit City Stores, Inc.

Electronics Giant Circuit City Stores Sends Its Software Out

Circuit City Stores, Inc., of Richmond, Virginia, is a large and highly successful electronics retailer. Its people are well informed about the products they sell—thanks partly to Circuit City's back office systems, which manage the merchandise so that salespeople always know what's in stock in their store as well as in other stores within the region.

Getting good products to sell and keeping salespeople up-to-date have never been problems for Circuit City. But getting enough good people to create all the application systems in the company's development plan proved just about impossible.

Finally, the company's IT directors faced the reality that in order to meet Circuit City's business needs, they would have to *outsource* selective computer applications, beginning with an accounting application. The company hired an external contractor, who, in turn, retained programmers working in offices in Bangalore, India, to write the computer code. The outsourcing contractor assumed full responsibility for meeting the specifications provided by Circuit City's IT staff and for on-time delivery at a specified price.

The experience was such a success for Circuit City that the company has incorporated outsourcing into its overall IT development strategy. This has proved to be an excellent way to gain access to high-quality personnel without having to hire them directly.

RETHINKING BUSINESS PRACTICES

Xerox's IT of the Future: Not a Copy of Its Legacy

XEROX Xerox Corp., the Stamford, Connecticut, company that redefined the way people around the world copy documents, has redefined its own manner of developing and managing information technology globally. In 1994, Xerox's chairman signed a $3.2 billion 10-year contract with the systems integration firm EDS Corp.

Xerox's decision to shift a substantial portion of its IT responsibility to EDS is unique in two ways: scope and intention. First, the Xerox-EDS contract is the largest ever *global* outsourcing contract. EDS has assumed responsibility for Xerox's information technology in the areas of computing, communications, and software management. To fulfill this huge responsibility, EDS has created a global strategic business unit that handles *only* Xerox IT activities. Some 1,700 of Xerox's 2,700 IT employees were shifted over to EDS, as was half of the $600 million Xerox was spending annually on information technology.

The other unique aspect of the Xerox decision is that it is viewed by top management as a means of transforming Xerox's IT activities. As soon as the company turned over the operation and maintenance of existing systems to EDS, it started to focus on new systems development initiatives. Outsourcing freed up Xerox's remaining systems development staff: no longer compelled to devote the vast majority of their time to maintaining existing systems (often termed *legacy* systems because they have been in use for years), they were able to devote themselves to development activities focused on the Xerox of the future.

Behind this effort is an IT structure that mirrors Xerox's goal of putting customers first. The technology and infrastructure that is taken for granted in the U.S. is not supported all over the world. Xerox relies on EDS to manage its systems changes and to maintain its large computer system. EDS handles global strategic decisions such as architecture and new applications developments internally allowing Xerox to focus on the needs of worldwide employees and customers.

In the process Xerox is rethinking—reengineering—its most basic business processes, giving particular attention to development of a global sales and marketing process that is seamless from one country and region of the world to another. Dispersed as it is, Xerox presents such a unified front that it has swept every major quality commendation from the Malcolm

operating systems that can be easily purchased and used with a variety of different computers or communications systems—and work with the different user interfaces. Windows and Unix are examples of open software systems: they can be used on a wide variety of computers, both stand-alone and shared.

interoperability
The perfect exchange of data and information in all forms (data, text, sound, and image, including animation) between the individual components of an application (hardware, software, network).

Interoperability is the perfect exchange of data and information in all forms (data, text, sound, and image, including animation) between individual components of an application (hardware, software, network). With interoperability, the same application can operate on two different kinds of computers, yet perform the same task and have identical-looking interfaces. In other words, the components can differ in their origin (manufacturer or supplier), size (e.g., desktop computer or mainframe system), operation (including communication protocol or individual software program), or location (in the same room or across the continent). Interoperability requires open systems.

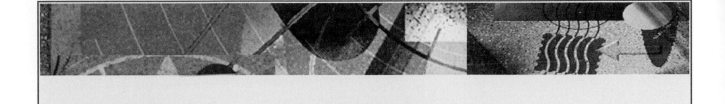

Baldrige Award to the Deming Prize. Xerox offers a consistent level of service to its customers, putting an overall strategy together and then tailoring it to local areas.

The IT transition is nearly complete and the system is running at 700 sites worldwide. It is a typical client/server system that features industry-standard Windows-based software. As a result, worldwide customer service reps can better serve remote regions.

Xerox's mix of information technology applications, along with supporting computer and communication systems, are also in transition. A new architecture—hardware, software, networks, and data and information—is being developed to support the company's worldwide business objectives. Open systems, interoperability, and client/server computing are key elements in the company's IT future.

The widely known spreadsheet package Lotus 1-2-3, for instance, will run on IBM-compatible and Macintosh desktop computers, on midrange computers, and on mainframes, even though these computers are quite different. Thus, Lotus 1-2-3 is said to be an interoperable software package. (Similarly, Lotus Notes, illustrated in the photo essay in Chapter 10, is also interoperable. The photo essay illustrates Notes running on a variety of different computers, interconnected to share information.)

Interoperability is closely related to software portability, another desirable characteristic associated with open systems. This means information technology applications and information can be moved relatively easily between computers of varying size (for example, mainframe, midrange, or microcomputer) and brands (for example, IBM, Apple, Compaq, and Dell). An important, but more subtle, benefit of software portability is that people also become somewhat portable. For instance, experts in the design and use of Lotus Notes applications can apply that expertise to systems running on any size or brand of computer. They are not constrained to a particular computer environment. (Prior to open systems, this was often a severe constraint on IT professionals.)

One of the reasons Microsoft's software is so widely used is because it is available to run on a variety of computer systems. Recognizing the desirability and benefits of open systems, interoperability, and software portability, there is widespread expectation that in the near future, Microsoft's Windows and NT products will be used on many computers besides desktop systems. This is not only a wish of Microsoft, but it is also the wish of many IT professionals responsible for developing and supporting their companies' business systems.

Business and individual IT users want to acquire software more quickly, owing in part to the rapid pace of business change and in part to the ever-increasing number of effective ways in which to use information technology. Moreover, the demand is high for more powerful capabilities, preferably at a lower cost.

So, even as information technology is aiding individuals and companies to be more innovative, IT professionals are continually seeking more innovative ways to develop software. The most promising innovation at the moment is the dramatic shift from the traditional view of software development as a craft to an approach known as software assembly that makes use of the principles of software reuse and object-oriented design.

Shifting Development Model

To illustrate the differences between the craft and component approaches to information systems development (Figure 12.1), we will use the analogy of the construction of a building.

CRAFT APPROACH.   Under the *craft approach,* a builder determines the size and principal features of the building (number of rooms, size of each room, height of ceilings, number of windows, location of doors, type of flooring, and so on). Then each item needed to construct the building is prepared: lumber is cut to the right size to create the frame, rafters, and beams (the structures supporting floors, walls, and ceilings).

The crafting continues as more visible features are designed. The size and appearance of each door are determined by considering how the room will be used and what items will be moved into and out of it. The size and appearance of windows are also deliberately chosen. Then the doors and windows are crafted from pieces of wood and glass (or whatever other materials are preferred). The process continues, step by step, until every item needed for the building project is identified, designed, crafted, and installed.

A crafted design provides a custom result with interesting individualized details. The problem with this approach is that it is both time-consuming and expensive. That is why the craft approach was abandoned for most construction in the industrialized world in favor of the assembly approach.

ASSEMBLY APPROACH.   In the construction industry today, the norm is the *assembly* of buildings based on extensive use of *components.*[1] The erection of a

[1]*Component method* here does not refer to prefabricated construction, in which all needed items are preselected, precut, and delivered together from a single source. The builder using the component method still chooses individual components and arranges to acquire them, possibly from a variety of sources.

FIGURE 12.1 *Home Building Via Craft Approach Versus Assembly Approach*
For the former, craftsmen make, by hand, each element of the roof. Under the assembly approach, preconstructed components are selected and lifted into place when needed.

building starts with a model outlining the structure's principal dimensions and features. Working from that model, contractors and subcontractors add key elements incrementally. Selections are made from catalogs of *predesigned* components: windows, doors, lighting fixtures, cabinets, and flooring (even the most lavish custom-designed facilities draw heavily on components). Few elements are created from scratch. Since crafting special components is extremely expensive and time-consuming, builders only craft custom components when catalog options are unsatisfactory. And then, careful advance scheduling is essential in order to avoid delays on other parts of the project.

The component-based modern construction industry suggests several practices that may be advantageous to IT professionals when they are creating information systems:

- *Division of labor,* or the specialization of activities.
- *Purchasing standardized components* from outside suppliers rather than crafting them individually.
- *Hiring specialized experts* to do substantial parts of the work.

As the assembly approach to IT becomes more widespread in businesses, the development of information systems will change in this direction.

Objects are components that are further refined. Objects contain data about themselves—data that tell how the object is to be processed. IT professionals term this feature *encapsulation,* meaning that the object includes information describing both the data and how the data are processed. The *Information Technology in Practice* feature entitled "At Reuters, Objects Aid Accuracy and Business Growth" describes how a 140-year-old news agency is capitalizing on object-oriented design principles to build information technology applications.

object
A component that contains data about itself and how it is to be processed.

Building IT with Components

When the concept of components is adapted to the IT world, components become functional units that can be plugged into a framework or surface, such as desktop windows (Figure 12.2). Individual components can be added incrementally to augment the application's utility. Each component can be inserted into the framework at the desired place. For example, the icon for a spreadsheet program can be dragged to the desired location or window on the computer user's desktop (the way a door can be inserted into a building at the desired location in a chosen wall).

One sign that the component approach is gaining in the IT environment is the appearance of program generation tools that enable the designer to specify boxes and option groups (Figure 12.3) without needing to write the program code to use them. Other examples are business elements (purchase orders and invoices) and control elements (such as communications interfaces) of desktop software packages. Just around the corner are catalogs containing hundreds of prewritten and packaged components available to developers (whose job will more and more focus on assembly of programs and applications).

Managing the Development Process

The development of shared systems is an important business activity because of the challenges it presents to the firm. When a firm embarks on a shared system development project, it must keep in mind several points:

1. A business is dependent on IT for its success.
2. Introducing a new system means introducing a change to the business.
3. Shared systems mean multiple viewpoints.
4. IT can create a competitive edge—or take it away.
5. Systems analysts (whose role we first discussed in Chapter 2) must understand the needs of business, but businesspeople must also understand the needs of systems analysts.
6. Both systems analysts and users must anticipate problems that can arise with the new system.
7. Systems analysts must design the system to use the computer and communications capabilities available within (or that can be acquired by) the organization.

Every development project must be managed well to achieve the desired results. But even a company that does a good job generally of managing projects can fail if it doesn't pay attention to the details of the specific project, as the ill-fated Confirm project described in the feature in the next section shows.

FIGURE 12.2

Design Tools Allow Developers to Insert Application Components into a Window

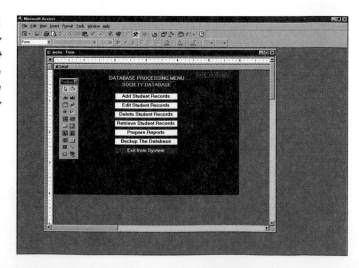

INFORMATION TECHNOLOGY IN PRACTICE

At Reuters, Objects Aid Accuracy and Business Growth

Reuters, a 140-year-old independent global news agency, provides information to financial and news organizations around the world: graphics, prices, photographs, and video clips. Its customers use that information to make multimillion-dollar investment decisions. An investor in Tokyo, for instance, may rely heavily on an on-line display of information retrieved from the Reuters system to determine whether to acquire a large block of stocks recently issued for public sale. Or a television producer in France may incorporate a Reuters report on falling prices on Le Bourse (the Paris Stock Exchange) into its nightly business news. Businesspersons like these expect the information supplied by Reuters to be both accurate and reliable. Customer confidence is essential to the company's image, so accuracy and reliability are critical components of the Reuters system.

More than 200,000 individuals in over 125 countries use the Reuters system. Reuters does not aim at just passing along well-presented information to these subscribers. Much of the information the agency transmits comes from various independent sources, and Reuters believes that to fully serve its customers, it must ensure that the information is accurate.

To guarantee reliability while at the same time ensuring that its systems can be adjusted quickly as trading and investment rules change, Reuters chose an object-oriented design. Here's how the systems work for investment activities.

Objects are types of investment instruments: securities, interest-bearing notes, derivatives, and so on. The data describing the investment are part of an object. So is the type of activity involving the object and its origin. Hence, a *derivative* object (a type of investment) will include details to identify that it was traded as an option (a type of derivative) at a specific time on, say, the Paris Bourse. Reuters also designed the object to contain rules that are used to ensure the details are correct. Some are quite simple: The *bid* price at which an institution will buy shares must be less that the *ask* price. Others are more complex, perhaps describing the manner in which a night trade (occurring after the exchange closes) is reported or specifying how to validate a put or call option.

Whenever Reuters receives information on an investment transaction, the system processes it using the rules contained in the object relating to that type

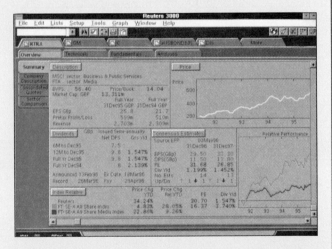

of transaction. The built-in processing logic helps validate the transaction for Reuters, ensuring that the agency will pass along only accurate information to its subscribers. Because the system has an object-oriented design, whenever rules change, the IT professionals responsible for the system need only change the object involved—which is much easier than having to check an entire system for possible adjustments to procedures. The object-oriented design helps both Reuters and its customers build their businesses. And after all, that's what business IT is all about.

Icon	Tool Name	Control Purpose on a Form or Report
↖	**Select Objects**	Select, move, size, and edit controls
A	**Label**	Display text, such as a title or instructions; an unbound control
ab|	**Text Box**	Display a label attached to a text box that contains a bound control or a calculated control
▢	**Option Group**	Display a group frame containing toggle buttons, option buttons, or check boxes; can use Control Wizards to create
▭	**Toggle Button**	Signal if a situation is true (button is selected or pushed down) or false
⊙	**Option Button**	Signal if a situation is true (black dot appears in the option button's center) or false; also called a radio button
⊠	**Check Box**	Signal if a situation is true (X appears in the check box) or false
▮	**Combo Box**	Display a drop-down list box, so that you can either type a value or select a value from the list; can use Control Wizards to create
▤	**List Box**	Display a list of values from which you can choose one value; can use Control Wizards to create

Using the option tool in Microsoft Access allows the designer to create an option component for processing

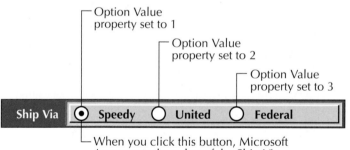

Option Value property set to 1

Option Value property set to 2

Option Value property set to 3

Ship Via ⊙ Speedy ○ United ○ Federal

When you click this button, Microsoft Access sets the value of the Ship Via option group to 1 and stores this number in the underlying table.

FIGURE 12.3 *Object Design Tools Enable Developers to Specify System Components*

A sample of object design tools included in the Microsoft Access database system.

The Origin of a Systems Project

systems development
The process of examining a business situation, designing a system solution to improve that situation, and acquiring the human, financial, and information technology resources needed to develop and implement the solution.

Systems development is the process of examining a business situation, designing a system solution to improve that situation, and acquiring the human, financial, and information technology resources needed to develop and implement the solution. **Project management** is the process of planning, organizing, integrating, and overseeing the development of an IT application to ensure that the project's objectives are achieved and that the system is implemented according to expectations. Before development can begin, a project proposal must be prepared by users or systems analysts and submitted to a steering committee.

Project Proposal

The **project proposal** is a critical element in launching the systems study. Although its form varies from firm to firm, the proposal should always answer the following questions:

- What specifically is the problem?
- What details describe the problem?
- How significant is the problem?
- What is a possible solution to the problem?
- How will information technology help to solve the problem?
- Who else knows about this problem and who else should be contacted?

Whether the proposal has been triggered by a single event or by a recurring situation is also an important consideration. For example, at AMR, parent of American Airlines and creator of the widely admired SABRE reservation system, managers and executives noticed that their major customers—business travelers and their travel agents—nearly always booked more than one type of reservation at a time. In addition to airline reservations, business travelers often require hotel and car rental reservations. AMR saw a business opportunity in creating a shared system capable of handling all types of reservations simultaneously. The *Information Technology in Practice* feature entitled "A SABRE-Toothed Tiger" describes the origin and success of the SABRE system at AMR as well as the failure of the ill-conceived Confirm project for handling all types of reservations.

Steering Committee Review

Most companies do not let individuals launch shared systems projects on their own. Rather, they direct that project proposals be submitted to a **steering committee.** The committee, usually made up of people from various functional areas of the business (e.g., executives in marketing, accounting, purchasing, inventory control, manufacturing, sales, and information systems), determines if the project is desirable and should be pursued.

The Systems Analyst

Recall that the term *systems analyst* is used very broadly to refer to a person who develops all or a portion of an IT application. However, IT professionals distinguish among systems analysts, systems designers, and programmer/analysts, all of whom have different responsibilities. **Systems analysts** are responsible for working with users to determine a system's requirements and to describe the features needed in the system. **Systems designers** are responsible for doing the technical work of designing the system and its software. **Programmer/analysts** are responsible for determining system requirements and developing and implementing the systems. In essence, they act as programmers, systems analysts, and systems designers.

In the business world, it is very often the systems analyst who sees the development of a shared IT application through, from original conception to finished product. For this reason, we focus primarily on the systems analyst's activities in the pages that follow.

---

project management
The process of planning, organizing, integrating, and overseeing the development of an IT application to ensure that the project's objectives are achieved and the system is implemented according to expectations.

project proposal
A proposal for a systems project prepared by users or systems analysts and submitted to a steering committee for approval.

steering committee
A group of people from various functional areas of a business that determines whether a systems development project proposal is desirable and should be pursued.

systems analyst
The IT professional responsible for working with users to determine a system's requirements and for describing the features needed in the system.

systems designer
The IT professional responsible for doing the technical work of designing the system and its software.

programmer/analyst
A person who has joint responsibility for determining system requirements and developing and implementing the systems.

INFORMATION TECHNOLOGY IN PRACTICE

A SABRE-Toothed Tiger

Sometimes a company's competitive advantage is tied into its ability to develop shared IT applications. Consider the experience of American Airlines (AA) of Dallas, Texas, which is recognized worldwide for its effective use of IT. The SABRE System developed by the airline has been a key ingredient in helping AA gain a competitive edge over other airlines.

SABRE was first conceived, in 1959, as an internal system that would link the airline's offices and ticket counters. Sixteen years later, AA CEO Robert Crandall and Chief Information Officer Max Hopper determined SABRE could be used as more than a communications system within the airline. They began marketing the system to travel agents, the people who sell the most tickets for the airline industry. After AA expanded SABRE's capabilities to make it a convenient tool for booking reservations on *all* airlines, a large portion of the country's travel agents were quickly convinced to use the system. AA also successfully implemented a policy of charging other airlines a nominal "booking fee" when travel agents made reservations on their flights through the SABRE system. Today, American receives millions of dollars of revenue annually because independent travel agents process flight reservations on other airlines through SABRE.

In the 1980s, when deregulation increased competition in the U.S. airline industry and changed it almost overnight, Crandall stepped forward again. Recognizing SABRE's potential for use in other kinds of programs, he came up with the American Advantage Frequent Flier program—a computer-based marketing strategy that encourages travelers to fly with American by rewarding them with points redeemable for free travel. American's frequent flier program has a membership of more than 11 million people and has created tremendous loyalty toward American in travelers. In addition to locking travelers into flying with American Airlines to obtain the benefits of its frequent flier program, the SABRE system allows the airline's management to adjust its fares rapidly in response to competitors' ticket prices.

But the story does not end there. Seeking to capitalize further on SABRE's enormous capabilities, AMR Information Services (AMRIS—AMR Corp. is the parent of American Airlines) in 1988 announced plans to create a hotel, car rental, and travel reservation system to be called Confirm. A budget of $125 million was established for the project. Four companies agreed to participate as partners in developing and using Confirm: AMR, Marriott, Hilton Hotels, and Budget Rent A Car. The partners formed the Interna-

The Systems Development Life Cycle

systems development life cycle (SDLC)
The six-phased set of activities that brings about a new IT application.

The proposal submitted to the steering committee is the first step in systems development. The **systems development life cycle (SDLC),** outlined in Figure 12.4, is the set of activities that brings about a new IT application. Like the process of developing a personal system (Chapter 9), the SDLC is a problem-solving process. It consists of six phases:

1. **Problem recognition/preliminary investigation**—defining and investigating the problem.
2. **Requirements determination**—understanding the current system and the new system's requirements.
3. **Systems design**—planning the new system.
4. **Development and construction**—creating the new system.

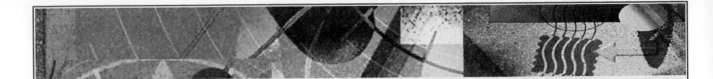

tional Reservations and Information Consortium (IN-TRICO) to oversee the development of Confirm and to market the system to the travel industry. The original plans for Confirm called for more than 3,000 programs running on two large mainframes at AMRIS's data center. The systems were to communicate with various hotel and rental-car airport reservations centers and to store data in a large, centralized database.

In October 1992, AMR announced that it was "suspending development" of Confirm. According to industry reports, the project was running well behind schedule and the partners disagreed about the system's features and functions—one partner had reportedly provided a set of specifications that stood literally six feet high. After the failure of the project, the partners made many charges and countercharges about their original expectations, the development process, the feasibility of the system, and the capabilities of development personnel.

SABRE was a success and Confirm a failure. Why? The Confirm concept was attractive and appeared to make creative use of IT. Yet, in the end, the project collapsed because the partners failed to manage the development of a shared IT system.

Reservations specialists at American Airlines use state-of-the-art headphones and the SABRE shared information system to book both domestic and international flights. American receives millions of dollars of revenue annually because independent travel agents process flight reservations on other airlines through SABRE also.

5. **Implementation**—converting to the new system.
6. **Evaluation and continuing evolution**—monitoring and adding value to the new system.

Each of these stages is discussed in detail in the sections that follow.

Problem Recognition/ Preliminary Investigation

Most businesses have more requests for systems development activities than they can possibly support. Hence, the first activity in the systems development life cycle—problem recognition/preliminary investigation—is conducted at the direction of the steering committee.

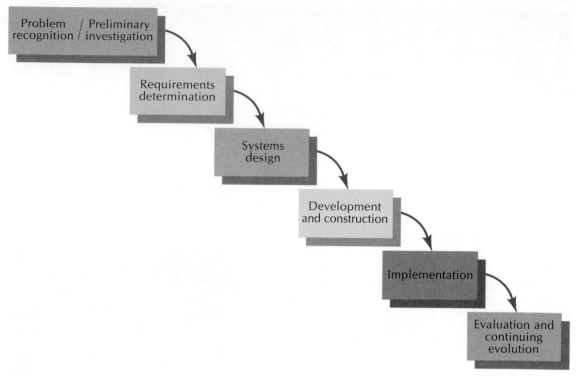

FIGURE 12.4 *The Systems Development Life Cycle*
The systems development life cycle begins with problem recognition but never really ends, for the new system must be continually monitored and evaluated after it has been put in place.

preliminary investigation

The first phase of the systems development life cycle, in which the merits and feasibility of a project proposal are determined.

The purpose of the **preliminary investigation** is to examine the project proposal in order (1) to evaluate its merits and (2) to determine whether it is feasible to launch a project that will address the issues it raises. During the preliminary investigation, systems analysts work to clarify the proposal, determine the size and scope of the project, assess the costs and benefits of alternative approaches, and determine the project's general feasibility. They then report their findings to the steering committee along with a recommendation.

Systems analysts assess three types of feasibility: operational, financial/economic, and technical feasibility.

OPERATIONAL FEASIBILITY. A project is judged *operationally feasible* if it will meet the business's operating requirements and will have a desirable effect on the company. If the project requires changes in current procedures, those changes must be acceptable for the project to be judged operationally feasible.

For example, United Parcel Service (UPS), the world's largest and most successful package delivery service, saw its business threatened by the growth of Federal Express's overnight service. UPS decided to examine the feasibility of expanding its business services to include both overnight package delivery and more effective use of its distribution and delivery capabilities. It conducted an investigation to determine if its operations, delivery procedures, and IT capabilities could be expanded to guarantee next-morning delivery. The company's executives and employees knew that developing a guaranteed-overnight business was desirable; they wanted to be sure it was feasible.

FINANCIAL AND ECONOMIC FEASIBILITY. Even if the proposed system is operationally feasible, it must be a good financial investment for the business to undertake it. In other words, the project's benefits should exceed its costs. Benefits would be increased business; lower costs; and fewer errors. The costs would be: the expense of conducting a full systems investigation; the cost of hardware, communications links, and software for the application being considered; and the cost to the business if the proposed system is *not* developed.

The UPS vision depends on information technology, not just for moving packages, but also for moving information. UPS executives recognized that enhancing communication between the drivers of its 50,000 trucks and the company's distribution centers was important for improving the UPS delivery system. They also wanted to provide customers with real-time information (see Chapter 2) about the location of their packages. A five-year $1.6 billion effort was launched to accomplish these goals. Because UPS is a successful, well-managed $23 billion company, an investment of this magnitude was financially feasible.

TECHNICAL FEASIBILITY. A project is *technically feasible* if the systems analyst can answer the following questions with "yes":

- Does the firm have the necessary computer and communications technology to do what the proposal suggests? If not, can it acquire this technology?
- Does the proposed hardware (whether currently installed or to be acquired) have the capacity to store and transmit the data and information required for the new system?
- Will the proposed system provide adequate responses to inquiries, regardless of the number of individuals who will use it?
- Can the system be expanded at a later date?
- Does the proposed system guarantee accuracy, reliability, ease of access, and data security?

To determine the technical feasibility of linking its customers, drivers, and distribution centers, UPS contacted the operators of the largest cellular networks (see Chapter 10). After much discussion, the company was convinced it could improve its distribution system with wireless communications. Working with four carriers—McCaw Cellular Communications, GTE Mobile Communications, PacTel Cellular, and Southwestern Bell Mobile Systems—UPS established a custom-designed nationwide network.

Thanks to the recently installed TotalTrack systems, UPS drivers are now connected to the cellular network through handheld computers attached to a combination cellular modem/telephone (Figure 12.5). The handheld computer automatically dials the closest carrier, which then interconnects to the UPS private network and the company's data center. Information about the pickup, delivery, or location of any package can be transmitted over the network.

UPS's cellular system was completed on time and within the $150 million budget allocation. Since implementing the system, UPS has transformed itself into a successful overnight package carrier while continuing to expand its highly efficient and profitable parcel service. It has duplicated virtually all of Federal Express's features and services in the overnight parcel business, including Saturday morning delivery. (Until recently, UPS delivered only Monday through Friday.) IT was the vehicle for turning the company's vision into reality. The UPS story will continue to evolve, making it an interesting company to watch for years to come.

Not all systems development proposals are feasible, of course. And not all proposals judged infeasible are worthless. Sometimes a proposal is sent back to the

FIGURE 12.5

United Parcel Service's Cellular Network for Package Tracking

UPS's new $150 million communications network has helped it compete with its major rival, Federal Express.

National cellular carrier transmits package information, via satellite, between the UPS data center, the regional cellular center, and UPS employees.

Regional cellular carrier transmits data and information to one of four national carriers.

UPS DATA CENTER

Package pickup and delivery information transmitted between driver's handheld computer and regional cellular carrier.

originator with a request for more information, then reexamined. At other times, the preliminary investigation of a proposal reveals opportunities to change business processes and activities in a way that both improves the business and eliminates the need to invest in a new information system. In these cases, the proposal and its preliminary investigation contributed to the business's ultimate goal: increased success for the organization.

Requirements Determination

requirement

A feature that must be included in a system.

A **requirement** is a feature that must be included in a system. This feature may be a way of capturing or processing information, a method of interacting with the system, a processing activity or result, a piece of information displayed or printed as a result of processing, or a function that can be performed to safeguard data and information. For UPS, the requirement was guaranteed overnight delivery and package tracking. For AMRIS, the requirement (never fulfilled) was the connection of business partners to allow them to share information and assist their customers.

requirements determination

The second phase of the systems development life cycle, in which the current business situation is studied to determine who is involved, what data and information are needed, and how the current system can be improved.

During the **requirements determination** phase of the systems development life cycle, the systems analyst studies the current business situation, collecting and analyzing data and information to determine who is involved, what data and information are used, and how the current system can be improved. Requirements determination should address either or both types of improvement: process improvement and business improvement.

process

A structured activity that leads to a set of results (output).

PROCESS IMPROVEMENT. A **process** is a structured activity that leads to a set of results (in systems terms, an *output*). The structure of the process specifies its sequence of activities and the flow of work from beginning to end. Processes cut

Volkswagen Parts On-Line in Mexico

Volkswagen is known around the world as a high-quality, moderately priced German automobile. Some six generations of drivers have grown up with Volkswagen AG's familiar logo and its ever-present Beetle model on the roads and in automobile showrooms.

Because there is such a high demand for Volkswagen cars, they are manufactured in several countries around the world, including Mexico. When the North American Free Trade Agreement (NAFTA) took effect, the potential U.S. market for Volkswagen automobiles made in Mexico prompted Volkswagen managers to take a new look at the company's operations there. They found that the manufacturing process at Volkswagen-Gedas NA, the company's Mexican subsidiary, was turning out high-quality cars, as they expected, but the spare parts operation (accounting for the sale of more than 1 million Volkswagen parts annually) was not of the same caliber.

Most Volkswagen dealers had to submit their parts orders on a diskette; only a few had on-line access to the company's ordering system. Processing and fulfillment often took two weeks, which was clearly unacceptable in the rapidly changing post-NAFTA business climate. Rapid development of a reliable parts ordering and fulfillment system for the 200 dealers in Mexico became the challenge for Volkswagen.

across business functions, spanning department and location boundaries. A company's order fulfillment process, for example, depends on the ability of its manufacturing, inventory, shipping, and accounting departments to work together to ship a customer's order and bill the account in a timely and accurate fashion.

Process improvement addresses the question, "Can we improve the way we work?" Before improvements to a system can be made, the systems analyst must know how activities are performed now, which procedures are effective, and which processes need improvement. Table 12.1 lists the questions that an analyst attempts to answer in evaluating a process. It is useful to think of the process as having a customer—an individual or a group who receives the benefits or results of the process. Depending on how well the process is performed, the customer will be satisfied or dissatisfied.

process improvement
An improvement in the way a business works.

The fast pace of business in the 1990s, coupled with the competitive pressures and customer expectations of high-quality products and services, is causing managers and executives in many organizations to review all their business processes. Reshaping business processes, often called *reengineering,* simultaneously seeks to remove barriers that prohibit an organization from providing better products and services and to help the organization capitalize on its strengths.

Reengineering is just one part of the "*re* phenomenon." Businesses are *re*designing, *re*tooling, *re*making, *re*shaping, *re*structuring, *re*organizing, *re*establishing, *re*building, and *re*positioning to gain an advantage in the extremely competitive global marketplace. IT plays an important role in reengineering business

TABLE 12.1 *Evaluating a Business Process*

- What is being done?
- How is it being done?
- How frequently does it occur?
- How great is the volume of transactions or decisions?
- How well is the task being performed?
- Does a problem exist?
- If a problem exists, how serious is it?
- If a problem exists, what is the underlying cause?
- Who is affected by the business process or work activity under consideration?

processes. The five steps involved in the reengineering process are outlined in Figure 12.6.

BUSINESS IMPROVEMENT. The capabilities of a business can be expanded through business improvement. Requirements determination addresses the question, "Can we improve our business?" The UPS example we've been using in this chapter illustrates clearly how information technology can improve a business.

IT plays a central role in business improvement in four general ways: it helps firms offer new products and services; it speeds up business processes; it reduces the cost of products and services; and it assists firms to enter new regions or markets.

Offering New Products and Services. This type of business improvement arises when businesses identify and then meet the previously unrecognized wants and needs of their existing or potential customers.

The Regional Bell Operating Companies (RBOCs) in the United States (Ameritech, Bell Atlantic, BellSouth, SBC, and U.S. West) and PTTs in Europe and the Far East are using their IT capabilities to offer many new services to customers. Among these new services are call forwarding (in which calls are automatically rerouted to the recipient's actual destination rather than to the number dialed) and call waiting (in which a signal alerts a customer that a call is waiting to come over a link already in use). For a small fee, weather and sports scores are also available over the same lines.

There are other new services in various stages of development by telephone companies, including the delivery of movies, the monitoring of home security systems, and the reading of electric and gas meters. Customers benefit from the new, more convenient services, and the telephone companies earn higher revenue and develop a larger customer base.

Speeding Up Business Processes. Compressing the time it takes to do business can increase efficiency or produce a substantial competitive advantage. As both Federal Express and UPS know well, the ability to move information quickly and effectively can give companies an edge in taking business from their competitors.

The benefits of speeding up business processes are not limited to service industries. Manufacturing companies have also reaped business advantages from speeding up their operations. When the time needed to complete a task is compressed,

Step 1: Review	During the review of business processes, the systems analyst should document activities in the current process, determine what value or benefits are added by performing the process, and identify opportunities for improvement.
Step 2: Redesign	Reengineering is often most successful when company personnel are able to take a fresh look at how they carry out activities. Challenging traditional assumptions about the reasons for doing things in a particular way often leads to process redesign. The frequent result is processes that are simpler, less time-consuming, and more effective than those they replaced.
Step 3: Reorchestrate	Redesign suggests new ways to do business. Reorchestration is the transition to those new ways. Realignment of responsibilities, adjustment of quality control procedures, and implementation of new methods are essential. Reorchestration also entails addressing the concerns of individuals who are directly affected by the changes. Failure to deal with human concerns may render reengineering efforts unsuccessful.
Step 4: Reassess	Measurement of results documents the impact of reengineering. Some changes may be better than expected, while others may need rethinking. Only by evaluating the results can the impact of the reengineering process be determined.
Step 5: Recycle	Reengineering is not a one-time activity. Because opportunities and the competitive environment change constantly, rethinking business processes is always an agenda item for an organization's leaders.

FIGURE 12.6
The Reengineering Process
Reengineering means overhauling business processes and organization structures that limit the competitiveness, efficiency, and effectiveness of the organization.

the risk of errors is reduced because decisions are made closer to the point when action is taken. And less risk usually means that businesses need to tie up fewer resources as a precaution against mistakes and poor cost or demand estimates.

Toyota Motor Corp. of Toyota City, Japan, competes worldwide on the basis of time. The company invented the "Toyota production system," which aims at using the same manufacturing process to make many different models of automobiles in small quantities. An essential component of this system is what has come to be known as *just-in-time production* (Figure 12.7). Toyota can take an order for a custom-manufactured automobile and deliver the vehicle within the same week. Many of Toyota's competitors require four to six weeks to manufacture and deliver a custom-ordered vehicle.

Toyota has compressed the manufacturing process by simplifying each step and by ensuring that the workers on the assembly line have all the information they need to assemble the car ordered by the customer. Doing things right the first time results in fewer delays and less time spent on reworking improperly assembled vehicles.

At Toyota, compressing time also means more accurate scheduling and closer relations with suppliers. The company uses IT to receive and assemble all dealers' orders electronically. The parts and assembly lists needed to build each vehicle are prepared by computers that retrieve details from the company's databases.

FIGURE 12.7

Just-in-Time Manufacturing at the Toyota Plant in Toyota City, Japan

Toyota's JIT system ensures that all assembly line workers have parts at hand when needed. The parts and assembly lists for each vehicle are prepared by computers that retrieve information from company databases. This information is shared through the company communications network with suppliers, who deliver the parts "just in time" for worker installation in the vehicle.

This information is then shared through Toyota's communications network with suppliers, who deliver the parts and assemblies, often several times daily, "just in time" for workers to install them in the vehicle. This system allows Toyota to deliver a customer's choice of automobile much faster than competitors can, even while maintaining high standards of quality. Scheduling parts delivery closer to manufacturing time also means the company needs less production space and ties up less of its money in inventory.

Reducing the Cost of Products and Services.   Reduced costs give companies great flexibility in their pricing policies. If a competitor decides to compete by lowering the price of a product, the company can respond and still make a profit. *Price wars* occur when businesses compete solely on the price they charge customers. In the end, the company that has the lowest costs is usually in the best position. (No business really wins in a price war—unless it is able to drive a competitor out of the industry—because reduced prices usually decrease profits, which are needed to finance future operations and expansion. Even the customer, who benefits from a price war in the short run, may lose out in the long run if companies drive each other out of business or if the survivor later raises prices.) IT, when used to help reduce costs of products or services, plays a central role in business improvement.

Entering New Regions or Markets.   Companies can improve their businesses by using their IT capabilities to enter new geographic regions. For example, both Federal Express and UPS found that a growing number of their business customers were expanding into new international regions. Accustomed to overnight package delivery in the United States, these customers expected the same capability abroad, whether in Canada or Mexico, Europe or the Far East. They also expected the same level of accountability—the same ability to find out the location of a package at any moment. After identifying these requirements, both companies expanded their delivery capabilities and the capabilities of their tracking systems to cover packages shipped to international destinations. The *Information Technology in Practice* feature entitled "IT comes to the Aid of Exporters" offers some advice for entrepreneurs interested in exporting their goods and services to international destinations.

Business improvement has the greatest impact when it enables a company to launch a new product or service that competitors cannot duplicate quickly or at all. Businesspeople call this type of improvement a *preemptive strike*. By launching a preemptive strike, a company can capture the market for the product or service, satisfying customers' desires so swiftly and to such an extent that they have no desire to switch to other products later.

American Airlines launched a preemptive strike when it implemented its computerized reservation system and related frequent flier program. Even though other airlines have tried to emulate this system, few have been successful. AMR retains approximately 50 percent of the U.S. market for travel agent and fee-based reservation processing, while the more than 50 remaining carriers fight it out for the rest.

Experience is an important factor in identifying systems requirements. Junior analysts tend to accept what they hear, see, or read about current business processes. But with seasoning, they recognize that processes change whenever an analyst becomes involved in a business situation because people tend to behave differently under scrutiny. They often change their actions to conform to the observer's expectations (a tendency called the *Hawthorne effect*). They may also make things look more difficult than they really are.

That is why experienced analysts use a variety of sources and methods to gather information. They compare the information obtained in one way or from one specific source with that obtained in other ways. They also seek to get inside the business or industry they are studying. Frequently, people will not inform an analyst of the details surrounding a business or industry practice. This is seldom an intentional withholding of information. Rather, the information is usually so integral to the process that the individual doesn't realize the systems analyst is not aware of it. Experienced analysts know how to get at this information.

Systems analysis entails more than simply gathering information and studying tools, techniques, and technologies. It requires gaining knowledge and insight and using these to identify and solve problems. ■

Systems Design

A system's *design* is the set of details that describe how the system will meet the requirements identified during requirements determination. The process of translating requirements into design specifications is known as **systems design.**

Systems design has three steps: preliminary (conceptual) design, prototyping, and detailed (physical) design.

PRELIMINARY (CONCEPTUAL) DESIGN.   The preliminary design of a system specifies its distinguishing characteristics, conceptualizing the functions it will perform and how they will occur. Current systems capabilities will influence the design.

The preliminary design typically specifies

- Whether the system will be distributed or centralized.
- Whether the system will be developed by the company's staff members or by outside contractors or by purchasing a software package.
- Whether processing will use on-line or batch procedures.
- Whether data communications networks will be developed.

systems design
The third phase of the systems development life cycle, in which requirements are translated into design specifications.

INFORMATION TECHNOLOGY IN PRACTICE

IT Comes to the Aid of Exporters

Thousands of small and midsize businesses are finding exporting a great way to increase sales. Consider the experiences of DMT Corp. and Interstate Engineering. DMT Corp., of Waukesha, Wisconsin, more than doubled sales by marketing its backup electrical generators to manufacturers in the Far East and Central and South America, where the electrical supply tends to be unreliable. And Interstate Engineering's sudden success at exporting to Germany, Italy, France, the United Kingdom, and Japan led to the cancellation of plans to lay off 10 to 15 percent of the company's 140 employees.

Unfortunately, too many U.S. companies hesitate to export because they are mystified by the requirements of international market research and bureaucratic red tape. This situation may change soon, however, thanks to a growing collection of IT-based assistance from both government and private sources.

Demystifying International Market Research

One of the most detailed resources of international market research is the National Trade Data Bank (NTDB), a CD-ROM issued every month by the U.S. Commerce Department. Each disk compiles and indexes more than 100,000 export-related documents, detailed export and import statistics from the Census Bureau, national income and product accounts from

Sales to foreign universities, research labs, and governments helped Linda and Robert Bernstein's SeaSpace Corp. grow from six to sixteen employees. The San Diego-based firm manufactures weather-satellite receiving systems. By 1992, 50% of the company's sales were coming from England, Germany, Italy, Japan, Korea, Portugal, Spain, and Taiwan.

- Whether applications will run on microcomputers, midrange systems, mainframes, or some combination of these.
- The data and information that will be generated and the reports that must be produced.
- The files or databases needed for the system to function.
- The number of users and locations supported by the system.
- The capacity of storage devices.
- The number of printers and communications links among individuals, customers, suppliers, and others who will interact with the system.
- The personnel needed to operate the system.

the Bureau of Economic Analysis, and world production figures from the Department of Agriculture. Although many libraries, private firms, and marketing consultants subscribe to the NTDB, its biggest fans may be the trade specialists who work for the federal government. Their job is to work directly with local companies to help them build their exports.

Another source of market information is the Export Hotline, a free service co-sponsored by AT&T, KPMG Peat Marwick, Delta Airlines, *Business Week, The Journal of Commerce,* the National Association of Manufacturers, the U.S. Council for International Business, and others. After callers use a voice mail system to enter their selection from a menu of 78 countries and 50 industries, the system taps into a database to produce a customized marketing report that is then faxed to the caller. The system can also generate a number of other documents, such as a country overview; an analysis of export, import, or investment issues; a list of key business contacts; direct marketing advice; shipping and transportation requirements; and tips on business travel, etiquette, and protocol.

Cutting Through Bureaucratic Red Tape

Of course, marketing is only half the battle. Exporters also have to meet the legal requirements of the countries in which they want to do business. Attempting to do so can lead to dealing with a flurry of bewildering forms, documents, and licenses. To simplify the process of getting an export license, the U.S. Commerce Department has created a trio of computer systems that can be accessed by phone. For general information, you call ELVIS—short for Export Licensing Voice Information System—a voice mail system that offers information on licensing procedures. If you call ELAIN, the Export License Application and Information Network, you can apply for an export license electronically over the CompuServe network. STELA, the System for Tracking Export License Applications, is an automated voice response system that lets you check on the status of your application.

Meanwhile, a growing number of entrepreneurs are creating export automation software—computer programs that can generate letter-perfect commercial invoices, country-of-origin certificates, packing slips, and export declaration forms in various languages. These programs can also help exporters comply with international and domestic regulations, such as the U.S. table-of-denial screenings that restrict the types of technology that can be sold in certain countries.

After the preliminary design is prepared, it is presented to the users and to the steering committee for approval. Any necessary changes are made before the design moves into the prototype phase.

Diamond Star Motors Corp., located in Normal, Illinois, began as a joint venture between Chrysler Corp. of Detroit, Michigan, and Japan's Mitsubishi Motors Corp. (MMC) in 1985. By 1991, Diamond Star had become a subsidiary of MMC. The company, which produces the Mitsubishi Eclipse and Galant, Eagle Talon, and Plymouth Laser, now has more than 3,200 employees.

Manufacturing activities at Diamond Star are patterned after Mitsubishi Motors' practices in Japan. Production associates begin their workday at 6:30 A.M. with

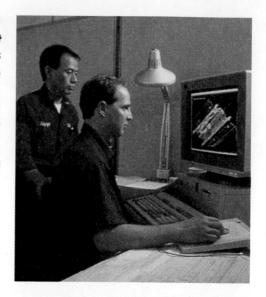

FIGURE 12.8

Shared IT Applications at Diamond Star Motors

All Diamond Star employees, including managers and assembly line workers, wear the same uniform. This standard is part of the company's team-oriented approach to automobile design and assembly. Using sophisticated design programs linked to the company's network, engineers can communicate directly with the assembly line to create prototypes of the parts they've designed.

stretching exercises (performed to the sound of music piped throughout the building). All employees, including managers and the 50-person Information Technology staff, wear the same uniform: gray pants and maroon shirts bearing the company logo over the left pocket and the employee's name over the right (Figure 12.8).

Originally, Diamond Star intended to duplicate the manufacturing and business processes of the Mitsubishi plant in Okazaki, Japan. It quickly determined, however, that copying that plant's computer and communications systems was much easier than transplanting its business processes and related IT applications. Analysts discovered, for example, how dramatically different Japanese finance and accounting practices are from those in the United States. For instance, Japanese companies often budget in six-month cycles—on the premise that shorter budget periods give businesspeople better control over resources, enable them to forecast more accurately, and allow them to respond more rapidly to fluctuations in business—while U.S. companies generally draw up 12-month annual budgets.

To launch the conceptual designs for the 30 new systems needed by the new company, Diamond Star's IT staff had to become familiar with the different cultures and business practices in the two countries. Some IT staff members spent time in Japan (from 2 to 10 weeks) to become familiar with the Japanese systems. In the end, not only did they design interfaces between each partner's computers to accommodate the different budgeting and reporting practices, but they also developed IT applications to run one of the most sophisticated automated manufacturing lines in the world. This line includes an on-line vehicle tracking system that tells workers the location of every vehicle, an on-line vendor broadcasting system designed to ensure that parts arrive just in time for installation in a vehicle, and more than 100 assembly line robots (550 plantwide). Diamond Star's assembly line is 20 percent automated (10 percent is the norm in most automotive plants with the same capacity) and a specially designed minicomputer helps to run and manage it. (We discuss these types of industrial applications in more detail in the next chapter.)

prototype
A working model of an IT application.

PROTOTYPING. A **prototype** is a working model of an IT application that, compared to a complete system, is relatively inexpensive to build. Although it usually does not contain all the features of, or perform all the functions that will be

FIGURE 12.9
Application Prototyping
IBM's Software Usability Laboratory allows systems design and development personnel to monitor people's reactions to a system prototype. Listening to future users' reactions to and concerns about the new system is an important component of the system development process.

included in, the final system, the prototype does have enough elements so that people can use the system and quickly determine what they like and dislike about it and what important features are missing from the design. If, for example, those using the prototype complain that the capabilities for certain types of processing or for handling exceptional situations are not built into the design, the system's requirements can be expanded.

The value of the component method shows up during prototyping. Developers can insert prewritten components into the prototype quickly and give the system to users. In fact, they can insert alternate components into the prototype to determine which design meets users' business needs most effectively.

Application prototyping has two primary uses. First, it is an effective method of clarifying the requirements that must be built into a system. Reviewing written specifications is not nearly so effective as working with the features firsthand. Second, prototypes are useful for evaluating a system's features. Users' reactions to methods of interacting with the system (through a keyboard or mouse, for example, or by touching a menu option with a finger) and the arrangement of information on a computer display can be gauged quickly and easily by watching an individual sit down at a workstation and actually use the application (Figure 12.9).

As Figure 12.10 shows, the prototype is part of an *evolutionary system*. New information acquired from users during prototyping can be applied to modify the physical design early in the development process. Modified prototypes can then be reevaluated. Making changes to a prototype is much less costly than altering an application once it has been fully developed and implemented.

DETAILED (PHYSICAL) DESIGN.   The detailed, or physical, design of a system specifies its features. The accompanying documentation consists of definitions explaining the characteristics of the system, its processing activities, and the reports and charts it can generate. Detailed design specifications, which might call for new program instructions to be written, new components to be created, or the use of prewritten components, usually are prepared in the following sequence:

- **Output: information and results.** Because output is the reason for developing a system in the first place, it is the starting point for the detailed design. In the output design, the type, contents, and formats of reports and display screens are defined using **layout descriptions**—charts that show the exact location of data and information on the screen and in a printed report

layout description
A chart that shows the exact location of data and information on a computer screen or in a printed report.

FIGURE 12.10

*Steps in the Development of
a System Prototype*

After preliminary investigation and
requirements determination, a
prototype is created. Like systems
themselves, prototypes undergo
evaluation, development, and
change.

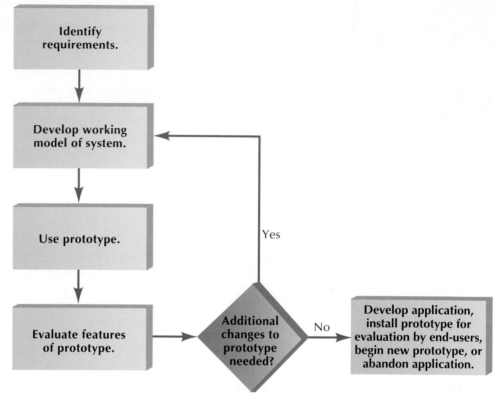

(Figure 12.11). If a prewritten output component is used (say, for a report or document, such as an invoice or payroll check), an output layout may already be suggested.

- **Input: data and information for processing.** Once they know the requirements, designers work back to determine what processing activities are needed to produce the output and which data and information will be provided as input by people using the system.

- **Stored data: databases and files.** If data are not keyed, scanned, or otherwise entered as input by a system user, and are not transmitted to a computer by an electronic link, they may be retrieved from a stored database or file. Figure 12.12 shows the various input components of a sales system and their origins, all of which are specified in the detailed design.

- **Processing and procedures.** Methods are determined for achieving computing results and arranging data and information into a desired sequence. These methods are the *processing requirements*. Also important is the establishment of procedures for the people using the system. Table 12.2 shows some important systems procedures specified during detailed design. These include actions taken to back up files and maintain system security.

- **Controls.** In a shared system, individual users have responsibilities for activities and specific actions. Controls describe these responsibilities. For example, if transactions are accumulated into batches before processing, control information describes how the batches are identified, when they are processed, what files and databases they use, and how the computer operator determines that the batches have been properly processed. In the American Airlines system, controls describe how the weekly batches of ticket payments submitted by each agent will be audited for accuracy and processed within the system.

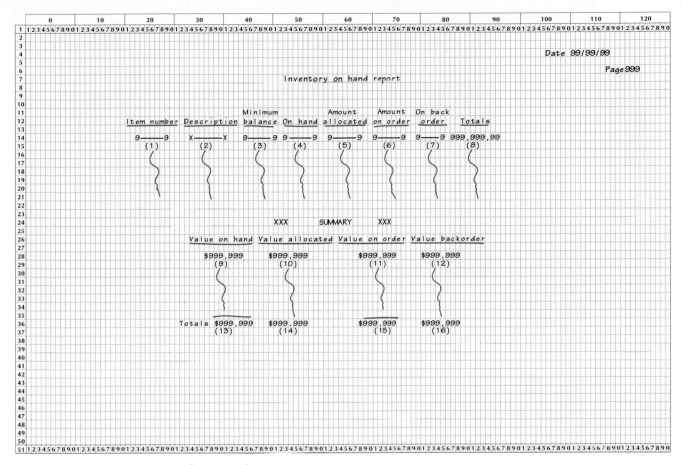

FIGURE 12.11   *Layout Form for Printed System Output*

Layout descriptions, sometimes drawn on paper and other times at the display screen, are used in physical design to show the exact location of data and information in a printed report and on screen. The layout form shown here was used to prepare the format of an inventory-on-hand report.

Confirm's design called for the crafting of over 3,000 programs because of the many different activities necessary to manage cross-country business transactions. Some of Confirm's many design requirements are detailed in Figure 12.13.

Throughout the design process for any system, designers examine many alternatives to ensure that the desired features are included, to meet every business requirement, and to fit within the budgetary constraints of the project.

Have you ever realized that good designs are hardly noticeable? When you get into an automobile, the car's physical features are pretty much the way you expect them to be. The speedometer, fuel gauge, and warning lights are in the same vicinity in most automobiles. So are the controls for the lights and windshield wipers. In each case, you reach for them without giving it a second thought. If the seat's position, steering wheel's tilt, or mirror's angle is not just right, you can make the necessary adjustments quickly and easily. These are all hallmarks of a good design.

TABLE 12.2 *Design of Systems Procedures*	
TYPE	DEFINITION
Data entry procedures	Procedures for capturing data and entering them into the system. Identify which data originate with specific documents, input devices, or individuals.
Run-time procedures	The steps the system's user or operator takes to achieve the desired results. Identify the files and programs that must be included with the system.
Error-handling procedures	The actions a user or operator must take when unexpected or unacceptable results occur. Describe the steps to take when an error is detected or processing is disrupted for any reason.
Security and backup procedures	The actions taken to protect the system, data, information, or programs against accidental or intentional damage. Specify when and how to make duplicate copies of data and programs or actions to take to prevent sabotage.

In contrast, a bad design is noticed almost immediately. You can probably think of instances when you had to fumble around to find the release for the hood, the gas tank cover, the ignition, or the headlight control switch. When the design is right, you don't give it a second thought; when it's wrong, your life is made more difficult. This is as true for computer and communications systems as it is for cars. ■

system construction
The fourth phase of the systems development life cycle, in which the system is actually built.

Development and Construction

During development and **system construction,** the system is actually built. That is, physical design specifications are turned into a functioning system. The prin-

FIGURE 12.12

Input Components of a Sales System and Their Origins

Data that are not entered by a user into the system may be automatically retrieved from a database or file stored in the system.

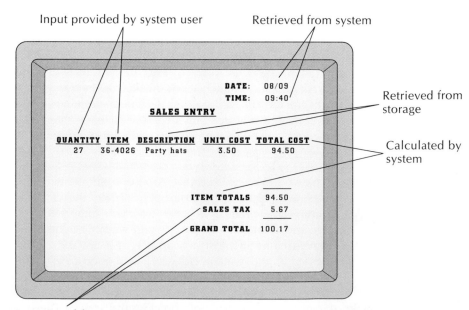

Input provided by system user   Retrieved from system

Retrieved from storage

Calculated by system

Tax rate retrieved from system; tax and grand total computed by system

Input	Output/Reports	Stored data	Processing/Procedures	Controls
•Entry of reservation details for airlines, automobiles, or hotels.	•Printed acknowledgments of reservations.	•Transactions already entered into the system.	•Descriptions of how transcaction data are used to update files and databases or generate reports.	•Methods for detecting invalid charges or credits.
•Entry of a wide variety of rates and charges for airline seats, automobiles, or hotel rooms.	•Printed tickets or invoices.	•Customer, travel agent, airline, automobile, or hotel characteristics.		•Steps for authorizing changes to charge rates and authorization codes in the system.
•Entry of changes to previously entered data and information.	•Printed reports summarizing the allocation of resources (airline seats, automobiles, or hotel rooms).	•Description of facilities, vehicles, or aircraft available to users of the system.	•Procedures for accepting, validating, and processing transactions.	•Description of facilities, vehicles, or aircraft available to users of the system.
•Entry of inquiries to retrieve information about a specific transaction, individual, flight, vehicle, or hotel.	•Printed current status information or historical descriptions of the business activities of a customer, travel agent, or hotel.		•Procedures for backing up the system to safeguard sensitve data and infomation.	
•Entry of requests to print reports, display information, or transmit details from one location to another.			•Procedures for restarting an application that is interrupted for any reason.	

FIGURE 12.13 *The Detailed Design of Confirm*

The design of AMRIS's Confirm system called for more than 3,000 programs. Some elements of the design, based on requirements determination, are listed here.

cipal activities of this phase of the systems development life cycle are the acquisition of software and services, computer programming, and testing (Figure 12.14).

ACQUISITION OF SOFTWARE AND SERVICES. Increasingly, systems incorporate prepackaged software and services originating outside the company. During construction and development, systems designers may acquire software packages that perform specific functions (e.g., data management, security, or backup) or special services (e.g., e-mail, electronic data interchange, or voice mail) and incorporate them into the overall system design.

Communications software and network services are usually acquired rather than developed in-house. During design and construction, systems analysts work with communications carriers to design the network characteristics (such as the locations to be interconnected, transmissions speeds, and management, backup, and error detection procedures).

PROGRAMMING. After the company has acquired software and services, computer programmers turn processing specifications into software. The software created for the system will perform its capture, generation, processing, storage and retrieval, and transmission functions.

Programming may be done in-house or by outside contractors. In the latter case, the contractor is given the specifications and prepares the necessary software according to a development and delivery schedule set up by the client firm. Depending on the system, portions of the software may be delivered as they are

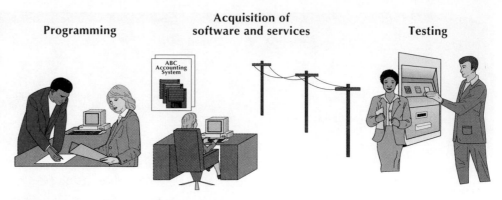

Programming	Acquisition of software and services		Testing
Have computer programs written by company personnel or by outside contractors.	Acquire and install prepackaged software purchased from outside sources.	Acquire communications links and network services needed for new system.	Test software, procedures, and features of new system.

completed, or the entire set of programs may arrive in one package when the development process is complete.

TESTING. Once the system is constructed, it must be tested to determine if it (1) performs according to specifications, (2) performs as users expect it to perform, and (3) detects errors that halt processing or produce erroneous results. During **software testing,** software programs are used with special experimental data files called **test data** to ensure that the software will not fail—that is, will not produce unexpected or incorrect results or interruptions in processing. The test data are created to determine whether the system will process them correctly. The systems analyst examines the processing results to see if they match expectations.

In **system testing,** the complete system—software, procedures, and guidelines—is tested. Also tested is the compatibility between different software modules that are to be used together in the system (e.g., a data input module, a communications module, and a report-writing module).

After UPS developed its wireless network, it performed many different tests. It checked (1) the reliability of the handheld computer in extremely hot and extremely cold temperatures and in both high and low humidity; (2) the clarity of network transmissions under different weather conditions; (3) the speed at which drivers could enter data through the keyboard; (4) the system's response rate if a large number of drivers entered data simultaneously; and (5) the system's response if a driver entered an unauthorized transaction code or entered only a portion of the data needed to process a transaction. UPS worked with a small number of drivers to test the system before deciding to go ahead and equip all 50,000 drivers with wireless devices.

software testing
The testing of software programs to ensure that the software will not produce unexpected or incorrect results or interruptions during processing.

test data
Experimental files used to test software.

system testing
The testing of a complete system—software, procedures, and guidelines.

IT professionals, particularly systems analysts and computer programmers, use the word *bug* to mean an error or an unintended result: "There's a bug in the software and it causes the program to fail if we report $0.00 sales for the day." They will then talk about "debugging" the program. What made them come up with that word, you may wonder.

Here's how it happened. Grace Murray Hopper, one of the pioneers in the computer field, was working in her laboratory one day, running a program she had developed. When the program produced an unexpected result, she tried to determine the cause. After rechecking the program's processing logic and convincing herself it was correct, she began looking elsewhere.

In those days—the 1940s and 1950s—computers were quite different. They did not use transistors and chips, but rather mechanical relays that opened and closed. Hopper glanced at one of the relays and saw that it was not fully closed, even though the program logic dictated that it should be. Upon closer scrutiny, she found that a moth had become trapped in the relay—and this intruder was preventing completion of the circuit and correct execution of the program. She pulled it out, and her program ran properly.

So the origin of the term *bug* was a real bug. ▨

Implementation

During the **implementation** phase of the systems development life cycle, the new system is installed and put into use. New systems often bring many changes to a business, including new business procedures, different individual responsibilities, and adjustments in the flow of information. Thus, three important aspects of implementation are training, site preparation, and conversion strategies.

implementation
The fifth phase of the systems development life cycle, in which the new system is installed and put to use.

TRAINING.   Even experienced computer users need to become familiar with the features of a new system. During **training,** IT professionals show people how to use the system and how to keep it running and reliable. Training covers all aspects of using the system, from routine procedures to periodic actions (e.g., replacing printer cartridges) to emergency operations (e.g., the steps to take if system security is breached).

We tend to think of "training" as the training of end-users who are part of a work group. But IT professionals also need training when a new application is installed because they often have to know both the user's procedures and the administrator's procedures to keep the network, server, or other components up and running.

training
The process by which people are taught how to use a system.

SITE PREPARATION.   Sometimes new systems require new equipment and furniture and the construction of additional facilities—for example, new electrical wiring, air-conditioning systems, lighting systems, and security systems. **Site preparation** includes these and all other activities involved in preparing for the installation of a new system.

Site preparation may be minimal or it may be extensive. If a new system requires the replacement of existing microcomputers with more powerful models, changes in the work site may not be needed. The old computers are simply unplugged and carried away and the new ones are installed in their place. But if a local area network is being installed in an office for the first time, site preparation may entail running communications cables, building a cable connection room, and installing cable plugs in the wall.

When UPS decided to install handheld computers and modem/telephone links in its delivery trucks, it had to train drivers how to use them, of course. But the company also had to prepare the connections and mount the devices in the trucks, as well as prepare communications facilities at its data center.

site preparation
The activities involved in preparing for the installation of a new system.

conversion plan

A description of all the activities that must occur to change over to a new system.

CONVERSION STRATEGIES.

A **conversion plan** describes all the activities that must occur to change over to a new system. It identifies the persons responsible for each activity, and includes a timetable for the completion of each event. The plan assigns responsibility for ensuring that each activity is completed, specifies and verifies dates on the conversion schedule, lists all databases and files to be converted, identifies all the data and information that are required to build databases and files for the system, lists all the new procedures that will go into use during conversion, and outlines all the controls that will be used to ensure that each activity occurs properly.

Analysts can choose from four conversion strategies in implementing the new system (Table 12.3). Each strategy has advantages and disadvantages.

1. When time is tight or when no dramatic changes are being made in work processes or responsibilities, the analyst may choose a **direct cut over strategy,** in which people stop using the old system and jump right into using the new one. This conversion method can be risky if there are any serious problems or misunderstandings about the new system. But it does offer a major benefit: when people are forced to use a new system right away rather than gradually, they tend to work hard to ensure its success.

direct cut over strategy

A conversion plan in which people abruptly stop using an old system and immediately begin using a new one.

parallel systems strategy

A conversion plan in which the old and the new system are used together for a period of time, with the old system being gradually phased out.

2. In a **parallel systems strategy,** both the old and new system are used together for a period of time, with the old system being gradually phased out. This conversion method offers the greatest security when people are unsure of the usefulness or reliability of the new system and appreciate the comfort of knowing they can fall back on the old one. Yet this advantage can also be a disadvantage if people feel the new system is taking away some of their important responsibilities or personal prestige. Then they may not try very hard to make it work. In fact, they may even want it to fail.

pilot conversion strategy

A conversion plan in which a working version of a new system is implemented in one group or department to test it before it is installed throughout the entire business.

3. The **pilot conversion strategy** is often used when the new system involves new business methods or drastic changes in work processes. Under this

TABLE 12.3 *Conversion Strategies*

METHOD	DESCRIPTION	ADVANTAGES	DISADVANTAGES
Direct cut over strategy	The old system is abruptly replaced by the new one. The organization relies fully on the new system immediately.	Forces users to make the new system work. There are immediate benefits from new methods and controls.	There is no other system to fall back on if difficulties arise with new system. Requires the most careful planning.
Parallel systems strategy	The old system is operated along with the new system for a period of time, but is phased out gradually.	Offers greatest security. The old system can take over if errors are found in the new system or if usage problems occur.	Doubles operating costs. The new system may not get a fair trial.
Pilot strategy	Working version of the new system is implemented in one part of the organization. Based on feedback, changes are made and the system is installed in the rest of the organization by one of the other methods.	Provides experience and testing before implementation.	May give the impression that the old system is unreliable and not error-free.
Phase-in strategy	The new system is gradually implemented across all users.	Allows some users to take advantage of the system early. Allows training and installation without unnecessary use of resources.	A long phase-in may cause user problems whether the project goes well (overenthusiasm) or not (resistance and lack of fair trial).

method, a working version of the system is implemented in one group or department. People know they are using a new system and that their experiences and suggestions may lead to changes in the system. When no more changes are needed and the system is judged complete, it is installed throughout the entire business. The advantage of this approach is that the system can be fully tested in one area of the business before it is put into full use throughout the company. But while pilot programs avoid the risk of encountering a problem that affects a large number of people in the company, it may give the impression that the old system is unreliable and therefore make those still using it uneasy.

4. When it is impossible to install a new system throughout an entire organization or department at one time, the **phase-in strategy** is used. The conversion of databases, training of personnel, and installation of hardware and software are staged over a period of time ranging from weeks to months, depending on the system. Some people begin to use the new system before others do. Thus, the phase-in method allows some users to take advantage of the system early on. The disadvantage is that long phase-ins can create user problems whether the project goes well or not—overenthusiasm if it seems to be going well, and refusal to give it a fair trial if it doesn't go well at first.

phase-in strategy
A conversion plan in which a new system is gradually phased in throughout the organization or department over a certain period of time.

UPS did not acquire its wireless communications capabilities all at once. Rather, it pilot-tested a few handheld computers and the cellular link to determine if they would work as expected. When evidence showed that they would, the company proceeded to roll out the system to all its drivers, region by region. The pilot test proved the concept and the technology worked; a phase-in of the system followed.

Evaluation and Continuing Evolution

Once the system is implemented, analysts perform systems evaluation to identify its strengths and weaknesses. They want to determine if the system can deliver the expected level of usability and usefulness and provide the anticipated benefits.

Open shared systems are often used for many years. However, during that time, the organization, the people using the system, and the business environment will change. Therefore, all systems need to undergo continuing development, with features added and capabilities augmented as new or improved technologies are introduced.

Given the complexity and time-intensiveness of the SDLC, there is a potential for significant error. The *Information Technology in Practice* feature entitled "The SDLC: Avoiding Problems Before They Occur" offers a list of the most common problems encountered in systems development. Forewarned is forearmed.

The Systems Analyst's Tools and Techniques

Systems analysts use a variety of techniques to collect data, including interviews, questionnaires, document examination, observation, and sampling. They also use tools like system flowcharts, dataflow diagrams, data dictionaries, and computer-aided system engineering to describe systems and document business processes. All these techniques and tools help systems analysts to become more productive and effective and deliver a better final product.

Data Collection Techniques

To determine system requirements, analysts use any combination of five data collection techniques: interviews, questionnaires, document examination, observation, and sampling.

1. **Interviews.** Analysts conduct interviews with a variety of persons (managers, staff members, employees, customers, and suppliers) to gather details about business processes. Interviews give the analyst the opportunity to learn why current procedures are followed and to hear suggestions for improvements. In a **structured interview,** the analyst prepares the questions in advance and asks each interviewee the same set of questions. In an **unstructured interview,** the analyst may also prepare questions in advance, but will often vary the line of questioning according to the participants' background and the answers they give to preceding questions. Unstructured interviews encourage interviewees to bring up ideas or worries that do not fit into any structured area of questioning.

2. **Questionnaires.** When an analyst must contact a large group of people, **questionnaires** can be a useful way to collect factual information and opinions. Analyzing the responses should give the analyst important insights into the system or business process and often identifies individuals who should be interviewed.

3. **Document examination.** Analysts should recognize that a great deal of important information already exists in company documents. **Document examination,** also called **record inspection,** is the review of manuals, reports, and correspondence about the system or opportunity under investigation. By inspecting samples of sales slips, order forms, and worksheets, analysts can also learn a great deal about how work is done and how errors are made.

4. **Observation.** If a systems analyst wants to know what steps an employee takes in performing a task, how long a task takes, or whether prescribed procedures are easy to use and work as expected, **observation**—actually watching the activities take place—may be the best way of collecting information. This technique often reveals information that cannot be obtained in any other way.

5. **Sampling.** With **sampling,** the analyst collects data and information at prescribed intervals, or may meet with some of the system's users to get a sense of the effectiveness of current procedures. For example, a sample of 10 percent of the staff who interact directly with customers may tell the analyst a great deal about the views held by the entire staff. Or the analyst could decide to examine one out of every ten orders to determine the kinds of items that are typically ordered and in what quantity.

Any of these techniques can yield valuable information about systems requirements. Most analysts use a combination of them to gain the best information possible.

If you were the analyst responsible for developing the UPS wireless system, what details would you have wanted and how would you have collected them? You probably would have used all the data collection techniques just described to gather the system information you needed. You might have conducted structured interviews with drivers, distribution center employees, and managers to determine the biggest problems in tracking and delivering packages. You might

INFORMATION TECHNOLOGY IN PRACTICE

The SDLC: Avoiding Problems Before They Occur

The U.S. General Accounting Office (GAO) is a federal agency charged with monitoring the performance of other federal agencies. Among the agencies it monitors are the National Weather Service, Federal Aviation Administration, Patent and Trademark Office, Department of Justice, Department of Education, NASA, Internal Revenue Service, Department of Defense, and Department of Veterans Affairs. Because the federal government uses many IT applications and dedicates large amounts of financial and human resources to each application, the GAO frequently examines the development of the applications to determine whether the projects are on schedule, within budget, and producing the intended results. Such information is highly useful both for evaluating project managers and for developing future IT projects.

The GAO has identified 10 problems that occur repeatedly in the development and use of IT applications. In order of frequency, they are as follows:

1. Inadequate management of the systems development life cycle.
2. Ineffective management information as a result of poor systems procedures.
3. Flaws in systems security, integrity, and reliability.
4. Inability of multiple systems to work together.
5. Inadequate resources to accomplish goals.
6. Cost overruns.
7. Schedule delays.
8. Systems not performing in the intended manner.
9. Inaccurate or incomplete data and information.
10. Difficulty in accessing data and information.

Such a list points up the importance of effective project management.

Improper management of the systems development life cycle can turn a systems project into a money-devouring monster. The best defense against cost overruns is strong project management from start to finish.

also have conducted unstructured interviews to solicit personal observations, opinions, and suggestions for capitalizing on previously unrecognized opportunities or responding to challenging problems.

In addition, you might have used questionnaires to survey a large number of people (including employees, customers, and suppliers) on very specific questions. Likes, dislikes, and the appropriateness of policies and procedures are among the issues you might have addressed through questionnaires.

Riding with drivers and working with distribution personnel would have given you firsthand information about the nature of these people's jobs and the situations they encounter daily. Observing the tasks they perform, the routines they follow, and the time it takes them to complete specific planned and unplanned tasks would have given you valuable insights into productivity.

Using the techniques of record inspection and sampling, you would have examined shipping notices and airbills as well as customer account records. These techniques would have allowed you to see which types of customers ship packages most often and on what days activities are heaviest.

Of course, your entire investigation probably began with a review of UPS's written procedures and policies describing the handling of packages.

System Flowcharts

system flowchart
A graphical description of a business process or procedure using standard symbols to show decision logic.

Of all the systems analyst's tools, system flowcharts are the easiest to use and understand. A **system flowchart** is a graphical description of a business process or procedure that uses standard symbols to show (1) the sequence of activities that take place in a process; (2) the data, information, or documents that are input to the process or generated (output) as a result of the process; and (3) the decisions that are made at each point in the process. Figure 12.15 describes the most commonly used symbols in system flowcharts.

System flowcharts describe *logic*—the decisions made within a process that determine which course of action will be followed. A sample system flowchart for order processing is shown in Figure 12.16. A more complex process would have several different process sequences.

FIGURE 12.15
Symbols Used in System Flowcharts

Process:
Indicates any processing performed by computer.

Document:
Indicates a printed document (input or output).

Predefined processing:
Indicates a process not specifically defined in the flowchart (defined in another flowchart).

Off-line storage:
Represents data stored off-line.

Decision:
Indicates a point in the process where a decision must be made to determine further action.

Magnetic disk:
Represents data stored on magnetic disk.

Manual operation:
Indicates an operation performed off-line.

Magnetic tape:
Represents data stored on magnetic tape.

Input/output:
Indicates an input/output operation.

Communication link:
Indicates transmission of data by any communication method.

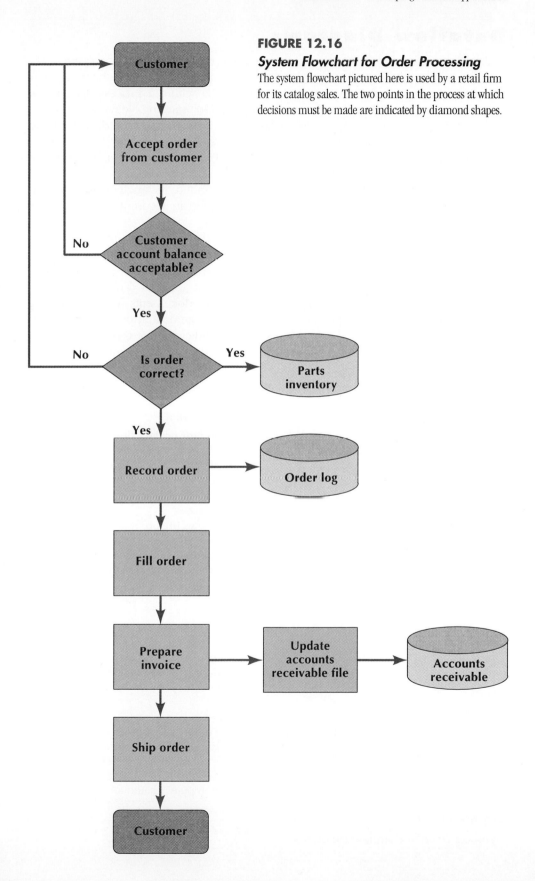

FIGURE 12.16
System Flowchart for Order Processing
The system flowchart pictured here is used by a retail firm
for its catalog sales. The two points in the process at which
decisions must be made are indicated by diamond shapes.

Dataflow Diagrams

A **dataflow diagram (DFD)** shows the movement of data through a system. The primary emphasis of a DFD is on the flow of data and information between people and processes and the changes that take place within a process. Like a system flowchart, a DFD shows data and information entering, leaving, or stored within the system, but unlike a system flowchart, it does not show decision logic. Different documents used within a system are represented in the DFD, but the conditions under which each is used are not. The DFD does not include anything not directly related to the *flow* of data.

DFDs use four symbols: arrows, circles or rounded rectangles, squares, and open rectangles. The functions of each are explained in Figure 12.17. The labels on each DFD symbol describe the system element.

Figure 12.18 is a dataflow diagram illustrating the order and invoice-handling procedure at a well-known mail-order company. Note that it describes the processes but does not indicate when they are performed (e.g., every Monday or on the 1st and 15th of each month). Dataflows or *vectors* (arrows) represent groups of data (order, payment, and shipment data), documents (orders, invoices, and other documents), or types of information (management approval/disapproval and so forth). Notice that the dataflows do not indicate *how* the information is carried; they do not tell us whether the information is communicated by tele-

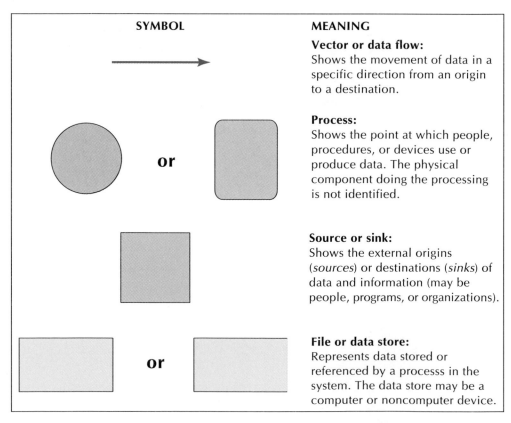

SYMBOL	MEANING
→	**Vector or data flow:** Shows the movement of data in a specific direction from an origin to a destination.
● or ▢	**Process:** Shows the point at which people, procedures, or devices use or produce data. The physical component doing the processing is not identified.
■	**Source or sink:** Shows the external origins (*sources*) or destinations (*sinks*) of data and information (may be people, programs, or organizations).
▭ or ▭	**File or data store:** Represents data stored or referenced by a processs in the system. The data store may be a computer or noncomputer device.

FIGURE 12.17
Symbols Used in Dataflow Diagrams

phone, e-mail, or personal messenger. This may surprise you. However, remember that the purpose of a DFD is to describe the movement of data, not the devices causing the movement.

Figure 12.18 shows that customers submit orders and payments ("settlement data") to the company. The principal information processes in this system, all identified by numbers, are entering orders (1.0), processing orders (2.0), producing invoices (3.0), posting payments (4.0), and maintaining accounts receivable (5.0). When orders are received from customers, they are approved or disapproved by management. Details of approved orders are processed and recorded in an order log. The order is then prepared in production for shipment. An invoice is also prepared, with one copy serving as a packing slip accompanying the order.

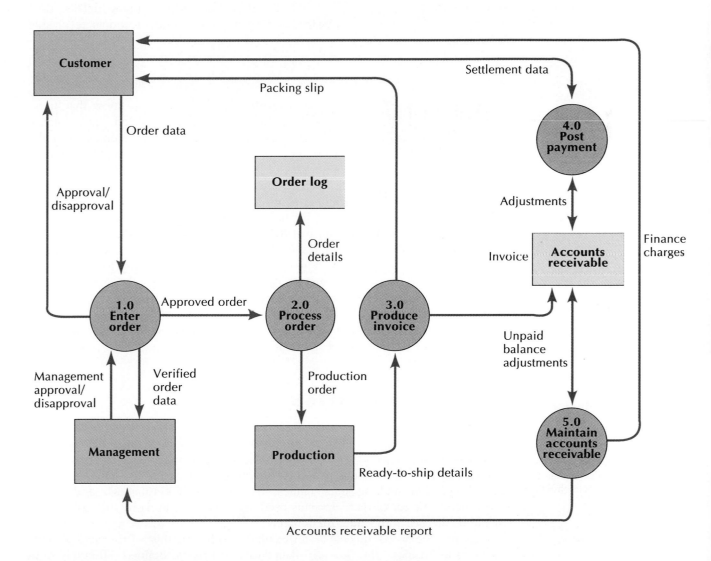

FIGURE 12.18 *Dataflow Diagram for Order and Invoice Handling at a Mail-Order Company*

This dataflow diagram includes five principal information processes: 1.0—order entry; 2.0—order processing; 3.0—invoice production; 4.0—posting of payments; and 5.0—maintenance of accounts receivable.

Another copy is used in preparing accounts receivable. Periodically, the records of accounts receivable are processed to adjust balances in accordance with payments and finance charges, as well as to provide management with an accounts receivable report.

LEVELS OF DFDs.   There are different levels of dataflow diagrams. A *system-level* DFD describes an entire system in summary form (Figure 12.18 is a system-level DFD). A second-level DFD "explodes" processes to show more detail. Processes in a second-level DFD may, in turn, be exploded further to show more details and subprocesses. This process of exploding processes in a dataflow diagram to show ever more detail is called **leveling.** Numbers on each DFD identify the diagram level. In Figure 12.19, which shows three exploded processes from the DFD in Figure 12.18, DFD 2.1 describes order-handling details, DFD 3.1 shows postpayment processing, and DFD 4.1 describes accounts receivable processing.

leveling
The process of exploding processes in a dataflow diagram to show more detail.

If you've ever watched one at work, you know that architects work from blueprints—exact detailed plans for the building they are designing. (The name comes from the white lettering on blue paper.) Every building's design consists of a series of blueprints, from the general to the very specific. Some show the shape of the building and its floor plan; others show locations of electrical outlets and ducts and pipes for heat and air flow.

A quick glance at a blueprint usually leaves those of us outside the profession overwhelmed by the symbols and technical terms. Yet, should you decide to build a house or create a layout for a new office, you can very easily learn what the key symbols and terms on an architect's blueprint mean (e.g., the size of a door, the positioning of windows, and the location of closets and storage areas). Think of system flowcharts and dataflow diagrams in the same way. They may appear quite abstract at first, yet if you learn how to read them, you will find that they provide a great deal of useful information. ▨

Data Dictionaries

data dictionary/ repository
A catalog that lists and describes all the types of data flowing through a system. Composed of data elements and a data structure.

data element
The component of a data dictionary that includes data names, alternate names, and length allowances.

data structure
The set of data elements used together and the name that collectively identifies the set.

When system analysts develop dataflow diagrams, they also typically create a **data dictionary** (sometimes called a **repository**), which is a catalog that lists and describes all the types of data flowing through a system. A data dictionary used in dataflow analysis contains two components: data elements and data structures. **Data elements** include data names, alternate names (aliases), and length allowances. The set of data elements used together and the name that collectively identifies the set is the **data structure.**

Let's use the word *invoice* as an example. Although this word has a specific meaning in business, the "invoice" data structure may be defined differently from one company to the next. The system in use at a particular company will have a data dictionary that defines the data elements that are included in that company's "invoice" data structure. (Whether "invoice" refers to a paper document or to an electronic format does not matter.) Figure 12.20 shows the data elements used by the Drazien Publishing Co.'s data dictionary to define *invoice*.

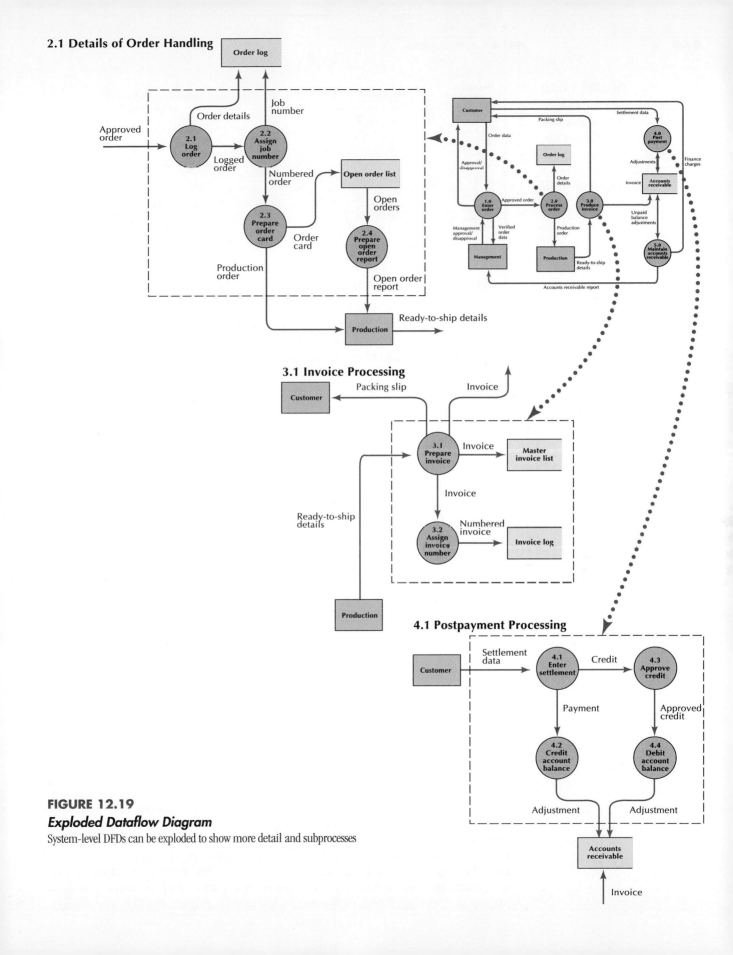

2.1 Details of Order Handling

3.1 Invoice Processing

4.1 Postpayment Processing

FIGURE 12.19
Exploded Dataflow Diagram
System-level DFDs can be exploded to show more detail and subprocesses

FIGURE 12.20
Data Structure for Invoice at the Drazien Publishing Co.

Eight data elements in Drazien's data dictionary define the term *invoice* as it is used at the company.

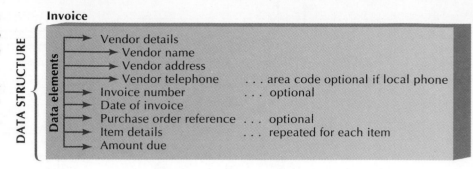

Analysts use data dictionaries for five reasons:

1. To manage detail in large systems.
2. To give a common meaning to all system elements.
3. To document the features of a system.
4. To facilitate evaluation of the system and determine where changes should be made.
5. To locate errors and to find omissions.

Because they define the meaning of each data element in a system, data dictionaries are an important accompaniment to DFDs. They are also an integral component of CASE tools, which we discuss in the next section.

Computer-Aided Systems Engineering (CASE)

computer-aided systems engineering/computer-aided software engineering (CASE) tools
A set of tools used in systems development to improve the consistency and quality of the system while automating many of the most tedious and time-consuming systems tasks.

The newest and most powerful tool available to the systems analyst uses a computer's vast processing and storage capabilities. These **computer-aided systems engineering** or **computer-aided software engineering tools,** also known as **CASE tools,** are designed to improve the consistency and quality of systems while automating many of the most tedious and time-consuming systems tasks. CASE tools are used both to develop systems and to design the system's software.

The characteristics, capabilities, and components of CASE tools vary among the different brands available for purchase, some of which are listed in Table 12.4. However, most CASE tools contain the following features:

- **Charting and diagramming tools.** Because systems analysts spend a great deal of time analyzing data and processes, CASE tools typically include the capability to produce dataflow programs (both system-level and exploded views), data structure diagrams, and system flowcharts.
- **Centralized information repository.** A *centralized information repository* is a dictionary containing the details of all system components (data items, dataflows, and processes). The repository also includes information describing the frequency and volume of each activity. For example, if the analyst needs to know the high and low estimates of the number of invoices likely to be processed on a given day, he can retrieve the information from the central repository.
- **Interface generators.** Recall that an *interface* is the means by which a person interacts with a computer. *Graphical interfaces,* such as those used by Microsoft Windows, OS/2, or the Apple Macintosh, employ pictures and images.

TABLE 12.4 *Leading CASE Tools*

CASE TOOL	DISTRIBUTED BY
Bachman Tools	Bachman and Associates
Easy CASE	European CASE Tools
IEF (Information Engineering Facility)	Texas Instruments
Intersolv	Intersolv
Method/Foundation	Andersen Consulting
Object Maker	Mark V Systems
Rational Rose	Rational Software Corp.
System Architect	Popkin Software and Systems Inc.

Text interfaces, such as those used by DOS, employ key words and phrases to instruct the system in processing. Interface generators provide the capability to prepare sample user interfaces so that the creator can examine their features before composing the final version. Interface generators allow analysts to present and evaluate many different interfaces and to make changes quickly and easily.

- **Code generators.** These tools automate the preparation of computer software. Although code generators are not yet perfected, many automate 75 to 80 percent of the computer programming needed to create a new system or application.
- **Project management tools.** As we've seen, development projects must be carefully managed to ensure that all tasks are completed properly and on time. Project management tools enable the project manager to schedule analysis and design activities, allocate people and other resources to each task, monitor schedules and personnel, and print schedules and reports summarizing the project's status. Figure 12.21 summarizes the features of CASE tools.

FRONT-END, BACK-END, AND INTEGRATED CASE.   As Figure 12.22 shows, CASE tools are often categorized by the SDLC activities they support. **Front-end CASE tools** automate the early (front-end) activities in systems development—namely, requirements determination and systems design. In these early phases, they help analysts describe process characteristics and record and analyze dataflows and processes. Front-end CASE tools' built-in charting capabilities relieve the analyst of the important but time-consuming task of drawing dataflow diagrams.

Back-end CASE tools automate the later (back-end) activities in systems development, developing detailed information from general system descriptions. Some back-end CASE tools are code generators, translation tools, and testing tools.

Integrated CASE (I-CASE) tools span activities throughout the entire systems development life cycle. They incorporate analysis, logical design, code generation, and database generation capabilities while maintaining an automated data dictionary. I-CASE is actually a family of tools, all accessible from the same computer program and display screen. A sample I-CASE screen is shown in Figure 12.23.

Because of the complexity of integrating all the activities of the systems development life cycle, only a few integrated CASE tools have been created. However,

front-end CASE tool

A CASE tool that automates the early (front-end) activities in systems development.

back-end CASE tool

A CASE tool that automates the later (back-end) activities in systems development.

integrated CASE (I-CASE) tool

A CASE tool that spans activities throughout the entire systems development life cycle.

FIGURE 12.21   *CASE Tool Features*

Although the capabilities of CASE tools differ among the packages available for purchase, most contain the features shown here.

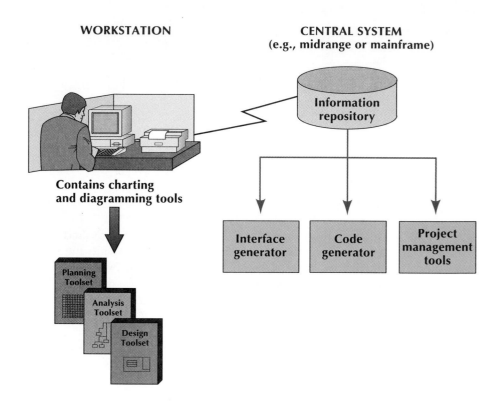

WORKSTATION

CENTRAL SYSTEM
(e.g., midrange or mainframe)

Information repository

Contains charting and diagramming tools

Planning Toolset

Analysis Toolset

Design Toolset

Interface generator

Code generator

Project management tools

FIGURE 12.22   *Types of CASE Tools*

SEQUENCE OF SYSTEMS DEVELOPMENT ACTIVITIES

Front-end development   **Back-end development**

Analysis ——— Design ——— Development and ——— Implementation ——— Evaluation and
(Preliminary investigation)   Construction   Continuing Evolution
(Requirements determination)

Front-end CASE tools   **Back-end CASE tools**
Analysis tools   Code generator tools
Charting tools   Translation tools
Tools for logical design   Testing tools

Integrated CASE tools

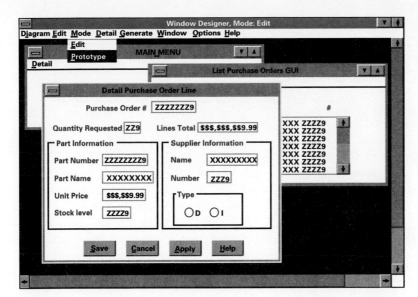

FIGURE 12.23

Display Screens of I-CASE Tool

Display contents are specified and arranged using the screen design tool. Data items are coded to show whether their contents will be numeric or character. Special codes that invoke specific actions are also shown on the display.

more integrated tools will probably emerge as IT professionals continue their quest for tools that link all the activities associated with systems development.

Although CASE tools offer many valuable features and can assist the systems analyst in myriad ways, they are not a substitute for a good systems analyst. A great deal of the analyst's work is based on understanding what questions to ask, deciding when to probe more deeply into a business situation, and knowing which people to contact and how to get information. Systems design is a creative activity: it takes insight and innovative ideas to produce a well-designed application, and these are not qualities that can be automated. Automated tools will not replace good analysts, but they can make good analysts even better and more effective. ■

IT Development Personnel

Because systems analysts are the central actors in the development of shared IT applications, we have focused on their activities throughout this chapter. In this section, we take a closer look at the job they do, the roles they play, and the skills that are critical to their success. We also discuss the other IT professionals with whom systems analysts work—the chief information officer, computer programmers, and outside contractors.

The Systems Analyst: The Key Roles

Systems analysts play several roles in business. As we have seen, they play a major *development role* in analyzing business activities and formulating solutions. But they also play an important *facilitating role*. Good analysts recognize the value of eliciting information from people who will use IT to perform a job or

Levi Strauss & Co. Learns the Value of Tailoring CASE Tools to Fit

Levi Strauss & Co. has a love-hate relationship with CASE tools. Although the company was one of the first and biggest customers for CASE tools, it found that its ambitions often exceeded the still-evolving capabilities of these tools. On one project, for example, the company set up teams of programmers with the idea that the teams could work simultaneously to develop a local area network. The problem: The time gained by automating some of the early steps was lost during the programming stage because the CASE tools were organized so that just one person could work on a section at a time. To counter this limitation, Levi Strauss's IT staff combined a variety of CASE tools from several companies—in effect, creating its own CASE tools. This led to another problem: Which glitches were caused by the ready-made CASE tools and which by the CASE tools developed in-house?

For all these problems, Levi Strauss is still committed to using CASE tools in its massive ongoing effort to make both process and business improvements by reengineering its operations around the world. CASE tools, the company believes, are simply the best way to help IT programmers develop the balance of business and technical skills they will need in the future.

manage a business process. These people, in fact, are the best sources of information about problems, solutions, and obstacles to solutions. Part of the analyst's job, then, is to facilitate the exchange of this information.

Developing and implementing information technology means change. People need to learn new or altered work processes (and perhaps even new computer and communications systems) and take on different responsibilities. Although change can be exciting, people often resist it, particularly if they do not see a reason for the change. Thus, the systems analyst's third role is the vitally important one of **change agent.** In this role, the analyst acts as a catalyst for change and as a liaison among different parties involved in the creation and implementation of change.

change agent
A person who acts as a catalyst for change.

FIGURE 12.24
Model of Change Agent's Role
In addition to working as a change agent, systems analysts play a development role and a facilitating role.

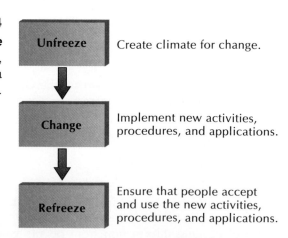

Unfreeze — Create climate for change.

Change — Implement new activities, procedures, and applications.

Refreeze — Ensure that people accept and use the new activities, procedures, and applications.

The change agent's role is often depicted in the form of a three-step model (Figure 12.24). These three steps are (1) *unfreeze*—communicate with people about the reason for change to reduce potential resistance; (2) *change*—implement new activities, procedures, and applications; and (3) *refreeze*—ensure that people accept and use the new processes and procedures. In each of these roles, the systems analyst is directly involved in the business. Developing information systems, therefore, demands knowledge about the business activities in which the applications will be used and how these systems can be changed to meet the business's needs.

Consider professional sports. In the United States (and in the Far East), the national pastime is baseball. In Europe and South America, it's soccer. Throughout the world, professional sports have become big business. And many teams not only use IT to manage their business but also employ IT professionals—including systems analysts.

Systems analysts in the baseball business have to know about more than computers, communications systems, and software if they are to contribute to the success of their organization. They also have to know the *business* of baseball and be prepared to change the hardware and software they use whenever a change is necessary to support the players, coaches, and team managers.

Take the Los Angeles Dodgers. The Dodgers' information technology department (yes, the team has an IT department) is responsible for maintaining applications that keep track of more than 300 major and minor league players throughout the Dodger organization. Each player is accounted for as a company asset. When the team acquires a player, its accounting system is adjusted to add him to the organization's list of assets. When another player is traded, a different transaction takes place. As the players' value to the organization changes, the records are adjusted to show this change in the asset value.

The Dodgers' systems analysts have also repeatedly modified the team's IT applications to handle new business practices: multiyear signing bonuses, salaries paid over many years (even after the player has retired or moved on to another team), special injury clauses, and incentive bonuses (paid for achieving a specified performance level).

PROFESSIONAL SKILLS. The most successful systems analysts have five important professional skills: problem-solving skills, the ability to focus on outcome, creativity, the ability to plan and run meetings, and excellent interpersonal communication skills.

- **Problem solving.** The problem-solving process, which we introduced in Chapter 1, seeks to close the gap between the current situation and the situation that is desired. Analysts play a key role in initiating the process by asking, "What is wrong?", "What is the cause of the problem?", and "What is the effect?"
- **Outcome thinking.** Good analysts complement their problem-solving skills with an ability to focus on outcome. They do this by asking: "What result is desired?", "Forgetting about constraints for a moment, what is the ideal result?", or "What is your vision of the way things should be?" This emphasis on outcome has the virtue of stressing the positive. More importantly, it recognizes the limitations of focusing solely on problems by pushing people to think about possibilities rather than impossibilities.
- **Creativity.** Creative people look at the same thing everyone else looks at, but they see something different. To be creative is to generate ideas, and that cannot be done without forgetting about constraints (at least temporarily), relaxing rules, and allowing alternatives to rise to the surface of the mind. Most of

CRITICAL CONNECTION 4

Welbro Constructors

Volunteer Systems Analyst Makes Orlando a "City of Light"

Profit-making businesses aren't the only organizations that can benefit from the process and business improvements spearheaded by a systems analyst. Just ask Ed Schrank. In 1991, he took a break from his job as a vice president at Welbro Constructors in Altamonte Springs, Florida, to become an "executive on loan" to the City of Light program in Orlando, Florida. An extension of President George Bush's Thousand Points of Light program, the Orlando program was intended to encourage communities to use volunteers and charitable donations to reduce the tax-supported aid to the needy.

Orlando's participation was sparked by its mayor, Bill Frederick, who realized that his city had many resources that were going to waste. A local business, say, might want to donate some used computers to a worthy charity. But how could it know who needs computers? And who would pick up the machines and train their new users? There was simply no way to match the supply of volunteer help with demand.

This was a problem made for an IT solution, thought Schrank. What Orlando needed was an "infostructure," an easy-to-use distributed computing system that would place basic PCs in churches, businesses, and schools, where volunteers could enter data about other volunteers and the skills and time they could offer. These data could then be transmitted to a database server (again, managed by volunteers), where a special program could play matchmaker. And with that realization, Schrank became a change agent, dedicated to mustering the resources needed to carry out his vision.

us are not born innovators, so we don't ordinarily consider ourselves highly creative. Yet, we recognize the power of good ideas and know how quickly they can turn a difficult situation into an exciting opportunity.

Good systems designs are often creative designs. UPS's decision to use wireless communications to link drivers to the company's data center was creative. It also made good business sense, because it allowed the company to offer new services that benefit customers and add to the company's business.

- **Meeting skills.** Recall that one of a systems analyst's roles is to facilitate information exchange. For this reason, knowing how to plan and run a meeting efficiently is a critical skill in the analyst's repertoire. Good meeting skills determine the value of the information that analysts capture from people involved in the meeting.

Good meetings begin with an agenda of the topics to be addressed and are structured in a way that allows all attendees to participate. Questions must be carefully crafted to elicit the desired information. Effective analysts also find ways to create enthusiasm among a meeting's participants, fostering an atmosphere in which people *want* to participate and share ideas.

More and more meetings today are using electronic support tools. Group conferencing networks (discussed in Chapter 10) and group support systems (which we discuss in the next chapter) tend to foster more interaction among people. In a regular group discussion, only one person speaks at a time, but through a network many people can express their ideas. Electronic meeting tools also keep components anonymous so that people feel free to speak up without worrying what other participants will think of their ideas. As the capabilities of these tools continue to evolve, electronic meeting systems are likely to become as important a tool in systems analysis and design as dataflow diagrams and flowcharts are today.

- **Communication skills.** Good communication skills are essential for effective person-to-person discussions. The analyst needs to be able to discuss ideas with users in their language (i.e., without lapsing into technical jargon), understand what they are saying (and recognize what they are *not* saying), and know how to assemble all this information. Indeed, the analyst's ability to listen to people and understand their ideas and opinions is critical to the success of shared IT applications. Misstated systems requirements resulting from misunderstandings about business activities account for over half the reasons that IT applications have to be changed after they've been implemented.

The Chief Information Officer

In many businesses, one person is given the responsibility for managing and developing the firm's information technology capabilities. In large organizations,

chief information officer (CIO)
The person given the responsibility of managing and developing the firm's information technology capabilities.

FIGURE 12.25 *Organization Chart for Typical Information Systems Department*
In large organizations, the chief information officer generally holds the rank of corporate vice president.

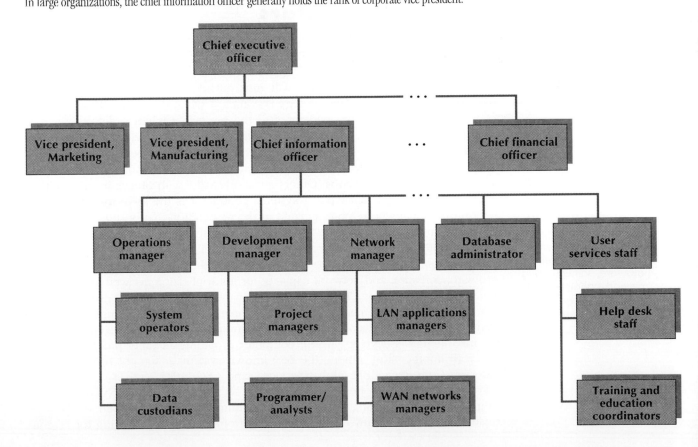

this person is often called the **chief information officer (CIO).** (Some firms use instead the title IT director or director of information systems.) The position generally has the corporate rank of vice president (Figure 12.25). In smaller businesses, the individual responsible for managing and developing the company's capabilities may have additional responsibilities. Hence, it is not uncommon to find IT management come under the controller, finance director, administrative coordinator, or operations manager in a smaller company.

Systems analysts generally work for a CIO or for a director of development, who, in turn, reports to the person responsible for managing the firm's IT capabilities. Communications about the firm's business plans flow to the analyst through these people. The quality of communication can be an important determinant of the firm's effective use of information technology for process or business improvement.

Computer Programmers

As we noted earlier, *programmers* are responsible for turning detailed specifications into computer software that processes data and information effectively and works with other computer programs (computer operating systems, network operating systems, database management systems, and so forth). They are also responsible for *documenting* the program, developing written explanations of how and why certain procedures are coded in specific ways and how the system can be used in the business. Analysts and programmers interact continually during the development of a system, usually serving jointly on the project team.

Systems Contractors

Most large organizations have computer programmers (or programmer/analysts) on permanent staff. Smaller firms often retain outside programming services on a contractual basis.

In some cases, an organization will hire outside consultants to manage the development of a system. This strategy is common when the organization chooses not to assign any of its own personnel to the project or when it determines that it will be more expedient to have a third party handle the development. The term **systems contractor** is used to describe all types of outside personnel who contract with a company to develop IT applications. Some contractors are very small—even one-person shops. Others are worldwide, with offices in many cities.

A particularly important type of systems contractor is the **systems integrator,** an IT professional whose job originated in the recognition that business uses information technology components from a variety of sources and with a diverse set of name plates (hence the importance of interoperability, discussed earlier in this chapter). Systems integrators are retained to take the responsibility for acquiring hardware, software, and network capacity for an application, as well as for implementing that application. They may play any number of roles: consultant, engineer, designer, procurement expert, programmer, system tester, implementer, or maintainer. They may even oversee the ongoing operation of the system. At times, systems integrators develop custom computer programs; at other times, they contract with another firm. Among the best-known systems integrator firms are EDS, Andersen Consulting, IBM Global Services, and CSC Index.

Systems contractors often become experts by gaining years of experience with companies before starting their own consulting firms or joining an established consulting firm. Yet, many others go directly from college into training for IT con-

systems contractor
An outside person or firm that contracts with a company to develop IT applications.

systems integrator
A type of systems contractor who is retained to take responsibility for acquiring hardware, software, and network capacity for an application, as well as for implementing the application.

sulting. Andersen Consulting, headquartered in Chicago, has its own way of educating its more than 45,000 employees about IT. New recruits hired by Andersen (at an average age of 25) spend their first three to four weeks training in the company's local office. Then they head off to one of Andersen's four training centers: St. Charles, Illinois; Manila, the Philippines; Singapore; or Veldhoven, the Netherlands. There they learn Andersen's methodologies for determining systems requirements, developing application specifications, and preparing computer programs.

"Personal people" is an Andersen credo. The firm recognizes that individuals are as different from one another as the countries, cultures, and corporations in which they work. Hence, Andersen seeks to draw out individual differences in its new hires and show them how to turn these personal qualities into strengths when dealing with clients. Trainees also learn valuable business skills: how to interact with clients, how to work on a project team, and how to understand a business or an industry. Not all the training is technical, however. New hires are often out in the woods near the training center, climbing rope ladders or planning strategies to make their team a winner in a competitive outdoor game.

Visits to the four centers are not just for new recruits because Andersen sees education as a career-long activity. Depending on the area in which he or she works, an Andersen consultant can expect to spend from 300 to 750 hours at one of these facilities every year. Continual improvement is a critical ingredient in the makeup of Andersen consultants and the systems they develop—and it should be a career objective for you, whether you work as a developer or a user of information technology.

A Final Word

Business benefits from IT only when the right combination of information technology is used in the best way for the particular company. Because the combination of IT resources that are most effective for one firm may not be as useful for another, the development process must be managed to ensure that both IT

SUMMARY OF LEARNING OBJECTIVES

1 **Describe the principal functions and roles of a systems analyst.** Systems analysts are responsible for working with users to determine a system's requirements and to describe the features needed in the system. The systems analyst sees the development of a shared IT application through, from original concept to finished product.

2 **Identify the characteristics of shared systems.** Shared systems are distinguished by the characteristics of openness and interoperability. *Open systems* utilize software programs that can run on different computer and communications hardware. They are built on *nonproprietary* operating

systems. An application is *interoperable* when it can run in an identical fashion on different computer systems.

3 **Discuss the changing process for developing information systems applications.** Application development is shifting from a *craft* approach, in which each feature is uniquely designed, to an *assembly* approach, in which prewritten components are selected and integrated into the structure of an application. Components are characterized by *reusable* designs, meaning that a component can be used in multiple systems.

4 Explain how a systems project begins and how its desirability is determined. A systems project begins with a *project proposal*. The proposal is a result of problem or opportunity recognition. The completed project proposal is submitted to a *steering committee,* usually made up of people from different functional areas of the business, which determines whether or not the project is desirable.

5 Describe the six phases of the systems development life cycle. There are six phases in the systems development life cycle: (1) problem recognition/preliminary investigation—the definition and investigation of the problem; (2) requirements determination—the process of understanding the current system and the new system's requirements; (3) systems design— planning the new system; (4) development and construction—creating the new system; (5) implementation—converting to the new system; and (6) evaluation and continuing evolution— monitoring and adding value to the new system.

6 Describe the tools and techniques available to systems analysts for collecting data and developing IT applications. Systems analysts use a variety of techniques to collect data. The most common of these are *interviews* (both structured and unstructured); *questionnaires; document ex-*

amination (also called *record inspection*); *observation;* and *sampling.* The tools most commonly used by systems analysts to design systems are *systems flowcharts*—graphical depictions of a business process or procedure that show decision logic; *dataflow diagrams (DFDs)*—graphs that show the movement of data through a system; *data dictionaries*—catalogs that list and describe all the types of data flowing through the system; and *computer-aided systems engineering (CASE) tools*—tools that automate many of the most tedious and time-consuming systems tasks.

7 Explain the roles of the four types of IT systems development professionals. In addition to their development and facilitating roles, *systems analysts* play the important role of change agent as they interact with the company's chief information officer, computer programmers, and systems contractors. The *chief information officer (CIO)* is the one person in an organization responsible for managing and developing the firm's information technology capabilities. *Computer programmers* are charged with turning detailed specifications into computer software and with documenting the program. *Systems contractors* are outside personnel who contract with a company to develop IT applications.

 # KEY TERMS

CRITICAL CONNECTIONS

1 Electronics Giant Circuit City Stores Sends Its Software Out

Circuit City Stores, Inc. Circuit City executives believe that outsourcing will play an increasingly important role in the future of IT at the company because they still cannot hire enough highly qualified professional staff to meet business needs. However, they recognize that not all projects should be outsourced. To be a candidate for outsourcing, a project must have well-articulated objectives and its specifications must be spelled out in detail. The company has also found that having the outsourcing firm develop completed portions of the project every few weeks is another important ingredient for success.

When a project is being developed away from company premises by persons who are not employees, some companies do not pay enough attention to the project. Circuit City found it necessary to closely manage development activities for outsourced applications. Even more important, the company discovered, was paying personal attention to the developers working on the project even though they are not permanent company employees. Outsourcing, it seems, is no substitute for the personal touch in systems development.

Questions for Discussion

1. What is outsourcing and why has it emerged as an important option in developing IT applications?

2. There is a view within some companies that says: "Outsourcing is no different from letting people do business-related work on their PC at home. In either case, they are away from the office. Yet, they can be quickly contacted by telephone or e-mail." Do you agree or disagree with this view of outsourcing? Explain the reasons for your answer.

2 Volkswagen Parts On-Line in Mexico

Volkswagen In designing a new spare parts order and fulfillment system in Mexico, Volkswagen turned to the World Wide Web. The design decided on provides for the submission of Volkswagen dealer orders from a PC running a Web browser. Orders are submitted over the Web directly to the spare parts center, and the system calls for shipments to the dealers within 24 hours instead of two weeks.

Service, not cost savings, was the driving force behind the new design. Yet, both dealer and company also wanted cost benefits. As use of the system grows, both expect to benefit from lower inventories and, consequently, lower inventory management costs.

Volkswagen's Web-based ordering system gives its users access to parts information anytime and anyplace there is a Web access point. By providing such good service behind the scenes, the business systems are supporting the Volkswagen name and increasing opportunities to sell Volkswagen cars.

Questions for Discussion

1. Were you surprised that Volkswagen decided to use the World Wide Web as a basis for its new parts system?

2. What features of the World Wide Web make it attractive or unattractive for widespread business use?

3. Why should more rapid parts fulfillment reduce inventory levels for both dealers and Volkswagen?

3 Levi Strauss & Co. Learns the Value of Tailoring CASE Tools to Fit

LEVI'S Levi Strauss's success in customizing CASE tools hasn't gone unnoticed. Other companies, such as The Gap, have been visiting Levi Strauss to study its techniques and get the kind of nitty-gritty tips missing from most vendor demonstrations.

Like the IT staff at Levi Strauss, the visiting IT professionals don't expect that CASE tools will ever completely automate the process of developing shared IT applications or eliminate the need for systems analysts. In fact, many IT professionals are expanding their definition of CASE from "a set of tools" to "a way of thinking"—a philosophy that forces them to model the business and take an enterprisewide view of the company's functions and information needs.

Questions for Discussion

1. Many companies report that one of the biggest obstacles to revamping a computer system to achieve process or business improvements is the time needed to retrain IT professionals, who have sometimes been educated to take a narrow, technical approach to their work. Why, then, do you think many of these same companies are adopting CASE tools?

2. Use Levi's experience to explain why "go slow" is becoming a rule in many companies that are adopting CASE tools. What other challenges might stand in the way of using CASE tools effectively, and what solutions would you suggest companies adopt to meet these challenges?

3. What should be an IT director's primary concerns in approving the adoption of CASE tools at his or her company?

4 Volunteer Systems Analyst Makes Orlando a "City of Light"

Welbro Constructors Ed Schrank also played developer and facilitator for the city of Orlando when he solicited professional services, as well as hardware and software donations, from the University of Central Florida, AT&T, IBM, and other businesses. The director of IS at the Orange County Property Appraiser's Office volunteered to become the project's technical director, and members of local computer clubs helped to install the donated computer workstations. The resulting system, dubbed the Orlando Community Connection, entered its final testing phase early in 1993, about the same time the local public television station began broadcasting training sessions for volunteer coordinators. The complete system is designed to match 250,000 volunteers with the needs of 5,000 agencies at the rate of 25,000 matches per month.

Questions for Discussion

1. The donations from AT&T included Conversance, a sophisticated and expensive telephone system that calls volunteers and uses synthesized speech to tell them of volunteer opportunities that might interest them. Volunteers can also call the system, which uses voice recognition to accept changes to the volunteers' personal information. Do you think this high-tech feature is appropriate for the Orlando Community Connection? What generalizations can you draw from this example regarding the costs of developing a shared IT application?

2. What professional skills did Schrank need to carry out his vision? Which do you think were most important? Why?

3. Orlando established the Executive on Loan program in 1991 to encourage business leaders to use their skills to develop service programs for the community. Would you support such programs? Why or why not?

Net_Work

A countless number of companies have created home pages on the World Wide Web. As you will quickly find whenever you browse the Web, some are more appealing and useful than others.

The best way to become familiar with good and poor designs is to examine them. In this Net_Work, you are asked to browse the home pages of companies on the Web to identify 10 firms that you believe have well-designed and useful Web sites.* In identifying well-designed sites, keep the following criteria in mind:

- **Content**—describes the usefulness of the information included at the company's Web site.
- **Ease of use**—describes (1) how easy or difficult it is to view information (text, graphics, animation, audio, video) on the company's pages and (2) how easy or difficult it is to navigate between the home page and other pages constituting the company's Web site.

- **Design and layout**—evaluates the extent to which the creation of the pages effectively and attractively illustrates and informs the viewer about the company and its products or services.
- **Use of Internet/WWW capabilities**—the extent to which the company utilized the features and capabilities of the World Wide Web in presenting information about itself and its products or services.

Then assemble your list of the 10 best users of the Web, indicating how they compare according to your evaluation criteria.

*You can choose the companies you wish to look at or draw them from the Fortune 500 list, a list of the 500 largest U.S. companies prepared each year by *Fortune* magazine, or from the Global Fortune 500 list. *Fortune* magazine's URL is: http://pathfinder.com/@@qffshQYAOJLZxYSB/fortune/1997/specials/f500/f500.html. You can reach it from www.pathfinder.com.

GROUP PROJECTS AND APPLICATIONS

Project 1

Many computer consulting firms offer companies help in developing shared IT applications. In small groups, contact a computer consulting firm in your area and ask a project manager to sit down with you and discuss the process of developing a shared IT application from scratch. Ideally, you will be talking about a project that the firm has just completed. Some questions to ask:

- What problem were you called in to solve?

- What kinds of different people worked on the project team? What are their skills and responsibilities?
- Did the development of the shared system follow the six-phase process outlined in Figure 12.5? Did any of these six phases occur simultaneously? If so, which ones?
- What were the biggest challenges encountered in designing the system?
- How did employees react to the system after it was set up? Did you need to go back and redesign any parts of it to accommodate employees' needs?

- What steps do you take to satisfy your customers? How do you continue to support the system after you've created it and trained the client's employees?

If possible, ask for copies of any flowcharts or dataflow diagrams the consulting firm used in developing the system, and share these with the class. Can other groups figure out the purpose of the shared application by examining these flowcharts?

Project 2

This is a group research project. Groups of four or five persons choose one of the following industries (each group should choose a different industry):

- Airlines
- Publishing
- Advertising
- Health and beauty aids
- Computers
- Women's apparel
- Management consulting
- Accounting
- TV production

Research the top three or four companies in each industry so you can answer the following questions:

- Does each of these companies have a chief information officer (CIO)?

- To whom does the CIO report?
- Within each industry, do those companies *with* a CIO perform better than those companies *without?*
- What is the CIO's background? What job did he or she hold in the company before becoming the CIO?
- What is the CIO's annual compensation package?
- What does the CIO see as his or her mission? Can the CIO point to any improvements he or she has made in the organization?

Present the results of your search to the class.

Project 3

The class breaks into an even-numbered set of groups. Half the groups brainstorm a new business they would like to start—one that will need to use a shared IT application. (You might choose to start a firm in one of the industries listed in Project 2.) The other groups take the role of IT consultants who have been hired to develop the system.

Role-play the meeting between the entrepreneurs and the consultants. The consultants should be prepared to ask questions regarding the entrepreneurs' goals, and the entrepreneurs should be willing to challenge the consultants to create an effective, efficient system within budgetary constraints and in a timely manner.

REVIEW QUESTIONS

1. What is systems development? How are systems projects initiated?

2. What are open shared systems? Why is the principle of openness desirable?

3. How do interoperable applications differ from those that do not have interoperability? What benefits does interoperability offer?

4. How do the craft and assembly approaches to systems development differ?

5. What role are software components playing in the development of information technology applications?

6. Discuss the desirability of the concept of reusability as it applies to software. What is the principal element that makes reusability possible?

7. Describe the purpose and contents of a systems development project proposal. Who initiates this proposal? Who reviews it?

8. Describe the purpose of a steering committee. Who serves on the committee? What role does the committee play in the development of an IT application?

9. What are the six phases of the systems development life cycle?

10. Describe the purpose of problem recognition and preliminary investigation. Who performs this investigation?

11. What three types of feasibility are assessed during the preliminary investigation phase of the systems development life cycle?

12. What is a systems requirement? What is requirements determination?

13. What is the difference between process improvement and business improvement? What is their relation to requirements determination?

14. Identify and discuss four types of business improvement that can be created through effective use of IT.

15. What are the differences between preliminary design, prototyping, and detailed design?

16. What three activities are involved in systems development and construction?

17. Discuss the purpose of testing. What is the difference between software testing and system testing?

18. What is implementation? List and describe three important aspects of implementation.

19. What four conversion strategies are available to systems analysts?

20. What is systems evaluation?

21. Name the five data collection techniques used by systems analysts.

22. Distinguish between a system flowchart and a dataflow diagram.

23. What is leveling? Why is it useful in documenting dataflows?

24. What are the two components of data dictionaries?

25. Describe the features that most CASE tools have. What are the three kinds of CASE tools?

26. What five skills should a systems analyst possess?

27. With which other IT professionals are systems analysts likely to work?

DISCUSSION QUESTIONS

1. Although computer downsizing is proceeding smoothly at MCA, Inc.—the $4 billion entertainment conglomerate based in Universal City, California—George A. Brenner, director of Corporate Information Services, admits, "Our users need a lot [of] handholding and cuddling. We've had to put a lot of effort into employee training in order to teach people to be more attentive to the power on their desktops." What professional skills did Brenner need to identify this problem and to deal with the challenge it presented? Explain your answer.

2. Should companies be advised to select a mission-critical application as their first client/server application, or should they select a small-scale test application initially to gain experience? Explain your answer.

3. Holiday Inn decided to retool its mainframe-based system after a client/server pilot project showed that the new system wasn't updating certain account information automatically. What information did Holiday Inn need to evaluate this shortcoming?

4. A growing number of companies have opened custom-designed laboratories for usability testing. At these labs, end-users can evaluate new IT systems and suggest improvements. Where and how do these usability tests fit into the system development life cycle?

SUGGESTED READINGS

Booch, Grady. *Object-Oriented Analysis and Design with Applications*. Redwood City, CA: Benjamin Cummings, 1994. This widely used text outlines the principles and characteristics of object-oriented development and applies them to the development of a wide variety of IT applications.

Davenport, Thomas H. *Process Innovation: Reengineering Work Through Information Technology*. Boston: Harvard Business School Press, 1993. This timely book discusses the necessity of reexamining the processes underlying an organization's day-to-day activities, highlighting questions and issues while presenting a framework for addressing process redesign issues. Includes many examples of firms that have succeeded or failed in combining business change and IT initiatives.

Gurbaxani, Vijay. "The New World of Information Technology Outsourcing." *Communications of the ACM 39* (July 1996): 45–46. In this brief article, part of a five-article set in this issue of the journal, the author profiles the landmark outsourcing agreement at Kodak, which triggered a series of similar agreements at other companies.

Hammer, Michael, and James Champy. *Reengineering the Corporation: A Manifesto for Business Revolution*. New York: HarperBusiness, 1993. This book is based on the thesis that corporations must undertake a radical reinvention of the way they work. The authors provide clear guidelines on the redesign of business processes, with special emphasis on the value of information technology in reengineering businesses.

Hammer, Michael. "Reengineering Work: Don't Automate, Obliterate." *Harvard Business Review 68* (July–August 1990): 104–112. The classic article that woke managers up to the need for rethinking the way they do business. It offers bold and challenging ideas that every executive and student of management must confront.

Harkness, Warren L., William J. Kettinger, and Albert H. Segers. "Sustaining Process Improvement and Innovation in the Information Services Function: Lessons Learned at the Bose Corporation." *MIS Quarterly 20* (September 1996): 349–368. The authors describe the creation of an enterprisewide source of process innovation and improvement to serve the worldwide customer base of famed Bose Corp.

Hopper, Max. "Rattling SABRE—New Ways to Compete on Information." *Harvard Business Review 68* (May–June 1990): 118–125. A thought-provoking article on the changing role of IT in business. Written by American Airlines' chief information officer, who inspired the company's SABRE computerized reservation system.

Keil, Mark. "Pulling the Plug: Software Project Management and the Problem of Project Escalation." *MIS Quarterly 19*

(December 1995): 421–448. An in-depth case study exploring the challenge of managing information technology projects that, once launched, seem to take on a life of their own. The article delves into the management and delivery of IT projects.

Majchrzak, Ann, and Qianwei Wang. "Breaking the Functional Mindset in Process Organizations." *Harvard Business Review 74* (September–October 1995): 92–99. The authors share their findings on the factors that contributed to or thwarted the successful reengineering of work processes in manufacturing firms. They show how culture, responsibility, and technology must fit together to create the desired level of success.

Martin, James. *Principles of Object-Oriented Analysis and Design*. Englewood Cliffs, N.J.: Prentice Hall, 1993. This book provides an easy-to-follow but comprehensive introduction to object-oriented design. It includes suggested standards for utilizing object techniques and adapts them to a variety of CASE tools and development methods.

Pancake, Cherri. "The Promise and Cost of Object Technology: A Five-Year Forecast." *Communications of the ACM 38* (October 1995): 33–49. This article reports on a meeting of leading industry and academic experts who came together to discuss the future of object-oriented applications and their development.

Porter, Michael E. *Competitive Advantage: Creating and Sustaining Superior Performance*. New York: Free Press, 1985. A definitive work for the manager trying to gain a competitive edge in the market. It shows how to choose a technological strategy that reflects both the company's capabilities and those of its competitors.

Stalk, George, Jr., and Thomas M. Hout. *Competing Against Time: How Time-Based Competition Is Reshaping Global Markets*. New York: Free Press, 1990. A fascinating book showing how time constraints and the need for speed-to-market are reshaping business practices and restructuring industry. The authors document how time consumption, like cost expenditure, can be managed and how virtually all businesses can use time as a competitive weapon.

Strebel, Paul. *Breakpoints: How Managers Exploit Radical Business Change*. Boston: Harvard Business School Press, 1992. Dramatic changes in markets, technologies, and politics are transforming the world, causing sudden shifts in business conditions. The discontinuities, or breakpoints, that result are opportunities for those who recognize them as such. This book tells the story of several companies that recognized these breakpoints as opportunities and redeveloped their business systems to capitalize on change at the expense of firms that did not.

CASE STUDY

Shoot-Out Whets Sara Lee's Appetite for Client/Server Computing

If you associate the name "Sara Lee" only with cheesecake, think again. Sara Lee Corp. also owns such familiar American brand names as Hanes (knit wear), L'eggs (hosiery), Isotoner (slippers and gloves), Coach (leather accessories), Ball Park (hot dogs), Mr. Turkey (poultry products), and Kiwi (shoe polish and pharmaceuticals). And since the 1980s, the company has been acquiring a number of European brands, including the Radox line of bath products favored in England since 1922; the Sanex bath products popular in Spain, Holland, Greece, and Portugal; Douwe Egbert's coffees, which are marketed under various brand names throughout Europe; Dim S.A., France's largest hosiery and underwear maker; and Vatter, Germany's largest hosiery maker.

Information technology plays an important part in improving efficiency, especially for a manufacturer like Sara Lee. That doesn't mean that Sara Lee's more than 100 divisions follow a single corporatewide standard for information systems, though. As the company's vice president of corporate systems told a *PC Week* writer, "Sara Lee has too diversified an environment and too

many types of operations to warrant [choosing] a single product or technology." Instead, Sara Lee's corporate IT staff acts as a team of consultants, taking the lead in evaluating new technology and compiling lists of suggested hardware and software options that divisions can use in developing their information systems.

Keeping on top of new technology is no small task. Over the space of eight months, for example, Sara Lee's IT staff visited all the top hardware and software makers to ask them about their future plans and to try to determine when the promise of client/server computing would be fulfilled.

Sara Lee is also a *PC Week* Lab Partner, one of a select group of corporations that work with *PC Week*'s technical experts and university researchers to test emerging technologies under real-world conditions. For example, Sara Lee teamed up with *PC Week* to sponsor an Industrial Automation Shoot-Out at North Carolina State University's College of Textiles. This two-week event followed months of preparation and involved hundreds of people, as well as contributions of time or

Sara Lee's U.S. brands...

...and its Eurobrands.

equipment from dozens of companies. The goal: to test a new generation of supervisory control and data acquisition (SCADA) software for client/server computing.

SCADA software monitors, controls, and coordinates factory operations, providing feedback that minimizes the number of decisions that workers need to make. Typically, this software has been part of costly closed systems using mainframes or midrange computers. (In contrast, IBM and IBM-compatible PCs are open systems, which means that any number of companies can provide peripherals and software that can be interconnected to work with their systems.)

Closed systems have some drawbacks. First is their price: buyers can't mix and match competitively priced hardware from various companies. Second, closed systems tend to be inflexible, making it cumbersome to shift production in response to market conditions.

Third, closed systems are islands of automation, blocking the sharing of data and information needed in computer-integrated manufacturing (CIM). CIM, which we discuss in detail in the next chapter, is the use of computer systems to share information and integrate all business functions, from marketing to manufacturing. CIM can make companies more nimble in responding to market opportunities, and is therefore a high priority for Sara Lee Corp.

Nimbleness was especially important to Sara Lee's textile divisions. The whole U.S. textile industry was hit hard by global competition in the late 1980s and early 1990s and was forced to cut layers of management and retrain workers to keep them productively employed. It also invested heavily in total quality management (TQM) programs. The industry is now much stronger, but to remain competitive, it needs the advantages of

CIM and it needs to determine whether client/server computing can deliver them. That's why Sara Lee and *PC Week* designed the Shoot-Out to simulate the textile-dyeing operations of a Sara Lee Knit Products plant.

The Shoot-Out was intended to answer some key questions: Can the operation of a billion-dollar facility be entrusted to the new technology? (Factory automation systems must collect, process, and present vast amounts of data in real time.) Is the user interface easy to use? (Workers faced with operational difficulties don't have time to decipher puzzling screen messages.) How well do the systems communicate with the devices that actually operate factory equipment and processes? The Shoot-Out team identified 200 judging criteria, which were then reviewed by IT professionals from more than 100 corporations.

Meanwhile, Shoot-Out team members were also working with Morton Machine Works, Inc., to develop a simulation of the textile-dyeing process. With the help of ZD Labs in Foster City, California, other team members gathered the donated equipment needed to create a high-speed LAN for the simulated manufacturing system.

A month before the test, the team sent the seven participating software manufacturers a description of the simulation and the tasks their software would have to perform. The Shoot-Out itself had two phases: a series of timed tests to perform specific tasks, followed by two-and-one-half-hour presentations to seven corporate judges representing a variety of industries. After all scoring was complete, Sara Lee executives identified three client/server packages they would suggest to the company's divisions.

Questions for Discussion

1. Why did Sara Lee go to the time, expense, and effort to co-sponsor the Shoot-Out? Why do you think the vendors chose to participate?

2. What does Sara Lee's participation in the Shoot-Out indicate about the relationship between corporate and divisional IT staff? How should the roles of these staff members differ?

3. After the Shoot-Out, the IT staff of the Knit Products Division decided to use one of the three recommended SCADA products in a pilot project at a new state-of-the-art dyeing facility in Greenwood, North Carolina. If all goes well, the division will eventually expand the system, replacing six or seven existing systems. Does this plan represent product improvement, process improvement, or both? Explain your answer.

CHAPTER
13

Business Information Systems and Information Technology in Industry

CHAPTER OUTLINE

Rethinking Common Practices

Business Information Systems

Transaction-Processing Systems • Management Reporting Systems • Decision Support Systems • Group Support Systems • Executive Support Systems • Expert Support Systems

Information Technology for Manufacturing Automation and Control

Material Requirements Planning (MRP) and Manufacturing Resource Planning (MRP II) • Computer-Aided Design and Computer-Aided Manufacturing (CAD/CAM) • Robots • Flexible Manufacturing • Computer Vision Systems

A Final Word

Case Study: IT: The Secret Ingredient at Mrs. Fields

Photo Essay: Saturn Sets New Automobile Standards, Capitalizing on Information Technology and Know-how

LEARNING OBJECTIVES

When you have completed this chapter, you should be able to

1 Define and explain the purpose of information systems.

2 Describe the six types of business information systems and know when each is used.

3 Summarize the purpose of computer-integrated manufacturing systems and manufacturing cells.

4 List and describe seven specialized types of computer-integrated manufacturing systems.

Rethinking Common Practices

By taking the time to rethink common practices, a company can reap tremendous business advantages. In the 1920s, Henry Ford made his company a spectacular success by manufacturing automobiles in a completely new way. Ford ignored the rules of car manufacturing used by his competitors and started from scratch. Rather than use a system in which workers performed many different tasks as they moved around the vehicle (the system in use at other automakers), Ford pioneered a new system—an assembly line on which the manufacturing work was broken down into separate tasks, with each being performed by people who specialized in that task. In the assembly line method of building automobiles, the partially completed auto was steadily transported by conveyor down an assembly line past the specialized workers, until it emerged, ready for some finishing touches, at the end of the line.

This new system used technology and time much more efficiently than the old system did and gave Ford a major competitive advantage. His company was able to turn out vehicles in a shorter time than its competitors, who still followed the old system. The assembly line method reduced the cost of manufacturing and improved the manufacturing management process.

Today, in the Information Age, many companies that are willing to rethink the rules of business rather than rely on common practices are also achieving a competitive advantage. IT is playing a major role in changing these rules by helping companies put processes together (rather than separating them, as the assembly lines of the Industrial Age did). Few of today's companies can start from scratch, as Ford did, but the most effective ones are redeveloping their business and work processes, combining them in such a way that makes the best use of both advanced technology and know-how.

In this chapter, we examine the activities of many successful companies that are using IT to run their business and to manage their manufacturing activities. We begin by looking at the various types of business information systems now in use throughout the business world. In the second part of the chapter, we focus on the applications of IT automation in manufacturing industries.

Business Information Systems

information system

A system in which data and information flow from one person or department to another.

business information system

The family of IT applications that underlies the activities of running and managing a business.

Recall that an **information system** is a system in which data and information flow from one person or department to another. Frequently, the term **business information system** is used to refer to the family of IT applications that underlies the activities of running and managing a business (including the people and procedures associated with the applications). Six types of information systems are commonly used in business: transaction-processing systems, management reporting systems, decision support systems, group support systems, executive support systems, and expert support systems.

Transaction-Processing Systems

Businesses exist by managing transactions, events that involve or affect the enterprise. Transactions are at the heart of every company's business process (Figure 13.1).

transaction-processing system (TPS)

A shared business information system that uses a combination of information technology and manual procedures to process data and information and to manage transactions.

Processing transactions efficiently and accurately is what keeps a business running smoothly. If a company cannot accept or fulfill orders, record its sales, manage its inventory, bill for its products or services, collect money, meet payroll needs, or maintain income tax records, it will not stay in business very long. A **transaction-processing system (TPS)** is a shared system that uses a combination of information technology and manual procedures to process data and information and to manage transactions. With a TPS, each transaction is handled according to standard company procedures. The characteristics of TPS are summarized in Table 13.1.

THE TPS AT PRICE CHOPPER SUPERMARKETS. In conjunction with its key suppliers, Price Chopper Supermarkets, a regional grocery chain in the northeastern United States, has developed an efficient TPS for processing delivery information. When deliveries arrive at a store, the driver connects a handheld computer to a communications cable on the loading dock outside the store. Invoices for the delivery are automatically transmitted to a store computer, which immediately checks the invoices for correct pricing and delivery authorization, using details downloaded daily from a purchasing and product authorization database at company headquarters.

Meanwhile, as the products are delivered into the store, the receiving manager counts the goods, entering the actual quantity delivered into another handheld computer connected to the store computer by FM radio signals (Figure 13.2). The computer immediately compares the driver's counts to the receiving manager's counts. Any discrepancy can be adjusted while the supplier is still at the delivery dock.

Each day, the invoices from the many deliveries made to the store are uploaded from the store computer to an accounts payable system at headquarters. This system processes each invoice to detect errors or discrepancies and notifies the store manager of any problems. After verification, the invoices go into the company's accounts payable cycle.

a) Stopping for fast food at a bodega in the "Little Havana" section of Miami.

b) Registering for the new semester's classes at the Registrar's office at Suffolk University.

c) Signing a lease at a Citroën dealership in Paris.

d) Purchasing tickets for a ride on a San Francisco cable car.

FIGURE 13.1

Business Transactions

Businesses exist by managing transactions, the events that involve or affect the enterprise. Transaction-processing systems can help to manage a wide variety of transactions, from registration for a university course to lease signings at an auto dealership

TABLE 13.1 *Characteristics of a Transaction-Processing System*
• Processes a high volume of similar business transactions.
• Supports multiple users in routine, everyday transactions.
• Utilizes relatively simple procedures to control processing and ensure accuracy.
• Produces documents and reports.
• Updates files and databases.

FIGURE 13.2

The Transaction-Processing System at Price Chopper Supermarkets

When deliveries arrive at Price Chopper Supermarkets, drivers use handheld computers to transmit invoices and pricing information to both the store's computer and company headquarters. Meanwhile, as the products are delivered into the store, the receiving manager counts the goods, entering the actual quantity delivered into another handheld computer connected to the store computer by FM radio signals.

THE TRANSACTION-PROCESSING SEQUENCE AND TPS OUTPUT AND REPORTS.

A transaction-processing system can process either on-line or in batches. (Review Chapter 2 if these terms are unclear to you.) Figure 13.3 summarizes the processing sequence and the five types of output produced during transaction processing: action documents, detail reports, summary reports, exception reports, and updated master data.

action document

A document designed to trigger a specific action or to signify that a transaction has taken place.

- **Action documents** are documents designed to trigger a specific action or to signify that a transaction has taken place. At Price Chopper, for example, invoices are action documents intended to result in the payment of money. When a utility company produces a customer's monthly bill, it, too, is creating an action document designed to result in the payment of money. Similarly, state motor vehicle departments process their files regularly to determine who must renew their car registrations during a particular month, then send out an action document prepared by the system. Airlines' reservation transactions lead to action documents in the form of printed tickets and, in some cases, boarding passes with the individual's seat assignment.

detail report/ transaction log

A report describing each processed transaction.

- A **detail report,** sometimes called a **transaction log,** contains data describing each processed transaction. It includes enough details to identify the transaction and its most important characteristics. For example, if the transaction is the payment of an invoice, the detail report will list the transaction and indicate the amount of money paid, the check number or cash reference, the date of the transaction, and the individual or company making the payment. If any questions arise during or after processing, the transaction log serves as a ready reference.

summary report

A report that shows the overall results of processing for a period of time or for a batch of transactions and includes a grand total for all listed transactions and the average transaction amount.

- A **summary report** shows the overall results of processing for a period of time or for a batch of transactions and includes a grand total for all listed transactions and the average transaction amount. It lists in summary form the transactions that took place. Different versions of the report may be produced for various recipients. For example, a grocery store may produce one summary report for the bookkeeper, another for the receiving manager, and others for department managers. If any of these people want additional data or information, they can request detailed reports, which also can be tailored to individuals.

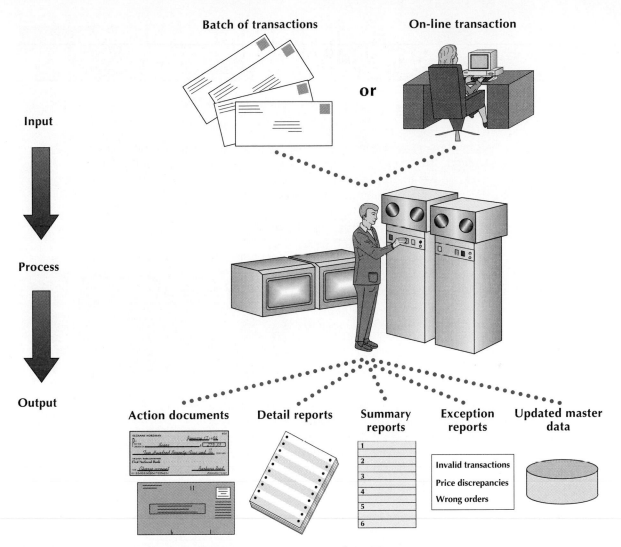

FIGURE 13.3   *The Transaction-Processing Sequence and TPS Output*

- An **exception report** lists unusual, erroneous, or unacceptable transactions or results. An exception is any activity that falls outside normal guidelines or expected conditions. One Price Chopper exception report, for example, lists supplier prices that are different from those in the database, items delivered that the store normally does not carry, and items delivered that were not ordered. The exception report is designed to call attention to the discrepancy and trigger an action to deal with it.

- Transaction-processing systems also generate **updated master data.** When a transaction is processed, all records in the system must be adjusted. When a customer makes a payment, for example, the database must be adjusted to show a decrease in that customer's account balance. When a supplier moves, the database must be updated to include the new address and telephone number. The people using the system should always be informed when master data change. In most cases, the detail report will include a summary of these changes.

exception report
A report that lists unusual, erroneous, or unacceptable transactions or results.

updated master data
An adjustment of all records in a system in response to a processed transaction.

EXPRESS   Express Selling on the Web

Columbus-based Express, a retailer of women's clothes (and a division of The Limited, Inc.), operates some 700 stores throughout the United States. Recently it expanded to conduct business around the world, but without opening a single store outside the United States.

Aware that approximately 50 percent of the world has Internet access, the company's executives determined that the Net was the key to overcoming geographic barriers to reach new customers. By opening an electronic storefront, complete with a colorful catalog, on the World Wide Web, Express could appeal to potential customers around the globe.

After advertising its storefront on the Web, using search engines such as Yahoo and Lycos, Express saw orders begin coming in from abroad. Customers used their Net browsers to locate the storefront, search through the electronic catalogs, and place orders. Distance did not matter—shoppers placed orders from South America, the United Kingdom, and elsewhere around the world.

Error-free transaction processing is essential. Because the data and information produced by transaction processing are used in the company's other business systems, a mistake in transaction processing can have a multiplier effect throughout the organization.

Management Reporting Systems

management reporting system/management information system (MIS)

A business information system designed to produce the information needed for successful management of a structured problem, process, department, or business.

A **management reporting system** is designed to provide managers with information useful in decision making or problem solving. For example, the manager of a furniture store needs to make many decisions concerning the purchase and replenishment of stock. These decisions include determining how much merchandise to order, whether a particular supplier is too expensive or carries low-quality products, and whether to continue offering certain products or services. The manager may also need to solve the problems of high labor costs or equipment repair costs. A management reporting system can help address these problems by retrieving and processing the data generated through transaction processing.

The processing done by a management reporting system may use either the actual "live" data in the system or a copy of the data. Working with a copy provides added security, protecting the master database from accidental or intentional damage or intrusion.

A person uses a management reporting system by requesting it to produce a certain report. Typically, the format and content of all reports are predetermined when the application is designed. The application simply retrieves the necessary data and information from a database or master file, processes them, and automatically presents the results in the specified format. For example, a Price Chopper district manager who wants to monitor the produce sales of all the stores in her district may have a report designed for that purpose and produced regularly. Each time it is prepared, the format will be the same, with the data and information reflecting recent business activity.

Management reporting systems are often called **management information systems (MIS)** because they are designed to produce information needed for successful management of a process, department, or business. They support recurring decisions when information needs have been determined in advance. Table 13.2 summarizes the characteristics of management information systems.

MIS REPORTS AT MCI. Management reporting systems usually generate reports automatically at specified time intervals, whether hourly, daily, weekly, monthly, quarterly, or annually. However, virtually all systems of this type include the capability to produce reports on demand.

MCI Communications Corp., the public long-distance carrier headquartered in Washington, D.C., gives the customers of its "virtual network" service three billing options. MCI will provide a record of all the customer's network transactions by (1) sending it electronically to the customer's designated computer center, where the details are printed out; (2) writing the data onto a magnetic tape or CD-ROM that is mailed to the customer; or (3) allowing the customer to download data from the MCI mainframe billing computer. MCI also provides its clients with management reporting software that allows them to process the data to produce over 20 standard reports. These reports enable managers to take four categories of action:

1. Monitor network usage and list the longest calls, the most expensive calls, and the most frequently used identification codes or calling card numbers (Figure 13.4).
2. Analyze calling history and patterns by identification code, calling card, and rate period (e.g., full-price day rate or reduced evening rate).
3. Report call frequencies, isolating the most frequently called numbers and area codes.
4. Summarize calling traffic by city, state, and country.

TABLE 13.2 *Characteristics of a Management Reporting System/Management Information System (MIS)*

- Uses data captured and stored as a result of transaction processing.
- Reports data and information rather than details of transaction processing.
- Assists managers in monitoring situations, evaluating conditions, and determining what actions need to be taken.
- Supports recurring decisions.
- Provides information in prespecified report formats, either in print or on-screen.

FIGURE 13.4
*MCI's Management
Reporting Software for
Clients*

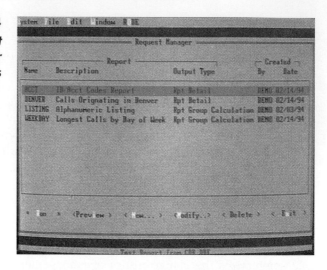

Printed on paper, the MIS reports for an average customer would fill 16 standard-sized boxes! MCI enables its customers to obtain information only in the form they desire, while ensuring that they have the information they need to manage their telephone use.

Decision Support Systems

**decision support system
(DSS)**

A business information system
designed to assist in decision
making where the decision
process is relatively
unstructured and only part of
the information needed is
structured in advance.

A **decision support system (DSS)** is a business information system designed to assist in decision making where the decision process is relatively unstructured and only part of the information needed is structured in advance. The DSS helps the individual to structure the problem by providing the needed information. Typically, the uniqueness of the issues and the breadth of the problems will require the system to retrieve and process data from several files and databases and to use data provided on-line by individual decision makers simultaneously.

Because information needs are not known at the beginning of a unique situation, the reports and displays generated by a DSS are not designed in advance. Instead, the user will generally request the processing of data and the generation of information through such inquiries as "How many _____ have this characteristic?", "Under what circumstances did this occur?", or "What if _____ occurs?" Frequently, getting some information raises additional questions, which, in turn, creates the need for more information. For this reason, a DSS must have greater flexibility than a management reporting system. The characteristics of decision support systems are summarized in Table 13.3.

There are three types of decision support systems:

1. An *institutional DSS* is an application that allows the user to both retrieve and generate information needed to address a general problem area (e.g., determining the viability of a merger or the price of a new product). The system contains a series of mathematical models that, when tailored to the characteristics of a specific problem, help in analyzing the situation. An institutional DSS is intended to be used on a continuing basis, even though the details of the situations in which it is used may vary.

2. *DSS generators* are used to create applications quickly. They are not complete applications themselves. A DSS generator consists of a series of high-level

TABLE 13.3 *Characteristics of a Decision Support System*

- Assists people who make decisions where information requirements are not known in advance.
- Supports problem solving and decision making where the situation is only partly structured.
- Provides information needed to define and solve the problem.
- Works both with files and databases and with people working on-line with the system.
- Provides information in a format determined by the recipient at the time of need.

commands that instruct the system to analyze data, simulate specific conditions, or produce reports quickly. A few commands can produce a great deal of valuable analysis and well-focused information.

3. *DSS tools* are designed for very specific capabilities. For example, one DSS tool may produce graphic displays of information in bar chart form. Another may analyze a file to determine categories of high and low business activity and variations in performance. Several DSS tools are generally used together, often with a DSS generator, to aid the problem solver in defining and then analyzing the problem.

The *Information Technology in Practice* feature entitled "Mining Data Provides an Edge for Sports Endeavors" shows how data mining, a capability some DSS provide, can boost management's effectiveness.

DSS IN THE U.S. CONGRESS. Every time the U.S. Congress sets out to reevaluate revenue generation and the tax system, it faces a different situation. The economy has changed, new legislation affecting revenues is in effect, and the spending needs of the government have altered. Before it can begin preparing a new tax package, Congress must determine the intent of the new legislation (e.g., raise more revenue, stimulate business spending on new plant and equipment, attract more investment to business research and development, or encourage more personal savings).

Analysts working for Congress can then use DSS generators to formulate models for evaluating a new tax or revenue proposal. For example, finding out that a change in investment tax credits will have an undesirable effect on the economy may cause them to adjust and then reevaluate a proposed tax credit. Alternatively, determining that a change in tax rates will affect middle-class savings negatively may cause them to readjust the proposed tax rates. Institutional DSS software makes it possible to change the components of the model easily, recalculating them to determine the likely effects of different proposals (Figure 13.5).

Keep in mind that every tax package is different. The creation of each new package involves determining what new information is needed. These characteristics suggest the need for a decision support system rather than an information or transaction-processing system, in which reporting needs have been predetermined.

Group Support Systems

A **group support system (GSS)** permits people to process and interpret information as a group, even if they are not working face-to-face. Like a DSS, a GSS supports people working in situations that are not fully structured. In these kinds

group support system (GSS)

A business information system that permits people to process and interpret information as a group, even if they are not working face-to-face.

INFORMATION TECHNOLOGY IN PRACTICE

Mining Data Provides an Edge for Sports Endeavors

In the summer of 1994, Mike and Brendan Moylan, co-owners of Sports Endeavors, Inc., in Hillsborough, North Carolina, saw the other shoe drop—and another, and another, and another. One of the buyers for their catalog company—they sell soccer and lacrosse equipment—had purchased 30,000 pairs of soccer shoes, expecting them to sell within two months. But by September, about 15,000 boxes of the cleated footgear were still languishing on the shelves. It wasn't until late fall that the brothers were able to unload the entire order. "That was our summer of enlightenment," says Mike, "When we were smaller, it was easy to know what customers wanted. And it didn't matter if we made a bad purchase. But by 1994, if we missed, we missed big."

That footless summer spurred the Moylans on a remarkably productive year. With the help of a consultant, they installed a database-marketing system that could systematically and precisely analyze sales trends to help them make smarter purchasing decisions. The system combines a database full of information about customers' buying habits with analytical software that, among other things, gives buyers

answers to key marketing questions: which products and colors sold best, which vendors were most profitable, which time of year was best for selling particular items, like sneakers. Armed with that knowledge, the buyers can revamp their sales approach. "With this system," says Brendan, the force behind the technology blitz, "we know we can grow."

It's a path big guys like American Express trod a long time ago: amassing large quantities of customer data in computerized form, then massaging the information to pinpoint their best customers and target them in a more personal way. In fact, through their highly sophisticated use of database marketing, big companies have come close to eliminating their small competitors' main advantage: a close, informed, flexible relationship with customers. . . .

The Moylans are a case in point. From the beginning—1984, when Mike set up shop at the tender age of 18—Sports Endeavors has worked hard to keep its finger on the customer's pulse. That was easy when the business was young, but as clients—and revenues—grew, it became harder and harder to keep track of who wanted to buy what when. That

of situations, an important part of problem solving involves conducting an analysis and determining what information is needed to make a decision.

Unlike in DSS systems, however, in GSS systems information is generated by the system in response to questions posed by group members. On-line interaction is an essential GSS feature. Individuals usually work at networked computer workstations, entering questions, ideas, suggestions, and comments that are shared electronically with other group members, sometimes anonymously. (We discussed an important part of group support systems, groupware software, in Chapter 10.)

Many companies have constructed specially designed group support rooms called *decision rooms* (Figure 13.6a). Similar in style to conference or board rooms, these facilities feature a large screen for display of information, individual workstations networked together, and a seating arrangement in which the group mem-

was one reason Mike brought Brendan into the business: while Mike had big ideas, Brendan had a knack for details and technology. It was Brendan who set as a priority building increasingly sophisticated database-marketing systems to follow and analyze sales and trends.

He had his work cut out for him. In 1990, the then $3-million Sports Endeavors had just one 286 PC, which it used in a distinctly low tech way: Six tele-

phone staffers took orders manually. A key-puncher typed the orders into the PC and then printed them out and delivered them to the shipping department. "We couldn't continue like that," says Brendan. . . .

Enter ProBit, a data warehousing program. . . . Expecting a slow beginning, the Moylans decided to focus first on forecasting. An example: based on an analysis of 20% growth in sales of Adidas watches in 1995, the company's four buyers were able to build a month-by-month sales plan for 1996.

They were also able to confirm some of their suspicions. Take suede sneakers in 1995. Buyers had noticed a decrease in demand, in favor of more trendy running shoes. But an analysis using ProBit revealed that sales had dropped by half. Now the catalog shows only a few suede-shoe styles, instead of the page of options it had featured before. Perhaps best of all, Sports Endeavors has reduced total inventory by three-quarters and sales have jumped to $25 million. "We're now able to anticipate what customers want and give it to them," says Brendan.

SOURCE: Excerpted from *Inc Technology,* No 2 (1996): 54–56.

bers can see one another. Another type of group support room uses a *remote decision network* (Figure 13.6b) format. Group members at remote locations are linked by a communications network that allows them to share databases, models, and GSS software. They enter their questions, ideas, and comments through a workstation; the network then displays these to other group members.

GSS sessions are typically managed by a facilitator who serves as an intermediary between the system and the group and who is responsible for administering the group's activities. The facilitator's job is to keep the group focused on the problem at hand, to ensure that no individual dominates the discussion, and to draw out ideas.

Unlike the other business information systems discussed so far, a GSS does not produce traditional printed reports. Rather, the questions, comments, and ideas of

FIGURE 13.5

Decision Support Systems in the U.S. Congress

The decision-making process in the U.S. Congress—which is sometimes considered agonizingly slow—has been helped along by a decision support system. Congressional analysts are now using DSS generators to evaluate the effects of new tax and revenue proposals on businesses, taxpayers, and the economy.

each group session are captured in a database that can later be printed and reviewed. Frequently, the most important result of a GSS session is a decision, or series of decisions, about how to solve a problem or capitalize on an opportunity. Table 13.4 summarizes the characteristics of group support systems.

GSS AT MARRIOTT. Business travelers are among Marriott Hotels' most important customers. One reason Marriott is so successful is that it meets the needs of these travelers, even though they change from year to year. Periodically, Marriott assembles handpicked hotel managers, heads of housekeeping, front desk personnel,

FIGURE 13.6   *Group Support Rooms*

Users of a GSS can be linked together in a decision room or through a remote decision network.

(a) Decision room

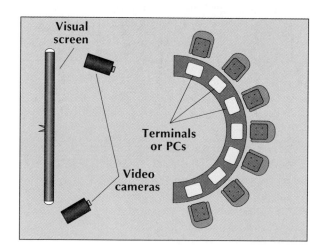

(b) Remote decision network

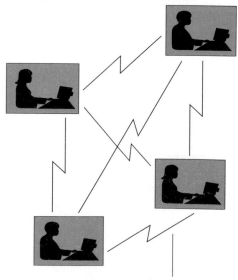

Communication may be through local or wide area network

DSS Takes the Guesswork Out of Building Energy-Efficient Homes

DSS

For years, energy designers and researchers have been devising techniques for building comfortable homes that can slash heating and cooling bills by 30 to 50 percent. But the techniques aren't flooding the market, partly because of resistance by the construction industry. Many builders, used to building "to code" or minimum standards, find it hard to justify the extra cost of energy-efficient construction. Others simply lack the engineering skills necessary to adopt the new techniques. This may change by the turn of the century, thanks to a number of programs designed to teach builders the new techniques and introduce them to a variety of new software tools.

Take the Energy Crafted Home Program, a trademarked program sponsored by several utilities and created with the help of a Harvard, Massachusetts, engineer. Most of the techniques taught at the program's seminars focus on ways to tighten the home's "envelope"—the boundary formed by the walls, ceilings, windows, and foundation. But make the envelope too tight, and you may let moisture or indoor pollutants build up. "Looking at a building as a total system is really too much for the human brain to encompass all at once," say some engineers. "But with the aid of computers we can do just that."

The two simplest decision support software tools designed for this purpose are Builder Guide, from the Passive Solar Industries Council, and REM/Design, which was created by Architectural Energy Corporation of Boulder, Colorado. Both programs rely on a description of the home, climate data, and local utility rates to calculate the home's annual peak heating and cooling loads, energy costs, and so on. With the aid of the software, builders can compare the potential costs and savings associated with alternate construction techniques and floor plans.

catering managers, room service coordinators, and bellmen to compare experiences regarding their guests. The meeting is conducted with a group support system, wherein hotel personnel enter their thoughts and criticisms regarding current capabilities and ideas for new services. For example, they may tell about encounters with guests in which they provided, or could not provide, an important service the guests wanted.

Because the entries are made anonymously, Marriott finds that the rank or pay level of the employee is not a deterrent to sharing ideas. (Without anonymity, hourly-wage desk attendants might feel intimidated by a hotel general manager.) When the ideas and comments are displayed visually, they are discussed openly, without knowledge of their origin, so the group can evaluate them honestly. You can probably see how such Marriott service features as voice mail, rentable portable computers, and cordless telephones might have originated through GSS sessions.

TABLE 13.4 *Characteristics of a Group Support System*

- Supports situations that are not fully structured.
- Assists in analyzing the problem under consideration.
- Is used by groups or teams rather than individuals.
- Emphasizes communication and generation of ideas and information.
- Permits communication among team members at different locations, who participate through communications networks.
- Involves a facilitator who keeps the group focused on the problem at hand and draws ideas out of group members.
- Generates a database of the group's questions, comments, and ideas rather than a traditional report.

Executive Support Systems

The activities of top-level executives in business and government are often quite different from those of middle managers and staff members. Rather than focusing on a single business process or an individual product or service line, as most middle managers do, executives spend most of their time meeting the challenges and opportunities that will affect the firm's future. When a serious problem arises—for example, an industrial accident or the potential loss of an important customer—they are also likely to be involved in determining the cause, dealing with the effect, and preventing the problem's recurrence. Executives also spend a good deal of their time on activities external to the company. Uncovering new

FIGURE 13.7 *How Executives Use Their Time*

Executives spend, on average, about 70 percent of their time in meetings.

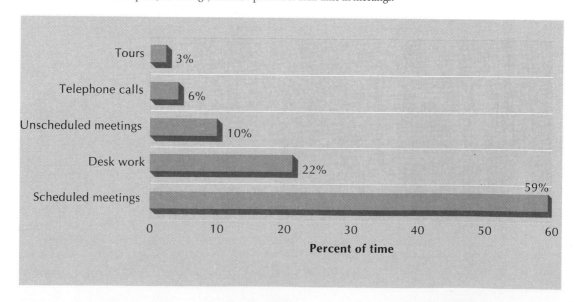

Coopers & Lybrand Boosts Productivity with Lotus Notes

If you've ever played telephone tag, you can understand the frustration building up at Coopers & Lybrand. Too often, auditing teams at this accounting giant spent hours trying to reach the few specialists at the firm capable of answering client's complex financial and tax questions. That's why Coopers & Lybrand was willing to take a gamble, becoming in 1991 one of the first firms to adopt Lotus Notes.

Lotus Notes helped to advance the concept of groupware—software that turns a network into an electronic conference room with on-line access to company databases and outside information services. (You encountered this concept in Chapter 10.) By early 1993, 500 Coopers & Lybrand professionals were using Notes to organize and share financial and tax information, including advice and analysis from outside specialists. Professional services were being completed faster and complex questions answered sooner. Within the year, Coopers & Lybrand was planning to install Notes for 2,000 client-service partners and staff.

market opportunities, monitoring the activities of competitors, and keeping an eye on impending legislation are among the executive's principal external concerns.

As you can probably guess, and as Figure 13.7 shows, executives spend much of their time in meetings. In fact, they spend very little time in their offices and have precious few moments of quiet time in which to contemplate the intricate plans and strategies they must put into effect. When they are in their offices, they need to be briefed on company developments quickly and in a way that provides them with useful and well-focused information. An **executive support system (ESS),** sometimes called an **executive information system (EIS),** is an interactive information system designed to fill exactly this need. An ESS encompasses a broad spectrum of company activities, presenting information on everything from entire business units to product and service lines to customers and suppliers.

Behind the scenes, the ESS software retrieves data and information from a variety of databases within or external to the company. The ESS usually displays information on the company's stock prices (if the stock is publicly traded), current orders booked, and market prices of important materials. (An airline executive will want to know the cost of fuel, for example, while an executive at an appliance manufacturer will undoubtedly monitor current steel prices.) The ESS also includes a communications link for retrieval of information from sources external to the company, such as Dow Jones News/Retrieval and similar services. Some systems also include DSS-like capabilities that let executives test "what if" strategies and compare alternatives. Often companies combine DSS, GSS, and ESS. A sample menu screen from an ESS appears in Figure 13.8.

ESS software includes powerful processing capabilities. These capabilities are necessary to boil down large volumes of performance details to a few screens

executive support system (ESS)/executive information system (EIS)
An interactive business information system designed to support executives that is capable of presenting summary information on company and industry activities.

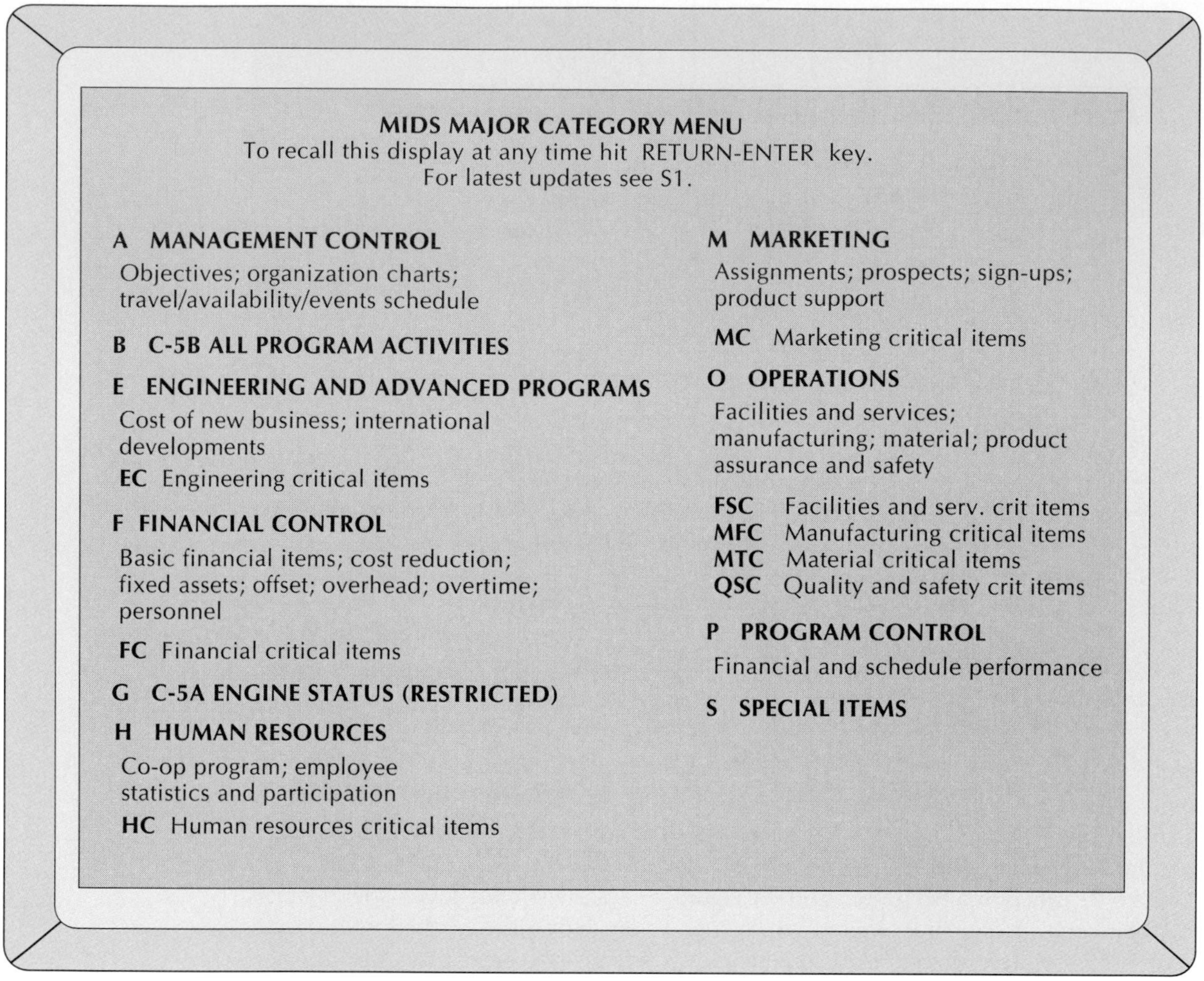

MIDS MAJOR CATEGORY MENU
To recall this display at any time hit RETURN-ENTER key.
For latest updates see S1.

A MANAGEMENT CONTROL
Objectives; organization charts;
travel/availability/events schedule

B C-5B ALL PROGRAM ACTIVITIES

E ENGINEERING AND ADVANCED PROGRAMS
Cost of new business; international
developments
EC Engineering critical items

F FINANCIAL CONTROL
Basic financial items; cost reduction;
fixed assets; offset; overhead; overtime;
personnel
FC Financial critical items

G C-5A ENGINE STATUS (RESTRICTED)

H HUMAN RESOURCES
Co-op program; employee
statistics and participation
HC Human resources critical items

M MARKETING
Assignments; prospects; sign-ups;
product support
MC Marketing critical items

O OPERATIONS
Facilities and services;
manufacturing; material; product
assurance and safety
FSC Facilities and serv. crit items
MFC Manufacturing critical items
MTC Material critical items
QSC Quality and safety crit items

P PROGRAM CONTROL
Financial and schedule performance

S SPECIAL ITEMS

FIGURE 13.8   *Main Menu of Executive Support System Showing Major Information Categories*
From the main menu of an ESS, executives can call up summary information on most categories of information relevant to their business.

that will allow the executive to grasp the status of events and assess key business indicators quickly. The summaries are usually presented in a standard format and rely heavily on business graphics to display results and relationships between business variables.

Although an ESS generally displays feature summaries only, the data supporting these summaries are quickly accessible. The report on each display screen is usually linked to detailed information that is available by clicking on an icon or entering a command. These supporting data can be presented in numeric or graphic form and displayed on-screen or printed. Table 13.5 summarizes the characteristics of an executive support system.

ESS AT WHIRLPOOL.   With sales of approximately $7 billion annually, Whirlpool Corp. of Benton Harbor, Michigan, is the largest appliance manufacturer in the

TABLE 13.5 *Characteristics of an Executive Support System*

- Offers quick, concise updates of business performance.
- Permits scanning of data and information on both internal activities and the external business environment.
- Highlights significant data and information in summary form.
- Allows the user to access data supporting the summary information.

United States and Brazil and the second largest in Europe, Canada, and Mexico. The company believes that its success depends on making information available to its executives—and its customers—quickly.

Global companies like Whirlpool, where international events affect day-to-day business operations, rely on IT to keep their executives in touch with one another and to help them make decisions. Whirlpool has developed an executive support system that lets executives retrieve data and information, regardless of their location, by clicking an icon to access data from commercial databases, Whirlpool databases, or the company's electronic mail system. If supply shipments to a particular region are unexpectedly disrupted, for example, an executive can use the system to determine the potential impact of the disruption and to devise alternatives to obtain supplies from other sources.

The system also includes a videoconferencing capability that allows managers from around the world to come together on-line. The system greatly reduces the need for travel while ensuring that decisions will continue to be made, even during difficult times. During the Persian Gulf War, for example, Whirlpool used its videoconferencing facilities to arrange a partnership with a European company —even though the war had temporarily forced Whirlpool's top management to curtail their travel plans. Whirlpool's executive support system is much more than a convenience. It's a proven management tool.

Expert Support Systems

An **expert support system,** or simply **expert system,** uses business rules, regulations, and databases to evaluate a situation or determine an appropriate course of action. These systems are designed to capture and apply consistently the expertise of a human specialist in a particular field. Because they are so specialized, expert systems are limited in application scope. Nonetheless, they are extremely powerful. They are commonly used in such diverse areas as medical diagnosis, manufacturing quality control, and financial planning. The *Information Technology in Practice* feature entitled "IT: ℞ for the U.S. Health-Care System?" describes some of the ways in which expert systems and other business information systems are being used to trim the costs of health care in the United States.

Expert systems usually process data provided by people interacting with the system through workstations. Alternatively, they may be part of a transaction-processing system, analyzing data and information included in business transactions. When automobile makers assemble vehicle order transactions, for example, they may use an expert system to review the orders' option packages to ensure they are appropriate. An expert system will know that if an automobile is built to include both air-conditioning and a towing package that will allow it to pull a trailer, it must have an oversize radiator, a heavy-duty alternator, and a

expert support system/expert system
A business information system that uses business rules, regulations, and databases to evaluate a situation or determine an appropriate course of action.

INFORMATION TECHNOLOGY IN PRACTICE

IT: Rx for the U.S. Health-Care System?

In 1970, it consumed just $74 billion, or 7.3 percent of U.S. GNP (gross national product). By 1990, however, its appetite had grown to $667 billion, or 13.4 percent of GNP. Unchecked, experts predict, it will devour $1,616 billion, or 16.4 percent of GNP, by the year 2000. "It" is the U.S. health-care system, and it's creating new opportunities for people who understand both health care and information technology.

Consider some of the ways that IT is being used in the health-care industry:

- *Speeding the release of new drugs.* Seriously ill patients and pharmaceutical companies both charge that the Food and Drug Administration (FDA) is too slow to approve new drugs. (The agency usually takes about 30 months to review an application and its 10,000 to 1 million pages of supporting data.) Over the last 10 years, though, a handful of pharmaceutical companies have shaved almost 9 months off the approval process by filing applications electronically.
- *Cutting through the red tape.* Experts estimate that transaction-processing systems using electronic data interchange (EDI) could save $4 billion to $10 billion a year in the processing of medical claims. The most ambitious effort to date may be the Healthcare Information Network, a nationwide network that uses toll-free telephone numbers to offer real-time processing of a variety of managed health-care transactions.
- *Deciding which treatments really work.* Although patients tend to be impressed by expensive treat-

ments, many doctors (and insurers) aren't always sure they improve survival rates. This doubt led Dr. Paul Ellwood to create InterStudy, a Minneapolis research organization dedicated to "outcomes management," a scorekeeping system for treatment options. This system is based on a database that collects survey data from both doctors and patients during and after treatment of 25 major illnesses, including diabetes, cataracts, and hypertension.

Outcomes management is also being used by the U.S. Agency for Health Care Policy and Research. One of its research teams, for example, is evaluating the relative effectiveness of bypass surgery, balloon angioplasty, and medication in treating coronary heart disease. Another team is looking at the 24 billion annually spent on treating lower-back pain in the United States.

- *Helping patients make better decisions.* Given a choice, informed patients may opt for less expensive treatments that promise as much or more relief than more expensive or risky treatments. That's the reasoning at the Foundation for Informed Medical Decision Making, which is producing a series of interactive videodisks that can be offered to patients in doctors' offices, hospitals, and HMOs (health maintenance organizations). The videodisks explain in plain English the latest findings of outcomes management for such maladies as early-stage breast cancer, mild hypertension, and lower-back pain.

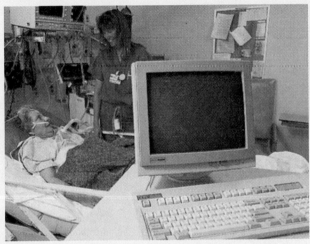

a) This computer at an Intermountain Health Care hospital in Salt Lake City delivers instant medical advice to a team of intensive care specialists.

b) A close-up of a screen from Intermountain's health-care information system.

Early results support the foundation's rationale. In the Denver region of the Kaiser Permanente HMO, where the foundation's videodisk on prostate enlargement has been used since 1989, surgery rates have dropped by 45 percent, saving the HMO $170,000 to $200,000 a year.

- *Giving doctors a helping hand.* Some medical problems are just too complex for doctors to handle unaided, especially in the high-pressure world of intensive care. In treating adult respiratory distress syndrome, for example, doctors have to balance hundreds of variables from moment to moment. That's why a research team created an expert system, dubbed HELP, to support doctors at Salt Lake City's LDS Hospital. The system is helping to eliminate the 25 to 35 percent added to hospital bills when caregivers have to correct such "mistakes" as postoperative infections. (Treating such an infection adds about $14,000 to a typical hospital bill.) After the HELP system was introduced, doctors were able to fine-tune the use of antibiotics, cutting the hospital's postoperative infection rate to less than half the national average.

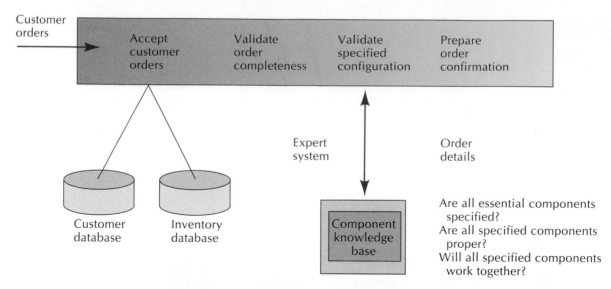

FIGURE 13.9   *Expert System Embedded in Order Entry Portion of an Auto Manufacturing System*

An expert system embedded in an auto manufacturing system will review all order details and report any discrepancy from the rules of manufacturing or good engineering.

transmission cooler. The expert system will review the order details and report any discrepancy from the rules, thereby preventing costly mistakes. In essence, the system incorporates the specialized knowledge of an auto design engineer to produce the finished product (Figure 13.9).

rule base/ knowledge base

A database of rules in an expert system.

The heart of most expert systems is a database of rules called a **rule base** or **knowledge base.** The rule base is often expressed in the form of IF–THEN statements. The expert system at the auto plant described in the last paragraph, for example, might include a rule that says:

> IF the vehicle requires a trailer package
> And it will have air-conditioning
> THEN check to ensure it will have the following components: oversize radiator, heavy-duty alternator, and transmission cooler.

The ultimate result of using an expert system is the diagnosis of a problem or determination of the cause of a problem. It may or may not include a recommendation for appropriate action. Expert systems generally do not produce formal detailed reports. (Table 13.6 summarizes the characteristics of an expert system.)

Mrs. Fields, the gourmet cookie franchiser, uses an expert system in its retail operations. For more information on how it works, see the Case Study at the end of this chapter.

TABLE 13.6   *Characteristics of an Expert Support System*

- Diagnoses problems and may recommend a course of action.
- Captures data and applies the expertise of a human specialist to a situation.
- Has a limited scope of application.
- Relies on rule base.
- Processes data entered by people interacting with the system as well as details retrieved from other information systems.

Information Technology for Manufacturing Automation and Control

The challenge and opportunity of managing a business unit or company today lie in removing the barriers that were erected when the Industrial Age brought about specialization. As we've seen throughout this book, information technology is helping companies integrate their business processes and revolutionizing the way businesses operate.

A similar revolution is taking place on the floors of manufacturing companies. Production systems have changed dramatically since Henry Ford redesigned his company's manufacturing processes. Today's factory finds people working in teams and relying heavily on computer and communications systems. **Computer-integrated manufacturing (CIM)** uses computers to link automated processes in a factory to reduce design time, increase machine utilization, shorten the manufacturing cycle, cut inventories, and increase product quality. In computer-integrated manufacturing, machines work together in groups known as **manufacturing cells.** Parts and materials are moved between cells by automated guide vehicles, automated machines, and materials-handling systems consisting of trolleys and carriers that move along guide wires or on conveyors. For most manufacturing companies today, the question is not *whether* to implement computers into their manufacturing processes, but *when*. The *Rethinking Business Practices* feature entitled "Computer Workstations Provide Visual Assembly Instructions" describes the impact the combination of creative thinking and desktop computers can have on a small business in the global automobile industry.

computer-integrated manufacturing (CIM)

A manufacturing system that uses computers to link automated processes in a factory to reduce design time, increase machine utilization, shorten the manufacturing cycle, cut inventories, and increase product quality.

manufacturing cell

A group of machines working together in computer-integrated manufacturing.

Companies in different parts of the world approach automation differently. Experts believe that U.S. and Japanese firms tend to address problems first at the level of the manufacturing floor, and then proceed to a full systems analysis and design effort. In contrast, the sequence in most European companies is to examine the full system first, and then break it down into individual processes and department functions. As a result, companies in different parts of the world have different priorities in using IT. Most Japanese firms implement CIM only when doing so is economically justifiable. Many U.S. companies follow a similar strategy, qualified by the American emphasis on short-term returns on investment. European companies tend to focus on long-term manufacturing strategies, installing systems without so much emphasis on short-term gain. ▉

In essence, CIM fits the IT model we've used throughout this book. (Recall that information technology has three components: computers, communications, and know-how; see Figure 1.3.) Computers are at the heart of many manufacturing systems and are the source of the artificial intelligence embedded in lathes and machine tools. Computers control the actions and movements of arms, wheels, gears, and conveyors, and examine process results. Database management systems store and retrieve manufacturing data and information, including product specifications, drawings, production procedures, setup instructions, and multimedia training documents.

Communications also play a central role in manufacturing industries. Wide area networks link factories across the country and interconnect work areas within the same facility. In fact, a special protocol called the **manufacturing automation protocol (MAP)** has been devised to assist factory designers in interconnecting

manufacturing automation protocol (MAP)

A protocol used by factory designers to provide a common language for the transmission of data.

RETHINKING BUSINESS PRACTICES

Computer Workstations Provide Visual Assembly Instructions

Talk about luck. If you can call an inexpensive system that has helped quadruple sales luck.

Back in 1990, Jess Anderson, president and general manager of a small, privately held manufacturing firm called Williams Technologies, Inc., had a dream. He wanted to turn his Summerville, S.C., plant, where workers take apart, clean and rebuild car and truck transmissions, into a flexible factory.

His vision is one every manufacturing executive in the world would like to achieve: to produce more varieties of products—in any quantity—and do it more quickly and accurately than before. Achieve it, and he'd have a great story to tell potential clients, Anderson thought.

Creating such a factory was no small feat. Each transmission has about 1,000 parts, which can be assembled in dozens of ways. Workers spent up to 53% of their time looking up assembly instructions in loose-leaf binders, Anderson says.

Anderson had envisioned a solution: computer workstations with instructions for building many different transmissions. But it remained just a vision until early 1991.

Then, because their daughters were friends, he invited Greg Allen and his family over for a barbecue. While the fajitas sizzled, Anderson described his dream system to Allen, a former photocopier salesman who taught himself programming, went into computer sales and opened a small custom software development shop. Allen said he'd come up with

something and returned a month later with a working prototype.

It was a "Eureka!" moment, Anderson recalls. He had "tripped across technologies that were exactly what I had in mind and somebody who could pull it off," he says. Anderson quickly brought in Allen as a consultant.

Allen was the only information systems professional on a seven-person development team that began work in May 1992. The first manufacturing line using the ProNet system went operational in January 1993. It went into widespread use a year later.

The system is remarkably inexpensive. Total cost for the pilot: $27,000, including $15,000 for 10 workstations. The system has grown but still runs on inexpensive software and equipment. The entire support staff consists of Allen, who is now a full-time Williams employee, and the one other member of Williams' IS department.

Did the system Allen helped create live up to Anderson's dream? "No question about that," says Anderson, who provided the following facts:

- **Productivity.** In two months, the ProNet pilot, a control valve body operation, was producing twice as many control valves with the same number of people. Today, Williams builds 450 transmissions a day, two times more than it did a year ago.

- **Flexibility.** ProNet has enabled its workforce to produce many different transmission models in

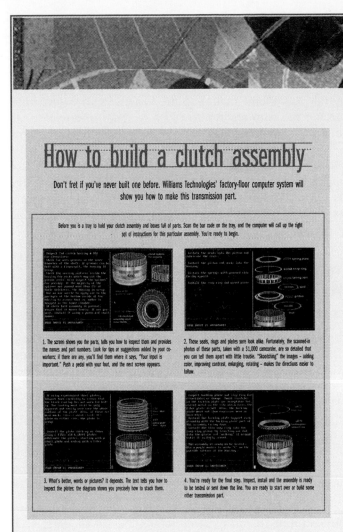

How to build a clutch assembly

Don't fret if you've never built one before. Williams Technologies' factory-floor computer system will show you how to make this transmission part.

Before you is a tray to hold your clutch assembly and boxes full of parts. Scan the bar code on the tray, and the computer will call up the right set of instructions for this particular assembly. You're ready to begin.

1. The screen shows you the parts, tells you how to inspect them and provides the names and part numbers. Look for tips or suggestions added by your co-workers; if there are any, you'll find them where it says, "Your input is important." Push a pedal with your foot, and the next screen appears.

2. Those seals, rings and plates sure look alike. Fortunately, the scanned-in photos of these parts, taken with a $1,000 camcorder, are so detailed that you can tell them apart with little trouble. "Skootching" the images - adding color, improving contrast, enlarging, rotating - makes the directions easier to follow.

3. What's better, words or pictures? It depends. The text tells you how to inspect the plates; the diagram shows you precisely how to stack them.

4. You're ready for the final step. Inspect, install and the assembly is ready to be tested or sent down the line. You are ready to start over or build some other transmission part.

- **Speed.** Cycle times have shortened. The average assembly time for all subassemblies and final assemblies has decreased from 150 seconds to 90 seconds.
- **Growth.** Besides the increase in sales, the number of employees has grown from 220 to more than 500. Williams Technologies has gone from one major customer—General Motors—to seven. They include Ford Motor Co., Mazda Motor Co., Hyundai Motor, Nissan Motor Co., Honda Motor Co., and Caterpillar, Inc. All work for GM and Nissan is done on ProNet, and Ford transmissions will soon be remanufactured using ProNet.

Ford, like GM, was impressed enough by ProNet to buy the system and launch its own pilot. "We saw how dramatically [ProNet] improved their operations," says Mark Femminaneo, an assembly and test engineer at Ford's transmission and new-products center in Livonia, Mich.

Because their facilities don't produce as many different transmissions as Williams, Femminaneo and Baumgart say a system such as ProNet probably makes the most sense as a training aid for them. But for managers who need to increase productivity and flexibility simultaneously, two lessons stick out: even low-cost computers can make great just-in-time instruction manuals, and rub a rabbit's foot before your dinner guests arrive. You might get lucky.

any quantity on one remanufacturing line. The biggest limitation appears to be the three months it takes to write and photograph instructions for a transmission. One customer vouches for the flexibility claims. "With ProNet, they have the capability of going in and rebalancing their people and output. They can respond to our schedule much quicker," says Al Baumgart, a senior systems analyst at the Allison Transmission division of General Motors Corp. in Indianapolis.

manufacturing tools, machines, and devices by providing a common language for the transmission of data.

The know-how needed for a successful CIM system is the same as that for any other IT application. All the people involved with the system—analysts, communications specialists, database administrators, and IT managers—are responsible for developing the procedures that keep the system in sync with business needs while safeguarding the firm against the loss of data, information, or processing capability. Using a CIM system properly means having the know-how to use the system to the firm's best advantage.

"Computer-integrated manufacturing" is a general, all-inclusive term used for computerized manufacturing systems. In this part of the chapter, we describe five specialized types of CIM: material requirements planning and manufacturing resource planning; computer-aided design and manufacturing; robots; flexible manufacturing; and computer vision systems.

Material Requirements Planning (MRP) and Manufacturing Resource Planning (MRP II)

material requirements planning (MRP)

A system that tracks the quantity of each part needed to manufacture a product; essentially, an important component of MRP II.

manufacturing resource planning (MRP II)

An advanced MRP system that ties together all the parts of an organization into the company's production activities.

Manufacturing management is as important to a company's success as the quality of the products it makes and the manner in which it produces them. **Material requirements planning (MRP)** is the core of the entire production management process. Most manufactured products are made from a range of individual components. MRP systems keep track of the quantity of each part needed to manufacture a product. They also coordinate scheduled manufacturing dates with the lead time needed to have components delivered and assembled.

Manufacturing resource planning (MRP II)[1] systems, which are essentially advanced versions of MRP systems that tie together all the parts of an organization into the company's production activities, include six essential subsystems (Figure 13.10):

1. **Bill of materials management.** A *bill of materials* is the list of parts used in manufacturing an item. A sample bill of materials and an assembly order for a swimming pool filtration system are shown in Figure 13.11. When a manufacturing company receives an order for a product, the system examines the bill of materials for the product and compares it to its current parts inventory. If necessary, additional parts will be procured so that the ordered product can be manufactured.

2. **Inventory management.** Inventory production schedulers keep track of what parts are on hand and on order. Using this information in conjunction with the bill of materials and the customer order, they determine which components must be ordered from suppliers. The manufacturing resource planning system helps inventory schedulers work with this information to determine the earliest date that manufacturing can begin.

3. **Production scheduling.** A company's production schedule specifies the planned use of its factory facilities and the quantity of items to be produced. Manufacturing resource planning allows production schedulers to examine the current schedule and to determine when additional activities can be incorporated into the schedule without overloading plant capacity.

---

[1]Another version of MRP, known as MRP III, has also been developed. This version adds a focus on distribution and logistics management.

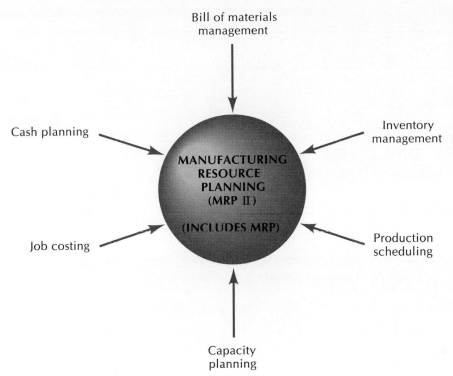

Bill of materials
management

Cash planning

Inventory
management

MANUFACTURING
RESOURCE
PLANNING
(MRP II)

(INCLUDES MRP)

Job costing

Production
scheduling

Capacity
planning

FIGURE 13.10

The Components of Manufacturing Resource Planning

Do not confuse manufacturing resource planning (MRP II) with material requirements planning (MRP). MRP is an important component of MRP II.

4. **Capacity planning.** Each tool, machine, production line, and worker in a factory has a capacity—usually measured in output per hour. Manufacturing resource planning helps schedulers to incorporate manufacturing capacity into their schedules.

5. **Job costing.** The level of costs and the sequence in which they will be incurred in manufacturing are extremely important to a business's bottom line. Manufacturing resource planning systems keep managers aware of both expected and unexpected costs throughout the production process.

6. **Cash planning.** Business planning includes ensuring that the company has sufficient cash flow to pay for materials and for workers. Manufacturing resource planning systems record the company's sources and uses of cash, both planned and actual.

Many types of report are produced by each component of the MRP II system. The systems are continually evolving to incorporate new features and additional capabilities. For this reason, they are often designated by generation number. For example, MRP II adds more capabilities for monitoring inventory of production resources to MRP.

MANUFACTURING RESOURCE PLANNING AT RAYCHEM. Raychem Corp.'s manufacturing facility outside of Vancouver, British Columbia, makes wiring systems that carry electrical power and control signals to various airplane devices. Because of the wide variety of aircraft designs in the industry, Raychem's manufacturing processes vary greatly. Planning production and managing the details with paper forms—the way all companies managed the production process in the past—is extremely time-consuming.

To cut down on the paper shuffling, Raychem has installed a paperless manufacturing system designed around client/server computing (review Chapter 11 if

Bill of Materials

Assembly number: 31436402
Assembly description: SWIMMING POOL FILTRATION SYSTEM
Drawing number:
Structure change: Drawing size:

Item number	Description	Type	Source	Unit of measure	Quantity/ assembly	Structure change	Dept. assembled in	Oper. assembled on

Assembly Order

Assembly number: 31436402
Assembly description: SWIMMING POOL FILTRATION SYSTEM
Order quantity: 50

Order number: 62566

Item number	Description	Unit of measure	Quantity per assembly	Expected quantity
531674	SCREW	01	6	300
531690	WASHER	01	5	250
728419	SCREW	01	5	250
1431478	SEAL	01	2	100
3519794	MOTOR	01	1	50
3572133	SPRING	01	2	100
31436130	PUMP SHAFT ASS'Y	01	1	50
31436301	SET COLLAR	01	1	50
31436315	CLAMP MOUNTING	01	1	50
31436338	SHIFTER COLLAR	01	1	50
31436345	SCREW	01	4	200

FIGURE 13.11   *Bill of Materials and Assembly Order for a Swimming Pool Filtration System*

A bill of materials is essentially a recipe for a product. It specifies the necessary ingredients, the order in which they should be combined, and how many of each ingredient are needed to make one batch of the product.

necessary). In this manufacturing resource planning system, production data and information are stored on servers that are accessible to a variety of workstations and manufacturing tools. The system is interconnected with a computer-aided design/computer-aided manufacturing (CAD/CAM) system (discussed in the next section). Both planners and designers work on-line, retrieving information from the system's databases and devising production plans to meet the diverse needs of the company and its customers. Because so much of the work is done through networked workstations, paper reports are not generated very often. Also included in Raychem's system is a rule-based expert system used to create wiring design and manufacturing specifications and a design database that allows designers to draw on previous specifications.

As production occurs, the system captures data on the amount of time needed to set up machines and assembly lines and the amount of scrap materials produced. These data are fed back into the materials-planning and job-costing subsystems to improve subsequent jobs.

Computer-Aided Design and Computer-Aided Manufacturing (CAD/CAM)

For many years, automated manufacturing systems were synonymous with MRP. Today, computer-aided design and computer-aided manufacturing are also important components of most manufacturing systems. Product designers and engineers working on **computer-aided design (CAD)** systems use a powerful computer graphics workstation outfitted with programs that allow them to draw design specifications on the display screen. Manipulating a light pen, scanner, or mouse, they can specify the product's dimensions and show its lines, indentations, and other features with precision. Each element of the design appears on the screen as it is specified. Changes can be made quickly by adding, removing, or altering details on the drawing (Figure 13.12).

Since CAD tools usually work in three dimensions, the designer can specify and see the height, width, and depth of the product right on the screen. Designs can be rotated, tilted, and turned upside down so that every angle is visible for inspection. When a design is complete, it is stored on disk, ready for review, editing, or printing at any time.

CAD designs are frequently transmitted to **computer-aided manufacturing (CAM)** systems, which rely on IT to automate and manage the manufacturing process directly. Using the CAD database, CAM software controls tools and

computer-aided design (CAD)
A system that uses a powerful computer graphics workstation to enable product designers and engineers to draw design specifications on a display screen.

computer-aided manufacturing (CAM)
A system that relies on IT to automate and manage the manufacturing process directly.

a) To improve its material handling and control system, Litton studied the design, spacing, and layout of the machinery in use on the manufacturing floor.

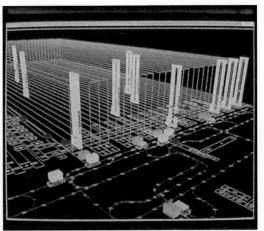

b) Litton's designers then created a 3-D graphic simulation of the manufacturing floor using CAD/CAM software. By manipulating the simulation on-screen, they were able to experiment with new floor layouts and manufacturing techniques without building costly prototypes.

FIGURE 13.12
CAD/CAM in Action at Litton Industries
Designers and engineers use computer-aided design and manufacturing programs to draw sophisticated design specifications on-screen. The photos shown here were prepared by Litton Industries as part of an investigation into improving its manufacturing systems.

machines on the factory floor to manufacture the product designed on the CAD system.

CAD/CAM systems require access to many computer and communications programs. For example, CAM systems obtain detailed product design information from the CAD databases and bills of materials from manufacturing resource planning systems. They communicate with the machines on shop floors by way of high-speed, sophisticated communications networks.

CAD/CAM AT DAYTON-WALTHER CORP.   Dayton-Walther Corp., located in Dayton, Ohio, manufactures truck, trailer, and automotive parts. To design these parts, it relies on a CAD/CAM system equipped with graphics workstations. Designers use a digitizing tablet to draw the points, lines, arcs, and other building blocks of each part on the computer screen. Once drawn, these images can be rotated, zoomed in on, or otherwise manipulated for close examination—all without ever touching paper, pencil, or drafting board.

To determine how well the designs will hold up under the stress of everyday use, engineers typically run the parts through a computer simulation. This process identifies any weak points in a part before it is put into production and installed in Dayton-Walther's products. For manufacturing, the CAD designs are turned over to computer-aided manufacturing devices. For example, a die model for a part is cut with a numerically controlled machine tool using information transmitted from the CAD system.

CAD/CAM often pays for itself quickly. Dayton-Walther's management estimates that its system paid for itself in less than a year—and that's not factoring in increased product quality and customer satisfaction.

Product design itself usually accounts for only 5 to 8 percent of a product's cost, but the decisions made by product designers typically account for 60 to 70 percent of a product's total cost. Discovering during actual production that a product is too difficult to build or that its constituent materials are too costly to use can mean serious problems. So can learning that the product contains features that will make it difficult to sell.

concurrent engineering
A design and manufacturing method in which team members work across their departmental functions to evaluate the activities of many departments and manage the product development process.

Concurrent engineering can solve these problems before they happen. In a concurrently engineered project, teams of people from different departments take a "process view" of the product—that is, they focus simultaneously on parts, components, manufacturing, and testing. Design engineers, cost experts, manufacturing engineers, and marketing staff members all work together to manage the design and development process. As each design detail is considered, so are its manufacturing, cost, and market characteristics. Ernst & Young, the U.S.-based international consulting firm, estimates that concurrent engineering typically shaves total product cost by 20 percent.

Concurrent engineering requires team members to work across their departmental functions to evaluate the activities of many departments. But this is just the beginning. Now emerging is the capability for companies to link their design teams, through communications networks and CAD systems, to machine tools located in a factory down the road or across the country. These factories can turn preliminary designs into prototypes that team members evaluate as part of the design process. ▪

Robots

A **robot** is a computer-controlled device that can physically manipulate its surroundings (Figure 13.13). On assembly lines, *pick-and-place robots* are usually programmed to carry out four functions: move to the location of a part, grasp the part, move to the location where the part will be used, and release their grip on the part. More sophisticated versions of robots, currently under development, will have the ability to *sense*—that is, to gather information about their immediate environment through a variety of sensing devices and to analyze this information and determine the proper course of action to take.

robot
A computer-controlled device that can physically manipulate its surroundings.

FIGURE 13.13
Robotics in Action
Don't let movies like *The Terminator* and *RoboCop* fool you. Although some robots have manipulator arms, grippers, and computer vision systems, they remain machines with no personality or will of their own. This constraint hasn't stopped them from being widely used, however.

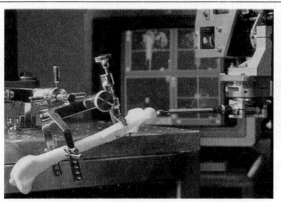

a) In veterinary medicine—Dr. Hap Paul developed a computer robot that drills a hole in a dog's femur so that a metal joint can be implanted to replace the natural joint.

b) In laboratories—Robots are widely used to select and move test tubes so that lab technicians do not have to come in contact with the tubes' contents.

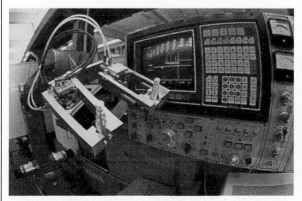

c) In manufacturing—Pick-and-place robots are frequently utilized to move parts into hard-to-reach areas.

d) In computer systems themselves—Mobile Robot Group's "Squirt" robot is used to repair the interior components of computers and other electronic systems.

CRITICAL CONNECTION 4

| Boeing | Boeing Takes Off with CAD Software |

Quick! What has more than 3 million parts and flies? It's the Boeing 777, the world's largest twin-engine jetliner. This is also the first commercial airplane ever to be designed completely with CAD software. (Boeing's huge system included 8 mainframe computers, 2,200 engineering workstations, and more than 5,400 engineering and technical employees during the peak design period.) In fact, because the plane was designed entirely on computer, engineers could "preassemble" it digitally, skipping the expensive and time-consuming stage of building physical mockups.

With the help of CAD software and powerful workstations, engineers can factor stress, inertia, and weight analysis—represented as colored, shaded, three-dimensional solids on their screens—into designs. But the software is also an important communications tool. With it, all the people on the design team have access to the same, consistent set of engineering drawings, so they can coordinate improvements and refinements as the design moves through the various stages. This capability is essential to Boeing's team-style approach to

Although the combination of increased computer power and decreased cost will undoubtedly lead to greater sophistication and capability in robots, don't expect robots to look like those you've seen in science-fiction movies. Industry has not yet given robots an "almost human" appearance, nor is it working terribly hard to do so. Most robots look exactly like what they are: programmable machines. Some have manipulator arms and grippers ("arms and fingers"), and others have computer vision systems ("eyes"; discussed below). But they remain machines—with no personality or will of their own.

Flexible Manufacturing

flexible manufacturing
A manufacturing system that automatically sets up machines for the next job, thus reducing setup time and making smaller job runs feasible.

CAM improves the efficiency of the entire manufacturing process by automatically setting up machines for the next job. This capability, known as **flexible manufacturing,** often reduces setup time by 75 percent while improving product quality by 75 to 90 percent. Shorter setup times make smaller job runs feasible, providing more flexibility in scheduling while also reducing manufacturing lead times and the amount of inventory kept on hand.

FLEXIBLE MANUFACTURING AT YAMAZAKI MACHINERY. Yamazaki Machinery of Oguchi, Japan, a manufacturer of machine tools, has been relying on flexible manufacturing systems since 1980. It built its first plant, consisting of two flexible manufacturing lines, at a cost of $18 million. When the company examined the impact of flexible manufacturing systems on profits, it determined that the return from such systems was overwhelming, as Table 13.7 shows.

TABLE 13.7		
	CONVENTIONAL PLANT	OGUCHI FLEXIBLE MANUFACTURING SYSTEM PLANT
Number of machines	68	18
Number of workers	215	12
Square feet occupied	103,000	30,000
Average days processing time per work piece:		
Line A	35	1.5
Line B	60	3.0

SOURCE: *Thomas G. Gunn, Manufacturing for Competitive Advantage (Cambridge: Ballinger, 1987), pp. 169–170. Copyright 1987 by Ballinger Publishing Company. Reprinted by permission of HarperCollins Publishers, Inc.*

The benefits from flexible systems accumulate year after year, not only saving the company money, but also giving it an edge over competitors that continue to use conventional manufacturing methods. The *Information Technology in Practice* feature entitled "Flexible Manufacturing Challenges Traditional Assumptions" gives additional examples of companies that have used flexible manufacturing for competitive advantage.

Computer Vision Systems

In manufacturing, product quality and consistency are essential for two reasons. First, customers today will not accept poor-quality products. They don't have to, because competition ensures that most manufactured products will be available from more than one company. Second, poor quality costs the company money and damages its profitability.

Computer vision systems are rapidly becoming an important tool to improve quality and consistency. Often used for recognition of parts and automated assembly of finished goods, these systems employ computer sensors to detect shapes, images, and varying levels of detail, which they then compare with data stored in memory. Depending on the logic programmed into the system, they can detect the presence or absence of a match and signal other devices in the manufacturing cell to take corrective action. Computer vision systems are also frequently used to scrutinize finished products to detect imperfections and defects.

computer vision system
A system that uses computer sensors to detect shapes, images, and varying levels of detail.

Vision capabilities are often embedded in robots. The integration of computer vision systems with robots increases the types of activities that robots can perform.

COMPUTER-INTEGRATED MANUFACTURING AT SATURN. At the Saturn automobile plant 35 miles south of Nashville, Tennessee, a 3,000-member team is living out one of the greatest experiments in manufacturing. After an investment of eight years and $3.5 billion, Saturn automobiles began rolling off the assembly line in 1991.

INFORMATION TECHNOLOGY IN PRACTICE

Flexible Manufacturing Challenges Traditional Assumptions

For Wendy Morita, the process is simple enough. She stops by the local Panasonic bicycle store and orders a custom-made bike from an attentive clerk. Two weeks later, she returns, happily paying anywhere from $545 to $3,200 for a bicycle that has been manufactured to her measurements, painted to her specifications, and embellished with her name. (By way of comparison, a standard model sells for between $210 and $510.) Little does she know that the bike was actually ready just three hours after her initial fitting, thanks to a fax machine that zapped her measurements to a small but high-tech factory. "We could have made the [delivery] time shorter," says Koji Nishikawa, head of sales, "but we want people to feel excited about waiting for something special."

Panasonic's secret—flexible manufacturing—is doing more than exciting a few bike owners. It's also inspiring manufacturing experts around the world to rethink some basic assumptions.

Assumption: Each production line should produce a single standardized product with limited variations. At Panasonic's bike factory, the single production line can produce 18 models of racing, road, and mountain bikes in 199 color patterns and almost any size. That's a grand total of about 11 million variations. And at Toshiba, workers can assemble 9 different word processors on the same line; on the next line, workers may be turning out 20 varieties of laptop computers. On a larger scale, Toyota uses "intelligent pallets," computer-controlled fixtures that work in rotation, picking up the parts for a specific model and holding them together as they are tack-welded by robots.

With these devices, Toyota routinely produces four body types or models on each line.

Assumption: Retooling the factory is an expensive and time-consuming task that always interrupts production. In a traditional factory, retooling for a new model can take anywhere from 3 to 12 months. At Toyota and Nissan plants, however, robots can be reprogrammed while the line keeps running. The physical changeover can be made in a single shift at Toyota plants.

Assumption: To maximize efficiency and return on investment, produce on a large scale. Traditional wisdom held that large production runs of standardized products would lower unit costs, which would, in turn, lower prices and pump up sales volume. Now, flexible manufacturers are showing that economies of scope—the ability to spread costs across many different products—can be just as beneficial. The reason? Flexible factories that produce customized products to order can command high prices. (Witness the premium price Wendy Morita paid for her new bike.)

Assumption: Inventory can be used as a buffer between production and demand. Driven by limited storage space, the Japanese pioneered the concept of just-in-time inventory—the delivery of parts and materials just as they are needed in manufacturing. (This frees up capital as well as space.) But flexible manufacturers are going beyond this: they are basing production on *actual* sales data and orders

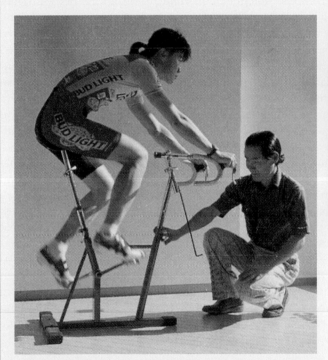

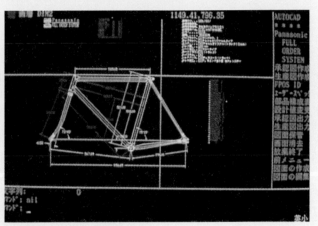

b) CAD software then produces a separate blueprint for each customized bicycle and transmits this to manufacturing.

a) The first step in creating a customized bicycle is a customer fitting.

rather than on sales *forecasts*. The secret here, of course, is IT. Consider Kao Corp., Japan's largest soap and cosmetics company. Its information system lets it make products to order and then deliver them within 24 hours.

Assumption: Mass production can meet the needs of a mass market. Henry Ford and hundreds of other industrialists made their fortunes selling mass-produced goods to a mass market.

Today's consumer is more demanding, though. Listen, for example, to Toshiba President Fumio Sato, who has been preaching the gospel of flexibility for over a decade: "Customers wanted choices. They wanted a washing machine or a TV set that was precisely right for their needs. We needed variety, not mass production." Wendy Morita—and millions of other consumers—would probably agree.

SOURCES: Susan Moffat, "Japan's New Personalized Production," *Fortune,* October 22, 1990, pp. 132–135; and Thomas A. Stewart, "Brace for Japan's Hot New Strategy," *Fortune,* September 21, 1992, pp. 62–74. Copyright © 1990 and 1992. All rights reserved.

The goal of General Motors, Saturn's parent company, was to use an innovative manufacturing process to build world-class small cars priced below comparable cars sold by Japanese automakers. To achieve this objective, GM's top managers were willing to break loose from GM's manufacturing traditions. They began the break by combing the world for the best, most efficient manufacturing practices. (Seeking out the world's best practices in any area is known as *benchmarking*. The best practice becomes a benchmark against which a firm can compare its own performance.) In designing their new system, Saturn's designers, managers, and executives borrowed ideas from such widely admired companies as Hewlett-Packard, Volvo, McDonald's, Nissan, and Kawasaki (along with 155 others).

The Saturn plant uses computer-integrated manufacturing and a hefty amount of automation. The typical Saturn has 10,000 or more parts. Hence, just making sure that all parts arrive in time for use is a challenge. Saturn makes its own engines, transmissions, body stampings, seats, and instrument panels—in fact, 65 percent of a Saturn car's parts are made right at the Saturn factory, so communication within the manufacturing site is critical. All of these tasks are made possible by IT and good manufacturing management systems.

Saturn's manufacturing cells, complete with robots (boasting computer vision systems) and automated guidance vehicles, can do only so much to make a quality automobile on time and within expected cost parameters, however. As in so many other companies, Saturn's success depends on its people and how deeply they are involved in and committed to the process. Saturn's management and assembly workers function as a team, sharing ideas and exchanging information. Information technology plays an important role by making the information accessible and interconnecting people and machines, but its role is secondary to that played by the people of Saturn.

The Saturn experiment seems to be working. Saturn automobiles are selling so far ahead of expectations that the company cannot make them fast enough, even after stepping up production. Cheered by the huge demand for Saturn cars from dealers and consumers, the company has several new models on the drawing board. For a guided tour of how IT is being used at Saturn, see the photo essay at the end of this chapter.

A Final Word

Information technology plays a pivotal role in the way companies develop or change their business practices. Whether in the office, on the manufacturing floor, or on the front line with customers and suppliers, information technology provides many advantages through its ability to capture, process, store, and distribute information. Clearly, starting from scratch has its advantages. But, once again, it is the organization's people and the know-how they possess that will determine whether a company can capitalize on the business opportunities presented by new IT capabilities.

SUMMARY OF LEARNING OBJECTIVES

1 **Define and explain the purpose of information systems.** An *information system* is a system in which data and information flow from one person or department to another. *Business information systems* are the IT applications that underlie the activities of running and managing a business.

2 **Describe the six types of business information systems and know when each is used.** There are six types of business information systems. *Transaction-processing systems (TPS)* are shared systems that use a combination of IT and manual procedures to process large volumes of data and information and to manage transactions. *Management reporting systems,* also called *management information systems (MIS),* are designed to provide managers with information useful in structured decision making or problem solving. *Decision support systems (DSS)* are used to assist in making decisions where the decision process is relatively unstructured and only part of the information needed is structured in advance. *Group support systems (GSS)* permit people to process and interpret information as a group, even if they are not working face-to-face. *Executive support systems (ESS),* also called *executive information systems (EIS),* are interactive information systems designed to brief company executives on company and industry developments quickly. *Expert support systems,* or simply *expert systems,* use business rules, regulations, and databases to evaluate a situation or determine an appropriate course of action.

3 **Summarize the purpose of computer-integrated manufacturing systems and manu-**

facturing cells. *Computer-integrated manufacturing (CIM)* uses computers to link automated processes in a factory to reduce design time, increase machine utilization, shorten the manufacturing cycle, and increase product quality. In CIM, machines work together in groups called *manufacturing cells.* Parts and materials are moved between cells by automated guide vehicles, automated machines, and materials-handling systems.

4 **List and describe seven specialized types of computer-integrated manufacturing (CIM) systems.** Seven types of CIM are used in manufacturing. *Material requirements planning (MRP) systems* keep track of the quantity of each part needed to manufacture a product. *Manufacturing resource planning (MRP II) systems* are advanced versions of MRP systems that tie together all the parts of an organization into the company's production activities. *Computer-aided design (CAD) systems* use computer graphics workstations outfitted with programs that allow designers and engineers to draw specifications on the display screen. *Computer-aided manufacturing (CAM) systems* rely on IT to automate and manage the manufacturing process directly. *Robots* are computer-controlled devices that can physically manipulate their surroundings. *Flexible manufacturing* improves the efficiency of the entire manufacturing process by automatically setting up machines for the next job. *Computer vision systems* use sensors to detect shapes, images, and varying levels of detail, which they then compare with data stored in memory.

KEY TERMS

CRITICAL CONNECTIONS

1   Express Selling on the Web

EXPRESS   When Express decided to create an electronic storefront, it knew it would need databases and backroom support systems capable of handling orders coming in from the Web. Databases had to be accessible on-line so the company could verify that the merchandise customers were ordering was in stock and available for immediate shipment.

Order transactions were accumulated into the company's sales and order database and linked to payments. Electronic payments via credit card transactions submitted over the Net required extra security. Charging shipping costs to distant customers demanded new thinking from a retailer accustomed to selling through ordinary "brick and mortar" malls. The company settled on a fixed shipping charge, regardless of the customer's location.

Experience has provided a wealth of new information to Express on how to do business electronically and how to develop information systems that support transactions originated on the Web. The company's newfound insights will help ensure that it is well positioned for the expected growth in on-line shopping.

Questions for Discussion

1. What advantages does an electronic storefront offer in comparison to traditional retail stores?
2. What factors might lead shoppers to visit and buy from electronic malls?
3. Drawing on the information in this Critical Connection, identify the new characteristics systems developers must add to support systems when business is conducted electronically.

2   DSS Takes the Guesswork Out of Building Energy-Efficient Homes

DSS   Decision support software like BuilderGuide and REM/Design offers builders the advantage of helping them "sell" the new techniques to home buyers by showing them the savings in energy costs. But this software also helps potential home owners, who may need a larger mortgage to cover the higher costs of energy-efficient construction. They may use the programs' output to qualify for an energy-efficient mortgage because the projected savings on utilities will leave them more money for a larger loan payment.

Questions for Discussion

1. Explain how BuilderGuide and REM/Design fit the definition of a decision support system.

2. The Energy Crafted Home Program is sponsored by a consortium of New England utility companies. Why do you think a utility company would sponsor a program designed to reduce energy consumption?

3. Output from software packages like BuilderGuide and REM/Design may eventually be used to create a national standard similar to the "energy guide" now found on all appliances. What might this mean for home builders as a professional group?

3 Coopers & Lybrand Boosts Productivity with Lotus Notes

Coopers & Lybrand Although Lotus Notes did boost productivity at Coopers & Lybrand, it took more than two years to install the system—the largest and most complex system of Notes applications in use—and then train a critical mass of professionals and support personnel to use it.

Part of the long lead time in installing business information systems can be traced to technical issues, such as the need to increase the capacity of the LAN or WAN used to run the software, deciding who controls key databases, and constructing the Notes applications themselves. But technology isn't the only challenge. Managers also need time to rethink their group processes and work habits. Otherwise, users may stumble into such nasty pitfalls as information overload, electronic chitchat, and too many on-line meetings.

Questions for Discussion

1. Explain how Lotus Notes typifies the characteristics of a group support system.

2. Many experts believe that on-line meetings shouldn't replace all face-to-face meetings. Can you suggest some guidelines for deciding whether a meeting can go on-line?

3. How might you use groupware to be sure employees do not lose sight of strategic goals and deadlines?

4 Boeing Takes Off with CAD Software

Boeing Boeing's commitment to CAD software goes back to the mid-1980s, when CAD was limited mainly to use in design work. By 1989, though, Boeing's management decided the company needed to go a step further—to "digital preassembly"—if it was going to make its billion-dollar investment in CAD pay off. In digital preassembly, parts that would once have been put together in an actual-size handmade mockup are assembled, instead, on the computer screen. When Boeing did this, at the end of the third design stage for the Boeing 777 in May 1991, it discovered 2,500 "interferences"—places where parts didn't fit together or fit so closely that they couldn't be reached by maintenance workers. By fixing such glitches on the screen, Boeing expected to minimize changes, errors, and the resulting rework by 5 percent—not bad on a multibillion-dollar project.

Questions for Discussion

1. How is Boeing's CAD-based engineering system similar to other business information systems? How is it different?

2. What would be your primary concern in installing a CAD system like Boeing's?

3. Why is engineering quality especially important to a company like Boeing?

Net Work

Individuals on the Internet can send and receive virtually anything that can be transmitted in digital form. Among the Net's most important capabilities is that of transferring files between computers. *File transfer protocol (FTP)** is an Internet program that provides the capability to download files from a remote computer or server to your computer.

To demonstrate the power of FTP sites, we will explore one particular site. Microsoft Corporation uses FTP to make a wide variety of software available to customers, which the company will transfer for free. Among the resources available at this site is a software library. Here's how you get to the FTP site:

1. Type the location: ftp://ftp.microsoft.com and press <enter>. (The address is entered where you usually see the URL: http:// . . .).

A directory of files, listed in a single column, will appear.

Included in the listing is a subdirectory *Softlib*. Click on *Softlib* and another directory will appear.
2. The new subdirectory contains an entry *softlib.exe*. If you click on the entry, a dialog box will appear on your screen along with a prompt to save a file.
3. If you click on SAVE, the FTP software will download the *softlib.exe* file and store it on your computer's hard drive.

By following these steps, you can transfer any file using the FTP method.

*When FTP sites are available to anyone, without restriction, they are known as *anonymous FTP sites*. To connect to an anonymous FTP, you log in, if prompted to do so, as *anonymous,* and then enter your e-mail address as the password.

GROUP PROJECTS AND APPLICATIONS

Project 1

With a partner or group, visit a company that uses one or more business information systems. Find out what exactly each of these systems does by interviewing various managers and employees using the following framework. Present your findings to the class.

SYSTEM TYPE	QUESTIONS TO ASK
Transaction-processing systems	• In what kinds of transactions does your company routinely engage?
	• What types of action documents does the system generate?
	• What types of exceptions show up in your exception reports?
Management reporting systems	• What types of reports does the system generate?
	• Where do the data in the management reporting system come from?
	• Which managers have access to the system?

SYSTEM TYPE	QUESTIONS TO ASK
Decision support systems	• What types of problems is the DSS designed to help solve?
	• Does the company use an institutional DSS?
	• Can you provide a recent example of a decision that has been made with the help of a DSS?
Group support systems	• How has the GSS helped employees improve their productivity?
	• How often do you use the GSS?
	• How large does the decision need to be for the GSS to be used?
	• Does your company have a decision room?
	• Who serves as facilitator during group meetings?
Executive support systems	• Who has access to the executive support system?
	• What types of information are included in the ESS?
Expert systems	• Who programmed the expert system? Is it updated as new knowledge comes to light?
	• Who uses the system, and for what reasons?
	• How much do workers rely on the expert system, and how much do they rely on their own experiences and hunches?

Project 2

Visit a manufacturing company that uses CAD/CAM technology. (Very often these companies are profiled in the business pages of your local newspaper.)

Spend some time on the shop floor, watching how the machines work.

- Does the company use robots?
- Flexible manufacturing?
- Computer vision systems?
- How expensive was the technology?
- Has it significantly improved productivity and profitability?

Present your findings in a two-page report. If possible, bring in photographs, brochures, or schematics to share with the class.

Project 3

Technology sometimes replaces human workers and this "unemployment" effect is occasionally cited as one of technology's drawbacks.

Conduct a debate on the pros and cons of technology. Two groups of four individuals each should debate the issue. The first group speaks in favor of technology, the second against it. After the first person from each side has spoken, the second questions the opponent's arguments, looking for holes and inconsistencies. The third individual attempts to answer these arguments. The fourth presents a summary of each side's arguments. Finally, the class votes on which team has offered the more compelling argument.

REVIEW QUESTIONS

1. What is an information system?
2. What is a transaction? Why is transaction processing so important to successful business processes? Why do businesses have transaction-processing systems?
3. Describe the five types of output produced during transaction processing.
4. Describe the characteristics of management reporting systems. What types of reports do they produce?

5. When do businesses use decision support systems? What are the three different types of decision support systems?

6. How do group support systems differ from decision support systems? When are group support systems used?

7. How do executive support systems help executives spend their time effectively? What types of information do executive support systems generate?

8. What is an expert system? Why are knowledge bases an essential component of expert systems?

9. Describe the purpose of computer-integrated manufacturing.

10. What is a manufacturing cell?

11. Why are manufacturing automation protocols (MAPs) important to the success of CIM?

12. Describe an MRP II system's capabilities and subsystems.

13. Explain the characteristics of CAD and CAM systems. Are CAD and CAM synonyms for one another?

14. What is concurrent engineering?

15. What are robots used for?

16. What competitive advantages does flexible manufacturing offer a company?

17. How are computer vision systems used to monitor and maintain quality?

DISCUSSION QUESTIONS

1. To help its marketing managers spot trends and identify opportunities for growth, Colgate-Palmolive Co. has installed Muse, a relational database system that consolidates sales data electronically collected from subsidiaries in about 160 countries and issues a summary report. What type of business information system is Muse? Explain your answer. How could Colgate's Muse system be used to support its manufacturing divisions?

2. A survey of IT managers by The Yankee Group, a market research firm, found that managers' primary goal for the late 1990s is the integration of manufacturing, engineering, and business groups. What business and IT trends do you think underlie this goal?

SUGGESTED READINGS

Christian, Flaviu. "Synchronous and Asynchronous Group Communication." *Communications of the ACM 39* (April 1996): 88–97. Part of a set of seven articles devoted to the topic of group communication, including descriptions of prototype applications. The author draws on experience in air traffic control to explore alternate ways to use IT in group support settings.

Clemons, Eric K. "Evaluation of Strategic Investments in Information Technology." *Communications of the ACM 34* (January 1991): 22–36. This article examines how information systems can make an enterprise more flexible, more responsive to customer needs, and more adaptable to rapidly changing conditions in competitive environments. Six lessons based on actual company experiences are presented as a guide to the successful use of information technology in business.

Earl, Michael J. "Experiences in Strategic Information Systems Planning." *MIS Quarterly 17* (March 1993): 1–24. Planning for information technology is a recurring theme in information systems literature. This article explores the IT planning experiences of 27 different firms and incorporates the results of extensive interviews with CEOs, senior user managers, CIOs, and information systems strategic planners.

Hammer, Michael, and James Champy. *Reengineering the Corporation*. New York: HarperBusiness, 1993. A widely read book that examines how businesses can rethink their most fundamental processes and the critical role IT plays in reengineering. The authors provide practical advice on ways to capitalize on IT's capabilities to change business processes and create opportunity.

Neiderman, Fred, Catherine M. Beise, and Peggy M. Beranek. "Issues and Concerns About Computer-Supported Meetings: The Facilitators' Perspective." *MIS Quarterly 20* (March 1996): 1–22. An in-depth study of the way successful facilitators use information technology when conducting electronic meetings involving group support systems.

Schneiderman, Ben, Maryam Alavi, Kent Norman, and Ellen Yu Borkowski. "Windows of Opportunity in Electronic Classrooms." *Communications of the ACM 38* (November 1995): 19–24. An insightful description of group technologies used to enhance the learning and education process on a university campus.

Tapscott, Don, and Art Caston. *Paradigm Shift: The New Promise of Information Technology*. New York: McGraw-Hill, 1993. A forward-looking book that explores how today's information technology can help an enterprise make the transition to higher-quality products and service, creating business success. It explains how to take action right away to achieve the short-term benefits of IT, while positioning the organization for long-term transformation.

Watson, Hugh J., and John Satzinger. "Guidelines for Designing EIS Interfaces: Meeting Executives' Information Needs." *Information Systems Management 11* (Fall 1994): 46–52. The authors present guidelines for using information technology to meet the unique information needs of executives. Corporate examples illustrate the guidelines in practice.

CASE STUDY

IT: The Secret Ingredient at Mrs. Fields

Millions of Americans have sampled a gourmet cookie or two from Mrs. Fields, Inc. Almost as many know the energetic Debbi Fields, either from her television appearances or from her autobiography, *One Smart Cookie,* which details how she and her husband, Randy, built their cookie empire. What most people don't realize, however, is the support role IT has played in the Mrs. Fields story.

The company's commitment to IT goes back to 1978. That's the year Mrs. Fields opened its second store and began thinking about a third, fourth, and fifth. It's also the year that Randy realized the company was at a crossroads. Could it continue to grow without selling franchises? A *franchise* is a license granted to someone (a *franchisee*) to use a brand name and a particular system for selling a company's products or services. It offers a company's founders (the *franchisers*) both advantages and disadvantages.

On the plus side, franchising provides a steady stream of risk-free revenue for the franchiser. In addition to the initial licensing fees (as much as $150,000 for a nationally known franchise), franchisees pay royalties (based on gross sales receipts) and cooperative advertising fees (to share advertising expenses), and assume full responsibility for daily operating expenses. Another plus for the franchiser is the franchise selling system, which provides a framework for delegating the management of far-flung outlets to franchisees, who are responsible for motivating employees and maintaining franchise standards.

Franchisers share some control and sales with their franchisees. However, rigid guidelines are often written into the franchise contract, a factor that can make it difficult to react quickly to changing market conditions. This factor worried Debbi and Randy Fields, who could see that competition was heating up in the gourmet cookie market. Equally worrisome was the risk that they would lose the special touch Debbi had brought to managing Mrs. Fields.

For these reasons, franchising offered both opportunities and challenges for Debbi and Randy. They knew they wanted to keep control of every outlet and preserve the quality of their product, but how? For Randy, a former programmer at IBM, the natural answer was IT.

Even before he began to think about specific hard-

The IT system created by Mrs. Fields, the PaperLess Management System, is now being used at other franchise operations, including Burger King and Fox Photo.

ware and software, Randy drew on his IT background to develop a vision of what he wanted IT to do for Mrs. Fields. The first goal was to control operating expenses. Cookies are a low-price, high-volume product. This means that managers need to keep an eagle eye on costs, to be sure they don't bake too few or too many cookies compared to demand, and to hold to Debbi's dictum that Mrs. Fields will sell no cookie more than two hours old. (Unsold cookies over that age are donated to charity.) A second, related, goal was to monitor individual store performance at headquarters and offer suggestions to franchisees for better decision making. Above all, Randy felt, machines that could handle rote tasks and paperwork should do exactly that so managers would be free to do what only people can do—namely, work with and motivate employees.

Out of this vision grew a *strategic system*—a computer system linking in-store PCs to a computer at headquarters, which merges store data with Debbi's management techniques to help store managers make more efficient decisions. Managers at headquarters can, in turn, monitor store performance. In fact, Debbi often calls store managers personally to congratulate them on meeting or exceeding sales quotas. The strategic system, dubbed the PaperLess Management System, is made up of more than 20 software modules. Here are 5 of the most important of them:

- *Daily Production Planner,* a combination "to-do list" and forecasting system that uses information about past sales, weather, and other conditions to project the amount of ingredients and dough needed on an hourly basis. The Planner monitors actual store traffic throughout the day. If traffic falls below projections, the Planner suggests alternatives, such as cutting back production or dispatching employees to pass out free samples (one of Debbi's favorite marketing techniques).
- *Sales Reporting and Analysis,* which compares the day's total sales to sales projections and other performance norms and suggests corrective actions to eliminate any shortfalls.
- *Labor Scheduler,* which draws on the company's extensive experience in managing minimum wage workers, the labor laws of a particular state, employee work preferences, and store characteristics to devise employee schedules (including work breaks)

that optimize service, minimize overtime, and maximize schedule flexibility.
- *Interviewing,* a half-hour computer-aided interview that provides a standardized, unbiased evaluation of a candidate and judges whether, based on past experience, he or she is likely to be successful at Mrs. Fields.
- *Skills Assessment and Computer-Aided Instruction,* a computer-based system that detects employee weaknesses and provides corrective training, as well as advanced instruction that prepares employees for advancement.

The strategic system was so successful for Mrs. Fields that, in 1988, that company created a separate division, the Fields Software Group (now Park City Group), to sell the PaperLess Management System to other retail operations. Fox Photo and Burger King were among the first customers.

Since then, Mrs. Fields has encountered challenging business conditions. Its meteoric growth (more than 700 stores) slowed when the recession of the early 1990s reduced demand for gourmet cookies and forced the company to adopt a recapitalization plan in 1993. Throughout the ups and downs of Mrs. Fields, however, Randy Fields' vision of IT has earned nothing but praise throughout the business world.

Questions for Discussion

1. Experts have written that computers will play three roles in the Information Age—those of assistant, adviser, and communicator. Describe how computers are used in these three roles at Mrs. Fields.

2. For years many organizations believed that there was a limit to the number of employees a manager could supervise effectively. This belief led to "tall" organizational charts with many levels of middle management. At Mrs. Fields, however, IT lets a headquarters staff of about 130 keep track of more than 5,000 employees at more than 700 stores. Why can Mrs. Fields function with this relatively small number of managers? What do you think this fact means for the organizational chart at Mrs. Fields and other companies in the Information Age?

SATURN

SETS NEW AUTOMOBILE STANDARDS

CAPITALIZING ON INFORMATION TECHNOLOGY AND KNOW-HOW

Information technology itself offers little competitive advantage to a company, but when combined with people's know-how, it can redefine the nature of a company's products and services and the way the company carries out its production activities. Together, information technology and know-how can produce a substantial advantage in the marketplace.

A grand experiment in rethinking American auto manufacturing with IT has captured the world's attention. Spring Hill, Tennessee—a small town just south of the U.S. country music capital of Nashville, and hundreds of miles away from Detroit, the U.S. automotive capital city—is home to the Saturn automobile. A division of General Motors, Saturn has creatively combined its people's capabilities with other resources to deliver a high-quality, low-cost automobile. The company invested over $3.5 billion to create the concept and build the factory from scratch. Now, more than 300,000 automobiles roll off the Spring Hill assembly line annually. This photo essay explores how Saturn is using IT to gain a competitive advantage in the cutthroat world of auto manufacturing and sales.

1 The know-how that comes from teamwork is a key element in Saturn's success. Throughout the eight-year process of developing the Saturn concept, designing the manufacturing facilities, and creating production processes, team meetings produced the most valuable and innovative ideas. Factory employees are organized into teams of 8 to 12 members to share in the making of wide-ranging decisions. These teams decide on and procure manufacturing equipment, hire co-workers, and establish assembly-line processes. They also have budget and supplier authority and can choose to reject parts from suppliers if they are too expensive or fail to meet worker-determined safety standards. More than than 150 teams share ideas and power with top management.

2 The world's best practices are used throughout the Saturn facility. A team of Saturn workers, dubbed the "Group of 99," traveled the world, racking up more than 2 million miles to visit and benchmark some 160 world-class companies. The names of the companies they visited read like a *Who's Who* of business innovation and success: Nissan, Kawasaki, Volvo, Daimler Benz, McDonald's, Hewlett Packard, and many more.

3 Manufacturing sleek-looking automobiles is one of the most challenging production efforts in the world. A typical automobile includes over 10,000 parts: the simplest nuts and bolts; molded sheet metal doors and fenders; complex engine and transmission assemblies; and precision sensors capable of detecting the most subtle changes in carburetion. IT components, in the form of microprocessors, circuit boards, and communication lines, perform the critical role of integrating the thousands of parts to provide the performance level demanded by buyers and technicians alike.

4 The mile-long Spring Hill plant is highly self-reliant, building approximately two-thirds of its parts on site.

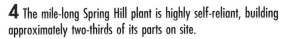

5 Lean production, a characteristic of Saturn manufacturing, was pioneered by Japan's Toyota Motor Corporation. Lean production uses "half the human effort in the factory, half the manufacturing space, half the investment tools, half the engineering hours to develop a new product."* IT is integrated into the Saturn's entire engineering and manufacturing process. Robots and computer networks work side-by-side with people, each taking care of the activities they do best.

*James P. Womack, Daniel T. Jones, and Daniel Ross, *The Machine that Changed the World* (New York: Rawson Associates, 1990).

6 In traditional automobile manufacturing practices, workers are virtually stationary with individual task responsibilities. Saturn employees saw these practices as an obsolete "toil and shuffle" process and rejected them in favor of teams who ride along with the cars they are manufacturing as the vehicles move down the "skillet" (a wooden conveyor). All team members have the responsibility to shut down the line if they spot a problem. Pulling the nearest emergency handle will stop the line instantly. The problem must be corrected before the line can be restarted.

7 Driving the first completed Saturn off the innovative assembly line was exciting for management, union leaders, and employees. Its public unveiling was a celebration for all Saturn workers because it proved the importance of combining the capabilities of people, process, technology, and know-how—all essential ingredients in innovation and successful goal achievement.

Drs. Junkins, Kwiatkowski, Cuervo, and Huang haven't been doctors long enough to know they're supposed to drive one of those overpriced luxury imports.

When Ed, Janet, Beth, and Jim emerged, successfully, from medical school, they felt the gratification of having achieved a lifelong goal, while also confronting a hard reality common to most young doctors—a ton of student loan debt. (You could buy five Saturns with what a new M.D. typically owes.)

In Ed's case, that hard reality also included his 10-year-old car—nobody could tell him how much time it had left. Since a pediatric resident's life is ruled by a beeper (and because you can't tell a sick kid that the tow truck was late), Ed bit the bullet and went looking for a new car.

While he was making the rounds of the car dealerships in town, Ed discovered Saturn. Where, along with the simple, painless way one shops at our showrooms, he liked the rather healthy range of standard features offered and (especially) the fact that the price of a Saturn did not put him into a state of shock.

Since then, mostly on his referral, many of Ed's colleagues have been filling the hospital parking lot with new Saturns. (Apparently, the people who pay most attention to a doctor's advice are other doctors.)

A Different Kind of Company. A Different Kind of Car.

8 Understanding the rules is important. But as Saturn has demonstrated, knowing when to break them and create new ones is critical. Just how confident is the company in the quality of its product? Saturn offers 24-hour roadside assistance should a breakdown occur. And it gives all purchasers a 30-day, 1500-mile money-back guarantee. If purchasers dislike the automobile for any reason, they get their money back.

9 The final—and perhaps most important—reviews for Saturn come from the experts, who praise Saturn for its solid workmanship, handsome interior and exterior design, and responsive handling.

THE I-75 CORRIDOR

At one time, all Japanese cars came from Japan, and people surmised that the quality of Japanese cars resulted from the commitment of Japan's manufacturing workers. Yet today, the leading Japanese automobile companies manufacture more automobiles in the United States than they do in Japan, and they do so with American workers.

The success along the I-75 corridor makes you wonder: Are Japanese automobiles manufactured by U.S. workers really Japanese? Or are they American? Or in this global world of business, is this question even relevant?

Opportunities for Business

Continuous Replenishment Means Never Having to Say You're Sorry

It's no secret that competition in business is reaching new heights. Consumers are more demanding—and often more fickle—than ever before. They want good service when they shop, and expect that the items they seek will be in stock. Stores that run out of stock may lose some customers, perhaps for good. Saying you're sorry in this case may not be enough.

Ever since the age of mass merchandising began, retailing managers and executives have been wrestling with twin dangers: (1) too much inventory on hand, with the risk that they will be stuck with it at season's end, and (2) being out of stock on an item sought by a potential customer. Information technology is enabling innovative retailers to cut way back on these risks.

Any business that makes, delivers, or sells a product is driven by the receipt and fulfillment of an order. Almost since its inception in business, information technology has been used to make companies and their workers more efficient at handling orders. When IT was introduced into order processing in the 1960s and 1970s, IT's role was to transform paper orders into electronic records that could be stored and retrieved as needed. Order-processing time was drastically reduced, even though most companies continued to use the traditional forms: purchase order, purchase order acknowledgment, purchase order change, and shipping notice. Throughout the

1980s and 1990s, businesses gradually began to rely on high-speed computer networks to transmit and receive orders electronically. *Electronic data interchange,* as the underlying technology was called (see Chapter 10), provided the means for manufacturer, distributor, shipper, and seller to agree on the contents of an order and to send and receive electronic versions of the order over communication networks. Both buyer and seller benefited because they no longer had to handle paper orders or key details into their computers. (The traditional order documents continued in use, but they were now electronic.) Once again, the need to handle and fulfill orders was dramatically reduced.

The 1990s are witnessing still another impressive change—to *continuous replenishment.* Rather than sending the manufacturer orders, sellers operating under continuous replenishment instead each day electronically transmit to the manufacturer actual sales

information—exact data on units sold for every item that manufacturer provides. The manufacturer processes this information, received over its communications network, to determine the quantity of each item ordered. Then it assembles the order, arranges for its shipment and delivery, and notifies the seller that a shipment is on the way.

By coupling their information technology capabilities, buyer and sellers have found they both benefit in six important ways:

- **Elimination of order documents.** Purchase orders, change forms, and acknowledgments are all unnecessary. Buyers no longer tell manufacturers to fill orders quickly and accurately, but rather "Never let us be out of stock."
- **Shorter order-processing cycle.** The time from initiation of the order to its receipt, processing, and fulfillment by delivery of merchandise to the buyer is typically reduced by a week or more.
- **Better prices for buyer.** The continuous replenishment *relationship* often means that the manufacturer is guaranteed a steady stream of business from the buyer, which lowers manufacturing costs and, therefore, the prices of the goods sold.
- **Lower costs for buyer and seller.** Regular and direct exchange of information eliminates costly paper documents and the need to have workers accept, review, and monitor individual orders.
- **More predictable demand for manufacturer.** Because information flows continually, there is less need to estimate what will sell. Rather, demand is

monitored daily, with computer applications playing a pivotal role.

- **Dramatic reduction in inventory levels.** Predictability leads to less guessing about the items that will be needed and what must be kept in stock in warehouses.

Much more data and information—sometimes as much as 100 times more—is transmitted between buyers and sellers who are participating in a continuous replenishment relationship than between those who are not. IT is critical to the success of this relationship, for without the ability of each party to exchange details automatically over networks, the entire process would crumble under its own volume and expense.

Questions for Discussion

1. What IT components are essential to carrying out a continuous replenishment strategy?

2. What are the risks of relying on continuous replenishment in business? At what points in the system must managers especially monitor potential problems?

3. Do you think continuous replenishment will become the norm in business? What factors will determine whether it does or does not?

4. What are the implications for brokers and distributors when manufacturer and seller exchange continuous replenishment information directly? If you were a broker or distributor, what would you do?

CHAPTER 14

Issues in Information Technology

CHAPTER OUTLINE

LEARNING OBJECTIVES

When you have completed this chapter, you should be able to

1   Explain how the term *privacy* applies to information technology and why privacy is an important issue in the late 1990s.

2   Describe the importance of ethics in the use of information technology and identify seven ethical issues associated with the use of IT in business.

3   Explain the IT professional's obligation to provide continued access to computers and networks and describe the four methods used to ensure IT reliability.

4   Discuss the legal issues surrounding software piracy and three methods that have been used to prevent software piracy.

5   Distinguish among copyrighted software, public domain software, and shareware.

6   Describe 10 ways to protect a system against intrusion.

7   Identify the three methods of virus detection used by virus detection software.

Are Cookies Dangerous to Your Health?

Surfing the Net can provide a wealth of information—not to mention amusement—about companies, products, and services. Best of all, you can visit company sites all over the world without physically leaving your desk. The Net will take you there. You surely know this.

There is another thing about surfing the Net you may not know: in the course of your travels along the Net's many links, you may pick up a few cookies. And *these* cookies may not be good for you. It depends on the intentions of their creator.

Cookies are bits of data and information that some Web servers store on your computer's hard drive during your visit to a Web site, so that when you return to that site, the server can read the cookies and in the process know how often you visit the site, which pages you look at, and what actions you take.[1]

How do these servers know it's *you* returning? Actually, you provide this information unknowingly. Net browsers have a

section listing your name, Internet address, and organization (it's usually found under the preferences section of the option menu on your browser). As you enter a site, the server software may request your browser to transmit your identity (or prompt you for the information before letting you continue). By combining your identity with information it reads from the cookie stored on your system from a previous visit, the server can tell who you are, when you last visited the site, how often you visit it, and what you like to see there.

Does this bother you? Should it bother you? Is this any different than a charitable organization noting the name and address on your check whenever you make a voluntary donation? (Your visit to a Web site is voluntary, too.)

---

[1] Not all Web sites deposit cookies on your hard drive. Some Web browsers, such as Netscape Communication Corp.'s Navigator version 3.0 and later, display a message alerting you that a cookie is present.

The spread of information technology throughout society is triggering new questions about the rights of individuals and organizations to have and use information. The *Rethinking Business Practices* feature entitled "At CNN, Watermarks Show When Copying Occurs" describes how the international broadcaster Cable News Network (CNN) uses digital markings to safeguard its programs from theft and reuse.

RETHINKING BUSINESS PRACTICES

At CNN, Watermarks Show When Copying Occurs

Thwarting counterfeiting and proving authenticity are centuries-old concerns, most often associated with currency and legal documents. However, these concerns have taken on new importance in the Information Age.

Atlanta-based Cable News Network (CNN) transmits its programs all over the globe, via satellite (see Case Study in Chapter 10). The network also produces special features that are shown only in selected regions of the world. Because of the uniqueness of each program, CNN needs to guard against unauthorized interception, copying, or rebroadcast. Hence, it takes all the usual and customary protection measures for its programs, including copyrighting the content and *scrambling* (i.e., encrypting) the transmittal signal.

Copyrighting and scrambling have been part of the programming process since CNN's origin. But both are merely protections, not guarantees, against unauthorized use. Since capturing, copying, and distributing copies of information, including digital transmissions, are tasks that information technology can do with ease, CNN decided to further protect its property *by making it visible whenever a program is copied.* To that end, it embraced the age-old practice of adding watermarks to its property—albeit in digital form.

Watermarks are faint words or symbols that have traditionally been used with paper stock. They become visible when the document is held up to the light. Since illegal copies of the document do not have the watermarks, watermarks are a useful device for certifying the origin, ownership, and authenticity of a work.

CNN's watermark—inserted throughout the entire length of each program—is a computer-generated digital signal consisting of the letters *CNN* appearing in the lower right-hand corner of the picture. It is embedded among the electronic signals of the program in a manner that does not interfere with the quality of the picture or the sound. Yet it is impossible to remove the watermark without damaging or erasing segments of the program. The watermark is therefore visible proof that a program has been copied.

In the Information Age, the value of intellectual property will continue to increase. So will unauthorized and illegal attempts at copying and duplication. Digital watermarks are an important weapon in the war against theft of intellectual property.

In this chapter, we examine five issues of public and private concern that have become more visible and more important with society's ever-increasing dependence on IT: privacy, ethics, reliability, piracy, and computer crime and system intrusion.

Privacy

You've probably filled out countless forms and applications in your life: applications for college or university admission, magazine subscription cards, credit card applications, job applications ... the list could go on and on. You've also provided information to local, state, and government bodies, including income tax agencies, the motor vehicles registration bureau, the health insurance bureau, and the social insurance coverage bureau.

Where is that information now? Who has control of it? Who has access to it and for what purpose? Is there a chance the data are being used in ways you did not intend or have not authorized? Who knows about your personal history because they have access to data you once provided to someone else?

What Is Privacy?

As used in the field of information technology, **privacy** refers to how personal information is collected, used, and protected. The privacy issue did not arise with the advent of computers; in an earlier time, the taking of photographs caused serious concern about the invasion of personal privacy. However, the enormous capabilities of IT to store and retrieve data have amplified the need to protect personal privacy. Some consumer advocates have suggested that privacy protection will be the leading consumer issue at the end of this century.

Some of the most heated privacy debates have been instigated by advances in telecommunications. Among the more controversial questions are the following:

- Is the use of automated equipment to originate phone calls or to collect caller information an invasion of privacy?
- Should telephone companies restrict the use of caller ID, which tells the recipient of a call the number of the calling party (Figure 4.1)?
- Is the telephone company's ability to know the location of an individual using a cellular phone an invasion of that person's privacy?

privacy
In IT, the term used to refer to how personal information is collected, used, and protected.

FIGURE 14.1
Caller ID
AT&T's Caller ID unit, which displays the telephone number of incoming callers, has been the subject of intense debate. Some units also display the caller's name. Do you have the right to know who is calling your home or business, or does the caller have the right to his or her privacy?

Privacy Legislation

To protect individual privacy, national legislatures have passed several important pieces of legislation. The principal U.S. privacy legislation is summarized in Table 14.1. All of these laws focus on government records and have little influence over individual companies except as they do business with the federal government.

In 1973, the U.S Department of Health, Education, and Welfare (now the Department of Health and Human Services) issued a publication entitled *A Code of Fair Information Practices* that set forth rules designed to protect personal privacy within government agencies. The code's guidelines state:

1. There must be no personal-data record-keeping system whose very existence is a secret.
2. There must be a way for people to access the information about them in a record and find out how that information is used.
3. There must be a way for people to prevent information about themselves obtained for one purpose from being used or made available for other purposes without their consent.

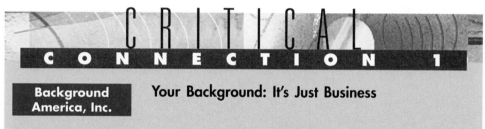

CONNECTION 1

| Background America, Inc. | Your Background: It's Just Business |

Background America, Inc., a professional investigation firm in Nashville, Tennessee, specializes in searching public records to locate information about people. If you apply for a job, your prospective employer may contact Background America to run a check on you. All the firm needs to do so is a check, usually for well under $100, and your signature.

Here's a sampling of the information Background America can assemble on you in that preemployment check:

Address verification
Credit check
Civil litigation, federal
Civil litigation, state
Driving record
Military record (if any)
National wants and warrants
Real property transactions
Social Security number verification

All these details are available to anyone who knows how to search public records.

Do you know what information Background America could find out about you during a preemployment search of these records?

TABLE 14.1 *Major U.S. Privacy Legislation*

LEGISLATION	DESCRIPTION
Fair Credit Reporting Act (1970)	Allows individuals access to their credit records, to receive printed reports of the contents free of charge, and to challenge the contents in the event of errors.
Freedom of Information Act (1970)	Allows citizens access to data that have been gathered about them by federal agencies.
Privacy Act of 1974	Allows people to determine what information is collected about them, to prevent records obtained for one purpose from being used for another purpose, to have access to—and copies made of—information about them, to correct or amend records, and to file civil suits for damages that occur through willful or intentional actions by individuals or organizations collecting the information.
Electronic Communications Privacy Act of 1986	Protects the privacy of electronic messages sent through public networks.

4. There must be a way for people to correct or amend a record of information about them.

5. Any organization creating, maintaining, using, or disseminating records of identifiable personal data must ensure their reliability and must take reasonable precautions to prevent misuse of the data.

The *Code of Fair Information Practices* served as the basis of the Privacy Act of 1974, the principal law governing privacy protection within the federal government.

Ethics

Most records stored by companies and other nongovernment organizations are not covered by existing privacy laws. Thus, a company's policy on privacy matters depends primarily on its ethical policies.

Ethics are the standards of conduct and moral behavior that people are expected to follow. *Personal ethics* pertain to people's day-to-day activities in private life; *business ethics* pertain to their actions in the world of business, including how they deal with colleagues, customers, and anyone else with whom their firm interacts. Some have argued that it is impossible to draw a boundary line between personal ethics and business ethics because one's personal ethics should always influence, and in the end outweigh, one's business ethics.

There is an important distinction between ethical behavior and legal behavior. Ethical behavior refers to *expected* actions, while legal behavior refers to *required* actions. An action may be legal but unethical, or ethical but illegal.

Companies today are challenged by many questions of ethics arising from the widespread use of information technology. These issues are not limited to IT professionals, but involve everyone in the company who provides data to, or uses information from, the company's IT systems.

ethics
The standards of conduct and moral behavior that people are expected to follow.

Ethics and IT Usage in Business

Among the most urgent ethical issues that business must confront today are the following:

- **Electronic mail privacy.** Do the contents of an e-mail system operated by a company, and intended for use by its employees, belong to the company? May the company do with those contents whatever it deems appropriate?
- **Software licenses.** What are the ethical requirements for acquiring and monitoring conformance to *software licenses,* which allow a company to use programs developed by another company? Are the ethical requirements here different from the legal requirements?
- **Software copyrights.** What are a company's obligations for determining who owns a software copyright? When is the company's obligation for enforcing software copyrights different from an individual's obligation to abide by a software copyright?
- **Hardware access.** Under what circumstances is access to a company's computer and communications hardware ethical? When is it unethical?
- **Intellectual property ownership.** When an information system contains ideas, writings, expressions, and other items considered to be the intellectual property of an individual, what obligations does the operator of the system have to safeguard the property? What *is* intellectual property and how is its ownership determined?
- **File access.** Under what circumstances is use of a file or database unethical?
- **Data ownership.** Who owns the data in a company's information system? The company, because it invested its resources to capture and store the data, or the individual or company described by the data?

Some IT directors and professionals dissent from the view that ethics in information technology is a major problem. Aside from questions related to computer software—and these are actually *legal* issues—most cannot recall more than a handful of instances when ethical problems have surfaced. Some researchers paint a contrasting picture, one that emphasizes the *threat* of ethics violations. They point out, for example that company business codes seldom address computing and communications issues. They also suggest that IT professionals generally do not take an active enough role in defining ethics as a critical concern in the Information Age, and that university and college faculty members need to do more to create an awareness in students that users of computer and communication systems have certain ethical responsibilities.

Both users and developers of information technology tend to focus primarily on IT's capabilities for assisting them in a particular business situation. They are so caught up in the power of IT that their first inclination is to ask: "Can IT help solve this problem?" or "Can IT do this?" And if the capabilities are affirmed, their position is implicitly, "If the system can do it and the payoff is right, then let's do it."

From an ethical standpoint, a more appropriate question to ask before developing an IT system is "*Should* the system do this?" If the answer is yes, then the system's capabilities can be determined. When ethics come first, implementing IT takes on a completely different perspective. ∎

An Ethics Challenge

To get an idea of the ethical challenges managers and employees face, consider how you would answer these 10 questions:

1. Is it right or wrong for managers to access the files or databases of people in their department or on their project team?
2. If data and information are stolen or illegally copied from a company's computer systems, should the IT director be held legally responsible for the loss?
3. If data and information are stolen or illegally copied by an outsider using the company's communications network, should the IT director be legally responsible for any resulting damage to the network?
4. If a company has a policy stating that its e-mail system is to be used only for company activities, does that company have the right to monitor its employees' e-mail messages?
5. Does a company have an obligation to inform its employees that their e-mail could be monitored?
6. Should IT directors be held accountable for software licensing violations by members of their department or development teams? If the copyright holder of a program decides to press charges for damages, including lost revenue, resulting from illegal copying of the software, should the IT director be liable for a fine or prison time if a court finds in favor of the software owner?
7. If an employee copies company software for personal use at home, should the company have the right to terminate the employee? If an employee copies company software for use at home to work on company business, but without receiving formal permission to do so, should that employee be terminated?
8. If an individual uses an illegal copy of copyrighted software without realizing either that it is an unauthorized copy or that it is copyrighted, should that individual be subject to legal action? Are people who discover that they have used an illegal copy ethically bound to report their infringement to the copyright owner?
9. Should a company be obligated to notify its employees in advance when a check will be made to see what software is loaded on their system and whether the company owns the software?
10. Do personal ethics take precedence over business ethics? If someone decides that a company's ethical practices are wrong based on his or her personal ethical standards and is fired for failing to follow company guidelines, should that person be compensated for the loss of his or her job?

This very short list could easily be expanded to include hundreds of similar questions. Users of information technology confront these kinds of questions daily, and "wrong" answers can have major consequences, as Epson America found out.

A QUESTION OF ETHICS AT EPSON AMERICA.   Until 1991, Alana Shoars (Figure 14.2) was e-mail administrator at Epson America, a well-known manufacturer of computer hardware in Torrance, California. In March 1991, Shoars filed suit against Epson, seeking $1 million in damages for wrongful termination, defamation, and invasion of privacy.[2] Then, in July 1991, Shoars filed a class-action suit against

---

[2]"Executive Report: IS Ethics," *Computerworld*, October 14, 1991, p. 84.

FIGURE 14.2
Alana Shoars: Questioning the Rules

Shoars' 1992 suit against Epson America alleged that she was fired for challenging the company's practice of monitoring and printing its employees' e-mail messages. The suit posed both legal and ethical questions: Does a company have the right to monitor its employees' computer transactions?

Epson, seeking $75 million for the 700 company employees and approximately 1,800 outsiders whose e-mail had allegedly been monitored by Epson.

In both suits, Shoars contended that she was fired by Epson because she challenged the company's practice of monitoring and printing its employees' e-mail messages. According to news reports, the company took the position "This is our computer—we'll monitor if we want to." In 1995, the suits were settled out of court (details of the settlement were not publicly disclosed), but this is an important issue that will not go away for some time to come.

DEVELOPING A CODE OF ETHICS.   Because it is impossible to list all the possible questions that could arise in a business situation, many companies have created a general *code of ethics* to guide the behavior of their employees. Among the IT professional groups that have established codes of ethics are the New York–based Association for Computing Machinery, part of whose code of ethics is reprinted in Figure 14.3, and the Association of the Institute for Certification of Computer Professionals in Des Plaines, Illinois.

Donn B. Parker, senior management consultant at SRI International in Menlo Park, California, and a leading expert on computer ethics, encourages IT professionals and users to adhere to the following ethical guidelines:

- **Informed consent.** When in doubt about the ethics of a particular action, inform those whom your action will affect of your intentions and obtain their consent before proceeding.
- **The "higher ethic."** Take the action that achieves the greater good.
- **Most restrictive action.** Use as your basis for deciding whether to take action (or avoid taking action) the assumption that the most severe damage that could happen will happen.
- **Kantian universality rule.** If an action (or failure to act) is not right for everyone to commit, then it is not right for anyone to commit.
- **Descartes' "change in" rule.** A sufficient change in degree produces a change in kind. Although many small losses may be acceptable individually, when added together, they may result in an unacceptable total loss.
- **The owner's conservative rule.** Assume that others will treat your assets as in the public domain. Explicitly declare that the products of your efforts and your property are either private or public in reasonably visible ways.
- **The user's conservative rule.** Assume that any tangible or intangible item belongs to somebody else unless an explicit declaration or convention identifies it as in the public domain or authorized for your use.

Code of Ethics and Professional Conduct
Association for Computing Machinery

General Moral Imperatives:
- Contribute to society and human well-being.
- Avoid harm to others.
- Be honest and trustworthy.
- Be fair and take action not to discriminate.
- Honor property rights including copyrights and patents.
- Give proper credit for intellectual property.
- Respect the privacy of others.
- Honor confidentiality.

More Specific Professional Responsibilities:
- Strive to achieve the highest quality, effectiveness, and dignity in both the process and products of professional work.
- Acquire and maintain professional competence.
- Know and respect existing laws pertaining to professional work.
- Accept and provide appropriate professional review.
- Give comprehensive and thorough evaluations of computer systems and their impacts, including analysis of *possible* risks.
- Honor contracts, agreements, and assigned responsibilities.
- Improve public understanding of computing and its consequences.
- Access computing and communication resources only when authorized to do so.

Organizational Leadership Imperatives:
- Articulate social responsibilities of members of an organizational unit and encourage full acceptance of those responsibilities.
- Manage personnel and resources to design and build information systems that enhance the quality of working life.
- Acknowledge and support proper and authorized uses of an organization's computing and communications resources.
- Ensure that users and those who will be affected by a system have their needs clearly articulated during the assessment and design of requirements. Later the system must be validated to meet requirements.
- Articulate and support policies that protect the dignity of users and others affected by a computing system.
- Create opportunities for members of the organization to learn the principles and limitations of computer systems.

SOURCE: Courtesy Association for Computing Machinery, Inc.

FIGURE 14.3

Excerpt from the Association for Computing Machinery's Code of Ethics

Leaders in many companies and professional associations agree that a code of ethics is necessary for every business, but they often disagree that a special code of ethics *for information technology* is needed. These people are not speaking against ethics in IT. Rather, they are pointing out that IT ethics must be part of the company's overall code of ethics because IT is so pervasive today that it is a major part of most companies' practices.

In recent years, the concept of social responsibility has been advanced as a counterpart to ethics. A company that exercises **social responsibility** attempts to balance its commitments—not only to its investors, but also to its employees, its customers, other businesses, and the community or communities in which it operates. McDonald's for example, established Ronald McDonald houses several years ago to provide lodging for families of sick children hospitalized away from their home areas. Sears and General Electric support artists and performers.

social responsibility
The concept that businesses need to balance their commitments to investors, employees, customers, other businesses, and the communities in which they operate.

One area of social responsibility that has received a great deal of attention lately is responsibility toward the environment. Do companies have a social obligation to help conserve the environment by purchasing computer equipment that uses less energy? Such equipment is now available, as the *Information Technology in Practice* feature entitled "EPA Spurs the Push for Green PCs" discusses.

Reliability

As companies become dependent on IT, they also become dependent on the continued availability of their computers and communications systems. With that dependence comes the expectation that the service provider—whether an in-house IT professional or a hired IT service—will take the necessary precautions to ensure that service cannot be interrupted. **Reliability** is the assurance the system will do what it should when it should.

There are currently no laws explicitly governing service reliability. However, because of the importance of IT to business operations, society generally treats service loss as a breach of trust.

Ensuring IT Service Reliability

Service reliability can be addressed at four levels: fault-tolerant computers, uninterruptable power supply systems, disaster recovery plans, and off-site backup facilities.

The most reliable system is one that never fails. **Fault-tolerant computers** are designed with duplicate components so that if one component fails (a fault), an identical component will take over—usually without the user's even realizing a fault has occurred. Many computers are not fault-tolerant, nor do they need to be. However, when applications must run 24 hours a day nonstop, the extra cost of a fault-tolerant computer is easily justified. Many bank automated teller systems and air control systems rely on fault-tolerant computers.

Because electrical power disruptions so often underlie a loss of computing capability, one of the most effective safeguards is the installation of **uninterruptable power supply (UPS) systems.** UPS systems ensure the continued flow of electricity, produced by private generators or from storage batteries, when the primary source fails. They are the second level of protection against computer failure. UPS systems have helped countless data centers ride out the many hurricanes that have struck the East Coast of the United States recently.

The third level of protection is the development of a disaster recovery plan. Organizations should always assume that service will be lost at some point. When this occurs, the objective is to minimize the loss. **Disaster recovery plans** are procedures for restoring data lost when a system stops functioning. For computer networks, they include procedures for bypassing a failed segment of a network by using other communications lines.

The fourth level of protection against computer failure is the creation of an **off-site backup facility.** This is a computer center, often owned by the company, away from the company's main facility (Figure 14.4). **Hot sites** are fully equipped computer centers to which a company takes its backup copies of data and software to resume processing. **Cold sites** are facilities outfitted with electrical power and environmental controls (heating and air-conditioning), ready for the company to install a computer system (Figure 14.5). Often several different

Margin glossary

reliability
The assurance that computers and communications systems will do what they should when they should.

fault-tolerant computer
A computer designed with duplicate components to ensure reliability.

uninterruptable power supply (UPS) system
A system that ensures the continued flow of electricity when the primary source of power fails.

disaster recovery plan
A procedure for restoring data lost when a system stops functioning.

off-site backup facility
A backup computer center located away from a company's main facility.

hot site
A fully equipped backup computer center to which a company can take its backup copies of data and software and resume processing.

cold site
A backup facility outfitted with electrical power and environmental controls so that it is ready for a company to install a computer system.

INFORMATION TECHNOLOGY IN PRACTICE

EPA Spurs the Push for Green PCs

All around the world, millions of PCs glow and whirr unattended while their users answer the phone, go to meetings, or even leave the office for the day. Unused but on-power PCs are costing U.S. consumers about $2 million a year, according to estimates from the U.S. Environmental Protection Agency. And then there are the indirect costs. To meet the electrical needs of PCs, power plants generate as much air pollution as 5 million cars do. If this trend continues, PC use (and nonuse) could add another 5 percent to the nation's demand for commercial electricity by the end of the decade.

To conserve some of this energy, the EPA has created the Energy Star program. This program, announced at a White House ceremony in June 1993, allows manufacturers to display a special Energy Star logo on PCs, monitors, or printers that fall into a "sleep" mode when not in use. To qualify, the machine's sleep mode has to use 30 watts of power or less; that's a 60 percent drop from what standard machines use today (70 to 200 watts every moment they are on). To encourage participation, the EPA launched a major ad campaign in popular consumer magazines. To set an example, during his first year in office President Clinton issued an executive order mandating that the U.S. government—the world's largest buyer of computer equipment—purchase only Energy Star equipment from that year on.

By August 1993, 70 major computer manufacturers had signed up to take part in the program. For most, it was a fairly easy transition: they simply adapted techniques designed to conserve the battery life of portable computers. These techniques include power management software, energy-conserving computer chips, energy-efficient power supplies, and screen-blanking software. (Ironically, "screen savers" that display flying toasters or Star Trek trivia do save

screens, but use 20 percent more energy than blank screens.)

Both the EPA and manufacturers are hoping the energy-conserving machines will appeal to consumers. Even if they aren't particularly concerned about the environment, they reason, users should like the idea of lower electric bills. IBM, for example, estimates that some of its new models can be operated for about $15 a year, versus the $150 to $250 electric bill required to run a conventional PC. The "green machines" should also appeal to computer buyers in Europe and Japan, where energy costs are high and climbing every year.

FIGURE 14.4
Disaster Recovery Facility
Most disaster recovery facilities are created to ensure an uninterrupted flow of electricity in case of emergency. The buildings are usually nondescript from the outside: what's inside (see Figure 14.5) is much more important. The 151,000-square-foot facility shown here houses multiple hot and cold sites.

FIGURE 14.5
Hot and Cold Sites
Given the need for computer reliability and the possibility of natural disasters, several companies have gone into the business of providing off-site backup facilities for companies that do not want to build their own. One of the most successful of these companies is Comdisco, whose rentable hot and cold sites are pictured here.

a) Hot sites are fully equipped computer centers to which companies take backup copies of their data and software to resume processing.

b) Cold sites are outfitted only with electrical power and environmental controls, but are ready for companies to install computer systems at a moment's notice.

companies share hot and cold sites, each assuming there is little likelihood that they will ever need to use the site at the same time.

A common mistake in reliability planning is to focus on internal concerns and overlook external causes. Because companies rely heavily on computer networks and outside software suppliers, the possibility of system failure caused by external sources must be considered. AT&T and Revlon found this out the hard way.

SYSTEM FAILURE AT AT&T. In 1991, AT&T suddenly and without warning encountered a series of telephone system breakdowns around the United States. During a two-week period, telephone service to approximately 10 million customers was disrupted. This caused serious problems for businesses that depend on telephone service for their daily transactions.

AT&T sprang into action as soon as it detected trouble, assigning more than 200 technicians and engineers to work around the clock to identify and remedy the mysterious bugs causing the loss of service. It turned out that the problem was not caused by AT&T but rather by a small supplier to the communications giant. This company's products had been incorporated into the AT&T network to control switching in the system at enough places around the United States so that when they began failing, the impact was felt nationwide. Neither AT&T nor its customers had ever experienced or planned for a failure of this type. AT&T's reputation for reliability was damaged in the short run, but its awareness of the impact of failure reached an all-time high.

DISRUPTION AT REVLON.   Ethical concerns and IT reliability issues come together quite often. They did so disastrously for Revlon, the internationally known maker of cosmetics headquartered in New York, several years ago.

Revlon signed a contract with software supplier Logisticon of Santa Clara, California, to use Logisticon's inventory management software. Then Revlon complained that the software was not performing according to expectations and informed Logisticon that it would withhold a $180,000 scheduled payment for one portion of the contract and intended to cancel outright the other portion of the contract, valued at $600,000.

Logisticon allegedly decided to "repossess" the software because Revlon had not made the scheduled payments. To do so, it gained access to Revlon's computers over the telephone and activated commands that disabled the software. Revlon charged Logisticon with activating viruses (discussed in detail later in this chapter) that had been planted in the software, making the data incomprehensible. (Logisticon acknowledged disabling the software, but denied using viruses or destroying Revlon's data.)

The disruption to Revlon's computers affected two main distribution centers in Phoenix, Arizona, and Edison, New Jersey, halting approximately $20 million in scheduled product deliveries and idling several hundred workers. Revlon termed Logisticon's actions "commercial terrorism."[3]

Software Piracy

Ethical issues apply as much to the use of software as they do to the characteristics of software that companies deliver. Like data and information, software is a valuable component of a business system: it is the element that oversees processing and transforms data into a useful form. Since commercial software is often perceived as expensive, it is often pirated.

Piracy is the making of illegal copies of copyrighted information. **Software piracy** is the making of illegal copies of software. Software piracy is one of the most serious issues in IT today because it is so widespread that it is responsible for an enormous loss of revenue to software originators. Manufacturers and software industry groups estimate that as many as seven illegal copies are made for every legal copy of software sold by retailers.

software piracy
The making of illegal copies of software.

Protecting Against Software Piracy

Although no software protection method is foolproof, three methods are widely used in the IT industry to avoid piracy: copyright protection, copy protection, and site licensing.

SOFTWARE COPYRIGHT PROTECTION.   A **copyright** protects original works against unauthorized use, including duplication, provided the owner visibly displays a notice of copyright on the product. The copyright notice is similar across many countries, although not all countries acknowledge the right of copyrighted ownership. Under the Universal Copyright Convention adopted by most nations, the copyright notice consists of three elements:

copyright
Legal protection of original works against unauthorized use, including duplication.

---

[3]"Revlon Sues Supplier over Software Disabling," *The New York Times*, October 25, 1990, pp. C1 and C4.

1. The symbol © (in the United States, the additional word Copyright or the abbreviation Copr. can also be used).
2. The year of first publication of the work.
3. The name of the copyright owner.

Copyright protection has been used for many years to protect books, magazines, music, and other original works (Figure 14.6). Today, it also applies to computer software, databases, RAM, and ROM, and is the principal legal protection against duplication or outright theft of original ideas embodied in computer programs. Well-known programs such as Lotus 1-2-3, Word for Windows, WordPerfect, Access, Paradox, and CC:Mail are copyrighted and therefore protected by law from unauthorized copying or use.[4]

FIGURE 14.6
Copyright Page

Copyright notices range in length from a single symbol, date, and name to an entire page of information. Copyright pages in books often contain information in addition to the copyright line. Included on the page shown here are (top to bottom): editorial staff credits, copyright information, printing information, the publication's international standard book number (ISBN), and international divisions of the publishing company.

Acquisition Editor: Stephanie Johnson
Editor-in-Chief: Natalie Anderson
Development Editor: Elisa Adams
Production Editor: Dee Josephson
Marketing Manager: Tamara Wederbrand
Supplements Editor: Lisamarie Brassini
Managing Editor: Dee Josephson
Design Director: Pat Smythe
Manufacturing Supervisor: Arnold Vila
Manufacturing Manager: Vincent Scelta
Cover & Interior Designer: Lorraine Castellano
Cover Illustration: Eric Kittelberger/Stock Illustration Source, Inc.
Photo Research: Melinda Alexander
Editorial Assistant: Dawn-Marie Reisner
Composition & Prepress: GTS Graphics, Inc.

 © 1998 by Prentice-Hall, Inc.
A Simon & Schuster Company
Upper Saddle River, NJ 07458

All rights reserved. No part of this book may be reproduced, in any form by any means, without permission in writing from the publisher.

This edition may be sold only in those countries to which it is consigned by Prentice-Hall International. It is not to be re-exported and it is not for sale in the U.S.A., Mexico, or Canada.

ISBN 0-13-906454-0

Prentice-Hall International (UK) Limited, *London*
Prentice-Hall of Australia Pty. Limited, *Sydney*
Prentice-Hall Canada, Inc., *Toronto*
Prentice-Hall Hispanoamericana, S.A., *Mexico*
Prentice-Hall of India Private Limited, *New Delhi*
Prentice-Hall of Japan, Inc., *Tokyo*
Simon & Schuster Asia Pte, Ltd., *Singapore*
Editora Prentice-Hall do Brasil, Ltda., *Rio de Janiero*
Prentice-Hall, Upper Saddle River, New Jersey

Printed in the United States of America
10 9 8 7 6 5 4 3 2 1

---

[4]Copyright owners can choose to allow others to use their copyrighted work. In such cases, a credit line indicating that use is authorized is attached to each copy of the work. Copyright owners may require the payment of a royalty for use of the work.

When Microsoft Corp. released new versions of its Windows and Windows 95 operating systems, it worked with law enforcement officials to seize pirated versions of the software. Even before the program was widely distributed, law enforcement officials had seized tens of thousands of illegally packaged copies. Diskettes, documentation, and the packaging itself were duplicated and wrapped in cellophane to look like the real thing.

COPY PROTECTION.   Software developers and vendors have tried many schemes to make software copying impossible. **Copy protection** schemes involve hardware or software features that defeat attempts to copy a program or make the copied software unreliable.

No copy protection scheme developed so far has proven foolproof. Even worse, copy protection has hindered the copying of software by individuals who have legally purchased a program and want to make a backup copy to protect against damage to the original copy. Making a backup copy is usually in most software license agreements. To avoid antagonizing users who have legally purchased the software, most software vendors have dropped attempts at copy protection. However, they still vigorously pursue legal action against software pirates under the copyright laws.

copy protection
A software protection scheme that defeats attempts to copy a program or makes the copied software unreliable.

SOFTWARE SITE LICENSING.   To assist large-volume users of programs and at the same time avoid software piracy, many software developers offer **site licenses.** Under these agreements, the purchaser (typically a company, university, or government agency) pays a fee to the manufacturer to make a specified number of copies of a particular program (and in some cases, its documentation). In turn, the buyer agrees to keep an accurate record of who makes the copies and the computer or network on which they are installed.

Both parties benefit from site licenses. Purchasers gain the convenience of making legal copies when necessary, and for an average cost that is substantially (usually more than 50 percent) lower than the retail cost of the software. Sellers gain large adoptions of their software programs while discouraging pirated use of their software within an organization.

site license
An agreement under which a software purchaser pays a fee to the manufacturer to make a specified number of copies of a particular program.

Public Domain Software

Not all software is copyrighted. Noncopyrighted software that can be used by the general public is known as **public domain software.** The individuals or companies who wrote, and therefore own, the software have chosen to make their programs available to anyone who wants to use them.

Shareware combines the best features of copyrighted software and public domain software. Like public domain software, shareware is given away and freely distributed. However, the developers retain ownership and ask users to register with them and to pay a nominal fee for using the program. Registering allows users to receive notices of updates to the programs, and the nominal fee supports the continued development of the software.

Sometimes a company or individual will offer software for a very small fee, often just $1. This small fee encourages people to use the software freely while simultaneously publicizing the issuer's claim of ownership. When you pay the $1, you are acknowledging that the issuer owns the software.

public domain software
Any noncopyrighted software that can be used by the general public.

shareware
Software that is given away and freely distributed. The developer retains ownership, asks users to register with the owner, and requests a nominal fee for using the program.

Software Publishing Assoc.

Software Police Out to Prove That Piracy Doesn't Pay

When you hear the term *police raid,* you probably think of a crackdown on illegal gambling or drugs. But some companies now associate the term with a crackdown on software piracy, thanks to the efforts of the Software Publishers Association (SPA). Since its founding in 1984, this Washington, D.C.–based group has been trying to stamp out illegal "softlifting," which costs its members an estimated $1 billion a year.

In most cases, the "software police" are tipped off when a current or ex-employee makes a call to the SPA's antipiracy hotline to report an instance of softlifting at a company. (The hotline gets about 20 to 30 such calls a day.) If the operator screening the call decides the tip is worth following up on, the SPA will try to verify the information through other sources. For example, it may ask the software publisher to count the number of registration records filed by the company named in the call. If the number falls well below the number of copies of the software in use at that company according to the tipster, the SPA will investigate further.

The next step is a letter to the suspect company, asking it to cooperate in a voluntary audit of its software. Ninety-five percent of the companies contacted cooperate fully, the SPA reports. But if the company does refuse to cooperate or simply ignores the letter, the SPA will seek legal assistance. Soon after, the company may get a surprise visit from the SPA, backed up by a federal marshal with a search warrant. Approximately 100 companies have been "raided" so far.

Computer Crime and System Intrusion

computer crime
The unauthorized use of a computer system or theft of system resources for personal use.

intrusion
Forced and unauthorized entry into a system.

The term **computer crime** encompasses any unauthorized use of a computer system (including software piracy) or theft of system resources for personal use (including computer processing time and network access time). It is also a crime to take any actions intended to alter data and programs or to damage or destroy data, software, or equipment. Table 14.2 lists the most common types of computer crime. All these crimes are committed through **intrusion,** the forced and unauthorized entry into a system. Throughout this book we have discussed the importance of putting data and physical security measures in place because these actions discourage intrusion.

Computer crime through intrusion can occur in one of two ways: either hackers break into a system, or software viruses inserted into a system destroy programs and data.

TABLE 14.2 *Types of Computer Crime*

Data diddling	Changing data and information before they enter a system.
Data leakage	Erasing or removing databases and files from a system without indicating that they were removed or leaving any trace they ever existed.
Eavesdropping	Using electronic surveillance devices to "listen in" on electronic transmissions or to capture contents of transmission.
Logic bomb	A program designed to execute when certain conditions occur. Designed to sabotage system data, programs, or processing (see also Time bomb).
Piggybacking	Gaining access to a system or process by using the passwords or access codes of an authorized system user. Alternatively, taking over a terminal or workstation in use by an authorized user, perhaps while he or she has stepped away from the system momentarily.
Salami (data) slicing	Developing or modifying software to capture small amounts ("slices") of money in a transaction and redirecting them to a hidden account. The amounts are so small they go unnoticed, but can accumulate to a substantial sum in large-volume transaction-processing systems.
Scavenging	Searching trash cans—either figuratively, through a computer system icon, or literally, in a computer center—to find discarded data and information or program details. Used to obtain confidential information or to learn the structure of a program.
Time bomb	A program designed to execute on a specific date. The program monitors the computer's internal clock/calendar. When the preset date arrives, the program comes to life, causing its damage.
Trapdoor	An illicit and unknown point of entry into a program or network that can be used to gain access to the system.
Trojan horse	A program that appears to do one thing, but actually does something very different. Named after the Trojan horse of ancient Greek lore because the program masquerades as a harmless application and then does its damage after it is loaded onto a disk or into computer memory.
Wiretapping	Using any device to capture data transmission electronically or to "listen" in on network conversations, especially those transmitted through wireless methods or over copper wire.
Zapping	Damaging or erasing data and information or programs. Usually possible because the criminal is able to bypass security systems.

Hackers

A **hacker** is a person who gains access to a system illegally. Hackers usually gain access to a system through a network, but sometimes they physically enter a computer or network facility.

Some people like to call themselves "hackers," referring not to their ability to break into computers and networks, but rather to their technical skill at computer programming and at making a system perform in innovative and productive ways. Criminal hackers who break into systems also have good technical skills, but have chosen to apply them in undesirable (often illegal) ways. When "computer whizzes" turn their attention to good deeds, the results can be in the best interests of society, as the *Information Technology in Practice* feature entitled "Working Miracles with 'Outdated' Computers" illustrates. When they decide to do damage, the results can be devastating.

hacker
A person who gains access to a system illegally.

INFORMATION TECHNOLOGY IN PRACTICE

Working Miracles with "Outdated" Computers

The U.S. Environmental Protection Agency estimates that as many as 10 million outdated computers hit the dumpsters every year. In a world of ever more sophisticated technology, it's been easy to overlook the potential uses of these older computers and their peripherals. But now the National Cristina Foundation is giving some of these "old" machines a new life and, in the process, offering hope and new opportunities to the disabled and the disadvantaged.

Bruce McMahan with his daughter, Cristina, who has cerebral palsy. The presence of computers in the classroom made such a difference for Cristina and her classmates that McMahan and Cristina's teacher, Yvette Marrin, decided they had to find a way to get similar technology to others in need.

number (1-800-274-7846), and it has non-profit status, which means all donations are tax deductible. Donations have ranged from a single machine to the $104,000 worth of equipment pledged by Packard Bell. Metropolitan Life donated 250 laptops when it bought new machines for its field agents. By 1993, the Cristina Foundation had "recycled" more than 100,000 used computers.

The idea for the foundation dates back to the 1980s when Bruce McMahan donated a used PC to a special education class attended by his daughter, Cristina. Dr. Yvette Marrin, the class's teacher, recalls, "When Bruce and I saw the miracles that happened in that class as people who couldn't hold a pencil were able to communicate for the first time in years, thanks to a couple of hundred dollars' worth of machine, we decided we had to share this miracle with others."

Today, Marrin is president of the Connecticut–based foundation, which actively campaigns for donations of used equipment that can be redirected to qualified schools and social service agencies. To make donating easy, the foundation maintains a toll-free

Like many charitable organizations, the Cristina Foundation needs to maintain a high profile in order to flourish. An energetic presence, Dr. Marrin makes sure the foundation has a booth at the major computer shows, where she and other "Cristinas" pass out pamphlets, answer questions, and take pledges. (People who visit the foundation's booth at the Las Vegas Comdex show might even meet Cristina McMahan, who now lives in California.)

Donations come in every day, but the Cristinas are always looking for more equipment and more volunteers. After all, there are still millions of old computers languishing in storerooms and clogging the nation's landfills. If you know of any—or if you'd like to volunteer at the foundation—why not give the National Cristina Foundation a call?

The number of hackers around the world has grown substantially over the past decade, primarily because of greater access to powerful desktop computers in schools, in offices, and at home. More computers, coupled with easily accessible network and communications capabilities, means more hackers of all ages. Consider these representative examples of hacking:[5]

- The United Press International (UPI) wire service reported that two Staten Island, New York, youths were arrested on charges of invading and disrupting the computerized voice mail system of a Massachusetts company. Their activities cost the firm $2.4 million. The youths used their home computer to dial into the system and obtain the system password. They then changed the passwords for various units in the system, resulting in the loss of important messages and numerous business transactions. The youths allegedly attacked the Massachusetts firm because it had failed to send them a poster that was supposed to accompany a paid subscription for a computer-game magazine published by the company.
- Australia's Compass Airline reported that its reservation system was being jammed. On one day alone, the new airline company received more than 25,000 calls. A computer had been used to dial the airline's reservation number repeatedly, then abort the call when the line was answered. The airline's CEO emphasized that Compass did not believe the culprit was a rival airline.
- *The Independent,* a London newspaper, reported that at least five British banks were blackmailed by a group of hackers who had broken into the banks' central computer over a six-month period. This was the largest and most sophisticated breach of computer security ever experienced by British banks. The electronic break-ins, with their implicit threats of stealing information or sabotaging the systems by planting false data or damaging the banks' complex information systems, could have caused chaos for the banks. The hackers demanded substantial sums of money in return for showing the banks how their systems were penetrated.

The increased frequency of hacking, coupled with the newness of computer crime as an issue of law, has forced governments to draw up special legislation. In 1984, the U.S. Congress passed the Computer Fraud and Abuse Act. This federal legislation, which is supplemented by state statutes, was a first step in positioning the judicial system to deal with the problem. Workshops and seminars are now offered to educate attorneys, judges, and other members of the judicial system about the challenges created by hackers and the problems their activities create. These workshops also explain proven strategies for prosecuting hackers.

PROTECTING AGAINST INTRUSION BY HACKERS. There is always the possibility that the person responsible for a computer crime is a disgruntled employee or former employee. Hence, when there is a breach of security, it is a good idea to look inside the company as well as outside.

Preventing unauthorized access to a system requires excellent physical security. Hiring honest, reliable people is an obvious starting point. Figure 14.7 illustrates 10 additional techniques helpful in deterring intrusion by hackers. These are as follows:

1. **Change access passwords frequently.** Users should be required to enter personal identification codes and individually assigned code words in order to access the system. Passwords should be kept strictly confidential.

[5]*Software Engineering Notes 16,* (January 1992): 20–22.

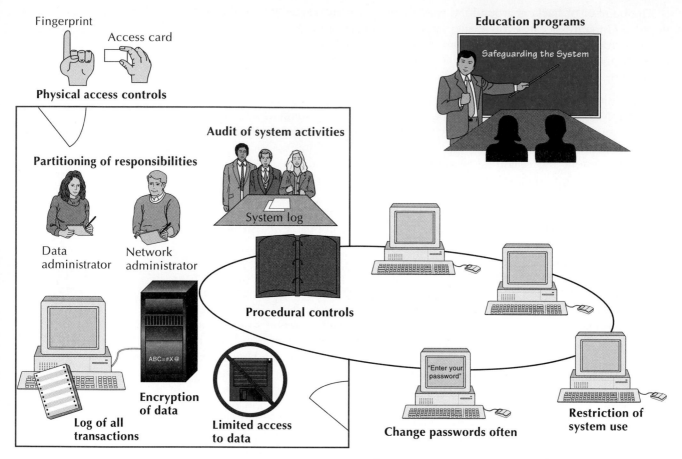

FIGURE 14.7   *Ten Protection Schemes to Deter Computer Hackers*

2. **Restrict system use.** Users should be given access to only the functions they need to use, rather than full-system access.

3. **Limit access to data.** Users should be allowed to access only the data they need to perform processing within their area of responsibility.

4. **Set up physical access controls.** Access cards and *biometric devices*—which recognize voice patterns, finger or palm prints, retinal eye patterns, and signatures—are among the most effective physical security systems (Figure 14.8). It is difficult to fool these systems.

5. **Partition responsibilities.** Critical functions involving high risk or high value in the data being processed should be separated so that more than one person must be involved to perform the processing. Database and network administrators should be given separate (but important) responsibilities for controlling access to the system.

6. **Encrypt data.** Changing the appearance of data through scrambling and coding makes it more difficult to use information even if a hacker is able to access it.

7. **Establish procedural controls.** When clearly stated security procedures guide users and IT staff members, it is more difficult to breach security.

a) Comdisco's security access cards are used widely through-out business and industry. Card keys are distributed to autho-rized individuals. The programming of the card key restricts the individual's access to only those areas he or she is autho-rized to enter.

b) Courtesy Recognition System's Handkey security system, used in many government buildings and prisons, reads palmprints.

FIGURE 14.8
Access Cards and Biometric Detection Devices
Access cards have been used as security devices for several years. Growing in popularity are biometric detection devices, which grant access to an area or system by recognizing physical characteristics.

Bank One's Checks Are an Image of Themselves

Bank One Corp., an industry leader, created its OneImage system to help its business customers view images of checks to be paid from their accounts. Like any business bank, Bank One is continually on the lookout for checks that are unusually large for a customer or contain anything out of the ordinary (such as old dates or blurred numbers). When these events occur, the bank contacts the customer issuing the check before it approves payment. In the past, when a customer wanted to see a check prior to payment, the Columbus, Ohio, bank faxed or couriered paper copies to the customer, a time-consuming process.

With OneImage, customers avoid that hassle by using the Internet's World Wide Web to access Bank One's Web site and view an image of their check. The image is retrieved from the bank's database and displayed on-line to the customer. All details, including signatures, handwritten notes, and payment amounts, are clearly visible as a result of the high-resolution scanning Bank One does when it captures a check's image for storage in the database. Since the bank's Web site is interactive, customers can send a message to the bank informing it of their "pay" or "no pay" decision.

8. **Institute educational programs.** There is no substitute for well-informed staff members. Security education programs stress the threat of intrusion, explain hackers' methods and tactics, and provide guidelines on how to respond when intrusions are detected.
9. **Audit system activities.** In an *audit,* independent parties review transactions and computer processing to analyze their origin and their impact on the system, as well as to determine that these activities were authorized and performed by authorized individuals.
10. **Log all transactions and user activities.** Keep a record of each activity and the individual responsible for that activity.

Some companies supplement these techniques with call-back security. Here's how it works: When callers dial into the system, they provide the telephone number from which they are calling. (The system may also sense the calling number automatically.) The person calling then hangs up, and the system, after verifying that the telephone number is valid and authorized, calls the person back. Call-back security adds a valuable layer of protection to the 10 techniques described above.

The *Information Technology in Practice* feature entitled "For the Best Security in Information Technology, RSA Security Makes the Code Public," discusses an innovative way of thwarting intruders seeking to capture electronic transmissions.

Despite these precautionary measures, some hackers do manage to break into even the best-guarded systems. When a hacker has penetrated a system, it is important to determine whether any damage or theft has occurred and to recognize that there is a *trapdoor*—an undetectable way of entering the system that bypasses the security system (see Table 14.2).

In detecting security breaches, noticing even the smallest "loose end" can be helpful, as Clifford Stoll found out.

CLIFFORD STOLL: HUNTING DOWN A HACKER.

When astrophysicist Clifford Stoll (Figure 14.9) joined the Lawrence Berkeley Laboratory, a university research laboratory outside of San Francisco, he knew he would be responsible for managing a dozen mainframe computers (interconnected to thousands of other systems over more than a dozen networks) and over 1,000 user accounts. An additional computer was dedicated to gathering statistics and sending monthly bills to the laboratory departments using the machines.

Stoll began his second day at work by reviewing the computer usage records for the previous day. He quickly found that the books did not balance: there was a 75-cent shortfall on a bill of several thousand dollars. Someone must have used a few seconds of computing time without paying for it.

Puzzled, he dug into the scrambled code of the accounting software. When he could not find an explanation for the discrepancy, Stoll became more puzzled. Several days later, Stoll found another accounting imbalance of a few cents and a five-minute discrepancy between the amount of computer time logged and the amount actually charged to user accounts. Digging further, Stoll decided that an intruder had entered a lab computer from a network. He thought the intruder had found a loophole in the system's security that would allow him to enter the system and become a "privileged user." You become a privileged user by logging onto the computer with the system manager's password. Once inside, you can establish new passwords, open access paths, and generally roam through the system, changing records and databases at will.

Stoll was a fan of a then-popular movie called *War Games,* in which a teenage

FIGURE 14.9

Clifford Stoll: Spy Catcher

Stoll, an astrophysicist, noticed a 75-cent discrepancy in the computer access time billed to his lab. He eventually traced the discrepancy to a mysterious secret agent in Pittsburgh, a spy ring in Germany, and the former Soviet Union's secret police.

hacker broke into a Pentagon computer and nearly started a global nuclear war. Stoll wasn't worried about someone getting in to damage the lab's computers, but he wondered if he was living through a real-life version of *War Games*. What did the hacker want and what were his intentions?

Stoll watched as the hacker came into the system repeatedly and erased his own tracks—except for the telltale accounting discrepancies. After monitoring the hacker's activities for several days, Stoll wrote a program that logged all the hacker's activities. He continued to let the intruder wander through the system while he carefully recorded every keystroke.

For over a year, Stoll stalked the elusive, methodical hacker as he prowled the Berkeley lab network and accessed the computer networks of more than a half-dozen national agencies, burrowing into sensitive information about military programs. Eventually, Stoll traced the hacker's origin to Hanover, Germany.

Next, Stoll set up a sting operation, tempting the intruder into accessing a set of data and then transmitting it to another location. The sting uncovered a spy ring in Germany linked to a mysterious agent in Pittsburgh. The spy ring was selling computer secrets to the former Soviet Union's secret police, the KGB, for cocaine and tens of thousands of dollars.

Stoll's experience, while extraordinary, points to the threat of criminal intrusion into ordinary computer systems. In his many television and newspaper inverviews, Stoll always makes the point that computer espionage is the most important IT security issue of the 1990s.

Computer Viruses

Sometimes intrusion occurs by way of software. A computer **virus** is a hidden program that alters, without the user's knowledge, the way a computer operates or modifies the data and programs stored on the computer. The virus is written by individuals intent on causing damage or wreaking havoc in a system. It is called a "virus" because it reproduces itself, passing from computer to computer when disks are shuttled from one computer to another. A virus can also enter a computer when a file to which it has attached itself is downloaded from a remote computer over a communications network. An infected disk or diskette will continue to spread the virus each time it is used, as Figure 14.10 shows.

Each virus has its own characteristics—its own "signature," as computer experts say. Some destroy irreplaceable data by writing gibberish over the disks they infect. Others take control of the operating system and stop it from functioning.

virus

A hidden program that alters, without the user's knowledge, the way a computer operates or that modifies the data and programs stored on the computer.

INFORMATION TECHNOLOGY IN PRACTICE

For the Best Security in Information Technology, RSA Security Makes the Code Public

Growth in the transmission of digital information has changed the encryption of data and information from an obscure specialty of spies, government agencies, and academics to an essential working tool for business. Electronic eavesdropping in general, and the scanning of documents in particular, leave no mark on the transaction. Hence, it is difficult to detect when there has been a compromise of data and information.

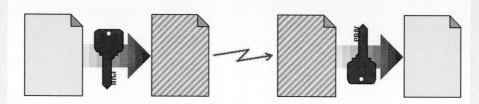

The RSA Public Key Concept

Anything encrypted with someone's RSA Public Key can only be decrypted with its corresponding Private Key, and vice-versa.

RSA Data Security, Inc., located in so-called Silicon Valley, south of San Francisco, came out with an innovation that has changed the way companies encrypt data and information. The company and its president, Jim Bidzos, control the patents for this crucial software that manages the scrambling and unscrambling of computer messages.

Before RSA's innovation, the traditional encryption system used a secret coding method (called a *key* or *cypher*) known only to the sender and the recipient. *Cryptography,* as this method is known, is very protective—so long as the key is safeguarded. Once the code is broken, or is no longer secret, transmissions using that coding method are no longer protected.

RSA uses a *public-key cryptography* method, which allows sender and receiver to exchange messages without getting together beforehand to determine the key. This method relies on *two* keys: a public key, available to anybody, and a private key,

known only to the recipient. The public key is used to *encode* the message. However, the message can be *decoded* and read only with the private key.

People wishing to receive coded messages can freely distribute the public key. Those corresponding with them use the public key to prepare their coded message. But only with the private key can the message be decoded.

The strength of RSA's coding methodology has been proven in the market, where some 5 million copies of the software have been sold. It has widespread support from the information technology industry, including such important firms as Apple Computer, AT&T, IBM, Lotus Development, Microsoft, Motorola, and Sun Microsystems.

The RSA Public Key Concept

Anything encrypted with someone's RSA Public Key can only be decrypted with its corresponding Private Key, and vice-versa.

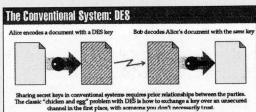

The Conventional System: DES

Alice encodes a document with a DES key   Bob decodes Alice's document with the *same* key

Sharing secret keys in conventional systems requires prior relationships between the parties. The classic "chicken and egg" problem with DES is how to exchange a key over an unsecured channel in the first place, with someone you don't necessarily trust.

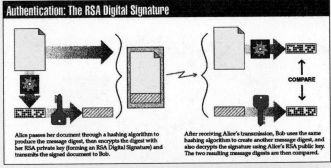

Authentication: The RSA Digital Signature

COMPARE

Alice passes her document through a hashing algorithm to produce the message digest, then encrypts the digest with her RSA private key (forming an RSA Digital Signature) and transmits the signed document to Bob.

After receiving Alice's transmission, Bob uses the same hashing algorithm to create another message digest, and also decrypts the signature using Alice's RSA public key. The two resulting message digests are then compared.

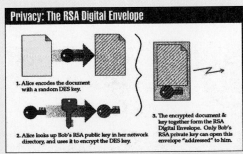

Privacy: The RSA Digital Envelope

1. Alice encodes the document with a random DES key.

2. Alice looks up Bob's RSA public key in her network directory, and uses it to encrypt the DES key.

3. The encrypted document & key together form the RSA Digital Envelope. Only Bob's RSA private key can open this envelope "addressed" to him.

Still others embed commands into the operating system, causing it to display messages on the computer screen. The worst forms of virus are much more subtle, moving through data and changing small amounts of detail in selected files so unnoticeably that they are difficult to detect.

All types of computers are vulnerable to viruses, but microcomputers are particularly vulnerable because most were not designed with computer security in mind. The next generation of PC is being developed with much greater concern for virus detection and security in general.

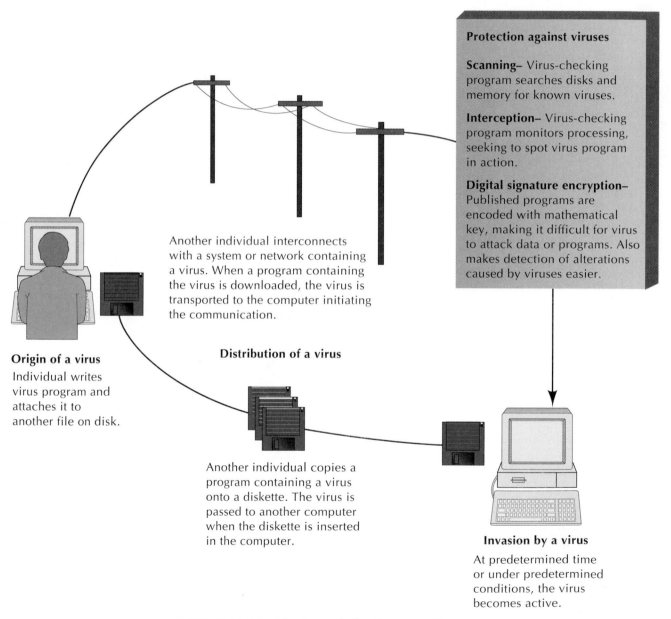

Protection against viruses

Scanning– Virus-checking program searches disks and memory for known viruses.

Interception– Virus-checking program monitors processing, seeking to spot virus program in action.

Digital signature encryption– Published programs are encoded with mathematical key, making it difficult for virus to attack data or programs. Also makes detection of alterations caused by viruses easier.

Another individual interconnects with a system or network containing a virus. When a program containing the virus is downloaded, the virus is transported to the computer initiating the communication.

Distribution of a virus

Origin of a virus
Individual writes virus program and attaches it to another file on disk.

Another individual copies a program containing a virus onto a diskette. The virus is passed to another computer when the diskette is inserted in the computer.

Invasion by a virus

At predetermined time or under predetermined conditions, the virus becomes active.

FIGURE 14.10   *The Spread of a Computer Virus*
Educational programs and the implementation of procedures are important steps in preventing the introduction and spread of viruses throughout a computer system.

Standing Guard on the Electronic Frontier

U.S. government officials have made news in recent years when they've arrested, indicted, and tried members of hacker groups bearing such exotic names as the Legion of Doom and Masters of Deception. But on a day-to-day basis, it's the company data security manager who patrols the electronic frontier, trying to ward off hackers and industrial spies. To do the job well, John A. Blackley says, takes two qualities: a love of change and polished sales skills. Blackley is a certified information systems professional with more than 10 years' experience on the electronic frontier.

Love of change serves data guardians well because they have to stay one step ahead of new technologies and other forces that threaten security. Excellent sales skills are needed to enlist the support of end-users who form the data security system's first line of defense. As Blackley describes it, "If we spend lots of money on access-control technology and do not educate our staff, we've wasted our money. And excellent negotiating skills are required because almost no one wants to set up another meeting just to hear about security." In fact, *Computerworld,* the leading newspaper of the computer industry, estimates that data security managers now spend over a third of their time "selling" data security programs and procedures.

VIRUS PROTECTION.   Although computer viruses are a fairly recent phenomenon, more than 1,200 of them are already known, some bearing such exotic names as the Michelangelo Virus and the Christmas Virus (Table 14.3).

To protect their systems against viruses, companies must buy virus detection software, programs that scan the computer's disks to detect the virus. There are three methods of virus detection: scanning, interception, and digital signature encryption.

Scanning programs search the computer and main memory to detect a virus. Most programs alert the user when a virus has been detected. The user can then signal the program to destroy the virus and, if possible, repair the data. *Detection programs* work behind the scenes, monitoring processing activities and signaling the user when a virus tries to infect the system. *Digital signature encryption,* an emerging technology, uses a mathematical coding scheme designed to foil a virus's attempt to attack programs and data.

STONED III AT NOVELL.   Detecting and stopping viruses early is critical to maintaining data integrity. Novell—a Provo, Utah, software publisher and the largest supplier of office networks for personal computers in the United States—found this out the hard way. A few years back, it had to send out letters to approximately 4,000 of its customers warning them that it had shipped them accidentally infected copies of a disk for updating their network software. The virus in question became known as "Stoned III." This virus is known for disabling every computer it infects.

TABLE 14.3 *Infamous Computer Viruses*

NAME	WHAT HAPPENS WHEN VICTIM USES AN INFECTED PROGRAM OR DISK
Stealth	Attacks the boot sector of a disk, causing the system to hang.
Stoned (aliases: *Hawaii, New Zealand, Marijuana, Smithsonian, Hamo*)	Possibly the most common virus in the United States. May display message, "Your PC is Stoned—LEGALIZE MARIJUANA." May damage disk directory and and file allocation table (FAT—a disk directory the computer needs to retrieve files).
Michelangelo	A mutation of the Stoned virus. Destroys contents of hard disk on March 6, the anniversary of the artist's birth in 1475. Gained national publicity in 1992, helping to raise public awareness of computer viruses.
Christmas (aliases: *XA1, XMAS*)	On April 1, the virus destroys the file allocation table. Between December 24 and January 1 of any year, the screen is filled with a picture of a Christmas tree.
Friday the 13th (aliases: *Jerusalem B, PLO Virus1808, 1813, Israeli Virus, Pay Day, Anarkia, Arab Star, Black Friday, Hebrew University, Mendoza*)	The first computer virus identified; caused widespread panic at Hebrew University of Jerusalem in July 1987. System slows dramatically. If virus is in memory on any Friday the 13th, it will delete every program executed. "Black Box" appears on the lower left side of the screen and scrolls up as the screen scrolls.
Whale (alias: *Mother Fish*)	A "stealth virus" that uses layers of encryption and can infect files in 32 different ways. Slows system down; display flickers. Decreases available memory by 9,984 bytes. Using system command to fix disk errors will damage files.
Casino (variant: *Casino B*)	On 15th of January, April, or August, screen displays a message that the FAT has been destroyed, even though the virus has saved a copy in memory. Offers user a "last chance to restore your precious data" by playing a slot machine game. If user loses, virus wipes out FAT. Casino-B variant destroys FAT whether user wins or loses game.
Falling Letters	Ten minutes after the virus is loaded into memory, all the characters on the screen fall to the bottom. Infects only floppy disks.
Disk Killer (alias: *Ogre*)	Damages disk; destroys files on floppy disks. May cause unexpected formatting of disk. Displays message: "Disk Killer . . . Warning! Don't turn off the power, or remove the diskette while disk killer is processing! PROCESSING! Now you can turn off the power." Once a certain number of disks have been infected, reformats hard drive, erasing all files.
MisSpeller (aliases: *Typo Boot, Mistake*)	Causes misspelled words in printed documents, even though the on-screen spellings are correct.
Zero Bug (alias: *Palette*)	Display shows a Smiley face character, which eats all the zeros.
Frère Jacques	Causes files to increase in size. System plays tune "Frère Jacques" on Fridays.
Code 252	Flashes screen message, "You are infected with a virus. Ha, Ha, Ha. Now erasing all disks. Ha, Ha, Ha," although no files are actually erased.
T4-A, T4-B	Damages or deletes application and system files by trying to change the startup code or overwriting the file.

SOURCES: Based on Central Point Software, Central Point Anti-Virus Users Manual, Chap. 8, "Virus Dictionary," pp. 71, 77, 79–80, 81, 82, 83, 85, 92, 98, 107, 110; Michele Hasson, "Virus Alert," MacUser, November 1992, pp. 268–269; and Christopher O'Malley, "Stalking Stealth Viruses," Popular Science, January 1993, pp. 54–58, 92.

Novell traced this debacle to a specific part of its manufacturing process, but admitted that it was unable to determine how the virus had infected its software in the first place. It later traced the origin of the virus to Europe just three months before the company produced and shipped infected disks. Somehow, the virus had traveled to the United States, on disk or via computer network, and crept into the Novell manufacturing process. To prevent a recurrence of this or similar problems, Novell acquired special digital-signature software that will make it far more difficult for viruses to spread undetected on the company's network software releases.

A Final Word

The issues discussed in this chapter affect everyone, either directly or indirectly. The most important points to take from these discussions are simple: Be aware of possible misuses and take responsibility for safeguarding the IT resources under your control.

SUMMARY OF LEARNING OBJECTIVES

1 **Explain how the term *privacy* applies to information technology and why privacy is an important issue in the late 1990s.** Privacy, as the term is used in information technology, refers to how personal information is collected, used, and protected. Although privacy has always been an important issue, the enormous capabilities of IT to store and retrieve data have amplified the need to protect personal privacy.

2 **Describe the importance of ethics in the use of information technology and identify seven ethical issues associated with the use of IT in business.** In the United States, most records kept by companies and nongovernment organizations are not covered by privacy laws. Therefore, people must rely on a company's ethical policies for protection of private information. Seven ethical issues that businesses must confront are electronic mail privacy, software licenses, software copyrights, hardware access, intellectual property ownership, file access, and data ownership.

3 **Explain the IT professional's obligation to provide continued access to computers and networks and describe the four methods used to ensure IT reliability.** As companies become dependent on IT, they become dependent on the availability of their computers and communications systems. With this dependence comes the expectation that the service provider—whether an IT professional or a hired IT service—will ensure that service cannot be interrupted.

Four methods are used to ensure IT reliability. *Fault-tolerant computers* are designed with duplicate components so that if one component fails, the duplicate automatically takes over. *Uninterruptable power supply systems* ensure the continued flow of electricity, produced from a backup source, when the primary source fails. *Disaster recovery plans* help to restore data lost when a system stops functioning. *Off-site backup facilities* provide a backup computer center away from the company's main facility.

4 **Discuss the legal issues surrounding software piracy and three methods that have been used to prevent software piracy.** *Software piracy* is the making of illegal copies of software. Three methods are used to protect against it. *Software copyright protection* safeguards original works against unauthorized use, including duplication, provided the owner visibly displays a notice of copyright on the product. *Copy protection* schemes either defeat attempts to copy a program or make the copied software unreliable. *Software site licensing* is used to assist large-volume users of programs and at the same time avert piracy by allowing purchasers of software to make a specified number of copies of a particular program.

5 **Distinguish among copyrighted software, public domain software, and shareware.** *Copyrighted software* protects original works against unauthorized use. *Public domain software* is any noncopyrighted software that can be used by the general public. *Shareware* combines the best features of copyrighted software and public domain software. It is given away and freely distributed by developers, but the developers retain ownership and ask users to register with them and pay a nominal fee for using the program.

6 **Describe 10 ways to protect a system against intrusion.** Ten common ways to protect a system against intrusion are as follows: change access passwords frequently; allow workers access to only the system functions they need to use; permit workers to access only the data that they need to use; establish physical security systems; separate critical processing functions so that more than one person must be involved in them; encrypt data by scrambling or coding information; adopt procedural controls; keep staff well informed through education programs; audit system activities; and keep a log of all transactions and user activities. Some systems also use call-back security.

7 **Identify the three methods of virus detection used by virus detection software.** All types of computers are vulnerable to *viruses,* hidden programs that alter (without the user's knowledge) the way a computer operates or that modify the data and programs stored on the computer. To protect against them, companies must buy and use virus detection software. There are three

methods of virus detection. *Scanning programs* search the computer and main memory to detect a virus. *Detection programs* monitor processing activities and signal the user when a virus tries to infect the system. *Digital signature encryption* uses a mathematical coding scheme designed to foil a virus's attempt to attack programs and data.

KEY TERMS

1 Your Background: It's Just Business

Background America, Inc. A great many publicly accessible documents and government agency databases and information sources are computerized, so you'd think searching them would be easy for Background America. However, most are *not* linked to a network or to the Internet, and thus cannot be searched from remote locations. Instead, someone must go to the right address and locate the room where the records reside. That can be a bit challenging, even for the pros!

Questions for Discussion

1. Are you concerned about the large amount of information that companies can find out about you (or

anyone) in public records? If so, what is behind your concern?

2. Does the Internet pose a *new* threat to personal privacy with respect to the use or distribution of public information?

3. Should use of the Internet to retrieve public information be regulated by law? What are the arguments for and against such regulations?

2 Software Police Out to Prove That Piracy Doesn't Pay

Software Publishers Assoc. One of the Software Publishers Association's goals is to prove that piracy doesn't pay. If it finds illegal software during a voluntary audit, for example, it will assess a fine equal to the cost of the software. In 1991, the SPA collected $3 million in fines. (The largest fine, $498,000, was paid by a company that had illegally copied 150 products published by 66 SPA members.) Then the "software police" will destroy every illegal copy. If the company wants to continue using the software (and the related data files), it has to buy legal copies.

The stakes are even higher if the company has refused to cooperate. Under U.S. copyright law, anyone who is convicted of willfully making an illegal copy of software can be fined up to $100,000. And commercial software piracy (the theft of at least 10 copies of a program, or more than $2,500 worth of software) is a felony that carries a prison term of up to five years and a fine of up to $250,000. At these rates, even the expensive software is a bargain.

Questions for Discussion

1. Some individuals try to justify software piracy by claiming that software costs "too much" or that they can't understand the copyright notices. How do you think the SPA or the courts would react to this argument? How would you answer this argument?

2. In defending themselves in court, some companies have claimed that they have an official antipiracy policy. As evidence, the provide a copy of a memo they circulated to their employees. Why do you think the courts have ruled that some of these companies' illegal activities were "willful"?

3. Boeing Co. in Seattle has a department of software accountability. This department maintains an inventory of all the company's software, including the hundreds of copies of CAD software used to design the company's products. Do you think Boeing's practice is a good model for business?

3   Bank One's Checks Are an Image of Themselves

BANK≡ONE.   Bank One was pleased with the way its OneImage program streamlined the check approval process for both bank and customer. But in order to be certain that its WWW-based system did not provide a loophole for new security problems, the bank introduced a security process that precedes the display of the check's image.

Each OneImage customer receives a security device the size of a pocket calculator. This device includes a chip that creates passwords for one-time use. Whenever a OneImage user accesses the Bank One WWW site, the server generates and transmits a password, called a *challenge*. The on-line customer must then enter the challenge into his or her security device, which displays a valid response. The customer keys the response into the workstation and transmits it over the Web. After the bank's system validates the response, it displays the check image for the customer's approval. This quick and easy challenge/response process dramatically increases the security of the approval transaction.

Questions for Discussion

1. What determines the success of the OneImage system?

2. What are the financial benefits of the OneImage system?

3. Why is it important for the OneImage security process to rely on one-use challenge passwords and responses?

4   Standing Guard on the Electronic Frontier

Security often seems an annoyance to companies setting up new systems. "After all," Blackley reports, "no one wants to hear that the new server can't be brought up on Monday because we don't know how to secure the data on it."

Another problem is that the IT professionals who end up in the data security field often have little or no formal training in security. Some industry groups are trying to rectify this situation. The International Information Systems Security Certification Consortium, for instance, was formed in 1989 to identify people well qualified to resolve current and future security issues. The consortium now certifies security experts on the basis of their work experience: a minimum of eight years in the data security area, with at least one year's experience in 4 of 17 specialties, such as physical security, access control, and cryptography (the art of writing and deciphering code). Future standards will be even more exacting: certification will require passing a two-part exam every three years.

Questions for Discussion

1. Why do you think security is such a "tough sell" at so many companies? How could IT managers work with the IT staff to make the sell easier?

2. Blackley says he spends a lot of time just roaming about the organization. What advantages does his "management by walking around" provide to the company?

3. Some IT professionals are skeptical of certification programs, arguing that test-taking skills are no substitute for real-world experience. What questions would you ask a person interviewing for the job of company data entry specialist? What skills would you seek in a person interviewing for a job as head of a government agency charged with evaluating proposals for computer services by outside suppliers?

Net Work

Among the most intense debates centered on the Internet are those concerning security of transactions and the protection of privacy. Hence, great efforts are being made to protect the identity of people using the Net to make purchases. Similarly, companies have developed various ways to ensure that individuals and companies alike can transact business over the Internet and exchange money or credit information securely. You may wish to review the discussion of on-line payments in Chapter 12.

Four different methods of securing transactions have come to the forefront. They include methods for exchange of cash as well as variations on credit card transactions. To review the differences among them, visit the following Web sites:

- **DigiCash** (http://www.digicash.com.nl). Provides new concept in payment systems, one that combines computerized convenience with security and privacy in a way that the company says "improves on paper cash."

- **First Virtual** (http://www.firstvirtual.com). First Virtual has devised a unique and innovative method to conduct secure on-line transactions. The company says it will "simply never ask you to put your credit card number or other sensitive financial data on the Internet."

- **CyberCash** (http://www.cybercash.com). An electronic wallet that can be used on the Internet is a distinguishing characteristic of this company's products.

- **Mastercard** (http://www.mastercard.com). This worldwide processor of credit card transactions has staked out its place on the Internet, promising that "when you do need cash, you can have instant access to it absolutely anywhere" through Mastercard.

After visiting each of these sites and reviewing the information provided there, do a comparison by answering the following questions:

1. What product does each company provide?
2. What are the distinguishing characteristics of each company's product?
3. Can these products be used only on the Internet?
4. Which products do you feel offer (1) the greatest security and privacy protection and (2) the greatest convenience for consumers?

GROUP PROJECTS AND APPLICATIONS

Project 1

In groups of five persons each, brainstorm a list of technology-based products and/or practices that may lead to a loss of privacy. Suggest how these items could have positive uses.

A designated person should collect each group's list, then write all the items on the blackboard. The class will then conduct a straw poll, with each person voting "for" or "against" each item.

After the poll, the class should discuss the following issue:

- What separates the "acceptable" technologies from the "unacceptable" technologies?

Project 2

Each individual should bring to class a "code of ethics" from a real-world company. Then break into small groups to discuss these individual codes, addressing the following questions:

- Does the code specifically mention the ethical use of technology? If not, write a paragraph to address the ethics of using technology in a responsible manner.

- Do you consider these codes to be generally effective? What, if anything, would you change about them?

Project 3—Group Research Project

It is widely known that software piracy is a major problem in the international arena. U.S. software companies have reported that millions of unauthorized copies of their most important products have turned up in European and Asian markets.

In groups of three, conduct some research into this growing problem. Each person in the group should research and report on one of the following topics:

- Software piracy in Asia.
- International law and policies regarding software piracy.
- Proposals to decrease software piracy.
- Built-in antipiracy protection in software.

Project 4

A recent *Fortune* cover story asked, "Who's Reading Your E-Mail?" Most companies have a policy stating that e-mail is considered a corporate asset and that employee privacy is therefore not guaranteed in this area.

Do employees have the right to privacy in their e-mail, or do employers have the right to read any documents prepared by their workers? Two groups of four students each should debate the issue. The first group takes the employers' perspective; the second group takes the employees' perspective. After the first student from each side has spoken, the second student questions the opponent's arguments, looking for holes and inconsistencies. The third student attempts to answer these arguments. The fourth student presents a summary of each side's arguments. Finally, the class votes on which team has offered the more compelling argument.

REVIEW QUESTIONS

1. What does the word *privacy* mean as applied to information technology? Why is privacy a concern among those using IT and those affected by the use of IT?

2. Describe the five privacy provisions outlined in the Code of Fair Information Practices.

3. What are ethics? Can personal ethics be separated from business ethics?

4. Identify and explain seven ethical issues related to the use of IT in business.

5. Describe the ethical guidelines that Donn B. Parker of SRI International encourages IT professionals and users to adopt.

6. Why do companies have an obligation to ensure continued access to computer and communications systems once they have been made available to users?

7. Describe the four methods of ensuring IT service reliability.

8. What is piracy? What is software piracy?

9. Describe three methods that companies can use to protect their software from piracy.

10. How does copy protection differ from copyright protection?

11. Describe the differences between copyrighted software and public domain software.

12. What is shareware?

13. What are hackers and what is their role in system intrusion? Is system intrusion a crime?

14. Describe 10 techniques for deterring computer intrusion by hackers.

15. What is a computer virus? How does a virus originate? How does it spread?

16. Name the three techniques used to detect the presence of a computer virus.

DISCUSSION QUESTIONS

1. It is fairly easy to eavesdrop on cellular and cordless phone conversations because most of these messages are carried on analog radio waves that can be picked up by inexpensive radio frequency scanners. For this reason, Apple Computer has instructed its employees never to discuss confidential matters over these devices. What might increased use of cellular phones mean to you as a private citizen? As a manager?

2. What ethical issues are raised by the practices of credit reporting agencies, such as TRW Information Services and Equifax Credit Information Services? Can you suggest any solutions for these issues?

3. In April 1992, a broken water pipe interrupted the electrical service at the Chicago Board of Trade

Clearing Corp. In less than an hour, the company's manager of quality assurance had to put her disaster recovery plan in action. This involved shifting people and computer tapes to a backup site in a nearby suburb, where they spent four days coordinating recovery activities that kept all normal business activities operating. Why are such plans essential for businesses? Do different types of businesses need different types of recovery plans?

4. In a recent survey, *PC Computing* magazine found that 64 percent of respondents thought it permissible for company managers to search employees' hard disks for illegal copies of software. Do you agree that this activity is permissible? Explain your answer.

SUGGESTED READINGS

Icove, David, Karl Seger, and William Von Storch. *Computer Crime: A Crime Fighter's Handbook.* Sebastopol, CA: O'Reilly & Associates, 1995. Spans the vast arena of computer crime. Begins with the questions "What is a computer crime?" and "What are the risks?" and then explores both personal and corporate security issues. Includes detailed descriptions of state and federal laws in this area, as well as guidelines for preventing computer crime and prosecuting criminals.

McLean, John. "The Specification and Modeling of Computer Security." *Computer,* January 1990, pp. 9–16. A technical analysis of ways to limit potential damage caused by Trojan horse programs.

Neumann, Peter G. "Distributed Systems Have Distributed Risks." *Communications of the ACM 39* (November 1996): 130. A concise but candid assessment of the challenges resulting from the increased reliance by firms and individuals on distributed systems.

Stoll, Clifford. *The Cuckoo's Egg.* New York: Doubleday, 1989. A fascinating first-person account of Cliff Stoll's tracking of a spy through a maze of computer espionage. Provides insight into the operations of national networks as well as the strengths and weaknesses of computer security systems.

Smith, H. Jeff, Sandra J. Milberg, and Sandra J. Burke. "Information Privacy: Measuring Individuals' Concerns About Organizational Practices." *MIS Quarterly 20* (June 1996): 167–196. A review of the academic literature on privacy leading to the creation of an instrument that can be used to assess privacy loss in organizations.

Straub, Detmar W., Jr. "Effective IS Security: An Empirical Study." *Information Systems Research 1* (September 1990): 255–276. This article concludes that IT security has not been a high priority for most managers. Data gathered from over 1,200 organizations suggest that many permit their installations to be either lightly protected or wholly unprotected.

Wolinsky, Carol, and James Sylvester. "Privacy in the Telecommunications Age." *Communications of the ACM 35* (February 1992): 23–25. Advances in telecommunications have brought many new services while raising issues of personal privacy. The authors explore both sides of some of these debates.

CASE STUDY

Facing Up to the Millennium Bug

Dates—those conventional combinations of day, month, and year—are essential to keeping track of our daily activities and time's march. Adults use them without a second thought. Early in their education, children learn how to use dates to mark time and calculate age. Dates are built into the tracking of business activities, travel plans, and special events. We use them to mark elapsed time and monitor approaching requirements. Other than the basic necessities, there are few things in one's personal or business life more fundamental than keeping track of dates.

Only a few people are yet aware that when the clock strikes midnight at points around the world on the last day of 1999, computers will crash, with catastrophic results. This failure will be triggered by decisions made about dates in the early days of computing—the 1950s through the 1970s. Unless sufficient corrective actions are taken before January 1, 2000—something experts seriously doubt will happen—the early computing decisions concerning dates could well turn into the most expensive and serious mistake in recent memory. How did this come about?

Expensive Space at a Premium

When computers were introduced into business, computer storage space was both very limited and expensive. Data were then typically fed into a computer on 80-column punched cards. Systems developers, seeking to minimize data entry to save storage space, as a matter of course stripped out the seemingly unnecessary century designation in dates.* "Why store 1965 when a date of 65 will mean the same thing?" By eliminating the century designation, "You get a 25 percent savings in storage usage every time a date is stored." So the logic of the time went.

The Millennium Bug

Here's a simple example that designers might have used in developing a date routine in 1975: Good systems design practice calls for storing a date and calculating age or elapsed time from the detail. For instance, in personnel records, an individual's year of birth is stored, and at any time that person's age can be determined merely by subtracting the current year from the year of birth. Thus, $1975 - 1932$ yields the age of 43 when 1932 is the year of birth. Actually, since designers usually stored only the last two digits, the subtraction would be: $75 - 32 = 43$.

The "millennium bug" is a direct outgrowth of this process. To see the effect, calculate the age in the year 2000 (a date designers were not thinking about in 1975) of someone born in 1932: $2000 - 1932 = 68$. This seems to work just fine—except that, following the conventions used by IT professionals in 1975, the computer version of this would be $00 - 32 = -68$. Results like this will throw computers into confusion, causing them to crash or function in unpredictable ways.

This simple age example is but one illustration of how the millennium bug will affect computers. There are so many other widespread uses of dates that the problem is much more ominous than the misdetermination of people's ages.

Widespread Impact

How could designers have failed to anticipate these consequences? For one thing, the end of the century seemed a long way off in the 1950s, when the conven-

tion of leaving out the century designation became established. For another, there was little expectation during the early days of computing that information technology would have such a widespread impact on our daily lives. Computers then were large mainframe systems, and their numbers were limited. They were used primarily by large companies and government agencies for record-keeping transactions. Since the invention of the microprocessor was not foreseen, nobody predicted that information technology would be embedded in everyday products and services, influencing our lives the way it does today.

Computers reference dates many times during business processing (e.g., sales and order transactions, accounting transactions, payment processing, personnel record keeping, administration of health care and medical treatment). Even more important are the microprocessors embedded in the vehicles, appliances, and electronic devices that surround us throughout the day. Your automobile, VCR, and auto-focus camera, for example, process date information in the course of their normal activities. So do the guidance systems on commercial and military aircraft. Even traffic lights are managed by dates, for the length of time signal lights are illuminated changes depending on whether it is a weekday or a weekend.

Eliminating the Millennium Bug

Estimates suggest that the *typical* company will have to invest between $50 million and $100 million to correct the date problem in their business systems. Large companies may have to spend billions. (Remember, these are only rough estimates, for no one really knows.)

Getting rid of the millennium bug comes down to these four questions:

1. *Can we find all the date references?* Date routines are included in software written by IT professionals within a company as well as in software purchased from a software developer. Computer operating systems, including those in your desktop PC and in the guidance system of an aircraft, contain an embedded chip that keeps track of date and time. How do we go about identifying routines when we may not even realize they are embedded in a system?
2. *Can we fix all the date references?* Are you aware that many elevators in skyscrapers have built-in microprocessors that both monitor ongoing performance and keep track of the date on which the next preventative maintenance activities should be performed? How do you go about fixing a date routine that is embedded in a silicon chip?

---

*Written numerically, dates are typically presented in the form MM/DD/YYYY or DD/MM/YYYY, for month (M), day (D), and year (YYYY).

3. *Can we fix the effect of* not *fixing a date reference?* If we can't fix the date routine, can we interrupt processing to avert erroneous calculations capable of causing computer crashes? How would we do this?

4. *What if the answer to questions 1–3 is "No!"?* What, then, will happen on January 1, 2000?

Some companies are hard at work on this problem. Others are either totally unaware of it or are taking the laissez-faire attitude that some magic solution will appear before the year 2000. One thing is certain: Every nation that depends on information technology will confront this problem because the millennium bug is not a respecter of international boundaries.

Questions for Discussion

1. Identify at least 10 products, services, or events where the calculation of dates is a requirement for normal activity.

2. Do *you* believe the millennium bug is a serious problem? Why or why not?

3. What action do you recommend be taken, if any, by national governments wishing to protect their citizens from the threat of the millennium bug?

4. Who is responsible for fixing this problem? Who would be liable for catastrophic events attributable to the millennium bug?

The Information Age: Next Steps

CHAPTER OUTLINE

LEARNING OBJECTIVES

When you have completed this chapter, you should be able to

1 Identify the "three C's" of information technology and discuss how the definition of IT is changing in the Information Age.

2 Describe the importance of consumer electronics as an element of IT.

3 Explain the expanded definition of "communications carrier."

4 Discuss the change in the definition of "software" to incorporate content as well as programs.

5 Explain why TV is an important type of IT and how interactive TV works.

6 Discuss how the IT industry is changing.

7 Distinguish between a communications infrastructure and an information superhighway and give two reasons why world leaders are seeking to develop information superhighways.

8 Describe six issues involved in designing and developing an information superhighway.

Cybersurgery—On the Brink

Just 48 hours after having surgery to remove a brain tumor, a well-known United States politician was back on the campaign trail, sporting a full head of hair, walking and talking normally, shaking hands, and bouncing children in his arms. Compared to the common perception of invasive cancer surgery, this, indeed, was a miracle. Fortunately, miracle medical treatments like the senator's cybersurgery will soon be the norm—all because advances in information technology and medicine are combining the skill of a surgeon and the pinpoint precision of a laser beam with the computer and communications capabilities of information technology.

A common cancer treatment method exposes cancerous tumors to radiation in order to kill the diseased tissue. Keeping the beam on target is critical because radiation will kill whatever tissue it strikes—both healthy and diseased cells. Cybersurgery uses a *cyberknife* (also called *X-knife* or *gamma knife,* or, more formally, *computer-mediated stereotaxic radiosurgery system.*) This device is a robotic arm that locks a radiation beam onto the tumor, continually readjusting the direction of the beam to compensate for the slightest movement of the patient. What enables the cyberknife to do this is a capability for matching computer-generated images of the area of surgery to video images of the patient. The continual matching detects any movement by the patient and triggers the necessary adjustment.

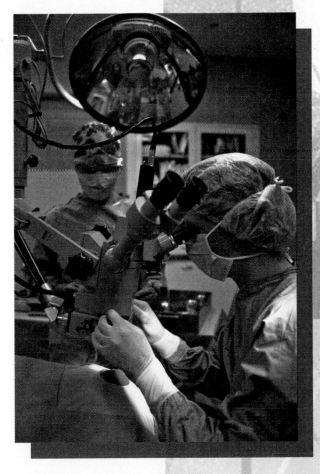

Leading university medical schools, including Stanford, Washington, and Iowa as well as the medical colleges of the universities of Georgia and Virginia, are well on their way to perfecting these techniques for general use. The potential uses of cybersurgery are tremendous, offering hope for patients seeking cures for such diseases as prostate and breast cancer. Another variation of cybersurgery combines the robotic system with laser beams that can make small, precise incisions, treat damaged organs and tissue, and even coagulate blood. These techniques not only provide a way for physicians to avoid invasive surgery (i.e., large incisions) and reduce the risk of bleeding, they also mean that bloodless surgery is within reach.

Information technology's reach extends far beyond business. It is radically changing the way we live and how we play as well as how we work. In this chapter, we discuss the next steps in the Information Age, steps that will cause the very definition of IT to be rewritten. In the first part of the chapter, we explore the evolving definition of IT and its components. In the second part, we examine the steps that nations are taking to capitalize on the opportunities IT presents.

New IT: The Convergence of Three Information Technologies

Throughout this book, we've examined the experiences of people, work groups, and companies that use information technology. The examples we've given have emphasized the role of two technologies: computers and communications networks—"the 2 C's of IT"—as well as the importance of know-how. But the definition of IT is changing through

- The incorporation of consumer electronics.
- A broadened definition of "communications carriers."
- A broadened definition of "software."
- The arrival of interactive television.
- A redefinition of the IT industry.

The Incorporation of Consumer Electronics

consumer electronics
Electronic devices used to satisfy people's needs and wants rather than to manufacture products or deliver services.

As we advance toward the twenty-first century, the definition of IT is being broadened through a convergence of three technologies. In addition to computers and communications systems, IT is evolving to encompass the "third C"— **consumer electronics,** those electronic devices created to satisfy people's needs and wants, rather than to manufacture products or deliver services (Figure 15.1). You are already familiar with the products in this category: television, camcorders, VCRs, laser disc players, stereo and sound systems (Figure 15.2), and photographic systems that use CDs rather than film. To the list of well-known computer and communications companies like IBM, Apple, Digital, Group Bull, Toshiba, and Hitachi, we'll add a few new names: Matsushita, Sony, Kodak, and Zenith.

We've already seen how multimedia is changing the face of IT, paving the way for the incorporation of consumer electronics. Many people have come to expect image, voice, and animation alongside data and text. As many more get into the multimedia phenomenon, video records and CD players will probably become part of information technology. When these and other types of consumer electronics are given processing power through chips and microprocessors, we'll see other changes as well.

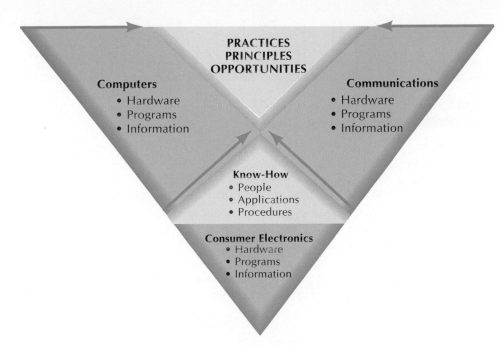

FIGURE 15.1

The Converging Forces of Information Technology
As the year 2000 approaches, the definition of IT is broadening to include not only computers and communications but also the "third C"—consumer electronics.

FIGURE 15.2 *Consumer Electronics: The Fourth Component of Information Technology*
Although consumer electronics are now used primarily to satisfy people's wants and needs rather than to manufacture products or deliver services, the definition of IT is evolving to include consumer electronics along with computers, communications, and know-how.

a) Zenith's SL3283 television offers advanced video-imaging capabilities for improved picture performance.

b) Sharp's VL-E30U videocamera fits in the palm of your hand and features a color screen.

c) Standard features in Zenith's VRA424 VCR include on-screen programming, one-year eight-event recording, and 181-channel capability.

d) Pioneer's CLD-V2400 laser disc player includes remote control and bar-coding capabilities.

e) RCA's tabletop stereo system consists of high-fidelity speakers, dual cassette deck, digital tuner with memory, control amplifier, multi-CD player with memory and oversampling features, and remote control.

| Gateway 2000 | Gateway 2000 Blurs the Line with New IT Products |

Whenever popular devices are used together by consumers, innovative manufacturers come up with a way to combine them into a single product. That's been the case with televisions and video recorders (VCRs). You can even buy a jumbo screen TV with its own built-in VCR. Another combination that is beginning to appear on the market is the cellular phone with a pager (cell phones that include a capability to receive e-mail are already on the market). And don't forget those combination printer/copier/fax machines. They're selling quickly.

Since the very meaning of information technology encompasses communications, computing, and consumer electronics, and since the Internet has become such an important means of communication for many people, the time seemed ripe for a single device that combines these capabilities. Gateway 2000, the South Dakota mail-order computer distributor, has started shipping just such a product. Its Destination system consists of a computer combined with a 31-inch television. Options include a built-in VCR and a high-quality stereo system.

Broadening the Definition of "Communications Carrier"

Today, the word *communications* is usually taken to mean telephone communications made possible by a communications carrier—the phone company or PTT. Yet the meaning of *carrier* extends beyond the telephone industry, as more people are realizing. Television networks and cable companies are becoming important parts of a nation's communications capacity. As we discussed in Chapter 10, communication cables can transport all types of digital and analog signals. Hence, computer data—as well as voice, video, and graphics signals—can be transported over the coaxial cables we associate with cable TV. Cable TV can carry much more than television programs.

In addition, the information technology underlying telephone transmission is growing more sophisticated. Telephone companies and PTTs have the capability to carry ordinary network TV programs over different types of communication links. Whether they will be allowed to do so depends on government policies. In most countries, national governments as well as regional public service commissions regulate telephone companies and must grant the traditional voice carriers permission to transmit video. Several legal barriers to such transmissions have been removed recently; attempts to overcome more of them are likely to be vigorous over the next several years.

The *Rethinking Business Practices* feature entitled "When Commerce Is Electronic" describes how communications innovations are changing the very definition of commerce. As this feature shows, new opportunities for reaching customers and for delivering products and services are emerging as a result.

RETHINKING BUSINESS PRACTICES

When Commerce Is Electronic

The U.S. Chamber of Commerce, Dun & Bradstreet, Chase Manhattan Bank, and publishing giant Simon and Schuster (among others) launched an electronic marketplace called the International Business Exchange in 1995. Virtually any product or service from all over the world can be traded on the Exchange. Anyone with a personal computer can join it and post messages describing the products or services they are offering or seeking. An electronic virtual agent matches buyers and sellers, allowing them to negotiate their own terms (anonymously, if desired). Verification of credit histories and other pretransaction services ensure that the sale and purchase meet both parties' requirements. In 1995, the year it was established, the Exchange had a base of 50,000 business participants. This base is expected to grow to more than 1.5 million by the end of the decade.

Conducting business electronically is becoming more accepted every year. As electronic commerce expands well beyond electronic data interchange (see Chapter 10) for conducting business over communications links, countless businesses are rethinking the way they initiate and carry out their day-to-day transactions.

The Internet is playing a crucial role in the expansion of electronic commerce, giving rise to the term *Internet commerce*. Its vast array of services can easily be adapted by commercial enterprises. Furthermore, its accessibility through either dedicated or dial-up connections involving home, office-based, or mobile personal computers means that anyone can interconnect to participate in business transactions.

What exactly do the growing capabilities of electronic commerce and the Internet mean for business? Here are some specific things a business can do through the Internet:

- Reach customers 24 hours a day.
- Place an illustrated catalog of products and services on-line for rapid access by potential customers.
- Deliver services and information-based products over communications links.
- Provide data and information in virtually any form (printed, spoken, animated) over a device at the recipient's location.
- Incorporate a wealth of data and information resources into any transaction or related decision.
- Provide search capabilities to locate data and information, companies and agencies, or people interconnected or accessible through communications links.
- Make or accept payment for the transaction over the same communication link, utilizing digital cash or traditional billing and payment services, all with acceptable authentication and encryption protection.

Electronic commerce is transforming business. Some cases in point: Hawaii's Best Espresso Co. (hoohana.aloha.net/~bec) closed its retail shop and turned it into a 100 percent World Wide Web business for sale of its varieties of rich, Hawaii-grown Kona coffee. CDNow: The Internet Music Store, of Penllyn, Pennsylvania (www.cdnow.com), offers every CD sold in the United States, with two-day delivery. Microsoft (www.microsoft.com) now delivers its software electronically, if the buyer chooses to bypass retailers.

Where will electronic commerce venture next? Your imagination is your guide, for people are increasingly finding that "If you can dream it, it will happen."

FIGURE 15.3

Akio Morita: IT Visionary

Morita, longtime chairman of Sony Corp., sees software as any element that gives value to hardware. His vision led Sony (once primarily a hardware company) to purchase two U.S. entertainment companies—Columbia Pictures and CBS Records.

Broadening the Definition of "Software"

In the computer industry, the term *software* has frequently been used to mean "computer programs," the set of instructions that controls a computer or communications network. As the convergence of technologies continues, the definition of this term is being broadened to include content. Akio Morita, longtime chairman of Sony Corp., viewed software for many years as any element that gives value to the hardware, a concept that extends the definition of software well beyond computer programs. Morita's views led Sony to purchase two U.S. entertainment companies: Columbia Pictures Entertainment, Inc., and CBS Records.

In describing Sony's decision to acquire CBS Records, Morita (Figure 15.3) explained his innovative views on software as content:

> We have been engaged in a joint venture with CBS Records since 1968. If it had not been for this venture, the search for a record company to agree to record on our compact disc would have been a "mission impossible," when one considers how apprehensive established record factories would have been toward the emergence of new hardware. If we did not realize the benefit of software as early as we did, I wonder how long it would have taken for the CD technology to be as appreciated as it is now. Sony, by combining CBS Sony audio software to our CD hardware, created a new industry—the CD industry. The music industry, as a result, has grown with the transition from records to CDs. This success in hardware-software synergy illustrates that hardware alone, no matter how good, is not sufficient for either expediency or enrichment of human life. Moreover, it supports Sony's belief in how a good relationship between software and hardware can promote the further growth of both industries.

For Sony, the software—that is, the music (which is really recorded data and information)—gives value to the hardware.

Software also means images. Always on the cutting edge of IT, Microsoft is now busy preparing CD libraries loaded with information, ranging from a *Musical Instruments* disc (an educational disc, as illustrated in Chapter 8, that recounts the history and sounds of musical instruments from all over the world) to a disc containing huge collections of photos of paintings by world-famous artists.

This broadening of the software concept marked a significant turning point for both Sony and Microsoft, and for IT in general. From now on, software will mean *content*—data and information—*as well as the means to manipulate it*. The world's art galleries, museums, filmmakers, recording companies, and television networks will be firmly tied to the IT industry. We've discussed examples of these industries' involvement in IT throughout this book, so it probably comes as no surprise to you that they have become an important part of the information technology industry. What we don't know is whether they will continue to provide simply content—that is, software—for the industry, or will choose to become players in other ways.

Interactive Television

Television is becoming an important information technology for three reasons:

1. Although the number of microcomputers in the home in all industrialized countries is large—30 to 35 million in the United States and growing (Figure

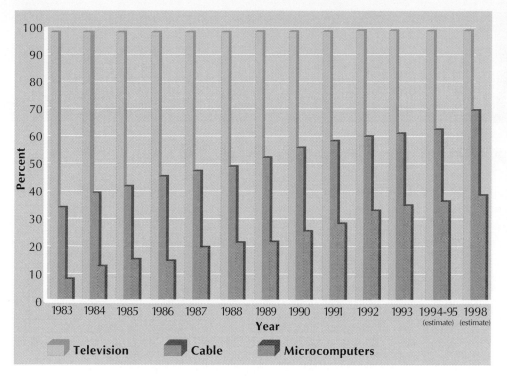

FIGURE 15.4

Percentage of U.S. Households with TVs, Cable Service, and Microcomputers, 1983–1993 and Projections

Although the percentage of U.S. households with televisions has held steady for the last decade, the percentage with microcomputers has increased 500 percent—from 7 percent in 1983 to 35 percent in 1993.

15.4)—the number of homes with television sets is typically two to three times larger. In addition, many homes have several TVs. In IT terms, the *installed base* of television sets is huge.

2. Television technology is advancing rapidly, with **high-definition television (HDTV)** emerging in Japan, Europe, and the United States (Figure 15.5). The U.S. version of HDTV uses digital technologies to present sound and images over television screens that are much higher in quality than those used by regular TV. (In Japan, HDTV research has relied on older analog technology.

high-definition television (HDTV)

A television system that uses digital technologies to present sound and images over high-quality television screens.

FIGURE 15.5

High-Definition TV

High-definition television images show the fine picture detail achieved by quadrupling the video information transmitted on current TV broadcasts. The HDTV technology used to produce these high-quality images was developed by Zenith and AT&T, two members of the "Grand Alliance" established to develop the U.S. HDTV standard.

INFORMATION TECHNOLOGY IN PRACTICE

Looking for Gold on Interactive TV

Interactive TV is good news for IT professionals, especially for the creative people who create entertaining multimedia and interactive television programs. *Morph's Outpost on the Digital Frontier,* a newsletter aimed at multimedia professionals, estimates that as many as 100,000 people were working in multimedia by 1993. There will be at least as many opportunities for people who understand what the new IT means for traditional businesses.

Consider the challenge of navigating hundreds of TV channels. *TV Guide,* one of the largest-circulation magazines in the United States, is working on an on-screen guide that will tell viewers what's on all those channels and how to find what they want to watch quickly. Time Warner, Viacom, AT&T, Microsoft, Apple Computer, Ameritech, InSight, and Discovery Communications are all developing software for interactive TV systems. Bell Atlantic's entry, Stargazer, uses a graphic image of an electronic mall that viewers can roam via remote control.

Here are a few other areas in which interactive TV is booming:

- **Retailing.** Spurred by the success of the Home Shopping Network and QVC Network, R. H. Macy, Nordstrom, Toys "R" Us, and others are building experimental TV networks offering online, on-demand interactive shopping. In time, some predict, your TV will be your gateway to an electronic mall with virtual mannequins created to match your measurements and coloring. By the year 2001, it is estimated, 17 percent of U.S. households will be spending almost $10 billion via interactive TV shopping. (By way of comparison, U.S. shoppers now spend $12 billion per year on catalog shopping, which is also expanding into interactive TV.)

- **Advertising and marketing.** Marketers who place commercials on the basis of television ratings (estimated number of viewers) will be adrift in a world where viewers aren't tied to a specific schedule or list of options. (In fact, viewers may eventually be able to watch commercial-free TV—for a fee, of course.) In this brave new world, marketers may turn to using demographic information to decide which household will see a commercial for an economy car and which will see an ad for a luxury model.

  Advertising is already competing with conven-

We described analog systems in Chapter 10). Television programs of all types, from sports to opera to comedy to the nightly news, will soon be shown in vivid color with high-resolution images.

3. If HDTV uses digital technology, drawing a line between the TV and the PC will be difficult. HDTV also means more uses of IT components, since HDTV allows the incorporation of communications cables and wireless transmission methods into the TV set. Communications links in TV sets means that vast amounts of data and information can be received and displayed. Digital data compression methods will make it possible for the viewer to choose from hundreds of different TV channels being transmitted across a single fiber-optic cable running from the street into the home, apartment, or office. As TV acquires both computer and communications capabilities, its functions will change. Now a device for displaying broadcast programs, it will become a device for transmitting information as well. **Interactive television (ITV)** will

interactive television (ITV)

A television with a keyboard, storage capability, and the capacity to transmit and receive vast amounts of information.

tional programming. A case in point is the steady rise of *infomercials*—program-long commercials that are entertaining enough to attract willing viewers. Bell Atlantic Corp., for example, has produced a half-hour sitcom about the Ringer family to tout a number of Bell Atlantic services. In the future, viewers may use infomercials to comparison-shop for cars and major appliances, instead of going from dealer to dealer.

- **Video rental and sales.** Many interactive TV experiments include some provision for video-on-demand. Instead of racing to the video store to find (or return) a copy of a new release, viewers can use their remote controls to select a video title and a start time from an on-screen menu. Pay-per-view charges go directly on a credit card or cable TV bill. At issue here is the $12 billion U.S. consumers spend on video rentals and, in all likelihood, some of the $12 billion they spend on video games every year. In the future, some predict, feature films might go directly to interactive TV, or they might debut simultaneously in theaters and, at a slightly higher cost, on interactive TV.

- **Education.** Many school districts already operate a "homework hotline" so that parents and students can confirm assignments and due dates. So it is only natural to extend these programs to interactive TV. In New Jersey, for example, the Department of Education is creating an interactive TV system that will let students respond to test questions by remote control. The system will then grade the tests, freeing the instructor to devote more time to working directly with students. An experiment at Northern Kentucky University that compared an on-line course with a traditional one found that the on-line course cost 30 percent less and was rated more highly by students, who got better grades than their counterparts in the traditional course.

- **Law.** Until the dust settles, look for some complex lawsuits over copyrights, program ownership, and distribution rights. Some companies are trying to jump the gun by actively buying digital or video rights. For example, Continuum Products, a Microsoft subsidiary, was created with one goal: to acquire nonexclusive digital rights to some of the world's most famous images.

be a television with a keyboard, storage capability, and the capacity to transmit, as well as receive, vast amounts of information. ITV is creating many opportunities for forward-thinking entrepreneurs, as the *Information Technology in Practice* feature entitled "Looking for Gold on Interactive TV" details.

INTERACTIVE SPORTS, COURTESY OF GROUPE VIDEOWAY. Here's how *Fortune* magazine projected the future of interactive TV:

While watching the San Francisco Giants, you'll be able to check the scores of other games under way, scan the lineups, or see a "baseball card" with the stats of any player. Switch to a . . . video on MTV [a cable television station featuring music videos]: You can send the artist fan mail, order the CD, or call up subtitles with the lyrics if you can't make out [the] words. Flip to *Beverly Hills 90210*. That cool blue blouse Brenda is wearing—you can

Philips Takes a Gamble on Multimedia

Philips

Multimedia got a boost in the early 1990s when Philips Electronics announced CD-Interactive (CD-I), a technology designed to "teach your old television some new tricks." The heart of the system is the Imagination Machine, a device that looks like a VCR. Hooked to a stereo, it plays conventional 5-inch music CDs. Hook it to a television set, though, and it plays CD-I discs, compact discs containing interactive video. Children playing a *Sesame Street* disc, for example, can use the remote control to open an on-screen book and read with Ernie, or they can stage an interactive arithmetic lesson with the whole Sesame Street gang. CD-I titles, which cost $25 to $50 each, range from education to games and "infotainment," such as a self-guided tour of the Smithsonian.

For Philips, the CD-I is a bold gamble with high stakes. In the past, this Dutch electronics giant developed the compact disc and the VCR with Japanese partners, only to see the Japanese go on to dominate the market. To survive as a global competitor, Philips had to prove that it could both develop cutting-edge technology *and* market it well. By moving early and fast, Philips hopes to capture enough of the multimedia market to make CD-I an industry standard. If that happens, Philips will be able to capitalize on the situation by licensing the technology to other manufacturers. But it will earn as much or more revenue selling CD-I discs produced by its subsidiary, Philips Interactive Media of America (PIMA).

order it for your teenager. Click. The latest stock quotes appear. Scrutinize a company's financials, then place a buy order directly with your broker.[1]

"Wishful thinking," you say. "Impossible," you think. But not in Montreal, Canada, where Groupe Videoway is giving sports fans a glimpse of the future today. There, interactive television combines computing, communications, and consumer electronics—all in a single system managed by a viewer through a simple converter box on top of the television set (Figure 15.6). Baseball fans can watch Montreal Expos games through the Groupe Videoway system. The converter is the interface to this system; it allows the viewer to choose four different angles from which to watch the next pitch. A flick of a key on a handheld remote control device changes the view you see, even as the pitch is in the air.

Groupe Videoway's system also allows the viewer to watch more than one image on the television screen (Figure 15.7). For example, the main window might show the action of a hockey game full-screen, while another window inserted below or to the right of the main screen displays information about a player, including statistics, career highlights, and perhaps current salary. Want to see the shot or save again? The Groupe Videoway system allows you to call up another window carrying instant replays, as well as a window showing the current score.

[1]Alan Deutschman, "Bill Gates' Next Challenge," *Fortune,* December 28, 1992, p. 41.

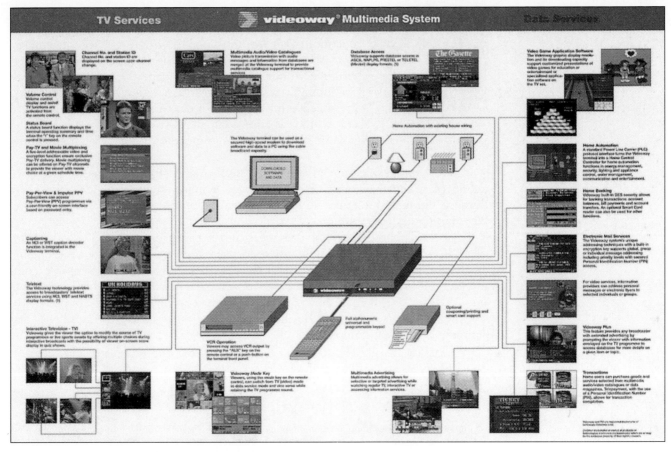

FIGURE 15.6   *The Groupe Videoway Multimedia System*

The Videoway Multimedia System provides a wide range of services and applications, from interactive TV and home shopping to electronic mail services and database access.

FIGURE 15.7

Groupe Videoway Interactive Sports

Using the Videoway Interactive Sports System, viewers can use a main screen to watch the game and multiple windows (inserted to the right of or below the main screen) to see close-ups of the action, call up instant replays, and display players' and game statistics and scores.

If you think all these advances in television, software, and consumer electronics mean more complexity, you're right. But more *complexity* is not the same as more *complication*. Many computer chips will be used to provide the services we've been discussing, manage the retrieval and storage of information, and carry out the processing needed for effective transmission of data and information. But these chips—that is, the computers—will be embedded in the system. The technology, not the individuals using the system, will handle the complex tasks.

Today's automobiles are also more complex, since there are more processes taking place simultaneously in the electrical system, engine, and drivetrain. Yet because the typical automobile has more than 20 embedded computers handling the sending and processing of data, driving is less complicated than ever.

Have you noticed that when you get into a car, even one you've never driven before, you intuitively know where to place the key, how to start the engine, and where to find the gearshift? That's the way the new combined computer/communications/consumer electronics systems will have to be. Since most people will only want to use them if they can do so without having to think about *how* to use them, these systems will be intuitive. If they are not, they will fail. It's that simple . . . and that complex. ▪

| Computertots | Computertots Puts Byte on Technophobia |

A recent survey by Dell Computer Corp. confirmed what many have long suspected: 55 percent of Americans are uncomfortable using digital alarm clocks, VCRs, answering machines, computers, compact disc players, or car phones. In fact, 25 percent of all U.S. adults have never used a computer, and 32 percent are actually afraid to use a PC. Although the scores for teens were much more encouraging, this survey did demonstrate how far many Americans have to go to feel at home with new IT technology.

To a growing number of preschoolers, though, using a computer is child's play, thanks to an innovative franchise chain called Computertots. Computertots brings computers, printers, instructors, and fun software to preschools, day-care centers, YMCAs, and other community centers. The service is free to the organizations; parents who want their children to participate pay $28 to $40 a month, depending on the child's age and the program length.

The program dates back to 1983, when two former special education teachers, Mary Rogers and Karen Marshall, founded Educational Computer Workshop (ECW) Corp. in a suburb of Washington, D.C. Their initial goal was to develop and market software that would carry out the principles of the Massachusetts Institute of Technology's computer projects for young children. From there, it was a relatively simple—and lucrative—step to sell ECW's lessons to preschools and day-care centers.

Redefining the IT Industry

The convergence of the three C's of IT will change both the meaning of IT and the capabilities we associate with it. But it will also change the IT industry as firms join forces to get the most value from their know-how.

Computer and chip vendors have already come together to form alliances, as evidenced by the partnership of IBM, Apple Computer, and Motorola in Talagent, a company whose goal is to develop a new generation of software for interacting with computers and multimedia systems. Microsoft, Intel, and General Instruments (a leading U.S. manufacturer of cable television decoder boxes) have combined forces to design a new control system for interactive television. Working together, they developed a system that makes it possible for viewers to select any of 500 television channels as they arrive via a single cable.

Cooperation will not be the trend in all parts of the IT industry, however. As we approach the year 2000, we can expect to see companies in the converging industries fighting it out. Public telephone companies and PTTs, cable television operators and television broadcast networks, all want to participate in the IT industry—traditionally viewed as the domain of computer hardware and software companies. Add the determination of the world's consumer electronics giants and the many newly emerging companies to innovate and capture market share, and you have the makings of rivalries as intense as that between Coke and Pepsi.

Toward an Information Superhighway

The Information Age has shown the world's leaders that a modern national telecommunications infrastructure is essential to maintaining and increasing personal, organizational, and national productivity. Most leaders also believe that such an infrastructure is essential for competing successfully in global commerce.

The demand for this infrastructure points toward a growing need for an additional resource: an information superhighway. Analogous to a highway that carries vehicular traffic, an **information superhighway** is a communications network spanning a nation, carrying data and information traffic. From a technical viewpoint, this national information superhighway would consist of fiber optics, satellites, and other communications links with huge amounts of transmission capacity. It would augment the quality of life by linking cities and people and serving as the gateway for the transfer of information in education, research, and commerce.

information superhighway
A communications network spanning a nation, carrying data and information traffic.

Communications Highway Infrastructure

What precisely is a **communications infrastructure?** The U.S. Office of Technology Assessment has offered this definition: "The communications infrastructure is the underlying structure of technical facilities and institutional arrangements that supports communication via telecommunication, broadcasting, film, audio and video recording, cable, print, and mail"[2] Note that this definition includes not only the hardware and program components of IT, but also, implicitly, the information, people, and procedures to develop, maintain, and apply the infrastructure for society's benefit.

communications infrastructure
The underlying structure of technical facilities and institutional arrangements that supports communication via telecommunications, broadcasting, film, audio and video recording, cable, print, and mail.

[2]U.S. Congress, Office of Technology Assessment, *Critical Connections: Communication for the Future*, OTA-CIT-407 (Washington, D.C.: U.S. Government Printing Office, 1990).

A national information infrastructure can be "national" only if it does not exclude potential users by limiting physical access or imposing economic barriers (i.e., the cost of the service). In the Information Age, it is in a nation's best interests to ensure that all of its industry and all of its citizens have the access they need.

Widespread acceptance of communications capabilities will produce some unforeseen advantages. For example, the *Information Technology in Practice* feature entitled "Through Visa Toward God" shows how a church in Spain is using an ATM to make contributing easier for parishioners.

 People frequently try to assess the benefits of investing in a service or building an element of infrastructure by measuring the potential improvement monetarily or statistically. "How will we save by taking this step?" "To what extent will productivity improve?" "How will the costs of production be reduced?" Although these kinds of questions are important, they ignore many equally important considerations that cannot be quantified or costed out.

A developed infrastructure is beneficial because it improves *other* services. New infrastructure can mean improved health care, better transportation, or higher achievements in education, for example. In many cases, it is impossible to fully quantify the benefits of investing in infrastructure, even though we know they're there. For instance, it is impossible to place a financial value on better health. We can describe the cost of poor health in terms of increased medical costs, but this is only one dimension of the health-care issue, and a very limited one at that. Measuring medical costs alone says nothing about the lower achievement levels, lower living standards, and lost career opportunities attributable to poor health.

The U.S. highway infrastructure produced completely new services and industries. After it was constructed, the interstate trucking system, United Parcel Service (UPS), Holiday Inns and the entire roadside motel industry, and interstate tourism grew. Clearly, building these highways did much more than help then-existing companies increase their revenues and productivity.

The right infrastructure is a foundation whose value cannot be accurately measured in dollars and cents. Rather, its value lies in the achievements and benefits it makes possible for people, organizations, and society. ▪

The Superhighway and National Competitive Advantage

In the Information Age, access to a global IT infrastructure, particularly through telecommunications, is at the heart of business and national competitiveness. In the business environment of the late 1990s, it is not enough for many companies to seek an edge only in their regional market, or even nationally. They must compete internationally, or at least keep an eye on global competitors, always prepared to develop a response to a rapidly surfacing challenge or opportunity.

National leaders are seeking to connect IT sites within their countries to encourage organizations to share information in a way that makes each organization more competitive internationally. In the United States, Vice President Al Gore is

INFORMATION TECHNOLOGY IN PRACTICE

Through Visa Toward God

Visa

So quipped a newspaper in Madrid reporting the story of an innovation at San Claudio's Church in Leon. The priests there had come upon an idea for increasing contributions: they installed a bank machine at the church's entrance. To use this electronic alms box, parishioners simply insert their bank card, key in the amount they wish to contribute, and continue on their way—with a printed receipt that is suitable for tax purposes.

The priests of San Claudio had decided that a church ATM was compatible with modern life and its own goals. Information technology had become a fact of life for San Claudio's parishioners, and the priests figured that in an age of "plastic money," electronic alms was the way to go.

This alms box, of course, only accepts contributions; it does not issue cash. The electronic contributions are transmitted automatically to the local sav-ings association that installed San Claudio's ATM. This innovative method of church collection eliminates theft, a growing concern for the priests since the traditional alms box had suffered repeated burglaries. It also makes it easier for people to contribute in an era when ATMs are so widely used.

Most parishioners accepted the innovation, although a few thought it inappropriate for a church. And the church received a good deal of publicity, which the priests hoped would spur further contributions. The newspaper article alone got many residents of other parts of the city to stop by the church just to see its electronic alms box. Even the archbishop sent a representative to check it out.

The idea seems to have gained his approval, for the cathedral in Leon now has its own ATM—dedicated to raising money to rebuild this thirteenth-century Gothic church.

promoting a national network of supercomputers located at major universities, research centers, and national laboratories. Gore's plan calls for interconnecting each node on the network by fiber optics, thus providing the capability for high-speed transfer of large quantities of data and information. It also calls for an evolutionary extension of current scientific networks in the United States.

Japan, Germany, and France are also developing initiatives for national information highways. Japan intends to have its network completed between 2010 and 2015. Some U.S. experts say that the United States is not moving quickly enough to do the same; at the current rate, they estimate, the U.S. information highway will not be complete until 2037. Nonetheless, the United States is much closer to a superhighway than are the nations of Latin America, many of which still lack basic phone service. (See the *Information Technology in Practice* feature entitled "Potholes on the Information Highway: A Challenge for Latin America.") A national initiative is under way to push for more rapid development of a U.S. information superhighway.

Questions in the Development of the Superhighway

Questions, questions. When you're taking the first few steps along a path that will eventually turn into a cross-country superhighway system, plenty of questions are bound to emerge. As each of these questions is answered, the highway will move one step closer to completion.

TECHNICAL QUESTIONS.   The developers of the information highway face many technical questions: Will the highway be built from glass fiber or rely on wireless satellite links? What minimum bandwidth will be needed? And what computer and communications technology will underlie the highway? Many believe that the Internet (see Chapters 3 and 10) is the obvious choice of foundation. But the rate of IT change is rapid and accelerating, so today's ideal solution may change even as the highway is being built, and some features will be obsolete even before they are developed and implemented.

Thoughts of developing a national information superhighway tend to turn naturally to technical issues like communication lines, transmission speeds, and network reliability. Addressing these issues properly is, of course, essential.

Often overlooked, however, are the storage needs that a superhighway will create. Keep in mind that the network will be used more for transmitting than for processing data and information. Thus, the data will need to be stored in the network so they are accessible on demand. This means that huge servers will be required. Imagine the complete video library of MGM, Columbia Pictures, and Paramount Pictures, plus every volume in the U.S. Library of Congress, all available on-line. Yet, all this information together is but a drop in the bucket compared to the full scope of data and information that consumers and service providers will expect to see stored on the national information superhighway. ▧

TIME AND COST OF DEVELOPMENT.   Every nation knows that the costs of developing an information superhighway will be high, although they are hard pressed to come up with an accurate figure since the project is likely to span decades. Many estimates of costs and development time for a U.S. information superhighway have been prepared, some running as high as $140 billion and 25 years, but no one knows for sure.

THE ROLE OF GOVERNMENT.   What role will the government play in developing the information superhighway? In most countries, national highway systems were developed under government supervision and according to government specifications. Should government play this sort of role for the information superhighway, too, or should IT industries make these decisions? Once the information superhighway is in place, should the government set and enforce standards? Should it regulate who can interconnect with the superhighway and for what purpose? Is the network more likely to be successful if it is managed by the government?

These issues are particularly tricky because there is no precedent for determining the respective roles of government and private enterprise in a project like the information superhighway. And, unfortunately, there may not be time to hear all of the arguments on both sides before a decision must be made.

INFORMATION TECHNOLOGY IN PRACTICE

Potholes on the Information Highway: A Challenge for Latin America

Imagine trying to order up phone service only to hear that you'll have to pay a few thousand dollars and be patient because the phone company has about a million orders on backlog. If you can't wait one to five years for a legal installation, you may head for the black market or bribe a phone company employee. If you already have phone service, you can expect intermittent cross-talk, static, howls, incomplete calls, or no dial tone—in which case you have to decide whether the line is merely out of order or has been commandeered by a black market entrepreneur, who physically snips existing lines and runs them to new locations, leaving you stuck with other people's bills. Now try to imagine using such a phone system to compete in the global economy.

This was the quandary the "Big Three" economies of Latin America—Mexico, Argentina, and Brazil—were in for many years. After long debate, all three countries' governments announced in 1990 plans to privatize, or sell public shares in, a number of state-owned industries—including banks, utilities, mines, airlines, mass transit systems, oil and steel companies, *and* telephone companies—to private or foreign investors. To make the shares attractive to investors, these governments guaranteed the new owners a monopoly for 4 to 10 years, provided they met ambitious schedules for making major capital improvements in these industries. Venezuela and Chile soon instituted a similar program.

For the nations' leaders, the policy shift was a gamble with three goals. First, they wanted to reduce government payrolls and redirect the savings into economic growth programs. Second, they wanted to generate capital for launching social programs and reducing their foreign debt. Third, they wanted to attract outside investment to modernize and manage their infrastructures. Telecommunications capabilities were especially important in their plans. Brazil's decaying phone system, for example, had led General Motors to move its Latin American headquarters from São Paulo, Brazil, to Miami, Florida.

By 1992, some of the world's leading telecommunications companies had bought major shares in the state-owned companies. Others, such as Motorola and AT&T, had signed contracts to build copper wire, fiber-optic, cellular, or two-way radio networks. (In many cases, cellular networks are the fastest way to provide basic phone service where none exists.) Financial institutions such as Citibank, Coopers & Lybrand, and Morgan Stanley provided financing, appraised assets, and negotiated terms.

Still, the new owners encountered some daunting technical challenges. In Mexico, 9 out of 10 families lacked basic phone service. In Venezuela, more than a million phone lines had faulty connections. In Brazil, only 7 percent of the public network had been upgraded to digital technology. In Argentina, there had been no capital improvements over the previous decade, and some switches dated back to 1913. In Chile, most industries had no phone service at all.

The new owners and their managers also faced social and political challenges, including employees who feared massive layoffs. In Venezuela, a GTE-led consortium had to deal with a failed military coup and violent nationalistic street demonstrations.

Despite all these risks and technical challenges, many investors have been delighted to find themselves profiting hugely from a telecommunications boom fed by Latin America's high demand for modern phone service. Where else in the world could they get double- and triple-digit returns on their investments?

CRITICAL CONNECTION 4

Bridging the Gaps in the Information Superhighway

Just one mile of fiber-optic cable. That's all Tom DeFanti wanted. DeFanti, co-director of an advanced virtual reality research center at the University of Illinois at Chicago, needed the one-mile cable to link his lab to AT&T's experimental fiber-optic network. The hookup promised opportunities for both parties. For DeFanti's researchers, it presented the opportunity to send virtual reality and multimedia transmissions to other research centers. For AT&T, it provided a great way to test an upgraded fiber-optic technology and get practical answers to the technical challenges of high-speed data transmission. That's why DeFanti was so frustrated by the one-mile gap between his lab and the AT&T lines that lie about a mile away.

This gap illustrates some of the challenges facing the creators of the information superhighway. Ironically, though, the biggest challenge isn't a technical one. In fact, the fiber-optic technology AT&T was testing may become an economical and practical way of upgrading the speed and bandwidth of today's telephone system, paving the way for multimedia and other data-intensive transmissions. A shortage of optical fibers isn't a challenge either. In fact, many telecommunications experts say the nation already has an information superhighway made up of miles of "dark fiber," unused fiber-optic cables installed by the telephone companies, just in case they ever need the extra capacity. Rather, the biggest challenge is deciding who controls the dark fiber and who has the right to use it: a question the government is attempting to answer.

SOURCE OF FUNDING.   Will companies and industries pay the cost of designing, developing, and running the national information superhighway? If not, is there any reason that taxpayers should fund such an initiative? For that matter, must government fund an information superhighway if private industry cannot?

The huge cost of constructing a national information superhighway makes it unlikely that any single private source will undertake the project or investment. At best, this suggests that without government financing and direction, the superhighway will ultimately comprise a collection of interconnected networks—a network of networks, so to speak.

universal service
The principle, established in telecommunications, whereby it is assured that anyone who wants a basic service can receive it at low cost.

PROVISION OF UNIVERSAL SERVICE.   The principle of **universal service** in the telephone industry, whereby it is assured that anyone who wants low-cost, basic phone service can receive it, has been guiding government-regulated telecommunications companies since the 1930s. Will the same principle apply to the information highway? If so, will carriers be obliged to interconnect everyone in their region for the same basic service rate? Should businesses pay more for the interconnection than households do? Many companies that provide communications service but are outside the regulated telephone industry, such as cable companies, are not bound by universal service rules. Will this situation change when an information superhighway is put in place?

DETERMINING SUCCESS. What will determine the success of the information superhighway? If success depends on the revenues generated by the highway, what will people and companies be willing to pay for using the highway? Or should the success of the highway be judged by the new services and indirect benefits it stimulates?

Part of the problem of determining success stems from mixed thoughts on when and why the network should be constructed in the first place. Should an information highway be built to stimulate demand for consumer and business services? Or should it be developed only as a result of demand for those services?

A Final Word

The growth of the automobile industry in the 1920s, '30s, and '40s brought about the development of the interstate highway system in the 1950s and '60s. It took decades to build the networks of highways that now crisscross the United States, but business has never been the same since.

Air travel came a little later, bringing with it even greater opportunities. Yet it took many years to build the infrastructure supporting each development in the air travel industry. Airport systems and air traffic control systems were developed relatively early in the era of flight, but only in recent decades did travel agents and computerized reservation systems emerge. When they did, they played a principal role in restructuring the industry and the way people viewed it for both business and pleasure.

We are only a few years into the Information Age. The resources and infrastructure needed to keep up with the momentum of information technology are still being developed. Even though IT's impact has already been tremendous, it is just the beginning. We need to look ahead, seeking to determine what *will be* and what *can be.*

In a few years, computers, communications systems, and consumer electronics will be one and the same. Computers will process all forms of data and information, without distinction between numeric data or animated images. Telephones will handle images as easily as they do sound. Television and other consumer electronics devices will function as both computers and communication systems. No one has ever lived through such a convergence of technologies before. It's clear that the real excitement of the Information Age will come from asking the right questions, and then using our know-how to determine the right answers. Onward!

SUMMARY OF LEARNING OBJECTIVES

1 Identify the "three C's" of information technology and discuss how the definition of IT is changing in the Information Age. The three C's of information technology are computers, communications networks, and consumer electronics. The definition of IT is evolving through the incorporation of consumer electronics, a broadened definition of "communications carrier," a broadened definition of "software," the arrival of interactive television, and the redefinition of the IT industry.

2 Describe the importance of consumer electronics as an element of IT. Multimedia is paving the way for the incorporation of consumer electronics—electronic devices used to satisfy people's needs and wants rather than to manufacture products or deliver services—into IT. Many people are coming to expect images, voice, and/or animation alongside data and text.

3 Explain the expanded definition of "communications carrier." With the advancement of technology the term *communications carrier* has come to refer to more than just the telephone company or PTT. Television networks and cable companies are becoming important parts of a nation's communications capacity because communication cables can transport all types of signals.

4 Discuss the change in the definition of "software" to incorporate content as well as programs. In the computer industry, *software* has often been used to mean "computer programs." Recently, software has come to mean *content*—data and information—*as well as the means to manipulate it*. Software can also be defined as any element that gives value to hardware.

5 Explain why TV is an important type of IT and how interactive TV works. Television is becoming an important type of IT for three reasons: (1) While many homes have microcomputers, many more have television sets. (2) Television technology is advancing rapidly. (3) If *high-definition TV*

(HDTV) uses digital technology (the U.S. standard), it will become difficult to draw a distinction between TV and the PC. If TV has both computer and communications capabilities, its functions will change. Interactive TV will be a television with a keyboard, storage capability, and the capacity to transmit and receive vast amounts of information.

6 Discuss how the IT industry is changing. The convergence of the three C's of IT is changing the IT industry as firms join forces to get the most from their know-how and the global economy becomes more competitive.

7 Distinguish between a communications infrastructure and an information superhighway and give two reasons why world leaders are seeking to develop information superhighways. A *communications infrastructure* is the underlying structure of technical facilities and institutional arrangements that supports communication via telecommunications, broadcasting, film, audio and video recording, cable, print, and mail. An *information superhighway* is a communications network spanning a nation, carrying data and information traffic. It consists of fiber optics, satellites, and other communications links with huge amounts of transmission capacity. Most world leaders believe that a modern national telecommunications infrastructure is essential to maintaining and increasing personal, organizational, and national productivity. They also believe that it is essential for competing successfully in global commerce.

8 Describe six issues involved in designing and developing an information superhighway. The six issues involved in developing an information superhighway are technical questions, time and cost, the role of the government, sources of funding, the provision of universal service, and the challenges of determining the success of the superhighway.

KEY TERMS

communications infrastructure
711
consumer electronics   700
high-definition television (HDTV)
705

information superhighway   711
interactive television (ITV)   706
universal service   716

CRITICAL CONNECTIONS

1   Gateway 2000 Blurs the Line with New IT Products

Gateway 2000   Internet access capability is built into televisions produced by Gateway 2000, Mitsubishi, Zenith, and others. And since telephone calls can be made over the Internet with little difficulty, these devices combine all our most popular methods of communication.

You can expect a continually expanding cafeteria line of new products that combine multiple functions from devices that used to be stand-alone products. At a growing rate, many will be wireless as well, meaning capable of communicating and computing from any location, anytime.

Questions for Discussion

1. What other devices would you like to see combined into a single product?

2. Imagine and then describe the benefits, or limitations, of viewing television if the device on which you are viewing programs can also send and receive data and information, including messages from the Internet.

3. Do you think people really want to receive telephone calls over a television? Explain the reasoning behind your answer, using an example to illustrate your position.

2   Philips Takes a Gamble on Multimedia

Philips   Philips' Imagination Machine and the CD-I format offer some clear advantages. Chief among them are simplicity and familiarity: most consumers have television sets and they understand the concept of a VCR-like device that can play prerecorded titles. Another plus is the emphasis on education software.

But the Imagination Machine also faces a number of marketing challenges. True, consumers are excited about multimedia, but they are also confused by the options. Is the Imagination Machine just another game? (It can play many Nintendo titles.) Is it intended to replace the trusty VCR? Or are consumers supposed to fiddle with the connections every time they want to record a show or play a videotape?

Price has been another challenge. The Imagination Machine's original list price was around $1,000. Faced with high interest but sluggish sales, Philips dropped the price; by the summer of 1993, the list price was about $600. In the meantime, PC makers had launched their own price war. Multimedia PCs, once a high-priced rarity, were being sold at a discount, tempting consumers who might never have considered the purchase of a computer.

Despite the competition, Philips continued to make inroads into the consumer market. Within a year, it had demonstrated CD-I disks with full-screen, full-motion video, which could be used to show feature films. Soon, PolyGram Records, a Philips subsidiary, was releasing music videos on CD-I. By the summer of 1993, a number of electronics companies had announced they would support the Philips format for feature movies, and Philips had persuaded Paramount Communications to offer *Top Gun* and other popular movies in the CD-I format.

Questions for Discussion

1. Which elements of Philips' strategy seem most effective to you? Least effective? Explain your answers.

2. By mid-1992, Philips had supplemented its consumer model of the CD-I with an expandable professional model geared to organizations that need to make interactive multimedia sales and training presentations. Many companies found Philips' hardware and software, which included a portable unit with a color screen and cost about $3,000, a cost-effective alternative to laser-disc–based systems costing about $13,000. What does this suggest to you about the marketplace for Philips CD-I products?

3. What does Philips' experience suggest about the near future of the Information Age for consumers? For manufacturers of consumer electronics and PCs? For the publishers of software?

3   Computertots Puts Byte on Technophobia

Computertots   By the end of 1993, Computertots had sold 130 franchises and was collecting revenues of more than $3 million—a doubling of both franchises and revenue over the previous year.

Many of the franchise owners are former corporate professionals who appreciate the franchise's support and elastic schedules. Deborah Cole, for example, is a single mother who began her career as a salesperson for IBM and later became a regional sales manager at a major software company. Today, she and her staff of 15 have brought Computertots to more than 700 children in Chicago-area day-care centers and schools. For the three- to five-year-olds, the half-hour sessions are filled with games, puzzles, graphics, and fun projects like using child-sized desktop publishing programs to create holiday greeting cards. The children are learning a lot about technology and terminology—and having lots of fun in the process.

Questions for Discussion

1. Why do you think so many adults are uncomfortable using information technology? What solutions can you suggest to remedy this situation?

2. What are the advantages of the Computertots program? The possible disadvantages?

3. Are private programs like Computertots sufficient to create the technological literacy the United States needs for the future? If not, how might U.S. technological literacy be improved?

4   Bridging the Gaps in the Information Superhighway

The one-mile gap that stymied DeFanti represents a physical gap between AT&T's long-distance lines and the local lines controlled by Ameritech (formerly Illinois Bell). But it also represents a marketing and regulatory gap between Ameritech and its competitors. Ameritech had dark fiber in the one-mile gap that DeFanti could have used to link up to AT&T's lines, but Ameritech had a policy against leasing dark fiber to organizations that could install activating equipment and then bypass the telephone company, thus cutting into its profits.

The prohibition dates back to the mid-1980s, when other telephone companies began leasing dark fiber to a few select large customers. After smaller customers complained to the Federal Communications Commission—and won—the telephone companies labeled the practice an experiment and tried to drop it. The issue didn't go away, though. In the summer of 1993, while DeFanti was struggling to find his mile of dark fiber, the FCC and a federal court in Washington, D.C., were grappling with the question of whether the FCC could require the telephone companies to provide dark-fiber services to potential competitors. Many experts predicted that the telephone companies would fight the dark-fiber issue until government regulations were eased, giving the telephone companies the right to offer new and lucrative communications services.

Questions for Discussion

1. What does the dark-fiber issue indicate about the role of government in building the information superhighway?

2. Should Ameritech be required to lease dark fiber? Present an argument in favor of the telephone companies and an argument in favor of their potential competitors.

3. At present, government regulators base telephone rates on the initial cost of the system and the amount individual customers use it. What changes might be required in the future when high-speed, high-capacity data lines are able to transmit millions of bits per second? Can you suggest a fair basis for the telephone bill of tomorrow?

Net Work

There is growing interest in buying and selling products and services over the Internet. Will this become an important sales and marketing channel? Who will use the Internet to shop, and what will they shop for? What new services will be possible because of the Internet's powerful multimedia and communications capabilities?

Electronic commerce is about buying and shopping over communications links like the Internet. To see how some companies have built a business around electronic commerce on the Internet, take a look at:

- Amazon.com books (http://www.amazon.com). The first massive bookseller, listing more than 1 million titles, to set up shop on the Internet.
- CDNow (http://www.cdnow.com). A seller of compact discs, providing more than 150,000 products from which its customers can choose.

- Internet Shopping Network (http://www.isn.com). An Internet source for more than 25,000 computer products, typically sold at discounts of 10 to 20 percent.

1. What services do these Internet merchants provide to assist their customers in finding and then purchasing products from them? Could these be provided if the companies were not doing business on the Internet?
2. Do you think these merchants' methods are representative of the way other companies must do business on the Internet?
3. In the future, what types of products and services do you think will be most commonly searched out or purchased over the Internet?
4. Why will or will not consumers typically turn to the Internet when they wish to shop for and purchase products or services?

GROUP PROJECTS AND APPLICATIONS

Project 1

Most issues of *Business Week* feature sections titled "Information Technology" and "Developments to Watch." The material in these sections is devoted to research, applications, and developments in information technology.

The class should divide into groups of four or five. Each group should scan the most recent issues of *Business Week* (or some other publication) and report to the entire class on a technology under development. What is the time frame for completion? How will this technology affect our lives?

Project 2

The backbone of the information superhighway is likely to be the Internet. In the past few years, the Net's popularity has exploded. Once a tool used by scientists and academics, it is now a household word. Many praise the Net as an egalitarian virtual community where information is available at one's fingertips and where people from all walks of life can meet and communicate.

Yet, like all new products and trends, the Net has its detractors. First of all, it is accessible only to those who can afford computers.

Second, access can be notoriously slow. Third, many social scientists fear that time spent on the Internet is becoming a substitute for normal face-to-face human interaction. Finally, for-profit businesses fear that it is simply impossible to make money on the Net.

Two groups of four persons each should debate the pros and cons of life on the Internet. The first group speaks in favor of the Net; the second group speaks against it. After the first person from each side has spoken, the second questions the opponent's arguments, looking for holes and inconsistencies. The third person attempts to answer these arguments. The fourth presents a summary of each side's argument. Finally, the class votes on which team has offered the more compelling argument.

REVIEW QUESTIONS

1. In what ways is the definition of information technology changing?

2. What is the "third C" of information technology and what is its relationship to multimedia?

3. In what way is the definition of "communications carrier" changing? Why?

4. In what way is the definition of "software" changing? What does this change mean for IT in general?

5. Discuss three reasons why television is becoming an important type of information technology.

6. What is high-definition television (HDTV)? How do U.S. developments in HDTV technology differ from those in Japan?

7. What is interactive TV?

8. How and why is the definition of the IT industry changing? What does this mean for consumers and businesses?

9. What is an information superhighway? Name two reasons why world leaders are seeking to develop an information superhighway.

10. What is a communications infrastructure?

11. Describe the relationship between an information superhighway and a nation's competitive advantage in global markets.

12. Give three examples of technical questions that the designers of an information superhighway must address.

13. Discuss the issues surrounding the role of government and the sources of funding in developing an information superhighway.

14. What is the principle of universal service and how does it relate to the information superhighway?

15. What criteria may be used to determine the success of an information superhighway?

DISCUSSION QUESTIONS

1. CUC, Inc., was losing money as a shop-by-PC service until it transformed itself into a buyers' club in which members shop by phone for discounts on travel, auto services, insurance, and more than 250,000 products. By 1993, CUC had 28 million members and was ready for a third transformation—into an interactive shopping network for the 70 million cable subscribers in the United States. Why do you think CUC is more successful as a phone-based service than it was as a PC-based service? What are its chances as an interactive TV service?

2. What might the success of CUC and other interactive shopping services mean for retail-dependent businesses, like commercial real estate? For society?

3. Many interactive TV experiments are being sponsored by cable companies like TCI, Inc., which al-

ready require a subscriber fee and may demand higher fees for the new interactive services. What are the pros and cons of such a fee-based service for cable and interactive TV?

4. AT&T recently cooperated with the telephone service provider in Mexico to build a digital network offering improved service for five major U.S.–Mexico border areas, including the free-trade zone containing many *maquiladoras* (United States–owned manufacturing plants located very close to the border in Mexico). Why would AT&T enter into such an agreement?

SUGGESTED READINGS

Davis, Stan, and Bill Davidson. *2020 Vision: Transform Your Business Today to Succeed in Tomorrow's Economy.* New York: Simon & Schuster, 1991. An excellent discussion of how computers and data communication networks are reshaping the structure of modern business, allowing firms to improve existing products and services and to create new ones.

Egan, B. L. *Information Superhighways: The Economics of Advanced Public Communication Networks.* Norwood, MA: Artech House, 1991. A comprehensive discussion of the issues, challenges, and opportunities surrounding the development of national communications networks.

Keen, Peter G. W. *Competing in Time: Using Telecommunications for Competitive Advantage.* Cambridge, MA: Ballinger, 1988. A balanced and practical analysis of the changing role of communications systems in business. Offers unique insights useful to both IT professionals and executive officers.

Kalakota, Ravi, and Andrew B. Whinston. *Frontiers of Electronic Commerce.* Reading, MA: Addison Wesley, 1996. An extensive, in-depth discussion of electronic commerce, including both technologies and applications. The book addresses consumer topics as well as inter- and intra-organizational uses of electronic commerce.

Malone, Thomas W., et al. "Intelligent Information-Sharing Systems." *Communications of the ACM 30* (May 1987): 390–402. A thought-provoking discussion of a prototype information system designed to support problem-solving needs. The system can be tailored to personal needs and is useful for screening and filtering information transmitted through communications systems.

Rayport, Jeffrey F., and John J. Sviokla. "Managing in the Marketspace." *Harvard Business Review 72* (November–December 1994): 141–150. Advances in information technology are causing businesses to transform not only how they operate but also where they do business. The authors introduce the idea of a *business marketspace,* and describe the many opportunities and challenges it presents in contrast to the traditional marketplace.

Senn, James A. "Capitalizing on Electronic Commerce: The Role of the Internet in Electronic Markets." *Information Systems Management 13* (Summer 1996): 15–24. Aimed at helping managers evaluate the business potential of electronic commerce and the characteristics of the Internet that make it a highly visible forum for conducting business electronically.

Stoll, Clifford. *Silicon Snake Oil.* New York: Doubleday, 1995. Stoll claims the much-heralded information superhighway will not turn out to be all it's cracked up to be. In his opinion, communications systems like the Internet do not have much relevancy to daily living. Not surprisingly, Stoll's book has sparked a nationwide debate on the role of networks in the future. Reading this book will enable you to decide for yourself.

Toffler, Alvin. *Powershift.* New York: Bantam Books, 1990. A groundbreaking book in which Toffler, one of today's leading futurists, describes how knowledge is creating tremendous shifts in power at both the local and global levels.

Wriston, Walter B. *The Twilight of Sovereignty.* New York: Free Press, 1992. A discussion of the effects of the worldwide information revolution, with a look to the future.

Finland: A Virtual Reality for the Future

It might be the long winter nights, or it might be the high education and literacy levels, the good standard of living, or the level of government spending on research and development. Whatever the explanation, Finland, the Nordic country buffering the old Soviet Union on one side and Western Europe on the other, by every measure leads the world in creating and living the electronic future. In this country of 5 million people—the most connected nation in the world—information technology is already a habit.

In Finland's virtual world, where linking up has replaced traditional ("real-world") methods of communication, being on-line is the norm. Socializing, shopping, and conducting ordinary business rely on electronic communications links. Chances are when a Finn wants to make a telephone call, he'll reach for his cellular telephone. The Internet is also the Finns' chosen medium for personal chats, business communication, and conducting research. Merita, the country's largest bank, has granted over 3 million customers secure access by computer. But Finland's success goes well beyond cell phones and the Internet.* "Electronic wallets"

and digital cash are commonly used to shop, purchase concert tickets, play in electronic arcades, and pay for education and training.

Many intertwining forces are responsible for Finland's information technology foundation. One is that the nation has the highest penetration of cellular telephones in the world: one-third of Finland's citizens

*Finland has more than 60 Internet hosts for every 1,000 people, more than double the comparable statistic for the United States. It leads the world in this respect.

carry cellular telephones. Fixed phones, the norm worldwide, are rapidly become obsolete in Finland. Even standard cellular telephones are regarded as "old-fashioned" compared to newer versions that send and receive e-mail and allow their owners to search the World Wide Web and participate in news groups and on-line conversations. Cellular calls are charged on a rate that is independent of the distance called within the country, effectively eliminating the traditional distinction between local and in-country long-distance rates. Only the caller pays for cellular calls, in contrast to other parts of the world (including the United States), where *both* caller and recipient pay a charge based on the length of the call. Finns can choose from several communications providers, including global satellite networks (GSM).

Nokia, the Finnish maker of world-class communications systems, headquartered in Helsinki, was the first company anywhere in the world to bring to market a handheld communications system that combines the capabilities of both a wireless telephone and a personal computer—all in a package the size of a cellular telephone.

In the mid-1990s, the state-owned Telecom Finland launched an Internet phone service: customers talk to one another at their computer terminals. This promises to become the most inexpensive way to make calls in the future.

Development of the country's IT capabilities has also benefited from the widespread belief in the potential of information technology and a willingness to make the necessary investments. The national government, municipalities, and Finnish computer makers have all subsidized a campaign to offer abundant links to computers and communications systems.

Olli-Pekka Heinonen, Finland's minister of education and a prominent proponent of information technology capabilities, has stated that the country is spending more than $400 million to educate 1 million students and adults on how to use the Internet and plans to connect all of the country's 5,000 schools to the Net by the year 2000. The overall objective: "A society where competence is based on knowledge, know-how and the creation of new economic wealth."[†]

"Virtual reality" is the image of the future in most of the developed nations. Finland has it today.

Questions for Discussion

1. What factors do you feel account for Finland's leading edge in the use of information technology in everyday activities? Why do you believe Finland has been able to develop these factors before other nations?

2. Do you believe Finland will continue to expand IT's use and extend its capabilities? In what ways?

3. What do you think it would be like to always have widespread information technology around you, from the moment you enter school? How would it change your education and the educational process?

[†]Youseff M. Ibrahim, "Finland: An Unlikely Home Base for Universal Use of Technology," *The New York Times*, January 20, 1997, p. A1.

Opportunities for Intrusion

Coping with Network Insecurity

Computer networks are an essential part of corporate and business activities. Customers, suppliers, and employees expect networks to be available and accessible to obtain and exchange information. Thus, it's no surprise that the number and use of computer networks are growing at an accelerating rate. Add in Internet and intranet usage, and it's impossible even to gauge the amount of network utilization.

Causes of Network Insecurity

As networks have grown, so has network insecurity. The twin aspects of network insecurity are security violations and inadequate protection mechanisms.

Security Violations Are Abundant

A study by the consultancy firm Ernst & Young revealed that more than half of the 1,300 large companies surveyed had in the past two years encountered information technology security violations in which they suffered a loss. When intrusion due to computer viruses was included, the proportion jumped to nearly 80 percent.

Even the most seemingly secure sites are vulnerable. For instance, hackers have broken into World Wide Web sites of the U.S. Department of Justice, the Federal Bureau of Investigation (FBI), and the Central Intelligence Agency (CIA).

Executives are well aware of the problem, so you would expect them to be striving to ensure that their companies are truly protected. However, the evidence suggests that they are not.

Protection Is Not Adequate

Most executives will admit—at least in private—that they are not confident their companies are protected against outside intrusion or security violations by dis-

gruntled employees (the source of more than one-third of all breaches of security). Most don't even know their level of vulnerability, for they have no IT staff members assigned to IT security. In even the largest companies, generally one or two persons have security responsibility—an altogether inadequate number given the number of networks and attached computers. Security provisions don't appear in the IT or corporate budgets either, since most companies do not spend money to train staff members or build adequate IT security systems. Apparently, at the great majority of firms, security is an afterthought.

Discovering Company Vulnerability

Some companies, eager to find out exactly where their exposure is, have hired experts to break into their systems. San Antonio, Texas–based WheelGroup specializes in this kind of work. It will examine a firm's systems and test protection mechanisms by attempting to enter the network, including the e-mail systems. Leave a handwritten password on the side of a monitor, and WheelGroup's team members will find it. Leave a computer on, and even though the monitor is off, the team typically finds that it is still connected to the company network—meaning its files and applications are accessible to anyone.

What characterizes an impenetrable system? When interviewed by *Fortune* magazine, a WheelGroup executive claimed that the company's teams *had yet to find a system or network anywhere that they could not pierce electronically.* "It's really very easy to do," according to the executive. "If it's a big network, it may take us an evening. Otherwise, it may take two hours."*

Questions for Discussion

1. Are you conscious of the possibility of intrusion

when you send, receive, or store information through a computer network? If so, what precautions do you take?

2. What instances of network insecurity have you personally encountered? How did the intrusion occur?

3. If most organizations don't have the resources or expertise to monitor the security of their own critical systems effectively, what should they do?

4. How should companies go about determining their security weaknesses? Do you think the best way is to hire an outside firm to break into the system?

5. Who is responsible if a company's network is accessed by an intruder? Do you think the IT director should be legally responsible for damages? Should shareholders of the company make the CEO responsible for damages due to security lapses?

*Richard Behar, "Who's Reading Your E-Mail," *Fortune 135* (February 3, 1997): 57–70.

Numbers above the timeline at the center of the page correspond to the photos and caption numbers in red boxes.

1 Lascaux cave paintings created

3 Johannes Gutenberg invents printing press

5 Baron Gottfried Wilhelm von Leibniz designs calculation machine (working version produced in 1694 from earlier plans)

6 Charles Babbage devises "difference engine" to mechanize calculation of trigonometric and logarithmic tables

Ts'ai invents paper ▲

1	2				3	4	5		6	7
15,000 - 10,000 BC	3500 BC	3200 BC	AD 105		AD 1400	1642	1671	1729	1812	1831

▼ Egyptians first use ink

▼ Electronic pulses first sent over a wire

2 Sumerians develop a system of writing

7 Joseph Henry builds first electromagnetic telegraph

4 Blaise Pascal invents the Pascaline adding machine

8 Alexander Graham Bell patents first telephone

10 Howard H. Aiken, Ph.D. candidate at Harvard University, devises Mark I, the first large-scale automatic digital calculator

Charles Babbage designs "Analytical Engine" ▲

Transatlantic telegraph cable is laid ▲

8

9

Scottish inventor John Baird demonstrates his invention, the television ▲

U.S. Congress passes the Communications Act of 1934, which creates the Federal Communications Commission (FCC), whose sole purpose is to regulate the U.S. telecommunications industry ▲

10

11

| 1834 | 1838 | 1866 | 1876 | 1890s | 1921 | 1926 | 1928 | 1934 | 1937 | 1939 |

▼ Samuel Morse develops Morse Code

▼ U.S. Congress passes the Graham Act, which recognizes and legitimizes AT&T's monopoly for providing telecommunications services in the U.S.

▼ First television programming begins in U.S.

9 Herman Hollerith, of the U.S. Bureau of the Census, devises punch card system and punch card machine

11 John Atanasoff (top) and Clifford Berry build the first electronic digital computer, nicknamed "ABC" (for Atanasoff-Berry computer)

THE FIRST TABULATING SYSTEM BY HOLLERITH COMPANY IN 1890

14 UNIVAC I, the first commercially used computer, announced

12 U.S. FCC devises rules for commercial television broadcasting

William Shockley, Walter Brattain, and John Bardeen announce their invention of the transistor at AT&T Bell Laboratories

First pocket radios are introduced to the U.S. market

12		**13**	▲		**14 & 15**		**16**	▲	**17**	**18**	**19**
1940	1945	1946	1948	1951-1958	1951	1952	1953	1954	1959-1964	1960	1963

▼ John von Neumann, at Princeton University, develops concept of stored program computer

▼ The vacuum tube (first) generation of computers

▼ UNIVAC I used to tabulate the U.S. national election vote, declaring Dwight D. Eisenhower to be the elected president only 45 minutes after the polls closed

▼ Digital Equipment Corporation builds the first successful minicomputer

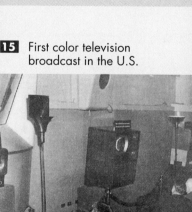

15 First color television broadcast in the U.S.

13 J. Prosper Eckert, graduate student, and Dr. John W. Mauchly develop the Electronic Numerical Integrator and Calculator (ENIAC) at the Moore School of Engineering, University of Pennsylvania

16 IBM begins manufacture of line of business computers

17 Transistor generation (second generation) of computers

19 Theodore H. Maiman operates first laser

21 Bill Gates (right) and Paul Allen found Microsoft

- Beginning of microminiaturized integrated circuit generation (fourth generation) of computers
- Robert Metcalf develops the first local area network (LAN) while at Xerox PARC
- U.S. FCC concludes a study known as Computer Inquiry I determining that, although the data processing and telecommunications industries are growing closer together, the data processing industry, which is unregulated, should not be subject to its control

IBM announces the System/360 line of computers—the first-ever family of compatible computers

Computer beats human opponent at chess for the first time

Intel introduces the 8080 microprocessor

Digital Research, Inc.'s Gary Kildall develops CP/M, first operating system for a microcomputer

20

21

22

| 1964 | 1965-1970 | 1967 | 1969 | 1971 | 1972 | 1974 | 1975 | 1976 | 1977 |

- Edgar F. Codd publishes the first in a series of papers defining relational databases
- Carterphone Decision by the FCC for the first time allows the attachment of non-telephone company devices to the telephone network
- Microwave Communications, Inc. (MCI) requires public telephone companies to interconnect the lines of private companies (like MCI) to the public telephone network, thereby giving their customers nationwide access

The first video game, Pong, becomes an overnight success

- Altair 8800, the world's first microcomputer system, is released as a kit to be assembled
- First user groups are formed
- Cray-1 supercomputer announced

- Commodore introduces PET microcomputer
- Tandy TRS-80 microcomputer introduced

18 COBOL specifications introduced; Grace Hopper, who coined the term "bug," is one member of the COBOL development team

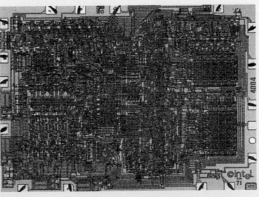

20 Integrated circuit generation (third generation) of computers

22 Apple II microcomputer debuts (created by Steve Wozniak, bottom, and Steve Jobs, right)

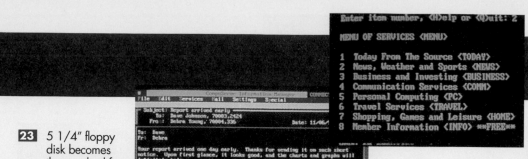

23 5 1/4" floppy disk becomes the standard for microcomputers

24 CompuServe and The Source on-line services begin operation

27 First compact disc (CD) player sold

- Microsoft agrees to develop MS-DOS for IBM's forthcoming PC
- First relational database management system, Oracle, announced
- Pac-Man video game introduced
- Cable News Network (CNN) is launched

- Lotus announces Lotus 1-2-3
- WordPerfect Corp. introduces WordPerfect, an instantly popular word processing system running on many different microcomputers under DOS
- *Time* magazine names the computer "Man of the Year"
- The U.S. Federal Government releases its Modified Final Judgment, stating that the monopolistic nature of AT&T is now detrimental to the development of telecommunications. On January 1, 1984, At&T must divest itself of all 22 of its associated operating companies in the Bell System

- Apple introduces the Macintosh microcomputer and along with it releases the first windows-based interface
- The 3 1/2" diskette debuts
- IBM unveils the IBM PC Portable and the PC-AT
- AT&T divests itself of the 22 Bell operating companies; 6 regional Bell operating companies (NYNEX, Bell Atlantic, Bell South, Southwestern Bell, U.S. West, and Pacific Telesis) are created

23	24	▲	25	▲	26 & 27	▲		
1978	1979	1980	1981	1982	1983	1984	1985	1986

- VisiCorp introduces the VisiCalc spreadsheet package (created by Dan Bricklin and Bob Frankston) for the Apple II

- Nintendo introduces its first arcade video game, Donkey Kong
- IBM introduces its first desktop computer, the Datamaster
- Adam Osborne introduces the first portable microcomputer, the Osborne 1
- Commercial mouse debuts with the Xerox Star office computer
- MicroPro, Inc. introduces WordStar, a word processing system running on many different microcomputers under DOS
  - FCC's Computer Inquiry II announces that computer companies can transmit data on the telephone network on an unregulated basis, that telephone companies can participate in data processing, and that basic telephone services will remain regulated but that enhanced services and equipment on the customer's premises will be deregulated

- Apple debuts its second family of computers, the Lisa
- IBM introduces the PC-XT, which uses the Intel 8086 chip, and the PC Jr.
- First inter-city fiber-optic phone system

- Intel debuts the 80386 chip
- Desktop publishing is born
- CD player sales surpass turntable sales

- IBM introduces the PC convertible microcomputer: part portable, part desktop PC
- Compaq unveils the first 32-bit PC, the Deskpro 386
- FCC's Computer Inquiry III allows the Bell operating companies and AT&T to offer enhanced services if they agree to a set of provisions, *open network architecture*, that entitle other companies to information about the network

25 IBM unveils the IBM PC

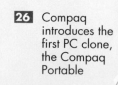

26 Compaq introduces the first PC clone, the Compaq Portable

28 Apple debuts the Macintosh II

29 IBM introduces the PS/2 series of microcomputers

30 Microsoft Windows 3.0 is released and, unlike earlier versions, is a runaway success. Windows 3.0 quickly becomes the dominant interface for IBM-compatible computers

32 U.S. President Clinton and Vice President Al Gore openly campaign for the development of a U.S. information superhighway

- Apple sues Microsoft and Hewlett Packard for copyright infringement over use of a windows interface
- Internet worm unleashed
- The Internet comprises 33,000 host computers

- Michael Hammer, in a landmark article in the *Harvard Business Review*, coins the term *re-engineering*, saying that IT should be used to rethink, rather than merely automate, business processes
- IBM debuts the PS/1 series
- U.S. Federal Trade Commission probes Microsoft for possible antitrust violations (but does not file a lawsuit)

- The University of Arizona (Jay Nunamaker and faculty colleagues) and Lotus both roll out software products inaugurating the era of groupware
- Pen computers introduced
- Object technology gains momentum and is critically examined for development in a wide variety of IT applications

- Bell Atlantic and TCI call off their decision to merge, citing uncertainties in the regulatory environment surrounding cable TV and telecommunications
- Netscape, a new Internet browser program, is developed by Marc Andreessen and Jim Clark

28 & 29 ▲	▲	▲	▲	▲	▲	**31 & 32** ▲	▲
1987	1988	1989	1990	1991	1992	1993	1994

▼ **30** ▼ **33**

- IBM and Microsoft announce joint development agreement for the OS/2 microcomputer operating system

- Adobe announces the Postscript standard for document and graphics printing

- Borland buys Ashton-Tate, creator of dBASE II-IV
- LAN software developer Novell and Digital Research, Inc. (DRI) merge

- IBM and Apple roll out highly successful notebook computers
- Intel announces the Pentium microprocessor
- Apple rolls out the Newton MessagePad, its highly anticipated personal digital assistant
- Internet comprises 1.8 million host computers
- U.S. cable giant Tele-Communications, Inc. (TCI) and Bell Atlantic announce a megamerger aimed at creating leadership in pursuit of the world of the information superhighway

31 Apple, IBM, and Motorola announce the Power PC RISC microprocessor

33 Apple rolls out the first PowerPC microcomputers

- The National Library of Medicine's Visible Man, the world's first computerized library of human anatomy, consisting of 1,800 thin cross sections of the body of a man donated to science, is made available on the Internet. The Visible Woman follows
- U.S. Semiconductor Industry Assoc. determines that Moore's Law (i.e., that the computing power on an equivalent size chip will double every 18 months) will break down in 2010
- The Internet is turned over to the public sector (partly because it can no longer be used for national security purposes)
- Supercomputer manufacturer Cray Computer files for bankruptcy
- Visa International announces the introduction of a new plastic card containing a microchip. The card is intended to replace cash for small purchases
- Netscape's initial public offering excites Wall Street investors, triggering a rapid escalation in the value of its own shares as well as other Internet stocks

36 U.S. Telecommunications Act of 1996 is signed, calling for competition in the sale of local telecommunications service

38 Michael Kingsley, journalist and cable television personality, leaves CNN to join Microsoft in Redmond, Washington, starting *Slate*, the first commercial on-line magazine

37 Turner Broadcasting and Time Warner win government approval for a $6.8 billion merger

40 Intel announces the Pentium II microprocessor

41 67 nations agree to freer markets in communications, signing a landmark agreement in which the nations agreed to open up their telecommunications markets to all rivals

- Time Warner decides to pull the plug at the end of 1997 on its Florida interactive TV network
- Microsoft rivals IBM, Sun Microsystems, Oracle Corp., and Netscape Communications Corp. endorse common methods to develop programs based on corporate computer networks and the Internet

36, 37, 38, 39

▲ **1995**   ▼ **1996**   ▲ **1997**

34 & 35

34 Microsoft releases Windows 95, containing an interface many observers claim was designed after the Apple Macintosh interface

35 James Gosling, engineer at Sun Microsystems, develops Java, a programming language designed to be independent of specific computer platforms. Potentially, a Java program can reside anywhere on the Internet and be executed by any program connected to the Internet

- Pacific Telesis and SBC Communications announce a $16.5 billion merger
- U.S. West acquires Continental Cablevision for $5.3 billion
- Nynex and Bell Atlantic announce a $21.3 billion merger
- IBM researcher devises a way to transmit information via a tiny pocket computer and current running through the human body
- IBM unveils plans for new mainframe computers that will use PC-like chips instead of customized circuit boards
- AT&T spins off Lucent Technologies and NCR
- BT and MCI Communications announce they will merge to create the world's first transatlantic telephone carrier
- AMR Corporation, parent company of American Airlines, announces it will make its technology division, SABRE, a separate unit
- MasterCard and Visa agree to promote a single payment method for Web-based electronic commerce

41

Microsoft® **Windows CE**

39 Microsoft rolls out Windows CE, a compact edition of Windows 95 designed for use on handheld, palmtop computers that enable transfer of information to and from desktop systems

Concise Dictionary of IT Terminology

accelerator board An add-in circuit board that increases a computer's processing speed.

action An instruction that tells a database how to process an object to produce specific information.

action document A document designed to trigger a specific action or to signify that a transaction has taken place.

add-in board A board that can be added to a computer to customize its features and capabilities.

address An identifiable location in memory where data are kept.

Agricultural Age The period up to the 1800s, when the majority of workers were farmers whose lives revolved around agriculture.

analog audio Sound transmitted by acoustic, mechanical, or electrical frequencies or waves; the normal version of sound.

anonymous FTP site A public FTP site that does not require you to use a special password to gain access.

application generation In a database system, the use of menus and simple commands to describe the application to a system program that creates the set of detailed commands.

application program/application A program or a combination of programs written for a specific use.

Archie A server that lists the contents of anonymous FTP sites.

architecture The structure of a communications network, which determines how the various components of the network are structured, how they interact, and when cooperation between the system's components is needed.

arithmetic/logic unit (ALU) The part of the CPU that performs arithmetic and logical operations.

attribute A category of data or information that describes an entity. Each attribute is a fact about the entity.

audio Sound. The two forms of audio are analog and digital.

audio response unit/speech synthesizer An output device that transforms data or information into sound.

authoring The sequence of activities used to create a multimedia production: deciding on purpose, content, and components, and incorporating them into a presentation.

authoring system The set of software tools used to create a multimedia presentation.

backbone network A transmission facility designed to move data and information at high speeds.

back-end CASE tool A CASE tool that automates the later (back-end) activities in systems development.

backup copies Extra copies of information or software made to protect against losses.

backup procedure A procedure that describes how and when to make extra copies of information or software to protect against losses.

bar code A computer-readable code consisting of bars or lines of varying widths or lengths.

batch processing The grouping and processing of all transactions at one time.

BIOS The computer's basic input/output system.

bitmapped image A paper photograph that has been digitized.

bit mapping A feature of some monitors that allows each dot on the monitor to be addressed or controlled individually. Graphics created through bit mapping are sharp and crisp.

block The writing of one or more records onto a section of magnetic tape.

board A hardware device onto which chips and their related circuitry are placed.

boot To turn on the computer system and let the built-in self-test run.

bridge A device that interconnects compatible LANs.

build The animation technique that displays text one line at a time in a multimedia slide presentation.

business graphics Charts, graphs, and maps that are created using special graphics packages that translate data into visual representations.

business information system The family of IT applications that underlies the activities of running and managing a business.

business processes Collections of activities, often spanning several departments, that take one or more kinds of input and create a result that is of value to a company's customers.

byte A storage location in memory; the amount of memory required to store one digit, letter, or character.

cache memory A form of high-speed memory that acts as a temporary holding/processing cell.

capture The process of compiling detailed records of activities.

CD-ROM disk Short for "compact disk—read only memory," an optical storage medium that permits storage of large amounts of information. CD-ROM disks can only be written to and cannot be erased.

cell In an electronic spreadsheet, the intersection of a row and a column.

cell address/cell reference The intersection of a particular row and column in an electronic spreadsheet.

cell pointer The cursor in an electronic spreadsheet.

cellular telephone A device used to send and receive voice communications and computer and fax transmissions while allowing users freedom of movement.

centralized architecture A communications architecture in which a computer at a central site hosts all of the network's hardware and software, performs all of the processing, and manages the network.

central processing unit (CPU)/ processor The computer hardware that executes program instructions and performs the computer's processing actions.

change agent A person who acts as a catalyst for change.

character addressing The precursor to bit mapping that allowed only full characters to be sent to and displayed on a VDT.

chat session A live interactive discussion where all parties are actually on the network, interacting through their computers.

chief information officer (CIO) The person given the responsibility of managing and developing the firm's information technology capabilities.

client In client-server computing, a desktop workstation.

client computer The computer that accesses the information stored on a server computer.

client-server computing A type of computing in which all data and information retrieval requests and responses pass over a network. Much of the processing is performed on the server and the results of the processing are transmitted to the client.

coaxial cable/co-ax A physical communications channel that uses one or more central wire conductors surrounded by an insulator and encased in either a wire mesh or metal sheathing.

cold site A backup facility outfitted with electrical power and environmental controls so that it is ready for a company to install a computer system.

columns The vertical elements in a spreadsheet.

common carrier A company that furnishes public communications facilities for voice and data transmission.

communication The sending and receiving of data and information over a communications network.

communications channel/communications medium The physical or cableless media that link the different components of a network.

communications infrastructure The underlying structure of technical facilities and institutional arrangements that supports communication via telecommunications, broadcasting, film, audio and video recording, cable, print, and mail.

communications network A set of locations, or nodes, consisting of hardware, programs, and information linked together as a system that transmits and receives data and information.

communications program A program that manages the interaction between a computer system and a communications network and the transmission of data, programs, and information over the network.

complex instruction set computing (CISC) A computing instruction set that moves data to and from main memory so often that it limits the use of registers.

computer An electronic system that can be instructed to accept, process, store, and present data and information.

computer-aided design (CAD) A system that uses a powerful computer graphics workstation to enable product designers and engineers to draw design specifications on a display screen.

computer-aided manufacturing (CAM) A system that relies on IT to automate and manage the manufacturing process directly.

computer-aided systems engineering/computer-aided software engineering (CASE) tools A set of tools used in systems development to improve the consistency and quality of the system while automating many of the most tedious and time-consuming systems tasks.

computer crime The unauthorized use of a computer system or theft of system resources for personal use.

computer engineer An IT professional who designs, develops, and oversees the manufacturing of computer equipment.

computer-integrated manufacturing (CIM) A manufacturing system that uses computers to link automated processes in a factory to reduce design time, increase machine utilization, shorten the manufacturing cycle, cut inventories, and increase product quality.

computer programming language A series of commands or codes that a computer can translate into the electronic pulses that underlie all computing activities.

computer vision system A system that uses computer sensors to detect shapes, images, and varying levels of detail.

concurrent data sharing A database procedure that allows several users to access the database simultaneously.

concurrent engineering A design and manufacturing method in which team members work across their departmental functions to evaluate the activities of many departments and manage the product development process.

configuration The specific combination of hardware and software in a system.

consumer electronics Electronic devices used to satisfy people's needs and wants rather than to manufacture products or deliver services.

content line/edit line The line of an electronic spreadsheet's control panel indicating the data or information being keyed into the active cell of the spreadsheet.

control unit   The part of the CPU that oversees and controls all computer activities according to the instructions it receives.

conversion plan   A description of all the activities that must occur to change over to a new system.

co-processor chip   A special-purpose chip mounted on a processor board; it is designed to handle common functions quickly and efficiently.

copy protection   A software protection scheme that defeats attempts to copy a program or makes the copied software unreliable.

copyright   Legal protection of original works against unauthorized use, including duplication.

current cell/active cell   In an electronic spreadsheet, the cell in which the user is currently working.

custom programming   In a database system, the writing of detailed procedures using the commands and functions built into the database management software.

custom software   Software written specially for a particular business.

data   Raw facts, figures, and details.

database   A collection of data and information describing items of interest to an organization.

database administration   The management of a database.

database administration procedures   The procedures associated with managing a database.

database administrator (DBA)   The IT professional responsible for managing all the activities and procedures related to an organization's database.

database application   A computerized database routine for collecting, retrieving, or manipulating data to meet recurring needs.

database directory   The component of a shared database that keeps track of data and information.

database management program   A program that allows users to store information as interrelated records that can be retrieved quickly.

database management system (DBMS)   A program that makes it possible for users to manage the data in a database in order to increase accessibility and productivity.

database management system (DBMS)   A program that makes it possible for users to manage the data in ways that increase accessibility and productivity.

data bus   A bus that moves data between the central processor and memory.

data center/computer center   A facility at which large and midrange computer systems are located. These systems are shared by many users who are interconnected with the system through communications links.

data communication   The transmission of data and information through a communications medium.

data definition language (DDL)   A tool that allows users to define a database.

data dictionary/repository   A catalog that lists and describes all the types of data flowing through a system. Composed of data elements and a data structure.

data element   The component of a data dictionary that includes data names, alternate names, and length allowances.

data entry   The process of populating a database with data and information.

data entry form   Custom-developed video display used to enter and change data in a database.

dataflow diagram (DFD)   A chart showing the movement of data through a system.

data item   A specific detail of an individual entity that is stored in a database.

data manipulation language (DML)   A tool that allows users to store, retrieve, and edit data in a database.

data processing   The process of handling data and transforming them into information.

data structure   The set of data elements used together and the name that collectively identifies the set.

deadlock   A situation in which each user of a database is waiting for the others to unlock a record.

decision support system (DSS)   A business information system designed to assist in decision making where the decision process is relatively unstructured and only part of the information needed is structured in advance.

desktop publishing (DTP) program   A program that combines text and image-handling features with document-design capabilities.

detail report/transaction log   A report describing each processed transaction.

development procedure   A procedure that explains how IT professionals should describe user needs and develop applications to meet those needs.

digital animation   A method for making an object appear to move across a computer screen.

digital audio   Sound transmitted by discrete binary pulses; the computerized version of sound.

digital camera   A device that captures a photographic image as a collection of tightly grouped dots that can be stored on disk or in memory.

digital video/digital motion video   The presentation of data and information as moving images that can be processed by computer or transmitted over communications networks.

digitizer   An input device that translates measured distances into digital values that the computer can process.

digitizing tablet   A device by which an image on paper can be translated into electronic form.

direct cut over strategy   A conversion plan in which people abruptly stop using an old system and immediately begin using a new one.

directory   A listing of information by category.

disaster recovery plan   A procedure for restoring data lost when a system stops functioning.

disk operating system (DOS)   An operating system whose components reside on a disk and are brought into computer memory as needed.

disk pack   A stack of disks, enclosed in a protective plastic cover, that can be lifted onto or off a disk drive.

distributed architecture   A communications architecture in which the computers reside at different locations and are interconnected by a communications network.

distributed database   A database that resides in more than one system in a distributed network. Each component of the database can be retrieved from any node in the network.

distributed processing   Processing in which an application runs on one or more locations of the network simultaneously.

division of labor   Separation of a work process into component tasks, with different workers specializing in each of the tasks.

documentation An instruction manual that accompanies software. Also, a technical, detailed written description of the specific facts of a program.

document examination/record inspection The review of company documents about a system or opportunity under investigation.

downloading The transfer of information from a central system to a desktop computer.

drive The device containing a secondary storage medium's read/write unit.

effectiveness The extent to which desirable results are achieved.

electronic bulletin board A network service application that allows messages and announcements to be posted and read. It is accessed by dialing a telephone number and interconnecting with the bulletin board through a modem.

electronic data interchange (EDI) A form of electronic communication that allows trading partners to exchange business transaction data in structured formats that can be processed by applications software.

electronic funds transfer (EFT) The movement of money over a network.

electronic mailbox An area of space on magnetic disk in a server or host computer that is allocated for storing an individual's e-mail.

electronic spreadsheet An automated version of the manual spreadsheet, created and maintained by a spreadsheet program.

e-mail/electronic mail A service that transports text messages from a sender to one or more receivers via computer.

entity A person, place, thing, event, or condition about which data and information are collected.

ethics The standards of conduct and moral behavior that people are expected to follow.

exception report A report that lists unusual, erroneous, or unacceptable transactions or results.

execution cycle (E-cycle) The last two steps of the machine cycle (execute and store), which produce processing results.

executive support system (ESS)/ executive information system (EIS) An interactive business information system designed to support executives that is capable of presenting summary information on company and industry activities.

expansion slot A slot inside a computer that allows a user to add an additional circuit board.

expert support system/expert system A business information system that uses business rules, regulations, and databases to evaluate a situation or determine an appropriate course of action.

fault-tolerant computer A computer designed with duplicate components to ensure reliability.

fiber-optic cable A physical communications channel that uses light and glass fibers.

fields The columns of a relation. Also called attributes.

file server A computer containing files that are available to all users interconnected on a local area network.

file transfer protocol (FTP) An Internet method that allows you to use a password to connect to another computer on the Net and transfer its files to your computer.

film recorder An output device that transforms an electronic image on a computer screen into a film image.

flash memory Memory that retains its contents even when electricity is turned off.

flatbed scanner A large image scanner that works like an office photocopier.

flexible manufacturing A manufacturing system that automatically sets up machines for the next job, thus reducing setup time and making smaller job runs feasible.

floppy disk/flexible disk A type of magnetic disk made of flexible plastic.

formula An electronic spreadsheet instruction describing how a specific computation should be performed.

fractal method An image compression method that stores images in pixel blocks and matches those blocks with fractal shapes whose identifying numbers constitute a mathematical formula that is used to regenerate the image.

front-end CASE tool A CASE tool that automates the early (front-end) activities in systems development.

front-end computer In a centralized system, a minicomputer loaded with special programs to handle all incoming and outgoing communications traffic.

function A formula built into electronic spreadsheet software that will automatically perform certain types of calculation.

functional distribution strategy A database distribution strategy in which the database is distributed according to business functions.

function key A key designed to assist the computer's user to enter data and information or to control processing.

gap In magnetic storage, a space left before and after a block so that the tape drive can stop without skipping over any data.

gateway A device that connects two otherwise incompatible networks, network nodes, or devices.

generation The process of organizing information into a useful form, whether as numbers, text, sound, or visual image.

geographic distribution strategy A database distribution strategy in which the database is located in a region where the data and information are used most frequently.

gigabyte/G-byte/GB/gig One billion bytes.

Gopher A server that organizes descriptions of information located on the Internet in the form of easy-to-use hierarchical menus.

graphical browser A type of browser used with the Web that displays both text and images within a page.

graphical user interface (GUI) A link to an operating system that allows users to use icons rather than command words to start processing.

graphics adapter card An interface board between a computer and monitor that is used to determine the monitor's resolution and use of color.

group support system (GSS) A business information system that permits people to process and interpret information as a group, even if they are not working face-to-face.

hacker A person who gains access to a system illegally.

handheld scanner An inexpensive handheld alternative to the flatbed image scanner.

hands-on system A system in which a user enters data and information, directs processing, and determines the types of output to be generated.

hard copy The paper output from a printer.

hard disk A type of secondary storage that uses nonflexible, nonremovable magnetic disks mounted inside the computer to store data or information.

hardware The computer and its associated equipment.

hardware/computer hardware/devices The computer and its associated equipment.

head crash The situation that occurs when the read/write heads that normally float close to a magnetic disk's surface actually touch the surface.

hibernation mode The time during which all tasks are suspended and memory data and processing details are stored on the hard disk.

high-definition television (HDTV) A television system that uses digital technologies to present sound and images over high-quality television screens.

home page The first page of a Web site, which identifies the site and provides information about the contents of electronic documents that are part of the site.

host-based computing Centralized computing.

hot site A fully equipped backup computer center to which a company can take its backup copies of data and software and resume processing.

hybrid network A communications architecture that combines centralized and distributed architectures to take advantage of the strengths of both.

hyperlinks Words and/or symbols highlighted by blinking, color, or underline that connect one document to another related document on the Web.

hypertext A multimedia text display system in which words or phrases are highlighted to signal that clicking on them will reveal additional information. Also called hyperlinks.

hypertext markup language (HTML) A set of commands that specifies the position, size, and color of text, the location of graphic information, and the incorporation of sound and video. HTML commands also identify the words or images that will serve as hyperlinks to other documents.

icon bar The line of an electronic spreadsheet's control panel that shows the icons (pictures) used to invoke frequently used commands.

illustration program A program in which the computer screen becomes a drawing board on which artists translate their ideas into visual form.

image compression A technique for reducing the size of stored images.

image scanning Examining an image and translating lines, dots, and marks into digital form.

impact printing A printing process in which the paper and the character being printed come into contact with each other.

implementation The fifth phase of the systems development life cycle, in which the new system is installed and put to use.

index A data file that contains identifying information about each record and its location in storage.

indexing A database system's capability to find fields and records in the database.

index key/search key A data item used by database management software to locate a specific record.

Industrial Age The period from the 1800s to 1957, when work processes were simplified through mechanization and automation.

information An organized, meaningful, and useful interpretation of data.

Information Age The period that began in 1957, in which the majority of workers are involved in the creation, distribution, and application of information.

information processing A general term for the computer activity that entails processing any type of information and transforming it into a different type of information.

information repository/repository A synonym for database.

information society A society in which more people work at handling information than at agriculture and manufacturing combined.

information superhighway A communications network spanning a nation, carrying data and information traffic.

information system A system in which data and information flow from one person or department to another.

information system/management information system (MIS) A business information system designed to produce the information needed for successful management of a structured problem, process, department, or business.

information technology (IT) A term used to refer to a wide variety of items and abilities used in the creation, storage, and dispersal of data and information. Its three main components are computers, communications networks, and know-how.

information technology professional A person who is responsible for acquiring, developing, maintaining, or operating the hardware associated with computers and communications networks.

infrared A cableless medium that transmits data and information in coded form by means of an infrared light beamed from one transceiver to another.

input The data or information entered into a computer or the process of entering data or information into the computer for processing, storage and retrieval, or transmission.

input device A device by which input is fed into a computer's central processor.

input/output controller A data controller with its own memory and processor that regulate the flow of data to and from peripheral devices.

input/output (I/O) bus A bus (electronic circuit) that moves data into and out of the processor.

installed memory The amount of memory included by a computer's manufacturer on its memory board.

instruction cycle (I-cycle) The first two steps of the machine cycle (fetch and decode), in which instructions are obtained and translated.

instructions Detailed descriptions of the actions to be carried out during input, processing, output, storage, and transmission.

integrated CASE (I-CASE) tool A CASE tool that spans activities throughout the entire systems development life cycle.

integrated circuit/chip/microchip A collection of thousands or millions of transistors placed on a small silicon chip.

integrating The process of packing more transistors onto a single chip.

interactive multimedia presentation A multimedia presentation in which information is presented dynamically—that is, it can be shown in many different sequences, depending on the viewer's instructions.

interactive television (ITV) A television with a keyboard, storage capability, and the capacity to transmit and receive vast amounts of information.

interface The means by which a person interacts with a computer.

Internet/Net A communication network that is itself a connection of many other networks.

internetworked The linking of several networks.

interoperability The perfect exchange of data and information in all forms (data, text, sound, and image, including animation) between the individual components of an application (hardware, software, network).

intrusion Forced and unauthorized entry into a system.

joystick An input device used to control the actions in computer games or simulations. The joystick extends vertically from a control box.

JPEG (Joint Photographic Expert Group) format An image compression method that stores images in pixel blocks embedded with information that makes possible the regeneration of the image.

jump To suspend the display of the current screen and immediately display a new screen; direct navigation.

keyboard The most common computer input device.

keywords A string of letters or words that indicates the subject to be searched.

kilobyte/K-byte/KB/K One thousand bytes.

know-how The capability to do something well.

knowledge An awareness and understanding of a set of information and how that information can be put to the best use.

knowledge workers Workers involved in the creation, distribution, and application of information.

label A piece of descriptive information pertaining to a row or column of an electronic spreadsheet.

laser printer A nonimpact printer that uses laser beams to print an entire page at once.

layout description A chart that shows the exact location of data and information on a computer screen or in a printed report.

leased line/dedicated line A communications line reserved from a carrier by a company for its exclusive use.

leveling The process of exploding processes in a dataflow diagram to show more detail.

light pen An input device that uses a light-sensitive cell to draw images and to select options from a menu of choices displayed on a computer screen.

local area network (LAN) A network that interconnects computers and communications devices within an office or series of offices; typically spans a distance of a few hundred feet to several miles.

machine cycle The four processing steps performed by the control unit: fetch, decode, execute, and store.

macro A time-saving miniprogram, identified by a name and a series of keystrokes, that is used to perform commonly repeated actions.

magnetic disk A general term referring to two types of storage disk: the flexible/floppy disk and the hard disk.

magnetic ink character recognition A form of optical character reading in which preprinted information written in magnetic ink is read optically or sensed magnetically.

magnetic tape A magnetic storage medium in which data are stored on large reels of tape.

mainframe Larger, faster, and more expensive than a midrange computer, this computer is used for several purposes simultaneously.

management reporting system/management information system (MIS) A business information system designed to produce the information needed for successful management of a structured problem, process, department, or business.

manufacturing automation protocol (MAP) A protocol used by factory designers to provide a common language for the transmission of data.

manufacturing cell A group of machines working together in computer-integrated manufacturing.

manufacturing resource planning (MRP II) An advanced MRP system that ties together all the parts of an organization into the company's production activities.

material requirements planning (MRP) A system that tracks the quantity of each part needed to manufacture a product; essentially, an important component of MRP II.

maximum memory The most memory that a processor can hold.

megabyte/M-byte/MB/meg One million bytes.

megaflops Millions of floating point operations per second—a measure of how many detailed arithmetic calculations the computer can perform per second.

megahertz (MHz) Millions of electric pulses per second—a measure of a computer's speed.

menu bar The line of an electronic spreadsheet's control panel that contains the commands for working with worksheets, creating graphics, and invoking special data-processing actions.

metropolitan area network (MAN) A network that transmits data and information over citywide distances and at greater speeds than a LAN.

microcode The instructions that coordinate the execution of the instructions to move data to and from memory.

microcomputer/personal computer/ PC A computer that is relatively compact and usually found on a table or desktop.

microprocessor The smallest type of processor, with all of the processing capabilities of the control unit and ALU located on a single chip.

microsecond One millionth of a second.

microwave A cableless medium that uses high-frequency radio signals to send data or information through the air.

MIDI (musical instrument digital interface) audio A form of digital audio in which objects containing sound created by musical instruments are stored in computer-processible form.

midrange computer/minicomputer A computer used to interconnect people and large sets of information. More powerful than a microcomputer, the minicomputer is usually dedicated to performing specific functions.

millions of instructions per second (MIPS) The number of instructions the processor can execute per second—a measure of processor speed.

millisecond One thousandth of a second.

mixing An editing process in which two or more audio files are integrated during playback.

model A plan that simulates the relationships between events or variables.

modem A device that connects a computer to a communications medium and translates the data or information from the computer into a form that can be transmitted over the channel. Used in WANs.

monochrome display A video screen display that shows information using a single foreground color on a contrasting background color (e.g., black on white).

mouse An input device with a small ball underneath that rotates, causing a corresponding movement of a pointer on a display screen.

multimedia PC A system that contains standard PC features but also has the capability to handle audio, video, animation, and graphics.

multimedia presentation The seamless integration, through information technology, of different forms of information, including text, sound, still and animated images, and motion video.

multimedia slide show A multimedia presentation in which information is displayed in a predetermined sequence, one slide at a time.

multimedia system A computer system that can process multiple types of information simultaneously.

multiple instruction/multiple data (MIMD) method A parallel-processing method that connects a number of processors that run different programs or parts of a program on different sets of data.

multiplexer A device that converts data from digital to analog form and vice versa in order to allow a single communications channel to carry simultaneous data transmissions from the many terminals that are sharing the channel.

multisync/multiscan monitors Monitors designed to work with a variety of graphics standards.

multiuser system A communications system in which more than one user share hardware, programs, information, people, and procedures.

nanosecond One billionth of a second.

navigation A capability of interactive multimedia presentations that allows the viewer to move around within the presentation.

network administration/network management The management of a network, consisting of those procedures and services that keep the network running properly.

network interface card A circuit board used in LANs to transmit digital data or information.

network operating system (NOS) A software program that runs in conjunction with the computer's operating system and applications programs and manages the network.

network services The applications available on a communications network.

node A communication station within a network.

nonconcurrent data sharing A database procedure that allows individuals to access a database only when no other person or application is processing the data.

nonimpact printing A printing process in which no physical contact occurs between the paper and the print device; the characters are produced on the paper through a heat, chemical, or spraying process.

notebook computer, laptop computer Smaller versions of microcomputers that are designed for portability. All of their components, except a printer, are included in a single unit.

object A component that contains data about itself and how it is to be processed.

object-oriented database A database that stores data and information about objects.

object-oriented programming Software development combining data and procedures into a single object.

observation The process of watching an activity take place to collect information about that activity.

off-site backup facility A backup computer center located away from a company's main facility.

open system A software system that performs on different computer and communications hardware.

operating system A combination of programs that coordinates the actions of a computer, including its peripheral devices and memory.

operations procedure A procedure that describes how a computer system or application is used, how often it can be used, who is authorized to use it, and where the results of processing should go.

optical character reader An OCR device that recognizes printed information rather than just dark marks.

optical character recognition (OCR) A technology by which devices read information on paper and convert it into computer-processible form.

optical code reader An OCR device used to read bar codes.

optical mark reader An OCR device that recognizes the location of dark marks on a special form as the form is scanned.

optical storage device A device that uses a beam of light produced by a

laser to read and write data and information.

output The results of inputting and processing data and information returned by the computer, either directly to the person using the system or to secondary storage.

output device A device that makes the results of processing available outside of the computer.

outsourcing A business practice in which firms use freelancers and consultants, rather than in-house staff, for selected activities.

palmtop computer The smallest and most portable computer, typically used for a limited number of functions, such as maintaining a personal calendar or address file.

parallel processing Processing in which a computer handles different parts of a problem by executing instructions simultaneously.

parallel systems strategy A conversion plan in which the old and the new system are used together for a period of time, with the old system being gradually phased out.

partitioning A method of database distribution in which different portions of the database reside at different nodes in the network.

PCMCIA card/PC card A card designed to expand a computer's memory.

pen-based computer A tabletlike computer controlled with a special pen.

peripheral equipment A general term used for any device that is attached to a computer system.

personal digital assistant (PDA) A portable computer generally used as a personal aid.

personal productivity software Software packages that permit activities to be completed more quickly, allow more activities to be completed in a particular period of time, or allow a task to be completed with fewer resources.

phase-in strategy A conversion plan in which a new system is gradually phased in throughout the organization or department over a certain period of time.

picosecond One trillionth of a second.

pilot conversion strategy A conversion plan in which a working version of a new system is implemented in one group or department to test it before it is installed throughout the entire business.

pixels   The dots used to create an image; the higher the number of dots, the better the resolution of the image.

platform   The computer foundation on which applications are built. The two most common platforms for PCs are IBM-compatibles and Apple Macintosh.

plotter   An output device that draws image information (such as charts, graphs, and blueprints) stroke by stroke.

plug and play   The ability to install devices into a computer when the computer itself makes any necessary internal adjustments.

pointing stick   A device that positions the cursor on the computer screen.

port   A connector through which input/output devices can be plugged into the computer.

Post, Telephone, and Telegraph (PTT)   A general term used for the government-controlled telephone company in a country other than the United States.

preliminary investigation   The first phase of the systems development life cycle, in which the merits and feasibility of a project proposal are determined.

primary storage/primary memory/ main memory/internal memory Storage within the computer itself. Primary memory holds data only temporarily, as the computer executes instructions.

privacy   In IT, the term used to refer to how personal information is collected, used, and protected.

private branch exchange (PBX)/ computer branch exchange (CBX) A private telephone system designed to handle the needs of the organization in which it is installed.

private network   A network made up of leased (dedicated) communications lines.

problem   A perceived difference between an existing condition and a desired condition.

problem solving   The process of recognizing a problem, identifying alternatives for solving it, and successfully implementing the chosen solution.

problem solving cycle The five-step sequence of activities designed to address and solve problems in a structured way.

procedure   A step-by-step process or a set of instructions for accomplishing specific results.

process   A structured activity that leads to a set of results (output).

process improvement   An improvement in the way a business works.

processing   The process of converting, analyzing, computing, and synthesizing all forms of data or information.

processor/central processing unit (CPU)   A set of electronic circuits that perform the computer's processing actions.

productivity   The relationship between the results of an activity (output) and the resources used to create those results (inputs).

program   A set of instructions that directs a computer to perform certain tasks and produce certain results.

programmer/analyst   A person who has joint responsibility for determining system requirements and developing and implementing the systems.

project management   The process of planning, organizing, integrating, and overseeing the development of an IT application to ensure that the project's objectives are achieved and the system is implemented according to expectations.

project proposal   A proposal for a systems project prepared by users or systems analysts and submitted to a steering committee for approval.

protocol   The rules and conventions guiding data communications, embedded as coded instructions in the network software.

prototype   A working model of an IT application.

public access network   A network maintained by common carriers for use by the general public.

public domain software   Any non-copyrighted software that can be used by the general public.

query   A question to be answered by accessing the data in a database.

query by example (QBE)   A query format in which the user fills in the blanks with simple commands or conditions.

query language   A computer language that forms database queries from a limited number of words.

questionnaire   A sheet of questions used to collect facts and opinions from a group of people.

radio wave transmission/radio frequency (RF) transmission   A cable-less medium that uses frequencies

rented from public radio networks to transmit data and information.

RAM disk   A disk created in primary memory that offers instant direct access to the data stored on it.

random-access memory (RAM) Memory that permits data or information to be written into or read from memory only as long as the computer is turned on.

random access storage/direct access storage   The process of retrieving a particular record of information from any track directly.

read only   A type of disk that information can be read from but not written onto.

read-only memory (ROM)   A type of storage that offers random access to memory and can hold data and information after the electric current to the computer has been turned off.

read/write head   A device that records data by magnetically aligning metallic particles on the medium. The write head records data and the read head retrieves them.

real-time processing   The processing of each transaction as it occurs.

record   A grouping of data items that consists of a set of data or information that describes an entity's specific occurrence.

record key   In a database, a designated field used to distinguish one record from another.

recording density   The number of characters per inch at which a drive writes data.

record locking   A concurrency procedure that prohibits another user from accessing or altering a record that is in use.

recovery procedure   An action taken when information or software must be restored.

reduced instruction set computing (RISC)   A computing instruction set that takes data for the execution of an instruction only from registers.

reengineering   The reshaping of business processes to remove barriers that prohibit an organization from providing better products and services and to help the organization capitalize on its strengths.

register   A temporary storage area in the processor that can move data and instructions more quickly than main memory can, and momentarily hold the data or instructions used in processing as well as the results that are generated.

relational database   A database in which the data are structured in a table format consisting of rows and columns.

relational operator   A symbol that tells a database system to make a comparison to call up the requested data.

relation/file   The table in a database that describes an entity.

reliability   The assurance that computers and communications systems will do what they should when they should.

reliability   The assurance that computers and communications systems will do what they should when they should.

replication   A method of database distribution in which one database contains data that are included in another database.

requirement   A feature that must be included in a system.

requirements determination   The second phase of the systems development life cycle, in which the current business situation is studied to determine who is involved, what data and information are needed, and how the current system can be improved.

resolution   The clarity or sharpness of an image.

retrieval   The process by which a computer locates and copies stored data or information for further processing or for transmission to another user.

RGB display   A video screen display with the ability to create 256 colors and several thousand variations on these colors by blending shades of red, green, and blue.

robot   A computer-controlled device that can physically manipulate its surroundings.

router   A device that interconnects compatible LANs.

rows   The horizontal elements in a spreadsheet.

rule base/knowledge base   A database of rules in an expert system.

sampling   The process of collecting data and information at prescribed intervals.

satellite   A cableless medium in which communications are beamed from a microwave station to a communications satellite in orbit above the earth and relayed to other earth stations.

scanning   The process of transforming written or printed data or information into a digital form that is entered directly into the computer.

schema   The structure of a database.

scroll bar   A bar located at the right or bottom of the computer screen that allows the user to move around the screen—up, down, left, or right.

search engine   A program invoked from within the browser that scans the network by using a keyword or phrase.

secondary storage   A storage medium that is external to the computer, but that can be read by the computer; a way of storing data and information outside the computer itself.

secondary storage/auxiliary storage   A storage medium that is external to the computer, but that can be read by the computer; a way of storing data and information outside the computer itself.

sector   A subdivision of a track on a magnetic disk; used to improve access to data or information.

security procedure   A procedure designed to safeguard data centers, communications networks, computers, and other IT components from accidental intrusion or intentional damage.

security software   Software that is designed to protect systems and data.

sensitivity analysis   The analytical process by which a computer determines what would happen if certain data change.

sequential processing   Processing in which the execution of one instruction is followed by the execution of another.

server   A computer that hosts a network and provides the resources that are shared on the network.

server computer   The computer that contains data and information that can be accessed by a client computer.

shared database   A database shared among many users and applications.

shared system   A system in which two or more users share computers, communications technology, and applications.

shareware   Software that is given away and freely distributed. The developer retains ownership, asks users to register with the owner, and requests a nominal fee for using the program.

single in-line memory module (SIMM)   A multiple-chip memory card inserted as a unit into a predesigned slot on a computer's system board.

single instruction/multiple data (SIMD) method   A parallel-processing method that executes the same instruction on many data values simultaneously.

single-user system or personal system   An IT system used by only one person. A system that stands alone and is not interconnected with other companies or shared by other people.

site license   An agreement under which a software purchaser pays a fee to the manufacturer to make a specified number of copies of a particular program.

site preparation   The activities involved in preparing for the installation of a new system.

social responsibility   The concept that businesses need to balance their commitments to investors, employees, customers, other businesses, and the communities in which they operate.

software   The general term for a set of instructions that controls a computer or a communications network.

software package   An application that focuses on a particular subject, such as word processing, and is sold to businesses and the general public.

software piracy   The making of illegal copies of software.

software testing   The testing of software programs to ensure that the software will not produce unexpected or incorrect results or interruptions during processing.

source data automation   A method of data entry in which details enter computers directly from their written or printed forms without the intermediate step of keying.

spoken information   Information that is conveyed by sound.

spreadsheet   A table of columns and rows used by people responsible for tracking revenues, expenses, profits, and losses.

spreadsheet program   A software package used to create electronic spreadsheets.

spreadsheet/worksheet   A table of columns and rows used by people responsible for tracking revenues, expenses, profits, and losses.

steering committee   A group of people from various functional areas of a business that determines whether a systems development project proposal is desirable and should be pursued.

still image   A paper photograph; an analog image.

storage   The computer process of retaining information for future use.

structured interview   An interview in which the questions are prepared in advance and each interviewee is asked the same set of questions.

summary report A report that shows the overall results of processing for a period of time or for a batch of transactions and includes a grand total for all listed transactions and the average transaction amount.

surfing Moving among a number of networks that are linked together, or internetworked.

switched network The complete set of public access networks, so named because the telephone company operates and maintains the switching centers that make it possible to transmit data and information.

system A set of components that interact to accomplish a purpose.

system board/mother board The system unit in a microcomputer, located on a board mounted on the bottom of a computer base.

system clock A circuit that generates electronic impulses at a fixed rate to synchronize processing activities.

system construction The fourth phase of the systems development life cycle, in which the system is actually built.

system flowchart A graphical description of a business process or procedure using standard symbols to show decision logic.

systems analyst The IT professional responsible for working with users to determine a system's requirements and for describing the features needed in the system.

systems contractor An outside person or firm that contracts with a company to develop IT applications.

systems design The third phase of the systems development life cycle, in which requirements are translated into design specifications.

systems designer The IT professional responsible for doing the technical work of designing the system and its software.

systems development The process of examining a business situation, designing a system solution to improve that situation, and acquiring the human, financial, and information technology resources needed to develop and implement the solution.

systems development life cycle (SDLC) The six-phased set of activities that brings about a new IT application.

systems engineer An IT professional who installs and maintains hardware.

systems integrator A type of systems contractor who is retained to take re-

sponsibility for acquiring hardware, software, and network capacity for an application, as well as for implementing the application.

systems programmer A software and hardware specialist who works with the physical details of a database and the computer's operating system.

system testing The testing of a complete system—software, procedures, and guidelines.

system unit The hardware unit that houses a computer's processor, memory chips, ports, and add-in boards.

T-carrier A very-high-speed channel designed for use as the backbone of a network and for point-to-point connection of locations.

teleprocessing The processing capability made possible by connecting desktop computers to a remote computer through telephone lines.

Telnet The means users employ to communicate with their own systems through the Internet when they are away from their home location.

template A worksheet containing row and column labels, and perhaps formulas, but not necessarily any values. It is distributed to people as a guide for analyzing problems or providing data.

terabyte/T-byte/TB One trillion bytes.

terminal A combination of keyboard and video screen that accepts input and displays it on the screen.

test data Experimental files used to test software.

text-based browser A type of browser used with the Web that displays only text information, either a line at a time or a full screen at once.

thumbnail The display of miniature images of each slide in a multimedia slide presentation so the designer can check them for sequence.

title bar The line of an electronic spreadsheet's control panel that contains the program name and sometimes the name of the file in use.

topology A network configuration, or the arrangement of the nodes or workstations of a network in relation to one another.

track The area in which data and information are stored on magnetic tape or disk.

trackball An input device that consists of a ball mounted on rollers. As the user rotates the ball in any direction, the computer senses the movement and

moves the cursor in the corresponding direction.

training The process by which people are taught how to use a system.

transaction-processing system (TPS) A shared business information system that uses a combination of information technology and manual procedures to process data and information and to manage transactions.

transceiver A combination transmitter and receiver that transmits and receives data and information.

transistor An electrical switch that can be in one of two states: open or closed.

transmission The computer process of distributing information over a communications network.

tuples The rows of a relation. Also called records.

twisted pair A physical communications channel that uses strands of copper wire twisted together in pairs to form a telephone wire.

Uniform Resource Locator (URL) A document's address on the WWW.

uninterruptable power supply (UPS) system A system that ensures the continued flow of electricity when the primary source of power fails.

Universal Product Code (UPC) A bar code that identifies a product by a series of vertical lines of varying widths representing a unique product number.

universal service The principle, established in telecommunications, whereby it is assured that anyone who wants a basic service can receive it at low cost.

unstructured interview An interview in which the questions may be prepared in advance, but follow-up questions vary, depending on the interviewees' background and answers.

updated master data An adjustment of all records in a system in response to a processed transaction.

uploading The process by which information is sent from a PC to a mainframe.

Usenet/User's Network A system of worldwide discussion groups, not an actual physical network.

users/end-users The people who use IT in their jobs or personal lives.

utility programs/utilities Special programs used to perform tasks that occur repeatedly during processing.

value A number that is entered into a cell of an electronic spreadsheet. It may be an integer, a decimal number, or a number in scientific format.

value-added network (VAN) A public data communications network that provides basic transmission facilities plus enhancements (e.g., temporary data storage and error detection).

Veronica An internet program that uses keywords to search Gopher menus.

very small aperture terminal (VSAT) A satellite earth station with an antenna diameter of under one meter.

videoconferencing A type of conferencing in which video cameras and microphones capture the sight and sound of participants for transmission over a network.

videodisk An optical read-only storage medium.

video display terminal (VDT)/monitor A computer's visual display.

videotex A two-way, interactive, text-only service operating on mainframe computers that combines a video screen with easy-to-follow instructions.

view A subset of one or more databases, created either by extracting copies of records from a database or by merging copies of records from multiple databases.

virtual company A company that joins with another company operationally, but not physically, to design and manufacture a product.

virus A hidden program that alters, without the user's knowledge, the way a computer operates or that modifies the data and programs stored on the computer.

voice input device An input device that can be attached to a computer to capture the spoken word in digital form.

voice mail A system that captures, stores, and transmits spoken messages using an ordinary telephone connected to a computer network.

wand An input device used to read a bar code and input this information directly into a computer.

WAVE audio A form of digital audio that captures sound through sampling.

Web browser Client computer program designed to locate and display information on the World Wide Web.

Web pages Interconnected electronic documents.

Wide Area Information Servers (WAIS) A retrieval method that searches databases on the Internet and creates a menu of articles and manuscripts containing the keywords provided.

wide area network (WAN) A network that connects sites dispersed across states, countries, or continents.

Winchester disk drive A disk drive that contains a read/write head, an access arm, and a disk in one sealed unit.

Windows A single-user operating system that allows several programs to be operated simultaneously.

word The number of bits a computer can process at one time.

work group conferencing A type of conferencing that uses a software package called groupware to interconnect participants' computers at their various locations. Participants interact through a microcomputer directly linked to a server and their comments are broadcast to all others taking part in the conference.

work processes The combination of activities that workers perform, the way they perform those activities, and the tools they use.

word-processing (WP) program A program that allows the user to enter, change (edit), move, store, and print text information.

worksheet area In an electronic spreadsheet, the rectangular grid of rows and columns that make up the worksheet.

workstation/client A desktop computer connected to a network.

World Wide Web (WWW)/the Web A set of interconnected electronic documents linked together over the Internet.

Credits

Benainous/Gamma-Liaison, Inc.; Gil Michael/Graceland; screen capture courtesy of Graceland, a division of Elvis Presley Enterprises, Inc.; **157** New Media Corporation; **158, 159** IBM Corporation; Action Tec Electronics; **160** logo and photographs courtesy of Carolina Power & Light; **161** IBM Corporation; Amdahl; **162** IBM Corporation; Intel Corporation; **164** IBM Corporation; Intel Corporation; **166** Sears, Roebuck and Co.; **167, 168** Intel Corporation/Photo Research Center; **169** *both*: High Techsplanations; **173** Gamma- Liaison, Inc.; **174** Wildfire Communications; **183** courtesy of YAHOO! Corporation; **187** *all*: DigiCash; **189** Ted Horowitz/Stock Market; Intel Corporation; **190** IBM Corporation; Chuck O'Rear/Intel Corporation; Intel Corporation; **191** National Semiconductor; IBM Corporation; National Semiconductor; Motorola Corporation; **192** Motorola Corporation; Motorola Corporation; SCI Systems, Inc.; Motorola Corporation; **193** SCI Systems, Inc.; *rest:* Intel Corporation.

■ **Chapter 5** **195** Hewlett-Packard Company; **197** NTSB/Federal Aviation Administration; Allied Signal, Inc.; **200** IBM Archives; **201** EMTEC Magnetics GmbH; Maxell Corporation of America **203** *bottom*: courtesy of Iomega; **206** Compton's New Media, Inc.; **208** courtesy of Royal Automobile Club; **209** Panasonic Communications Systems Division; IBM Corporation; **210** Yamaha Systems Technology, Inc; **211** IBM Corporation; **213** Churchill & Klehr/Simon & Schuster/PH College; **216** IBM Corporation; Bill Pappas/Diebold, Inc.; IBM Corporation; **217** McKesson Corporation; **218** Scantron Corporation; **219** courtesy of Doubleday Direct, Inc.; **222** IBM Corporation; **223** MicroTouch Systems, Inc.; Logitech, Inc.; **224** Logitech, Inc.; Toshiba Corporation; Churchill & Klehr/Simon & Schuster/PH College; Joseph Nettig/Stock Boston; **225** Eastman Kodak Company; **227** Truevision; Sony Electronics, Inc.; **228** Tulare County Department of Public Social Services; **229** *both:* IBM Archives; **230** John Greenleigh/Apple Computer, Inc.; NEC Technologies, Inc.; **233** Redrawn from *The Way Things Work* by David Macaulay, pp. 348-349. Compilation copyright © 1988 by Doling Kindersley, Ltd. Text copyright © 1988 by David Macaulay and Neil Ardley. Ilustrations copyright © 1988 by David Macaulay. Reprinted by permission of Houghton Mifflin Co. and Dorling Kindersley, Ltd.; **234** Tektronix, Inc.; Churchill & Klehr/Simon & Schuster/PH College; Hewlett-Packard Company; Eltron International, Inc.; **235** Hewlett-Packard Company; **236** Panasonic Communications Systems Division; IBM Corporation; Dataproducts Corp.; **237** Lufthansa German Airlines; **239** *top photos:* Michael Newman/PhotoEdit; Hewlett-Packard Company; **240** Mirus Industries Corporation; **248** logo courtesy of Talbott Studio; Robert Holmgren; **249** Frank S. Balthis Photography; **250** logo and photograph courtesy of NCI Network Computer, Inc.

■ **Chapter 6** **253** Lotus Development Corp.; Bettmann; Telegraph Colour Library/FPG International; **257** courtesy of Lotus Development Corp.; **260** Jon McNally/Times Staff Photographer/Contra Costa Newspapers; Maxis; **262** cour-

tesy of Microsoft Corporation; **263** Lotus Development Corporation; Microsoft Corporation; **264, 267, 268** courtesy of Microsoft Corporation; **271** courtesy of Lotus Development Corporation; **272, 274** courtesy of Microsoft Corporation; **277** courtesy of Lotus Development Corporation; **278** courtesy of Microsoft Corporation; **279** Teri Stratford; **280** courtesy of Microsoft Corporation; **281** "The Outs of Spreadsheet Power" by Daniel Gasteiger from *PC Computing*, June 1990, p. 110. Copyright © 1990 by Ziff-Davis Publishing, Co. Reprinted by permission. **286, 287** courtesy of Lotus Development Corporation; **298** Jim Egan/Jim Egan Photography.

■ **Chapter 7** **301** Lloyd Gallman; **304, 305** Finagle-A-Bagel; **307** PictureWare, Inc.; **310, 311** *all:* courtesy of Topaz International, Ltd.; **317** Brian Wood; **320** logo courtesy of Farmland Industries; **322, 324, 326** courtesy of Microsoft Corporation; **335** logos courtesy of Haven Corporation; **336** Gregory D. Baker/Gregory D. Baker Photography; **337** *all:* courtesy of Firefighters Bookstore.

■ **Chapter 8** **339** David Burnett/Contact Press Images; **341** SuperStock, Inc.; Tony Stewart & R. Baxter/Tony Stone Images; Sylvain Grandadam/Tony Stone Images; **344** Jenny Thomas/Simon & Schuster/PH College; **345** *all:* Nicholas Arroyo/Simon & Schuster/PH College; **347** General Accident Insurance; **349** Chris Covey/Simon & Schuster/PH College; **350** *both:* The Learning Company, Inc.; **351** Sony Computer Entertainment America; Namco America; Jean Pierre Arnet/Sygma; **352** Gamma-Liaison, Inc.; Gabe Palmer/The Stock Market; Corel Corporation; Gamma-Liaison, Inc.; **353** *all:* courtesy of Microsoft Corporation; **354** Time-Life Syndication; Frank LaBua/Simon & Schuster/PH College; **356** courtesy of Microsoft Corporation; courtesy of Lotus Development Corporation; courtesy of Asymetrix Corporation; **357- 363** *all:* courtesy of Microsoft Corporation; **364** logo courtesy of UBS Union Bank of Switzerland; **365** courtesy of Asymetrix Corporation; **366, 368** screen captures courtesy of Microsoft Corporation; **371** photos by Churchill & Klehr/Simon & Schuster/PH College; **372** *all:* courtesy of Eastman Kodak Company; **374** *all:* Churchill & Klehr/Simon & Schuster/PH College; **376** Courtesy of Adobe Systems Incorporated; **377** courtesy of Joni Carter; **379** Hans Hammar-skjold/Vasamuseet - The Vasa Museum; **388** Courtesy of ESPN, Inc.; **389** Kobal Collection; **390** Gamma-Liaison, Inc.; Sally Corporation; **391, 392, 393** *all:* Sally Corporation.

■ **Chapter 9** **395** Hellmuth, Obata & Kassabaum, Inc.; **396** Jeff Goldberg/Hellmuth, Obata & Kassabaum, Inc.; **398** Rick Taylor Photography; **399** America Online, Inc.; **400** Fredrich Cantor/Onyx/Outline Press Syndicate, Inc.; logo courtesy of National Institutes of Health; **403** Teri Stratford; **406** logo courtesy of American Greetings Corporation; **408, 409** courtesy of OmniForms; **410** SuperStock, Inc.; **414** Richard Passmore/Tony Stone Images; **418** David Simson/Stock Boston; **430, 431** courtesy of Freightliner Corporation; **432** IBM Corporation; Donna Cox, Robert Patterson, NCSA, University of Illinois; **433** Ken M. Johns/Photo Researchers, Inc.; ChromoSohm/Photo Researchers, Inc.; Teri Stratford; Dell Computer Corporation; **434** Michael A. Keller/Uniphoto;

Intel Corporation; Dell Computer Corporation; **435** Teri Stratford; Superstock; Peter Poulides.

■ **Chapter 10** **439** David R. Frazier Photolibrary, Inc.; **440** logo courtesy of France Telecom Intelmatique; photograph by Owen Franken/Stock Boston; **442, 443** logo and photographs courtesy of Levi Strauss & Co.; **450** Eli Reichman; **451** logo courtesy of Mellon Bank Corporation; **452** Phil Schofield Photography; courtesy of Microsoft Corporation; **455** Churchill & Klehr/Simon & Schuster/PH College; **457** The Image Reader; **465** AT&T Archives; AT&T Bell Laboratories; Sperry Corporation; **468** *top two:* Schneider National, Inc.; Steve Weber/Stock Boston; **469** VideOcart, Inc.; **470** United Technologies-Otis Elevators; **473** *top two:* Hayes Microcomputer Products, Inc. - World Headquarters; IBM Corporation; **475** logo courtesy of Peapod, Inc.; **482** From *The Way Things Work* by David Macaulay. Compilation copyright © 1988 by Dorling Kindersley, Ltd. Illustrations copyright © 1988 by David Macaulay. Reprinted by permission of Houghton Mifflin Co. and Dorling Kindersley, Ltd.; **487** logo courtesy of Delta Air Lines; **495** logo courtesy of CNN Cable News Network, Inc.; **496** Forbes Magazine; **498-501** courtesy of Lotus Development Corporation.

■ **Chapter 11** **503** *both:* Sonic Air; **506** logo courtesy of National Car Rental; photo by Raymond Reuter/Sygma; **517, 518** Tony Freeman/PhotoEdit; **524** *both:* David Male Photography/Burlington Coat Factory; **528, 529** courtesy of Glass's Information Services, Ltd.; **539** Telegraph Colour Library/FPG International; **540** Hubert Raguet/Gamma-Liaison, Inc.; **542** Gamma-Liaison, Inc.; David Young-Wolff/PhotoEdit; **543** J. Greenberg/The Image Works; Teri Stratford; *remaining photographs:* Etienne de Malglaive/Gamma-Liaison, Inc.; **544** Bill Gallery/Stock Boston; John Madere; Nubar Alexananian/Stock Boston; Etienne de Malglaive/Gamma-Liaison, Inc.; B. Roland/The Image Works; Kenneth Gabrielsen Photography/Gamma-Liaison, Inc.; **545** Federal Express; John Madere.

■ **Chapter 12** **547** Churchill & Klehr/Simon & Schuster/PH College; R. Lord/The Image Works; **550** logo courtesy of Xerox Corporation; **551** Rank Xerox Ltd.; **553** M. Siluk/The Image Works; Mark E. Gibson/The Stock Market; **554** courtesy of Microsoft Corporation; **555** logo and screen capture courtesy of Reuters America, Inc.; **556** Courtesy of Microsoft Corporation; **559** courtesy of American Airlines; **566** Tom Wagner/SABA Press Photos, Inc.; **568** Christopher Covatta/Gamma-Liaison, Inc.; **570** Diamond Star Motors, Inc.; **571** IBM Corporation; **581** Michael Witte; **605, 606** *all:* courtesy of Sara Lee Corporation.

■ **Chapter 13** **609** Corbis-Bettmann; **611** David Dietz/Stock Boston; Richard Pasley/Stock Boston; Greg Meadows/Stock Boston; Mike Mazzaschi/Stock Boston; **612** Bill Houlton, Intermec; **614** logo courtesy of The Limited, Inc.; photo by Churchill & Klehr/Simon & Schuster/PH College; **616** courtesy of MCI Communications Corp.; **619** text from "Precision Marketing" in *Inc. Technology #2.* Copyright © 1996 by Goldhirsh Group, Inc., 38 Commercial

Wharf, Boston, MA. Reprinted by permission.; photo by Nancy Pierce/Black Star; **620** Mark Reinstein/FPG International; **627** *both:* Tim Kelly; **630, 631** text and illustration from "Picture This" by Allan E. Alter in *Computerworld,* April 29, 1996. Copyright © 1996 by Computerworld, Inc., Framingham, MA. Reprinted by permission of Computerworld.; **635** *both:* Lon Harding; **637** Ken Kobre/Words & Pictures; Ted Horowitz/The Stock Market; Richard Nowitz/The Stock Market; Louis Psihoyos/Matrix International; **639** From *Manufacturing for Competitive Advantage* by Thomas G. Gunn. Copyright © 1987 by Ballinger Publishing Company. Reprinted by permission of HarperCollins Publishers, Inc.; **641** *both:* Louis Psihoyos/Matrix International; **650** logo courtesy of Mrs. Fields; photo from *The Arizona Daily Star;* **652** *both:* Saturn Media Center; **653** Andy Sacks/Tony Stone Images; *rest:* Saturn Media Center; **654** *four photos:* Saturn Media Center; AP/Wide World Photos; Time; **655** Saturn Media Center; Saturn Media Center; courtesy of Auto Alliance; courtesy of Toyota Motor Manufacturing, Kentucky, Inc.; courtesy of Honda of America Mfg.; courtesy of Honda of America Mfg.; courtesy of Nissan Corp.

■ **Chapter 14** **659** Randy Faris/Westlight; **660** David Young-Wolff/PhotoEdit; **661** AT&T Archives; **666** Bob Riha/Gamma-Liaison, Inc.; **669** T. Taylor/AST Research, Inc.; **670** *all:* Comdisco Disaster Recovery Services; **677** National Cristina Foundation; **679** Comdisco Disaster Recovery Services; Recognition Systems, Inc.; **681** Gamma-Liaison, Inc.; **682, 683** *all:* RSA Data Security, Inc.; **695** Richard Russo/Media Image Resource Alliance.

■ **Chapter 15** **699** Jon Riley/The Stock Shop, Inc./Medichrome; **701** courtesy of Zenith Electronics Corporation; Sharp Electronics Corporation; courtesy of Zenith Electronics Corporation; Pioneer Electronics; Thomson Consumer Electronics, Inc.; **704** Carlo Carino/SABA Press Photos, Inc.; **705** Sources: *Statistical Abstract of the United States, 1992;* Television Bureau of Advertising, Inc. Research Department, Electronic Industries Assn., Marketing Services Research Center; Zenith Electronics Corporation; **709** *both:* Le Groupe Videotron Itee; **725** *both:* Nokia Americas.

■ **Appendix** **728** D. Mazonowicz/Art Resource; Erich Lessing/Art Resource; Ewing Galloway; IBM Archives; *rest:* Bettmann Archives; **729** AT&T Archives; Bell Telephone Systems; IBM Archives; Hollerith Company; IBM Archives; Iowa State University Archives; Iowa State University Archives; Iowa State University Archives; **730** Neal Peters Collection; Neal Peters Collection; Neal Peters Collection; Sperry Corporation; Sperry Corporation; Bettmann; Melgar Photography, Inc.; *rest:* AP/Wide World Photos; **731** IBM Archives; James S. Davis/Dava Still Media Depository; UPI/Bettmann; Melgar Photography, Inc.; *rest:* AP/Wide World Photos; **732** IBM Archives; CompuServe, Inc.; The Source Information Network; IBM Archives; courtesy of Compaq Computer Corporation; Ted Morrison/Still Life Stock; Courtesy of Apple Computer, Inc.; **733** IBM Archives;

Microsoft Corporation; Microsoft Corporation; IBM Archives; IBM Archives; Corbis-Bettmann; Courtesy of Apple Computer, Inc./Photographed by John Greenleigh; Courtesy of the Apple Computer, Inc.; **734** AP/Wide World Photos; Sun Microsystems, Inc.; AP/Wide World Photos; Porter Gifford/Gamma Liaison, Inc.; Dan Lamont/Matrix 1996, Matrix International; Microsoft Corporation; AP/Wide World Photos; AP/Wide World Photos.

Indexes

■ Subject Index

▪ Name, Company, and Product Index